Wolfgang Amade Mozart.

After the Family picture in the Mozarteum
at Salzburg.

LIFE OF MOZART

BY

OTTO JAHN.

TRANSLATED FROM THE GERMAN BY

PAULINE D. TOWNSEND.

WITH A PREFACE BY

GEORGE GROVE, Esq., D.C.L.

IN THREE VOLUMES
VOL. II.

COOPER SQUARE PUBLISHERS, INC.
New York
1970

LONDON :

NOVELLO, EWER AND CO.,

PRINTERS.

Originally Published 1891
Published 1970 by Cooper Square Publishers, Inc.
59 Fourth Avenue, New York, N. Y. 10003
Standard Book No. 8154-0343-7
Library of Congress Catalog Card No. 78-125917

Printed in the United States of America

CONTENTS.

—⚜—

CHAPTER XVIII.

FRENCH OPERA.

MOZART and his mother left Mannheim on March 14, and arrived in Paris on the 23rd, after a journey of nine days and a-half. "We thought we should never get through it," writes Wolfgang (March 24, 1778),[1] "and I never in my life was so tired. You can imagine what it was to leave Mannheim and all our dear, good friends there, and to be obliged to exist for ten days without a single soul even to speak to. God be praised, however, we are now at our journey's end. I am in hopes that, with His help, all will go well. To-day we mean to take a fiacre and go to call on Grimm and Wendling. Early to-morrow I shall go to the Electoral Minister, Herr von Sickingen, who is a great connoisseur and lover of music, and to whom I have letters of introduction from Herr von Gemmingen and Herr Cannabich." L. Mozart was full of hope concerning this visit to Paris, and believed that Wolfgang could not fail to gain fame and, as a consequence, money in the French capital. He remembered the brilliant reception which had been given to him and his children fourteen years before, and he was convinced that a like support would be accorded to the youth who had fulfilled his early promise to a degree that to an intelligent observer must appear even more wonderful than his precocious performances as a child. He counted upon the support and assistance of many distinguished and influential persons, whose favour they had already experienced, and more especially on the tried friendship of Grimm, who had formerly given them the benefit of all his knowledge and power, and with whom they had continued in connection ever since. Grimm had lately passed through Salzburg with two

---

[1] Ed. Fournier, Mozart à Paris (Revue Franç., 1856, II., t. 7, p. 28).

friends, and was pleased to hear his " Amadeo," as he called Wolfgang. He chanced to arrive at Augsburg on the evening of Wolfgang's concert there, and was present at it without making himself known, since he was in haste, and had heard that Wolfgang was on his way to Paris. L. Mozart, who placed great confidence in Grimm's friendship and experience, had made no secret to him of his precarious position in Salzburg, and of how greatly Wolfgang was in need of support ; he commended his son entirely to Grimm's favour (April 6, 1778) :—

I recommend you most emphatically to endeavour by childlike confidence to merit, or rather to preserve, the favour, love, and friendship of the Baron von Grimm ; to take counsel with him on every point, and to do nothing hastily or from impulse ; in all things be careful of your own interests, which are those of us all. Life in Paris is very different from life in Germany, and the French ways of expressing oneself politely, of introducing oneself, of craving patronage, &c., are quite peculiar ; so much so, that Baron von Grimm used always to instruct me as to what I should say, and how I should express myself. Be sure you tell him, with my best compliments, that I have reminded you of this, and he will tell you that I am right.

But, clever as he was, L. Mozart had miscalculated on several points. He did not reflect that Grimm had grown older, more indolent, and more stately, and that even formerly a tact and obsequiousness had been required in order to turn the great man's friendship to account, which, natural as they were to himself, his son never did and never would acquire. He had not sufficiently realised that the attention of the public is far more easily attracted by what is strange and wonderful, than by the greatest intellectual and artistic endowments. This was peculiarly the case in Paris, where interest in musical performances only amounted to enthusiasm when some unusual circumstance accompanied them. True, such enthusiasm was at its height at the time of Mozart's visit, but his father could not see that this very fact was against a young man who had so little of the art of ingratiating himself with others. To us it must ever appear as an extraordinary coincidence that Mozart, fresh from Mannheim, and the efforts there being made for the establishment of a national German opera, should have come to Paris at the very height of the struggle between Italian opera and the French opera, as reformed by Gluck, a struggle which appeared to be on the point of being fought out. In neither case did his strong feelings on the subject tempt him to take an active part; he maintained the attitude of a neutral observer, in preparation for the tasks to which he might be appointed.

If we are clearly to apprehend the musical situation, we must remind ourselves in order of the circumstances which had brought it about.

Jean Baptiste de Lully (1633-1687), a native of Florence, had gained such distinction by his violin-playing and ballet music, that in 1652 he was appointed kapellmeister by Louis XIV., and in 1672 he received full power to establish and direct the Académie Royale de Musique. Not only was he the founder of this still existing institution,[2] but he established by its means the grand opera in France. Faithful to the traditions of his birthplace, Florence, he kept in view the first attempts which had been made in Italy to revive ancient tragedy in opera (Vol. I., p. 154 et seq.). As in Italy, so in Paris, operatic performances were originally designed for court festivals; Lully's privilege consisted in his being allowed to give public representations of operas, " even of those which had been produced at court " ("même celles qui auront été représentés devant Nous "). They were preceded by ballets, in which the connection of the action was indicated by vocal scenes; but the singing was quite subordinate to the long succession of dances, in which the distinguished part of the audience, and even the king himself, took part. Dances, therefore, became an essential ingredient of the opera, and it was the task of the poet and the composers to give them appropriate connection with the plot; to this day, as is well known, the ballet is the special prerogative of the Grand-Opéra at Paris. It was not less important to maintain the reputation of the most brilliant court in the

---

[2] Cf. [Noinville] Histoire du Théâtre de l'Opéra en France (Paris, 1753; 2nd Edit., 1757). Castil-Blaze, L'Académie Imp. de Musique de 1645 à 1855 (Paris, 1855, I., II.).

world by means of variety and magnificence of scenery, costumes, machinery, &c.; in this respect, also, the Grand-Opéra has kept true to its traditions.

But whilst in Italy the musical, and especially the vocal element of the opera had always the upper hand, in Paris the dramatic element held its ground with good success. It was the easier for Lully to found a national opera in Paris, since he found a poet ready to hand in Quinault, who had the genius to clothe his mythological subjects in the dramatic and poetical dress of his own day. To us, indeed, his productions seem far apart from the spirit of ancient tragedy, and more rhetorical and epigrammatic than poetical in their conception. But his operas (or rather tragedies) expressed truly the spirit of the age, and they became more distinctively national in proportion as the reign of Louis XIV. came to be considered as the golden age of France. It was Lully's task to give musical expression to the national spirit, and in this he succeeded to the admiration of his contemporaries and of posterity. His music is closely connected with those first attempts in Italy. We find none of the set forms of the later opera seria, no regular arie, no duets, no ensembles. The words are for the most part simply rendered in recitative. There is sometimes a figured bass accompaniment; but even then it is not the free movement of Italian recitative, but is much more precisely apportioned, and the harmonies of the accompaniment change more frequently. When the sentiment becomes rather more elevated, a sort of compromise is effected between recitative and song. The words are rendered with a declamatory spoken accent; and not only are they strictly in time, but the harmonies are so arranged that a full orchestral chord is given to every note of the song. The melodies are therefore limited in every respect; the phrases are generally too small in compass to be well carried out, and hang loosely together without any proper design; it was difficult to develop an elaborate musical form out of such elements as these. Independent songs occur seldom, and then only in the most precise of forms, tending generally to dance melodies (airs). When several voices unite they alternate with each other; or if they sing together note follows note, with only exceptionally real ensemble passages. The choruses are formed by a simple harmony in several parts, the soprano not being always appointed to give the melody. The orchestra, except in the dance music, has seldom any independent significance, but simply gives the full harmony to every note of the bass. Instrumental effect is seldom aimed at, and the different instruments are only occasionally employed singly. Lully's merit chiefly consists in his having accentuated his music in a manner which suited the French language, and also in his having succeeded in throwing a certain amount of characteristic pathos into some of his passages. It is comprehensible that at first, musical cultivation being in its infancy, this quality should be most readily felt and acknowledged ; but in every art, and especially in music, it is the fate of individual characteristics to become the soonest incomprehensible, and, therefore, unpleasing. For this reason, the reaction against Lully's music attacked just this mode of treating the text. It was considered monotonous, tiresome, and heavy; and the isolated significant phrases having lost their power to please, were compared with the plain-song (plain-chant) of church psalmody.[3]

The delivery of the vocalists, male and female, is described as dreadful ; monotonous droning alternating with violent shrieks and exaggerated accent (*urlo francese*).[4]

Notwithstanding all this, Lully's operas held undisputed possession of the stage during his life,[5] and even after his death, a sure proof that his success was not merely the result of the favour personally accorded to him. The composers whose operas found favour after his (such as Campra, Colasse, Desmarets, Blamont, and Mouret) are of less im-

---

[3] Grimm, Corr. inéd., p. 222 ; cf. Corr. Litt., I., p. 93. The following is not bad (Corr. Litt., II., p. 205) : " M. Hasse, qui avait entendu parler de la légèreté et de la pétulance françaises, ne se lassait point, lorsqu'il fut en ce pays-ci, d'admirer la patience avec laquelle on écoutait à l'Opéra une musique lourde et monotone." Goldoni amusingly describes the impression made upon him by the French opera (Mém., II., p. 182).

[4] Grimm, Corr. Litt., XV., p. 283 ; cf. IV., p. 165. Grétry gives more particular instances of the faults of the old style (Mém., I., p. 301).

[5] The last performance of one of Lully's operas (" Thésée ") was in 1778.

portance historically, because they all copied his manner. Any part of their works which pointed to the influence of the opera seria, as it was being formed in the Neapolitan school, was rejected by the national vanity.[6]

Jean Phil. Rameau (1683-1764) came to Paris from the provinces as an established musician in 1721. He succeeded by his force of character, and the powerful protection of the Farmer-General, La Popelinière, in placing his operas on a level with those of Lully in the public estimation. When he produced his " Hippolyte et Aricie " in 1732, he was met by the most determined opposition on the part of Lully's supporters ; but the very decided success of his acknowledged masterpiece, " Castor et Pollux," in 1737,[7] placed him, if not above Lully, certainly on an equality with him during the remainder of his career. His opponents became gradually reconciled to his supremacy, and acknowledged that French music had not been essentially altered by Rameau, only developed and perfected.[8] And there can be no question that this was the case. Before Rameau had produced any operas he had made his reputation as an organist and instrumental composer, and more especially as the founder of a theory of harmony. On this latter point his operas also show considerable progress — the harmonic treatment is rich and varied, though sometimes the straining after novelty and effect

---

[6] Raguenet, Parallèle des Italiens et François en ce qui regarde la Musique et les Opéras (Paris, 1702), translated into German, with notes, and the rejoinder of Freneuse de la Vieuville (Bonnet, Histoire de la Musique, p. 425 ; Bourdelot, Hist. de la Mus., I., p. 291), in Mattheson's Critica Musica (Hamburg, 1712), I., p. 91, and in Marpurg's Krit. Briefen, I., pp. 65, 89, 113, 398. Freneuse, Comparaison de la Mus. Ital. et de la Mus. Franç. Brussels, 1705 (in Bourdelot's Hist. de la Mus., 1725 and 1743, II.-IV.). Raguenet, Défense du Parallèle (Paris, 1705).

[7] La Harpe, Corresp. Litt., II., p. 302.

[8] When Grimm first came to Paris he wrote to Gottsched : " M. Rameau is rightly considered by all connoisseurs to be the greatest musician who has ever lived " (Danzel Gottsched, p. 349). His opinion soon changed, but the account he afterwards gives of Rameau (Corr. Litt., IV., p. 80), prejudiced as it is, recognises Rameau's merits, though without giving him the credit of them. In his Lettre sur " Omphale " (1752, Corr. Litt., XV., p. 281), Grimm gave a detailed criticism in a very moderate tone. A good account of him may be found in Ad. Adam's Derniers Souvenirs d'un Musicien, p. 39.

leads to affectation and over-elaboration. Rameau's accompaniments are free and independent; the orchestra is used with striking effect by means of variety of tone-colouring in the instruments as well as of independent subjects, which serve to accent the details. Rameau's employment of the orchestra shows a marked improvement, not only on Lully, but even on Italian opera as then existing. In the same way we find the choruses released from the fetters of strict thorough-bass, and the parts moving freely and expressively. In the lyrical portions of the opera, much is evidently due to the advance in the art of solo singing, both rhythm and melody move more freely, and embellishment is not wholly wanting. But Rameau has not avowedly adopted the Italian style, although he spent a short part of his youth in Italy. The accepted forms of Italian opera are entirely disregarded, both in the choruses and solos. The slow, uniform progress of Lully's operas becomes freer and more animated in Rameau's, the dramatic expression has more energy and life, and the music has more of individual colouring; but the foundation remains. The same is the case with the treatment of the dialogue. It is still severe, stately, recitative-like singing in varied measure, but Rameau's harmonic art is displayed in his incomparably greater power of expression. Rameau's opera, notwithstanding its independent invention and advance in artistic feeling, is the natural development of Lully's principles, not a revolution against them. It was debated at the time with much warmth whether Rameau's peculiarities were to be accepted as improvements, or to be looked upon as injudicious attempts at novelty. The points which then excited the liveliest interest now seem to us most trivial. But the main fact is not to be denied, that Rameau, by the efforts of his own genius, constructed a national French opera upon the foundations laid by Lully, and that the further development of the grand opera proceeded along the lines laid down by him. Not only can the framework and design of these early operas be recognised in the grand opera of the present day, but French dramatic music, spite of many transformations, betrays its relationship with the early masters in many

II. B

peculiarities of melody, rhythm and harmony; a sure proof that national feeling lies at the root of the traditions.

The well-wishers of the national French opera were right in settling their disputes about Lully and Rameau by the recognition of them both ; for both alike were threatened by a formidable irruption of Italian taste, which now so completely governed the remainder of Europe that France could not fail to be in some measure affected by it. In August, 1752, a company of Italian singers came to Paris under the direction of a certain Bambini, and having received permission to represent comic operas (intermezzi) in the hall of the Grand Opéra, were called "Les Bouffons."[9] Their first representation of Pergolese's "Serva Padrona" was a failure, but subsequently it was applauded with enthusiasm. The chief singers of the company, Manelli and Anna Tonelli, were highly esteemed both for their singing and acting, although they did not reach to the highest level of Italian opera; the others were indifferent.[10] But they were Italian throats, Italian ways of singing and acting which lent all their powers to the interpretation of opera buffa, with its polished, pleasing form, simply and easily grasped harmonies, and sustained melodies. They found in Paris an appreciative audience, and very soon even the Parisian orchestra, where the conductor beat time audibly,[11] while the Italian conductor only directed from the clavier, was described, in comparison to the Italian, as a company of uneducated musicians whose great aim was to make as much noise as possible. The supporters of the national school of music naturally took up arms against the

---

[9] Hiller, Wöch. Nachr., 1770, p. 331. Schelle, N. Ztschr. f. Mus., LVII., p. 211; LVIII., p. 119.

[10] According to Castil-Blaze (L'Opéra Italien, p. 144), the operas produced by the Bouffons were, "La Serva Padrona," by Pergolese; "Il Giocatore," by Orlandini: "Il Maestro di Musica," by Al. Scarlatti; "La Finta Cameriera," by Atella; "La Donna Superba," by Rinaldo da Capua; "La Scaltra Governatrice," by Cocchi; "Il Cinese Rimpatriato," by Selletti; "La Zingara," by Rinaldo da Capua; "Gli Artigiani Arrichiti," by Latilla; "Il Paratajo," by Jomelli; "Bertoldo in Corte," by Ciampi; "I Viaggiatori," by Leo.

[11] The Italian opera was conducted from the pianoforte only, while in the French opera time was beaten audibly with a stick. Cf. Grétry, Mém., I., p. 39.

Italian enthusiasts, and so arose the well-known struggle between the "coin du roi" (nationalists) and the "coin de la reine" (Italians).[12]

Grimm, who always manifested great interest in musical matters, had become acquainted with Italian opera in Germany, and afterwards in Paris, where he took up his abode in 1749; his intercourse with Rousseau and other sympathetic friends increased his partiality for it. His burlesque of "Le Petit Prophète de Boehmischbroda" (1753), which foretold in the biblical prophetic style the downfall of good taste if Paris were not converted to Italian music,[13] proved a powerful ally to Italian music; he was joined by Diderot, who, like all the encyclopedists, was personally antagonistic to Rameau on account of his attack on the "Encyclopédie."[14] Jean Jacques Rousseau, who in his "Devin du Village" had shown the delighted public how far the treasures of the Italian opera could be turned to good account in the French (Vol. I., p. 87 et seq.), threw all the weight of his influence into the scale of the Bouffonists; not content with mercilessly exposing the shortcomings of the French opera, he undertook to prove that the French language was unfitted for composition, and French music altogether an impossibility.[15] The enraged musicians threatened to punish this daring outrage on the nation[16] with horsewhipping, assassination, or even the Bastille; but a flood of angry discussion was all that actually resulted.[17] Those, however, whose interests were

---

[12] The heads of the parties had their regular places below the box of the King and Queen.

[13] It was republished (Corr. Litt., XV., p. 315,) and translated into German (N. Ztschr. f. Mus., IV., p. 63, where it is wrongly ascribed to Rousseau). Grimm speaks of its extraordinary success to Gottsched, and Frau Gottsched speaks of an imitation of it directed against Weisse's operetta, "Der Teufel ist los" (Danzel Gottsched, p. 350).

[14] The account which he gives to Rameau's nephew of his uncle and Italian music is graphic enough (Goethe, XXIII., p. 208).

[15] This was in the well-known Lettre sur la Musique Française (1753), to which the Lettre d'un symphoniste de l'Académie Royale de Musique à ses camarades de l'orchestre (1753) was a witty after-piece.

[16] Grétry, Mém., I., p. 279.

[17] Rousseau, Confessions l., VIII. Grimm, Corr. Litt., I., p. 92. Fétis, Curios. Hist. de la Mus., p. 107.

attacked, especially the proprietors and singers of the opera-house, took such measures as obliged the Italian singers to quit Paris in March, 1754.[18]

It may well be wondered at that men like Rousseau[19] and Diderot,[20] who upheld simplicity and nature as the true canons of art, should have evinced a preference for Italian music. For though doubtless the Italian style was grounded originally on the nature of music, it had already become conventional, and far removed from what the philosophers called natural. At the same time it must be remembered that their partiality always turned in the direction of opera buffa, which sought from its commencement to free itself from the conventional restraint of opera seria (Vol. I., p. 203). Then, too, the musical element, as distinguished from the poetical or dramatic, had always been the foundation of Italian opera, and an opposition directed against the French opera, with its poetical and dramatic proclivities, would be sure to uphold the purely musical development of the Italians, even though the exaggerations into which it was carried might be displeasing to the philosophers.

The influence of the Bouffons survived their departure. The Comédie Italienne (aux Italiens) produced Italian comedies in masquerade, French comedies, and parodies of operas, the charm of which consisted mainly in their vocal parts, on which account they were called opéras comiques.[21] A dangerous rival to the Comédie Italienne was the Théâtre de la Foire, whose representations took place originally on

---

[18] Grimm, Corr. Litt., I., p. 114.

[19] Rousseau had apparently a natural musical talent, which was quickened by Italian music; his logical reflections sometimes led him into error, but he remained accessible to new musical impressions, even when they contradicted his expressed opinions.

[20] Diderot appears to have had some musical taste, but not much cultivation, and in this respect Grimm had some influence upon his opinions, as he certainly had upon Grimm's in more important matters. The article " Poème lyrique" in the Encyclopédie (publ. Corr. Litt., XV., p. 349), is a curious mixture of Italian taste, and of reflections after Diderot's manner: the views it upholds are often warped and superficial.

[21] Grimm, Corr. Litt., VI., p. 229. The parodies are collected in Les Parodies du Nouveau Théâtre Italien (Paris, 1738, I.-IV.). Supplément aux Parodies (Paris, 1763, I. III.).

the Feasts of St. Germain, St. Laurent, and St. Ovide. The two companies were always inimical, and the "Comédiens de la Foire" were from time to time suppressed by their stronger rival,[22] but always revived, until at last in 1762 the two companies were amalgamated.[23] In this soil was planted opera buffa, and, favoured by circumstances, it grew into a great national institution.[24] Translations and adaptations of favourite Italian operas satisfied the public at first, and were decried by the Bouffonists as travesties of the original.[25] But very soon, especially after the brilliant success of Vade's "Les Troqueurs" in 1753, a new school of composers sought to reconcile the excellencies of the Italian music, especially in singing, with the exigencies of the national taste. It was difficult at first to break loose from the defined outline and simple design of the intermezzi, but gradually the French taste became apparent in the greater connection and interest of the plot, and the delicacy and wit of the composition. The lively interest of the public induced poets of talent, such as Favart, Sedaine, and Marmontel, to devote themselves to operatic writing, and the French comic opera soon surpassed the opera buffa, from a dramatic as well as a musical point of view. These various impulses were all the more lasting since they were founded on the national character.[26]

Egidio Romoaldo Duni (1709-1775), born and educated in Naples, having made his reputation on the Italian stage, was led by his connection with the court at Parma, which was French in manners and in taste, to compose French operettas, as, for instance, "Ninette à la Cour." The applause with which they were received induced him to go to Paris in 1757, where he made an exceptionally favourable *début* with the "Peintre Amoureux," and during the next

---

[22] Favart, Mém., I., p. XVII.

[23] Favart, Mém., I., pp. 203, 214, 228, 233.

[24] [D'Orville] Histoire de l'Opéra Bouffon (Amst., 1760). [Desboulmiers] Histoire du Théâtre de l'Opéra-Comique (Paris, 1769, I., II.). Fétis, Curios. Hist. de la Mus., p. 342. Castil-Blaze, Acad. Imp. de la Mus., I., p. 216.

[25] Grimm, Corr. Litt., VII., p. 289.

[26] Goldoni concedes the superiority of the opéra-comique over the Italian buffa (Mém., II., p. 227).

thirteen years produced a succession of comic operas, the easy style and simple form of which secured them both the favour of the public and the imitation of untrained French composers.[27]

Duni was followed by Pierre Alex. Monsigny (1729-1817),[28] a dilettante, who was so excited by the performances of the Bouffons that he applied himself to the study of music, and at once began to compose operas. In 1759 he put his first opera, " Les Aveux Indiscrets," on the stage, and this was rapidly succeeded by others. Sedaine was so interested in Monsigny that he intrusted all his operatic librettos to him.[29] A wider sphere was opened to him with the three-act opera, " Le Roi et le Fermier," which was the commencement of the most brilliant success. It must be allowed that the co-öperation of a poet to whom even Grimm allows all the qualities of a good librettist[30] was an important element in this success; but Monsigny's work was quite on a level with that of his collaborateur. His music expresses with instinctive truth the most amiable side of the French character. Monsigny not only had at his command a wealth of pleasing sympathetic melodies, but possessed as decided a talent for pathos as for light comedy, and a sure perception of dramatic effect, combined with life, delicacy, and grace. His natural feeling for beauty of form concealed the want of thorough artistic training,[31] and his operas were universally admired, some of them, such as " Le Déserteur,"[32] acquiring more extended fame.

---

[27] Grimm, Corr. Litt., IV., p. 164; VII., p. 126. After 1765 he thought his style " un peu vieux et faible, mais ailleurs plein de finesse, de charme, de grace, et de vérité. C'est toujours malgré sa faiblesse l'homme chez lequel nos jeunes compositeurs devraient aller à l'école" (Corr. Litt., IV., p. 414). He afterwards exhorts Philidor and Grétry to yield the field to him with honour (Corr. Litt., V., pp. 140, 369; VI., p. 63).

[28] A. Adam, Derniers Souvenirs d'un Musicien, p. 107.

[29] Grimm, Corr. Litt., VI., p. 61.

[30] Grimm, Corr. Litt., III., p. 136.

[31] Grimm judged him so severely (Corr. inéd., p. 219; cf. Corr. Litt., III., p. 136; VI., p. 208; IX., p. 463); that one suspects personal dislike. Madame de Genlis rightly protested against his severity (Mém., II., p. 22).

[32] Grimm, even in this case, ascribed all the merit to the poet (Corr. Litt., VI., pp. 197, 206); Madame de Genlis, on the contrary, maintained that Monsigny's music caused one to overlook the improbabilities of the piece (Mém., II., p. 21).

A better theoretical musician was Franç. André (Danican) Philidor (1727-1795), who enjoyed the reputation of extraordinary genius as a chess-player before appearing as a composer with his first opera, "Blaise le Savetier," in 1759.[83] His fame as a musician was soon established, and he ruled the comic stage with Duni and Monsigny until Grétry took possession of it. He was reproached with justice for too great a display of musical scholarship, and for making his accompaniments too prominent.[84] He had more force and energy than Monsigny, with greater power of passionate expression, but his fun is coarser, and he is inferior in grace and tenderness. He finally abandoned music, partly from disinclination to enter into rivalry with Grétry, and partly from his passion for chess.

It was characteristic that comic opera, the outcome of vaudeville and chanson, should have been nursed in its infancy by composers like Duni, who had no pretensions to great genius, Monsigny, who was half a dilettante, and Philidor, who only composed music as a pastime. André Ern. Grétry, on the contrary (1741-1813), threw himself into the pursuit with all his powers, and with zealous ardour. He it was who perfected the comic opera, making it, what it still remains, the representative of the French national character in the province of dramatic music. As a boy, he had delighted in the performances of Italian opera singers in his native town of Liège, and as a youth he had been in Rome during the most brilliant part of Piccinni's career, had studied there for several years, and at last produced an intermezzo, " Le Vindemiatrici," which was well received, and gained even Piccinni's approval. In Paris, although Monsigny and Philidor received him kindly, he had to contend with difficulties ; but

---

[83] G. Allen, Life of Philidor (Philadelphia, 1863). At first Grimm thought his music no better than other French music (Corr. Litt., II., p. 346 ; III., p. 89) ; after 1764 he notes his increasing progress (III., p. 401 ; IV., p. 200), and praises him highly in 1768 (VI., p. 14). He was accused of stealing from Italian masters, but Grimm retorted that it required great talent to steal in such a way (V., p. 25 ; VI., p. 145). Later on Grimm considered that Philidor inclined too much to Gluck's manner (IX., p. 378 ; X., p. 358), and finally he declared that Philidor had grown feeble (XII., p. 468 ; XIII., p. 137).

[84] Tagebuch der Mannh. Schaub., I., p. 264.

after the complete success of his opera "Le Huron," in
1768,[85] even his remarkable fertility in production could hardly
satisfy the demands of the public for his works. Marmontel,
Sedaine, and other poets offered him libretti which were in
themselves pledges of success. The idea that dramatic
poetry should represent human nature in its naked reality,
which had emanated from the encyclopedists, found its reali-
sation in the drama of common life, and had considerable
influence on the development of the comic opera.

The strict line of demarcation between opera seria and
buffa did not exist in Paris. The effort to give more dramatic
interest and freer scope to operatic music led to the por-
trayal of the deeper and noble emotions, and opera approached
more and more nearly to serious comedy in plot, situations,
and psychological intention. Merriment gradually ceased to
be the predominating element, and became nothing more
than a flavouring thrown in; it was replaced by that mixture
of seriousness and playfulness which, in opposition to the
former prohibition of any amalgamation of different styles,
was now considered as the true expression of music.[86]
A characteristic distinction between comic and serious
opera in France was the adoption by the former of spoken
dialogue instead of recitative.[87] Any attempt to imitate the
free, declamatory recitative of the Italians would have been
thought too daring, and was perhaps actually prohibited by
the privileges of the Grand-Opéra. But in renouncing recitative, the dialogue gained the freedom of witty and sparkling
conversation, without which the French cannot exist; and
this note, once struck, soon regulated the whole character of

---

[85] Marmontel relates the affair more circumstantially (Mém., IX.; Œuvr.,
II., p. 72).

[86] Grimm discusses this question after the manner of Diderot, on the
production of "Le Déserteur," the first comic opera of the kind (Corr. Litt., VI.,
p. 212). Madame du Deffand thought the exhibition of passion in "Le
Déserteur" of very doubtful propriety (Corr. inéd., I., p. 175).

[87] Grimm condemns the "barbarous fashion" of mixing spoken dialogue and
song in the comic opera, and asserts that there can be no great composers in
France until real recitative is made use of (Corr. Litt., IV., p. 166; VI.,
pp. 120, 209).

operatic music, which, elevated as it may be, nevertheless starts from the idea of a conversation.

No one could be better fitted than Grétry for the development of such a style as this.[88] His was a pliant and amiable nature, but not a great one. He was excitable and susceptible to any emotion, but without depth; his wit was delicate and versatile, and he possessed the power of giving it the most striking and appropriate expression. He was determined that his music should always faithfully render some definite emotion, even to the minutest detail of the dramatic situation and characters. He held that a composer could only attain this end by working himself up into a pitch of intense excitement,[89] and living for the time in the drama that was under his hands.[40] The actual means which he employed was song, that is, melody. He learnt the art of tuneful song from the Italians,[41] and made its expressiveness depend upon intonation in delivery, which it is the composer's part to suggest and control.[42] He laid great stress upon true and strongly accentuated declamation,[43] which he had studied under good actors.[44] This lent a liveliness and piquancy to his musical style,[45] and rendered it essentially French.[46]

---

[88] He has given a detailed account of his education, of the suggestions for his works and of his views on dramatic music in his Mémoires ou Essais sur la Musique (Paris, 1789; Brussels 1829, I.-III.). The naïveté of intense vanity is apparent everywhere. His opinions show some power of observation, but are for the most part trivial and arbitrary.

[89] He describes his way of working to the celebrated physician Tronchin (Mém., I., p. 21): "Je lis, je relis vingt fois les paroles que je veux peindre avec des sons; il me faut plusieurs jours pour échauffer ma tête; enfin je perds l'appétit, mes yeux s'enflamment, l'imagination se monte, alors je fais un opéra en trois semaines ou un mois." He maintains that this excitement is more likely to lead a composer aright than attention to rules (I., pp. 168, 204).

[40] Prince Henry of Prussia paid him the most appropriate compliment in the words: "Vous avez le courage d'oublier que vous êtes musicien pour être poète" (Mém., I., p. 121, cf., p. 346).

[41] Mém., I., p. 112.

[42] Mém., I., pp. 141, 238 ; III., p. 144.

[43] Mém., I., p. 169.

[44] Mém., I., pp. 146, 170.

[45] Mém., I., p. 231.

[46] He declared the French language to be the one best suited to music (I., p. 400), although he does not conceal its difficulties (I., p. 134), and demonstrates that France is destined to be pre-eminent in music.

Grétry accomplished wonders for musical form, as far as grace and freshness, lively emotion and wit go, but his powers did not attain to anything truly great or important to art. The art of melodious expression was developed by him almost to the exclusion of other means, such as rich and well-chosen harmonies,[47] artistic accompaniments, and instrumental effects, all of which he treated as subordinate and unimportant.

He inveighs against the misuse of the instruments, especially of the wind instruments, which Gluck's example had introduced, even if he were not personally responsible for it;[48] but he recommends· the moderate use of them for characterisation,[49] and prides himself on his very questionable invention in his "Andromaque" of assigning special instruments to the recitatives of each principal character—Andromache, for instance, having always three flutes.[50] A saying of Grétry's, that in opera song is the statue, and the orchestra the pedestal, and that Mozart sometimes put the pedestal on the stage, has often been repeated. Whether this is authentic or not, the fact remains that Grétry's neglect of the orchestra was not altogether of set purpose, but that this branch of artistic education was unknown to him and interested him as little as did the minute elaboration and hard study which are dear to all first-rate musicians. His idea that a musician of genius may spoil his inventive powers by too much study is truly comical; what he tells of his own studies shows how shallow they were, and his productions are all of a piece. On the other hand he lays great weight upon reflection, which does not properly concern music at all; but his simplicity, which almost amounted to barrenness, served to heighten his truly excellent qualities, and to make him the popular idol he was. It is quite conceivable that the encyclopedists, who were the champions of Italian music, should have seen in him the man who united beauty and melody with Italian truth and characteristic expression. Diderot wrote unde:

---

[47] Mém., I., p. 212; cf. pp. 224, 260.
[48] Mém., I., p. 339; II., p. 45.
[49] Mém., I., pp. 237, 375.
[50] Mém., I., p. 356.

Grétry's portrait the motto: "Irritat, mulcet, falsis terroribus implet, ut magus ";[51] Rousseau thanked him for having reopened his heart to emotion by his music;[52] Grimm, who had received him with approbation from the first,[53] declared during the heat of the struggle between Gluckists and Piccinnists that connoisseurs and others were all agreed that no composer had succeeded like Grétry in fitting Italian melody to the French language, and in satisfying the national taste for wit and delicacy.[54] Suard and Arnaud, Gluck's supporters, stood by Grétry,[55] as well as Marmontel, who was opposed to Gluck.[56] And with what enthusiasm the public received his operas! Many of them—to mention only "Zemire" and "Azor"—made their way throughout Europe, and had unquestionably much influence on the formation of musical taste.

While comic opera was thus flourishing more and more richly and abundantly, the grand opera was confined almost exclusively to Lully and Rameau; it might almost seem that it had reached its limits, and that the interest of the public was henceforth to be centred on comic opera.[57] But fresh trials awaited the grand opera. Doubtless the light breezes which sprang from the reformed comic opera were precursors of the coming storm; but the actual impulse to it was not given in Paris itself.

Christ. Wilh. Gluck (1714-1787), after doing good service

---

[51] Mém., II., p. 10. He sometimes gave him good advice (I., p. 215) and Grétry embraced his views (III., p. 377).

[52] Grétry, Mém., I., p. 270; cf. II., p. 331.

[53] Grimm says, after the performance of "Le Huron" (Corr. Litt., VI., p. 34): "M. Grétry est un jeune homme qui fait ici son coup d'essai; mais ce coup d'essai est le chef-d'œuvre d'un maître, qui élève l'auteur sans contradiction au premier rang." His praise of the "Lucile" (VI., p. 122) and the "Tableau parlant" (VI., p. 251) was equally strong, and he accompanied it with a respectful and appreciative criticism.

[54] Grimm, Corr. Litt., X., p. 228.

[55] Grétry, Mém., I., p. 150.

[56] He himself examines the grounds on which his music has become naturalised in France, "sans me faire des partisans enthousiastes et sans exciter des ces disputes puériles, telles que nous en avons vu (Mém., I., p. 169).

[57] It is almost comical to observe the pertinacity with which the Grand-Opéra brought out its old pieces, to be as pertinaciously attacked by Grimm.

to Italian opera in Italy and London, went to Vienna in
1748, and there wrote, partly for the Prince of Hildburghausen, partly and chiefly for the imperial court, a succession of Italian operas of no very striking originality. It was
precisely the time when the traditional forms were becoming
more and more conventional formulas, and when the vocal
art was demanding the sacrifice of simplicity, nature, and
truth to the whim of each virtuoso. The decadence of operatic music, which Metastasio bitterly laments (Vol. I., p. 163),
inspired Gluck with the desire to lead it back to its first
principles. He was a man of earnest thougnt and strong
will. The tendency of German literature to give dignity
and importance to poetry did not pass by him unnoticed,
and he was a warm admirer of Klopstock, whose odes he
set to music.[58] The efforts then being made to raise the
German stage in Vienna had an influence on him, and his
own first attempts at reformation were greeted with loud
applause by Sonnenfels.

Gluck has professed his principles of dramatic composition
in the well-known dedication to his "Alceste." He declares
his opposition to the abuses introduced by the vanity of
singers and the servility of composers, by which the most
beautiful and stately drama becomes the most tiresome ; he
refused to interrupt the action at a wrong time by a ritornello, to sacrifice expression to a run or a cadenza, to neglect
the second part of a song when the situation demands that
peculiar stress shall be laid on it, in obedience to the custom
which requires the fourfold repetition of the words of the first
part, or to give an ending to the song against the sense of
the text ; his overtures were to be characteristic of the drama
which was to follow, and to prepare the minds of the spectators for it. His fundamental law of operatic music was
its due subordination to the words, so that every turn in the
action should be suitably expressed, without any superfluous
adornment, just as colour gives life and expression to a

---

[58] A collection of Klopstock's odes, set to music by Gluck has often been
published ; he had the " Herrmannsschlacht" ready in his head, according to his
habit, but it was never written out. For Gluck's intercourse with Klopstock in
Karlsruhe, see Strauss, Kl. Schr., p. 42.

sketch. He professed his highest aim to be simple beauty;[59] he condemned all difficulties which hinder clearness, all novelties which do not proceed from the necessities of the situation; he set aside all rule in order to obtain true effects.

There can hardly be a doubt as to the justice of these principles in general, and we are only concerned with the result of their adoption on musical progress.[60] Our remarks on a style of music which professes itself the handmaid of poetry, and is content with giving the fittest expression to verse, must be prefaced by some notice of the poets who supplied the verse.

Ranieri de' Calsabigi came to Vienna in 1761, after making himself known by an edition of Metastasio's works, with an æsthetic introduction proving their perfection as tragedies and operas; he had also written several libretti for operas and cantatas. He had formed an idea that music fitted for dramatic poetry must approach as nearly as possible to natural, ener- getic declamation; for since declamation was only unperfected music, dramatic song could only be elaborated declamation enriched by the harmonies of the accompaniment. The poetry for such music must be intense, forcible, passionate, moving, and harmonious, and it could not fail of its result. Full of this idea he wrote "Orfeo," and submitted it to Count Durazzo; the latter wished it to be put on the stage, and recommended Gluck as the composer who could best carry out the intentions of the poet. Calsàbigi declaimed his "Orfeo" repeatedly before Gluck, and noted his decla- mation in the text-book with signs which he illustrated by remarks.[61] Gluck, while giving full justice to the impulse

---

[59] It is worthy of note how certain intellectual currents, running through an age, take simultaneous effect in different spheres. The tendency to individuality in art, to truth and nature, which was due to the encyclopedists, made itself manifest side by side with the principle of simple beauty which Winckelmann laid down as characteristic of ancient art.

[60] Planelli, Dell' Opera in Musica (Neap., 1772), p. 148, approves of Gluck's principles, and the latter praises Planelli's performance of "Alceste"; Vinc. Manfredini (Regole Arm., p. 163) takes much exception to it.

[61] Schelle has (N. Ztschr. f. Mus., LIX., p. 42) published Calsabigi's letter (Mercure de France, Aug. 21, 1784), in which the latter, who considered himself neglected, represents his relations with Gluck.

which he had received from his poet,[62] could only partially
yield to his whimsical exaggeration of declamatory music.
But Calsabigi's ideas accorded with his own so far as to
aid him in giving them clearness and precision.

Gluck's demands on the musical drama went farther and
deeper than Calsabigi's comprehension and powers could
reach.[63]   But in the meantime he accepted what was offered
to him, and so were produced "Orfeo ed Euridice" (1762),
"Alceste" (1767), and "Paride ed Elena" (1769).

Not one of these works betrays any apprehension of true
tragedy, any trace of the antique mind; when the poet seeks
to escape from the rhetoric of Italian poetry, he draws not
from the Greek but from the French tragedy.   Nor do the
operas possess any proper dramatic interest.   Instead of
having a well-connected, symmetrical plot, they consist of a
succession of detached situations closely resembling each
other, which are too often repeated, while in details they are
too broad and rhetorical.   Gluck's principle of making music
the simple exponent of the poet's words was calculated to
give them dignity and influence.   Gluck possessed not only
boldness and energy united with intellectual acuteness; he
had, what is a rare quality at all times, a deep perception of
true grandeur. But although Calsabigi strove to simplify his
plots and to excite the deeper and more powerful emotions of
his audience, of *greatness* there was no trace in his librettos.
Gluck, perceiving the latent capabilities which the poet had
failed to develop, brought them out, as it were, instinctively,
and while he believed himself to be following the poet, he
was in reality himself creating all that was great and new
in the work.   His fame will be immortal, and rests upon the
stately breadth of his designs, upon the simple truth of his
representations—in short, upon the greatness of his artistic
genius.   His weakness consisted in his one-sided tendency

---

[62] Mém. pour servir a l'Hist. de la révolution opérée dans la Musique par
Gluck, p. 8.

[63] Calsabigi retracted his opinion on the opera in the letter prefixed to his
"Elfrida" in 1794. At that time he believed in Paesiello as the true philosophical
composer.

to characterisation, a tendency in no way identical with those qualities which made his reputation.

Gluck does not abandon any of the accepted forms in his Italian operas; he rather, in many respects, revives older traditions. His strict treatment of the aria, the simplicity of his melodies, and the moderation of his adornments, together with his careful recitative, and especially his correct expression, were certainly variations on the then ruling taste, but not innovations on the earlier method. But in his desire to replace by accurate musical characterisation the ear-flattering artificial degeneration of operatic singing, he made use of stronger means than had hitherto been known. His harmonies in especial are not only more important and interesting in themselves, but they are used of set purpose for dramatic characterisation. In a similar manner the orchestra is made of higher use. The instruments are treated according to their individualities, not as combining to a purely musical effect, but as giving by their tone-colouring definite expression to a variety of moods; light and shade are carefully adjusted, and much lively execution is allotted to the orchestra. The effect is still further heightened by the frequent use of the chorus, which is intricately treated, and so becomes a powerful factor in the musical characterisation.

Gluck extended his care to the details of scenery, to marches and dances; everything was to be in accordance with and characteristic of the situation. Here he had been preceded by Jean George Noverre (1727-1810) who, in his "Lettres sur la Danse et sur les Ballets" in 1760, strove for a reformation in the ballet on the same principles which Gluck employed for the opera. He condemned stereotyped forms of set dances, and demanded a plot for the ballet; expression should be the task of the dancer, with nature for his model, and the ballet-master should be both poet and painter. The ballets which he produced upon these principles at Stuttgart until 1764, then at Vienna, and after 1776 at Paris, were finished productions of a very pure taste, and effected a complete revolution in the art of dancing.

Gluck laid great stress upon recitative. He almost entirely abandoned the customary plain recitative, and used accom-

panied recitative as most fitting for the dignified language
of musical drama. Truth and power of expression are combined with a wealth of delicate and characteristic detail, and
Gluck rarely falls into the error of destroying the impression
of the whole by over-elaboration of detail; his nature was
averse to all forms of triviality.

But here again the one-sided application of Gluck's
principle becomes a weakness. As, according to his view,
music is to be subservient to the words, he follows with his
strongly marked recitative every turn of the dialogue, rhetorical and inflated as it might be, so that he not only employs
all the resources of his art on an unworthy object, but
fritters away the interest, on which he makes claims at once
too extensive and too rapidly succeeding one another. Musical
representation works immediately upon the mind and the
emotions, and can do this so much more strongly and vividly
than verse, which, however forcibly declaimed, appeals primarily to the intellect and the imagination, that a painful
incongruity occurs when music, with all her resources of
accurate characterisation, follows step by step the words of
the poet. It is therefore an error to suppose that the music
must always yield to the words; "as in a correct and well-
composed picture," adds Gluck, "the animation of the
colouring and of well-disposed light and shade vivifies the
forms without distorting the outlines." But the true painter
does not colour or illumine the naked outline; he considers
the form in its total effect as a piece of colouring, and it
exists for him only in this totality, which it is his object to
represent. The distinction between form and colour is only
technically important, and does not affect artistic perception
and production. In the same way the musician has something more to do with respect to the words of his text than
to colour given outlines. The conceptions which the poet
has formed, with the consciousness that they could only
attain complete independence by their combination with
music, must be absorbed by the musician, and reproduced in
the forms appointed by the nature of his art.

The exaggerations attending on all forms of opposition
and attempted reformation will not suffice to explain this

important error.[64] In dealing with so great and powerful a mind as Gluck's we must go deeper, and seek for the cause in his artistic organisation alone. An ardent admirer of Gluck has pronounced[65] that he was "more intellectually than musically great"; and certainly his musical productions do not correspond to the energy of his feelings and his will. His organisation fitted him for a reformer; as a creative artist his weakness became apparent. Gluck's works are not exactly one-sided; he expressed every variety of passion with equal skill, and he is never wanting in grace and charm; but he cannot be said to be rich or spontaneous. The lofty sentiment which he expresses in firm and comprehensive melodies is natural to him, but his exact and confined mode of composition is in part the result of his limited power of invention. The final cause of his desire to deprive music of her rights as an independent art in favour of verse lies in this weakness of his musical organisation. Closely connected with this is another phenomenon. It has been justly remarked[66] that Gluck's powers of characterisation extend only to soliloquies, that he failed to give proper expression to the dialogue proper, the contrast of voices and characters which, either in opposition or agreement, demonstrate their different natures; the polyphonal power of music, in its intellectual sense, remained undeveloped by Gluck. Failing in this, he failed in the highest object of music, by virtue of which alone she can make any claim to dramatic force. The fact that Gluck did not feel himself impelled to express his dramatic situations after this fashion is a proof that his imagination was more easily stirred poetically than musically. The narrow limits within which he occasionally confines even the music whose expression is intended to be purely lyrical may be traced to the same source. For Gluck did not think it necessary that action on the musical stage should maintain the same uninterrupted

---

[64] Berlioz rightly protests against Gluck's views (Voy. Mus., II., p. 269; À Travers Chants, p. 150). Cf. Hanslick, Vom Musikalisch-Schönen, p. 24.

[65] A. B. Marx, Musik des neunzehnten Jahrh., p. 82.

[66] Marx ibid., p. 183; he modified his opinion afterwards (Gluck u. d. Opera, II., p. 67.

II.

flow as in real life. He thought it far more important to give a well-sustained musical representation of some one mood or disposition; and the more broadly such moods were indicated by the poet the better he was pleased. It is true that even then he keeps within the limits of the strictest form, but he is fond of employing frequent repetition, particularly when the chorus and a solo voice are set in opposition to each other. This way of rendering a dramatic idea is often of powerful effect; but, considered from an artistic point of view, it should be subordinated to the design of a grandly conceived composition expanding into a living organism.

It cannot be denied, therefore, that Gluck failed in the working out of his subjects, and that he sometimes betrays a certain amount of weakness as well in the structure of his compositions as in their details. It was not for want of industry or care; it was that he did not feel the necessity for mastering this important side of musical representation, and the fact affords fresh testimony of the singularity of his musical organisation.

Gluck's first opera, "Orfeo ed Euridice," adheres most closely to the usual Italian style, and was indeed successfully performed in Italy.[67] Of action in this opera there is hardly any; the introduction of Cupid at the beginning and the end gives it the cold allegorical character of the then customary festival entertainments. The broadly represented situations in which Orpheus mourns for Eurydice, and charms by his music the demons of the lower world, form the main portions of the opera; and they are expressed with striking fidelity and fervour of sentiment, as well as with great force and beauty. The use which is made of the chorus, and the cultivation of the orchestra, betoken great and important advances on the older style. The opera was well received by connoisseurs, both in Vienna and Paris,[68] but it does not appear to have been regarded as the inauguration of a reformation

---

[67] It failed in Naples in 1774 (Galiani, Corr. inéd., II., p. 96).

[68] Count Durazzo had the score printed there; Favart tells him how highly Mondonville and Philidor thought of the opera. (Favart, Mém., II., pp. 67, 102, 180).

in music; indeed, during the next few years Gluck composed several Italian operas quite after the old fashion.

"Alceste," however, is an avowed attempt towards a reformation of dramatic music, and it manifests the settled purpose and the complete individuality of the master. The poet offers nothing but a succession of situations without any progressive action; the situations turn exclusively on the decision of Alceste, and are employed less as psychological developments of character than as opportunities for a rhetorical representation of certain frames of mind. The character of Hercules is omitted, and the task of deliverance is entrusted to Apollo as an apparition in the clouds; this destroys an effective contrast; and the two confidants retain a suspicious likeness to the *parte seconde* of Italian opera. But Gluck considered the separate scenes not only with regard to their fitness for musical treatment; he felt firm ground in which he might strike root. It testifies to his marvellous energy of mind that no weakness was discernible in the repetition of such closely allied situations, and that he had always new shades of expression and climacteric effects at his command. The connection with the forms of Italian opera is not by any means completely severed; an unprejudiced survey discovers numerous traces of this, and many of the main features of the composition are the results of the particular way in which Gluck made use of these forms.

The Vienna public received the opera with indifference, but the critics welcomed it eagerly as the inauguration of a new era. Unhappily the critics were not by any means competent judges; Sonnenfels and Riedel were not cultivated musical connoisseurs.[69] The opera scarcely reached a more extended circle; in Italy little notice was taken of it; Frederick the Great had several portions of it performed before him without finding any enjoyment in them;[70] North German

---

[69] Sonnenfels, Briefe üb. d. Wien. Schaubühne (Ges. Schr., V., p. 155; Hiller, Wöch. Nachr., 1768, p. 127). Riedel, Ueber die Musik des Ritter Gluck, p. IX.

[70] Allgem. deutsche Bibl., X., 2 p. 31. Nicolai, Reise, IV., p. 529. Reichardt relates (A. M. Z., XV., p. 612; Schletterer Reichardt, I., p. 264) that the King afterwards expressed himself in violent terms against Gluck. Cf. A. M. Z., III., p. 187.

critics, while doing full justice to the new work, raised objections to some of the essential points of Gluck's principles, as carried out in it.[71] Gluck remarks with some resentment, in his dedication to " Paride ed Elena," on the lukewarmness of the public, and the want of insight and justice on the part of the critics ; he goes on to blame the cowardice and stupidity of musicians, none of whom had ventured to follow his lead, and proudly declares his intention of maintaining his principles, to the correctness of which this new opera was to testify on altogether new grounds. This was an unlucky announcement, for " Paride ed Elena " gave no proof of Gluck's exceptional powers. The subject, a sufficiently poor one, is deprived of every vestige of interest by the interposition of Cupid in disguise between the lovers —a fiction which turns the whole drama into an absurdity. The meagre story is spun out into five acts, while to the love scenes, which are wanting in any true passion, independent choruses and dances are attached, calling for nothing beyond outward display. Gluck's genius for depicting the wider and deeper emotions found no task fitted to its powers, and the inclination to mere grace and superficiality was one altogether foreign to his nature. Beauties of detail do not suffice in the consideration of a work of art. The opera was a failure, however, and it does not appear to have been reproduced.

Perhaps Gluck would now have paused in his endeavours,[72] had not new prospects opened which seemed to promise good results. A Frenchman named Du Rollet, attached to the embassy at Vienna, and an enthusiast for poetry and music, asserted that the tendency of Gluck's principles was in essentials the same as that of French opera style. He therefore assured him that in Paris only would his reforma-

---

[71] Agricola criticised "Alceste" in the Allgem. deutschen Bibliothek (X., 2 p. 29, XIV., 1 p. 3; also in Forkel's Musik. Krit. Bibl., I., p. 174) in a pedantic, trivial spirit, but not ill-naturedly.

[72] Calsabigi says that he wrote the libretti for " Semiramide " and " Ipermnestra " on Gluck's commission, and they were afterwards taken as the foundation of Salieri's "Danaides " (Cramer, Magaz. d. Mus., I., p. 366; N. Ztschr, f. Mus. LIX., p. 42).

tion meet with approval, and urged that a true tragedy ought always to be the foundation of an opera. As an example, he suggested Racine's "Iphigénie en Aulide," and commissioned him to arrange it as an opera, and to take the preliminary steps for its production in Paris. Gluck accepted the proposal without hesitation.

The circumstances were, in fact, very favourable. The principal difficulty against which Gluck had hitherto to contend, viz., the deep-rooted partiality for Italian music and its accepted forms, did not exist in Paris ; for opera seria in its developed form had made as little way there as the display of fine execution, and even lovers of Italian music would have been loth to introduce its abuses and exaggerations of set purpose. French opera, on the contrary, in accordance with the genius of the nation, made its first principle dramatic and characteristic expression, which could only be attained by correct yet free treatment of musical forms, and by well-considered treatment of recitative. Choruses, too, which were for Gluck an important aid to climax and dramatic effect, were indispensable in French opera ; and since Rameau's time the orchestra had been successfully employed as a means of characteristic expression. But the French school had hitherto failed to combine dignity and beauty with their dramatic force and expression; and here Gluck's Italian training enabled him to supply the deficiency. As far as comic opera was concerned, Grétry had preceded him with similar efforts, and had accustomed the ear of the Parisians to the mingling of French and Italian music. But to carry out such a reformation in the grand opera required a man of commanding qualities; and such an one Gluck had proved himself to be.

The choice of subjects was a happy one. Racine's tragedy was known as a masterpiece to the whole nation, and unless the adaptation were very clumsily made, success for the poetic share of the opera was assured. The advance on earlier operas is a very decided one. An important event forms the centre of the plot, dramatic contrasts, passions, and characters, are effectively portrayed. It is true that the spirit of the age of Louis XIV. runs through it all;[73] we have Greeks in patches and powder, Monseigneur Achille and Princesse Iphigénie behave with becoming courtesy and gallantry, and even the artistic representation is made subordinate to the ceremonial. But Gluck had been trained among these impressions, the forms were not irksome to him, and the greatness of his artistic individuality is nowhere more plainly seen than in his power of exhibiting at momentous crises, the purely human and poetic emotions stripped of their outward disguise, and reflecting the ideal spirit of antique art by means of music in a way of which the poet had never dreamed. Gluck did not venture to depart from the national form of the versification; he was well aware that he must yield to the demands of French taste if he wished to influence the French on his main points. He not only strove to conform to external conditions, as, for instance, to the great extension of the ballet,[74] endeavouring to turn them to his own ends; he carefully studied the language, in order to declaim it and treat it musically in a way suitable to its character; he also eagerly studied the operas of his predecessors, Lully and Rameau, that he might adopt all that was truly and genuinely national in them. The influence of these studies may be recognised even in details; but Gluck turned to account whatever he adopted in a perfectly free and independent manner, and developed it still further. His most important innovation was the substitution of free Italian recitative, with the grand capabilities for characteristic expression given to it by Gluck himself, for the old "psalmodie." He changed throughout the fundamental character of the musical representation, and here he had no predecessors; for the treatment of the several parts of the composition after the Italian style, comic opera had, as we have seen, in some degree prepared the way. A

---

[73] This is correctly put forward by Marx (Musik des neunzehnten Jahrhunderts, p. 84).

[74] His admirable ballet music was slow in making its way in Paris; it was so confidently assumed that the French were the first masters in the world for ballet music, that a foreigner had to contend against much prejudice. La Harpe remarks that want of success in this respect was in Gluck's favour, for that his system, consistently carried out, would exclude ballet.

further advance, brought about by the greater vividness of
the dramatic impersonations, was the cultivation of ensemble
pieces; but this, as has been already remarked, is the
weakest side of Gluck's performances.

Although Gluck's "Iphigénie" might rightfully claim to
have perfected the French grand opera in its national sense,
yet it was a difficult undertaking to gain recognition for this
fact in Paris, and to produce there the work of a foreign, if
not of an unknown composer.   Du Rollet published a letter
to D'Auvergne, one of the directors of the Grand-Opéra, in the
" Mercure de France " (October, 1772), in which he acquaints
him of Gluck's wish to produce his " Iphigénie" in Paris.
He laid stress on Gluck's having preferred the French language and music to the Italian, and declared that his composition of Racine's masterpiece was altogether after the
French taste; he hoped in this way to gain the favour of
the public and the theatre management. As this met with no
response, Gluck himself published a letter in the " Mercure "
(February, 1773), in which, without undue submission, he
reiterates the wish; he wastes great praise on J. J. Rousseau,
who was destined to be the most determined opponent of
the French language and music.   At last Gluck succeeded
in gaining the interest of the Dauphiness, Marie Antoinette,
all difficulties were overcome, and in the autumn of 1773
Gluck went to Paris to put his opera in rehearsal.[75] Again
hindrances were thrown in his way which it required all the
force and vigour of his character to overcome.   The hardest
struggle was with the vocalists, male and female, and with
the orchestra; they must be attached to him at all costs.
But he was an implacable conductor,[76] and never gave way
before a storm.[77] After six months rehearsing, " Iphigénie "
was performed (February 14, 1774); the success of the first
performance was not brilliant, but the second quite confirmed the victory.   Gluck had succeeded (an important
point in Paris) in raising public expectation to a high pitch

---

[75] Interesting details of this visit are given by Frz. M. Rudhart, Gluck in
Paris (Munich, 1864).
[76] Burney, Reise, II., p. 253. Cf. Cramer's Magazin, 1783, p. 561.
[77] Madame de Genlis, Mém., II., p. 248.

beforehand, and he found zealous supporters among the journalists, especially the Abbé Arnaud; the opposition engendered by the enthusiastic partisanship of his admirers was in his favour in so far that it prevented the interest of the public from becoming faint.[78]

Opposition came, as might have been expected, from both sides;[79] the followers of Lully and Rameau would not grant any progress made, and saw in Gluck's innovations nothing but the harmful influence of Italian music,[80] while the partisans of the Italians looked upon Gluck's music as essentially identical with the "old French," and complained of the "tudesque" modifications of the Italian style.[81] As usual, neither party was satisfied with the concessions made to it, and still less would either acknowledge that its strong places had been overthrown. J. J. Rousseau alone acknowledged himself vanquished; and as he had previously done justice to Grétry's efforts, so he now extolled Gluck's music as being genuinely dramatic.[82] Not so Grimm. He was too well versed in Italian music not to perceive that if Gluck's ideas became prevalent, those forms which he held to be essential would soon be annihilated; Gluck's operas appeared to him a revival of the old French style, which would

---

[78] A number of pamphlets and newspaper articles of this and following years are collected in Mémoires pour servir à l'Histoire de la révolution opérée dans la musique par M. le Chev. Gluck (à Naples et à Paris, 1781), partly translated by Siegmeyer: Ueber Gluck und seine Werke (Berlin, 1823). Here again the dispute is chiefly carried on by men of literary rather than musical knowledge (Madame de Genlis, Mém., II., p. 250). The first favourable notices were at once translated by Riedel and published with an enthusiastic preface, Ueber die Musik des Ritters Gluck (Vienna 1775). This called forth Forkel's criticism (Musik. Krit. Bibl., I., p. 53). He was incapable of appreciating Gluck's true greatness, and as partial and philistine as other Berlin critics of that day; he was spiteful besides; but some of his remarks are true enough. The personal animosity which Forkel afterwards threw into his attacks is quite repulsive.

[79] Grimm, Corr. Litt., VIII., p. 320.

[80] Grimm, Corr. Litt., VIII., p. 321; IX., pp. 34, 350.

[81] Grimm, Corr. Litt., VIII., pp. 321, 427; IX., p. 350.

[82] Grimm, Corr. Litt., VIII., p. 321. Garat, Mém. sur M. Suard, II., p. 238. La Harpe, Corr. Litt., I., p. 86. Rudhart, Gluck in Paris, p. 10. A speaking testimony of his reverence for Gluck is the " Réponse sur un morceau de l'Orphée de M. le Chev. Gluck," and the unfinished " Observations sur l'Alceste Italien de M. le Chev. Gluck," where some striking observations are made.

only hinder or retard the triumph of the Italian. It is true that out of deference to public opinion, and to that of many of his friends and of Gluck's royal patroness, he does not express himself very positively on the subject, but his real views cannot be mistaken.[83]

With just discrimination the directors had declared that they would not risk appearing before the public with one of Gluck's operas ; if he would write six, they might have a chance of success. Gluck himself was aware that if he was to succeed in the long run, his " Iphigénie" must not be left long alone. He rapidly revised and elaborated "Orphée et Euridice," not at all to the advantage of the opera, in which he was induced, quite against his principles, to insert a long bravura aria by Bertoni.[84] It was performed on August 2, 1774, with great success,[85] and was followed on February 27, 1775, by a one-act opera, " L'Arbre Enchanté," and on August 11, 1775, by an opera in three acts, " La Cythère Assiégée," neither of which had any lasting effect. In order to insure a fresh and lasting success Gluck took in hand his "Alceste" anew. The text was thoroughly revised by Du Rollet, with the adoption of Rousseau's suggestions, especially in the second act ; Hercules is introduced again, but not very skilfully.[86] Gluck's revision was a very thorough one ; the old music was transposed, curtailed, or lengthened, the details altered, and new passages inserted,.generally with admirable discrimination.[87] Then, in order to put new works in direct competition with his old compositions, he undertook to set operas by Quinault to music unaltered, and chose " Roland" and "Armida."

While Gluck was engaged on these works in Vienna, the

---

[83] Grimm, Corr. Litt., VIII., pp. 78, 322. When he remarked that Gluck influenced other composers, such as Grétry, he turned the full sharpness of his criticism upon them.

[84] Berlioz, À Travers Chants, p. 127.

[85] Mdlle. de l'Espinasse, in Stendsal, Vie de Rossini, p. 607. As might be expected, Grimm bestowed his highest praise upon "Orphée" (Corr. Litt., VIII., p. 390).

[86] Winterfeld, Zur Gesch. heil. Tonk., II., p. 308.

[87] Berlioz, Voy. Mus., II., p. 279; À Travers Chants, p. 142. Schelle, N. Ztschr. f. Mus., LV., p. 205. LVI., p. 1.

supporters of Italian music, who were now convinced of the
possibility of procuring foreign composers for the grand
opera, sought on their side to oppose a rival to Gluck. Some
time previously Madame Dubarry had been induced by La
Borde's influence to obtain the presence in Paris of Piccinni,
the most esteemed of Italian composers.[88] The Neapolitan
ambassador, the Marquis Caraccioli, by his intellect and
position a powerful patron of the arts and sciences, had been
mainly instrumental in summoning Piccinni; and the young
Queen, Marie Antoinette, who saw no necessity for bending
her inclinations to party interests in the matter of music,
and who, like her brother the Emperor, was personally
attached to Italian music, gave her consent to Piccinni's
appointment.

Marmontel declared himself ready to adapt an opera by
Quinault for Piccinni, of whose music he announced himself
the champion.[89] When Gluck heard that the work selected
was the "Roland," on which he was already at work, he
published a letter ("Année Littéraire," 1776), in which he
bitterly complained of this affront, and violently assailed his
adversaries.

Open war was now declared between the critics of the
Gluckists and the Piccinnists, and carried on in pamphlets,
journal articles, and epigrams, with so much violence that
even the public were led into a partisanship more eager
than had ever before arisen from a question of art.[90] The
leaders of the Piccinnists were Marmontel and La Harpe,
while Gluck's faithful partisans were Arnaud and Suard, who
appeared as the Anonymous of Vaugirard.[91] Grimm took no
direct share in the contest; but his comments on it show him,

---

[88] Galiani, Corr. inéd., II., p. 106.

[89] Marmontel, Mém. Litt., IX.; Œuvr., II., p. 110.

[90] Grimm, Corr. Litt., IX., p. 348. Dorat describes very comically in an
Irishman's letter the party-fight in the pit (Coup d'Œil sur la Littér., I., p. 211).
Amusing incidents were not wanting. At one concert a song by Gluck was
announced; as it began the Piccinnists ostentatiously left the hall. and the
Gluckists applauded noisily; it afterwards appeared that the song was by
Jomelli (Grimm, Corr. Litt., X., p. 440).

[91] An account of the whole dispute from this side is given by Garat, Mém.
Hist. sur M. Suard, II., p. 231.

in spite of apparent impartiality, to have been decidedly on the side of Piccinni.

The first performance of "Alceste," on April 23, 1776, was a failure, and it only gained in public favour by slow degrees.[92] "Iphigénie," too, which was reproduced, was severely criticised. But this severity served but to increase public sympathy, and Gluck's operas drew full houses, and became more and more unmistakably popular.

Piccinni arrived in Paris quite at the end of 1776. He was welcomed by all the composers, Grétry alone failing to pay his respects to him. For this he was severely censured, since on first coming to Paris he had announced himself as a pupil of Piccinni, which he was not.[93] Strange and unknown in Paris, Piccinni took a great distaste to its harsh climate, its unaccustomed way of living. His ignorance of the French language isolated him and debarred him from any personal share in the contest of which he was the subject.

His easy-going and peace-loving temperament prevented his wishing to join in the fray, while for Gluck's passionate nature it was a satisfaction to give vent to angry vituperation in the public journals.

Marmontel relates how he had to instruct Piccinni in French by reading him his opera every day as a task, and translating what Piccinni had to compose.[94] Thus slowly proceeded the work of the dissatisfied maestro, and every day he doubted of its success more and more.[95]

Gluck began the rehearsals of his "Armide" in July, 1777, and it was performed on September 23. The opera, on which Gluck had built such confident hopes of success, was very coolly received.[96] Its failure was owing partly to

---

[92] Grimm, Corr. Litt., X., p. 34. Schelle, N. Ztschr. f. Mus., LV., p. 197.

[93] Grimm, Corr. Litt., IX., p. 352. Galiani, Corr. inéd., II., p. 292.

[94] Marmontel, Mém. Litt., IX.; Œuvr., II., p. 115. P. L. Ginguené, Not. sur Piccinni, p. 25.

[95] Grimm, Corr. Litt., IX., p. 352. Galiani, Corr. inéd., II., p. 291.

[96] To Marie Antoinette's question as to whether his opera, "Armida," was finished, and how he liked it, Gluck is said to have answered composedly: "Madame, il est bientôt fini, et vraiment ce sera superbe!" (Madame Campan, Mém., 7 p. 131.)

the dangerous rivalry of Lully, partly to the fact that the subject was not suited to his genius,[97] and partly also to the premonitory shadow of Piccinni's new work. Justice was not done to " Armide " until later.[98]

La Harpe attacked it bitterly, and Gluck, in a violent retort, called for the aid of the Anonymous of Vaugirard, which did not tarry. Then began the rehearsals of Piccinni's opera, and the storm of partisanship was let loose.[99] Piccinni was incapable of restraining it. While his friends espoused his cause with zeal, while Gluck himself sought to restrain the singers and the orchestra,[100] Piccinni looked sorrowfully to heaven and sighed, " Ah ! toutte va male, toutte !" Firmly convinced that the opera would be a failure, and resolved to return to Naples on the following day, he went to the first performance (January, 1778), consoling his family with the assurance that a cultivated nation like the French would do a composer no bodily harm, even if they did not admire his operas—and experienced a brilliant triumph.[101]

CHAPTER XIX.

PARIS, 1778.

SUCH was the condition of musical affairs at the time of Mozart's arrival in Paris. The successes on either side, and the violence of partisan controversy, had, as might have been expected, prevented any decisive conclusion of the dispute. We know now that Gluck remained master of the field, and that the influence of Lully and Rameau sinking henceforth into oblivion, Gluck determined the character of French opera in all its essential points as it still exists, in spite of its many Italian modifications. But at the time of

---

[97] Grimm, Corr. Litt., IX., p. 428.

[98] Grimm, Corr. Litt., IX., p. 469.

[99] Grimm gives a minute and amusing account of all this.

[100] So Grimm says. His friendliness towards Piccinni is confirmed by Galiani (Corr. inéd., II., p. 248), and Madame de Genlis (Mém., II., p. 248). Cf. Ginguené, Not. sur Piccinni, p. 45.

[101] Grimm, Corr. Litt., IX., p. 500; X., p. 23.

which we are speaking the Gluckists and Piccinnists were carrying on the warfare with greater bitterness than ever, and the old national party, although pushed into the background, was seeking to free itself from both influences.[1]

The interest of the public was more eagerly excited than ever, but, as usual, more for the sake of the literary scandal and personal animosity than with any love of art, and when audiences flocked to the opera they desired not to enjoy but to participate in what was going on.

This was an unfortunate state of things for a young composer whose object was to acquire an honourable position for himself; he must, in order to be heard at all, attach himself to one or other party, and so lose his independence, the only true foundation of excellence. To put an end to the dispute by forcing the combatants to acknowledge a success greater than that of either was at this juncture beyond the power of even a transcendent genius ; and Mozart brought nothing with him to Paris but his genius.

He had failed in obtaining an introduction to the Queen Marie Antoinette from Vienna, and access to the circle of the nobility was no easy matter. Mozart had little to expect from the support of his fellow-artists, for they were all ranged against each other, and had enough to do to fight their own battles. Gluck had left Paris when Mozart entered it ; he renewed his acquaintance with Piccinni, whom he had known in Italy (Vol. I., p. 111), and was polite in his greetings when he met him at the Concert Spirituel and elsewhere ; but there the intercourse ended. "I know my affairs, and he his, and that suffices " (July 9, 1778).

We find no traces of any acquaintance with Grétry, who never mentions Mozart in his "Mémoires." He was resigned to professional envy, and had already experienced his full share of it; but in Paris at that time the "gens de lettres " were the arbiters of taste and fashion. Pamphlets and critical articles, epigrams and *bon mots*, proceeding from

---

[1] [Goudard] Le Brigandage de la Musique Italienne (Amsterdam, 1780) is directed against Italian musicians, but includes in this category " Le Général Gluck et son Lieutenant-Général Piccinni et tous les autres noms en *ini*."

the literary circle, ruled public opinion, and a thorough
knowledge of music was, as a rule, the last requirement
thought of by those who strove to influence its progress.

It was a new world to Wolfgang, in which he would have
found it difficult to move successfully and uprightly, even if
he had gained access to its favour.

Grimm, who might have introduced him, was himself a
partisan, and esteemed only by his own party; besides
which, he could not fail soon to discover that Mozart was
the last man in the world for this kind of intercourse. Nevertheless, he received him very kindly, and sought to make
him known wherever he could; they were always quite of
accord in their opinions of French music. "Baron Grimm
and I," writes Mozart (April 5, 1778), "often pour out our
wrath over the music of the present day, but in private, be it
understood; in public, it is all 'bravo, bravissimo,' and clapping one's hands till the fingers burn." And in another letter
he says: "What annoys me is that the French have improved their taste just enough to enable them to listen to
good music. But their own is still very bad. Ay! upon my
word, but it is! and their singing! *oimè!* If they would
only let Italian songs alone, I could forgive their Frenchified
chirruping; but it is really unpardonable so to spoil good
music."

Mozart's outward circumstances were not pleasant. In
order to economise (for his mother found everything in
Paris half as dear again as elsewhere) they took a dark,
uncomfortable lodging, so small that Wolfgang could not get
his clavier into it. But their life was rendered considerably
more cheerful by the presence of their Mannheim friends.
"Wendling," writes the mother (April 5) (there is no
more talk of his irreligion), "has prepared Wolfgang's way
for him, and has now introduced him to all his friends. He
is a true benefactor, and M. von Grimm has promised him
to use all his influence, which is greater than Wendling's, to
make Wolfgang known." In Paris, too, Mozart became
better acquainted with Raaff, and learned to value him as
an artist and as a friend. This was greatly owing to the
interest Raaff took in the Weber family; he appreciated

Aloysia's talents, promised to give her lessons, and approved of Mozart's liking for her; this was all the greater consolation since he dared not speak openly on the subject to his father, although he did not attempt to conceal his correspondence with the Weber family. Nor could his wishes and feelings fail to be perceived when he wrote (July 3, 1778) :—

I have never been backward, and never will be. I will always use my powers to the uttermost. God can make all things good. I have something in my mind, for which I pray to God daily; if it is His Divine will it will come to pass; if not, I am content. I have at least done my best. If all goes well, and things turn out as I wish, then you must do your share, or the whole business will fall through; I trust to your kindness to do it. Do not attempt to discover my meaning, for the immediate favour I have to beg of you is to let me keep my ideas to myself until the right time comes.

He does not seem to have been very hopeful (March 29, 1778) :—

I am pretty well, thank God : but for the rest, I often scarcely know or care for anything ; I am quite indifferent, and take little pleasure in anything. What most supports and invigorates me is the thought that you, dear father, and my dear sister are safe and well, that I am an honest German; and that although I cannot always say what I like, I can always think what I like—which is the main point.

In a mood like this the encouragement of musical compatriots would be doubly grateful to him. This was freely bestowed on him by the ambassador from the Palatinate, Count von Sickingen, to whom Gemmingen and Cannabich had given him letters, and Raaff a personal introduction :—

He is a charming man, a passionate lover and true judge of music. I spent eight hours with him quite alone; we were at the clavier morning and afternoon, and up to ten o'clock in the evening, all the time making, praising, admiring, altering, discussing, and criticising nothing but music : he has about thirty operatic scores.

He maintained this acquaintance zealously, often dining with the Count, and spending the evening over his own compositions with so much interest that the time went without their knowing it (June 12, 1778).

The Mannheim friends were engaged for the Concert Spirituel, which had been founded in 1725. Anne Danican Philidor, elder brother to the composer already mentioned, was accorded the privilege, on payment of a fixed sum, of giving about four-and-twenty concerts in the course of the year, on festivals when there was no grand opera. They were given in a hall of the Tuileries, and consisted of instrumental music, and sacred or classical compositions for chorus or solo singing.[2] Wolfgang was introduced to the director, Jean le Gros (1739-1793), and at once received from him a commission, with which he acquaints his father (April 5, 1778) :—

The kapellmeister, Holzbauer, has sent a Miserere; but the Mannheim chorus being weak and bad, while here it is good and strong, his choruses make no effect; therefore M. le Gros has commissioned me to write other choruses. Holzbauer's introductory chorus remains; the first by me is "Quoniam iniquitatem meam ego," &c., allegro; the second, adagio, "Ecce enim in iniquitatibus"; then, allegro, "Ecce enim veritatem dilexisti," up to "ossa humiliata." Then an andante for soprano, tenor and bass soli, "Cor mundum crea"; and "Redde mihi lætitiam," allegro as far as "te convertentur." Then I have done a recitative for the basses, "Libera me de sanguinibus," because it is followed by a bass song by Holzbauer, "Domine, labia mea." In the same way, because "Sacrificium Deo, spiritus" is an andante tenor air for Raaff, with solo oboe and bassoon, I have added a little recitative, "Quoniam si voluisses," also with oboe and bassoon concertante: recitatives are very much in vogue here. "Benigne fac" up to "muri Jerusalem," andante moderato, chorus. Then "Tunc acceptabis" to "super altare tuum vitulos," allegro, tenor solo (Le Gros), and chorus together.[3] I must say I am glad I have finished this work, for it is confoundedly awkward when one is in a hurry with work and cannot write at home. But it is finished, thank God, and will, I think, make an effect. M. Gossec, whom you must know, told M. Le Gros, after seeing my first chorus, that it was charming, and would certainly tell in performance; that the words were well arranged, and admirably set to music. He is a good friend of mine, but a dry, reserved man.

That this scampering work (for Mozart was only a few

---

[2] Histoire du Théâtre de l'Opéra en France, I., p. 164. Fétis, Curios. Hist. de la Mus., p. 325. Burney gives a detailed account of a "Concert Spirituel" at which he was present in 1770 (Reise, I., p. 11).

[3] Nothing is known of this music, so far as I am aware; Mozart does not seem to have kept it himself, and therefore did not bring it to Salzburg.

days over it) should form his *début* before the French public caused his father great uneasiness; but it was uncalled for, for in his next letter Wolfgang informs him (March 1, 1778) :—

I must tell you, by the way, that my chorus work came to nothing. Holzbauer's Miserere is too long as it is, and did not please; besides which, they only performed two of my choruses instead of four, and left out the best. It did not much matter, for many people did not know that they were mine, and many more never heard of me. Notwithstanding, they were highly applauded at rehearsal, and, what is more important (for I do not think much of Parisian applause), I liked them myself.

Another work was occasioned by the presence of the Mannheim performers, with whom was associated the celebrated hornist, Joh. Punto (1748-1803), who in Mozart's opinion " played magnificently." Mozart set to work at a Sinfonie Concertante for flute (Wendling), oboe (Ramm), French horn (Punto), and bassoon (Ritter), which was to be performed at one of the concerts. But he was soon obliged to write to his father (May 1, 1778) :—

There is another " hickl-hackl " with the Sinfonie Concertante. I believe there is something behind, for I have my enemies here, as where have I not had them ? It is a good sign, however. I was obliged to write the symphony in great haste, worked hard at it, and thoroughly satisfied the four performers. Le Gros had it four days for copying, and I always found it lying in the same place. At last, the day but one before the concert, I did not find it; searched about among the music, and found it hidden away. I could do nothing but ask Le Gros, " *À propos*, have you given the Sinfonie Concertante to be copied ? " " No, I forgot it." Of course I could not order him to have it copied and played, so said nothing. The day it should have been performed I went to the concert; Ramm and Punto came up to me in a rage, and asked why my sinfonie concertante was not played. " I do not know; this is the first I have heard of it." Ramm was furious, and abused Le Gros in French, saying that it was unhandsome of him, &c. What annoyed me most in the whole affair was Le Gros not telling me a word about it, as if I was to know nothing of it. If he had only made an apology, that the time was too short, or anything; but no, not a word.[4] I think Cambini, an Italian

---

[4] This Sinfonie Concertante is lost beyond recovery. Mozart sold it to Le Gros, and kept no copy; he must have thought he could write it again from memory; but apparently cared the less to do so as there were no virtuosi in Salzburg able to perform the symphony.

II.   D

composer here, is at the bottom of it, for I was the innocent cause of his being extinguished on his first introduction to Le Gros. He has written some pretty quartets, one of which I had heard at Mannheim; I praised it to him, and played the beginning; Ritter, Ramm, and Punto were there, and they left me no peace, insisting that I should go on, and make up myself what I could not remember. So I did it, and Cambini was quite beside himself, and could not refrain from saying, " Questa è una gran testa!" But it must have been sorely against the grain with him.

The father was of the same opinion, and warned Wolfgang that Cambini would not be the only one who would seek to injure him; but he must not allow himself to be disconcerted (April 29, 1778). Wolfgang expressed himself with considerable dissatisfaction :—

If this were a place where the people had ears to hear, and a heart to feel, and just a little understanding and taste for music, I would laugh from my heart at all these things; but, as far as music is concerned, I am among a set of dolts and blockheads. How can it be otherwise? They are just the same in all their transactions, love-affairs, and passions. There is no place in the world like Paris. You must not think that I exaggerate in speaking so of the music here. Ask whom you will (only not a native Frenchman), and they will tell you the same. Well, I am here, and must make the best of it, for your sake. I shall thank the Almighty if I come out of it with unvitiated taste. I pray to God daily to give me grace to stand firm, and do honour to myself and the German nation, and that He will grant me success, so that I may make plenty of money, help you out of all your present troubles, and that we may meet once more, and all live happily together again.

Through the good offices of Grimm, Mozart was recommended to the Duc de Guines, who had been recalled from his post as Ambassador in London after his notorious lawsuit with secretary Tort[5] in 1776, and. stood high in favour with the Queen.[6] L. Mozart wrote (March 28, 1778) :[7]—

My dear Son,—I beg that you will do your best to gain the friendship of the Duc de Guines, and to keep well with him; I have frequently read in the papers of his high place in the royal favour; the Queen being now *enceinte*, there are sure to be grand festivities when the child is born; you may get something to do, and make your fortune; for in these cases everything depends upon the pleasure of the Queen.

---

[5] L. de Lomenie, Beaumarchais, II., p. 89.   Dutens, Mém., II., p. 59. Madame du Deffand, Lettr., III , p. 172, 297.

[6] Madame du Deffand, Lettr., IV., p. 107.

[7] The Dauphin was born on December 11, 1778.

The Duke was amusing and fond of music;[8] as Mozart himself says, he played the flute inimitably, and his daughter the harp magnificently.[9] He gave Mozart a commission to compose a concerto for flute and harp. These were exactly the two instruments which Mozart could not endure.[10] But this did not prevent his accomplishing his task to the perfect satisfaction of the Duke. The concerto (299 K.) is in C major, with accompaniments for a small orchestra, and consists of the usual three movements. In conformity with the nature of the instruments the character of the concerto is cheerful and graceful, and it is excellent of its kind. Each movement is well and compactly formed, and has an abundance of rich melody, enhanced in effect by the harmonic treatment, the varied character of the accompaniment, and the alternation of the solo instruments. The thematic treatment is only lightly sketched in so as to keep the interest alive; but in the middle movement of the first part the harmonic arrangement betrays a master-hand; at its close a fresh melody is introduced, as was then the rule, in order to excite the attention anew. Especially graceful and tender is the Andantino, accompanied only by a quartet. The solo instruments are brilliant without being particularly difficult; the orchestra is discreetly made use of to support the delicate solo instruments without interfering with their effect; but the easy setting *à jour* is elaborated in detail with great skill and decision, both as regards the sound effects and the passages and turns of the accompaniment.

Besides this, Mozart gave the Duke's daughter two hours' lessons in composition daily, for which generous payment might be expected. He describes the lessons minutely (May 14, 1778) :—

She has talent and even genius, but especially has she a marvellous memory : she knows two hundred pieces, and can play them all by heart.

---

[8] Madame de Genlis, Mém., I., p. 288.

[9] She married M. de Chartus (afterwards Duc de Castries) in the summer of 1778, with a dowry from the King, and died in childbirth (Madame du Deffand, Lettr., IV., p. 52).

[10] Jos. Frank narrates in his Reminiscences (Prutz, Deutsch. Mus., II., p. 28): " Once when we were talking of instruments, Mozart said that he detested the harp and the flute."

She is, however, very doubtful whether she has any talent for composition, particularly as regards ideas and imagination; but her father—
who, between ourselves, is a little infatuated about her—says she has
plenty of ideas, but is over-modest, and has too little confidence in herself. Well, we shall see. If she does not get any ideas or imagination
(at present she has absolutely none) it is all in vain, for, God knows, I
cannot give them to her. Her father has no intention of making her
into a great composer. "I do not wish her," says he, "to write operas,
concertos, songs, or symphonies, but only grand sonatas for her instrument and mine." To-day I gave her her fourth lesson, and, as far as
regards the rules of composition and exercises, I am fairly satisfied.
She has supplied a very good bass to the first minuet which I set her.
She is beginning now to write in three parts. She does it, but she gets
ennuyée. I cannot help it, for I cannot possibly take her farther. Even
if she had genius it would be too soon, and unhappily she has none—
everything must be done artificially. She has no ideas, and so nothing
comes of it. I have tried her in every sort of way. Among other things, it
came into my head to write down a very simple minuet, and to try if she
could write a variation on it. No; it was in vain. "Well," I thought,
"she does not know how to begin;" so I began to vary the first bar, and
told her to go on with it, and keep the same idea; and at last she managed
it. When that was done, I told her to begin something herself, only
the first part of a melody. She reflected for a quarter of an hour, but
nothing came of it. Then I wrote the first four bars of a minuet, and
said, "See what a donkey I am; I have begun a minuet, and cannot
even finish the first part. Be so kind as to do it for me." She thought
it was impossible. At last, after much trouble, something came to
light; and I was very glad of it. Then I made her complete the minuet
—only the first part, of course. I have given her nothing to do at home
but to alter my four bars, and make something out of them—to invent a
new beginning, even if the harmony is the same, so long as the melody
is altered. I shall see to-morrow what she has made of it.

The father was justly astonished at the demands made by
Wolfgang on the talent of his pupil, and on the earnestness
with which he threw himself into his task (May 28, 1778) :—

You write that you have just given Mdlle. de Guines her fourth lesson,
and you want her to write down her own ideas; do you think that
everybody has your genius ? It will come in time. She has a good
memory; let her *steal*, or more politely, *adapt ;* it does no harm at the
beginning, until courage comes. Your plan of variations is a good one,
only persevere. If M. le Duc sees anything, however small, by his
daughter, he will be delighted. It is really an excellent acquaintance.

But Wolfgang had not the art of cultivating such acquaintances any more than of giving lessons in composition to young ladies of no talent; he wrote later that she was thoroughly stupid and thoroughly lazy (July 9, 1778), and in conclusion the Duke offered him two louis-d'or, which he indignantly rejected.

He had some other pupils, and might have had more had not the distances in Paris been so great that his time was too much curtailed thereby; he complains (July 31, 1778) :—

It is no joke to give lessons here. You must not think that it is laziness; no! but it is quite against my nature, my way of life. You know that I, so to speak, live in music; that I am busy at it the whole day, planning, studying, considering. Lessons come in the way of this; I shall certainly have some hours free, but I need them rather for rest than for work.

Highly distasteful to him also were visits to people of rank, and attempts to gain their favour. He enumerates all the disagreeables of it (May 1, 1778) :—

You write that I should pay plenty of visits to make new acquaintances and renew old ones. It is really impossible. To go on foot takes too long and makes one too dirty, for Paris is inconceivably filthy; and to drive costs four or five livres a day, and all for nothing; the people pay compliments and nothing more; engage me for such or such a day, and then I play, and they say " Oh! c'est un prodige, c'est inconcevable, c'est étonnant!" and then adieu. I have already spent money enough in that way, and often uselessly, for the people have been out. No one can know the annoyance of it who is not here. Paris is very much altered; the French are not nearly so polite as they were fourteen years ago; they approach very near to rudeness now, and are dreadfully arrogant.

The example which he gives his father sufficiently justifies his complaints, and is as significant of the impertinence of the nobility towards artists as of Mozart's powerlessness to resent such behaviour :—

M. Grimm gave me a letter to Madame la Duchesse de Chabot,[11] and I went there. The purport of the letter was principally to recommend me

---

[11] The Duchesse de Chabot, daughter of Lord Stafford, mentioned as an acquaintance by Grimm and Madame Epinay (Galiani, Corr. inéd., II., p. 305).

to the Duchesse de Bourbon [12] (then in a convent),[13] and to bring me again
to her remembrance. A week passed without any notice taken; but, as
she had already commanded my presence in that time, I went. I was
left to wait half an hour in an icily cold, very large room, with no stove
or means of heating it. At last the Duchesse de Chabot came in,
and politely begged me to make allowances for the clavier, since she had
none in good order; would I try it? I said I should have been delighted
to play something, but that I could not feel my fingers for the cold, and
I begged her to allow me to go to a room where at least there was a
stove. " Oh, oui, monsieur; vous avez raison," was her only answer.
Then she sat down and began to draw for at least an hour with some other
gentlemen, who all sat round a great table. I had the honour of standing waiting this hour. The doors and windows were open; very soon,
not only my hands, but my feet and whole body were stiff with cold, and
my head began to ache. No one spoke to me, and I did not know what
to do for cold, headache, and fatigue. At last, to cut it short, I played
on the wretched, miserable pianoforte. The most vexatious part of all
was that Madame and all the gentlemen went on with their employment
without a moment's pause or notice, so that I played for the walls and
chairs. All these things put together were too much for my patience.
I began the Fischer variations, played the half, and got up. Then
followed no end of *éloges*. I said what was quite true, that I could do
myself no credit with such a clavier, and that I should be very pleased
to appoint another day when I could have a better clavier. But she did
not consent, and I was obliged to wait another half-hour, till her husband
came in.[14] But he sat down beside me, and listened with all attention;
and then I—I forgot cold, and headache, and annoyance, and played on
the wretched clavier as you know I can play when I am in a good
humour. Give me the best clavier in Europe, but with an audience who
do not or will not understand and feel with me when I play, and I lose
all pleasure in it. I told the whole affair to M. Grimm.

Wolfgang tells his father (May 14, 1778) of a prospect of
a settled position, in which, however, he was disappointed :—

Rudolph (the French horn-player) is in the royal service here, and
very friendly to me. He has offered me the place of organist at
Versailles, if I like to take it. It brings in 2,000 livres a year, but I
should have to live six months at Versailles, the other six where I

---

[12] She was the daughter of the Duke of Orleans, sister to the then Duc de
Chartres, the future Egalité. A short time previously a duel, of which she was
the occasion, between the Duc de Bourbon and the Comte d'Artois, had made
a great stir (Du Deffand, Lettr., IV., p. 28. Grimm, Corr. Litt., X., p. 1.)

[13] That is on his first visit to Paris. The Duchess entered a convent in her
fifteenth year, and remained there several years (Genlis, Mém., III., p. 84).

[14] Cf. Madame de Genlis, Mém., I., p. 289; II., p. 185.

chose. I must ask the advice of my friends, for 2,000 livres is no such great sum. It would be if it were in German coin, but not here; it makes 83 louis-d'or and 8 livres a year; that is, 915 florins 45 kreutzers of our money (a large sum), but only 333 dollars and 2 livres here, which is not much. It is dreadful how soon a dollar goes! I cannot be surprised at people thinking so little of a louis-d'or here, for it is very little; four dollars, or a louis-d'or, which is the same thing, are gone directly.

His father, who considered a settled position of such importance that a certain amount of concession should be made for it, advised .him to reflect well on the proposal, if indeed Rudolph (1730-1812), who had been a member of the band since 1763, had sufficient influence to bring it about (May 28, 1778) :—

You must not reject it at once. You must consider that the 83 louis-d'or are earned in six months; that you have half the year for other work; that it probably is a permanent post, whether you are ill or well; that you can give it up when you like; that you are *at Court, consequently* daily under the eyes of the King and Queen, and so much the nearer your fortune; that you may be promoted to one of the two kapell-meisters' places; that in time, if promotion is the rule, you may become clavier-master to the royal family, which would be a lucrative post; that there would be nothing to hinder your writing for the theatre, concert spirituel, &c., and printing music with dedications to your grand acquaintance among the ministers who frequent Versailles, especially in summer; that Versailles itself is a small town, or at all events, has many respectable inhabitants, among whom pupils would surely be found; and that, finally, this is the surest way to the favour and protection of the queen. Read this to the Baron von Grimm, and ask his opinion.

But Grimm took Wolfgang's view of the matter, expressed in his answer to his father (July 3, 1778) :—

My inclination has never turned towards Versailles; I took the advice of Baron Grimm, and others of my best friends, and they all thought with me. It is small pay. I should have to waste half the year in a place where nothing else could be earned, and where my talents would be buried. For to be in the royal service is to be forgotten in Paris— and then to be only organist! I should like a good post extremely, but nothing less than kapellmeister—and well paid.

Mozart's absorbing desire was to have an opportunity of distinguishing himself as a composer, above all things by an opera. There seemed a fair prospect of doing this soon after his arrival in Paris. He had renewed his acquaintance with Noverre (p. 145), who, after giving up the direction of the ballet at Vienna in 1775, had, through the Queen's influence, been appointed ballet-master to the Grand-Opéra in 1776.[15] He took such a liking for Mozart that he not only invited him to his table as often as he chose, but commissioned him to write an opera. He proposed as a good subject, "Alexander and Roxane," and set a librettist to work at the adaptation of it. The first act was ready at the beginning of April; and a month later Mozart was in hopes of receiving the whole text. It had then to be submitted to the approbation of the director of the Grand-Opéra, De Vismes; but this did not seem to offer any difficulty, Noverre's influence being powerful with the director.

As soon as L. Mozart heard of the prospect of an opera, he wrote (April 12, 1778) :—

I strongly advise you, before writing for the French stage, to hear their operas, and find what pleases them. In this way you will become quite a Frenchman, and I hope you will be specially careful to accustom yourself to the proper accent of the language.

And he continues to impress upon him (April 29, 1778) :—

Now that you tell me you are about to write an opera, follow my advice, and reflect that your whole reputation hangs on your first piece. Listen before you write, and study the national taste; listen to their operas, and examine them. I know your wonderful powers of imitation. Do not write hurriedly—no sensible composer does that. Study the words beforehand with Baron von Grimm and Noverre; make sketches, and let them hear them. It is always done: Voltaire reads his poems to his friends, hears their judgments, and follows their suggestions. Your honour and profit depend upon it; and as soon as we have money we will go to Italy again.

Wolfgang was aware of the difficulties which lay before him, especially with regard to the language and the vocalists, and expressed himself energetically on both points (July 9, 1778) :—

If I do get as far as writing an opera, I shall have trouble enough over it; that I do not mind, for I am used to it, if only this cursed French

---

[15] Grimm, Corr. Litt., IX., p. 174.

language were not so utterly opposed to music! It is truly miserable; German is divine in comparison. And then the vocalists, male and female! they have no right to the name, for they do not sing, but shriek and howl, and all from the nose and the throat.

In spite of all this, he was eager to set to work (July 31, 1778):—

I assure you that I shall be only too pleased if I do succeed in writing an opera. The language is the invention of the devil, that is true; and the same difficulties are before me that beset all composers; but I feel as well able as any one else to surmount them; in fact, when I tell myself that all goes well with my opera, I feel a fire within me, and my limbs tingle with the desire to make the French know, honour, and fear the German nation more.

In the meantime L. Mozart heard that at the very time when Noverre was interesting himself so warmly in Wolfgang's opera, he had engaged him to write the music for a ballet which was coming out (May 14, 1778). When, after a considerable lapse of time, the father inquired what had become of this ballet, and what he had made by it, Wolfgang had almost forgotten the subject (July 9, 1778):—

As to Noverre's ballet, I only wrote that perhaps he would be making a new one. He just wanted half a ballet, and for that I provided the music; that is, there were six pieces by other people in it, consisting of poor, miserable French songs; I did the overture and contredanses, altogether about twelve pieces. The ballet has been performed four times with great applause.[16] But now I mean to do nothing without being sure beforehand what I am to get for it, for this was only as a good turn to Noverre.

But such "good turns" were precisely what Noverre had in view. It suited him, as it did Le Gros, to have at command the services of a young artist eager to compose and ready to accept hope and patronage in lieu of payment, whose name it was not necessary to risk bringing before the public, since he was only employed as a stop-gap. But it would be a very different and far more serious thing for them to bring forward an original work, such as an opera, by this

---

[16] Noverre's ballet "Les Petits Riens" was given in June, 1778 (in Italian by Italian singers), and was praised by Grimm, but without mention of the music (Corr. Litt., X., p. 53). This composition has also been irrecoverably lost.

same unknown young man.   In case of failure the protectors
would share the responsibilities of the *protégé*, while success
would bring fame and profit to the latter alone.   Nothing
shows more clearly Mozart's unsuspecting nature than his
explanation of the long delay of his libretto (July 9, 1778):—

> It is always so with an opera.   It is so hard to find a good poem ; the
> old ones, which are the best, are not in the modern style, and the new
> ones are good for nothing; for poetry, which was the only thing the
> French had to be proud of, gets worse every day, and the poetry of the
> opera is just thé part that must be good, for they do not understand
> the music.   There are only two operas *in aria* which I could write—one
> in two acts, the other in three.   The one in two acts is " Alexander and
> Roxane," but the poet who is writing it is still in the country.   That in
> three acts is " Demofoonte " (by Metastasio), translated and mixed with
> choruses and dances, and specially arranged for the French theatre,
> and this I have not yet been able to see.

The father saw through it all more plainly, and cautioned
Wolfgang, if he wanted to succeed with an opera in Paris,
to make himself known beforehand (August 27, 1778):—

> You must make a name for yourself.   When did Gluck, when did
> Piccinni, when did all these people come forward ?   Gluck is not less
> than sixty, and it is twenty-six or twenty-seven years since he was first
> spoken of; and can you really imagine that the French public, or even the
> manager of the theatre, can be convinced of your powers of composition
> without having heard anything by you in their lives, or knowing you,
> except in your childhood as an excellent clavier-player and preco-
> cious genius ?   You must exert yourself, and make yourself known as
> a composer in every branch; make opportunities, and be indefatigable
> in making friends and in urging them on; wake them up when their
> energies slacken, and do not take for granted that they have done all
> they say they have.   I should have written long ago to M. de Noverre if
> I had known his title and address.

But this way of pushing his talents was completely foreign
to Wolfgang's nature; and so it followed, in the natural
course of things, that after a delay of months Noverre declared that he might be able to help him to a libretto, but
could not insure the opera being performed when it was
ready.

One success, however, was to be granted him in Paris.
He had naturally ceased to visit Le Gros since the latter

had so ruthlessly rejected his Sinfonie Concertante, but had been every day with Raaff, who lived in the same house. He had chanced to meet Le Gros there, who made the politest apologies, and begged him again to write a symphony for the Concert Spirituel. How could Mozart resist such a petition? On June 12 he took the symphony which he had just finished to Count Sickingen, where Raaff was. He continues:—

They were both highly pleased. I myself am quite satisfied with it. Whether it will please generally I do not know; and, truth to say, I care very little; for whom have I to please? The *very few* intelligent Frenchmen that there are I can answer for; as for the stupid ones, it does not signify much whether they are pleased or not. But I am in hopes that even the donkeys will find something to admire. I have not omitted the *premier coup d'archet!*—and that is enough for them. What a fuss they make about that, to be sure! *Was Teufel!* I see no difference. They just begin together, as they do elsewhere. It is quite ludicrous.[17]

The symphony pleased unusually, however, as he tells his father (July 3, 1778):—

It was performed on Corpus Christi day with all applause. I hear that a notice of it has appeared in the "Courrier de l'Europe." I was very unhappy over the rehearsal, for I never heard anything worse in my life; you cannot imagine how they scraped and scrambled over the symphony twice. I was really unhappy; I should like to have rehearsed it again, but there are so many things, that there was no time. So I went to bed with a heavy heart and a discontented and angry spirit. The day before, I decided not to go to the concert; but it was a fine evening, and I determined at last to go, but with the intention, if it went as ill as at the rehearsal, of going into the orchestra, taking the violin out of the hands of M. La Houssaye, and conducting myself. I prayed for God's grace that it might go well, for it is all to His honour and glory; and, *ecce!* the symphony began. Raaff stood close to me, and

---

[17] The imposing effect of the simultaneous attack of a fine orchestra was the occasion of this catchword. Raaff told Mozart of a piquant *bon mot à propos* of the term. He was asked by a Frenchman, at Munich or some other place: "Monsieur, vous avez été à Paris?" "Oui." "Est-ce que vous étiez au Concert Spirituel?" "Oui." "Que dites-vous du premier coup d'archet? avez-vous entendu le premier coup d'archet?" "Oui, j'ai entendu le premier et le dernier." "Comment, le dernier? qui veut dire cela?" "Mais oui, le premier et le dernier, et le dernier même m'a donné plus de plaisir."

in the middle of the first allegro was a passage that I knew was sure
to please; the whole audience was struck, and there was great applause.
I knew when I was writing it that it would make an effect, so I brought
it in again at the end, *da capo*. The andante pleased also, but especially
the last allegro. I had heard that all the last allegros here, like the
first, begin with all the instruments together, and generally in unison;
so I began with the violins alone *piano* for eight bars, followed at once
by a *forte*. The audience (as I had anticipated) cried "Hush!" at the
piano, but directly the *forte* began they took to clapping. As soon as the
symphony was over I went into the Palais-Royal, took an ice, told my
beads as I had vowed, and went home.

So brilliant a success was not wanting in more lasting
results: "M. Le Gros has taken a tremendous fancy to me,"
he writes (July 9, 1778); and he was commissioned to write
a French oratorio for performance at the Concert Spirituel
during the following Lent:—

My symphony was unanimously applauded; and Le Gros is so pleased
with it that he calls it his best symphony.[18] Only the andante does not
hit his taste; he says there are too many changes of key in it, and it
is too long; but the real truth is that the audience forgot to clap their
hands so loud as for the first and last movements; the andante is more
admired than any other part by myself, and by all connoisseurs, as well
as by the majority of the audience; it is just the contrary of what Le
Gros says, being unaffected and short. But for his satisfaction (and
that of others, according to him) I have written another. Either is
good of its kind, for they differ greatly; perhaps, on the whole, I prefer
the second one.

The symphony (297 K.), well known by the name of the
French or Parisian Symphony, was repeated with the new
andante on August 15. It consists of three movements in the
customary form, except that none of the parts are repeated
entire, although they are perfectly distinct. This was a concession to the Parisian taste. Wolfgang writes to his father
(September 11, 1778) that his earlier symphonies would not
please there: "We in Germany have a taste for lengthy
performances, but in point of fact, it is better to be short and

---

[18] Mozart speaks in a later letter (September 11, 1778) of two symphonies
which had been much admired, and of which the last was performed on
September 8. With this agrees his assertion (October 3, 1778) that he had
sold to Le Gros two overtures (*i. e.*, symphonies) and the Sinfonie Concertante.
There are no further traces of this symphony.

good." The first and last movements are unusually animated
and restless, with an almost unbroken rapidity of movement;
and the different subjects offer no contrasts as to character,
being all in the same light, restless style. Thematic elaboration is only hinted at, except in the well worked-out middle
movement of the finale. Melodies are scattered through
the whole in great abundance, often connected with each
other in a highly original and attractive manner. Suspense
is kept up by strong contrasts of *forte* and *piano*, by sudden
breaks and imperceptible modulations, and by striking harmonic effects. The general impression given by both movements is animated and brilliant, but they are more calculated
to stir the intellect than to awaken the deeper emotions, and
are therefore well suited to a Parisian audience. The same
is the case with the tender and beautiful andante, which only
now and then, surreptitiously as it were, betrays the existence of deep feeling. There are, as has been seen, two
versions of the andante, both still existing in Mozart's handwriting—the second considerably shorter than the first. The
leading part is minutely given throughout the score of the
whole piece (which is marked *andantino*), besides a fixed
subject being indicated for the bass, and in some places for
the other instruments. After thus laying down, as it were,
the ground plan, he proceeded to details, making few alterations beyond some slight abbreviations. When, in working
out the movement, he came to a passage which seemed to
him tedious or superfluous, he struck it out, and went on
with the next. This has been the case with several unimportant passages, and with one longer one, a transition to
the theme by means of an imitative passage (after page 36,
bar 6, of the score); soon after, too, a middle passage with
flute and oboe solos is cut out. After thus elaborating the
movement, he hastily copied it all, as it is now printed.[19] The
later andante is printed in a Parisian edition of the symphony;[20] it is far less important than the first, and was

---

[19] Mozart has made considerable abbreviations in the first movement of this
symphony, while working out the score in the manner described above.
[20] Süddeutsche Mus. Ztg., 1857, No. 44, p. 175.

rightly rejected by Mozart. It is worthy of remark that the violoncello is employed as a leading instrument.

The orchestral workmanship shows that Mozart had not listened to the Mannheim band in vain; the different instruments form a well-ordered whole, in which each has its individual significance. It is only necessary to examine the thematic arrangement in the last movement (score, page 54) to perceive how skilfully the effect of varied tone-colouring is taken into account, while at the same time, by means of contrapuntal treatment, due prominence is given to the purely melodious element. It may well be imagined that Mozart would not let slip the opportunity of trying the splendid effect of a symphony with flutes, oboes, and clarinets (Vol. I., p. 385). But the clarinets are sparely used as a foreign importation, and, together with the trumpets and drums, are altogether omitted from the andante. Large demands are made on the executive delicacy of the orchestra, and in many places the whole effect depends on a well-managed *crescendo*, as it had never done in previous works; in fact, it is not too much to say that many of the subjects would not have been conceived as they are, without the prospect of their performance by a well-organised orchestra.

During this interval Mozart also completed the clavier sonatas, with violin accompaniment, which he had begun at Mannheim (301-306 K.), the fourth bearing the inscription " á Paris," and busied himself to find a publisher for them who would pay him well.[21] He found leisure, also, to compose a capriccio for his sister's birthday.

Thus we see Mozart, disliking Paris and the Parisians, deriving little practical gain from all his exertions, and yet striving in his own way to attain the position which was his due, when an event occurred which plunged himself and his family into the deepest grief. Paris had never agreed with the Frau Mozart. Their lodging in the " Hôtel des quatre fils d'Aymon," in the Rue du Gros-Chenet—a musical quarter

---

[21] The father writes to Breitkopf (August 10, 1781): " The six sonatas dedicated to the Elector Palatine were published by M. Sieber, in Paris. He paid my son for them fifteen louis neuf, thirty copies and a free dedication."

—was bad, as well as the living, and she sat all day " as if under arrest," Wolfgang's affairs necessitating his almost constant absence. She was ill for three weeks in May, and intended, on her recovery, to seek out better lodgings, and manage the housekeeping herself. But in June she fell ill again ; she was bled, and wrote afterwards to her husband (June 12, 1778) that she was very weak, and had pains in her arm and her eyes, but that on the whole she was better. But the improvement was only apparent, and her illness took a serious turn; the physician whom Grimm sent in gave up hope, and after a fortnight of the deepest anxiety, which Wolfgang passed at his mother's bedside, she gently passed away on July 3. His only support at this trying time was a musician named Heina, who had known his father in former days, and had often, with his wife, visited Frau Mozart in her solitude. Wolfgang's first thought was to break the news gently to his father, who was ill prepared for so crushing a blow. He wrote to him at once, saying that his mother was ill, and that her condition excited alarm ; at the same time he acquainted their true friend Bullinger with the whole truth, and begged him to break the dreadful news to his father as gently as possible. In a few days, when he knew that this had been done, he wrote again himself in detail, offering all the consolation he could, and strove to turn his father's thoughts from the sad subject to the consideration of his own prospects. This letter[22] affords a fresh example of the deep and tender love which bound parents and children together, and of Wolfgang's own sentiments and turn of mind. The consolations he offers, and the form in which he expresses them, are those of one who has himself passed through all the sad experiences of life ; but to his father, whose teaching had tended to produce this effect, his expressions were justified and correct. With a natural and genuine sorrow for his irreparable loss is combined a manly composure, which sought not to obtain relief by indulging in sorrow, but to look forward calmly and steadily to the future and its duties.

---

[22] A fac-simile of the letter to Bullinger will be found at the end of the third volume.

As a loving son, he set himself to the filial task of comforting
and supporting his father.   After hearing that the latter was
aware of his wife's death, and resigned to God's will, Wolfgang answers (July 31, 1778):—

Sad as your letter made me, I was beyond measure pleased to find
that you take everything in a right spirit, and that I need not be uneasy
about my dear father and my darling sister.   My impulse after reading
your letter was to fall on my knees and thank God for His mercy.   I am
well and strong again now, and have only occasional fits of melancholy,
for which the best remedy is writing or receiving letters—that restores
my spirits again at once.

He felt, and with justice, that his father's anxiety on his
account would now be redoubled.   In keeping him informed
of all his exertions and successes he satisfied his own longing
to confide in his father, and gave the latter just that kind of
interest and occupation of the mind which would serve to
dispel his grief.   It is touching to see the pains he takes to
keep his father informed of all that he thinks will interest
him, and how a certain irritability which had occasionally,
and under the circumstances excusably, betrayed itself in
his former letters, now completely disappears before the expression of tender affection : even the handwriting, which had
been blamed as careless and untidy by his father, becomes
neater and better.   Trifles such as these are often the clearest
expression of deep and refined feeling.

When the heavy blow fell, Wolfgang was alone, his Mannheim friends having left Paris ; his father might well be apprehensive lest he should neglect the proper care of himself
and his affairs.   But Grimm now came forward; he, or more
properly, as Mozart delares, his friend Madame D'Epinay,
offered him an asylum in their house,[28] and a place at their
table, and he willingly agreed, as soon as he was convinced
that he should cause neither appreciable expense nor inconvenience.   He soon found himself obliged occasionally to
borrow small sums of Grimm, which gradually mounted

---

[28] Mémoires et Correspondance de Madame d'Epinay (Paris, 1818). Cf. Grimm,
Corr. Litt., XI., 468.   Madame de Genlis, Mém., III., p. 99.   Sainte-Beuve,
Causeries du Lundi, II., p. 146.

"piecemeal" to fifteen louis-d'or; Grimm reassures the father by telling him that repayment may be indefinitely postponed. But Wolfgang soon found the way of life in Grimm's household not at all to his mind, and wrote of it as "stupid and dull." And, indeed, a greater contrast cannot well be imagined than when, from the house whence issued with scrupulous devotion bulletins of Voltaire's health, contradictory reports of his religious condition, and finally the announcement of his death (May 30, 1778), Wolfgang should write to his father (July 3, 1778) : " I will tell you a piece of news, which perhaps you know already; that godless fellow and arch-scoundrel Voltaire is dead, like a dog, like a brute beast —that is his reward!" The condescending patronage with which he was treated soon became intolerable to him, and he complains of Grimm's way of furthering his interests in Paris as better fitted to a child than a grown man. We can well imagine that Grimm, like Mozart's own father, desired that he should make acquaintances, should gain access to distinguished families as a teacher and clavier-player, and should seek to win the favour of the fashion-leading part of the community; no doubt, too, Grimm felt it his duty to remonstrate openly with Wolfgang for what he considered his indolence and indifference. It is impossible to deny the good sense and proper appreciation of the position of all Grimm's remarks, but they were resented by Mozart on account of the tone of superiority with which they were enforced. Grimm was indeed openly opposed to Mozart, and told him frankly that he would never succeed in Paris—he was not active, and did not go about enough ; and he wrote the same thing to Wolfgang's father.[24]

---

[24] Grimm's letter to L. Mozart, which the latter forwarded to his son (August 13, 1778), runs as follows: " Il est *zu treuherzig*, peu actif, trop aisé à attraper, trop peu occupé des moyens qui peuvent conduire à la fortune. Ici, pour percer, il faut être retors, entreprenant, audacieux. Je lui voudrais pour sa fortune la moitié moins de talent et le double plus d'entregent, et je n'en serais pas embarrassé. Au reste, il ne peut tenter ici que deux chemins pour se faire un sort. Le premier est de donner des leçons de clavecin; mais sans compter qu'on n'a des écoliers qu'avec beaucoup d'activité et même de charlatanerie, je ne sais s'il aurait assez de santé pour soutenir ce métier, car c'est une chose très fatiguante de courir les quatre coins de Paris et de s'épuiser à parler pour

II.   E

It soon became apparent that Grimm was not really of opinion that Mozart's talents were of such an order as to offer him a career in Paris; he said that he could not believe that Wolfgang would be able to write a French opera likely to succeed, and referred him for instruction to the Italians. " He is always wanting me," writes Mozart (September 11, 1778), "to follow Piccinni or Caribaldi (Vol. I., p. 77), in fact, he belongs to the foreign party—he is false—and tries to put me down in every way." He longed above all things to write an opera to show Grimm " that I can do as much as his dear Piccinni, although I am only a German." Grimm's character was not a simple one;[25] he had both won and kept for himself under adverse circumstances an influential position, which was no easy matter in Paris at any time. Queer stories were told of him,[26] and his love of truth was not implicitly relied on.[27] Rousseau describes him as perfidious and egotistical. Madame D'Epinay, on the other hand, extols him as a disinterested friend, and others speak of his benevolence and ready sympathy.[28] There is, at any rate, no reason to suspect that he meant otherwise than well by Mozart, although he did not appreciate his genius, and interested himself more for the father's sake than the son's. He had striven for years to assert the supremacy of Italian music, and his ideal was Italian opera performed in Paris by Italian singers in the Italian language. When De Vismes, who was anxious to propitiate all parties, engaged a company of Italian

---

montres. Et puis ce métier ne lui plaît pas, parcequ'il l'empêchera d'écrire, ce qu'il aime par-dessus tout. Il pourrait donc s'y livrer tout à fait; mais en ce pays ici le gros du public ne se connaît pas en musique. On donne par conséquent tout aux noms, et le mérite de l'ouvrage ne peut être jugé que par un très petit nombre. Le public est dans ce moment si ridiculement partagé entre Piccinni et Gluck que tous les raisonnements qu'on entend sur la musique font pitié. Il est donc très difficile pour votre fils pour réuissir entre ces deux partis. Vous voyez, mon cher maître, que dans un pays où tant de musiciens médiocres et détestables même ont fait des fortunes immenses, je crains fort que M. votre fils ne se tire pas seulement d'affaire."

[25] Cf. the account by Sainte-Beuve, Causeries du Lundi, VII., p. 226; II., p. 158.

[26] Merck, Briefe, II., p. 282.

[27] Madame de Genlis, Mém., IV., p. 3.

[28] Jacobs, in Hoffmann's Lebensbilder ber. Humanisten, p. 15.

singers,[29] Grimm hailed the auspicious day on which Caribaldi, Baglioni, and Chiavacci appeared in Piccinni's "Finte Gemelle" (June 11, 1778).[30] It is therefore quite conceivable that he renounced all interest in Mozart's artistic future as soon as he was convinced of his falling off from purely Italian notions, and it is interesting to us to have so clear an indication that even thus early in his career Mozart had set himself in opposition to the Italian school. He had long since learnt all that it had to teach, and he fully recognised the fact that it was his mission to carry on the reform set on foot by Gluck and Grétry, at the same time retaining all that was valuable in the Italian teaching.

A confirmation of this is found in a later expression of opinion made by Mozart to Joseph Frank, who found him engaged in the study of French scores, and asked him if it would not be better to devote himself to Italian compositions; whereupon Mozart answered : " As far as melody is concerned, yes; but as far as dramatic effect is concerned, no ; besides, the scores which you see here are by Gluck, Piccinni, Salieri, as well as Grétry, and have nothing French but the words."[31] This view was confirmed by his stay in Paris, a stay quite as fruitful for his artistic development as that at Mannheim had been. Grimm's accounts show that Mozart had opportunities for hearing the operas of numerous French composers. Besides Gluck's "Armide" which was still new, "Orpheus," "Alceste," and "Iphigenia in Aulis," which had been revived, Piccinni's "Roland," Grétry's "Matroco," "Les Trois Ages de l'Opéra," and "Le Jugement de Midas" were given, as well as Philidor's "Ernelinde," Dezaide's "Zulima," Gossec's "Fête du Village," Rousseau's "Devin du Village." Added to these were Piccinni's Italian opera "Le Finte Gemelle," and doubtless many others of which we know nothing. It may well excite wonder that Mozart's letters to his father describe

---

[29] Grimm, Corr. Litt., X., pp. 37, 112, 162. La Harpe, Corr. Litt., II., p. 249.

[30] Grimm, Corr. Litt., X., p. 52.

[31] Prutz, Deutsches Museum, II., p. 28.

none of the new artistic impressions which he must have
received in Paris. But, apart from the fact that personal
affairs naturally held the first place in his home correspondence, it must be remembered that abstract reflections
on art and its relation to individual artists were not at that
time the fashion, and were besides quite foreign to Mozart's
nature. His æsthetic remarks and judgments whether they
treated of technical questions or of executive effects, are
mostly founded on concrete phenomena. The practical
directness of his productive power, set in motion by every
impulse of his artistic nature, prevented his fathoming the
latest psychical conditions of artistic activity, or tracing the
delicate threads which connect the inner consciousness of
the artist with his external impressions, or analysing the
secret processes of the soul which precede the production of
a work of art. He does not seem any more actively
conscious of the effect wrought upon him by the works of
others. Some men's impressions of a great work are
involuntary, and they seek later to comprehend the grounds
of their enjoyment; others strive consciously to grasp the
idea of the work and to incorporate it into their being; but
to the man of creative genius alone is it given to preserve
his own totality while absorbing all that is good in the
works of other artists.

Without ever losing his own individuality, an artist of
true genius absorbs impressions from nature and from other
works of art than his own, and constructs them anew from
his inner consciousness. He accepts and assimilates whatever is calculated to nourish his formative power, and rejects
with intuitive right judgment all that is foreign to his nature.
Just as in the production of a true work of art invention
and labour, inspiration and execution, willing and doing, are
inseparably interwoven, so in the consideration by a genius
of the works of other men and other ages, delighted appreciation is combined with criticism, ready apprehension col-
lects materials for original work in its truest sense ; it is a
natural process, which perfects itself in the mind of the
artist without any conscious action on his part.

Therefore the judgment that one artist pronounces on

another is not always in perfect accord with the influence which has been brought to bear on himself by that other. The deeper the influence penetrates into the roots of an artist's inner being, the more will it become part and parcel of his productive powers, and the consciousness of any outside influence will be rapidly lost. It remains for future historical inquirers to ascertain and define the influence of the intellectual current of the age on the individual, and the mutual action on each other of exceptional phenomena.

Small as the visible results of Mozart's stay in Paris might be, and far as he remained from the object with which he had undertaken the journey, it yet enabled him, with great gain to his progress as an artist, to free himself from the Italian school, after such a thorough study of its principles as convinced him of the value of the element of dramatic construction which lay concealed in it. It may indeed be considered as a fortunate circumstance that no sooner had this conviction taken root in him than he turned his back on party disputes and left the place which was of all others the least fitted to encourage the quiet steady progress of genius.

L. Mozart had other and very different reasons for wishing to shorten Wolfgang's stay in Paris as much as he had hitherto desired to prolong it. With his wife's death he had lost the assurance that Wolfgang's life in Paris would be of no detriment to his moral nature. Indulgent as she had been to her son, in this respect her influence was unbounded; and now it might be feared that Wolfgang's easy-going nature would lead him into bad company. Grimm's account convinced him that Wolfgang had no prospects of success in Paris, the less so as he took no pains to conceal his dislike of the place. His dearest wish at this time was to be appointed Kapellmeister to the Elector of Bavaria; he hoped thus to be able to improve the position of the Weber family, and to claim Aloysia as his own. The project was not disapproved of by his father (who, however, was told nothing of the last item); on the contrary, he wrote to Padre Martini describing the state of affairs, and earnestly

requesting him directly and through Raaff to gain the
Elector for Wolfgang; this the Padre readily undertook.
As for Raaff, his friendship for Mozart and the interest
which he took in Aloysia Weber were incentives enough for
exertion, and Mozart had other influential friends among
the musicians, besides being able to count on the support of
Count Sickingen.

In Munich especially, where there was no German operatic
composer of merit—Holzbauer being too old to have much
influence—the need of a kapellmeister and composer was
strongly felt; but the circumstances were very unfavourable.
After it had been finally decided that the court should be
removed from Mannheim to Munich, and all had been prepared for the move, threatenings of war threw everything
into confusion again. Wolfgang felt this a heavy blow to
the interests of the Webers, concerning whom he writes to
his father (July 31, 1778) :—

The day before yesterday my dear friend Weber wrote to me, among
other things, that the day after the Elector's arrival it was announced
that he intended to take up his residence at Munich. This news came
like a thunderbolt to Mannheim, and the joy which had been testified
by the illuminations of the day before was suddenly extinguished
(p. 404). The court musicians were all informed that they were at
liberty to follow the court to Munich, or to remain in Mannheim with
their present salary; each one was to send in his written and sealed
decision to the Intendant within fourteen days. Weber, whose miserable
circumstances you know, wrote as follows: " My decayed circumstances
put it out of my power to follow my gracious master to Munich, however
earnestly I may wish to do so." Before this happened there was a
grand concert at court, and poor Mdlle. Weber felt her enemies' malice;
she was not invited to sing—no one knows why. Immediately afterwards was a concert at Herr von Gemmingen's, and Count Seeau was
present. She sang two of my songs, and was fortunate enough to please,
in spite of the wretched foreigners (the Munich singers). She is much
injured by these infamous slanderers, who say that her singing is deteriorating. But Cannabich, when the songs were over, said to her,
" Mademoiselle, I hope that you will go on deteriorating after this
fashion! I will write to Herr Mozart to-morrow, and acquaint him with
your success." As the matter now stands, if war had not broken out, the
court would have removed to Munich; Count Seeau, who positively *will
have* Mdlle. Weber, had arranged everything so as to take her, and there
was hope that the circumstances of the whole family would improve in

consequence. But now the Munich journey is no more talked of, and the unfortunate Webers may have to wait here long enough, their debts growing heavier day by day. If I could only help them! My dear father, I recommend them to you with my whole heart. If they had only 1,000 florins a year to depend upon!

Thereupon his father reminds him that his anxiety about the Webers is unbecoming, as long as he does not bestow the same care on himself and his own family (August 27, 1778). Besides there was no prospect for him in Munich at present, and his father therefore wished him to remain in Paris, at all events until the matter was decided.[82]

In the midst of this uncertainty a favourable prospect opened in Salzburg itself. Since Adlgasser's death it had become more and more evident at court that Wolfgang's recall would be of all things most advantageous; it was signified to L. Mozart through Bullinger that, as he doubtless wished to retain his son near him, the court would be prepared to give him a monthly salary of fifty florins as organist and concertmeister, and he might look forward with certainty to being made kapellmeister; but the Archbishop could not make the first advances. Bullinger duly performed his mission, but L. Mozart, who well knew the perplexity the Archbishop was in, required that the proposition should be made direct to him. So, therefore, it was obliged to be; and the diplomatic skill, "worthy of a Ulysses" as Wolfgang says, with which L. Mozart contrived to hold his ground and to avail himself of his strong position in an interview with the canon, Count Joseph Stahremberg, is minutely described by himself (June 29, 1778) :—

When I arrived no one was there but his brother the major, who is staying with him to recover from the fright into which he has been thrown by Prussian powder and shot. He told me that an organist had been recommended to him, but he would not accept him without being sure that he was good. He wished to know if I was acquainted with him —Mandl, or some such name, he did not remember what. "Oh, you stupid fellow!" thought I; "is it likely that an order or a request should be received from Vienna with reference to a candidate whose

---

[82] Both the father and son, especially the former, follow closely the course of political and military events, and communicate them to each other.

name is not even mentioned." As if I could not guess that all this was
by way of inducing me to mention my son! But not I! no, not a syllable.
I said I had not the honour of knowing any such person, and that I
would never venture to recommend any one to our prince, since it would
be difficult to find any one who would altogether suit him. "Yes," said
he, "I cannot recommend him any one; it is far too difficult! Your son
should be here now!" "Bravo! the bait has taken," thought I; "what
a pity that this man is not a minister of state or an ambassador!" Then
I said, "We will speak plainly. Is it not the case that all possible
measures were taken to drive my son out of Salzburg?" I began at the
beginning and enumerated every past circumstance, so that his brother
was quite astonished, but he himself could not deny the truth of a single
point, and at length told his brother that young Mozart had been the
wonder of all who came to Salzburg. He wanted to persuade me to
write to my son; but I said that I would not do so—it would be labour
in vain, for that unless I could tell him what income he might expect, my
son would laugh at the proposition; Adlgasser's salary would be totally
insufficient. Indeed, even if his Grace the Archbishop were to offer him
fifty florins a-month, it would be doubtful whether he would accept it.
We all three left the house together, for they were going to the riding-
school, and I accompanied them. We spoke on the subject all the way,
and I held to what I had said; he held to my son as the only candidate
for him. The fact is, that the Archbishop can hear of no other good
organist who is also a good clavier-player; he says now (but only to his
favourites) that Beecké was a charlatan and a buffoon, and that Mozart
excels all others; he would rather have him whom he knows than
some one else highly paid whom he does not know. He cannot promise
any one (as he would have to do if he gave a smaller salary) an income
by pupils, since there are but few, and those are mine, I having the
name of giving as good lessons as any man. Here then is the affair in
full swing. I do not write, my dear Wolfgang, with the intention of
inducing you to return to Salzburg, for I place no reliance on the words
of the Archbishop, and I have not yet spoken to his sister the Countess;[33]
I rather avoided the opportunity of meeting her; for she would take the
least word as consent and petition. They must come to me, and if anything is to be done, I must have a clear and advantageous proposal
made, which can hardly be expected. We must wait, and hold fast to
our point.

Wolfgang, who disliked Salzburg more even than Paris, at
first took no notice of all this. But the death of the old kapellmeister Lolli, coinciding with that of his mother, brought

---

[33] The Archbishop's sister, Marie Franziska (b. 1746), who had married
Oliver, Count von Wallis, had a residence assigned her in the archiepiscopal
palace, and kept up a sort of regal state.

matters in Salzburg to a crisis, and under the circumstances
L. Mozart was more than ever convinced that Wolfgang
should have a good position there.   Good old Bullinger was
again employed as a mediator to reconcile Wolfgang to
the idea. He wrote to his young friend that he would be
wronging his family by refusing so advantageous a position
as that now offered to him, and that life might be endurable
even in so small a place as Salzburg.   He mentioned casu-
ally that the Archbishop intended engaging a new singer,
and hints that his choice might be turned towards Aloysia
Weber.   Thereupon Wolfgang wrote candidly to Bullinger
(August 7, 1778) :—

You know how hateful Salzburg is to me!—not alone on account of
the unjust treatment received there by both my father and myself—
though that in itself is enough to make one wish to wipe the place clean
out of one's memory.   But even supposing that things turned out so
that we could live *well*—living *well* and living *happily* are two things,
and the latter I should never be able to do without the aid of magic—it
would be against the natural order of things !   It would be the greatest
pleasure to me to embrace my dear father and sister, and the sooner
the better ; but I cannot deny that my joy would be doubled if the reunion took place anywhere but in Salzburg. I should have far more
hope of living happily and contentedly.

He goes on to explain that it is not because Salzburg is
small that he dreads returning to it, but because it offers no
field for his talent, music being but little esteemed there ; he
remarks with bitter satire how the Archbishop pretends to
seek with much parade for a kapellmeister and a prima
donna, and in reality does nothing.

Soon after his father gives him further information as to
the position of affairs (August 27, 1778) :—

I have written to you already that your recall here is desired, and
they beat about the bush with me for a long time without getting me to
commit myself; until at last, after Lolli's death, I was obliged to tell the
Countess that I had addressed a petition to the Archbishop, which,
however, simply appealed to his favour by drawing attention to my long
and uncomplaining services. The conversation then turned upon you,
and I expressed myself as frankly upon all necessary points as I had
previously done to Count Stahremberg.   At last she asked me whether
you would come if the Archbishop were to give me Lolli's post, and you
Adlgasser's, which, as I had already calculated, would bring us in

together one thousand florins a year; I could do nothing else but answer that I had no doubt that if this happened you would consent for love of me, especially as the Countess declared that there was not the least doubt that the Archbishop would allow you to travel in Italy every second year, since he himself had said how important it was to hear something new from time to time, and that he would furnish you with good letters of introduction. If this were to happen, we might reckon securely on one hundred and fifteen florins a-month; and, as things now are, on more than one hundred and twenty florins. We should be better off than in any other place where living is twice as dear, and, not having to look so closely after money, we should be able to think more of amusement. But I am far from thinking the affair a certainty, for I know how hard such a decision will be to the Archbishop. You have the entire goodwill and sympathy of the Countess, that is certain; and it is equally certain that old Arco, Count Stahremberg, and the Bishop of Königsgrätz, are all anxious to bring the matter to a conclusion. But there are reasons, as is always the case; and, as I have always told you, the Countess and old Arco are afraid of my leaving also. They have no one to succeed me as a clavier-teacher: I have the name of teaching well—and, indeed, the proofs are there. They know of no one; and, should a teacher come from Vienna, is it likely that he would give lessons for four florins or a ducat the dozen, when anywhere else he would have two or three ducats? This sets them all in perplexity. But, as I have said before, I do not reckon on it, because I know the Archbishop. It may be true that he sincerely wishes to secure you; but he cannot make up his mind, especially when it concerns *giving*.

Probably Wolfgang counted on this fact, and refrained on that account from treating the matter seriously. Just at this time his discomfort in Paris was lightened by a pleasant event. His old London friend Bach, (Vol. I., p. 39), had been invited to write an opera ("Amadis") for Paris. "The French are asses, and always will be," remarks Wolfgang thereupon (July 9, 1778); "they can do nothing themselves, but are obliged to have recourse to foreigners. Bach came to Paris to make the necessary arrangements, and Wolfgang wrote (August 27, 1778):—

Herr Bach has been in Paris for the last fortnight. He is going to write a French opera. He has come to hear the singers; then he goes back to London, writes the opera, and returns to put it on the stage.[34] You may imagine his joy and mine at our meeting. Perhaps mine is

---

[34] Grimm, Corr. Litt., X., p. 236.

more sincere, but it must be acknowledged that he is an honest man, and does people justice. I love him, as you know, from my heart, and have a high esteem for him. As for him, he does not flatter or exaggerate as some do,·but both to myself and others he praises me seriously and sincerely.

Bach had introduced Wolfgang to the Marshal de Noailles,[85] and the latter had invited them both, as well as Bach's " bosom friend " Tenducci (Vol. I., p. 41), to St. Germain. There they spent some pleasant days together, and it need hardly be said that Mozart composed a scena for Tenducci, with pianoforte, oboe, horn, and bassoon accompaniment, the instruments being taken by dependents of the Marshal, chiefly Germans, who played well.[86]

Meanwhile the time for decision drew near. The Salzburg authorities had made a definite proposal to L. Mozart, as he had wished, and he wrote to his son in a way which hardly left him a choice (August 31, 1778) :—

You do not like Paris, and I scarcely think you are wrong. My heart and mind have been troubled for you until now, and I have been obliged to play a very ticklish part, concealing my anxiety under the semblance of light-heartedness, in order to give the impression that you were in the best of circumstances and had money in abundance, although I well knew to the contrary. I was very doubtful of gaining my point because, as you know, the step we took and your hasty resignation left us little to hope from our haughty Archbishop. But my clever management has carried me through, and the Archbishop has agreed to all my terms, both for you and myself. You are to have five hundred florins, and he expressed regret at not being able to make you kapellmeister at once. You are to be allowed to act as my deputy when the work is beyond me, or I am unfit to do it. He said he had always intended to give you a better post, &c.; in fact, to my amazement, he made the politest apologies. More than that! he has given five florins additional to Paris,[87] so that he may take the heaviest duties, and enable you to act as concertmeister again. So that

---

[85] There were two Marshals of the name, the Duke and the Count de Noailles: I do not know which of the two is here meant. The first was the father of the Countess de Tessé, Mozart's early patroness (Vol. I., p. 35), and, like her, was interested in literature and art (Lomenie, Beaumarchais, I., p. 206).

[86] Tenducci must have taken this composition with him to London. Burney (Barrington's Miscellanies, p. 289) praises it as a masterpiece of invention and technical execution (Pohl, Mozart und Haydn in London, p. 121).

[87] Anton Paris was the third court organist in Salzburg.

we shall get altogether, as I told you before, an income of one thousand
florins. Now I should like to know whether you think my head is
worth anything, and whether or not I have done my best for you. I
have thought of everything. The Archbishop has declared himself
prepared to let you travel where you will, if you want to write an opera.
He apologised for his refusal last year by saying that he could not bear
his subjects to go about begging. Now Salzburg is a middle point
between Munich, Vienna, and Italy. It will be easier to get a commission for an opera in Munich than to get an official post, for German
composers are scarce. The Elector's death has put a stop to all
appointments, and war is breaking out again. The Duke of Zweibrücken[38] is no great lover of music. But I would rather you did not
leave Paris until I have the signed agreement in my hand. The Prince
and the whole court are wonderfully taken with Mdlle. Weber, and are
absolutely determined to hear her. She must stay with us. Her father
seems to me to have no head. I will manage the affair for them if they
choose to follow my advice. You must speak the word for her here,
for there is another singer wanted for operatic performances.

He was now so sure of the affair that he concluded his
letter with the words, "My next letter will tell you when to
set off."

L. Mozart was not mistaken in his son; however great
the sacrifice it entailed upon him, he prepared to yield to the
will of his father. "When I read your letter," he answered
(September 11, 1778), "I trembled with joy, for I felt myself
already in your embrace. It is true, as you will acknowledge,
that it is not much of a prospect for me; but when I look forward to seeing you, and embracing my dearest sister, I think
of no other prospect." He did not conceal from his father
his repugnance to the idea of a residence at Salzburg, on
account of the want of congenial society, the unmusical tone
of the place, and the little confidence placed by the Archbishop in sensible and cultivated people. His consolation
was the permission to travel, without which he would hardly
have made up his mind to come. "A man of mediocre talent
remains mediocre whether he travels or not; but a man of
superior talent (which I cannot without hypocrisy deny myself
to be) becomes bad if he always remains in the same place."
The possibility that Aloysia Weber might come to Salzburg

---

[38] The heir-apparent, afterwards King Max I.

filled him with joy; for, indeed, if the Archbishop really wanted a prima donna, he could not have a better one. He is already troubled by the thought "that if people come from Salzburg for the Carnival, and ' Rosamund ' is played, poor Mdlle. Weber will perhaps not please, or at least will not be judged of as she deserves, for she has a wretched part —almost a *persona muta*—to sing a few bars between the choruses " (Vol. I., p. 403). "When I am in Salzburg," he continues, " I shall certainly not fail to intercede with all zeal for my dear friend ; and in the meantime I earnestly hope you will do your best for her—you cannot give your son any greater pleasure." He begs for permission to take Mannheim on his way home, in order to visit the Webers.

L. Mozart, knowing how deep and well-founded an antipathy Wolfgang had for Salzburg, sought to convince him that he would find himself in a much better position there now than formerly. " Our assured income," he wrote (September 3, 1778), " is what I have written to you, and your mode of life will not come in the way of your studies and any other work. You are not to play the violin at court, but you have full power of direction at the clavier." This was an important point to Wolfgang, and his father recurs to it again (September 24, 1778) :—

Formerly you were really nothing but a violinist, and that only as concertmeister; now you are concertmeister and court organist, and your chief duty is to accompany at the clavier. You will not think it any disgrace to play the violin as an *amateur* in the first symphony, since you will do it in company with the Archbishop himself, and all the court nobility. Herr Haydn is a man whose musical merit you will readily acknowledge—should you stigmatise him as a " court fiddler " because, in his capacity as concertmeister, he plays the viola in the smaller concerts? It is all by way of amusement; and I would lay a wager that, rather than hear your compositions bungled, you would set to yourself with a will."

He consoles him also by reminding him that the concerts at court are short, from seven o'clock to a quarter past eight, and that seldom more than four pieces are performed—a symphony, an aria, a symphony or concerto, and another aria (September 17, 1778). Since the pay-

ment of their debts did not press, they could pay off annually
a few hundred gulden, and live easily and comfortably.
"You will find amusement enough here; for when one
has not to look at every kreutzer, it makes many things
possible.   We can go to all the balls at the Town-Hall
during the Carnival.   The Munich theatrical company are
to come at the end of September, and to remain here the
whole winter with comedies and operettas.   Then there is
our quoit-playing every Sunday, and if we choose to go into
society it will come to us; everything is altered when one
has a better income."   But the father knew that the point
on which Wolfgang would be most open to persuasion was
not the prospect of Salzburg gaieties, but that of a union with
his beloved Mdlle. Weber; and he goes on to speak on this
subject too.   Not only does he say, " You will soon be asked
about Mdlle. Weber when you are here; I have praised her
continually, and I will do all I can to gain her a hearing,"
but he continues: " As to Mdlle. Weber, you must not
imagine that I disapprove of the acquaintance.   All young
people must make fools of themselves.   You are welcome to
continue your correspondence without interference from me.
Nay, more!   I will give you a piece of advice.   Every one
knows you here.   You had better address your letters to
Mdlle. Weber under cover to some one else, and receive them
in the same way, unless you think my prudence a sufficient
safeguard."
    The paternal permission to make a fool of himself was
calculated to hurt the lover's tenderest feelings, and he does
not disguise that this is the case in narrating a proof of the
genuine attachment of the Webers for him.   " The poor
things," he writes (October 15, 1778), " were all in great
anxiety on my account.   They thought I was dead, not
having heard from me for a whole month, owing to the loss
of a letter; they were confirmed in their opinion because of
a report in Mannheim that my dear mother had died of an
infectious illness.   They all prayed for my soul, and the
dear girl went every day to the church of the Capucins.
You will laugh, no doubt? but not I; it touches me; I cannot help it."   About the same time he received the news

that Aloysia had obtained an operatic engagement at Munich with a good salary,[39] and he expresses the mingled feelings with which he heard it simply and truly :—

I am as pleased at Mdlle. Weber's, or rather at my dear Aloysia's appointment as any one who has taken such a warm interest in her affairs was sure to be ; but I can no longer expect the fulfilment of my earnest wish that she should settle in Salzburg, for the Archbishop would never give her what she is to have in Munich. All I can hope for is that she will sometimes come to Salzburg to sing in operas.

This turn in affairs must have strengthened Mozart's secret wish to obtain an appointment under the Elector of Bavaria, and his determination to do all he could towards this end on his journey through Mannheim and Munich, and to "turn a cold shoulder" on the Archbishop. His father had nothing to oppose to such a project except the uncertainty of its prospects ; he sought, therefore, to convince Wolfgang that his only right course now was to accept the certainty offered to him, and to keep Munich in view for a future time. He gave him definite instructions on the point (September 3, 1778) :—

Since the Electoral Court is expected in Munich on September 15, you can speak yourself to your friend Count Seeau, and perhaps to the Elector himself on your journey through. You can say that your father wishes you to return to Salzburg, and that the Prince has offered you a salary of seven or eight hundred florins (add on two or three hundred) as concertmeister; that you have accepted it from filial duty to your father, although you know he has always wished to see you in the electoral service. But, N.B., no more than this ! You may want to write an opera in Munich, and you can do so best from here; it cannot fail to be so, for German operatic composers are very scarce. Schweitzer and Holzbauer will not write every year; and should Michl write one, he will soon be out-Michled. Should there be those who throw doubts and difficulties in the way, you have friends in the profession who will stand up for you; and this court will also bring out something during the year. In short you will be at hand.

It was now quite necessary that Wolfgang should leave Paris; and in anticipating what he had to expect in Salzburg, he began to feel what he was leaving in Paris. He

---

[39] Aloysia received a salary of 1,000 florins, her father 400 florins, together with 200 florins as prompter, as Mozart afterwards learnt at Mannheim.

was angry with Grimm, who desired that he should be ready
for his journey in a week, which was impossible, since he
had still claims on the Duc de Guines and on Le Gros, and
must wait to correct the proofs of his sonatas, and to sell
the compositions he had with him.[40]   He had no small desire
to write six more trios, for which he might expect good payment.   Grimm's evident wish that he should go, and his
offer to pay the journey to Strasburg (which seemed to the
father a proof of friendship) was considered by Wolfgang as
distrust and insincerity.   Grimm no doubt wished to be
relieved of the responsibility he had undertaken as soon as
possible, and may have offended his *protégé* by too open an
expression of his desire ; but there is no doubt that he acted
according to the mind of the father, and in the sincere
opinion that the unpractical and vacillating young man
required decided treatment.   But Wolfgang was so firmly
convinced that his departure from Paris was premature,
that he wrote to his father from Strasburg (October 15,
1778), that it was the greatest folly in the world to go to Salzburg now, and only his love to his father had induced him
to set aside the representations of his friends.   He had been
praised for this, but with the remark that—

If my father had known my present good circumstances and prospects,
and had not believed the reports of certain false friends, he would not
have written to me in a way that I could not withstand.   And I think
myself that if I had not been so annoyed in the house where I was
staying, and if the whole thing had not come upon me like a thunderbolt, so that there was no time to consider it in cool blood, I should
certainly have begged you to have a little more patience, and to leave
me in Paris ; I assure you I should have gained both money and fame,
and been able to extricate you from all your embarrassments.   But it

---

[40] He hoped to sell his three pianoforte concertos (238, 246, 271, K.) to the
engraver of his sonatas for ready money, and if possible his six difficult piano
sonatas (279-284 K.).   Whether he succeeded or not I do not know, but they
do not seem to have been engraved.   His father advised him to insure his
connection with the Parisian publishers for the future.   In a letter to Breitkopf
(August 10, 1781), he mentions Trois airs variés pour le clavecin ou fortepiano,
engraved by Heyna, in Paris.   These are the variations on Fischer's Minuet
(179 K.) ; on an air from Salieri's " Fiera di Venezia," " Mio caro Adone "
(180 K.), mentioned in a letter to his father (December 28, 1778) ; and on " Je
suis Lindor," from Beaumarchais' " Barbier de Seville " (354 K.).

is done now.   Do not imagine that I repent the step, for only you, my dear father, only you can sweeten for me the bitterness of Salzburg, and we shall do it—I know we shall; but I must frankly own that I should come to Salzburg with a lighter heart if I did not know that I was to be in the service of the court.   The idea is intolerable to me.

In the meantime business was wound up, the mother's property and the heavy baggage was sent direct to Salzburg; and on September 26 Wolfgang left Paris, having gained much experience but little satisfaction, as depressed and out of humour as he had entered it.

CHAPTER XX.

THE RETURN HOME.

WOLFGANG'S father expected that he would perform his homeward journey without any unnecessary delay, and his anxiety became serious when day after day passed and he received no tidings of his son's approach to Strasburg.

"I confessed and communicated together with your sister," he writes (October 19, 1778), "and earnestly prayed for your preservation; good old Bullinger prayed for you daily in the holy mass."   The fact was, that instead of providing Mozart with means to travel by the diligence, which accomplished the journey to Strasburg in a week, Grimm had satisfied himself with an ordinary conveyance, which occupied twelve days on the road.   Mozart's patience was tired out in a week, and he halted at Nancy.   Here he met with a German merchant, the best man in the world, who at once conceived a paternal attachment for him, and wept at the idea of their parting.   With this new friend Wolfgang determined to travel to Strasburg as soon as an opportunity of doing so cheaply should occur.   They were obliged to wait a considerable time, and it was the middle of October before they reached Strasburg :—

Things are not promising here; but the day after to-morrow (Saturday, October 17) I intend, *quite alone* (to avoid expense), to give a subscription concert to certain friends and connoisseurs; if I had engaged any other instruments it would, with the lighting, have cost me more than three louis-d'or; and who knows if it will bring in so much ?

II.   F

It was a shrewd guess, for his next letter had to announce three louis-d'or as the exact sum made by this "little model of a concert":—

But the principal receipts were in "bravos" and "bravissimos," which resounded from all sides. Prince Max of Zweibrücken, too, honoured the concert with his presence. I need scarely say that every one was pleased. I should have left Strasburg immediately after this, but I was advised to stay until the following Saturday, and give a grand concert in the theatre. At this I made the identical same sum, to the amazement and indignation and shame of all Strasburg. I must say, however, that my ears ached as much from the applauding and hand-clapping as if the theatre had been crammed full. Every one present openly and loudly denounced the conduct of their fellow-townsmen; and I told them all that if I could have imagined that I should have so small an audience, I would gladly have given the concert gratis, for the pleasure of seeing the theatre full. Indeed, I should have preferred it; for nothing can be more dismal than to lay a table for eighty guests and receive only three—and then it was so cold! But I soon grew warm; and in order to show my gentlemen of Strasburg that I was not put out, I played a great deal for my own entertainment; I gave them a concerto more than I had promised, and improvised for a long time at the end. Well, it is over and done with, and at least I have gained the reputation and honour.

Besides the concerts, he played publicly on the two best of Silbermann's organs in the Neue Kirche and the Thomas Kirche, and the roads being flooded and his departure for the present impossible, he resolved to give another concert on his fête-day, October 31. This he did at the solicitation and for the gratification of his friends Frank, De Beyer, &c., and the result was—*one* louis-d'or. No wonder that he was obliged to raise money in order to continue his journey, a fact which he remembered years after with indignation.

By the advice of friends who had made the journey he continued his way by diligence viâ Mannheim; the better roads and more comfortable carriage amply compensating for the *détour*. At Mannheim he alighted on November 6, and was welcomed with acclamations by his friends. The journey viâ Mannheim seemed to Leopold Mozart a most senseless proceeding on Wolfgang's part; the Weber family and all his best friends had migrated to Munich, and there was nothing to be gained by the visit.

He stayed with Madame Cannabich, who had not yet left, and who was never tired of hearing about himself; all his acquaintance tore him in pieces, for " as I love Mannheim, so Mannheim loves me." The old associations woke in him the old hopes and wishes. The Mannheim people were anxious to believe that the Elector could not stand the coarse manners of the Bavarians, and would soon be tired of Munich. It was reported that Madame Toscani and Madame Urban had been so hissed that the Elector had leant over his box and cried "Hush!" As this had no effect, Count Seeau had begged some officers not to make so much noise, since it displeased the Elector; but they answered, that they had paid for their admission to the theatre, and no one had any right to give them orders there. Every one was convinced that the Elector would soon bring the court back to Mannheim, and Wolfgang was only too ready to believe the assurances of his friends that when this took place, a fixed appointment would certainly be offered to him. Between Mannheim and Salzburg—what a difference! " The Archbishop," he wrote to his father (November 12, 1778), " cannot give me an equivalent for the slavery in Salzburg. I should feel nothing but delight were I only going to pay you a visit: but the idea of settling myself for good within that beggarly court is pain and grief to me." At Mannheim there were already prospects of immediate employment, besides — and what did he want more? — the opportunity for dramatic composition. Amid the universal desolation which was spread over Mannheim by the removal of the electoral court to Munich, patriotic men were not wanting who strove to resuscitate the intellectual and material prosperity of the town. Heribert von Dalberg failed indeed in his project for removing Heidelberg University to Mannheim, but he gained the express support of the Elector to the establishment of a theatre for carrying out the idea of an established national drama (Vol. I., p. 369).[1] Dalberg undertook the management with zeal and intelli-

---

[1] Dalberg's papers are preserved in the Royal Library at Munich. Koffka, Iffland u. Dalberg, p. 8.

gence, and both the choice of pieces and the manner of representation were considered entirely from an artistic point of view.

The Mannheim theatre first attained its peculiar importance and celebrity in the autumn of 1779, when the principal members of the Gotha Court company, with Iffland among them, were engaged at Mannheim.[2] When Mozart was on his way back from Paris Seyler was there with his company, which was only available for operetta and vaudeville. But higher notions were in the air; the idea of a German national opera had never been abandoned, and to enlist in its service such a composer as Mozart was a prospect not to be despised. How ready he was for the service we know. He had not been in Mannheim a week when he wrote, full of enthusiasm, to his father (November 12, 1778) :—

I have a chance of earning forty louis-d'or here! I should be obliged to stay six weeks or, at the longest, two months. The Seyler troupe are here; no doubt you know them by reputation. Herr Dalberg is manager, and refuses to let me go until I have composed a duodrama for him. I have made no objection, for I have always wished to write a drama of this kind. I do not remember if I told you anything about these duodramas when I was here before. I have been present at the performance of one of them twice with the greatest pleasure. In fact, I never was more surprised! for I had always imagined such a piece would have no effect. You know that the performers do not sing, but declaim, and the music is like an obbligato recitative. Sometimes speaking is interposed with first-rate effect. What I saw was "Medea," by Benda. He wrote another, "Ariadne on Naxos," both excellent. You know that Benda was always my favourite among the Lutheran kapellmeisters. I like these two works so much that I carry them about with me. Now you may imagine my joy at having to do just what I wished. Do you know what I should like? To have recitatives of this kind in opera, and only sometimes, when the words are readily expressible in music, to have them sung.

The duodrama which he was thus burning to compose was "Semiramis," and the poet was his friend and patron, Herr von Gemmingen (Vol. I., p. 429). It was he probably who wished Mozart to remain to compose "Semiramis," for Dalberg

---

had other views for him. He had written an opera ("Cora ")[3] which he much wished to have composed. He had already applied to Gluck and to Schweitzer,[4] but not feeling sure of either of them, he now sought to secure Mozart. The latter wrote to him (Mannheim, November 24, 1778) :—

Monsieur le Baron,—I have already waited upon you twice without having had the honour of finding you at liberty; yesterday I believe you were at home, but I was not able to speak with you. I must therefore ask you to pardon me for troubling you with a few lines, for it is very important to me that I should explain myself fully to you. Monsieur le Baron, you know that I am not mercenary, especially when I am in a position to be of service to so great a lover and so true a connoisseur of music as yourself. On the other hand, I feel certain that you would not desire that I should be in any way injured by the transaction; I am therefore bold enough to make my final proposition on the matter, since I cannot possibly remain longer in uncertainty. I undertake, for twenty-five louis-d'or, to write a monodrama, to remain here two months longer, to arrange everything, attend the rehearsals, &c.; but with this proviso, that, let what will happen, I shall be paid by the end of January. That I shall be free of the theatre is a matter of course.[5] This, Monsieur le Baron, is the utmost I can offer; if you consider it, I think you will see that I am acting very moderately. As far as your opera is concerned, I assure you that I should like above all things to set it to music. That I could not undertake such a work as that for twenty-five louis-d'or, you will readily allow; for it would contain at the most moderate computation quite as much work again as a monodrama; the only thing that would make me hesitate to undertake it is that, as you tell me, Gluck and Schweitzer are already writing it. But even supposing that you offered me fifty louis-d'or for it, I would as an honest man dissuade you from it. What is to become of an opera without singers, either male or female? At the same time, if there were any prospect of its being well produced I would not refuse to undertake the work from regard for you; and it would be no trifle, I give you my word of honour. Now I have told you my ideas clearly and straightforwardly, and I must beg for a speedy decision. If I could have an answer to-day I should be all the better pleased, for I have heard that some one is going to travel alone to Munich next Thursday, and I would gladly profit by the opportunity.

[3] "Cora, a Musical Drama," appeared to a contributor to the Pfälz. Schaubühne" unsuited for composition and representation.

[4] Gluck's letters in reference to this are printed in the Süddeutschen Musikzeitung, 1854, p. 174. Dalberg's Correspondenz for 1778 also mentions that Schweitzer was occupied with the composition of " Cora."

[5] Brandes affirms that the actors, when not performing, had to pay entrance-money (Selbstbiogr., II., p. 277).

Mozart would hardly have left Mannheim as long as a glimmer of hope remained—he, who was so overjoyed at finding employment there that he wrote to his father (November 12, 1778) : "They are arranging an Académie des Amateurs here, like the one in Paris. Herr Franzl is to lead the violins, and I am writing them a concerto for clavier and violin."[6] But his father, who was very dissatisfied with the "foolish fancy" for remaining in Mannheim, came to the point, and represented to him (November 19, 1778) how impossible it would be for the Elector to return to Mannheim. It was especially undesirable now to seek a post in the Bavarian service, since the death of Karl Theodor had "let loose on the world a whole army of artists, who are in Mannheim and Munich seeking a mode of livelihood. The Duke of Zweibrücken himself had an orchestra of thirty-six performers, and the former Mannheim establishment cost 80,000 florins." He cares nothing for the "possible earning of 40 louis-d'or," but emphatically orders : "Set off as soon as you receive this !" And to meet any conceivable remonstrance, he once more sets plainly forth the true position of affairs (November 23, 1778) :—

There are two things of which your head is full and which obscure your true judgment. The first and principal is your love for Mdlle. Weber, to which I am not altogether opposed. I was not formerly, when her father was poor, and why should I be so now when she may make your fortune instead of you hers ? I conjecture that her father is aware of your love, since all Mannheim knows it, since Herr Fiala (oboist in Salzburg) has heard it, since Herr Bullinger, who teaches at Count Lodron's, told me of it. He travelled with some Mannheim musicians from Ellwang (where he was in the vacation), and they could talk of nothing but your cleverness, compositions, and love for Mdlle. Weber.

In Salzburg, the father goes on, he would be so near Munich that he could easily go there, or Mdlle. Weber could come to Salzburg, where she might stay with them. Opportunities would not be wanting. Fiala had told the Archbishop a great deal about Mdlle. Weber's singing and Wolf-

---

[6] It does not appear to have been finished; the autograph of the first 117 bars is in the possession of M. Dubrunfeut, in Paris.

gang's good prospects in Mannheim. He might also invite his other friends—Cannabich, Wendling, Ritter, Ramm. They would all find hospitable welcome in his father's house:—

Most especially will your acceptance of the present office (which is the second subject of which your head is full) be your only certain opportunity for revisiting Italy, which is what I have more at heart than anything else. And your acceptance is indispensably necessary, unless you have the abominable and unfilial desire to bring scorn and derision on your anxious father—on that father who has sacrificed every hour of his life to his children to bring them credit and honour. I am not in a position to pay my debts, which now amount in all to one thousand florins, unless you lighten the payment by the receipt of your salary. I can then certainly pay off four hundred florins a year, and live comfortably with you two. I should like, if it is the will of God, to live a few years more, and to pay my debts, and then you may, if you choose, run your head against the wall at once. But no! your heart is good. You are not wicked, only thoughtless—it will all come!

This was not to be withstood. Wolfgang wrote that he would set off on December 9, but he still declined to travel the shortest way (December 3, 1778): "I must tell you what a good opportunity I have for a travelling companion next Wednesday—no other than the Bishop of Kaysersheim. One of my friends mentioned me to him; he remembered my name, and expressed great pleasure at the idea of travelling with me; he is a thoroughly kind, good man, although he is a priest and a prelate. So that I shall go viâ Kaysersheim, instead of Stuttgart."

The farewell to Mannheim was a sad one, both to Mozart and his friends. Madame Cannabich, who had earned the right to be considered as his best and truest friend, and who placed implicit confidence in him, was specially sorrowful; she refused to rise for his early departure, feeling unequal to the leave-taking, and he crept silently away that he might not add to her distress.

He was loth to give up his monodrama: "I am now writing," he says (December 3, 1778), " to please Herr von Gemmingen and myself, the first act of the declamatory opera which I was to have finished here; as it is, I shall take it with me, and go on with it at home; my eagerness for this kind of composition is uncontrollable."[7]

The Bishop took such an "extraordinary liking" for him that he was persuaded to stay at Kaysersheim, and to make an expedition with his host to Munich, where he arrived on December 25. Here he looked forward to some pleasant days in the society of all his Mannheim friends, and above all to reunion with his beloved Aloysia. In order that nothing might be wanting to his pleasure he begged his cousin to come to Munich, and hinted that she might have an important part to play there: he had no doubt of the success of his suit. But he almost immediately after received a letter from his father, ordering him in the most positive manner to set out by the first diligence in January, and not on any account to be persuaded by Cannabich to make a further postponement. L. Mozart foresaw that Wolfgang would make another effort to escape the slavery in Salzburg, and that his friends would encourage him to hope for a place under the Court at Munich. In anticipation of this he once more laid plainly before him that the settlement in Salzburg would afford the only possibility of putting their affairs in order. This representation arrived very inopportunely for Wolfgang. Cannabich and Raaff were, in point of fact, working "hand and foot" for him. By their advice he had already undertaken to write a mass for the Elector, and the sonatas (Vol. I., p. 415; II., p. 70) which he had dedicated to the Electress had arrived just in time to be presented by him in person; and in the midst of

---

[7] Gemmingen's "Semiramis" was not, as far as I am aware, printed; and I know nothing further of Mozart's composition. We find on p. 137 of the Theaterkalender for 1779: "Mozard . . . Kapellmeister zu Salzburg; *setzt* an 'Semiramis,' einem musikalischen Drama des Frh. von Gemmingen"; which must be a private communication. In following years it is regularly included among Mozart's finished compositions, but I have found no notice of its performance nor any other mention of it except that Gerber includes it among Leopold Mozart's posthumous works, with "Bastien and Bastienne" and the "Verstellte Gärtnerin." I mention this only to illustrate the fact that many of Mozart's earlier works were ascribed to L. Mozart after his death. But "Semiramis" was undoubtedly Mozart's own composition. How it happened that it did not remain in his hands, and pass into André's possession with his papers, I cannot explain.

all this his father's letter dashed his hopes to the ground, and added to his gloomy anticipations of life in Salzburg the fear that he would not be kindly received. He opened his heart to their old friend the flautist Becke (Vol. I., p. 228), who moved him still further by his account of the kindness and indulgence of his father. "I have never written so badly before," he writes to his father (December 29, 1778); "I cannot do it; my heart is too much inclined for weeping. I hope you will soon write and console me."

Becke also wrote on behalf of Wolfgang :—

He burns with desire to embrace his dearest and best-beloved father, as soon as his present circumstances will allow of it; he almost makes me lose my composure, for I was an hour or more in quieting his tears. He has the best heart in the world! I have never seen a child with a more loving and tender affection for his father than your son. He has a little misgiving lest your reception of him should not be as tender as he could wish; but I hope quite otherwise from your fatherly heart. His heart is so pure, so childlike, so open to me; how much more so will it not be to his father! No one can hear him speak without doing him justice as the best-intentioned, most earnest, and most honourable of men.

L. Mozart answered at once that his son might rely on the most loving welcome, and that everything would be done to entertain him; the autumn festivities and quoit prize-meetings had been postponed on his account. But he bids him observe that his long delay, the appointment being already four months old, is beginning to make the Archbishop impatient, and it must not go so far as to cause him to draw back in his turn.

To this Wolfgang answered (January 8, 1779) :—

I assure you, my dear father, that I feel only pleasure in coming to you (not to Salzburg) now that I see by your last letter that you have learnt to know me better. There has been no other cause for this last postponement of my journey home than the doubt I felt (which, when I could no longer contain myself, I confided to my friend Becke) as to my reception. What other cause could there be? I know that I am not guilty of anything that should make me feel your reproaches. I have committed no fault (for I call that only a fault which is not becoming to an honourable man and a Christian). I look forward with delight to many pleasant and happy days, but only in the society of you and my dear sister. I give you my honour that I cannot endure Salzburg and its inhabitants (that is, natives of Salzburg). Their speech and their way of living are thoroughly distasteful to me.

Mozart had other causes than this for despondency; before he left Munich he was destined to be painfully undeceived. He had been kindly welcomed by the Webers, who insisted on his staying with them; Aloysia had made striking progress as a vocalist, and Mozart, as might well be expected from him, rendered anew his musical homage to her by writing for her (li 8 di Gennaio, 1779) a grand aria (316 K.). He had designedly chosen as a subject the recitative and air with which Alceste first enters in Gluck's Italian opera; Schweitzer's "Alceste" had been performed in Munich, so that Mozart entered the lists with both composers. In order to provide his friends, Ramm and Ritter, with a piece of brilliant execution, he made the oboe and bassoon accompany obbligato, and emulate the voice part. The song is admirably adapted for a bravura piece, affording to the singer an opportunity for the display of varied powers and great compass, together with artistic cultivation of the voice. The recitative may be considered as an attempt at dramatic delivery of a grand and dignified kind; the song itself affords in both its parts, Andante sostenuto e cantabile, and Allegro assai, the most charming instances of sustained singing and brilliant execution. It is written for a high soprano, seldom going so low as 🎼 generally upwards from 🎼 What is expected of the singer in the way of compass and volubility may be judged by passages such as—

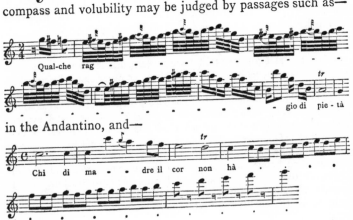

in the Andantino, and—

in the Allegro. But the importance of this song does not
depend alone on the brilliancy of its passages.

The recitative, undeniably the most important section of
the composition, is second to none of Mozart's later recitatives
in depth and truth of expression and noble beauty, and is
richly provided with unexpected harmonic changes, such as
he used more sparingly in later songs. The very first entry
of the voice is striking and beautiful, with a long and
pathetic prelude :—

and the close of the recitative is equally effective:—

If this carefully and minutely elaborated recitative be compared with Gluck's simple secco recitative there can be no doubt that Mozart's is far superior, both in fertility of invention and marked characterisation. But it must not be left out of account that if Mozart, treating the recitative and air as one independent whole, was right to emphasise and elaborate details, Gluck had to consider the situation in its connection with a greater whole; in which respect his simple but expressive recitative is quite in its right place. The song itself in depth of tragic pathos is not altogether on a level with the recitative. It consists of two movements, an Andantino and an Allegro, very nearly equal in length and compass, and each of them independently arranged and elaborated. The motifs in both are simple and expressive (especially the passionate middle part of the Allegro in C minor), but in performance the attention to bravura, necessitated by the emulation of the wind instruments, detracts from the intensity and earnestness of tone. The treatment is masterly, both of the voice and the two instruments, whether considered singly or in relation to each other; it is equally so of the orchestra (quartet and horns), which forms a foundation for the free movement of the solo parts. In the hands of a first-rate performer the song could not fail to have a brilliant and striking effect. But the exclusive reference to individual talents and executive powers detracted of necessity from the dramatic effect, and if the composer had given full sway to his passions the harmony he calculated on between his work and the performer would have been lost. As far as we can judge of Aloysia Weber as a singer from the songs composed for her by Mozart, the powerful rendering of violent and fiery passion was not her forte. Her delivery cannot be said to have been wanting in depth of feeling, and yet a certain moderation seems to have been peculiar to her, which Mozart turned to account as an element of artistic harmony.[8]   This song was a parting salutation to Aloysia Weber. A touching memorial of the parting is preserved in the voice part of a song ("Ah se in ciel") written by Mozart's hand in 1788 (538 K.). At the close of it she has written the words: "Nei giorni tuoi felici pensa qualche volta al Popoli di Tessaglia."

L. Mozart, with his custom of reckoning on the selfish-

---

[8] A somewhat extraordinary musical enthusiast, Frh. von Boecklin, writes of Aloysia that she "performed marvels with her delicate throat," and that her voice resembled a Cremona violin, and her singing was more expressive and affecting than that of Mara (Beitr. zur Geschichte der Musik, p. 18).

ness of mankind, had already expressed apprehension lest Weber, now that he no longer required Wolfgang's good offices, should cease to desire his friendship. This was not indeed the case, but he found a great change in Aloysia's sentiments. " She appeared no longer to recognise him for whom she had once wept. So Mozart sat down to the clavier and sang loud : ' Ich lass das Mädel gern, das mich nicht will.' "[9] This renunciation might satisfy his pride, but not his heart; his love was too true and deep to evaporate as lightly as the whim of a woman whose true character he learnt to know later. And yet he wrote from Vienna to his father (May 16, 1781) : " I was a fool about Lange's wife, that is certain ; but who is not when he is in love ? I loved her in very deed, and I feel that she is not yet indifferent to me. A good thing for me that her husband is a jealous fool and never lets her out of his sight, so that I seldom see her ! " On January 7, 1779, Mozart was presented to the Electress by Cannabich, and handed her the sonatas he had composed for her ; she conversed with him very graciously for a good half-hour. A few days after, he saw Schweitzer's " Alceste," which was the Carnival opera, and at last, after repeated injunctions from his father, he set out for Salzburg in the comfortable carriage of his fellow-traveller, a Salzburg merchant named Gschwendner.

CHAPTER XXI.

COURT SERVICE IN SALZBURG.

MOZART was welcomed to the paternal roof with open arms ; everything was prepared for his reception ; " a convenient cupboard and the clavichord were placed in his room," the cook Theresa had cooked capons without number, the high steward Count von Firmian (Vol. I., p. 345) offered him his horses, and Dr. Prexl also placed his " beautiful

---

[9] So Nissen narrates (p. 415), and further informs us that Mozart came to Munich with black buttons on his red coat, after the French fashion of showing mourning. Aloysia does not seem to have liked this.

bay mare" at his disposal; in short, Mozart's return home was a happy and triumphant event to all the good friends of his youth. We know the feelings with which he returned. Disappointed in his hopes of rapid and brilliant success, he returned to the old condition of things, and the yoke must have pressed on him all the more heavily now that his illusions were dispelled and he no longer saw a prospect of shaking it off. He had buried his mother in a foreign land, and his warm true heart had been deceived in its first love; in poverty he returned to his father's house. He was not in a position to see as clearly as we do how powerfully his added experience of life and manifold artistic impressions had contributed to his moral and mental development, and he could scarcely be expected to look to this development for the strength and courage necessary to face the future.

The commencement of his residence in Salzburg was cheered by the presence of his lively young cousin; she had followed him from Munich on his entreaties, to pay a visit of some weeks to her uncle. Mozart's amiability and cordial manners renewed many pleasant intimacies, but the actual cause of his distaste to Salzburg, viz., the want of cultivation and of a disinterested love of art among its inhabitants, remained as before, and his long absence was likely to make him feel it all the more sensibly. The Archbishop, compelled by circumstances and his surroundings to recall Mozart, had not by any means forgiven his voluntary resignation of his former office, and the disinclination to return which Mozart had so evidently displayed, was certainly not calculated to appease his ill-will. We shall soon learn the kind of treatment which Mozart had to expect from him. The Salzburg public are described by Wolfgang in a letter to his father (May 26, 1781): "When I play in Salzburg, or when any of my compositions are performed, the audience might just as well be chairs or tables." He declares that, although he actually loves work far better than idleness, the want of congenial intercourse and inspiring surroundings make it often almost impossible for him to set to work at composition. "And why? Because my mind is not at ease." Again, he says (April 8, 1781): "To dawdle away one's youth in such a wretched hole is sad enough, and harmful besides." This and similar expressions might lead one to suppose that Mozart had neglected composition during these years, but a survey of the works which are known to us suffices to dispel this idea.

His musical activity took as a matter of course, in all essential points, the same direction as formerly; his official position as concertmeister and as court and cathedral organist (for so he was entered in the Salzburg Court Calendar), gave occasion for instrumental and church compositions, the style and materials of which were as restricted as before.

The first instrumental composition, in G major (318 K.), dated April 26, 1779, seems to have been written for some very special occasion. The orchestra is strongly appointed (besides the quartet there are two flutes, two oboes, two bassoons, four horns in G and D, and two trumpets in C), and used for effects which must have startled the Salzburgers. It is in the form now usual for overtures, but out of date for concert symphonies, viz.: three connected movements, Allegro spiritoso 4-4, which contains, besides the principal energetic motif with which it begins, and which constantly recurs in different ways, two independent, quieter motifs in succession: Andante 3-8, gentle and soft, somewhat longer than is usual for middle movements, but simple and without thematic elaboration; it leads back to the first Allegro, shortened (by the omission of the second subordinate subject) and modified in the elaboration. The individual and dramatic character of this composition, expressed most particularly in the commencement and the close of it, makes it probable that it was written as an introduction to a drama. We shall see that there was no lack of occasion for such works.

Also belonging to this period are two symphonies in the usual three movements.[1] The earlier, in B major (319 K.,

---

[1] The minuet movement in symphonies was not liked in Salzburg. The minuet of the Symphony in B flat major was written later (to judge by the handwriting) for a performance in Vienna, and appended on a separate leaf. Mozart began a minuet to the C major symphony, but only finished the first part, and crossed it out in the score. The effort not to make the symphony too long is evident throughout, and especially in the non-repetition of the first movement, although it is completely detached.

part 11), composed in the summer (July 9) of 1779, was evidently the results of "a pleased frame of mind"; it is a genuine product of Mozart's humour, lively, cheerful and full of grace and feeling. The second, a year later (August 29, 1780), in C major (338 K., part 10), is grander in conception and more serious in tone. This is particularly noticeable in the first movement; a constant propensity to fall into the minor key blends strength and decision with an expression not so much of melancholy as of consolation. In perfect harmony of conception, the simple and fervent Andante di molto combines exceeding tenderness with a quiet depth of tone. The contrasting instrumentation is very effective in this work; the first movement is powerful and brilliant, but in the second only stringed instruments (with doubled tenors) are employed. The last movement is animated throughout, and sometimes the orchestral treatment is rapid and impetuous.

A Serenade in D major (320 K.) belongs also to 1779, composed probably for some special festival, and (except that the march is omitted) quite in the style of the early already-noticed serenades[2] (Vol. I., p. 301). A short Adagio serves as introduction to a brilliant Allegro, arranged exactly like the first movement of a symphony, and worked out at considerable length; to this follows a minuet. Then there is inserted a concertante, described as such in the title, consisting of two movements, an Andante grazioso 3-4, and a rondo, Allegro ma non troppo 2-4, both in G major.[3] In earlier days, when Mozart figured as a violin-player, a violin solo played the chief part in such compositions; but now the wind instruments, two flutes, two oboes, and two bassoons are employed concertante; the stringed instruments and horns form the accompaniment proper. These two pieces are elaborated with great care and accuracy, and are clear and perspicuous as well as tender and graceful;

---

[2] The first movement (Adagio, Allegro con spirito), the Andantino and the Finale are (not quite correctly) printed as an independent symphony. (Breitkopf and Härtel, 7.)

[3] André possessed a careful copy of these two pieces, inscribed by Mozart "Sinfonia Concertante," as if for their special performance at a concert in Vienna, March 20, 1783.

II.   G

the rondo is somewhat lighter in tone than the first movement. Of bravura, properly so called, there is none to be
found, and the ornamental passages are confined to moderate amplifications of the melodies. The instruments are
solo in that they bear the principal part throughout, concertante in that they emulate each other in manifold and
changing combinations; their strife is playful, with sometimes almost a mischievous tone.

The Andantino which follows offers a strong contrast to
both movements of the concertante. This is marked at once
by the fact that the stringed instruments are here put forward as the exponents of the musical idea, while the very
sparely used wind instruments only emphasise certain sharp
points of detail. But the contrast is deeper than this; the
light and sunshiny mood of the two previous movements
accentuates the serious melancholy of the Andantino, which
seems to tell not of the pain of an existing passion, but of
the inner peace of a sorrow overcome. After a less noticeable minuet[4] the serenade closes with a long elaborate Presto,
an important movement full of life and force; the most
emphatic contrapuntal arrangement of the principal theme
is in the middle passage; it is lively and original, as well as
technically correct.

The melodies and subjects of these works show unmistakable progress; they are of maturer invention, have more
musical substance, if the expression may be allowed, more
delicacy and nobility of apprehension. Technical progress is
visible in the greater freedom of the contrapuntal treatment,
which had already been fully developed in Mozart's vocal
compositions. This is most obviously apparent in those
parts where thematic elaboration predominates, which are
richer and freer than hitherto. There are also many motifs
which owe their importance mainly to their contrapuntal
treatment. But, above all, we recognise Mozart's sure tact
in preserving the limits that prevent the interest in the dif-

---

[4] The customary attempt to give a peculiar charm to the trio of the minuet
by means of unusual instrumentation is here apparent in the solos for the flute
in the first trio and for the horn in the second. In Mozart's autograph score
the flute part is left blank: was the player to improvise?

ferent combinations of counterpoint to which a motive can be subjected from becoming essentially technical, and losing its artistic character.

Equally surely has his genius preserved him from the mistake of ascribing any absolute value to the contrapuntal method, or favouring the logical element which lies in it to the disadvantage of sensuous beauty. He makes use of the forms of counterpoint only to arrest the attention and to heighten the interest, without wearying the mind, intruding a foreign element into the original essence of the work, or neglecting beauty of form ; Mozart never forgets that music must be melodious. Therefore a receptive although uncultivated hearer receives a pleasing impression from artistic and even intricate passages, without at all suspecting the difficulties which he enjoys.

But the influence of the contrapuntal method reaches far deeper than well-defined and scholastic forms, just as a well-considered discourse does not consist merely in the observance of syllogistic forms. The principle of the free movement of the separate members of one whole penetrates the minutest divisions; and the combined effects of creative ability and artistic cultivation are nowhere so well displayed as in the independent construction of the separate elements which go to form the whole work. We admire Mozart's art in devising his plan, in accurately distributing his principal parts, and in disposing his lights and shades; but where he is in truth inexhaustible is in his power of strewing round a wealth of small touches which assist the characterisation and give to each part its peculiar effect and, in some respect, the justification of its existence. This power, which always seems to have something at command beyond the necessities of the case (although, in fact, every detail which seems to be the chance expression of individual vigour is conditioned of necessity by the whole conception), is the prerogative of genuine creative genius. It approaches the eternal power of nature, whose apparent prodigality is revealed to the deeper view as the wisest economy, or rather as the unruffled harmony of a great whole. So a statue by Phidias suggests to the spectator the impression of animated

G 2

nature, because it not merely puts before his eyes in general features a representation of the bodily form of man, but suggests to him the totality of the muscular movements which are in a living body in incessant activity. It is in art as in nature : the further we penetrate the fewer and less complex become the governing forces and impulses. Many details may be considered as trifling until it is asked whether they, in their place, have the required effect as part of the whole. When a work of art gives an effect of an artistic whole, in a way which cannot be explained by a consideration of its apparently, insignificant parts, this may be taken as the surest proof that the artist worked downwards from his conception of a great whole to the minutest details of his work. We must not undervalue, on the other hand, Mozart's more exact knowledge and freer use than formerly of external means. His residence in Mannheim had given him an altogether new conception of the performance of a good orchestra, both as to sound-effects and execution. The result is present in these compositions, although Salzburg surroundings and customs limited him greatly in his choice of means. It may be that for these reasons his instrumental combinations show no marked progress on former works, but the skilful use of the forces at his command become all the more apparent.

It is remarkable how, without any alteration in the instrumentation as a whole, the body of sound has become richer and fuller, the result of a more careful consideration of the particular nature of each instrument. This is most striking in the management of the wind instruments. The bassoons predominate throughout, independently treated, whereas formerly they only strengthened the bass ; and the use of the horns, with their long-sustained notes, shows marked progress. The combination of the wind instruments, sometimes in opposition to the stringed instruments, sometimes in unison with them, is another advance. Effective as are the wind instruments in combination, they are still more so in the delicacy of their individual features, and the perfection of their treatment could not fail to influence that of the stringed instruments, which show the same higher conception of what orchestral performances ought to be.

The Mannheim experiences were not without result either in respect to the executive delivery of the orchestra. Mozart must have been particularly impressed with the effect of *crescendo*, for almost in every passage we meet with phrases built upon a long-drawn *crescendo*. The contrast between *piano* and *forte* is also made the most of. Regular alternations of long passages *forte* and *piano* were formerly the custom, but now we have a rapid succession of very varied shades, *fortissimo* and *pianissimo* being also brought into use. But all these are only the outward signs of a higher intellectual apprehension, for which it was necessary also to give credit to the performers ; the composer, far from relying only on external effect, makes it the mere expression of the deeper meaning and intrinsic value of his compositions; it is from this point of view that the progress made by Mozart in the manipulation of his artistic materials acquires its true worth in the eyes of a musical critic.

We may imagine that Mozart found it no easy task to substitute a completely new style of execution for the time-honoured customs of the Salzburg band. The energy with which he was able at a later date to inspire the Leipzig orchestra, wedded as it was to its own traditions, gives some indication of his way of proceeding as a young man at Salzburg. His cousin used to hold forth later on Mozart's eccentric behaviour when conducting, and we may imagine that she witnessed some of the extraordinary scenes she describes during her present visit to Salzburg.

Mozart never appeared again as a violin-player, and we therefore find no compositions for the violin belonging to this period. After such an expression of opinion concerning the Salzburg public as that noted above, we cannot wonder that he was not over-anxious to appear before them as a clavier-player. We doubtless owe the Concerto for two claviers with orchestral accompaniment in E flat major (365 K., part 17) to his wish to play a duet with his sister.[5]

---

[5] I do not know André's authority for his assertion that it was composed in 1780, but it appears to me to be justified. Mozart sends from Vienna (June 27, 1781) for " The Sonata à quatre mains in B, and the two Concertos for two claviers," and he writes later on that he had played the Concerto à duo with

In design and treatment it is essentially similar to the earlier triple concerto. There is no intention apparent of making the two instruments independent; the players emulate each other in the delivery of the melodies and passages, sometimes together, sometimes in succession, often breaking off in rapid changes and interruptions ; the melodies are sometimes simply repeated, sometimes with variations so divided between the two instruments that neither can be said to have the advantage over the other. There are somewhat greater difficulties of execution than have been usual hitherto, a few passages, for instance, in octaves and thirds, but very modest ones ; the passages generally have more variety and elegance. The orchestra is simply and judiciously, but very delicately treated, the wind instruments in sustained chords, as a foundation for the clavier passages ; the effect of the *crescendo* and a greater attention to light and shade show the influence of Mannheim. Altogether the concerto is a well-arranged composition, clear and melodious, as well as accurately constructed, with a free, cheerful expression, which is most strikingly shown in the fresh gaiety of the last movement.

As organist, Mozart was under the necessity of playing the organ at festivals, but as a rule only for accompaniments and for interludes at set places, which gave him opportunities for improvising—his special delight. We have some organ sonatas with orchestral accompaniments belonging to this time (328, 329, 336, K.), quite in the style of those already noticed (Vol. I., p. 286); compositions after the fashion of the first movement of a sonata, without a trace of ecclesiastical severity, either in the technical construction, which is very light, or in the style, which is brilliant and cheerful. The organ occurs as an obbligato instrument only in one of these sonatas (329 K.), which is the most elaborated, but still very moderate in style, and without any florid passages.

Frl. Auernhammer at a concert (November 24, 1781). Two clarinets were added to the original accompaniment, on a flyleaf, for this performance. The second concerto which is mentioned is no doubt that originally written for three claviers, and afterwards for two (p. 331).

Of more important church compositions there belong to this period two Masses in C major, of which the earlier (317 K.) is one of Mozart's best-known works of the kind, bearing date March 23, 1779, and the later (337 K.) was written in March, 1780.[6] They are quite after the prescribed manner, not too long, not too serious, and yet not light; in no respect difficult or important, and closely allied in substance and treatment to the earlier works which have already been analysed (Vol. I., pp. 263 et seq.). The easy invention, never at a loss for fitting expression, the talent for organisation which arranges the parts into a connected and coherent whole, the technical sureness which gives to every detail its due share of interest—above all, the inexhaustible gift of melody and symmetry: all these qualities are here to be found, and it is by their aid that, in spite of hampering circumstances, such great and healthy work was done.

Nevertheless, these Masses show more plainly even than earlier works of the same kind how the fetters of outward control check the impulses of inner strength and feeling. We see Mozart as it were in court dress; he is expert enough to move in it with tolerable freedom, but he is disguised rather than clothed. Conventional influence is most apparent in the instrumentation, which, as a whole, is little different from that of the earlier works. Some passages are remarkable even in their instrumentation; for instance, the Et incarnatus and Crucifixus of the first Mass have an expressive violin passage, and in the second the treatment of the wind instruments in the Crucifixus and Resurrexit, and the organ, oboe, and bassoon in emulation with the voice in the Agnus Dei, remind us of Mannheim.

But these are details, and in its general features the tone-colouring of the orchestra is the same as formerly; rapid violin passages predominate, the trombone follows the voice regularly and *forte*, and so on. But in other respects original features are not wanting, nor even passages of surprising beauty, to which belongs, for instance, the unusually melodious close of the first Mass, in which the Benedictus,

---

[6] The Credo as far as the "Et in spiritum" was afterwards laid aside; it was in 3-4, with the doubtful superscription, "Tempo di ciacconna."

contrary to custom in a serious choral movement, is in strict counterpoint. These are signs of a great genius, which make us regret all the more that the whole work is not dictated and inspired by the same spirit. To this period also, according to the handwriting, belongs a Kyrie sketched by Mozart and not preserved quite complete (323 K.), which has been completed and printed as a Regina cœli by Stadler. It is characterised by a rapid sextole passage which is distributed among the wind instruments in uninterrupted movement. The voices take their own independent course throughout. Among other unfinished attempts by Mozart preserved in the Mozarteum at Salzburg, and both by the handwriting and instrumentation, as well as from other reasons, to be referred to this time, we may particularise the beginning of a Mass with obbligato organ (Anh., 13 K.) and the beginning (two pages) of a Kyrie (Anh., 16 K.), which is in such strict counterpoint that the Mass, if it had been finished, would have been among the most elaborate of them all. But Mozart had neither inducement nor the means for producing such compositions in Salzburg.

Two Vespers by Mozart (321, 339, K.), of the years 1779 and 1780, have much the same resemblance in substance and compass to masses that litanies had at an earlier period, but they stand higher in many respects.

Five psalms and the Virgin's hymn of praise form the part of the Vespers which is in varied chant; every division ends with the doxology, and is complete in itself. In the Litany the principal part is framed in, as it were, by two equally original and characteristic movements, the Kyrie and Agnus; the Vespers, on the other hand consist of six separate movements which have no connection, either actual or artistic. More striking differences of key are therefore permissible than is generally the case with the movements of one composition,[7] and it was possible to put together at pleasure

---

[7] The Dixit and Magnificat of the first vesper is in C major, Confitebor in E minor, Beatus vir in B flat major, Laudate pueri in F major, Laudate Dominum in A flat major. The Dixit and Magnificat of the second vesper are also in C major, Confitebor in E flat major, Beatus vir in G major, Laudate pueri in D minor, Laudate Dominum in F major.

psalms belonging to different compositions, sometimes even by different composers. The Dixit and Magnificat, as the two corner-posts, were considered the principal parts ; they were generally specially composed, and others inserted between them. As the words of the doxology (Gloria Patri) recur at the close of each movement, it would have been natural that the idea should arise of giving them the same musical rendering, and suggesting a relation between the different movements by this kind of refrain. But they are, on the contrary, in close connection with the words to which they serve as a conclusion, so as to characterise the use of the general formula as dependent on the special nature of each case. For the most part, therefore, a principal subject of the piece which it concludes is utilised for the doxology, and it is astonishing of what a variety of appropriate and expressive musical renderings these words are capable.

A settled custom became established, both as to the general conception and the distinguishing characteristics of these compositions, which was closely followed even by Mozart. In the main, the conception and treatment resembled those of the litanies; the effort is evident to reconcile the requirements of Divine service with the prevailing and somewhat trivial musical taste of the times. But the vespers preserved the dignity and solemnity of church music more strictly than the litanies. There is no sign of a leaning to operatic style, concessions to bravura are sparely and exceptionally made, the orchestra preserves the simplicity of the traditional church orchestra,[8] and limited scope is allowed even to grace and pleasing fancies. Nevertheless, the expression of dignity and solemnity shows the influence of a time which did not exact from sacred art the absorption of the inner man in the sacred and the divine, but was satisfied with a decent ob-

---

[8] The accompaniment consists, besides the organ (which is only once obbligato), of two violins and bass, trumpets and drums (these last only in the Dixit and Magnificat), and trombones in unison with the choir. The tenors invariably go with the bass; but, a rare occurence, the violoncello is frequently distinct from the double-bass. Once a very simple solo for the bassoon, *ad libitum*, occurs.

servance of the forms of external homage. It was left to the artist, who had a deeper spiritual craving, and such a delicate artistic sense as forbade the use of form without substance, to give a higher tone to his work. In this sense we may include by far the larger portions of these vespers among Mozart's great works.

As concerns the musical construction in detail, a narrow mode of treatment resulted throughout from the conditions of worship; the words had to be composed straight through, just as in short Masses. A broader rendering of separate portions which might seem to lend themselves to musical expression was not admitted, and the endeavour after a dramatic characterisation of certain points did not come within the artistic usages of the time. The important point, therefore, was not to render the words in music, so as to give a new and fitting expression to each detail, but to invent characteristic motifs for the important points which should be suitable for further elaboration, and which, in spite of individual distinction, should spring from the fundamental conception of the whole work. The task of the composer is not made easier by the words of the psalms; they do not offer a good basis for musical construction, nor are the ideas conveyed in them generally such as would incite to musical production. The composer must therefore be original in no ordinary degree, and it is excusable if he now and then handles the rules and forms of his art with a certain amount of abruptness, and even makes verbal expression subservient to them, so far as it can be done without harmful pressure.

In order to introduce variety among these closely allied compositions a certain type had been formed, which was not exactly the inevitable consequence of the effort to satisfy the rules of art and of good taste, but, as in the litanies, exercised considerable influence over the treatment of the text. The two vespers we are considering are very similar in form and workmanship. Various parts are treated in both with marked preference, and it is scarcely possible to place one before the other in merit, except that perhaps the earlier one is the more serious.

The first psalm, Dixit Dominus, is formed into an ani-

mated, restless movement, full of strength and dignity;
while the same tone predominates in both, there is more
fire and brilliancy in the first composition, more mildness
and tranquillity in the second. The kind of treatment may
be compared to that of the Gloria and Credo of the Mass.
Without any sustained thematic elaboration, certain principal motifs are maintained and emphasised in different
ways. The animated string passages are not only in varied
harmonic combinations, but often in counterpoint, either
imitative or a combination of the different subjects. The
voices are free and independent, but with a few trifling exceptions they are treated harmonically ; solo voices sometimes alternate with the chorus, but without any special
prominence.

The second psalm, Confitebor tibi, Domine, is in the earlier
Vesper (321 K.), a chorale with solo intermixed, accompanied
only by the organ and stringed instruments (E minor 3-4).
This mature and beautiful composition approaches the Mass
in F major (Vol. I., p. 257) both in tender and fervent sentiment
and in simplicity and purity of form. But there the treatment
is contrapuntal throughout, here it is essentially harmonic.
The independent progress of the voices displays a succession
of rich and startling harmonies in animated but natural
development ; notwithstanding many suspensions and unexpected turns, they are always clear and melodious, and
always the true and natural expression of the sentiment to
be conveyed.[9] The frame of mind represented is not one of
fanatical remorse, but rather of a soul penetrated with the
feeling of guilt, and impelled to acknowledge it with shame
and anguish. The moderate expression of such a mood,
which might easily pass over into the sentimental, coincides
with the symmetry of form observable in the main features
as well as in the details of the work. The corresponding
movement of the second Vesper (339 K.) is not to be placed
on the same level as this. It maintains on the whole the
tone of the first movement, with an increase of earnestness,

---

[9] The simple but sometimes independent accompaniment, especially of the
violins, is very beautiful, and heightens the effect, as it does in the Mass.

and is a clever and melodious composition, with good effect
in its place ; but the poetical beauty of the other is altogether
wanting.

The third psalm, Beatus vir, has least original colouring.
It is in both Vespers a lively, powerful, one might almost
say, cheerful movement, suggestive of the Gloria or Credo of
more than one mass, but without the solemnity which
characterises them. Here, too, solo voices alternate with
the chorus[10] without interrupting the steady flow of the composition. In the earlier work there are some beautiful
harmonic effects; in the later, contrapuntal phrases sometimes
occur; an animated rapid accompaniment by the violins is
common to both.

As in the Litany, the Pignus futuræ gloriæ, so in the
Vesper the fourth psalm, Laudate pueri, was treated in
severe counterpoint, and here it was that a thoroughly trained
church composer made good his claim to the title. In the
first of the Vespers that we are considering this psalm[11] is a
clever piece of counterpoint, original in form, and deviating
from the strict regularity which usually characterises Mozart.

It begins with an infinite canon. The twelve bars melody
for the soprano—

is imitated three bars later by the alto in unison. Then
follows the tenor an octave higher, and then the bass in
unison. After the completion of the melody the soprano
again takes it up, alto and tenor follow. The regular
progress of the canon is then broken by a complete final
cadenza, in which all the voices unite on the last note of the
bass melody. A short theme introduced by the bass—

---

[10] In the second vesper a long triplet passage is given to the solo soprano at
the words " Cornu eius exaltabitur," but nothing further comes of it.

[11] Printed as an offertory, " Amavit eus Dominus " (Vienna: Diabelli).

A so - lis or - tu us - que ad . . oc - ca - sum,

is imitated by the other parts in similar or in contrary motion,
and soon passes over into a short passage ending in D
minor. Hereupon the soprano interposes with a new and
characteristic melody—

Quis si - cut Do - mi - nus De - us nos - ter,

the first bars of which are taken up by the other voices;
but instead of a further elaboration, a new theme is introduced by the alto, followed by a counter-theme, which are
both imitated together—

Qui in all - - - tis ha - bi - tat in al - tis ha-

whereupon the alto raises a new melody, which is figured
by the other parts in imitation as Cantus firmus, and
closes in A minor. Then the alto begins with the previous
soprano subject, but now in F major; the soprano follows
with the second, but the imitative figuring soon gives place
to a fine harmonic elaboration, followed by the third
passage; the imitative parts maintain the same character,
and the alto has now another Cantus firmus. To this at
last is appended a long coda, formed of detachments of
previous subjects, variously elaborated in stretto and contrary
motion, ending in organ point on the dominant. It cannot
fail to be remarked how tuneful and melodious, as well as
independent, characteristic, and striking in their effect are
the different parts. The melodies which compose the Cantus
firmus may have been, in part at least, borrowed from church
tones. Far more ambitious is the contrapuntal work in the
second Vesper,[12] which consists of a close succession of diffi-

---

[12] Printed as an offertory, " Sancti et iusti " (Vienna: Diabelli).

cult problems solved after the severest and most rigorous rules.   After the first regular enunciation of the theme—

there occurs a second motif—

which is at first treated freely, and issues into a short harmonic passage, which is afterwards used again as an interlude.   Then the two motifs are combined—

and elaborated together, after which this section closes on the chord of the dominant in a stretto arrangement of the chief subject, while the violins take up the subordinate motif.   When the chief subject has again asserted itself, there follows its inversion as a counter-subject—

and regular elaboration, ending in the above interlude, after which the subject and its inversion appear together as an organ point on the fundamental tone, while the violins proceed with an independent accompaniment:—

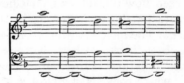

After the previous stretto has again occurred on the chord of the dominant the two first subjects reappear in new original climacteric treatment, divided between the voices and the accompaniment:—

A free conclusion brings the artistic and forcible work to an end.

As if for refreshment after this effort, the fifth psalm, Laudate Dominum, is treated as a solo movement of a pleasing character. In the earlier vesper it is a soprano solo with organ obbligato, not certainly set in prescribed aria form, but in its brilliant passages and easy grouping of the melodies more akin to secular music than any other of Mozart's church compositions of this period. In the second vesper the psalm has a more solemn character, but even here it is a mild and tender soprano solo, somewhat pastoral in tone, and supported by a solo bassoon; simple throughout, and with a fine climax at the close, the doxology being sung by the chorus.

The Virgin's hymn of praise, " Magnificat anima mea," which forms the conclusion of the Vespers, is by its form the part best fitted for musical rendering. But the connection in which it here stands with the preceding psalms obliges a corresponding treatment both as to extent and conception. We must not therefore look either for a comprehensive treatment giving free development to the details of the separate sentences, such as is to be found in the Magnificats of some great masters, or for such an amount of dramatic characterisation as the words give scope for. The text is tersely and precisely treated, with the avowed intention of concluding the work with a movement in contrast to the first psalm. This is evident not only in the external arrangement, which introduces trumpets and drums, and returns to the original key, but in the technical treatment and the closely allied tone of expression. The expression of firm and cheerful confidence, which is common to both, is naturally accentuated in the Magnificat in accordance with the text, and the lively expectation of the first psalm is now turned into thanksgiving for its fulfilment. The technical treatment of the Magnificat is consistently more important and animated, especially in the extended use of the forms of counterpoint; but in the main the two compositions have the same tone and colour, and the same condensed and impulsive style. The words "Magnificat anima mea Dominum" form a solemn introduction as a short slow movement; "Et exultavit" is in quicker tempo, which is maintained to the end, chorus and solo alternating in the usual way. Here again it is to be noticed that different points are accentuated in the earlier Magnificat chiefly by harmonic means, in the second chiefly by counterpoint.

Having in these works followed Mozart's steady upward progress along the path which he had previously entered on, a progress maintained against most unfavourable surroundings, let us now turn to his attempts in the new province of music as an adjunct to the drama. Remembering his intense desire to write for the stage, a desire which had been increased by the manifold influences of his travels, we shall not be surprised that even theatrical undertakings in Salzburg offered him the opportunity he sought. When he returned home a theatrical company was performing under Böhm's management; in 1780 we find Shikaneder there with his travelling *troupe*, a friend of the Mozart family, joining in their quoit contests and quite ready to turn Wolfgang's talents to his own advantage.[18] Two great works owe their origin to these performances, although the exact time of their production cannot now be ascertained.

---

[18] Wolfgang had promised to compose an aria for him, but had not done so when he was summoned to Munich for "Idomeneo"; reproached by his father, he found time in the full swing of his work at "Idomeneo" to write this aria and send it to Salzburg (November 22, 1780).

The first is the music to "Thamos, King of Egypt"
(345 K.), an heroic drama, by Baron Tob. Phil. von Gebler,
who, in spite of his exalted position, had devoted himself
zealously since 1769 to the reform of the Vienna theatre.[14]
The contents of the piece need be given but briefly, since it
is as good as lost:[15]—

Menes, King of Egypt, has been deposed by a usurper, Rameses, and
as it is thought, assassinated; but he is living under the name of Sethos
as high priest of the Temple of the Sun, the secret being known only to
the priest Hammon and the general Phanes. After the death of Rameses
his son Thamos is heir to the throne. The day arrives when Thamos
attains majority, is to be invested with the diadem, and to select a bride.
The friends of Menes seek in vain to persuade him to dispute the
throne. He will not oppose the noble youth whom he loves and
esteems. But Pheron, a prince and confidant of Thamos has, in
conjunction with Mirza, the chief of the virgins of the sun, organised
a conspiracy against Thamos, and won over a portion of the army.
Tharsis, daughter of Menes, who is believed by all, even her father, to
be dead, has been brought up by Mirza under the name of Sais. It is
arranged that she shall be proclaimed rightful heir to the throne,
and as she will then have the right to choose her consort, Mirza
will secure her beforehand for Pheron. When she discovers that
Sais loves Thamos, and he her, she induces Sais to believe that
Thamos prefers her playmate Myris, and Sais is generous enough
to sacrifice her love and her hopes of the throne to her friend. Equally
nobly Thamos rejects all suspicions against Pheron, and awards him
supreme command. As the time for action draws near, Pheron
discloses to Sethos, whom he takes for a devoted follower of Menes,
and consequently for an enemy to Thamos, the secret of Sais'
existence and his own plans. Sethos prepares secretly to save Thamos.
Sais also, after being pledged to silence by an oath, is initiated into the
secret by Mirza and Pheron, and directed to choose Pheron. She
declines to give a decided answer, and Pheron announces to Mirza his
determination to seize the throne by force in case of extremity. Sais,
who believes herself not loved by Thamos, and will not therefore
choose him as consort, but will not deprive him of the throne, takes
the solemn and irrevocable oath as virgin of the sun. Thamos enters,
and they discover to their sorrow their mutual love. Sethos, entering,
enlightens Thamos as to the treachery of Pheron, without disclosing
the parentage of Sais. Pheron, disturbed by the report that Menes is

---

[14] The Wien. Ztg. (1786, No. 31) contains an obituary notice. Cf. Gervinus,
Gesch. d. Poet. Nat. Litt., IV., p. 590.
[15] Published in Vienna, 1774, Frankfort, 1775, and in Freih. von Gebler's
Theatralischen Werken (Prague and Dresden 1772), III., p. 305.

still living, comes to take council of Sethos, and adheres to his treacherous design. In solemn assembly Thamos is about to be declared king, when Mirza reveals the fact that Sais is the lost Tharsis, and heiress to the throne. Thamos is the first to offer her his homage. When she is constrained to choose between Thamos and Pheron she declares herself bound by her oath, and announces Thamos as the possessor of the throne. Then Pheron calls his followers to arms, but Sethos steps forward and discloses himself as Menes; whereupon all fall at his feet in joyful emotion. Pheron is disarmed and led off, Mirza stabs herself, Menes, as father and ruler, releases Sais from her oath, unites her with Thamos, and places the pair on the throne. A message arrives that Pheron has been struck with lightning by Divine judgment, and the piece ends.

Mozart wrote music to this drama at Salzburg in 1779 or 1780, according to the evidence of the handwriting and paper of the score, as well as of the treatment of the orchestra.[16] It consisted at first of four instrumental movements which were played between the acts, and one which formed the conclusion of the whole piece. It was not a new idea to compose appropriate music to a drama of importance instead of the usual indifferent or inappropriate instrumental movements. Joh. Ad. Scheibe (1708-1776) wrote music for "Polyeucte" and "Mithridate" in 1738, and afterwards wrote an article on this kind of music in the "Kritischen Musicus." He maintained that the overture should be composed with reference to the whole piece, and should lead up to its commencement; that the symphonies between the acts should be connected both with the act which preceded and that which followed, so as to lead the audience insensibly from the one frame of mind to the other. The closing symphony should be in close relationship to the end of the piece, so as to intensify the impression made by the *dénouement* upon the audience. He con-

---

[16] Confirmed by an expression of Mozart to his father, written from Vienna (February 15, 1783): "I am really sorry that I cannot make use of the music to "Thamos." The piece, having failed here, is destined to be never again performed. If it were, it would be solely on account of the music, and that is scarcely likely. It is certainly a pity!" Mozart gave his music, in 1786, to the needy theatrical manager Bulla, who made a good profit by it (Nissen, p. 685); "König Thamos" was given the same year in Berlin (Teichmann's Litt. Nachl., p. 40). The whole composition was successfully performed at Frankfort in the winter of 1865, with a connecting poem by Gisb. von Vincke.

sidered a change of instruments particularly necessary, in order to keep up the attention of the audience; but care must be taken to select the most appropriate instruments for each movement, so as to express what had to be expressed in the most effective manner possible.

Scheibe was followed by Joh. Christ. Hertel (1726-1789) with the music to Cronegk's "Olint and Sophronia,"[17] and by others (among them Agricola) with the music to "Semiramis" (after Voltaire), which Lessing thought worthy of an analysis, and declared his opinion that the *entr'actes* should have no reference to the following act, but should only amplify and conclude what had gone before.[18] Vogler's overture and *entr'actes* to "Hamlet" were given in Mannheim in 1779.[19] Even in Salzburg M. Haydn had composed in 1777 special music for the performance of Voltaire's "Zaire" by French actors, which was received with great applause.[20]

The music to "King Thamos" has, curiously enough, no overture, which is perhaps accounted for by the fact that the play begins with a chorus, and so is opened by music.[21] Each *entr'acte* is in connection with the last scene of the preceding act, and seeks to express the same set of emotions by means of music; Mozart has each time noted down what seemed to him the prevailing idea to be represented. Thus, he writes concerning the first movement: "The first act ends with the determination of Mirza and Pheron to place the latter

---

[17] Cf. Schmid, Nekrolog, I., p. 363.

[18] Lessing, Hamb. Dramat. St., 26 (Werke, VI., p. 115).

[19] Betracht. d. Mannh. Tonsch., I., p. 313; III., p. 253.

[20] "Haydn's *entr'actes* (to 'Zaire') are really fine," writes L. Mozart (October 6, 1777). "One of them was an arioso with variations for violoncelli, flutes, oboe, &c., and next after a *piano* variation came one with Turkish music so suddenly and unexpectedly that all the women started, and there was a general titter. Between the fourth and fifth acts was a cantabile with recitatives for the English horn, and then the arioso again, which accorded very well with the sadness of the preceding scene and with the following act."

[21] It might be supposed that the overture before mentioned (Vol. II., p. 86) was intended for this play, and the date of the composition agrees with this supposition. But the paper differs from that of the other instrumental movements, and Mozart was exact and careful in these matters. Something also of the solemn dignity characteristic of the choruses might be looked for in an overture to "König Thamos"; in other respects it is not unsuitable.

on the throne." Upon the last words of Mirza—"Mirza, a woman, trembles not. Thou art a man; conquer, or die!"— the orchestra strikes in with three solemn chords, the effect heightened by long pauses; then begins a restless and agitated Allegro (in C minor). The prevailing tone is one of excitement, and those who were in the theatre might well receive the suggestion of Mirza, as an eager passionate woman, inciting Pheron to action; but the characterisation is not very striking. It is only noticeable that the separate phrases of the subject are shorter and in greater contrast than is usual with Mozart; otherwise we have before us a movement in two parts, with a coda arranged in the ordinary manner, but not elaborated.

The second act has, if possible, a still more general application: "The noble nature of Thamos is displayed at the end of the second act; the third act opens with Thamos and the traitor Pheron," and the dialogue wherein Thamos declares his belief in Pheron's fidelity, and resigns Sais to him, while Pheron continues to dissemble. Here, too, Mozart has written an ordinary movement in two parts (Andante, E flat major); but he has resorted to the expedient of denoting the character of the two personages by means of distinct subjects, which he indicates by superscriptions:—

THAMOS' Noble Nature.

It is easy to be seen here that musical contrast is the main point, and that the characterisation is very general, quite apart from the fact that integrity and hypocrisy cannot be expressed in music, as Mozart was well aware, in spite of his naïve superscriptions. The inadequacy of such

characterisation is shown in the second part, where both
characters occur together :—

Here the expression has become still more general, and we
have only the musical development of a given subject, not
the progress of a dramatic situation ; more than this it is out
of the province of the musician to give.

The suggestions for the music of the third *entr'acte* are
more promising. The music is connected in the first place
with the last scene: "The third act closes with the
treacherous dialogue between Mirza and Pheron," expressed
by means of an agitated, strongly accented Allegro, which,
however, soon breaks off, and dies away. Thereupon
the music turns to the fourth act, which begins with the
vow of the deluded Sais. Here the influence of the melodrama upon Mozart becomes apparent, for he follows with
his music every turn in the monologue of Sais, indicating
each by a superscription. We may, indeed, doubt whether
he had not some idea of a melodramatic delivery of the
music, although there are no pauses left for spoken sentences, and the flow of the music, notwithstanding frequent
changes of time is uninterrupted. This movement would
be most open to the adverse criticism of Lessing, for it
anticipates the whole of the following scene. In itself it
is the most expressive and the most successful ; in spite of
its division into separate points it preserves connection and

unity, and a tone of tender grace such as becomes a bashful maiden.

The fourth *entr'acte* is again an animated movement (Allegro vivace assai) which is to depict "the universal confusion" with which the fourth act concludes. We can recognise in the wild, restless subject, in opposition to which is placed another full of dignity and reserve, the intended contrast between the conspirators and Thamos with his followers ; but we need, of course, to be told what it is that the music means to represent.

Since the spectators were in a position to transfer the factitious presumption from the stage to the music, a general characterisation would suffice for them. The music therefore fulfils its primary aim, but it has undertaken a task which lies beyond its province, and a previous knowledge of the subject treated is indispensable to the due appreciation of it ; in this way the music is as dependent as though it were a setting to words without the advantage of the direct intelligibleness given to it by words.

The closing movement describes "Pheron's despair, blasphemy, and death." As this situation coincides with a fearful thunderstorm, the musical characterisation is confined to a representation of it without any dramatic detail ; it is a wildly forcible movement, and the effect accords well with the suggested idea.[22]

It is unquestionable that Mozart, excited by the melodrama, has set himself eagerly to express dramatic details in music, and yet in almost every case the exigencies of musical construction have been too much for him. The impressions he has received from the drama become only impulses, leading him to accent more sharply and set in stronger contrast the various points of his composition ; the special points of the dramatic situations are not fully brought out in the music. This is in great measure the fault of the play, which affords few powerful or effective suggestions to the composer either through its characters or its situations ;

---

[22] The usual Salzburg orchestra is kept in view for these movements: strings, oboes, bassoons, and horns ; and for the three entr'actes (I., IV., V.), trumpets and drums.

great poetical or dramatic power would no doubt have called forth other music. That such a play should have been received with interest and applause,[23] that it should have incited Mozart to composition, is a speaking proof of the taste of the time. Shakespeare and Goethe had not yet penetrated the intellectual atmosphere in which Mozart had grown up; before poetry could assert its sway in the province of music it had to express and realise the demand for a characterisation bringing to view the most individual traits of human character.

Gebler had sought to invest his drama with peculiar dignity by providing it with choruses, for which Racine's " Athalie " may have furnished him with an example. The play begins with a solemn sacrifice in the Temple of the Sun, the priests and virgins singing hymns to the Godhead ; in the same way, at the beginning of the fifth act, the coronation of the king is introduced by a sacrifice, the priests and virgins again singing a hymn.[24] These choruses gave Mozart opportunity for a magnificent style of composition, with all the brilliancy that external support could give.

The hymns were well-known ones with Latin words inserted later, for which, however, a German translation was again substituted. Our judgment as to style and conception

---

[23] Wieland enthusiastically praises the completed drama (Auswahl, Denkw., Briefe, II., pp. 14, 26). Soon afterwards (p. 27) he wished the conclusion altered, and complained that the virtuous people were unreal, and the wicked ones veritable demons. Ramler, Sulzer, Thümmel, also spoke highly in praise of " König Thamos " (Schlegel, Deutsch. Mus., IV., pp. 139, 153, 159). It was at once translated into French (Wieland, Auswahl. Denkw. Briefe, II., p. 30), and into Italian in 1780, by J. S. von Berghoff, secretary to Prince Colloredo. A handsomely bound copy of this translation is preserved with Mozart's score ; it was probably sent to the Archbishop, and Mozart may have thought of adapting his choruses to the Italian version.

[24] Schweitzer professed to discern in the composer to the choruses which Gebler sent to Ramler and Wieland a beginner of great promise. That this talented beginner was not Mozart (although he was in Vienna in the summer of 1773) no one who casts a glance over the choruses will for a moment doubt. " Two choruses to the play of ' Thamos ' by Mozart, scored for the piano by C. Zulehner," were published by Simrock, in Bonn, and are certainly not genuine. The fact that Mozart was known to have written an anonymous composition for the stage no doubt caused this one to be attributed to him.

will naturally be affected by the fact that the hymns were written for the theatre, and not as church music proper; and yet these very hymns have been widely circulated by countless performances in churches, and are made to serve as the principal evidence of Mozart's style of church music. There is no question that their whole conception is grander, freer, and more imposing than that of any of his masses belonging to that period, but this is because he felt himself unfettered by conventional restrictions. A solemn act of worship was represented on the stage, the expression of reverence to the Supreme Being was heightened in effect by the Egyptian surroundings; and Mozart's endeavour was to render the consequent emotions with all possible truth and force. But he was fully conscious that the expression must be *dramatic*. Therefore everything was avoided that directly suggested the church, and an impression of splendour and brilliancy was given which in this fashion was foreign to the church; above all the subjective points of sentiment are thrown into strong relief, and forcibly expressed. But although there is an essential difference between these choruses and Mozart's contemporary church music, yet we cannot fail to perceive a certain amount of resemblance in the manner in which the solemnity and importance of religious ceremony is rendered both here and in the "Zauberflöte." The drama itself has some resemblance to the "Zauberflöte," both in its deistic-humanitarian tendency and its Egyptian costume and sun-worship. Freemasonry may have exerted some influence over Gebler's mind[25]—it could have had none at that time over Mozart.

In the music to the "Zauberflöte" everything, more especially the power of concentrating ideas in the strictest forms, shows mature development, while here we are aware of the youthful genius, rejoiced at the opportunity of pouring forth his best in full measure, and thereby satisfying his nature to the utmost. The consideration of these choruses explains his joy at finding the chorus in Paris strong and good

---

[25] Gebler was Grand Master of the district lodge, " zum neuen Bund," in 1784 (Lewis, Gesch. d. Freimaurerei in Oesterreich, p. 162).

(Vol. I., p. 429), and choruses, his "most favourite compositions," well performed and much thought of; we can imagine what he would have made of the choruses if he had written a grand opera in Paris. They leave Gebler's words (out of which, according to Wieland, Gluck could have made something excellent) so far behind that the music and the poetry, considered from an artistic point of view, seem to belong to different periods. For actual representation they are no doubt too grandly and broadly conceived and executed; they overpower the whole drama with their weight. The impression of solemnity and grandeur produced on the mind by symbolic ceremonies is rendered with dignity, and at the same time with fire and energy. The chorus and orchestra unite to give the effect of splendour and magnificence, and startling harmonies are borne along as if on an irresistible stream; the lighter subordinate subjects (divided between male and female chorus as well as solo voices) are less marked. The style and treatment of the choruses have afforded a precedent for many similar works in later days; so also has the way in which the choruses and a full orchestra are united so as to give a massive effect, both of arrangement and construction. Mozart himself had no opportunity of again uniting chorus and orchestra on a large scale, and proceeding further in the same direction; Haydn in his oratorios inherited this portion of Mozart's genius, and numerous efforts have since been made to accomplish what Mozart began.

The orchestra is provided with all the external advantages that Salzburg could offer; no instruments employed at a later date are wanting, except the clarinet, which Mozart missed so sensibly. It is organised and constructed exactly as we find it at the present day; the wind instruments of wood and brass and the stringed instruments are united in definite groups, but in perfect freedom of treatment. Most striking is Mozart's progress in his treatment of the brass instruments. The trombones are no longer with the voices, and where they support them they do it in an independent manner, generally by sustained chords. But they also take their own place in the orchestra, the horns and trumpets united with them, and

then again the horns combine with the wood-wind instruments; while the trumpets, with the drums, occasionally
assert their peculiar character. In the same way, the other
wind instruments are combined among themselves, as well
as with the other instruments; it is in accordance with their
nature that the rendering of the more delicate details should
fall to their share. Such an extended employment of the
wind instruments must naturally have influenced the treatment of the strings. These are independently and forcibly
placed in contrast with the wind instruments, so that, while
the latter heighten the colouring, the former determine the
fundamental character of the work and maintain unity of
tone. In short, all important effects which can be produced by
different combinations of the instruments are here brought
into use, not merely as sound effects produced by changes of
tone colouring, but as the means of giving due expression to
musical ideas.

The chorus also takes a different position in conjunction
with an orchestra such as this. It is no longer the principal
object in the sense of making everything else subservient to
itself; but the independence of the instruments renders it
freer in its own motion. Since so much was left to be
rendered by the orchestra, the chorus was able to characterise what belonged essentially to it all the more sharply
and strongly; and the powerful and effective orchestra called
forth all the strength of the chorus that they might keep
pace with each other. For this there was requisite, besides
an intensified meaning in the subjects, a free and melodious
treatment, which made the separate voices the foundation
for the display of natural and forcible effects of sound. To
satisfy these varied conditions in detail, and to unite them
harmoniously into combined effect, has been Mozart's successfully executed task. Let any one place those earlier
works, in which the voices supply the harmonies to a continuous violin passage and a *basso continuo* side by side with
these hymns where an independent chorus, complete in itself,
is united with an equally independent and carefully arranged
orchestra, so as to form a compact and solid whole, and what
an extraordinary progress is apparent !

Mozart, who executed this work with loving care, composed both choruses twice over. The first chorus, in the earlier and completely carried-out attempt, has essentially the same features as the later, only the solo parts are simpler and without the delicate accompaniment which gives them their chief charm. The voices are only altered in the details of the main portions of the chorus, but the orchestra is subjected to a thorough elaboration. At first there were no flutes, and the addition of these has given to the oboes a different position and in many ways caused a different grouping of the instruments. But, apart from this, there are so many improvements in detail that this work may be considered as a regular study in instrumentation. The difference between the two versions of the second chorus are more essential. Only the beginning and the fundamental ideas of some of the subjects in the first attempt are identical with the later elaboration. The working-out is quite different, not only much shorter, but in every respect scantier and less important ; and more especially are the orchestral parts far removed from their present rich perfection. Mozart did not even finish this first attempt ; it breaks off in the middle of the last passage, although only a few bars are wanting. The difference in the elaboration proves once more that the true gift of an artist consists in the unerring judgment with which, after no matter how many experiments in the process of his work, he seizes in the end on what is best for his purpose. It is instructive to follow the progress of development from the earlier ideas and attempts—in the second chorus the main features are more carefully perfected, in the first the details.

The magnificent effect of these two choruses seems to have suggested the idea of bringing the drama to an impressive close by means of another chorus. In the place of the instrumental movement which represented Pheron's death, there was introduced a short exhortation by the High Priest to fear the Divine wrath, which is taken up by the chorus, and passes into joyful trust in the protection of the Almighty.

Mozart's composition (to words provided by a Salzburg

local poet—perhaps by Schachtner)[26] is altogether worthy of the two first hymns. The bass solo of the High Priest foreshadows the Commendatore in "Don Giovanni." The chorus which follows gives the right expression of humble reverence on the part of the bystanders; and the cheerful dignity of the conclusion is quite appropriate when we take into account that the chorus was intended for the stage and not for the church.

Another composition falling within Mozart's present residence at Salzburg is a German operetta, for which honest Schachtner provided the libretto. It was almost finished when Mozart went to Munich in November, 1780.

His father wrote (December 11, 1780) that nothing could then be done with "Schachtner's play" on account of the public mourning at Vienna. This was all the better, since "the music was not quite ready." But Wolfgang begs him (January 18, 1781) to bring with him "Schachtner's operetta." "People come to see Cannabich, with whom the hearing of such things does not come *mal à propos*." Later on the father revived the idea of producing the operetta in Vienna, but Wolfgang answered (April 18, 1781): "Nothing can be done with Schachtner's operetta, for the same reason that I have often given before. I could not contradict Stephanie; I could only say that the piece—except the long dialogues, which could easily be altered—was very good, but not suited for Vienna, where they only care for comic pieces."

There can be no doubt that this is the opera[27] in two acts, without a title, preserved in Mozart's carefully executed original score, and complete all but the overture and the conclusion (344 K.), which was published by André, with the

---

[26] This concluding chorus is wanting in Gebler's works, and in the Italian translation thus proving its Salzburg origin.

[27] As early as 1799 the following inquiry was made in the Intelligenz-Blatt of the A. M. Z., II., p. 21: "Among Mozart's posthumous works has been found a German vaudeville, written apparently in 1778 or 1779; it is without a title, and contains the following characters: Gomaz, Zaide, Sultan, Zaram, Soliman, Osmin, &c. Any person acquainted with the title of this work, or with the fact of its having been printed, is requested to communicate with the editor of this paper." The inquiry appears to have remained unanswered.

suitable title of "Zaide."[28]   The handwriting, style, and
instrumentation, as well as some special circumstances to
be presently noted, prove this beyond a doubt.   The plot
may be conjectured in its general features by the songs and
music : [29]—

Gomaz has been betrayed into the power of the Sultan Soliman and
set to servile tasks.   He has won the love of Zaide, who is in the
seraglio of the Sultan, but the passion of the latter for her affords little
hope to the lovers.   Finding Gomaz, overcome with toil, asleep in the
garden, she leaves him her likeness.   This leads to a declaration of
their mutual love.   To them attaches himself Alazim, the Sultan's
favourite, and apparently the overseer of the slaves, who represents
the humane and enlightened Mussulman.   He procures for them
Turkish dresses, and accompanies them in their flight.   At the beginning of the second act we find the Sultan in violent wrath at the
treachery he has just discovered.   He rages against the fugitives,
whom Zaram undertakes to pursue and capture.   They are, in fact,
soon brought back, and Soliman is not moved to clemency either by the
prayers and constancy of Zaide, or by the exhortations of Alazim.   In
what way a happy *dénouement* is at last brought about cannot be
conjectured.[30]

This serious operetta is written in the manner and after
the scale of the vaudeville of the time; it does not depend
upon the executive powers of the performers nor upon large
expedients, and the standard throughout is a modest one.
The orchestral combinations prove that it was intended for
performance in Salzburg, and the treatment of the separate
parts may have had reference to the available *personnel*.

---

[28] "Zaide," Oper in zwei Acten von W. A. Mozart.   Score (and pianoforte
arrangement).   Offenbach : Joh. André.   André has added an overture and a
closing chorus for the purpose of performance, to which there can be no
objection.   Mozart's composition is given intact, but the text has been altered
by C. Gollmick.   Schachtner's libretto is truly insufferable, but it is indispensable to the critical examination of Mozart's music.

[29] Schachtner has evidently imitated a French original, but I have not been
able to discover it.   I have failed to procure an opera entitled "Zaide," in three
acts, by La Mare, composed by Royer (1739).

[30] The resemblance of some situations to the "Entführung" is as striking as
the difference of the two works on the whole.   An Osmin appears as a
secondary character, and sings a comic aria in the second act, which seems to
have no immediate connection with the action.   The disclosure of the flight
was made in the original by Zaram, not by Osmin.

Zaide lays no claim to anything but a certain amount of
fluency.   The part of the Sultan requires a strong pene-
trating voice, but for the rest the requirements of the music
are well within the compass of ordinary theatrical singers;
musical feeling, and a natural, correct judgment Mozart
always displays, because they were in fact a part of himself
which could not be laid aside.

In the construction of the songs the traditional arrangement of the Italian aria is not closely adhered to.   An effort
is evident to make use of the fundamental law requiring contrasting motifs to be compacted into a whole, in developing the
individuality of the characters and of the dramatic situations.
Nevertheless, the influence of the old tradition is visible in
many phenomena, such as the change of tempo, the long
ritornelli, the division of the different motifs by regular
rests, and their amplification.   Yet it is no longer servile
obedience to an external type, but an evident determination
to evolve the form out of the given situation.

Every artist, no matter how many-sided his genius, feels
his nature impelled in a certain direction in which his creative strength works freely and independently, while other
paths remain strange to him or are altogether closed.   Experience and cultivation go far to equalise his powers, but
they are powerless to alter the original impulse.   Now
dramatic representation makes demands upon the artist for
the satisfaction of which he must not indeed overstep the
bounds of his individuality—that no man can do with im-
punity—but he must stretch them to their extremest limits.
Here it is that he seeks aid from the poet.   The latter can
elevate the musician by the strength and vividness of his
situation and characters, by the style and vigour of his
language, while it needs but little to stimulate his musical
production to activity.   This aid was denied to Mozart when
as a young man he first sought to write dramatic music in
its true sense.   The first act of the opera before us has no
events except the love passages between Gomaz and Zaide,
which take their peculiar tone from the mixture of pity for
suffering innocence and from the danger threatening in the
background.   Here Mozart is quite in his element.   The

tendency and fervour of his own sentiments are involuntarily
expressed; but, graceful and interesting as is this first act,
the poetical expression of the words discovers nothing of the
more delicate features of the music. Again, in the second
act, the Sultan raging in jealousy, Zaide at first beseeching,
then also furious, Alazim moralising—these are elements in
the treatment of which Mozart might well look for aid from
the poet. And here it was that the poet left him in the
lurch altogether. We fancy ourselves in a marionette-show
when the Sultan sings:—

> Ich bin so bös als gut,
>   Ich lohne die Verdienste
>   Mit reichlichem Gewinnste;
> Doch reizt man meine Wuth,
>   So hab' ich auch wohl Waffen
>   Das Laster zu bestrafen,
> Und diese fordern Blut.

And Zaide:—

> Tiger! wetze deine Klauen,
>   Freu' dich der erschlichnen Beut'!
> Straf' ein thörichtes Vertrauen
>   Auf verstellte Zärtlichkeit!
> Komm nur schnell und tödt' uns beide,
>   Saug' der Unschuld warmes Blut,
> Reiss' das Herz vom Eingeweide
>   Und ersättge deine Wuth!

The music totters under the weight of such words as
these. The songs, which follow one after the other, are
indeed well conceived and carefully executed, and even for
the most part characteristic; but their characterisation
is all external, and when suggested by different touches
in the text it is rarely happy. There is a want of harmony
and balance, as well as of impulse and warmth, so that
the really beautiful separate ideas have no proportionate
effect. It is remarkable that these songs are all too long,
and their cadenzas are especially tedious, as if quantity was
to make up for quality. Further adherence to the antiquated
aria form is particularly noticeable; as if, when the musical
construction no longer proceeded directly from the impulse

of the dramatic situation, the old forms involuntarily asserted their sway. The quartet (16) in which the musical and dramatic interest is, as it were, concentrated, contrasts very favourably with the solo songs. The *dramatis personæ* are all happily characterised; the Sultan, implacable in his anger, Gomaz seeking to console *Zaide*, who, in her turn, strives to purchase his life by the sacrifice of her own, and Alazim, overcome with grief at being unable to see a way out of the complications that he himself has brought about. Here too we have a conflict of opposing emotions faithfully and accurately delineated, and all directed to one central point; it is, in fact, a situation which fulfils all the essential conditions of musical representation. Here then Mozart is in his element. The different characters are drawn with a steady hand, every emotion is definitely and accurately expressed, and the elements thus gained are employed as materials for a construction which is as faithful to the laws of musical organisation as to the requirements of the dramatic situation. The quartet thus fulfils the two essential conditions of dramatic music, and reveals itself as a consistent and harmonious piece of work, the separate motifs of which are beautiful and expressive, while the interest is kept alive by alternation and climax, and a vivid dramatic picture is produced by the artistic treatment of musical forms. The grouping of the voices in manifold variety of combination displays, as if on a ground plan, a symmetrical, well-disposed musical edifice. As they proceed they develop out of the simplest situations the most varied shades of sentiment, so that the music carries into the innermost recesses of the mind and heart what the words have merely hinted at. Even the actual musical formulas, such as the entry of the voices in imitation, produce, in the right place, such a direct and vivid effect that they appear to have been invented for the special case. As to the main conception on which the construction of the quartet rests, it might, if the violent rage of the Sultan were considered as the chief point, have been made more passionate and agitated without overstepping truth of expression; but Mozart has in preference emphasised the more fervid and reserved emo-

II.   I

tions of the other characters, to which the expression of
anger must be subordinated. This conception has perhaps
been suggested by the greater ease which it afforded for the
introduction of the necessary reconciliation of the characters;
partly, also, a more quiet and contained piece might appear
to be of better effect after so many lively and agitated songs;
it is certain, however, that it was the conception most in
accordance with Mozart's nature as an artist.

Equally in accord with the situation, but not by any means
so deep and expressive, is the terzet (8) which brings the first
act to a conclusion. In this there is no conflict of sentiment;
Zaide, Gomaz and Alazim are happy in the feeling of mutual
love and friendship, and in the hope of a speedy deliverance;
the fear lest their plan of escape should fail casts only a
passing shadow on their cheerful frame of mind.[31] The music
therefore expresses content and happiness with great tenderness and the purest melody, especially in the first movement.
The duet between Zaide and Gomaz (5), whose love is not
a stormy passion, but the devotion of two noble beings, expresses in the most delightful manner the purity and openness of a happy affection.

There are not wanting, either, such delicate features of
detail as characterise the genuine musical dramatist. For
instance, in Gomaz' song (6), when he is divided between
gratitude to Alazim and impatience to hasten to Zaide, there
is charming humour in his confusion, particularly at the
words " doch ich muss dich schnell verlassen," and "lass
dich küssen, lass dich drücken," which in no way interferes
with the more serious sentiment of the song as a whole.
The union of humour and sentiment at the close is excellent.
While the accompaniment continues the last subject, Gomaz,
who had rushed off in hot haste, turns back, and sings once
more with heartfelt emotion: " Herr und Freund, wie dank'
ich dir!" There is a pretty touch in Osmin's air (11)
where the purely musical return to the theme is used to
express recurring bursts of hearty laughter.

The workmanship of the opera, both as regards the treat-

---

[31] This part did not satisfy Mozart, and he composed it again.

ment of the voices and of the orchestra, is, as might be
expected, thorough and sure. The orchestra deserves special
notice. We find only the instruments in use at Salzburg,
and the wind instruments are sparingly employed. The
flutes and oboes generally alternate, but they are together
and in conjunction with bassoons and horns in the quartet(16)
and in one of the Sultan's airs (12); trumpets and drums
are only used in the Sultan's raging scene (9). Many songs
(1, 11, 13) are accompanied by stringed instruments alone.
The hand of a master is recognisable throughout, in the
life and movement which we follow with unflagging interest,
in the force and beauty of the sound effects, and in the delicacy
of the lights and shades. Many touches recall later works of
Mozart ; but these for the most part consist in turns of
expression, in the treatment of the accompaniment, &c. One
decided reminiscence is not without interest. The quartet
is introduced by a short passage for the wind instruments,
which recurs several times in the course of the piece, whereupon the voices enter as follows :—

This motif occurred to Mozart again in the "Entführung,"

I 2

where it appears in the song of Constanze, "Traurigkeit ward mir zum Loose" (10) in the following form :—

The alternate rendering of the subject by the voices and accompaniment, and the alternation between the wind instruments, give it a new charm; and it is not without intention that the instrumentation here is less full than in the former case.

One peculiarity of this operetta is the introduction of melodrama. J. J. Rousseau, in his production of "Pygmalion" at Lyons in 1770 and Paris in 1775, gave the first example of a dramatic piece in which spoken dialogue was interspersed with music in the nature of obbligato recitatives.[32] The attempt thus to render music effective as a means of dramatic expression was successful, although the critics raised objections to the union of music and speech.[33] Inde-

[32] Castil-Blaze, Molière Musicien, II., p. 423.
[33] La Harpe, Corr. Litt., I., p. 280.

pendently of Rousseau's experiment, it had occurred to Brandes in 1772 at Weimar to adapt Gerstenberg's cantate "Ariadne " as a melodrama for his wife, who was an excellent actress, but no musician. Schweitzer undertook the composition, but owing to the interruption caused by his "Alceste " he did not finish it.[84] When Brandes removed to Gotha in 1775, he transferred " Ariadne " to Georg Benda, with whose music it was then produced.[85] The extraordinary success it met with suggested to Gotter the idea of writing the melodrama " Medea " for Madame Seyler, the rival of Madame Brandes; this also was composed by Benda.[86] The success of the melodramas was universal and extraordinary.[87] Critics might object to the principle as they pleased,[88] the public was not to be reasoned out of its enthusiasm, which was shared even by many connoisseurs.[89] That the success was mainly due to Benda's expressive music, which all joined in praising, admits of no doubt, and none of his successors have been able to produce a similar effect.[40]

Mozart's idea of substituting melodrama for accompanied recitative in German opera was a kindred one (Vol. II., p. 74), and the same idea is evident in other directions.[41] It is put into practice in " Zaide." Two important monologues are melodramatically treated; one by Gomaz at the beginning of the first, and another by Soliman at the beginning of

---

[84] Brande's Lebensgesch., II., pp. 140, 157.

[85] Brande's Lebensgesch., II., pp. 173, 184. Reichardt says (Kunstmag., I , p. 86; Mus. Alman., 1796, G. Benda) that Benda was the first to propose it; but this seems incorrect.

[86] Brande's Lebensgesch., II., p. 193. Teutsch. Mercur, 1775, III., p. 276.

[87] Brande's " Ariadne " was successfully performed in Paris in 1781 (Grimm, Corr. Litt., X., p. 450).

[88] Eberhard, Neue Verm. Schr. (Halle, 1788), p. 1. N. Bibl. d. Schön Wiss , XXXVII., p. 177. Forkel, Krit. Bibl., III., p. 250. Tagebuch d. Mannheim, Schaub., I., p. 327. Nachtr. zu Sulzer's Theorie., III, p. 318. Herder was of opinion that music and declamation met at every point; they could not unite (Böttiger, Litt. Zust., I., p. 126).

[89] Reichardt, Kunstmag., I., p. 86. Rintel, Zelter, p. 100. Cf. Huber, Tamira, p. 79.

[40] A list of melodramas is given by Schletterer, Das Deutsche Singspiel, p. 225.

[41] Reichardt, Geist des Musik. Kunstmag., p. 102. Knigge, Ephemer. f Theat. u. Litt. (1785, II., p. 100).

the second act.[42]   Benda's composition has evidently been
taken as a model ; the music in short periods, often only in
detached chords, follows each turn of the monologue, and
seeks to give expression to the lightest shades of sentiment.
The musical treatment is essentially different from that of
obbligato recitative, where the independent instrumental
passages are connected partly by the recitative itself, which
is always sung, partly by the harmonies of the accompaniment ; in the melodrama, on the other hand, every
passage, even the smallest, is treated as distinctly apart.
In the recitatives, again, which are sung, the lighter
shades of sentiment may be rendered by cadence, rhythm,
or harmony, without the intervention of any instrumental
passages. In the melodrama this is impossible, and in
order to accentuate details, the continuity of the dialogue
must be sacrificed ; another decided and almost inevitable
drawback is the dependence upon details for characterisation, which is thereby often out of proportion.   In this
way, spoken dialogue loses its chief means of effect—
that is, its continuity of idea—while nothing is gained for
musical unity, which ought to make up for all deficiencies by
the steady maintenance of a sustained mood.   For, impelled
as Mozart might be by his nature to gather into a whole
the shattered members of this musical representation by
means of rhythmical combinations and harmonic progressions,
this was only possible to a limited degree, and musical construction in its proper sense can only exist in those few
places where the music is independent of the melodrama.
The main point, however, cannot be denied, which is that the
words and the music are not here so blended that each part
is richly repaid for what it sacrifices by its union with the
other, but that each is continually asserting itself in opposition to the other, so that both are in fact the losers.   To

---

[42] It is particularly to be regretted that the original words for these melodramatic scenes have not been printed. The alterations in Soliman's monologue
are not so essential, but Gomaz's monologue is entirely transformed. In the
original text he was absorbed by his unpleasant position ; when he prays for
refreshing slumber, and the music represents his repeated starting up from rest,
the altered version puts love-ravings for Zaide into his mouth.

this may be added the great difficulty of satisfying the requirements of music, together with those of declamatory speech, and of filling the pauses with suitable gestures and movements, the amount of histrionic art necessary being rarely possessed by singers. Benda's melodramas were written for distinguished actresses, whose forte lay in their declamation and action; the situations were selected with this view, the dialogue was constructed in accordance with it; in fact, each scene was self-contained, not incorporated as a component part of a greater whole. Objections of this kind must have acted upon Mozart at a later time; at all events, he never again employed melodrama, not even in the " Zauberflöte," when the occasion seemed ready to hand. It was nevertheless often introduced into operas—and partially also into plays—with very good effect. But the effect relies chiefly either on the material impressions of sound or upon the delicate and intellectual treatment of the musical interludes, suggesting familiar ideas, sentiments, or fancies, which exist in the minds of the speakers, though they are incapable of expression in speech.[43] These are certainly admirable points in their place, but they can scarcely serve as organising principles in a work of art; the melodrama must be content to take its place as a subordinate and connecting member if it is to have its true effect.

Mozart never took up this opera again, and he was right. It could only have been rendered fit for the stage by complete reconstruction. The first act, however graceful the music may be, has too little variety in its treatment and tone to gain favour on the stage; the second is, as we have seen, barely tolerable. After the composition of the "Entführung," "Zaide" was heard of no more, partly on account of the similarity of subject and accessories, partly because it was so far surpassed in every respect that it could not fail to fall henceforth into oblivion.[44]

---

[43] It will suffice to remind the reader of the fine melodrama in " Fidelio."

[44] " Zaide" was performed in Frankfort on January 27, 1866, and though naturally not a stage success, it was a most welcome instruction to those who brought historical interest to bear upon it.

CHAPTER XXII.

"IDOMENEO."

ALTHOUGH in his earlier years Mozart's career had, as we have seen, been hindered by the circumstances to which he was forced to succumb at Salzburg, yet the severe discipline to which he was subjected must have been in many respects useful during his period of education. Since his return from his travels, however, his Salzburg surroundings were utterly oppressive and distasteful to him. His time of training was over; what he now required was freedom, work worthy of his powers, and the means of producing all that he was able and willing to produce. But of all this Salzburg could give nothing, and want of appreciation and mistrust, in addition to external obstacles, almost caused Mozart to lose heart and spirit, and throw up his post. His longing looks were naturally turned in whatever direction deliverance might seem to lie, and he considered it a fortunate circumstance when he was commissioned to write the opera for the Carnival of 1781 at Munich. The interest he had excited in Karl Theodor and his consort rendered it comparatively easy for Mozart's friends among the court singers and musicians to direct the choice so that it should fall on him; the Archbishop had promised leave of absence too distinctly to be able to draw back, nor would his many obligations to the Bavarian court have rendered a refusal possible. An entirely new opera was desired on this occasion, and the Abbot Giambatt. Varesco, who had been court chaplain at Salzburg since 1766, was commissioned to write the libretto; he could take counsel with Mozart, who knew the Munich company well, and by obeying his suggestions make the text quite according to his mind, so that a work not unworthy of the brilliant fame of the Munich Opera might be expected. When a translation of the text was called for later, Mozart proposed his old friend Schachtner, who was employed to do it; and Leopold Mozart could write with some pride to Breitkopf (August 10, 1781): " It is remarkable that every part of the work is by persons residing in Salzburg: the poetry by the court chaplain, Abbate Varesco, the music by my son, and the German translation by Herr Schachtner."

Varesco's "Idomeneo" was modelled on the opera "Idomenée," written by Danchet and composed by Campra, first performed in 1712 and revived in 1731.[1]

The *dramatis personæ* are as follows: —

Idomeneo, re di Creta	Il Signor Raaff (virtuoso di camera).
Idamante, suo figlio	Il Signor dal Prato.
Ilia, principessa Trojano, figlia di Priamo	La Sign. Dorothea Wendling (virtuosa di camera).
Elettra, principessa, figlia d'Agamemnon, re d'Argo	La Sign. Elisabetta Wendling, (virtuosa di camera).
Arbace, confidente del re	Il Signor Domenico de Panzacchi (virtuoso di camera).
Gran Sacerdote di Nettuno	Il Signor Giovanni Valesi (virtuoso di camera).

The plot is briefly as follows:—

Idomeneo, King of Crete, after the siege of Troy, has wandered a long way from his home, where his son, Idamante, grown to man's estate during his absence, awaits him in filial love. Electra, daughter of Agamemnon, banished by the people of Argus on account of the matricide of Orestes, has taken refuge with Idamante, and becomes deeply enamoured of him. But Ilia, daughter of Priam, who, with other Trojan captives, has been sent to Crete by Idomeneo, has conceived a passion for Idamante, which he returns. At the opening of the opera we find Ilia struggling with her love for the enemy of her fatherland (aria, 2). Idamante approaches her joyfully. He has received tidings that his father's fleet is in sight, and has sent his old confidant, Arbace, to bring more exact intelligence. On this joyful day he gives freedom to all the Trojan captives, and declares his love for Ilia, which she, although reluctantly, rejects; whereupon he bewails himself in an aria (3). The captive Trojans are led in and loosed from their fetters,

---

[1] Dict. des Théâtres, III., p. 126. An edition by Christoph Balard appeared in 1712, and the text is printed (Rec. des Opéras, XII., 1).

giving occasion for a joyful chorus. Electra comes and expresses
dissatisfaction at the liberation of so many enemies. Then follows
Arbace with intelligence (which is mistaken) of the shipwreck of
Idomeneo. Idamante departs overwhelmed with grief. Electra remains behind and gives vent to her jealousy and despair in a song
(aria, 5). The scene changes to the sea-coast, and the fleet of Idomeneo
is seen threatened by a storm, and driven on to the rocks, the mariners
lamenting and beseeching aid. Neptune appears and commands the
winds to depart. Idomeneo prays for his help, but the god casts
threatening glances on him, and disappears. The sea being calmed,
Idomeneo lands and declares that, during the storm, he has vowed to
sacrifice to Neptune the first person who shall meet him on shore. He
trembles at the rashness of his vow, and anxiously looks for the sacrifice
he is to make (aria, 6). Idamante enters, having sought solitude as ease
to his grief. He offers shelter to the stranger, whom he fails to recognise.
In the course of conversation it transpires that he is mourning for his
father Idomeneo. Whereupon Idomeneo makes himself known, but
overcome by the horror of his situation, he departs, forbidding Idamante to follow him. The latter, ignorant of the cause, is inconsolable
at his father's rejection of his proffered love and services (aria, 8). An
intermezzo of suitable character follows the first act. The warriors of
Idomeneo disembark to a march (9), are welcomed by their wives and
children, and "express their joy in a grand figure-dance, ending with a
chorus (10)."

At the beginning of the second act Idomeneo is in conversation
with Arbace. He communicates to him his fearful vow, from the fulfilment of which he wishes to escape. Arbace represents to him that this
is impossible. But when he hears that Idamante is to be the sacrifice,
he counsels his being sent to a distant country, and that during his
banishment they should seek to appease the wrath of Neptune. Idomeneo decides upon commanding Idamante to accompany Electra to
Argos, and there ascend the throne, and commissions Arbace to bid
him prepare for the journey. Arbace promises obedience (aria, 11), and
departs. Ilia now appears, expresses delight at Idomeneo's safety, and,
while extolling Idamante's goodness, declares her own gratitude and
submission (aria, 12). Her warmth causes Idomeneo to suspect their
love, and his grief and confusion are thereby augmented (aria, 13).
Electra, entering, thanks him for his care. He leaves her alone, and
she expresses her joy at the fulfilment of her dearest wishes (aria, 14).
The warriors assemble in the harbour to the sound of a march (15).
Electra appears with her followers, the sea is calm, and all look forward
to a fortunate voyage (chorus, 16). Idomeneo dismisses Idamante, who
sees in this command a fresh proof of his father's inexplicable displeasure. They express their opposing sentiments in a terzet (17).
As they prepare to embark, a terrific storm arises, and a huge sea-
monster rises from the waves. This convinces Idòmeneo that his

disobedience has offended Neptune, and he determines to die himself, and not to sacrifice the innocent. " The storm continues to rage, the Cretans fly, and the act closes with the expression of their fear and horror by singing and pantomimic dancing."

Ilia opens the third act, bewailing her unhappy love (aria, 19). Idamante surprises her, and declares his resolve to seek death in combat with the monster who is laying waste the land; this leads to a disclosure of her love, and the two express their happiness in a duet (20). Idomeneo, entering with Electra, discovers them; he cannot bring himself to acknowledge to Idamante the true cause of his mysterious behaviour, but commands him anew to leave Crete at once, and seek an asylum in a distant land. The various emotions of those present are expressed in a quartet (21). Idamante having departed, Arbace enters and announces that the people are hurrying with the high priest at their head to demand deliverance from the monster; Idomeneo goes to meet them, and Arbace expresses his earnest wish for the happiness of his ruler (aria, 22). On an open space in front of the castle the high priest appears with the multitude; he describes the ravages of the monster, which can only be terminated by the fulfilment of Idomeneo's vow, and demands to know the name of the promised victim (23). When Idomeneo names his son as the sacrifice, horror seizes the people (chorus, 24). During a march (25) Idomeneo with his subjects enters the temple of Neptune, and while the priests prepare for the sacrifice they offer their solemn prayers to the god (26); cries of joy are heard from afar, and Arbace hastens in and announces that Idamante has slain the monster in heroic combat. Idamante is presently borne in by priests and warriors, crowned and in white robes; he now knows his father's vow, and satisfied as to his feelings towards him, he is ready to fall a joyful sacrifice to the angry god (aria, 27). As Idomeneo is in the act of striking the fatal blow, Ilia hastens in and restrains him; she insists upon taking the place of her lover, and a tender strife arises between them, which Idomeneo listens to with emotion, Electra with rage and jealousy. As Ilia kneels before the altar, " a great subterranean disturbance is heard, the statue of Neptune totters, the high priest stands entranced before the altar, all are amazed and motionless from fear, while a deep and majestic voice declares the will of the gods ": Idomeneo is to renounce the throne, which Idamante is to ascend, and to be united to Ilia (28). At this unexpected issue, Electra breaks into violent anger, and " goes off raging"; Idomeneo arranges everything according to the divine will (30), and expresses his grateful joy (aria, 31); Idamante is crowned in a pantomimic ballet, during which the chorus sing a joyful conclusion to the opera (32).[2]

---

[2] Idomeneus's vow, his unwillingness to sacrifice his son, the consequent pestilence, and his dethronement by the people, are found in ancient writers; the rest is modern.

Varesco omitted the prologue of his original, and reduced the five acts to the customary three. He also left out altogether the divinities and allegorical personages, which were somewhat prominent in the French text ; and of three confidants he retained only Arbace. For the rest he follows the progress of the plot pretty closely, only judiciously omitting the love of Idomeneo for Ilia, and altering the conclusion. In the original, Idomeneo, after voluntarily raising his son to the throne, and bestowing on him the hand of Ilia, is stricken with madness by Nemesis, and slays Idamante with the sacrificial axe. He is then prevented from committing suicide, but Ilia falls by her own hand. Metastasio had weaned Italian opera from such horrors. Varesco naturally looked to opera seria as the foundation of his adaptation,[3] but he endeavoured at the same time to make use of the distinctive features of French opera. This is evident in his care for variety of scenery and machinery, in the marches and processions which occur in every act, and in the pantomimic dances which are made subservient to the plot. Further, the frequent introduction of the chorus was evidently suggested by French opera, and a marked progress displayed in the fact that the chorus was not employed merely to heighten the pomp of the piece, but took part in the action at critical moments, and expressed important dramatic situations. The ensembles, too, are not placed in regular succession at the end of the acts, without reference to the plot ; they occur naturally as the piece proceeds, and have a dramatic signification of their own. Such movements are indeed rarely introduced, and not all the suitable points are made use of for them ; no attempt is made either to unite the several connected points of the plot into a musical whole in the finale, but rather each separate situation has its own independent musical treatment.[4] On the other hand, there

---

[3] I owe to the courtesy of Herr Reg. Lenz, of Munich, the original libretto with the dialogues in full, not abbreviated as they afterwards were for composition : " Idomeneo, dramma per musica, da rappresentarsi nel teatro nuovo di corte per comando di S. A. S. E. Carlo Teodoro, nel Carnovale, 1781 " (Munich : Frz. Jos. Thuille.).

[4] A regular finale to an opera seria was first introduced by Giov. Gammerra in his " Pirro " (1787) ; so says Manfredini (Reg. Armon., p. 121), who disliked this mixture of styles.

is an evident intention to give the piece a tragic tone
rather than that of the then prevalent effeminate tenderness, and to invest the characters with a psychological
interest, and the plot with natural development and climax.
It must be admitted that the success is but partial. Varesco
was no poet, and the spirit of French tragedy was not
calculated to raise him to a higher sphere than that of
Italian opera. Conventionality predominates, passion and
emotion find but unnatural expression, pedantry and exaggeration, both alike untrue, jostle each other; and the plot
hangs on such slender threads that, in spite of the strong
passions which are set in motion, it awakens no lively interest.
The weak points both of French and Italian opera are here
combined; but there are other faults belonging more especially to the latter. Such, for example, is the giving of the
part of Idamante to a male soprano, and employing the bass
voice only for the subordinate part of the Oracle. Idomeneo
is tenor, according to traditional usage, and stands almost
alone against three soprano voices, for Arbaces as second
tenor acts only as a stop-gap, and the high priest only
appears once in an obbligato recitative. Generally speaking
the airs do not form the culminating point of a dramatic
situation, but only close it with a kind of point. Frequently
they have only a commonplace phrase or an elaborated
image for their subject, and all their individuality is bestowed
upon them by the music. Varesco is nevertheless a practised
verse-maker, who has employed, not without skill, the
materials he found ready to hand, but is far removed from
Metastasio's delicacy and grace.

With all its drawbacks the advantage of a settled tradition
is very visible, the external arrangements, such as the distribution among the characters of the different pieces being
carefully carried out. In short, if "Idomeneo" is compared
with Mozart's earlier operas, the progress in the choice and
treatment of material is very marked. Such an absolute
blending of the essential features of French and Italian
opera as is aimed at does not indeed take place; a compromise between the two had first to be made. It can
scarcely be doubted that Mozart had a share in the construction of the libretto in its more important parts, and that

his experiences in Mannheim and Paris had qualified him for the task; but his influence was not felt in the details of the work.

When the libretto was ready, and part of the music composed, Mozart repaired to Munich, according to custom, to finish the opera on the spot. After a journey in the post-carriage, "which shook the soul out of one's body," and gave him not an instant's sleep, he wrote to his father (November 8, 1780), "Joyful and glad was my arrival!" There was plenty to be done: the opera was to be rehearsed, to be put on the stage, and the greater part of it was still unwritten. How much of it he took with him ready to Munich is not precisely known; probably the majority of the recitatives, the first act, and perhaps part of the second; at all events his first letters mention some of the songs as already composed.

He was able to set to work with a good heart, for he was met with goodwill on all sides. Count Seeau was altogether at his service; and when they sometimes fell out, and Mozart was provoked to be rude, it was always the Count who gave way. The Elector received him very graciously. "I had almost forgotten the best!" he writes (November 15, 1780); "Count Seeau presented me *en passant* to the Elector last Sunday, after mass; he was very gracious, and said, 'I am glad to see you here again.' And when I said that I would endeavour to deserve the approbation of his highness, he patted me on the shoulder and said, 'Oh, I have no doubt it will all go very well indeed.' *A piano piano si va lontano!*" The nobility, too, were favourably disposed towards him. Cannabich introduced him to the Countess Baumgarten, who was then the favourite of the Elector. "My friend is everything in this house," he writes (November 13, 1780), "and I, too, now; it is the best and most useful house here for me, and so far all has gone, and by God's help will go, well with me." He was able, therefore, to satisfy his father as to the success of the opera (November 24, 1780): "Have no care as to my opera, dear father; I hope there will be no hitch. A little cabal is opposed to it, but it will certainly come to grief, for all the best and most powerful houses of the nobility are in my favour, as well as the principal musicians, especially Cannabich."[5]

There was, at all events, no opposition to be feared on the part of the singers or the orchestra; they and Mozart were mutually anxious to satisfy each other. But their joint labours and the requirements of the stage showed many alterations in the text to be necessary, and Varesco must have been often appealed to to undertake these, or to sanction proposed changes. Among the performers for whom he wrote, Dal Prato gave him some real trouble. Soon after his arrival he had " a piece of roguery " to narrate (November 8, 1780) : " I have not indeed the honour of knowing the heroic Dal Prato, but according to the description Ceccarelli must be better than he ; for sometimes his breath fails in the middle of a song, and, *nota bene*, he was never on the stage, and Raaff is like a statue. Now, you may imagine the scene in the first act (the meeting of Idomeneo and Idamante." Further acquaintance with Dal Prato justified the reports concerning him. "My *molto amato Castrato dal Prato*," he writes (November 15, 1780), "requires teaching the whole opera "; "he has to learn his part like a child, and has not a pennyworth of method " (November 22, 1780). He was the stumbling block also in the quartet, which had to be rehearsed six times before it went right. " The fellow can do nothing," complains Mozart (December 30, 1780) ; " his voice would not be so bad if he did not sing in his throat and head, but he is absolutely without intonation or method or sentiment, and sings like the best among the boys who come to be heard when they seek admission to a choir."

He had trouble of quite another kind with his "dear old friend" Raaff. He was exceedingly fanciful, and Mozart made many alterations out of love for him and consideration for his gray hairs (December 27, 1780) :—

---

[5] Aloysia Weber was no longer in Munich; she had removed with her family to Vienna, where the good offices of the imperial ambassador, Count Hardeck, had procured her an engagement as prima donna. It is an error to suppose that this visit of Mozart to Munich had anything to do with his relations to Aloysia.

Let me tell you that Raaff is the best and honestest man in the world, but so wedded to his old jog-trot ideas that it is enough to drive one crazy. Consequently it is very difficult to write for him; very easy, too, I grant you, if one is content to write songs such as, for example, the first, "Vedrommi intorno," &c. If you could only hear it—it is good, and it is pretty; but if I had written it for *Zonca* I should have made it much better fitted to the words. I had a good deal of trouble with him about the quartet. The oftener I hear this quartet the more effective it appears to me, and every one that has heard it likes it. Only Raaff thinks it will be wanting in effect; he said to me, "Non c' è da spianar la voce." As if there should not be more speaking than singing in a quartet! But he knows nothing about these things. I only said, "My dear friend! if there was only one note in this quartet that I thought should be altered, I would do it; but I am better satisfied with it than with any other piece in the opera, and when you have once heard it together, you will alter your mind. I have done my best to please you with your two songs, and so I will with the third, with good hopes of succeeding; but as far as regards the terzets and quartets, the composer should be allowed his own way." That satisfied him.

After the rehearsal Raaff "gladly acknowledged himself in the wrong, and had no more doubt as to the good effect of the quartet" (December 30, 1780). When Mozart had "shown him the paces" of his first air, he was quite satisfied with it (November 15, 1780); and equally so with the air in the second act (December 1, 1780):—

He is as much in love with his song as a younger man might be with his fair lady: he sings it at night before he goes to sleep, and in the morning as soon as he wakes. He said to Baron Viereck and Herr von Castel, "I have always been used to have a hand in my own part, in the recitatives as well as the songs; but I have left this just as it was. There is not a note that does not suit me exactly." *Enfin*, he is as happy as a king over it.

Some ill-natured speeches were made in spite of all this, as Mozart writes to his father (December 27, 1780):—

À propos! Becke tells me that he wrote to you again after the last rehearsal but one, and told you among other things that Raaff's song in the second act is not written for the words. "They tell me," he said, "that you know too little of Italian. Is it so?" "You should have asked me, and then written! I can assure you that he who told you this knows very little Italian himself." The song goes exceedingly well with the words. One hears the "mare" and the "mare funesto;" and the passages lead up to "minacciar" in a way that thoroughly expresses "minacciar"—a threatening; in fact, it is the finest song in the opera, and meets with universal approval.

The two other male vocalists belonged to the old Munich opera. "Honest old Panzacchi" had been an excellent singer and a good actor in his time, but his best days were over; and Valesi, too, who had a well-deserved reputation as a tenor, had almost given up the stage, and devoted himself to teaching. L. Mozart had reason, therefore, to write (November 11, 1780): "What you tell me of your vocalists is sad, and shows that everything must depend on the composition."

There were no difficulties this time with the female vocalists. Both the Wendlings were friendly and amenable—they went Mozart's way, and were contented with everything he did. "Madame Dorothea Wendling is *arci-contentissima* with her scena, and wanted to hear it three times over," he wrote home (November 8, 1780), and they were quite in accord about the second song. "Lisel Wendling," he wrote soon after (November 15, 1780), "sang her two songs half-a-dozen times; she is thoroughly pleased; I have it from a third person that both the Wendlings have praised their songs very highly."

Mozart kept up with great industry the work of rehearsing and composing (a song for Schikaneder was composed meanwhile, Vol. II., p. 102), although he was suffering from a severe cold. The homely remedies which his father ordered brought some alleviation of it, but, as he was obliged to continue writing, the cure was a slow one.

At Munich he fell in with Mara, who had not long left Berlin. "She is not so fortunate as to please me," he writes (November 13, 1780); "she does too little to come up to the Bastardina (Vol. I., p. 112), which is her ambition, and she does too much to touch the heart like a Weber, or an expressive singer." He was even less edified by the behaviour of the husband and wife than by Madame Mara's singing, and writes at a later date (November 24, 1780) of the "pride, insolence, and effrontery which were visible in their countenances." When Mara was to sing at a court concert, after the first symphony "I saw her lord and master creep behind her with a violoncello in his hand; I thought it was going to be a song with obbligato violoncello. Old Danzi, a very good accompanist, is first violoncellist here ; all at once old Toeschi—conductor when Cannabich is not there—said to Danzi, who is his son-in-law, by the way, ' Stand up, and let Mara take your place.' But Cannabich heard him, and cried, ' Danzi, stay where you are! The Elector likes his own people to play.' And the song proceeded. Herr Mara stood meekly with his violoncello in his hand behind his wife." The song which Mara was singing had a second part, but she went out during the ritornello without acquainting the orchestra, "with her native air of effrontery," and afterwards complained to the Elector.[6] He answered : "Madame, you sang like an angel, although your husband did not accompany you," and referred her to Count Seeau.

The first act was rehearsed at the end of November, and Mozart was able to report to his father such success as raised the general expectation to a still higher pitch (December 1, 1780) :—

The rehearsal went off remarkably well. There were only six violins in all, but the proper wind instruments. No spectators were admitted but Seeau's sister and young Count Seinsheim. I cannot tell you how delighted and astonished every one was. It was only what I expected, for I assure you I went to this rehearsal with as light a heart as if it had been a banquet. Count Seinsheim said to me : "I assure you I expected much from you, but this I did not expect." The Cannabich family and all who know them are true friends of mine. I went home with Cannabich after the rehearsal. Madame Cannabich met us and embraced me, full of pleasure that the rehearsal had gone off so well ; then came Ramm and Lang half out of their minds with delight. The good lady, my true friend, being alone in the house with her sick Rose, had been full of anxiety for me. Ramm said to me (if you knew him you would call him a true German, for he says to your face exactly what he thinks) : "You may believe me when I say that no music ever made such an impression on me ; and I thought fifty times what a pleasure it will be to your father to hear this opera." But enough of this! My cold was made rather worse by the rehearsal. One cannot help getting overheated when fame and honour are at stake, however cold-blooded one may naturally be.

---

6 Similar stories were told elsewhere of the Maras (Cf. Forkel's Musik. Alman., 1789, p. 122; and the account of Mara in Zelter's Briefw. mit Goethe, III., p. 418; VI., p. 149).

Wolfgang's father received other confirmation of the success, which he did not withhold from his son:—

Fiala showed me a letter from Becke which is very eulogistic of the music of your first act. He writes that tears of joy and pleasure came to his eyes when he heard the music, and that every one declared it was the finest music they had ever heard—all so new and beautiful, &c. He says that the second act is about to be rehearsed, that he will write to me himself, &c. Well, God be thanked, this all looks well.

L. Mozart, who had been wont to exhort Wolfgang not to procrastinate, as indeed he often did at Salzburg, was now concerned to hear of his obstinate cold, the more so as his sister was suffering from a chest complaint, and he begs him to take care of himself; he was not to hurry over the third act, it would be ready quite in good time. Ready, as he always was, with good advice, he warns him to remember that an opera should not only please connoisseurs (December 11, 1780): "I recommend you not to think in your work only of the musical public, but also of the unmusical. You know that there are a hundred ignorant people for every ten true connoisseurs, so do not forget what is called *popular*, and tickle the long ears." But Wolfgang will not listen to this. "As to what is called popular," he answers (December 16, 1780), "do not be afraid, there is music in my opera for all sorts of people—only none for long ears." Meantime the work of rehearsing went steadily forward. On December 16, in the afternoon, the first and second acts were rehearsed at Count Seeau's, the parts being doubled, so that there were twelve violins. All went well, as Wolfgang reported (December 19, 1780):—

The orchestra and all the audience gladly acknowledged that, contrary to their expectations, the second act was superior both in novelty and expression to the first. Next Saturday the second act is to be rehearsed again, but in a large room in the palace, which I have long desired, for the room at Count Seeau's is far too small. The Elector is to listen *incognito* in an adjoining apartment. "We must rehearse for dear life then," said Cannabich to me. At the last rehearsal he was bathed in perspiration. You will judge from my letters that I am well and hearty. It is a great thing to come to the end of a great and laborious work, and to feel that one leaves it with honour and fame; this I have almost done, for now nothing is wanting but three songs, and the last chorus of the third act, the overture and the ballet—" et adieu partie!"

The next rehearsal gave even greater satisfaction (December 27, 1780) :—

The last rehearsal was splendid; it was in a large room in the palace, and the Elector was present. This time we had the whole orchestra (that belongs to the opera-house, of course). After the first act the Elector said " Bravo ! " out loud ; and when I went to pay my respects to him, he said, " This opera will be charming—it will certainly do you honour." As he was not sure of being able to remain to the end, we let him hear the concerted song, and the storm at the beginning of the second act. These he also approved of in the most kindly manner, and said, laughing, " No one would imagine that such great things could come out of such a little head." The other day at his early reception, too, he praised my opera very much.

In the evening at court the Elector again spoke in high praise of the music, and Mozart learnt from a sure source that he had said after the rehearsal, " I was quite taken by surprise—no music ever had such an effect on me—it is truly magnificent."

The news of this success reached Salzburg bit by bit. " All the town is talking of the excellence of your opera," his father tells him (December 25, 1780). " Baron Lerbach set it going; the chancellor s wife told me that she had heard from him that the opera was wonderfully well spoken of everywhere. Then came Becke's letter to Fiala, which he gave to be read everywhere." Becke wrote to L. Mozart himself that " the storm chorus in the second act is so powerful that none could hear it, even in the greatest heat of summer, without turning as cold as ice ;" and he praises Dorothea Wendling's concerted song very much. The violinist Esser from Mayence, who had given concerts in Salzburg, wrote from Augsburg concerning the two acts of the opera which he had heard : " Che abbia sentito una musica ottima e particolare, universalmente applaudita." " In short," writes the father, " it would be tedious to tell you all the compliments paid to you. I hope that the third act will have as good an effect, and I do so the more confidently, since all the best situations are here, and the subterranean voices must be startling and terrifying.[7] I hope to be able to say, ' Finis coronat opus.' "

---

[7] " The accompaniment to the subterranean voices," writes Wolfgang (January 3, 1781), " is in only five parts, namely, three trombones and two

To this his son answers, over head and ears in work
(December 30, 1780): "The third act will be thought *at
least* as good as the other two: I like it infinitely better, and
you may justly say, ' Finis coronat opus.' "   But there was
plenty to do meantime.   "Head and hands," he writes
(January 3, 1781), "are full of the third act, so that I should
not be surprised if I were to turn into a third act myself.   It
alone has cost me more trouble than the whole opera, for
there is not a scene in it that has not peculiar interest."
He had the satisfaction of finding after the rehearsal that it
really was considered to surpass the other two acts.

Mozart's anxious father strove to draw his attention to
every point that might contribute to success, and particularly cautioned him to keep on good terms with the
orchestra (December 25, 1780).   Experience of Salzburg
must necessarily have shown him the importance of this : —

Try to keep your orchestra in good humour—flatter them, and make
them devoted to you by praising them; I know your way of writing,
and the unceasing and close attention it exacts from all the instruments;
it is no joke for the orchestra to be kept on the stretch of their attention
for three hours and more.   Every one, even the worst fiddler, is touched
by being praised *tête-à-tête*, and becomes more and more attentive and
zealous; and these courtesies cost you nothing but a few words.   But
you know it all yourself; I only tell you because such things are often
forgotten at rehearsal, and you will need the friendship and zeal of the
whole orchestra when the opera is in scena.   The position is then
altered, and the player's attention must be much more intent.   You
know that they cannot all be friendly towards you.   There is always a
but and an *if* to be met with.   You say people doubted whether the
second act would come up to the first.   This doubt being relieved, few
will have misgivings for the third act.   But I will wager my head that
there will be some who will doubt whether the music will be as effective
in the theatre as in a room ; and in that case the greatest zeal and
goodwill are necessary on the part of the orchestra.

But the opera was not ready yet; there was to be no
ballet, only a divertissement fitting into the plot, and this
Mozart was, as he expressed it, to have the honour of composing (December 30, 1780).   "I am very glad of it," he
adds, "for then the music will be by *one* master."   He was

---

horns, which proceed from the same place as the voices.   The orchestra is
silent at this place."   This arrangement was not carried out without opposition
from Count Seeau.

hard at work at the "cursed dances" until the middle of January, and had no time to think of anything else, not even of his own health. It was not until January 18 that he could write: " Laus Deo, at last I have come to an end of it !"

Amid rehearsals and anxious labours, the day of representation drew near. L. Mozart had been concerned lest the death of the Empress Maria Theresa on November 29, 1780, should put a stop to it, but Wolfgang reassured him by saying that none of the theatres had been closed on this account. Soon after he was terrified by a rumour that the Electress was dangerously ill, but discovered this to be a "lie from beginning to end." At first January 20, 1781, was fixed for the performance, then the 22nd, and finally January 29 ; the last rehearsal was to be on the 27th, Wolfgang's birthday; he was pleased at the postponements : " The opera can be oftener and more carefully rehearsed."

The fame of " Idomeneo," which had reached Salzburg even before its performance, was a great source of satisfaction to Mozart's friends; Dr. Prexl, for instance (Vol. II., p. 84), wrote to him of the " inexpressible satisfaction " with which he had learnt the honour done by Wolfgang to Salzburg, and more than one friend undertook the journey to Munich in order to be present ; among these were Frau Robini and her family, two Fräulein Barisani, and Fiala, from the Kapelle. L. Mozart, who was " as pleased as a child about the excellence of the orchestra," intended to go to Munich with his daughter as soon as he could arrange to be absent. But as he dared not risk a refusal from the Archbishop, and it was rumoured that the latter meditated a journey to Vienna, he waited his time. It suited him very well that the first performance was postponed until Hieronymus had actually left Salzburg. This being so, he set out on January 26 to be present at the last rehearsal and the performance. Wolfgang had arranged that his father and sister should find accommodation at his own lodging (in the Burggasse), if they would be contented to live for the time " like gipsies or soldiers."

The arrival of Mozart's father and sister at Munich brings us to a detailed account of the performance of " Idomeneo " and its success. The " Munich Literary and Miscellaneous News" (February 1, 1781, No. XIX., p. 76) announced it briefly as follows :—

> On the 29th ult. the opera of " Idomeneo " was performed for the first time in the new opera-house. The adaptation, music, and translation all proceed from Salzburg. The scenery, including a view of the harbour and Neptune's temple, are among the masterpieces of our well-known theatrical architect, the Herr Councillor Lorenz Quaglio.[8]

All that we read, however, of the success of the opera in rehearsal leaves us no doubt that it met with a very favourable reception.

As to the sum received by Mozart in payment for " Idomeneo " we know nothing ; but it cannot have been a large one, or L. Mozart would not have written (December 11, 1780) : " How about the score ? will it not be copied ? You must be careful as to this, for *with such a payment the score cannot be given up*." To which Wolfgang answered (December 16, 1780) : " I made no ceremony as to the copying of the score, but spoke openly on the subject to the Count. It was always the custom in Mannheim (where the kapell-meister was well paid besides) to give up the score to the composer." The original score, in three volumes, is written in a very neat but rapid hand, with scarcely any alterations except a few in the recitatives. As usual, the different numbers are written separately and then put together ; the double-bass part was written larger, as in other scores, for the convenience of the bass-player at the clavier. The score was to have been printed at the time, as appears from a letter of L. Mozart to Breitkopf (August 10, 1781) : " We were advised to publish the opera, printed or engraved, either in full score or clavier score. Subscribers were promised for some thirty copies, among whom was his highness Prince Max of Zweibrücken, but my son's journey to Vienna and the intervening events caused us to postpone the whole affair." The music for the ballet which was given with " Idomeneo " has not yet been printed (367 K.).

Mozart seems to have set great value on " Idomeneo "

---

[8] The notice was also published in the Augsburgischen Ordinari-Postzeitung (February 5, 1781, No. 31), Rudhart, Gesch. d. Oper zu München, I., p. 168.

(366 K.), even in later years ;[9] it is certain that soon after he
had made good his footing in Vienna he exerted himself to
have it placed on the stage, for which purpose he intended
entirely to remodel it. Unfortunately this project fell
through, and when in 1786 a company of distinguished
amateurs performed the opera at the residence of Prince
Karl Auersperg, Mozart contented himself with several alterations, but did not attempt a complete remodelling. Later,
and more especially quite recently, " Idomeneo " has been
given from time to time on different stages, without exciting
as much interest in the general public as the better-known
works of Mozart ; the judgment of connoisseurs, on the
other hand, has always distinguished it.[10] Both phenomena
are comprehensible on a close examination of the distinctive
features of the work.

Ulibicheff remarks with great justice that it is easy to
distinguish in " Idomeneo " where Mozart has still clung
to the formulas of the opera seria, where he strives to
imitate Gluck and the French opera, and where he gives free
play to his own independent impulses as an artist. These
indications are, of course, not to be met with accurately
marked out in the different pieces, Mozart's individuality,
in the perfection to which it had now attained, being
throughout the very pith of the work.

We have seen that the libretto unites the characteristics
of Italian and French opera as far as style is concerned, but
that the determining element is the Italian style. We
have seen further that the singers, with the exception of the
two female characters, belonged to the Italian school, which
fact tended to the maintenance of Italian form.

It might therefore be expected that Mozart, especially in
the songs, should set out from the traditional forms, and only

---

[9] So says Rochlitz (A. M. Z., I., p. 51). His authorities, however, are on
the main points untrustworthy.

[10] Reichardt, who was usually rather inclined to depreciate Mozart, gives an
appreciative criticism of " Idomeneo," and speaks of it as the purest work of
art which Mozart ever completed (Berl. Mus. Ztg., 1806, p. 11). Seyfried's
criticism of the opera is insignificant (Cäcilia, XX., p. 178), but Ulibicheff's
remarks are often striking, and show much delicate perception (Nouv. Biogr.,
II., p. 94).

attempt to modify them as far as was possible. But the influence of the French original on the opera lay deeper than this, and was impressed on its poetry, language, and nationality, Italian as these all were in external form. Let us consider the songs. The effort is evident to give a more individual expression to the sentiment arising from the dramatic situation than was usual even with Metastasio; but the form and construction are only modified, and have retained the specific character of Italian poetry. The rhetoric differs altogether from the rhetoric of French poetry. Indirectly, too, language by its rhythm and accent affects musical construction, and the distinctions between the Italian and French language are strikingly apparent, not only in the recitatives, which are governed by the musical character of the language, but in the formation of the melodies, where language must be taken into account as an essential element. But deepest of all lies the difference in the conceptions and ideas of the two nations. The emotions and passions of different nations vary not only in intensity but in mode of expression, and where a truly national art has developed itself this special character is stamped on all its productions. The Italians express their feelings vividly and accent them strongly, and not only so, but their instinctive love of formula calls forth sharply defined characterisation and favours typical developments, as is shown, for instance, in their singularly perfect talent for pantomimic representations. This tendency has had a marked influence on the development of music, particularly of dramatic music, in Italy. It still bears a national character, which is not only stamped on it in certain forms and turns of expression, but which is the artistic expression of emotions springing from the very nature of the people. Whoever has heard Italian music performed both by Italian and German singers will readily be convinced that the difference rests not only on style and method, but still more essentially on the peculiarities of the Italian national character. It should not therefore be matter for surprise that music which to Germans appears false or unnatural should make a much deeper impression on Italians than the merely sensual one which strikes the ear.

Mozart's "Idomeneo" bears this distinctive Italian colouring, as do all his Italian operas, not only in the employment of Italian technicalities and mechanism, but in the living breath and fragrance which nothing but an absorption into the national spirit could bestow. Even as a boy he displayed a delicate sense of national distinctions, when in "Bastien und Bastienne" and the "Finta Semplice" he defined so sharply the limits of German vaudeville and of opera buffa. If "Zaide" is compared with "Idomeneo," the fundamental distinctions of conception and style are not less definitely marked ; and the same was the case later in the "Entführung" and the "Zauberflöte," in "Figaro," "Don Giovanni," "Così fan Tutte," and "Tito." To give only one example : one of the most beautiful and affecting scenes that Mozart ever wrote is that in which Idomeneo, at the request of the high priest, indicates his son as the sacrifice demanded by the gods, and all the people break out into lamentations; and yet this chorus (24) is a most unmistakable instance of the Italian form and style. Places like "Già regna la morte" appear typical of similar modes of expression which occur so frequently in Italian operas. But the Italian mould in which Mozart's work is cast, and on which the harmony of the whole depends, is not consciously put forward as a national colouring. It proceeds from such an intimate acquaintance with the Italian style as was then considered the proper foundation for musical studies, and was only possible so long as Italian music bore actual sway in German churches and theatres, and found no contradiction in the national consciousness. This sway was undisputed in South Germany during Mozart's youth and period of artistic development. The musical atmosphere in which he grew up, the elements of culture which were offered to him, were thoroughly Italian; and Italian conceptions and fashions had become second nature to him as to all other German artists who took part in the development of Italian opera during the last century. The relation in which an artistic genius stands to his time and nation is difficult to grasp. Far from shunning the influences of either, his genius displays itself in his power of representing their significant features and tendencies with force and vigour, amounting even to one-sidedness; and then again it sets itself in opposition to them, and struggles until it rules and determines them anew. It would be a hard task indeed to fathom the nature of an artist to that point where the threads of his personal powers and proclivities, and those of the cultivation of his time and nation, are so interwoven that they appear as the root of his artistic individuality; we must be content with tracing onward the path of his development.

Although Mozart's training had so imbued him with the spirit of Italian music that its essence appeared to him as the essence of music itself, yet he transformed the elements which he had so absorbed with the whole force of his individuality. He did not consciously adopt them as national, neither did he oppose them from motives of patriotism, and seek to substitute a German style. His individuality joined issue with the elements of an art ready to hand in full development, and produced works of art which were genuinely Italian, and also genuinely Mozart. The fresh new life which had awakened in German poetry, and which first caused a consciousness of national existence to show itself in the realm of art, touched Mozart at a time when his musical education was already firmly grounded. He could therefore without self-contradiction continue along the trodden path, and carry on the development of the Italian opera as a settled form of art, which he had made his own in the truest sense. But the impulse of German art laid hold, as we shall see, of his innermost being, and gave him clear consciousness of his capabilities as a German artist. Granted that the German element of his nature—with which he could never dispense—remained latent and inactive while he appropriated Italian art as his own, yet all that he so took was treated as his own free property and turned to account with German thought and feeling. While thus the German school of music was partly founded, partly endued with new life by him, he brought Italian opera to a climax as far as its universal application was concerned; after Mozart it becomes more exclusively national. Like every genius who has made his mark in the history of art, he casts his glance over the past as well as into the future. To him it was given to concentrate the living elements of Italian music into works of mature perfection in art, and, setting to work with freshly tempered force, to turn to account the youthful impulses of German music, and lead them towards the goal of artistic freedom and beauty.

Thus, in Idomeneo we recognise the genuinely Italian character of the opera seria, brought to its highest perfection by the force of Mozart's perfectly cultivated individuality; but in details we still perceive the ascendency of traditional form, to which the artist was obliged to yield.

It is most unmistakably present in the two songs allotted to Arbace. The part of confidant was intended both musically and dramatically as a stop-gap; it served as a foil for the more important characters, and was a principal adjunct in the production of that *chiaroscuro* which was considered as essential to scenic effect. On this account Arbace's two songs (11, 22) are not woven into the dramatic web of the opera either in words or music. Some concessions were doubtless made to Panzacchi, a clever and accomplished singer of the old school, and there is no lack of runs, jumps, and similar feats for display of execution. The songs follow the old fashion in other ways also (except that they have only one tempo, and a structure modified accordingly), as, for instance, in the introduction of cadenzas; a very long ritornello of the second song is afterwards shortened at both ends. But in order to give them some musical interest, the accompaniment, although weak in instrumentation, is carefully worked out in counterpoint, especially in the second song. The preceding accompanied recitative, in composing which Mozart plainly had Panzacchi in view, is fine and expressive.

Dal Prato also, for whom the part of Idamante was intended, had only the knowledge of an Italian singer, and that in no considerable degree. Mozart was again, therefore, fettered by tradition, and could venture little to render the song more original and lifelike. In all the three songs for this character (3, 8, 27), the old type is clearly to be recognised. The first, if the singer had had a powerful execution, which he avowedly had not, would probably have been an ordinary bravura song; it has the general plan of one, but is without bravura passages. The emphasis is laid on the accompaniment, which is independent and interesting throughout; the constant use of the wind instruments supplies it with fine sound effects. The frequent changes of time, the construction of the song being in all other respects very regular, is intended to give animation to the expression. The second air is shorter, to suit the situation, more lively and energetic in expression, but equally dependent on the accompaniment for originality and interest. The third adheres to the old form by the introduction of a slow middle movement (Larghetto 3-4) and the accompaniment is simpler ; but the song as a whole is conciser than was the fashion foimerly.

Raaff's advanced age would have prevented his satisfying any very great expectations; but he was also, as Mozart complained, " so wedded to his old jog-trot ideas that it was enough to drive one crazy." He was obliged therefore in the very important part of Idomeneo to submit to much that was against his convictions and inclinations. But Raaff was an accomplished and sensible singer, from whom much could be looked for in respect of delivery and expression. His first air (6) vividly expresses deep and painful feeling in two tolerably short and precise movements, an andantino sostenuto 3-4, and allegro di molto (5); it is dramatically quite in its place, and gives opportunity to the singer to display a well-trained voice. The detached, sharply defined motifs, united by interludes, remind us of the old style, but they are very cleverly arranged and carried out, and the treatment of the wind instruments gives a splendidly sonorous and yet subdued effect to the orchestra, which was then quite novel, and must have been remarkably impressive. The second air (13) is a long bravura song in one movement (allegro maestoso) in the grand style. Mozart calls it "the most splendid song" of the opera; and protests vigorously against the idea that it was not written "for the words"; but more was demanded from the singer than Raaff was able to give. It has the proper heroic character of the opera seria, and affords opportunity for the display of vocal art in sustained passages, long notes, and bravura passages. The last are completely obsolete; but Mozart was right to think well of the song; it is full of expression and character, interesting through its rich and brilliant accompaniment, and containing, especially in the middle movement, surprising beauties of harmony. How striking and expressive is, for instance, this harmonic transition :—

The third air (30), which Mozart endeavoured to write to please his old friend, is on that very account quite after the old pattern; it has great resemblance to the song which Mozart had so accurately fitted to Raaff at Mannheim (p. 408). The chief movement is a broadly sustained adagio, simple and noble in tone, and giving opportunity to the singer to display sustained singing, the effect of which is enhanced by a figured accompaniment, shared between the strings and the wind instruments; the middle movement, allegretto 3-8, is of less importance. A sketch which has been preserved of this song affords a good example of Mozart's method of work; the ritornellos, the voice and the bass are all fully noted. Probably he submitted the sketch to Raaff before elaborating the song; it coincides in all but a few unimportant alterations with the later elaboration. He wished at first to compose the words of the middle movement in the same time and measure as the first movement; after four bars, however, which he erased, he wrote the middle movement as it at present stands.

In spite of the restrictions laid upon him in this far from inconsiderable part of the opera, Mozart's progress since the "Re Pastore" is very marked. What we now find is not the struggle of youthful genius against obsolete and hampering forms, but a conscious compliance with them, on definite grounds, by means of which the composer strives to extract all the good possible from his unfavourable circumstances, and knows exactly how far he can go. It is difficult, however, now that the tradition of these forms is wholly lost, to decide with certainty how much is due to the insensible effect of custom, and how much to the conscious labour of the artist. Those pieces in which Mozart could act without control make an entirely different impression.

To these belong the parts of Ilia and Electra. Bravura has a decided place in the conception of the latter, but with an individual colouring of passion which Mozart has made free use of as the characterising element. The two great airs (5, 29) are the vivid expression of a glowing impulsive nature, which is raised by an admixture of haughty dignity above that vulgarity into which violent outbreaks of jealousy and revenge so readily fall. In spite of the text, which puts the traditional bombastic pathos into the mouth of Electra (29)—

> D' Oreste, d' Ajace
> Hò in seno i tormenti,
> D' Aletto la face
> Già morte mi dà.
> Squarciatemi il core
> Ceraste, serpenti!

the composer has succeeded in infusing character and individuality into the song.

The two songs are allied in subject, but their treatment is

different. While in the first passion ferments, as it were, and breaks forth in separate bursts, the second is a continuous stream of wild rage, and calls for the more particular employment of the higher notes of the voice. Purely executive display is not sought after, with the exception of one passage going up to C in alt, and very expressive, if well sung, but a passionate, well-declaimed delivery is taken for granted throughout. Occasionally the voice part is more declamatory than melodious, and the effect is provided for by a rapid succession of striking harmonies. How wonderfully affecting, for instance, is the passionate outcry:—

The orchestra has an altogether novel function as a means of musical characterisation. It goes its independent way side by side with the voice, interesting by virtue of the singular vitality of its accompanying passages and its own motifs, and its masterly tone-colouring gives body and force to the whole composition. In the first air all is restless motion—we have the flutes in broken chords, flashes of sound like lightning from the wind instruments, and only at certain points are the forces united into a concentrated expression of emotion. How striking, again, is the effect in the last song when, after the long torturing shake passage for the violins,[11] the united orchestra bursts forth into a very transport of revengeful feeling.[12]

Electra's middle song (14) is in strong contrast to the passionate outbursts of the other two ; here her happy love seems to fill her very being. She breathes forth a calm serenity and tender sweetness, as if there could be no place in her heart for jealousy and revenge. The voice part, with the exception of one ornamental passage resembling the string quartet accompaniment, is very simple ; rightly delivered the expression of satisfied affection will be found quite in accord with Electra's character.

In the character of Ilia, Mozart has followed his natural bent ; it is full of sentiment, tender and graceful, without any violent passion. It was played by the excellent actress and singer, Dorothea Wendling; here Mozart had free scope, and in her songs (2, 12, 19) we find the finest expression of his manner as an artist. In the first air (2) we find the simplest means lying ready to hand employed to give dramatic effect ; such, for instance, is the alternation of major and minor key for the principal subject, the climax produced by its repetition, the different ways in which the exclamation " Grecia !" is treated, &c. Not only are we affected by the charm of beautiful and graceful ideas, but the expedients of formal construction become the natural

---

[11] I should not like to assert that this tremolo passage was not suggested by the words; just as in Idomeneo's aria (13) the words " fuor del mar ho un mar in seno " have suggested the billowy motif of the accompaniment.

[12] The recitative preceding this aria was originally (as the libretto shows) much longer and more fully composed; many pages were cut out for performance and some small alterations were made.

expression of the innermost feelings of the heart. The second air (12) is a cavatina, having two verses repeated with trifling alterations, and accompanied by four obbligato wind instruments, viz.: flute, oboe, horn, and bassoon, besides the string quartet. Mozart's old Mannheim friends, Wendling, Ramm, Lang, and Ritter were together again, and he was delighted to write a piece that should do honour to them and to him.

There can be no question as to his success. The first impression is one of the purest melody, filling the musical listener with perfect satisfaction. A nearer examination shows as much to admire in the simplicity of the artistic structure (the symmetry of which in reading the score is displayed as it were on a ground plan) and in the delicate use of sound effects, as in the tenderness and grace of the conception. Let us consider the situation. Ilia comes to thank Idomeneo for the kindness which she, as a captive, has received in Crete. She is embarassed by the remembrance that she has lost her father and her fatherland, that Idomeneo is her ruler, and the father of Idamante, and, more than all, by the consciousness of her love for Idamante; and yet this very love sheds for her a rosy light on all around.

She begins, then, with a composed, almost reverential address, and as her feelings grow more intense, the remembrance of her sorrows returns; but all gives way to the one feeling: "or gioja e contento," in which she altogether loses herself. Such a combination of different elements into a harmonious whole constitutes a true work of art, and it must needs be found beautiful as long as the principles of music remain what they are. The situation of the last air (19) is less striking; it is the longing sigh of a deserted lover; but the main features of Ilia's character have already been so clearly defined that her singular charm is as indelibly impressed here as elsewhere. It is only necessary to compare the air (14), in which Electra expresses her tenderest feelings, to perceive how the essential distinctions between the two women are characterised by the music.

The duet for the two lovers (20 B) is interesting and pleasing, but not very striking; in form and change of tempo, as well as in conception and treatment, it adheres to the old-established custom of making a love duet light and graceful. It proceeds in unbroken movement and precise form throughout, and there is no true bravura.

The terzet (17) is more striking, noble, and simple, and of fine musical effect, but the dramatic situation is not brought to expression in the full energy of which it is capable. It is certainly placed with design between a succession of pleasing situations and of more agitated ones; its calm and earnest mood fitly concludes what has gone before and prepares the mind for what is to follow, without unduly diminishing the effect of surprise. In the situation, as here presented, the three characters are all in a depressed and anxious mood, which restrains any lively outburst of emotion, and justifies the moderation of the musical rendering.

The quartet (21) takes a higher place as regards invention and characterisation; Mozart himself preferred it, and rejected any interference from the singers in its composition as decidedly as he gave way to them in the songs. It is not an easy task to write a quartet for three sopranos and a tenor, but Mozart's accurate knowledge of the capabilities of the voices, and his skilful combinations, enabled him to command the most original and beautiful sound effects. We must admire, too, his genius in marking out a distinct plan, within the limits of which he moves at his ease, and in giving sharp touches of character without disturbing the unity of the piece.

Ilia and Idamante stand in natural contrast to Idomeneo and Electra, and each individual is accurately characterised. This is most apparent where they all sing together, and gives life and significance to the music. Besides the independent treatment of the voices, the quartet is especially distinguished by harmonic beauties of an uncommon kind, and undeniably belongs to Mozart's finest performances. His wife relates that once, when singing in this quartet, he was so deeply affected that he was obliged to desist, and for a long time would not look at the composition again.[13] The

---

[13] Hogarth, Mem. of the Opera, II., p. 198.

L 2

conclusion is original and appropriate. Idamante's commencement is that of a man who has made up his mind : "Andrò ramingo e solo," however, dies away with the words "morte cercando" into gloomy meditations. At the close he again announces, "Andrò ramingo e solo," and leaves the scene while the orchestra continues to express gloom and sadness, dying away gradually into silence.[14]

The chorus forms a principal feature of "Idomeneo." There is an important difference, however, between those choruses which actually belong to the plot and express the meaning of the situation with emphasis, and those which are only superficially connected with the plot, and serve principally for ornament. These last are mostly in connection with the ballet, and should be placed side by side with the ballet music. Such are the first chorus (4), during which the Trojan captives are loosed from their fetters, the closing chorus during Idamante's coronation, and most especially the chorus at the end of the first act (10), in which we should not fail to recognise dance music, even without the superscription " Ciaconna " and the express indication of the libretto. The orchestra has a more independent part here than in the two other choruses. The character of them all is fresh and cheerful; as with a man rejoicing in the fulness of his health and strength, everything is stirring and full of sound and bustle, so it is with these choruses, which, without any striking qualities, are thoroughly effective where they stand. The charming chorus previous to the embarkation of Electra and Idamante is more characteristic, and seems to mirror the cheerful heavens and the calm sea, together with Electra's happy frame of mind. Very happy in expression are the verses which Electra sings between the choruses—simple, clear, and full of grace and delicacy.

---

[14] Another musical surprise at the close of Electra's second aria is expressive of the dramatic situation. The last note of the voice passes into a march heard in the distance, and beginning with the second part, so that the audience is at once transported into the midst of it. Mozart has employed the same musical expedient in the march in " Figaro," and Spohr in the minuet at the beginning of " Faust."

But the remaining choruses, which are more properly dramatic, are incomparably more important, grand, and earnest. The first (5), representing the shipwreck of "Idomeneo," is a double chorus for male voices. One chorus in the distance is in four parts—the other, nearer, is in two parts; the former is mostly in unison, the latter imitative; each chorus is complete in itself, and quite independent of the other, but the two together form an artistic, clearly apprehended whole. The orchestra contrasts with it as a solid mass, the stringed instruments belonging more especially to the second, and the wind instruments to the first chorus. It falls to the orchestra to depict the storm, and there are plenty of chromatic scales for the purpose, but the effect depends chiefly on bold and forcible harmonies. How little Mozart shunned difficulties and obstacles may be proved by several parts of this scene, the following passage among others :—

Still more powerful are the choruses which close the second act. Again there arises a storm, the sea-monster appears, and horror seizes the people. While the orchestra is in constant agitation, the chorus interposes *en masse*, partly in full chords, partly in effective unison. The succession of striking harmonies reaches its height in the four-times repeated ques-

tion " il reo qual è ? " which closes with a pause on a dis·
sonant chord, repeated, like an echo, by all the wind instruments. Such a magnificent and agitating effect as is attained
by this concentration into one point of every musical expedient, without overstepping the boundaries of the beautiful,
had scarcely been heard in any opera, and Mozart himself
never surpassed it.   The concluding chorus, which follows
an accompanied recitative for Idomeneo, is of an entirely
different character, expressive of a flight, winged by fear and
horror. The 12-8 time, seldom used by Mozart, is suited to the
expression of haste and agitation, and so also is the generally
independent and partially imitative treatment of the voices.
They only unite sometimes into an outcry of horror, otherwise they make detached exclamations, and each goes his
way in hurried confusion until all are dispersed.

The chorus in the third act (24) expresses a totally different
sentiment in equally grand style.   When, after the effective
appeal of the High Priest, Idomeneo discloses his obligation
to sacrifice his son, the people, still discontented and mur-
muring, are struck with grief and horror.   The intensity
and almost over-wealth of beauty with which these emotions
are expressed give the music, as we have already remarked,
the national stamp of the Italian opera. We may learn from
this chorus how in a true work of art the universal emotions
of the human heart may be blended with the peculiarities of
national and individual life and transported into the realm of
pure art.   The effect of unison at the words " già regna la
morte," expressing the depressed murmur of the people, is
wonderfully fine; the chromatic triplet passage of the accompaniment seeks meanwhile in vain to raise the fainting spirits
higher.   This motif passes finely into the calm confidence of
the High Priest's prayer, and the touchingly beautiful orchestral conclusion lets a ray of light on to this dispirited mood.
But the climax has not yet reached its highest point. After a
simple but wonderfully effective march, there follows a prayer
for Idomeneo and the Priest which is a complete masterpiece, whether we consider its truthful expression of emotion,
its rich and original orchestral accompaniment, or the combination in it of the various elements which produce the

total effect. We can here merely indicate the short chorus of priests, which remains in unison in the one key of C, while the instruments (the strings *pizzicato* in a harplike movement, the wind instruments in characteristic passages) proceed in varied harmonies from C minor to F major, whereupon the voices sink to F and keep this key, while the orchestra gives out the solemn and quieting chords of the so-called church ending (B minor, F major).

It is much to be regretted that after this chorus the opera follows the usual course of opera seria, and leaves important dramatic situations unused for the purposes of musical representation. If, according to the original design, the remaining chief situations had been wrought together into a duet for Ilia and Idamante and a quartet, we should then possess masterpieces of grand dramatic music at the close of the opera; instead of this separate songs have been detached from their context in order to satisfy the singers.

The grandiose and free treatment of the choruses, both in the voice parts and the accompaniments, places them almost on a level with those of " König Thamos "; but a more condensed and pregnant style of music was required in the opera than in " König Thamos," where the connection with the drama was loose and superficial. Mindful of this consideration, Mozart, while giving the choruses free scope for musical execution, never allows them to stand independent of and apart from the words.

A reminiscence of French opera is evident in the treatment of the recitatives as well as in the important part allotted to the chorus. The groundwork of the dialogue is, as usual, in secco recitative, but accompanied recitative is more often employed as introductory to the songs than formerly, and it is also made use of as the most fitting vehicle for passionate or agitated soliloquies, such as that of Idomeneo after the appearance of the monster (18), or for solemn and pathetic appeals, such as that of the High Priest (22); also at different points of the dialogue where the sentiment rises above the tone of ordinary speech, the accompanied recitative interrupts the secco for a longer or shorter interval, and gives the dialogue increased power and animation. The treatment of this kind of recitative is always free. It passes from sharply accented declamation into more or less elaborate melodious song. In the same way the orchestra sometimes serves simply as supporting accompaniment, sometimes suggests in an interlude or carries out more fully the expression of feeling excited by the words. A truly inexhaustible wealth of striking and, from many points of view, interesting features and beautiful motifs displays itself in these recitatives. Very fine, for instance, is the anticipation in Electra's recitative (p. 171, score) of the principal subject of the following song. How suggestive it is when Idomeneo, Ilia having just left him, expresses the conviction that she loves Idamante, in the characteristic motif of her song, by which doubtless she has betrayed her love, weaving it in the most striking manner into the interlude of his soliloquy! (p. 146, score). The variety and wealth of harmonic transitions in these recitatives is astonishing. Mozart's originality is displayed by the way in which he gathers to a point the scattered and fugitive emotions of the various parts, so as to form a consistent whole. There is not a note which stands alone, every separate touch becomes for him a motif, capable of further development, and each in its own measure contributes to express the situation; the subjects are not strung upon a thread, they are moulded into a homogeneous entity. The effect of the melodrama lingers in the dramatic character of the instrumental interludes, which is sharply emphasised by the great variety of orchestral tone-colouring. An example of such character-painting is afforded by the prelude to the High Priest's recitative (23), which is in close connection with the scene which is being enacted on the stage. It begins maestoso, with a rapid flourish of trumpets, drums, and horns—the King enters with his followers; then a largo (of two bars length), stringed instruments and bassoons; the priests enter; finally an agitated passage for the violins; the people throng tumultuously upon the stage. Then also we have not only the stringed quartet, with occasional use of one or other wind instrument, in the recitatives, but, wherever it seems advisable the whole orchestra is employed; the wind instruments serving to accent and light up the most varied combinations.

This brings us to one of the most remarkable features of "Idomeneo," which at the time rendered the work a true phenomenon, and which even now excites admiration and appears worthy of study : the treatment of the orchestra. It was to be expected that Mozart, having at his disposal a well-appointed and excellently trained orchestra, would develop with partiality the instrumental side of his great work. In point of fact, the orchestral portions of "Idomeneo" are richer, more brilliant, and more carefully carried out, even to the smallest details, than was ever again the case in his later works. The composition of the orchestra is quite the same as that which he employed in after-times, except that he occasionally has four horns, as on some former occasions (Vol. I., p. 304; II., p. 86), but not in Vienna. He disposed freely of all the forces at his command, not contenting himself any longer with accentuating different parts by means of richer instrumentation, but maintaining throughout a more brilliant and forcible instrumental colouring, and allowing the choice and use of means to be determined only by the particular subject which was to be represented. In this manner he kept himself within the bounds of moderation, and reserved certain resources for definite effects; for instance, flutes are employed only in the storm (18), trombones only for the oracle (28). In the choruses to "König Thamos," on the contrary, the trombones are in frequent use, as they were later with similar effect in the "Zauberflöte." So decidedly had Mozart even at that time fixed the character of this instrument. But he was particularly careful so to distribute his effects that the ear should never be either over-excited or over-fatigued. For instance, in the two storm scenes (5, 18) there are no trumpets and drums; they first occur in the flight scene, which is quite different in character; and again in the dance choruses (10, 32), when festive brilliancy is required ; also in the mourning chorus, where they are muffled, which modifies the effect in a very original manner. These observations might advantageously be carried into detail; but it will suffice here to point out that Mozart's

moderation in the use of his instrumental forces, any unusual
enrichment being more easily perceived in this quarter than
in any other, arises neither from meagreness of invention
nor from a calculated singularity, but that he adopts it with
clear views and firm control of his own powers.   Mozart has
in " Idomeneo " laid the foundation of all modern instrumentation, which has since only been developed in detail,
unhappily over-developed and perverted.   But the most
delicate perception of material sound effect can only produce superficial results; it should serve merely as a co-
operating element in true artistic production.[15]   The instruments in the hands of an artist are only transmitters of the
musical idea in its fixed construction and embodiment, and
the same loving care which the master displays over harmonious and thematic elaboration or characteristic expression
appears in his efforts to work on the senses of his hearers by
means of beautiful orchestral effects.   But, although the
orchestra is perfectly independent, it must not be forgotten
that it works side by side with the voices, serving as foreground and background for them, and never made so prominent as to cause the voices to appear only like the accessories
in a landscape.

Three marches are characteristic, each in its own way.   The
first (9) is a brilliant festival march, belonging by its style
to the ballet which follows ; the second (15), which is introduced in the charming way already noticed, is mainly effective by its gradual approach, new instruments falling in at
each repetition and adding to its force and tone-colouring.
At first the trumpets and drums are muted, as in the concluding chorus in " König Thamos." The simplest and most

---

[15] As one example among many, I may quote Idomeneo's prayer (26). The
pizzicato violin accompaniment, imitating the harp, is enlivened by the
division of the passage among the strings; then comes an independent
fully appointed passage for the wind instruments, with an harmonic movement increasing to a climax, which has an original colouring by means of its
peculiar sound effects. And the repetition shows us a new development of the
previously given elements. A partiality for certain passages for the wind
instruments, mostly in thirds and sixths, is apparent both in " Idomeneo "
and in the choruses to " König Thamos"; it is observable elsewhere, but in
moderation.

beautiful of the marches is the third (25), which fills a necessary pause in the scenic arrangements, but which is full of beautiful expression. The employment of the violoncellos is very original; they go for the most part with the double-basses, but two octaves higher, which produces an excellent effect.

The music to the ballet may most fitly be noticed here. It consists of the following numbers :—

1. Chaconne (D major), " Pas de deux de Madame Hartig et M. Antoine," " Pas de seul de Madame Falgera," an elaborate movement, with which is connected an equally elaborate Larghetto (B flat major). " Pas de seul pour Madame Hartig." To a tolerably long Annonce succeeds the Chaconne " pour le Ballet," partly repeated, and concluding with a *crescendo*.

2. " Pas de seul de M. Le Grand " (D major). This begins with a pathetic Intrade (Largo) leading to a neat and compact Allegretto, which was omitted in performance. This is followed by a very animated Più allegro, and concluded by another Più allegro " pour le Ballet," with a twice-repeated triplet passage in long-drawn *crescendo* rising from *pp* to *ff*, intensified by suspensions, and which is enough to make one giddy.

3. Passepied (B flat major) " pour Madame Redwen," short and simple, but very neat and graceful, and quite in dance form.

4. Gavotte (G major), not elaborated, delicate and graceful ; a very good effect is produced by the simple imitation of the violoncello, which is carried out in harmony in the third part.

5. Passecaille (E flat major). This piece was intended for further elaboration with a Pas de seul " for M. Antoine," and a Pas de deux (Madame Falgera et M. Le Grand), but it was considered too long. Mozart only planned two longer portions without completing them, and in performance the whole Pas de deux was omitted.

The traditional style of the different dances, as they are known to us from the suites of Handel and Bach, has been preserved in their rhythmical structure, and also in other characteristics; the Passepied, for instance, would have its own place in every suite, and so also would the Gavotte.

Besides this, the whole of the ballet music in "Idomeneo" is similar to corresponding movements in the opera, fresh, melodious, and appropriate throughout. But it is easy to see that Mozart was aware that the delicate details and the orchestral treatment that are present throughout the opera would not be in place here. It is true that he has done justice to himself in the free and flowing arrangement of parts and the animated grouping of the instruments, and true also that delicate harmonious transitions constantly betray the hand of a master; but he was well aware that he must depend chiefly for light and shade on sharp pregnant rhythm and strong emphasis. With this view, trumpets and drums are not spared, but the orchestra, with the exception of some separate strong strokes, is seldom used *en masse;* there are few attempts after peculiar effects through unusual instrumental combinations, and only in the Gavotte does a solo violoncello occur, and that in very modest fashion. The influence of the ballet-master is apparent from the fact that there are many more erasures and alterations in this than in any other part of the opera.

In the overture, a magnificent piece, Mozart altogether abandoned the old forms. It is in one lively movement, and maintains its character as an introduction by not coming to a proper conclusion, but passing immediately into the first scene. A certain typical tone of heroic solemnity is heard in the first bars, and reiterated more than once afterwards; but the whole is governed by a severe earnestness, expressed by the frequent occurrence of the minor key, and by the strong but beautiful dissonances. The middle subject, on the contrary, begins a gentle plaint in A minor, which is calmed and relieved by the wonderfully beautiful introduction of the key of C major, enhanced in effect by variety of tone-colouring.

If we gather together the results of our observations of "Idomeneo," we cannot fail to discern in it the work of a master who has arrived at the maturity of his powers while still in the full bloom of youth. It was only his

submission to those restraints which seemed unavoidable,
which prevented his freeing the opera seria from the conven-
tionalities which formed, indeed, no essential part of its being.
Even had he succeeded in doing so, it would have involved
no renunciation of its national character, which, as we have
seen, in no way fettered Mozart's individuality. But, since
in the improvements he made he was indebted to French
opera, and especially to Gluck, the question arises how much,
and in what way, Mozart had learnt from the great Parisian
master. It is not merely unquestionable that Gluck exerted
a general influence over Mozart's opinions and tendencies,
but the traces of a close study of his works, and especially
of "Alceste," may be easily discovered. He had been
present as a boy at the first representation of "Alceste."
Its influence is apparent in many details, such as the harmonic treatment of the oracle, and the use of sustained
chords for the horns and trombones in the accompaniment
to the appeal of the High Priest. The march in "Alceste"
has served as a model for the style, if not for the execution,
of the last march in "Idomeneo." The High Priest's soliloquy is altogether analogous in plan and treatment to that
of Gluck's High Priest; again, the recurring subject of the
interlude—

reminds us of the corresponding one in "Alceste"—

and other similarities may be detected. More important is
the similarity of dramatic style, which is especially evident
in the treatment of the recitatives, and in the share taken
by the orchestra in the characterisation. But that Mozart
learnt from Gluck only as one master learns from another,
and that he turned his borrowed pound to rich account, it
needs but a closer consideration of these details, as well as

of the whole work, to make plain. We must not underrate the wholesome and powerful effect which grand and important works must have made upon him, and the enlightenment and correction of his views as to the nature of the opera thereby obtained. But we must also remember that Mozart received these impressions and this instruction into a nature self-dependent and productive, and that his artistic cultivation enabled him to appropriate only what was in accordance with his nature. Gluck sets aside the fixed expressions of operatic form as far as is practicable, in order to gaih perfect freedom of dramatic action; Mozart, on the other hand, strives to spare these forms, and so to mould and develop them that they may themselves serve as vehicles for dramatic expression. This he does not because he clings to what is old and established, but with the just perception that these forms contain an essential element of artistic construction which is capable of development. Mozart never seeks, as Gluck did, to forget that he is a musician; on the contrary, he remembers it at every point of his artstic production, and could not ignore the fact if he would. In opposition to the one-sided requirements of dramatic characterisation, he falls back upon the principles of musical construction, which are far from contradicting such requirements, and are in fact the higher power which establishes them. On these grounds we assert that Mozart's creative power in music (to which we must first turn our glance in judging an artist) was more universal and deeper than that of Gluck; that he surpassed him in artistic cultivation and discipline will be doubted by no one who compares the technical work, the disposition of the orchestra, &c., in "Idomeneo" with Gluck's operas. This judgment does not exclude the fact that some of Gluck's performances as an artist are not only grand and striking, but surpass kindred works by Mozart. But if the laws and nature of art are once perceived, a more certain rule is provided for the judgment of the work of art as well as of the artist; and here Mozart may bear away the palm.

Mozart's leave of absence was not extorted from the Archbishop without difficulty, and it was limited to six weeks.

The better satisfied he became with his life in Munich, where he found friends, appreciation, and enlightenment, the more appalling grew the prospect of returning to Salzburg, and he was in terror lest the Archbishop should recall him even before the performance of the opera. With this idea he writes to his father (December 16, 1780):—

À propos! how about the Archbishop? Next Monday I shall have been absent from Salzburg for six weeks. You know, my dear father, that it is only for love of you that I remain in Salzburg, for, by heaven! if it rested with me I would have torn up the agreement and resigned my appointment before I left home this time. It is not Salzburg, but the prince and the proud nobility who become more insupportable to me every day. I should hail with delight a letter informing me that he no longer needed my services. The patronage I have here would assure me of present and future means of support, without taking into account the chances by death, which none ought to count upon, but which is no bad friend to a man in search of employment. But anything in the world to please you—and it would come all the easier to me if I could get away now and then for a little to take breath. You know how hard it was to get away this time, and that without some great cause there is no possibility of it again. Come to Munich and hear my opera, and then tell me if I am wrong to feel unhappy when I think of Salzburg.

His father seeks to reassure him as to the leave of absence (December 25, 1780):—

As regards the six weeks, I have decided not to take any steps in the matter, but if I hear anything on the subject I shall certainly answer that we understood you were to remain in Munich six weeks after the composition of the opera, for its rehearsal and production, but that I could not imagine that his highness would suppose that such an opera could be composed, copied, and performed in six weeks, &c.

It would not, however, have been a matter of regret to L. Mozart if Wolfgang could have met with a good situation in Munich. Wolfgang himself had been rendered full of hope from the gracious reception of the Elector, and wrote to his father that if he succeeded in settling in Munich, he (the father) must not long remain in Salzburg, but must follow him thither. He was very anxious to demonstrate in Munich that he could write other things besides operas, and he turned his church music to account. With this object he wrote to his father (November 13, 1780):—

Be so kind as to send me the scores of the two Masses that I have at home, and also the Mass in B flat major (275 K.), for Count Seeau has promised to speak of them to the Elector. I should like to make myself known in this style. I have just heard a Mass by Grua (kapell-meister in 1779, died 1826); it would be easy to compose half-a-dozen a day of that kind of thing.

Mozart also appears to have tried to win favour with the Elector by a new church composition; at least a grand Kyrie in D minor (341 K.), judging by the character of the composition and the distribution of the orchestra, can only have been written during this stay in Munich. The orchestra consists of the usual string quartet, and in addition two flutes, two oboes, two clarinets, two bassoons, four horns (in D and F), two trumpets, and drums; there is no grouping of the kind that is found in "Idomeneo." Whether this is a fragment of a Mass which was never completed, or whether it was intended for insertion in another work, cannot now be decided. It is tolerably long, but elaborated without much thematic treatment, the elements of the construction and flow being more rhythmical and harmonic, and taking their principal charm from the independent and richly elaborated orchestral accompaniment. Among Mozart's sacred compositions his Kyries are specially distinguished by an originality of tone-colouring and peculiarly melodious treatment, which are extremely well suited to the melancholy tone of the movement before us. Much of it points to the Requiem, and opens the door to conjecture as to the path which Mozart would have pursued had he devoted himself specially to church music.

Another great work, apparently written for the Munich Kapelle, is a grand serenata for wind instruments (361 K.),[16] with the date 1780, which he must have taken with him, since he would hardly have undertaken so important a work while engaged on "Idomeneo." The serenata is for two oboes, two clarinets, two viols, four horns, two bassoons, violoncello, and double-bass. The instruments, and the task appointed for them, point rather to the Munich orchestra

[16] For the quintet on which it was founded see p. 94. The serenata was afterwards made use of in many combinations.

than to that of Salzburg. Compositions for wind instruments alone, called Harmonie-Musik, were then much in favour, and Mozart may have wished to recommend himself by producing an important piece of the kind, which would place the performances of the band in a brilliant light.[17]

In form the serenata resembles those written for the complete orchestra. It begins with a solemn Largo, which serves as introduction to a Molto allegro, worked out very like the first movement of a symphony. This is followed by a Minue with two trios, than a broadly planned Adagio, and again a Minuet with three trios. To this is joined a Romanze (adagio), simple and lyrical, in two parts, interrupted by an Allegretto leading again to the Adagio, which is repeated and concluded by a coda. Then comes an Andante with six variations, and the finale, consisting of a cheerful Rondo. It is no easy task to write such a succession of pieces for wind instruments, for the tone-colouring, although striking and agreeable, must be moderately and carefully treated. People were certainly more accustomed to this kind of music at the time, but even at the present day the serenata does not produce a sense of fatigue. It has an interest as a proof of the minute study which Mozart bestowed on all instrumental forces, whereby he acquired that complete mastery of the orchestra which is displayed in " Idomeneo."

But the work has a higher significance than that of a mere study of instrumentation, as is shown by the admiration it has excited in many places quite recently. The charm of the composition depends greatly upon the certainty with which the peculiar style of each instrument is made use of; but this forms only one side of the artistic construction of the idea, and the full force and beauty of the instrumental effects are only perceived when they are considered as a means of representing each part of the whole work in its due proportion.

---

[17] Schinck (Litterar. Fragm., II., p. 286) describes a concert of Stadler's in Vienna, 1784: " I have heard a piece for wind instruments by Herr Mozart to-day. Magnificent ! It consisted of thirteen instruments, and at every instrument a master ! The effect was grand and magnificent beyond description ! "

Great delicacy and diversity are shown in the grouping and treatment of the different instruments. The first players naturally undertake the chief parts, the accompaniment falling to the secondary players, but the disposition of parts is so free and independent that the difference is not always apparent.[18] All the movements are well planned and constructed, rich in delicate and interesting touches of harmonic or thematic elaboration, and in general fresh and tuneful.

The crown of them is the Adagio,[19] in which the musical expression of deep and earnest feeling rises to a purity and height which is impossible to the specified representations of certain frames of mind now in fashion. We here attain, by means of artistic catharsis, as Aristotle calls it (*purging, purifying*), to an absolute freedom and satisfaction, which it is granted to man to feel only in the perfect harmony and beauty of art. The means by which this highest of all effects is reached are so simple that a dissection of them would only be a confirmation of the old scripture that the letter killeth and the spirit giveth life.[20]

As long as Mozart was engaged on the composition and study of his opera he had no time for recreation, and his visits were confined to the Cannabich family. After the performance he refreshed himself by entering with his father and sister into the Carnival gaieties, and by cheerful intercourse with his friends. But the latter did not allow him to remain long in idleness. To please his good friend Ramm he wrote a quartet for oboe, violin, tenor, and violoncello (370 K.), obbligato throughout for the oboe, but otherwise easy and light in design and execution. For his patroness the Countess Baumgarten (Vol. II., p. 132) he composed, on March 8,

---

[18] The violoncello and double-bass have, properly speaking, no independent part; they only strengthen the fundamental bass, which would not be sufficiently prominent with the second bassoons alone.

[19] This Adagio has been arranged to an offertory, " Quis te comprehendat " (Coblenz: Falkenberg).

[20] It has already been remarked that a relationship exists between the melodies of Mozart's instrumental works, and those of his German—never of his Italian—operas; there are in this serenata suggestions here and there of the " Entführung," which was composed soon after.

1781, a concert aria (369 K.), "Misera dove son" (from Metastasio's "Ezio," III., 12), which gives a favourable idea of the vocal performances of this lady. It makes no great demands on the compass of the voice or execution, but the recitative and air are both earnest and serious, and require in every respect an excellent delivery. The instrumentation is simple, only flutes and horns being added to the quartet.

Mozart's longer stay in Munich was rendered possible by the Archbishop's journey to Vienna, which was probably occasioned by the death of the Empress. He wished to appear with all the pomp of a spiritual prince, and took with him a considerable retinue of courtiers and servants, as well as some of his most distinguished musicians. Wolfgang rejoiced at this fortunate circumstance, and enjoyed himself so much in Munich that he confessed later to his father (May 26, 1781) :—

In Munich, it is true, I was a little too gay, but I can assure you on my honour that before the opera was on the boards I went to no theatre and visited no one but Cannabich. I exceeded a little afterwards, I own, but it was through youthful folly. I thought to myself, "Where are you to go to ? To Salzburg. Well, then, enjoy yourself while you can ! "

His father was full of thought for him even now ; he wrote from Munich to Breitkopf (February 12, 1781) :—

I have long desired that you should publish some work by my son. You will not, I am sure, judge of him now by the clavier sonatas which he wrote while still a child. You cannot have seen a note of what he has written for some years past, unless it may be the six sonatas for clavier and violin which were engraved at Paris (Vol. I., p. 415). We have allowed very little to appear. You might make the experiment with a couple of symphonies or clavier sonatas, or else with quartets, trios, &c. You should only give us a few copies in return, as I am anxious that you should see my son's manner of work. But do not imagine that I wish to over-persuade you. The thought has frequently occurred to me, because I see so much published and in print that moves me to pity.

Wolfgang did not return to Salzburg. His gay life in Munich was interrupted by a summons from the Archbishop to Vienna. There he accordingly arrived on March 12, and there his destiny was to be fulfilled.

M 2

CHAPTER XXIII.

RELEASE.

THE summons to Vienna appeared like the fulfilment of Mozart's ardent and long-deferred wish; but his relation to the Archbishop, among whose followers he was obliged to consider himself, was only too well calculated to turn his delight into disappointment. He had apparently the best opportunity of gaining admission to the most distinguished society, and of earning fame and money in a city where music was the prevailing means of entertainment. But the Archbishop, desirous as he was to shine by virtue of the extraordinary performers and composers who were in his service, found equal satisfaction in keeping them constantly in mind that they *were* in his service. It was the custom for princes when they were invited out to be attended by the members of their suite ;[1] and the musicians were summoned also to provide music in strange houses. The Archbishop did not hesitate to show off Mozart, as well as Ceccarelli and Brunetti, in this way, as his own private performers; but as often as Mozart found an advantageous opportunity for being heard independently, he refused him permission and treated him in all respects like a servant in his house. It can be imagined how Mozart felt himself aggrieved by such undignified treatment, after the full freedom and recognition of his talents which he had enjoyed in Munich, and within reach of such brilliant successes as he might have had in Vienna. His letters to his father show how he must have longed to throw off his galling chains, and give us a lively picture of his position and feelings :—

Yesterday, March 16 (1781), I arrived, God be praised, quite alone, in a post-chaise, at nine o'clock in the morning. . . . Now about the Archbishop. I have a charming room in the same house as the Archbishop. Brunetti and Ceccarelli are lodged in another house. *Che*

---

[1] Nicolai, Reise, V., p. 231.

distinzione! My neighbour, Herr von Kleinmayern (Director of the Council), overwhelmed me with civilities on my arrival. He is really a very pleasant fellow. We dine at twelve midday, a little too early for me, unfortunately. The two valets in attendance, the controller (E. M. Kölnberger), Herr Zezi (the court quartermaster), the confectioner, two cooks, Ceccarelli, Brunetti, and *my littleness* all dine together. The two valets sit at the head of the table, and I have the honour to be placed above the cooks. I can imagine myself in Salzburg. During dinner there is a good deal of coarse silly joking, but not with me, for I do not speak a word but what I am obliged, and that with the greatest circumspection. When I have had my dinner I go my way. There is no evening meal provided, but we each receive three ducats, and that you know goes a long way! The Archbishop is glad enough to glorify himself with his people—takes their services and gives them nothing in return. Yesterday we had music at four o'clock, when at least twenty persons of the high nobility were present. Ceccarelli has already sung at Palfy's (the Archbishop's brother-in-law). To-day we are to go to Prince Gallitzin (the Russian ambassador), who was present yesterday. I shall wait to see if I am paid anything; if not I shall go to the Archbishop and tell him straight out that if he will not allow me to earn anything for myself he must pay me, for that I cannot live on my own money.

L. Mozart, who saw the storm coming, sought to pacify his son by telling him that as the Archbishop had summoned him to Vienna in order to glorify himself by his performances, he would certainly take care to give him opportunities for display; but Wolfgang answers (March 24, 1781) :—

You say that the Archbishop's vanity is tickled by having me in his possession; this may be true, but of what use is it to me? It is not a thing to live by. And believe me that he only stands in the way of my preferment. How does he treat me? Herr von Kleinmayern and Boenike (secretary and councillor) have a special table with the illustrious Count Arco; it would be a distinction to sit at this table, instead of being with the valets—who, when they are not taking the first places at table, light the candles, shut the doors, and remain in the antechambers—and with the cooks! And when we go to a concert anywhere, the valet waits outside until the Salzburgers arrive, and then lets them know by a footman that they have permission to enter. Brunetti told me all this, and I thought as I listened, "Only wait till I come!"

The other day when we went to Prince Gallitzin, Brunetti said to me in his nice way, "Mind you are here at six o'clock this evening, and we will go together to Prince Gallitzin's : Angelbauer will conduct you. I replied, "Very well; but if I am not here at six punctually, do not wait for me; we shall be sure to meet there. So I purposely went alone, and when I arrived, there stood Monsieur Angelbauer ready to inform Monsieur the footman that he might show me in. But I took not the least notice either of the valet or the footman, but went straight through into the music-room, all the doors being open, and up to the Prince, to whom, after paying my respects, I stood talking for some time. I had quite forgotten Brunetti and Ceccarelli, for they kept out of sight behind the orchestra, and stood leaning against the wall, without venturing a step forward.

The Archbishop also made his musicians play for old Prince Rudolf Colloredo, his father, for which they received five ducats, and the demands he made on Mozart for his own concerts are shown by a letter to the father (April 8, 1781) :—

To day we had a concert (for I am writing at eleven o'clock at night) at which three pieces by me were performed (new ones, of course)—a rondo to a concerto for Brunetti,[2] a sonata with violin accompaniment for myself, which I composed last night between eleven and twelve o'clock; but I had only time to write the accompaniment part for Brunetti, and I played my own part out of my head;[3] and then a rondo for Ceccarelli, which was encored.[4]

For all this he received from the Archbishop, who had at least paid him four ducats for the first concert, nothing at all. This might pass, but shortly afterwards he writes (April 11, 1781): " What makes me half desperate is that the same evening that we had that confounded concert the Countess Thun invited me. Of course I could not go, and who do you think was there ? The Emperor ! Adamberger

---

[2] This rondo (373 K.) was composed, according to the autograph, on April 2, 1781, for Brunetti; it is in C major (allegretto grazioso 2-4,) accompanied by the quartet, two oboes, and two horns, and is simple and graceful without much demand of execution.

[3] The unfinished allegro movement in B flat major (372 K.), begun on March 24, 1781, probably belongs to this sonata, which was not afterwards written down.

[4] The words of the rondo (374 K., Concertarien, No. 5), "A questo seno," appear to have been taken from an opera called " Zeira." A short recitative introduces the rondo, of which the theme is thrice repeated and closes with a coda. The song is simple throughout, without any passages, and for a voice of moderate compass; the accompaniment (the quartet, two oboes and two horns) is also easy. It is plain that Ceccarelli was a singer of no pretensions. The cantilene, however, is expressive, and there are some original harmonic touches.

Madame Weigl[5] were there, and each had fifty ducats—and what an opportunity!"

He was right, certainly, in saying that the Archbishop stood in the way of his preferment, for he had very few opportunities for winning fame or success. He renewed his old acquaintance with the Messmer family (pp. 86, 145), with Herr von Auerhammer and his fat daughter, and with the old kapellmeister, Bono. Bono allowed a symphony by Mozart to be rehearsed in his house, which, as he reports (April 11, 1781), went splendidly and was a great success. "Forty violins played; the wind instruments were all doubled."

He had no difficulty, either, in gaining admission to the most distinguished musical circles:—

I go this evening (March 24) with Herr von Kleinmayern to one of his friends—the Councillor Braun—who, every one tells me, is a great amateur of the clavier.[6] I have already dined twice with the Countess Thun, and go there almost every day. She is the most charming and amiable woman that I have ever seen, and she thinks a great deal of me. I have also dined with Count Cobenzl (court and state vice-chancellor). My principal object now is to make myself favourably known to the Emperor, for I am determined that he shall know me. I should like to play through my opera to him, and then some good fugues—that is what he has most taste for. Oh! if I had only known that I was to be in Vienna during Lent, I would have written a little oratorio, and performed it for my own benefit, as is the custom here. I could easily have written it beforehand, for I know all the voices here. How I should like to give a public concert! but it would not be allowed, I know for certain; for, just imagine! you know that there is a Society here which gives concerts for the benefit of the widows of musicians, and every one at all connected with music plays there gratis. The orchestra is 180 strong.[7] No one who pretends to any philanthropy refuses to play when the Society calls upon him to do so; it is a sure way also to the favour of the Emperor and of the public. Starzer was

---

[5] The mother of the composer, at that time prima donna at the German Theatre (Jahrb. d. Tonkunst, 1796, p. 69).

[6] "The Imperial Councillor, Von Braun, is one of our greatest musical connoisseurs. He thinks very highly of the compositions of the great Ph. Emanuel Bach; and here he is opposed by the majority of the public in Vienna." (Nicolai, Reise, IV., p. 556.)

[7] There was a chorus of 200 voices for Dittersdorf's "Esther," 1772 (Selbst-biogr., p. 203). K. R[isbeck] speaks of 400 assistants (Briefe, I., p. 276).

commissioned to request me to play, and I willingly agreed, subject to the consent of my Prince, of which I had little doubt, seeing that it was a religious kind of performance, and gratuitous. He refused his permission, however, and all the nobility have taken it ill of him. I am only sorry on this account: the Emperor is to be in the proscenium box, and I should have preluded quite alone, and then played a fugue and the variations, "Je suis Lindor." [8] The Countess Thun would have lent me her beautiful pianoforte by Stein for the purpose. Whenever I have played the variations in public they have been greatly applauded. They are easily understood, and every one finds something to his taste.

In this instance, however, the Archbishop was obliged to give way. The institution for the widows and orphans of Vienna musicians, founded by the kapellmeister Florian Gassmann, in 1771, enjoyed the highest patronage; and the four concerts given annually for its benefit—two during Advent, and two in Passion week—were as well supported by celebrated composers and performers as by the public. Starzer went to the concert at Prince Gallitzin's, and he and all the nobility teased the Archbishop so long for his consent that he could not withhold it. "I am so glad!" exclaims Mozart, when he informs his father of this. The programme of the thirty-fourth concert for the benefit of the Society of Musicians at Vienna, on April 3, 1781, contained the following: [9]—

The Herr Ritter W. A. Mozart will then perform alone on the pianoforte. He visited Vienna as a child of seven years old, and then excited the universal admiration of the public by his compositions, his insight into the art of music, and his extraordinary facility of touch and execution.

His success was all that could be desired. "After yesterday," he writes (April 4), "I may well say that I am satisfied with the Vienna public. I played at the concert for the widows' institution, and was obliged to begin twice over, because there was no end to the applause." He refers to it again in his next letter (April 8): "That which most pleased and surprised me was the total silence, and then in

---

[8] At his concert in Leipzig he played these variations again after an improvised fantasia (354 K.).

[9] Neue Wien. Musikzeitg., 1852, No. 35.

the middle of my playing bursts of applause and bravos. For Vienna, where there are so many and such good clavier-players, it has been really a wonderful success."

After this, his prospects, if he could succeed in giving a concert on his own account, were sufficiently brilliant; and ladies of rank offered themselves to dispose of the tickets for him. "What should I not make if I were to give a concert for myself, now that the Vienna public knows me! But the Archbishop will not allow it; he wishes his people to have loss rather than profit in his service." He contemplated shortly sending his musicians back to Salzburg; if Mozart were to be obliged to leave Vienna before he had established himself in the favour of the public, and to find himself in Salzburg again, with no hope of any further leave of absence, there would be an end to all his future prospects. Brunetti had told him that Count Arco had communicated to him the Archbishop's directions that they were to receive their travelling money, and to set out on the following Sunday; if any wished to remain longer he might do so, but he must live on his own means. Mozart declared that until Count Arco himself told him that he was to go he would entirely ignore it, and then he would tell him his mind on the subject. He would certainly remain in Vienna; he thought that if he could find only two pupils (he had one already in the Countess Rumbeck), he should be better off than in Salzburg; with a successful concert, and some profitable invitations into society, it could not be but that he should send money home, while his father would be drawing pay for them both, and would be relieved from his support. "Oh! I will turn the tables on the Archbishop in the most delightful manner, and as politely as possible, for he cannot do me any harm."

The father was horrified at this news. He had a well-founded distrust of Wolfgang's financial plans, which were always built upon an uncertain future, and he feared that a complete rupture with the Archbishop would be the consequence of such a step, that he would lose his situation and be liable for the expenses of the journey to the capital; he earnestly begged his son to reflect well on the feasibility of his project. " Dear father," runs the answer, " I love you very dearly, as you may see from my renouncing for your sake my dearest wishes and desires; for if it were not for you, I declare on my honour I would not delay an instant, but would quit my service, give a grand concert, set to work with pupils, and in a year I should be succeeding so well in Vienna that I should be earning at least a thousand dollars per annum. I assure you it is very hard for me so to set aside my hopes of fortune. I am young, as you say—true, but to dawdle away one's youth in such a miserable hole is sad enough, and hurtful besides."

The threatened departure was postponed for a time, for the Archbishop required his performers in Vienna; then it was said that they were to return home on April 22. " When I think," wrote Wolfgang (April 11, 1781) " of leaving Vienna without at least a thousand florins in my pocket, my heart sinks within me. Am I to throw away a thousand gulden because of a malicious prince who does what he likes with me for a miserable four hundred florins? I should make quite that by a concert." And now he was to come to the knowledge that not only had he laboured in vain for the Archbishop, but that he had thereby lost the opportunity of introducing himself to the notice of the Emperor. " I cannot quite say to the Emperor that if he wants to hear me he must make haste about it, for that I am going away on such a day—one has to wait for these things. And here I cannot and must not stay, unless I give a concert, for although I should be better off here than at home, if I had only two pupils, it helps one along to have a thousand or twelve hundred florins in one's purse. And he will not allow it, the misanthrope—I must call him so, for so he is, as the whole of the nobility say." There were favourable prospects, too, of a permanent settlement in Vienna at no very distant date. The kapellmeister, Bono, was very old; after his death Salieri would succeed him, and Starzer would take Salieri's place—for Starzer there was as yet no successor— could a better be found than Mozart ?

Again his father warned him not to make uncertain plans, but to hold fast to what was secure, and to bear what was

unavoidable ; he warned him also against incautious expressions "which could only do harm." Wolfgang could only
answer that his father was partly right and partly wrong ;
" but that in which you are right far outweighs that in which
you are wrong, therefore I will certainly come, and with the
greatest pleasure, since I am fully convinced that you would
never come in the way of my advancement " (April 18, 1781).
But it was hard to submit to the will of his father, and the
Archbishop's continual insults did not make it any easier.
He writes (April 28, 1781) :—

You are expecting me with pleasure, my dearest father! That is in
fact the one consideration which has brought me to the point of leaving
Vienna, for the whole world may know that the Archbishop of Salzburg
has only to thank you, my best of fathers, that he did not lose me
yesterday for ever (I mean, of course, from his suite). Yesterday we
had a concert, probably the last. The concert went very well, and, in
spite of all the hindrances put in my way by his archiepiscopal grace, I
had a better orchestra than Brunetti, as Ceccarelli can tell you; but
the worry and trouble I had to arrange it all can be told better than
written. But if, as I hope will not be the case, the same thing should
happen again, I should certainly lose patience, and you would as
certainly forgive me. And I must beg for your permission, my dear
father, to return to Vienna next Lent. It depends upon you, not on the
Archbishop ; for even if he refuses permission I shall go : it will do me
no harm, not a bit ! Oh, if he could read this, how glad I should be !
But you must give your consent in your next letter, for it is only on
this condition that I return to Salzburg—and I must keep my word to
the ladies here. Stephanie will give me a German opera to write. I
shall expect your answer to this. When and how I shall set out I
cannot tell you at present. It is lamentable that we are so kept in the
dark by our lord and master. All at once it will be, "Allons! weg!"
First we are told that a carriage is being made in which the controller
Ceccarelli and I are to travel; then that we are to go by the diligence;
then that we are to have the money for the diligence, and travel as we
choose (which, indeed, I should like best of all) ; first we are to go in a
week, then in a fortnight; then in three weeks, then again sooner.
Good heavens ! one does not know where one is with it all, and there is
no help for it. Yesterday the ladies kept me quite an hour at the clavier,
after the concert; I believe I should be sitting there still if I had not
managed to steal away.

Again he writes later (June 13, 1781) :—

At the last concert, when it was all over, I played variations for a
whole hour (the Archbishop gave me the subject), and the applause was

so great that, if the Archbishop has ever so little of a human heart, he must have been pleased; and instead of showing me approbation and content—or at least taking no notice of me—he treats me like a beggar, and tells me to my face that I must take more pains, that he could get a hundred who would serve him better than I do.

Mozart's passionate excitement had risen to such a pitch that a drop was sufficient to overflow the cup of his wrath; the Archbishop paid no heed, and affairs came to an inevitable crisis. The following letter (May 9, 1781) shows how far Hieronymus thought he might go with his dependents :—

I am still overflowing with gall, and you, my best and very dear father, will certainly sympathise with me. My patience has been tried for a long time; at last it has given way. I have no longer the misfortune to be in the Salzburg service. To-day was the happy one of my release. Now listen. Twice already the ——— I do not know what to call him—has used the most impertinent and coarsest language to my face, which I refrained from writing to you that I might not distress you, and which nothing but my love and duty to you prevented me from chastising on the spot. He called me a scoundrel—a miserable fellow —told me he would send me packing—and I bore it all; allowed not my own honour alone, but yours, to be so affronted because you wished it. So I was silent. Well, listen. A week ago the courier came up on a sudden and told me I was to leave immediately. The others all had the day fixed, but I had not. So I packed up my things as quickly as I could, and old Madame Weber was so kind as to offer me her house. There I have a pretty room, and I am with obliging people who are ready to provide me with everything that I require, but could not get if I were living alone. I appointed my journey for Wednesday (that is to-day, the 9th), by stage-coach, but I could not collect the money owing to me in time, so I postponed my journey until Saturday. Being seen about to-day one of the valets told me that the Archbishop had a parcel to give me. I asked if there was any hurry, and he replied that it was of the greatest importance. "Then I am sorry not to be able to oblige his grace, for (owing to the above reasons) I cannot set out before Saturday. I am out of the house, living on my own means, and it is therefore quite evident that I cannot go until I am ready, for no one will care to collect my debts for me." Kleinmayern, Moll, Boeneke, and the two valets thought I was right. When I went in to him (I must tell you that Schlaucka had advised me to excuse myself by saying I had already taken my seat in the coach—that would have most weight with him)— when I went in to him, then, he began at once :—*Archbishop:* "Well, when are you going, fellow?" *Mozart:* "I wished to go to-night, but I could not secure a seat." Then out it came, all in a breath—that I was the most miserable fellow he knew—no one served him so badly as

I did. He advised me to be off to-day, or he would write home to stop my pay. There was no getting in a word, it went on like a flood. I listened to it all calmly. He lied to my face by saying that I had five hundred florins salary[10]—called me the most opprobrious names—oh, I really cannot bring myself to write you all! At last, when my blood was boiling, I could hold out no longer, and said : "Then your Serene Highness is not satisfied with me ?" "What! do you mean to threaten me, you rascal, you villain ? There is the door; I will have nothing more to do with such a wretched fellow!" At last I said, "Neither will I with you." "Then be off!" As I went I said, "Let it be so then; to-morrow you shall hear from me by letter." Tell me now, dear father, should I not have had to say this sooner or later ? Now listen. My honour comes before everything to me, and I know that it is so with you also. Have no care for me. I am so certain of success here that I might have resigned even without a cause. As I have had very good cause, and that three times, it is no fault of mine; *au contraire*, I was a cowardly rascal twice, and the third time I could not be so again. As long as the Archbishop is here I will give no concert. Your idea that I shall lower myself in the opinion of the Emperor or of the nobility is entirely mistaken. The Archbishop is hated here, and most of all by the Emperor. That is his real grievance, that the Emperor has not invited him to Laxenburg. I will send you some calculations as to money by the next post to convince you that I shall not starve here. For the rest I entreat you to keep up your spirits, for I consider that my good fortune is beginning now, and I hope that it will be yours also. Write to me privately that you are pleased—for indeed you may be so—and find fault heartily with me in public, so that no blame may attach to you. But if the Archbishop offers you the least impertinence come to me at once in Vienna. We can all three live on my earnings, I assure you on my word, but I would rather you held out a year longer. Do not write to me any more at the Residence or by the mail. I want to hear nothing more of Salzburg. I hate the Archbishop to frenzy. But write to me here, and tell me you are pleased, for only that is now wanting to make my happiness complete.

He carried out his determination, and writes to his father again on May 12 :—

You know by my last letter that I sent in my resignation to the Prince on May 9, because he himself ordered it : for in two previous audiences he had said to me, "Take yourself off, if you will not serve me properly!" He will certainly deny it, but it is as true as the heavens above us. What wonder, then, that after being abused and vilified till I was quite

---

[10] So it had been promised (Vol. II., p. 65); but Mozart asserts repeatedly that he only had a salary of 400 florins (Vol. II., pp. 176, 181).

beside myself, I ended by taking him at his word. The following day I gave Count Arco a petition to be presented to His Grace the Archbishop, asking for the money for the journey—fifteen florins ten kreutzers for the diligence, and two ducats for current expenses. He refused to take either, and assured me I could not resign without obtaining the consent of my father. "That is your duty," said he. I assured him that I knew my duty to my father as well as he and perhaps better, and that I should be sorry if it were necessary to learn it from him at this time of day. "Very well, then," said he, "if he is satisfied you may demand your dismissal, and if not—you may also demand it." A fine distinction, truly! All that the Archbishop said to me in the three audiences—especially in the last—and the language used by this truly worthy man of God, had so strong a physical effect on me that I was obliged to leave the opera at the end of the first act, and go home to bed; for I was quite feverish, trembled in every limb, and tottered along the street like a drunkard. I remained the next day (yesterday) in the house, and kept my bed in the morning because I had taken the tamarind-water. My lord Count has had the kindness to write some fine things of me to his father (High Chamberlain), which you have doubtless had to swallow by this time. There will be some fabulous accounts, but when one writes a comedy one must turn and twist things so as to gain applause, without sticking to the truth of the affair, and you must take the obsequiousness of the Count into account. I will tell you without getting warm about it (for I have no wish to injure my health, and I am sorry enough when I am forced to be angry), I will tell you plainly the principal reproach made to me on account of my service. I did not know that I was to be a valet, and that undid me. I should have dawdled away a couple of hours every morning in the antechamber; I was in fact often told that I ought to show myself, but I could never remember that this was part of my duty, and contented myself with coming punctually when I was summoned by the Archbishop. Now I will briefly convey to you my unalterable determination, so that the whole world may hear it. If I was offered two thousand florins by the Archbishop of Salzburg, and only one thousand florins in any other place, I would go to the other place; for instead of the other one thousand florins I should enjoy health and contentment of mind. I pray you, therefore—by all the fatherly love that you have shown me in so rich a measure from my childhood, and for which I can never be sufficiently grateful—not to write to me on this matter, but to bury it in the deepest oblivion if you want to see your son cheerful and well; a word would be quite enough to rekindle my anger—and yours, if you were in my place, as I am sure you will acknowledge.

The same day on which Mozart sent this letter through the post he wrote another to his father by a safe opportunity, in which he once more seeks to persuade him of the justice of his fixed resolve to leave the Archbishop's service, and of his own good prospects in Vienna :—

In the letter which you will have received by post I spoke as though we were in the presence of the Archbishop; now I speak to you quite alone, my dear father. We will be silent once for all on the subject of the Archbishop's conduct to me from the beginning of his reign—of the unceasing abuse, the impertinence and bad language which he has addressed to my face, of the unquestionable right I have to forsake his service—not a word can be said against all this. I will only speak now of what has really induced me to leave him, laying aside all personal grounds of offence.

I have made the highest and most valuable acquaintances here that can be. I am treated with favour and distinction in the best houses of the nobility, and I am paid for it into the bargain; and shall I sacrifice all this for four hundred florins in Salzburg, without prospects, without encouragement, and unable to help you in any way, as I certainly shall hope to do here? What would be the end of it? It would come to the same thing. I should either fret myself to death or leave the service. I need say no more, you know it all yourself; I will only add that my story is known to the whole of Vienna, and all the nobility advise me not to suffer myself to be led about any longer. He will try to get over you with good words, my dear father—they are serpents, vipers! It is always so with such despicable creatures, they are so haughty and proud as to disgust one, and then they cringe and fawn—horrible. The two valets-de-chambre understand the whole villainy of the affair. Schlaucka said to somebody: "I cannot say I think Mozart at all in the wrong: he is quite right. I would have done just the same myself! He treated him like a beggar; I heard it myself. Shameful!" The Archbishop acknowledges to being in the wrong now; but had he not opportunities enough for acknowledging it before? And did he alter his conduct? Not a bit. Then away with all that! If I had not been afraid of doing you some harm I would have brought it to an end long ago. But, after all, what harm can he do you? None. If you know that I am doing well you can dispense with the Archbishop's favour. He cannot deprive you of your salary as long as you perform your duties, and I will answer for it that I shall do well, otherwise I should not have taken this step. Nevertheless I acknowledge that after this insult I should have resigned, if I had had to beg my bread. If you are at all afraid, make a show of anger against me—blame me as much as you like in your letters, if only we two know how the matter really stands. But do not be deceived by flattery. Be upon your guard!

But L. Mozart did not see the affair in this light, and was far from "strengthening his decision instead of dissuading him from it," as Wolfgang hoped. He considered the renun-

ciation of the Salzburg situation as the first step to ruin, and
hoped to check the passionate indignation of his son and
bring him back to the path of reason, as he considered it.
But he had not calculated on the fact that Wolfgang was no
longer an inexperienced youth, leaving his father's house for
the first time. The oppressive circumstances of his late
residence in Salzburg, and the clear insight into his own
powers and capabilities which he had acquired in Munich,
had given him a consciousness of the necessity of judging
for himself, which had been strengthened by the contrast
between the unworthy treatment of the Archbishop and the
brilliant reception he had met with on the part of the musical
public of Vienna. He saw clearly that the time had arrived
when he must hold his own, even in opposition to his father.
His comfort and convenience he was ready and willing to
sacrifice to his father's wishes, but his honour and the credit
of his whole existence were now at stake, and these he must
save at all risks. He withstood, therefore, all his father's
remonstrances and reproaches without betraying his
wounded feelings. To his father's objection that he had
never understood how to take care of his money, Wolfgang
answers (May 21, 1781) :—

> Believe me, I have quite changed in that respect. Next to health, I
> know of nothing more necessary than money. I am indeed no niggard
> —I should find it very hard to be niggardly—and yet people consider
> me more inclined to thrift than extravagance, which is surely enough
> for a beginning. Thanks be to my pupils, I have as much as I want;
> but I will not have many pupils, I prefer few, and to be better paid than
> other teachers.

He was more affected by the allusion to the obligation
he was under to his father, by reason of the debts incurred
by the latter on his behalf, especially since his father added
that he would soon forget his family in Vienna, as his
Aloysia had done. He answered (June 9, 1781) :—

> Your comparison of me to Madame Lange amazed me, and I was
> troubled by it the whole day. This girl lived dependent on her parents
> while she could earn nothing, and as soon as the time arrived when she
> might have shown her gratitude (her father died before she had received
> a kreutzer) she left her poor mother, took up with an actor, married

him, and her mother has not a farthing from them.[11] Good heavens!
my one anxiety, God knows, is to help you and us all; how often must
I write that I can do it better here than in Salzburg? I beseech you,
my dear, good father, write me no more such letters, for they serve no
purpose but to annoy and trouble me; and if I am to go on composing
as I do, I must keep a cool head and a calm mind.

He sent his father at the same time thirty ducats, with an
apology for not being able to spare more at present, and in
following years we find repeated mention of money sent
home.

It had been reported to L. Mozart that Wolfgang was
living a somewhat dissipated life in Vienna ; Herr von Moll,
in particular, " made a wry face, and said he hoped he
would soon come to himself and return to Salzburg, for he
only remained in Vienna for the sake of bad connections."
It was reported to his father that Wolfgang had had dealings
with a person of bad reputation, but he was able to reassure
his father on this point. L. Mozart had been rendered
uneasy, too, on the subject of his son's attention to religious
duties. Wolfgang begs him to be under no apprehension,
he is, no doubt, " a foolish young fellow," but he would wish
for his consolation that no one was more so than he. Eating
meat on fast-days he thought no sin, " for fasting I consider
to be abstaining—eating less than at other times," but he
never made a boast of this; he heard mass every Sunday
and holy-day, and as often as possible on ordinary days.
" Altogether you may rest assured that I have not deserted
my religion. You, perhaps, believe things of me that are
not true, for my chief fault is that I cannot always act *in*

---

11 The representations of Aloysia's mother, which Mozart afterwards learned
to receive with caution, may have had some influence on his judgment of
Aloysia. The account given by her husband, Jos. Lange, is very different. He
narrates in his autobiography (p. 116) that they conceived an attachment for
each other soon after Aloysia's arrival in Vienna : " She had the misfortune to
lose her father by a fit of apoplexy. Her inconsolable grief, and my care for her
family, drew us closer together; my sympathy lightened her sorrowing heart,
and she consented to marry me, hoping to find in her husband the friend she
had lost in her father. As she had contributed to the support of her family by
the exercise of her talent, she continued to make her mother an annual allowance
of 700 gulden, and paid her an advance of 900 gulden which had been made to
the family by the court."

appearance as I ought to act " (June 13, 1781). Wolfgang's renewed intercourse with the Weber family appeared to his father of ill omen ; he dreaded another love affair. This also his son repudiates (May 16, 1781):—

> What you write concerning the Weber family is, I assure you, without foundation. I was a fool about Madame Lange, that is true; but who is not when he is in love? I loved her in very deed, and I still feel that she is not altogether indifferent to me. Luckily for me her husband is a jealous fool, and never leaves her alone, so that I rarely see her. Believe me also that old Madame Weber is a very obliging person, and that I only fail in showing her the attention her obligingness deserves; I have not time for it.

When finally his father went so far as to demand that Wolfgang should sacrifice his honour by recalling his resignation, he answered in the full consciousness of the justice of his position (May 19, 1781) :—

> I scarcely know how to write to you, my dear father, for I cannot recover from my astonishment, and I shall never be able to do so as long as you continue so to write and to think. I must acknowledge that I scarcely recognise my father in some of the passages of your letter! It is a father who writes, certainly, but not the best, most loving father, the one most anxious for his own honour and that of his children—in a word, not *my* father. But it must have been a dream. You are awake by this time, and need no reply from me on the various points of your letter in order to be convinced that I cannot, now less than ever, depart from my resolution. You say the only way to preserve my honour is to renounce my intention. How can you utter such a contradiction? You could not have realised, in writing this, that such a renunciation would turn me into one of the most cowardly fellows in the world. All Vienna knows that I have left the Archbishop, knows the reason to be my injured honour, knows of the thrice-repeated insults of the Archbishop ; and am I all at once to retract my word and belie myself? Shall I announce myself as a scoundrel, and the Archbishop as a worthy prince? The first no man shall ever do, and I least of all ; and the second no one can do but God himself, if He should deign to enlighten him. To please you, my dear father, I would renounce my happiness, my health, and life itself, but my honour comes before all with me, and so it must with you. My dearest, best of fathers, demand of me what you will, only not that—anything but that. The very thought makes me tremble with rage.

The Archbishop was not a little taken aback by the firmness with which Mozart held to his resolve, but which he only strengthened by his continual abuse, without bringing the Viennese round to his side. They all looked upon him as a " haughty, ill-bred priest, despised by everybody," while Mozart was " an agreeable fellow." The Archbishop imagined that Mozart's father would bring his son to a sense of his duty; Count Arco, who had received a letter from the elder Mozart, proposed an interview, in the hope of persuading him in a friendly way. Mozart remained all the firmer when he had convinced himself that his father in Salzburg had nothing to fear. He begged for an audience to take leave, but this was three times refused, because it was feared to irritate the Archbishop, and Mozart's submission was still hoped for. The latter was beside himself when he heard that the Archbishop was to leave next day, and that he had not been informed of it. He drew up a fresh memorial, in which he explained that he had waited four weeks for a final audience; as this had been postponed so long from reasons unknown to him, he had no resource but to beg for it himself at the last moment. When he found himself in the antechamber, in pursuance of this intention (June 8), and prayed for an audience, Count Arco put the finishing touch to the brutalities suffered by Mozart. After loading him with abusive epithets, *he pushed him towards the door with his foot!* "This happened in the antechamber—there was therefore nothing for it but to make my escape, for I did not wish to forget the respect due to the Prince's apartments, although Arco had done so." Whether this affront was offered by command of the Archbishop, Mozart did not know certainly; but, in any case, the servant was worthy of his master, and neither of them could foresee the ineffaceable stigma that would thereby be attached to their names. Mozart boiled over with rage; he answered his father that he should return the insult in kind the next time he met Count Arco, even if it were in the public streets :—

I shall demand no satisfaction at the hands of the Archbishop, for he would not be in a position to offer it me in the way that I shall take it; but I shall at once write to the Count what he has to expect from me the first time I am so fortunate as to meet him, wherever it may be, unless it should be some place to which I owe respect.

N 2

The father was alarmed at such threats addressed to a nobleman ; but Wolfgang answered (July 20, 1781) :—

The heart shows the true nobleman, and, although I am no Count, I am more honourable perhaps than many a Count; and whether it be a footman or a Count, whoever insults me is a scoundrel. I shall begin by representing to him how low and ungentlemanly his conduct was ; but I shall conclude by telling him that he may certainly expect a thrashing from me the first time I meet him.

His father having remarked that the matter might perhaps be arranged by the intervention of a lady or of some other person of rank, Mozart answered that this was not necessary: "I shall take counsel only of my good sense and my heart, and shall do what is right and proper."   It was only with reluctance, and because he saw no other way of pacifying his father, that he consented to forego the threatening letter to Count Arco.

CHAPTER XXIV.

FIRST ATTEMPTS IN VIENNA.

WHEN Mozart's withdrawal from the service of the Archbishop had become an established fact, the latter was anxious to show the world that it lay in his power to attract equally distinguished artists to his service, and he offered a salary of one thousand gulden to Leop. Kozeluch, who was considered the first clavier-player in Vienna, if he would come to Salzburg. Kozeluch refused, as Mozart wrote to his father (July 4, 1781), because he was better off in Vienna, and he had said to his friends : "The affair with Mozart is what chiefly alarms me ; if he could let such a man as that leave him, what would become of me ? "

L. Mozart, much against his will, was obliged to reconcile himself to the step his son had taken.[1] He was full of

---

[1] He wrote to Breitkopf (August 10, 1781): "My son is no longer in the service of this court. He was summoned to Vienna by our Prince, who was there, we being in Munich. But his highness lost no opportunity of insulting and ill-treating my son, who, on the other hand, received much honour from all the high nobility of Vienna. My son was therefore easily persuaded to forsake his ill-rewarded service, and to remain in Vienna."

anxiety, caused by his conviction of Wolfgang's incapacity in matters relating to his own advancement, by his fear lest he should not be able to withstand the seductions of the pleasure-loving capital, and also, perhaps, by an unconscious feeling of annoyance at his son's independent demeanour. This caused him to express his affectionate and really justifiable concern in so perverse a manner that, instead of lightening Wolfgang's difficult position, he embittered his life with reproaches and objections, which were generally exaggerated, and often entirely unreasonable; for he was weak enough to place easy faith in rumours and gossip. He had so long been accustomed to undertake the care of all Wolfgang's affairs that he could not bring himself quietly to resign all interference in them. Mozart did not allow himself to be over-persuaded; he held fast to his independence, as well as to his reverence and love for his father, whose reproofs and accusations he repeatedly disclaimed.

At first, indeed, the father's gloomy forebodings seemed more likely to be verified than the brilliant hopes of the son. Summer had arrived, most of the nobility had gone to their country seats, and there was little to be done in the way of lessons or concerts. The Countess Rumbeck (*née* Cobenzl), who was afterwards considered a first-rate clavier-player,[2] remained his only pupil, since he would not abate his price of six ducats; but he managed to exist in spite of all. He consoled himself by the reflection that it was the dull season, and that he must employ his leisure by preparing for the winter. He worked diligently at six sonatas for the clavier, which were to be published by subscription; the Countess Thun and other ladies of rank undertook to collect subscriptions. They secured seventeen during the summer, and hoped for more in the autumn. He set to work to arrange a concert to be given during Advent; Rossi wrote the words for an Italian cantata which was to be composed for the occasion. But what lay nearest his heart was the composition of an opera in Vienna; his conviction of his vocation as a dramatic composer having been strengthened

---

[2] Jahrb. d. Tonkunst, 1796, p. 51.

by the performances at the Vienna theatre, and the lively interest taken in them by the public. " My only entertainment," he writes to his sister (July 4, 1781), " consists in the theatre. I wish you could see a tragedy performed here ! I know no other theatre where every kind of play is given to perfection. Every part, even the smallest and the worst, is well filled." The performances of the Vienna stage had, in point of fact, reached the highest level of excellence known at that time.[8]

Since the time when the stage had joined in the struggle which ended in the triumph of German literature and art over buffoonery and extemporised pieces, the theatre had remained the gathering-point of literary interests. The best authors of the day wrote for the stage with the avowed object of improving taste and aiding the spread of culture; such were Klemm, Heufeld, Ayrenhoff, and Gebler, and their efforts were ably seconded by such actors as Müller and the brothers Stephanie.[4]

The new and difficult task appointed for them spurred the actors to extraordinary efforts. A general feeling of sympathy and esteem began to replace the contempt in which the dramatic art had been held, and the stage was soon looked upon as the gauge of a nation's moral and intellectual cultivation. This elevation of the art as a whole benefited the artists as individuals, the interdict which society had laid upon them was removed, and actors became favoured members of the best and most cultivated circles.[5] The Vienna theatre in especial, since Joseph II. in the year 1776 had saved it from the weakening influence of variable private patronage, and had constituted it the court and national theatre, had rapidly reached to an unprecedented height of excellence. This monarch looked upon the theatre as an important means of national cultivation, took a lively interest in it, and shared himself in its practical management; he also watched over the talents and the destinies

---

[8] Devrient, Gesch. der Deutsch. Schauspielkunst, III., p. 117.

[4] Cf. Sonnenfels' programme of his theatrical management in the year 1770, in Müller's Abschied von der Bühne, p. 73.

[5] Müller, Abschied, p. 79. Lange, Selbstbiogr., p. 25.

of his actors with shrewd penetration and warm sympathy.[6] He was careful, by lowering the prices of admission,[7] to make attendance at the theatre more general than it had hitherto been; and an entertainment, which had borne almost exclusively the character of a court festival or an assembly of persons of rank, was thus placed within the reach of the citizen class.[8] Literary criticism too, let loose by the introduction of the liberty of the press, turned its attention to the drama, and enlightened the general reader on the quality of the entertainment afforded to him by the author and by the actor. In this way a public was educated without reference to rank or class, to whom the poet and musician could appeal as an independent artist, instead of ministering as heretofore exclusively to the entertainment of his patrons—a state of affairs which must have had important influence on the position of artists, more especially of musicians.

The theatrical public of Vienna at the time of which we are speaking had the reputation of being attentive, discerning, and appreciative, ready and liberal in its acknowledgment of what was good.[9] And in truth it had cause. Shortly before Mozart came to Vienna, Schröder and his wife had set the crown on admirable acting; and associated with them were Müller, Lange, Weidman, Brockmann, Jacquet, Bergopzoomer, the brothers Stephanie, Mesdames Weidner, Adamberger, Jacquet, Sacco, Stierle, Rouseul—affording proof that Mozart did not overrate the talent of his contemporaries.[10]

In the same spirit in which he had founded the national theatre Joseph II. abolished the costly spectacular ballet and the Italian opera. In the place of the latter he instituted a " national vaudeville," as he called the German

---

[6] Lange, Selbstbiogr., p. 65. Meyer, C. Schröder, I., p. 361.

[7] Müller, Abschied, p. 95. A. M. Z., XXIV., p. 253.

[8] Carl Pichler, Denkwürdigkeiten, I., p. 78.

[9] Meyer, I., pp. 361, 375.

[10] A survey and account of the Vienna stage of the time will be found in K. R[isbeck], Briefe über Deutschland, I., p. 258. Nicolai, Reise, IV., p. 587. Meyer, C. Schröder, I., p. 355.

opera.[11]   In December, 1777, he resolved to make a modest beginning with the forces which he had at his command. Umlauf, tenorist in the orchestra, had written the little operetta of " Die Bergknappen," in which only four characters appeared.   The principal part was intended for Mdlle. Cavalieri, the second for Madame Stierle ; the male parts were to be undertaken by Ruprecht, the tenor singer, and Fuchs, the bass ; the chorus was composed of church choristers, and the management was entrusted to Müller, the actor.   The rehearsals were very carefully made, and the Emperor having expressed his satisfaction at a dress rehearsal, the German opera was opened with " Die Bergknappen " on February 18, 1778.   The performance was highly successful,[12] and in the course of the following year fourteen operas or vaudevilles were performed, partly translations, with Italian or French music, such as "Robert und Kalliste" ("La Sposa Fedele"), by Guglielmi; "Röschen und Colas," by Monsigny ; " Lucile," " Silvain," " Der Hausfreund," by Grétry; "Anton und Antonette," by Gossec ; and partly original pieces composed in Vienna, such as " Die Apotheke," by Umlauf; " Die Kinder der Natur," by Aspelmeyer ; " Frühling und Liebe," by Ulbrich ; and " Diesmal hat der Mann den Willen," by Ordonnez.

The only singer of lasting reputation who took part in the first opera was Katharina Cavalieri (1761-1801).   Daughter of a poor schoolmaster named Cavalier in Währing, her talent was perceived and cultivated by Salieri, and she appeared in Italian opera as early as 1775.   She soon became a bravura singer of the first rank.[13]   It was clearly necessary that she should be well supported if the opera was to compete with the drama proper.   The first wife of the

---

[11] An accurate account of the state of German opera is given by Müller (Abschied von der Bühne, p. 253). Cf. A. M. Z., XXIV., p. 254. K. R[isbeck] (Briefe über Deutschland, I., p. 269) says that the members of the opera were looked down upon by those of the old comedy, and there were almost daily ridiculous displays of jealousy and ill-nature.

[12] Forkel, Musik. Krit. Bibl., II., p. 392.

[13] Sonnleithner, Recensionen, 1862, No. II., p. 18.

actor Lange, Mariane Schindler, was secured; but after having achieved great success in Grétry's "Hausfreund" and "Lucile," and bidding fair to become a main support of the opera, both by her singing and her acting, she died in the winter of 1779.[14] The following summer, through the intervention of the ambassador, Count Hardeck, Aloysia Weber was summoned from Munich, and took her place, not only on the stage, but in the affections of Lange, who shortly after made her his second wife. Aloysia Weber made her *début* in the part of the Rosenmädchen of Salency, and was received with general approbation.[15] It was evident, therefore, that Mozart was not blinded by youthful inclination when he declared her one of the first singers of her time, a judgment which posterity has ratified. The second parts had been allotted before her arrival to Theresa Teyber, afterwards Madame Arnold, who pleased by her fresh, youthful voice, while that of Madame Fischer (*née* Strasser), from Mannheim, a clever singer and good actress, was already somewhat past. In the summer of 1781 they had been joined by Madame Bernasconi (p. 130), by the desire, as it was said, of Gluck, who had used the influence of Count Dietrichstein to press her on the Emperor; but the position was not well suited to her talent. Mozart gives his opinion as follows (August 29, 1781):—

In the great parts of tragedy Bernasconi remains inimitable. But small operettas are not in her style at all; and then (as she acknowledges herself) she is more Italian than German, speaks on the stage with the same Viennese accent as in common life (just imagine!), and when she occasionally makes an effort it is as if one heard a princess declaim in a marionette theatre. And she sings so badly that no one will consent to compose for her.

And even before this (June 27, 1781) he had written derisively:—

She has three hundred ducats salary because she sings all her songs a division higher than they are written. It is really a great art, for she keeps well in tune. She has now promised to sing them half a tone higher, and then of course she will be paid more.

----

[14] Lange, Selbstbiogr., p. 104. Müller, Abschied, pp. 259, 261.
[15] Theaterkal., 1781, p. 183.

There were male singers also, who were quite on an
equality with these female vocalists. Soon after the opening of the opera the tenors Souter and Dauer, a whimsical
actor with a fine voice,[16] were engaged, and at a later date
Adamberger, one of the most admirable tenors, a singer of
artistic style and cultivation, and a "very respectable" actor
of lovers' parts. Fischer was secured as a bass; the compass, strength, and beauty of his voice and his artistic cultivation, both as a singer and an actor, placed him in the
very first rank among the singers of Germany. With him
were associated Günther and Schmidt as bass singers, and
Saal as a baritone.[17]   There were thus all the materials
required for the production of German operas, except a composer who could write them. Umlauf and some others
who imitated him were not the men for such an undertaking. Gluck had composed nothing since his "Iphigenia
in Taurus," and contented himself with putting on the stage,
in 1780, "Die Pilgrimme von Mekka," a comic opera which
had been written for Vienna with French words ("La Ren-
contre Imprévue") in 1764, and which was often played in its
German adaptation.[18]   In the following year, by the express
command of the Emperor Joseph, Salieri wrote a German
comic opera, "Der Rauchfangkehrer"[19] ("The Chimney-
Sweep"), the text of which, by Dr. Auernbrugger, was unusually bad;[20] but Salieri was too much of an Italian to have

---

[16] Müller, Abschied, pp. 181, 189, 194.

[17] The *personnel* of the opera from 1781 to 1783, which, with their salaries,
I have borrowed from Meyer (C. Schröder, I., p. 356), was as follows:—*Male
singers:* Adamberger (2,133 fl. 30 kr.), Souter (1,200 fl.), Dauer (?), Fischer
(1,200 fl.), Günther (1,200 fl.), Schmidt (1,200 fl.), Ruprecht (700 fl.), Hoffmann
(600 fl.), Frankenberger (400 fl.), Saal (800 fl.). *Female singers:* Mdlle. Cavalieri (1,200 fl.), Madame Lange (1,706 fl. 20 kr.), Madame Fischer (1,200 fl.),
Mdlle. Teyber (800 fl.), Mdlle. Haselbeck (600 fl.), Mdlle. Brenner (400 fl.),
Madame Saal (800 fl.) .Madame Bernasconi (500 ducats). The orchestra, under
the leadership of Kapellmeister Umlauf, consisted of six first and six second
violins, four tenors, three violoncelli, three double-basses, two flutes, two oboes,
two clarinets, two bassoons, four horns, two trumpets, and drums. The total
pay amounted to 16,124 florins.

[18] Schmid, Gluck, p. 107.

[19] Mosel, Ant. Salieri, p. 72.

[20] Cramer, Magazin der Musik, I., p. 353. Auernbrugger was further known
to fame as a physician, and his daughters Franziska and Mariane were distinguished pianoforte-players.

much effect on German opera. The operetta was assiduously
cultivated in North Germany, and a long list of those which
were produced might be given. But the contrast between
North and South Germany, founded on their political and
religious differences, was visible unpleasantly enough in
literature and art, and had a marked influence on their
musical sympathies and antipathies.[21]   Nicolai relates that
he had heard in Vienna many genuine and accomplished
musical connoisseurs speak of Ph. Em. Bach not only with
indifference, but with absolute dislike, and place Kozeluch
and Steffan before all other clavier-players.[22]   Adamberger,
when asked his opinion concerning a celebrated singer from
North Germany, answered that she sang like a Lutheran;
and on being pressed for an explanation, replied, " I call it
singing like a Lutheran to have a beautiful voice as the gift
of nature, and even to have received a good musical education, as is frequently the case in North Germany, but to
show no signs of study in the Italian school of music, through
which alone the true art of singing can be learnt."[23]

There was little demand in Vienna, therefore, for the
compositions which Hiller's successful enterprise with German opera had brought into being ; the works of men such
as Benda, Schweitzer, Wolf, Neefe, André, and Reichard;
their operas were not performed, and still less was there
any prospect of a field for their future labours in Vienna.
Schweitzer was not summoned, in spite of Wieland's pressing recommendation (Vol. I., p. 406). G. Benda had shown
himself not disinclined to remove to Vienna,[24] and report had
pointed to him as probable kapellmeister in 1778,[25] but he had
never been seriously thought of.   It appeared, therefore, that
a most fitting career stood open for Mozart, and he himself
wished nothing more than to prove his powers in this
branch of his art.   He had brought with him his operetta

[21] In Forkel's Musik. Alman., 1784, p. 189, the question as to why the music
of Viennese composers should be liked in North Germany, but the music of
North Germany should be disliked in Vienna, is treated of in a contribution for
Vienna, showing the two different standpoints.

[22] Nicolai, Reise, IV., p. 556.

[23] Allg. Wiener Musikztg., 1821, p. 56.

[24] Müller, Abschied, p. 185.

[25] Forkel, Musik. Bibl., III., p. 340.

" Zaide," in the hope of having it performed. The libretto, as he had feared, proved a stumbling-block (Vol. II., p. 115); but the younger Stephanie, at that time inspector of the opera, formed so favourable an opinion of the music, that he promised to give Mozart a new and good piece, which he was to compose for the Vienna stage. His father warned him that Stephanie was not to be depended upon; and he was right. Stephanie the younger was an arrogant, selfish man, who had made himself hated everywhere by his intrigues and pretensions. Mozart knew that he was in ill repute, and was upon his guard. He resolved to write no opera without the express commission of Count Rosenberg, who had had supreme direction of the theatre since 1776; but Stephanie continued friendly, and there seemed no actual cause for personal distrust. Count Rosenberg had received Mozart well whenever he had waited upon him, and had joined in the applause of other connoisseurs upon the occasion of the performance of "Idomeneo" at the house of Countess Thun, Van Swieten and Sonnenfels being also among the audience. It was not long, therefore, before Mozart was able to announce to his father the good news (June 9, 1781) that Count Rosenberg had commissioned Schröder, the distinguished actor, to look out a good libretto, which was to be given to Mozart for composition. A few days afterwards Stephanie told him of a piece he had found in four acts, of which the first was excellent, but the others fell off, so that it was doubtful whether Schröder would undertake the adaptation of it. " They may settle that between them," wrote Wolfgang (June 16, 1781). The book was rejected, but the matter did not rest; the Emperor was evidently anxious to give Mozart an opportunity of trying his powers as a German operatic composer; and at the end of July the latter found himself at the goal of his wishes, and able to inform his father (August 1, 1781):—

Yesterday young Stephanie gave me a book for composition. It is very good; the subject is Turkish, and it is called " Belmont und Constanze," or " Die Entführung aus dem Serail." The overture, the chorus in the first act, and the concluding chorus I shall compose in Turkish music. Mdlle. Cavalieri, Mdlle. Teyber, M. Fischer, M. Adamberger, M. Dauer, and M. Walter are to sing in the opera. I am so delighted at having it to compose that the first songs for Cavalieri and Adamberger and the terzet at the close of the first act are already finished. The time given is short, certainly, for it is to be performed in the middle of September, but the attendant circumstances will be all the more favourable. And indeed everything combines to raise my spirits, so that I hasten to my writing-table with the greatest eagerness, and it is with difficulty I tear myself away.

The favourable circumstances which made Mozart so hopeful chiefly consisted in the expected visit of the Grand Duke Paul and his wife; the opera was to be among the festivities given in their honour, and it was safely to be expected that the Emperor and Count Rosenberg would consider it to his credit if he prepared the work in such haste for them; but all this was to be a secret. It was now very convenient to him to be in a house with good friends who would provide him with dinner and supper, and so enable him to sit writing all day. "You know of old how hungry I get when I am composing." He continued in this whirl of excitement, and was able to write on August 8 :—

I have just finished the chorus of Janizaries. Adamberger, Cavalieri, and Fischer are thoroughly pleased with their songs. I let the Countess Thun hear as much as is ready. She told me afterwards that she was ready to stake her life on it that what I had written so far would please. On this point, however, I listen to no man's praise or blame before the whole has been heard or seen, but I follow entirely my own feelings—only you may see from it how greatly she was pleased with the music herself.

On August 22 he wrote that the first act was finished; soon after he learnt, to his relief, that the Grand Duke was not coming until November, so that he could write his opera "with greater deliberation" (September 5, 1781). Shortly afterwards he informs his father (September 26, 1781) :—

The first act was ready three weeks ago, and an aria in the second act and the drinking duet, which consists of nothing but my Turkish tattoo; but I cannot do any more at present, the whole thing being upset, and by my own desire. At the beginning of the third act there is a charming quintet, or rather finale, and this I mean to transfer to the end of the second act. But it will necessitate considerable alterations and the introduction of a fresh intrigue, and Stephanie is over head and ears in work.

Another circumstance also interfered with the completion
of Mozart's opera. It was proposed in honour of the distinguished visitors to perform two of Gluck's operas, viz.:
" Iphigenia " in a German adaptation, and " Alceste " in
Italian, " in order," as a contemporary announcement puts
it, " to show what we Germans are able to accomplish." [26]
Certainly the choice was well made with this object in view,
although it was said in Vienna, as Mozart wrote to his
father (August 29, 1781), that it had been difficult to persuade
the Emperor into it, for he was at heart as little partial to
Gluck as to Gluck's favourite singer, Bernasconi.[27] The projected performance of these operas disturbed all Mozart's
calculations. The applause which had been bestowed on
his " Idomeneo " by capable and influential judges, and the
readiness of the singers to appear in it, had raised the hope
of producing it on this occasion in a German adaptation,
which would have involved alterations in the composition;
but a third grand opera would have been too much, and it
could not have been studied together with Gluck's. Even
the comic opera had to be temporarily laid aside until
Gluck's two operas were ready—" and there is plenty of
study to be got through still," he wrote to his father (October
6, 1781). He was at work at it again in the middle of
November; but the original intention of having it completed
by the arrival of the Grand Duke was no longer feasible.
On November 21 " that grand animal, the Grand Duke,"
arrived under the name of Count von Narden, and on the
25th a brilliant festival was given at Schönbrunn. " To-
morrow 'Alceste' is given at Schönbrunn,"[28] writes Mozart,

[26] Cramer, Magazin der Musik, I., p. 353, where it is erroneously stated that
Gluck's "Alceste," " Iphigenia in Tauris," and " Orpheus " were given in Italian.
Cf. Müller, Abschied, p. 270. A. M. Z., XIV., p. 268. The German translation
of " Iphigenia " was by Alxinger (Forkel, Musik. Alman., 1783, p. 153).

[27] Reichardt describes his interview with Joseph II., in the summer of 1783
(A. M. Z., XV., p. 667. Schletterer, Reichardt, p. 326) : " The Archduke
Maximilian led the conversation on Gluck, whom they both considered as a
great tragedian: but now and then the Emperor was not so much in favour of
Gluck's operas as could have been wished."

[28] Wien Ztg.,1781, No. 95, Anh. "Alceste " was repeated on December 13 (Ibid.,
No.100), December 27 (No.104); " Iphigenia " was played on December 9 (No. 99),
and on January 3, 1782; " Orpheus " was performed in Italian (Ibid., 1782, No. 2).

sorrowfully (November 24, 1781). "I have been looking up Russian popular songs, in order to play variations on them."

Shortly before the arrival of the Grand Duke, the Duke of Würtemberg, with his consort, the Princess Elizabeth, intended bride of the Archduke Franz, and her brother, Prince Ferdinand, had entered Vienna. "The Duke is a charming man, and the Duchess and Princess also; but the Prince is an octogenarian stick, and a real blockhead," was Mozart's concise description (November 17, 1781); but the arrival of the trio opened a favourable prospect for him. The Princess, who had come to have the finishing touches put to her education in Vienna, required a teacher of music, and this position, which, besides making a welcome addition to his income, would bring him into contact with very influential persons, Mozart hoped to obtain. His chief supporter was the Emperor's youngest brother, the Archduke Maximilian, at that time Coadjutor of the Elector of Cologne. The Archduke was musical, and had an excellent band of wind instruments in his pay;[29] he had a favourable remembrance of Mozart from his visit to Salzburg in 1775, and proved a very warm patron. Mozart wrote to his father (November 1781):—

Yesterday at three o'clock I was summoned by the Archduke. When I went in he was standing in the first room by the stove, and he came straight up to me and asked if I had anything to do to-day? "No, your royal highness, nothing at all; but even were it otherwise, I should be delighted to place my time at the disposal of your Royal Highness." "No, no; I do not want to disturb anybody." Then he said that he had a mind to give a concert in the evening at the Würtemberg court, and would like me to play something and to accompany the songs; I was to go to him again at six o'clock. I played there last evening accordingly.

At the same time, Mozart could not conceal from himself that the Archduke had changed very much to his disadvantage :—

Before he was a priest he was much wittier and more intellectual, and spoke less but more sensibly. You should see him now! Stupidity stares out of his eyes, he talks and chatters without stopping, and all in a sort of falsetto voice; he has a swollen neck; in short, the whole man is transformed!

---

[29] A. M. Z., XV., p. 668. Schletterer, Reichardt, I., p. 327.

Nevertheless he continued to patronise Mozart, drew him out on every occasion, and if he had only been Elector of Cologne, Mozart would have been kapellmeister by this time, as he told his father. He had used his influence with the Princess to take Mozart as her music-master, but received for answer that if it depended on herself she would certainly have chosen him, but the Emperor—" he cares for no one but Salieri," cries Mozart in disgust—had recommended Salieri to her on account of his singing, and she felt obliged to engage him, to her great regret.

It was quite true that Salieri stood high in the favour of Joseph II. He had been pupil of the Emperor's special favourite Gassmann, and had in a sense grown up under the royal eye;[80] he was regularly engaged at the imperial private concerts, and retained possession of his patron's favour by means both of his music and his personal demeanour. It was plain, therefore, that the preference for Salieri shown by the Emperor on this occasion did not arise from any ill-will towards Mozart; he was in close personal intercourse with Salieri, and esteemed him highly as a vocal composer, while Mozart was only known to him as a clavier-player. As such he had great admiration for him, and Mozart informed his father (December 26, 1781), that the Emperor had lately " passed the greatest *éloge* on him in the words ' C'est un talent décidé.'"

He had also (on December 14) commanded Mozart to play at court, and had arranged for him a contest of skill with Clementi, who had come to Vienna with the reputation of a clavier-player of unheard-of excellence. Clementi relates the encounter to his pupil L. Berger:[81]—

I had only been a few days in Vienna when I received an invitation to play before the Emperor on the pianoforte. On entering the music-room I beheld an individual whose elegant attire led me to mistake him for an imperial valet-de-chambre. But we had no sooner entered into conversation than it turned on musical topics, and we soon recognised in each other with sincere pleasure brother artists—Mozart and Clementi.

[80] Mosel, Salieri, p. 22.

[81] Ludwig Berger's narrative was taken from the lips of his teacher in 1806, and is identical with Mozart's own account (Cäcilia, X., p. 238; A. M. Z., XXXI., p. 467). Other accounts differ somewhat, as usual in such cases.

Mozart continues the description of the scene (January 16, 1782) :—

> After we had paid each other all manner of compliments, the Emperor gave the signal that Clementi should begin. "La santa chiesa cattolica!" said the Emperor—Clementi being a native of Rome. He preluded, and played a sonata.

"It is worthy of note here," says Berger, "that Clementi was peculiarly fond of extemporising long and very interesting and elaborate interludes and cadenzas in the pauses of his sonatas ; it was this propensity which led him to select a sonata for performance which lent itself easily to such treatment, although in every other respect this sonata stands behind his earlier compositions of the same kind. It was the following—

and we have perhaps to thank this subject for the allegro in the overture to the 'Zauberflöte,' a composition never surpassed of its kind : "[82]—

> The Emperor then said to me : "Allons, d'rauf los!" (" Now then, fire away!") I preluded, and played some variations. Then the Grand Duchess[83] produced some sonatas by Paesiello (in his own miserable manuscript),[84] of which I was to play the allegro and Clementi the andante and rondo. Then we each took a subject and carried it out on two pianofortes. By the way, I had borrowed the Countess Thun's pianoforte for myself, but only played upon it when I played alone. The Emperor wished it to be so. The other instrument was out of tune, and had three of its keys sticking. "Never mind," said the Emperor. I look upon it that the Emperor knows my musical powers and knowledge, and wishes to do me justice in the eyes of the foreigners. I know upon very good authority that he was thoroughly satisfied with me.

---

[82] Clementi thought it advisable on the republication of this sonata to assert his prior claims, as follows : "Cette sonate, avec la toccata qui la suit, a été jouée par l'auteur devant Sa M. J. Joseph II., en 1781, Mozart étant présent." There can be no doubt that Mozart was conscious of the reminiscence.

[83] Bridi's account says that the Emperor had laid a wager with the Grand Duchess that Mozart would surpass Clementi, and won it.

[84] Paesiello composed sonatas and capricci for the Grand Duchess.

II.   O

Dittersdorf confirms this view, and extracts the following from a conversation with Joseph II. : [85]—

Emperor: "Have you heard Mozart?" *Myself:* "Three times already." *Emperor:* "How do you like him?" *Myself:* "As every connoisseur *must* like him." *Emperor:* "Have you heard Clementi also?" *Myself:* "I have heard him also." *Emperor:* "Some people prefer him to Mozart, which makes Greybig wild. What is your opinion? speak out." *Myself:* "In Clementi's playing there is merely art, but in Mozart's both art and taste." *Emperor:* "That is just what I said myself."

After the competition, the Emperor sent Mozart fifty ducats, " which were very acceptable at the time."

Clementi was delighted with Mozart's playing :—

I had never heard so delicate and graceful an execution. I was especially delighted with an adagio, and with several of his extemporised variations. The Emperor gave the subject, and we varied it, alternately accompanying each other.

On the other hand, Mozart's judgment of Clementi was sharp and severe:—

Clementi is a good player, and that is all one can say. He plays well as far as the execution of his right hand is concerned. His forte lies in passages in thirds. But he has not an atom of taste or feeling, in fact he is a mere mechanist.

When his sister in Salzburg had made acquaintance with Clementi's sonatas, he wrote to her (June 7, 1783):—

Now I must say a word to my sister on the subject of Clementi's sonatas. Every one who plays them must be aware that as compositions they are valueless. There are no striking passages, except the sixths and octaves, and I should strongly advise you not to be too much taken with these, for they are the ruin of a firm and quiet hand, and would soon deprive it of its lightness, flexibility, and flowing rapidity. For what is the object of these passages after all? They must be executed with the utmost rapidity (which not even Clementi himself can accomplish), and a lamentable hash is the result—nothing else in the world. Clementi is a charlatan, *like all the Italians!* He writes *presto* on a sonata, or even *prestissimo* or *alla breve*, and plays it *allegro* in three-four time. I have heard him do it! What he does

---

[85] Dittersdorf, Selbstbiogr., p. 236.

really well are passages in thirds—he worked at them day and night in London—but he can do nothing else, and he has not the least execution or taste, and far less any sentiment in his playing.[86]

In justification of this censure, Berger mentions Clementi having told him that, at the time of which Mozart writes, he devoted his attention to brilliant execution, and in particular to double runs and extemporised passages; it was only later that he adopted a more expressive style, which was perfected by the study of the best vocal music of the day, and by the gradual improvements made in the instrument known as the English pianoforte, the primitive construction of which had been too defective to allow of an expressive legato execution. Berger remarks further that Mozart's honourable and upright character prevents any suspicion of underhand motives for the severity of his judgment.

Mozart sought to gain favour with the Emperor by securing the support of his groom of the chamber, Strack, who possessed great influence in musical affairs. He tells his father (November 3, 1781) that on his name-day (October 31), which he had celebrated at the house of Baroness Waldstätten, he had been surprised by a serenade of his own composition (375 K.), which he had composed on St. Theresa's day (October 15) for the daughter-in-law of the court painter, Hickl. "The chief reason I wrote it," he continues, "was to let Herr von Strack, who goes there almost daily, hear something of mine, and I made it somewhat serious accordingly; it was very much admired." He ventured at a later date to count upon Strack as his friend with the Emperor, although, as he cautiously adds, "the courtier is never to be trusted" (January 23, 1782). The report having reached Salzburg that the Emperor intended taking Mozart into his service, he answers his father (April 10, 1782):—

The reason that I have not written to you about it is because I know nothing of it myself. It is certain, however, that the whole town is full of it, and that I am congratulated on all sides; I would fain believe, too, that the Emperor has been spoken to on the subject, and

---

[86] This criticism belongs to the toccata rather than to the sonata; it is marked *prestissimo*, and is a brilliant study of passages in thirds and fourths.

has it in his mind, but so far I have not heard a word. It has gone so far that the Emperor is thinking of it, and that without my having moved a step in the matter. I have been sundry times to see Herr von Strack (who is on my side) both to keep him in mind of me, and because I like him ; but not often enough to be tiresome or to appear to have any motive in it ; and he must acknowledge as an honest man that he has not heard a word from me which could give him occasion to say that I wished to remain, far less to be engaged by the Emperor. We talk of nothing but music. It is of his own free will and quite disinterestedly that he speaks of me to the Emperor. Since it has gone so far without my co-operation, it may come to something. If one appears anxious, there is less chance of a good salary, for the Emperor is certainly a niggard. If he wants to have me, he must pay me for it ; for the honour of being in the Emperor's service does not go very far with me.

Joseph II. was accustomed to have a concert in his own apartments every afternoon.[37] He generally dined alone in the music-room, which did not usually occupy more than a quarter of an hour ; if there was no important business to be transacted, the concert began as soon as the cloth was removed, and lasted for about an hour, so that the Emperor might visit the theatre. Three times a week there was a grand concert, at which Gassmann,[38] and later Salieri, or sometimes Umlauf, were expected to appear ; there was no audience, and the Archduke Maximilian, when he was present, took an active part in the performance. Joseph II. possessed a thorough musical education,[39] and preferred the severe style (Vol. I., p. 368) ; his fine bass voice had been trained in the Italian school,[40] and he played the violoncello and viola, as well as the clavier ; he also read both vocal and instrumental music with great facility, and was a skilful player from score. Usually separate pieces were selected from operas and oratorios ; the Emperor accompanied from the score on the clavier, and also took a tenor or bass part— a pathetic one by preference.[41] The pieces chosen were some-

---

37 The account which follows is founded on an accurate account of Joseph's chamber concerts (Musik. Corresp., 1790, p. 27).

88 Mosel, Salieri, p. 22.

89 Mosel, Ibid., p. 71.

40 A. M. Z., XXIV., p. 285.

41 The A. M. Z., XV., p. 512, narrates an apocryphal anecdote to the effect that the Emperor Joseph once wrote a song, and secretly inserted it in a

times old favourites of the Emperor, sometimes new works
with which he thus became acquainted; the operas which
were afterwards to be performed were generally gone through
in this way by the Emperor and the Archduke Maximilian.[42]
The pieces were generally played and sung at sight; it
amused the Emperor to put the executants on their trial,
and he was delighted at the confusion which often ensued;
the more energetic and distracted the conductor Kreibich
became, the more heartily the Emperor laughed.[43]

At the ordinary concerts the Emperor only took part in the
quartet. The first violin was played by Kreibich (or Greybig),
"a man who was made for a conductor; he has a capital
insight into the theory of music, but, unfortunately for his
art, affects a certain degree of charlatanry. His timidity
prevents his executing solo parts with distinctness and
elegance, and his bowing is not sufficiently round and firm."
This nervousness, joined to a pompous manner, made him
the butt of the jokes and squibs of the musical circle,[44] and
though not at all ill-natured, he was not in a position to
make his opinion of value, but allowed himself to be made
the tool of others, who were willing enough to let him appear
to the Emperor and the public as the leader of all that
related to the chamber music. With him were associated
the violinists Woborzil, who led the orchestra in the German
opera, Hoffmann, Ponheim, and Krottendorfer, mediocre
artists and unimportant men; of the last it was only said
that he flattered Strack, and was his marionette. Strack
was in fact the soul of these concerts; he had the direction
of the musicians, played the violoncello, and was present on
every occasion, while the others took it by turns; this,
together with his personal position, gave him overpowering
influence with the Emperor. "You know the kind of men

---

little Italian opera which he gave in his private theatre at Schönbrunn. On
his asking Mozart what he thought of the song, the latter, "with childlike
frankness and gaiety," replied, "The song is good, but he that wrote it is
better."

[42] A. M. Z., XV., p. 66. Reichardt, Mus. Monatschr., 1792, p. 57.

[43] A characteristic scene is related by Mosel (Salieri, p. 130).

[44] Dittersdorf tells a story which illustrates this (Selbstbiogr., p. 241)

who, as Schiller says, come in as makeshifts when any one is wanted. Strack has always been with Joseph, and has used his opportunities so well that, in the musical line, he can do exactly as he likes."

It was a fact that good music, especially good instrumental music, was seldom performed in the closet. If a quartet was played it was by a second-rate composer, and the masters who were then founding a new epoch in this province, Haydn—for whose "tricks" the Emperor did not care much[45]—and Mozart, together with their imitators, Pleyel and Kozeluch, were excluded, or as good as excluded. This was considered to be owing to Strack's influence, and it was wondered at that Salieri, "the idol of the Emperor," who invariably took part in the private concerts, did not assert his opinion; but he "was too politic to come into collision with the shadow of his Emperor."

How far, after all, was Salieri capable of influencing the music of his day? Joseph's taste had been formed on the tradition of Italian music, represented by Hasse and Piccinni, and his predilections retained the same direction. His wish to develop a national school of music proceeded from rational conviction; and, though he was intellectually capable of appreciating the works of Gluck and Mozart, they were not really after his own heart. He had avowedly accustomed himself to look for entertainment in music, and was overpowered by the independent power and fulness which Gluck, Haydn, and Mozart brought to bear upon their art. Salieri had no reason for combating the Emperor's inclinations, since they were also his own. He skilfully sought to turn to account the acquisitions which music had made in various directions, and to make Italian opera capable of satisfying the demands of a more enlightened taste. With the exception of the operas written for Paris, in which he consciously followed Gluck's manner, he remained throughout true to the tradition of Italian opera, introduced no new element into it, and did not possess

---

[45] Reichardt, A. M. Z., XV., p. 667 (Schletterer, Reichardt, p. 325; Griesinger Biogr. Not. über Jos. Haydn, p. 63).

originality enough to make an indelible mark on the music of the day. But it was just this mediocrity of talent, skill, and taste which won for him the favour of his imperial master and of the public; it would have required the possession of a singular union of moral and artistic greatness and magnanimity to acknowledge rising genius as superior to his own, and to bow himself down before it—and Salieri was not capable of this. He is described as a benevolent and good-tempered man, amiable in his private life, and adorned with the well-deserved fame of noble and generous actions;[46] but these good qualities did not preserve from envy either his reputation or his position. In the year 1780 he had just returned from a lengthened tour in Italy, which had brought him new fame and honour, and had confirmed him in the favour of the Emperor; at this point Mozart made his appearance as a rival, dangerous by reason of his brilliant powers of execution, which most readily win the applause of the multitude, as well as by his compositions. The "Entführung" threatening to throw Salieri's "Rauchfangkehrer" completely into the shade, and "Idomeneo" establishing its composer as a formidable competitor on his own ground, it was impossible that Salieri, who instinctively felt Mozart's superiority, could long pretend indifference to it. There was no interruption of their personal intercourse.[47] Mozart was friendly and unconstrained in his behaviour to his fellow-artists, "even to Salieri, who could not bear him," as Frau Sophie Haibl, Mozart's sister-in-law, relates, and Salieri was "too politic" to make any show of his dislike to Mozart. It was understood in Vienna, however, that he did dislike him, and that he secretly strove to check his progress, not only by depreciatory criticism,[48] but by every

---

[46] Besides Mosel's Biography cf. the account by Rochlitz (Für Freunde der Tonkunst, IV., p. 342; A. M. Z., XXVII., p. 412).

[47] A. Hüttenbrenner, a pupil of Salieri, relates upon his authority (A. M. Z., XXVII., p. 797) that Mozart often came to Salieri, saying: "Lieber Papa (?) geben sie mir einige alte Partituren aus der Hofbibliothek (?), ich will sie bei Ihnen durchblättern"; and that he often ate his midday meal during these studies.

[48] Mosel (Salieri, p. 211) confines this to silence on the merits of Mozart's works. But although Salieri occasionally spoke in praise of Mozart in afteryears (Hüttenbrenner, A. M. Z., XXVII., p. 797; Rochlitz, Für Freunde der

sort of obstacle thrown in his way from the very first. Salieri had been appointed maestro to the Princess Elizabeth, but he was unable to instruct her on the clavier, and Mozart had clearly the next claim. "He may take the trouble," writes he to his father (August 31, 1782), "to do me harm in this matter, but the Emperor knows me; the princess would have liked to learn from me from the first, and I know that my name stands in the book where the list of all those appointed to her service is kept." But Salieri was much too cautious to allow Mozart to attain to such a position. An unknown musician named Summerer was appointed teacher of the clavier to the Princess Elizabeth. Mozart consoled himself, when he heard that the salary was only four hundred florins, by the reflection that it would not leave much over when the waiting, travelling, and other expenses contingent on such a service had been paid for (October 12, 1782).

Under these circumstances Salieri and Strack were naturally sworn allies in the Emperor's music room, and resisted together the introduction of any elements which would undermine their influence by giving the Emperor's taste a new direction. Although, therefore, Mozart was encouraged by the Emperor's expressions of liking for him, more especially as "great rulers are not too fond of saying such things for fear of a dagger-thrust from an envious rival," yet the obstacles which he had to overcome in the surroundings of the Emperor were likely to prove too powerful for him. The Emperor's parsimony also restrained him from adding another kapellmeister to those who were already in receipt of salaries from the court.

Another chance of such a fixed situation as his father was continually urging upon him to secure offered itself through Prince Aloys Liechtenstein, the eldest son of the reigning prince, whose income was estimated at 900,000 imperial

---

Tonkunst, IV., p. 345), I have heard upon trustworthy authority in Vienna, that Salieri, even in his old age, when among confidential friends, expressed, with a passion that was painful to his hearers, the most unjust judgments on Mozart's compositions. Thayer's attempt to justify Salieri (A. M. Z., 1865, p. 241) led me to make a searching examination of the facts.

gulden.[49] He proposed enrolling a band of wind instruments
in his service, and wished to engage Mozart to arrange
pieces for it.   For this he could not expect a high salary, but
it would be a certain one, for he had quite resolved to accept
none but a permanent engagement.   But this hope, too, was
disappointed,[50] and he continued to exist on the uncertain
proceeds of lessons, concerts, and composition.

The state of affairs improved somewhat in the winter.
He had constant pupils in the Countess Rumbeck and Frau
von Trattnern, to whom was added later the Countess Zichy.
He gave each of them a lesson daily, and received six ducats
for twelve, which sufficed for absolute necessities.   Six
sonatas for clavier and violin, for which his patronesses had
opened a subscription of three ducats, were completed and
printed in November, 1781.[51]

In Lent he gave a concert, at which, following the advice
of his patrons, he played selections from " Idomeneo " and
his concerto in D major (175 K.), for which he had composed a new rondo (382 K.).   The rondo "made a great
sensation," and was sent to Salzburg, with a request that
it might be treasured as a jewel.   " I wrote it especially for
myself, and no one else shall play it except my dear sister "
(March 2, 1782).   As a conclusion he played a fantasia.
He had been advised to do this because he would be thereby
most certain of outrivalling Clementi, who was giving a
concert at about the same time.[52]   Mozart had plenty of
invitations to play at other people's concerts and in society,
on which occasions a new composition had generally to be
written.   At Auernhammer's concert, for instance, he played
with the daughter a " sonata for two " (381 K.), which he

---

[49] K. R[isbeck], Briefe, I., p. 272.

[50] " A cantata composed for Prince Aloys von Lichtenstein by W. A. Mozart,"
of which there is a copy in the Royal Library in Berlin, is certainly not by
Mozart (242 Anh. K.).

[51] The Wien. Zeit.,.1781, No. 98, announces "Six sonatas for the piano
with accompaniment for the violin by the well-known and celebrated master,
Wolfgang Amade Mozart, Op. 2, 5 fl." (296, 376-380, K.).   No. 2 (in C major)
was composed in Mannheim (p. 400), and No. 4 (in B flat major) was previously
known to his sister, as he writes to her (June 4, 1781).

[52] Clementi left Vienna at the beginning of May, 1782.

had composed on purpose, and which " was a great success"
(November 24, 1781). He wrote easier pieces for his pupils.
" I must close my letter" he writes (June 20, 1781), "for I
have to prepare some variations for a pupil"; and soon after
he wrote to his sister (July 4, 1781): " I have written three
airs with variations, which are not worth the trouble of
sending alone. I will wait until there is something to
accompany them."

His time was fully occupied, therefore, and he had no
difficulty in proving the injustice of his sister's reproaches to
him for not writing oftener (February 13, 1782) :—

You must not conclude that you do not give me pleasure by writing
to me because I do not always answer you. I always look forward with
great pleasure to receiving a letter from you, my dear sister. If I were
not prevented by pressing engagements, God knows I would always
answer you. Is it true that I have never answered you ? It certainly
has not been from forgetfulness nor carelessness, but from simple
impossibility ! Bad enough, you will say, but do I write often, even to
my father ? You both know Vienna. You ought to know that a man
who has no regular income must work day and night in such a city.
Our father, when he has finished his church service, and you, when you
have dismissed your few pupils, can do as you like all the rest of the
day, and you may write letters long enough to contain the whole
litany, if you like ; but I can do no such thing. I gave my father a
description of my mode of life a short time ago. I will repeat it for you
now. At six o'clock my barber comes, at seven I am dressed, and write
until nine. From nine o'clock till one I give lessons, then I dine, if I
am not invited out, in which case we dine at two or even three o'clock,
as we shall to-day and to-morrow at the Countess Zichy's and Countess
Thun's. I cannot begin to work again till five or six o'clock, and am
often even then prevented by a concert; if not, I write. The continual
concerts, and the uncertainty as to whether I shall be called away here
or there, prevent my writing in the evening; so it is my custom (especially when I come home early) to compose something before I go to bed.
I often write on until one o'clock, and am up again at six ! My dearest
sister, if you really believe that I can forget you or my father, then—
but no ! God knows it, and that is enough for me ; let Him punish me
if I ever forget you.

Instances are not wanting of his affection and thought for
his father and sister. He sends his father (March 23, 1782)
a snuffbox and a pair of watch ribbons : " The snuffbox is a
good one, and the picture on it is from an English story ;

the watch ribbons are not very valuable, but they are high fashion here just now." He did not buy either of them, he adds for his father's consolation, but was presented with them by Count Szapary. To his sister also he sent different bits of finery, and begged her to intrust him with any commission in Vienna; he also testified the warmest sympathy in her love affairs. He did not forget his old Salzburg friends in Vienna—begs for news of them from his sister, "the walking register of Salzburg," and wished still to be considered as an active member of the quoit club.

During these manifold occupations the opera had still the first place in his thoughts, but it was at a standstill owing to the production of Gluck's two operas and the numerous alterations which were necessary in the libretto; he hoped that it would he ready for representation, however, directly after Easter. This was not the case, but on May 8 he writes: "Yesterday I was with the Countess Thun, and ran over the second act for her; she is as pleased with it as she was with the first"; and on May 29: "Next Monday is to be the first rehearsal; I must admit that I am delighted with this opera."

And he had good cause to be so, for its ultimate success was assured. But he had to fight against strong cabals, and it needed the express command of the Emperor to bring the opera to performance on July 13. High as had been the expectations of the public, they were fully justified by the result. "The house was crammed full, there was no end to the applause and cheering, and performances followed one another in quick succession."[53] After having given his father a short account of the first performance, he reports more fully on the second (July 20, 1782):—

Yesterday my opera was given for the second time. Can you believe that the opposition was even stronger than on the first evening? The whole of the first act was drowned, but they could not prevent the bravos after every song. My hope was in the closing terzet, but

---

[53] "The 'Entführung,'" says a notice from Vienna in Cramer's Magazin, I., p. 352, "is full of beauties. It surpassed public expectation, and the delicate taste and novelty of the work were so enchanting as to call forth loud and general applause."

Fischer had been rendered nervous, and went wrong, as did Dauer, and Adamberger alone could not put things right; so that the whole effect was lost; and this time it was not encored. I was beside myself with rage, and so was Adamberger; we agreed that the opera should not be given again without a rehéarsal for the singers. In the second act the two duets were encored, and also Belmonte's rondo, "Wenn der Freude Thränen fliessen," &c. The theatre was almost more crowded than on the first performance; the day before not a seat was to be had either on the *noble parterre* or in the third story, and not a single box. The opera has brought twelve hundred florins in the two days.

In the next letter (July 27, 1782), he continues :—

My opera was given yesterday (St. Ann's day) in honour of all Nannerls, for the third time, and the theatre, in spite of the stifling heat, was again crammed full. It was to have been played again next Friday, but I have protested, for I do not want it to be run to death. People are quite foolish about the opera, I must say. But it does one good to receive such applause.

Notwithstanding this, it was given again on July 30, and also on the Friday, and the theatre " swarmed with people in every part."

Mozart was busily employed in arranging his opera for harmony (wind) music, when he received a commission from the Haffner family in Salzburg (Vol. I., p. 153) to compose a new serenata. L. Mozart had first been applied to, and he thought it becoming that Wolfgang should lighten his father's labours by undertaking a work which cost him no exertion, and would be of direct advantage to his father. He therefore begged him to write a serenata without delay, for the time was approaching when it was to be performed. Wolfgang was quite ready to consent, inconvenient as it might be to him (July 20, 1782) :—

I have certainly enough to do, for by Sunday week my opera must be arranged for wind instruments, or some one else will get the start of me, and reap the profit; and now I have to write a new symphony! I hardly see how it will be possible. You would not believe how difficult it is to arrange a work like this for harmony, so that it may preserve its effects, and yet be suitable for wind instruments. Well, I must give up my nights to it, for it cannot be done any other way; and to you, my dear father, they shall be devoted. You shall certainly receive something every post-day, and I will work as quickly as I can, and as well as I can compatibly with such haste.

He kept his word, although not quite so soon as he himself wished.   In his next letter he writes (July 27, 1782):—

You will make a wry face when you see only the first allegro; but it could not be helped, for I was called upon to compose a serenade in great haste—but only for wind instruments, or else I could have used it for you.   On Wednesday, the 31st, I will send the two minuets, the andante, and the last movement: if I can I will send a march also; if not, you must take that belonging to the Haffner music, which is very little known (249 K.).   I have written it in D, because you prefer it.

But the serenata was not ready within the next few days, for he says in his letter of July 31:—

You see that my will is good, but if one cannot do a thing—why one cannot !   I cannot slur over anything, so it will be next post-day before I can send you the whole symphony.

A week later he wrote (August 7, 1782):—

Herewith I send you a short march (probably 445 K.).   I hope all will arrive in good time, and that you will find it to your taste.   The first allegro must be fiery, and the last as quick as possible.

Six months later, when he had this symphony sent back to him for performance at one of his concerts, he wrote to his father (February 15, 1783): " The new Haffner symphony has quite astonished me, for I did not remember a word of it, and it must be very effective."   These little incidents show us the true Mozart, in his good-nature and readiness to oblige his father, and in his power of productiveness and elasticity of mind; he excuses himself for not having the symphony ready in a fortnight—and that at a time when not only his opera, but also his courtship and marriage were filling his head and his heart—and then he is astonished at himself for having done the thing so well.[54]   The serenata which was thus composed is the lovely one in C minor (388 K.).

Meanwhile the opera pursued its successful course; in the

---

[54] This symphony (385 K., part 5) with the superscription, " à Vienna nel mese di Juglio, 1782," has only a minuet, and no march.   The second minuet was written on separate sheets, and not preserved, not being used in Vienna. Mozart afterwards added two flutes and two clarinets to the first and last movements for the performance in Vienna; these are wanting in the printed score.

course of the year it was performed sixteen times; and in the beginning of October, when the Archduke and his wife returned to Vienna, on their homeward journey, the "Entführung" was given in their honour, "on which occasion I thought it as well to sit at the piano again and conduct," he writes to his father (October 19, 1782), "partly to wake up the somewhat slumbering energies of the orchestra, partly to show the great people present that I am the father of my offspring."

Kaiser Joseph had attained the object of his ambition; the German opera was established ; but he scarcely seemed to appreciate the importance of the movement thus set on foot. His criticism on the "Entführung"—"Too fine for our ears, and an immense number of notes, my dear Mozart!" (referring, no doubt, to the accompaniment, which was also found fault with by Dittersdorf as overpowering the voices)[55]—is indicative of his taste. Mozart's spirited answer, "Just as many notes, your majesty, as are necessary," was worthy of an artist.[56] Generally speaking, the opera received unmitigated praise. Prince Kaunitz, an accomplished amateur and passionate friend of the theatre,[57] sent for the young composer, received him in the most flattering manner, and remained henceforth his friend and patron. The veteran Gluck, the most distinguished person in the musical world, expressed a desire to hear the opera which was making so much sensation ; it was performed at his request, as Mozart writes to his father (August 7, 1782), although it had been given only a few days before; he paid the composer many compliments on it, and invited him to dinner.

The opera had decided Mozart's musical position in Vienna;[58] it speedily caused his fame to spread throughout Germany. The Prussian minister, Baron Riedesel—the well-

---

[55] Dittersdorf, Selbstbiogr., p. 237.

[56] The truth of this anecdote is vouched for by Niemetschek, who narrates it (p. 34). Napoleon is said to have received a similar answer from Cherubini, who certainly did not borrow it from Mozart (A. M. Z., XXXVI., p. 21; cf., II., p. 735).

[57] Many instances are given in Lange's Selbstbiogr., p. 98   Müller, Abschied, p. 100; Meyer, L. Schröder, I., pp. 341, 343, 346.

[58] It remained on the Vienna repertory until the German opera was quite extinguished in 1778 ; it was revived on September 23, 1801.

known traveller and friend of Winckelmann—begged Mozart for a copy of the score for performance in Berlin, for which he was to receive suitable remuneration. This was the more flattering, since André's version of the "Entführung" had been well received in Berlin only the year before. Mozart had sent the original score to his father immediately after the first performance, that he might become acquainted with the composition before seeing the opera, which he was not to do until the end of 1784, in Salzburg:—

> I have just promised to have it copied. As I have not got the opera I am obliged to borrow it from the copyist, which is very inconvenient, since I never can keep it three days together; the Emperor continually sends for it, as he did yesterday, and it is so often performed; it has been performed ten times since August 16. My idea was, therefore, to have it copied in Salzburg, where it can be done more secretly and cheaper.

The father, who watched his son's proceedings with jealousy and suspicion, thought he detected something underhand in the objection to have the copying done in Vienna. He had reminded his son, *à propos* of "Idomeneo," that the score should remain the property of the composer (Vol. II., p. 141); and he now cautioned him as to whether he had the right to dispose of the score, would it not cause unpleasantness in Vienna, and that for the sake of an uncertain verbal promise of payment. To this Wolfgang answered (October 5, 1782):—

> I waited on the Baron von Riedesel myself; he is a charming man, and I promised him (in the belief that the opera was already in the hands of the copyist) that he should have it at the end of this month, or at the latest at the beginning of November. I must beg you to take care that I have it by that time. To relieve you of all anxiety, which I thankfully acknowledge as a proof of your fatherly love, I cannot say anything more convincing than that I am under great obligation to the Baron for having asked me for the opera, instead of going direct to the copyist (as is the custom in Italy), who would have given it to him directly for ready money; and besides this, I should have been very sorry if my talent could be paid for in that way—especially by a hundred ducats![59] This time (because there is no occasion) I shall say nothing

---

[59] Even this sum appears to have been thought excessive; at least Schröder wrote to Dalberg (May 22, 1784): "Mozart received fifty ducats for the 'Entführung aus dem Serail'; he would compose no opera under this price." At a later time, one hundred ducats was the usual price for an opera (Dittersdorf, Selbstbiogr., p. 241).

about it; if it is performed, as it is certain to be (and that is what pleases me most about it), it will be known soon enough, and my enemies will have no excuse for ridiculing me, and treating me as a poor fellow; they will be quite ready to ask me for another opera if I will write it, but I do not know that I shall; certainly not if I am to be paid one hundred ducats, and see the theatre make four times that sum in a fortnight. I shall bring out my next opera at my own expense, make at least twelve hundred florins in three representations, and then the management may have it for fifty ducats. If not, I shall be paid, and can produce it anywhere. Meanwhile I hope you will never find in me the least trace of any evil intentions. I would fain not be a bad fellow, but I do not want to be a stupid one who lets other people reap the advantage of his labour and study, and gives up his rightful claim to his own works.

The father's distrustful prudence prevented his putting the work in hand at once, and such haste was then necessary that no copyist in Salzburg would undertake it; Mozart had no resource but to explain the cause of the delay to the ambassador. But in the end the score was copied in Salzburg. The "Entführung" was performed the following year at Prague with extraordinary success.[60] "I cannot describe the applause and sensation which it excited at Vienna from my own observation," says Niemetschek; "but I was a witness of the enthusiasm with which it was received at Prague by connoisseurs and non-connoisseurs. It made what one had hitherto heard and known appear not to be music at all! Every one was transported—amazed at the novel harmonies, and at the original passages for the wind instruments." It was given at Leipzig in 1783;[61] at Mannheim,[62] Salzburg, and Schwedt in 1784;[63] at Cassel in 1785;[64] at Berlin not until 1788.[65] The applause was great on all occasions, and very soon the smaller stages sought to master the favourite piece. The actor Philipp Hasenhuth used to relate how the theatrical manager

---

[60] Cramer, Magazin der Musik, I., p. 999.

[61] Raisonnirendes, Theaterjourn. von der Leipzig. Michaelmesse, 1783, p. 32.

[62] Koffka, Iffland und Dalberg, p. 136.

[63] Berl. Litt. u. Theat. Ztg., 1784, II., p. 160.

[64] Lyncker, Gesch. d. Theat. u. d. Musik, in Kassel, p. 316.

[65] Chronik. von Berlin, II., p. 440. Teichmann's Litt. Nachl., p. 45.

Wilhelm, at Baden,[66] in 1783 or 1784, undertook the production of the "Entführung" with a very weak company. At the rehearsal of the quartet there was no tenor-player; Hasenhuth, who had just begun to learn the violin, and hardly knew one string from another, was put down to the tenor. A little man who had come in as a spectator sat down by him, and when he saw the deficiency, seized a viola and they played together. But the little man soon showed his impatience of his stumbling neighbour, and giving vent to his anger more and more plainly as the quartet proceeded, he ended by flinging away the viola, exclaiming, "The man is a veritable donkey!" (Der Herr ist ein wahrer Krautesel!), and running out of the room. The opera, however, was a great success; and the well-satisfied manager gave his company a farewell supper, to which, hearing that Mozart was in Baden, he invited the composer. Hasenhuth was astonished to recognise in him the tenor-player at the rehearsal, but Mozart relieved him from all awkwardness by saying good-humouredly, "I was somewhat impolite when we last met, but I did not know who you were, and the devil himself could not have stood the wrong notes!" The judgment of contemporary critics of the opera was almost unanimously of accord with that of the public.[67]

It is not probable that Mozart obtained any share of the rich profits which accrued from the production of his opera on these various stages. He was even cheated out of the production of a clavier score. "Now it has come to pass exactly as I foretold to my son," wrote L. Mozart to his daughter (December 16, 1785); "the 'Entführung aus dem Serail' has appeared in clavier score at Augsburg, and has also been printed at Mayence. Since March, when he began it, my son has not found time to finish it. He has lost his time, and Torricella (who was to publish it at Vienna) his profits."[68]

---

[66] Ant. Hasenhuth's Leben., p. 94.

[67] Cramer's Magazin f. Musik, II., 2, p. 1056, and B. A. Weber, in Knigge's Dramaturg. Blättern, 1788, II., p. 21, give favourable notices. Both these journals were among Mozart's little collection of books.

[68] Two fragments of Mozart's pianoforte score of Constanze's and Blondchen's songs (11 and 12) are preserved in his handwriting. The piano score of the first act is noticed in the Wien. Ztg., 1785, No. 98.

CHAPTER XXV.

"DIE ENTFÜHRUNG AUS DEM SERAIL."

THE gradual decline of the German festival and "spektakel" operas was consummated in 1742, when Gottsched, who had waged incessant war against them throughout his career, had the satisfaction of chronicling the opera of "Atalanta," in Dresden, as the last of its kind;[1] but they were succeeded by a sort of aftergrowth in the form of the operetta.[2] The theatrical managers could not altogether dispense with similar means of attraction, and attempts were made to introduce the musical intermezzo, together with the now fairly well-established ballet. In 1743 Schönemann produced in Berlin Coffey's "Devil to Pay" ("Der Teufel ist los"), adapted by Von Barck, with the English melodies;[3] but this attempt, as well as the performance of Schürer's vaudeville "Doris," in Dresden, in 1747,[4] remained without result. In 1752 Koch, of Leipzig, who had had recourse to the performance of Italian intermezzi,[5] commissioned Chr. Fel. Weisse to make a new adaptation of Coffey's "Devil to Pay, or the Bewitched Wives," which was set to music by Standfuss, the assistant-manager of Koch's company.[6] Gottsched and his wife renewed the old strife against this attempt, but were completely defeated.[7] The second part of the opera "Der Teufel ist los"—"Der Lustige Schuster"—was produced by Koch, in 1759, at Lubeck.[8] But not until his return to

---

[1] Gottsched, Nöthiger Vorrath, p. 314.

[2] Schletterer, Das Deutsche Singspiel, p. 110.

[3] Chronologie des Deutschen Theaters, p. 109. Plümicke, Entwurf e. Theatergesch. von Berlin, p. 193.

[4] Fürstenau, Zur Gesch. der Musik zu Dresden, II., p. 246.

[5] Chronol., p. 159; Cäcilia, VIII., p. 277.

[6] Weisse, Selbstbiogr., pp. 25, 41; Blümner, Gesch. d. Theat. in Leipzig, p. 98.

[7] Blümner, ibid. Danzel, Gottsched, p. 172.

[8] Chronol., p. 202

Leipzig, in 1765, did he give his serious attention to vaude-ville. Weisse revised his old opera of " Der Teufel ist los," which, with partially new music by Hiller, was performed in 1766, and received with fresh applause.[9] Koch found in Joh. Ad. Hiller what had always hitherto been wanting, viz., a composer of good musical and general education, having a decided talent for light, easy, and characteristic music (more especially comic music), and full of zeal for the elevation of the national art. He endeavoured to make another step in advance, and by the composition of Schieb-ler's romantic poem of " Lisuart and Dariolette " (performed November 25, 1766) to lay the foundation of serious German opera.[10] Educated in the tradition of Hasse and Graun, with the additional influence of Ph. Em. Bach, he followed with interest the attempts to gain favour for Italian music in Paris by reconciling it with the demands of French taste ; and he wished to establish a national German opera on the same principles. He denied that the German language was un-fitted for song, if only the poet would take the trouble of accommodating it to the music, and if artists were trained for German singing with as much care as for Italian. Since German taste was more Italian than French, but the French were superior to the Italians in dramatic treatment, a French plan in Italian form was most likely to be approved of by Germans.[11] The insufficient appointments of the Leipzig stage must, however, have dissuaded him from any idea of a grand opera. To this was added his connection with Weisse, who during his residence in Paris had taken a lively interest in the comic opera, and had exerted himself to transplant it into Germany.[12]

His first opera, " Lottchen am Hofe," after " Ninette à la Cour," and " Die Liebe auf dem Lande," after " Annette et

---

[9] Chronol., p. 247.

[10] Blümner, Gesch. d. Theat. in Leipzig, p. 159. Hiller, Wochentl. Nachr., I., p. 219; II., pp. 135, 150. N. Bibl. d. Schön. Wiss., 1767, IV., p. 178. [Reichardt] Briefe e. Aufm. Reis., II., p. 23. Meyer, L. Schröder, I., p. 131. Goethe, Werke, XVII., p. 295.

[11] Hiller, Wöch. Nachr., I., p. 253 ; III., p. 59.

[12] Weisse, Selbstbiogr., p. 102.

Lubin" and " La Clochette," had so great a success in 1767 and 1768 that they prepared the way for other similar attempts.[13] These simple dramas, which occupied the mind without exerting it, and moved the feelings without unduly exciting them, were so much in keeping with Weisse's own nature that he was able to give them characteristic and appropriate form. They opened a field, too, for Hiller's simple hearty spirit, embodied in a popular form, which made his style appeal at once to the multitude; while an endeavour after higher things would only have turned him into an imitator of Hasse. A rapid succession of operas by Weisse and Hiller, which were received with unanimous approbation, and spread with incredible rapidity, soon established a definite type of German operetta, and raised up a host of imitators. The interest of the public, especially in North Germany, was almost exclusively confined to operetta,[14] so that in Berlin, for instance, during the years 1781-83, 117, 141, and 151 operettas were performed.[15] This implies an extraordinary production. Besides translations from French operettas by Duni, Philidor, Monsigny, Grétry, and Italian intermezzi, there were innumerable German vaudevilles, for the most part also founded on foreign originals.[16] Some idea may be formed of the fertility of these composers, by the fact that between 1765 and 1785, Hiller composed 13 operas, Wolf 18, Neefe 10, Holly 13, André 22, Schweitzer 16, Stegmann 10, G. Benda 8 ; to whom may be added a host of other less productive and less celebrated composers.

This activity had indeed drawbacks, for it was practised with great ease, and many amateurs of very inferior musical education intruded themselves among the operatic musicians.[17] The careless dilettantism of the poet went hand in hand

---

[13] Hiller, Lebensbeschr. berühmter Musikgelehrten, p. 311.

[14] Cf. Deutsch. Museum, 1779, II., p. 268. Plümicke, Entwurf e. Theatergesch. von Berlin, p. 205. The contrary is reported of Cassel as a rare exception (Berl. Litt. u. Theat.-Ztg., 1783, II., p. 409).

[15] L. Schneider, Gesch. d. Oper in Berlin, p. 209.

[16] The constitution of the operatic repertory of the time is shown in the review of the operettas performed in Berlin from 1771-1787 by Schneider (Ibid., p. 206.).

[17] Reichardt, Ueb. d. Com. Oper., p. 20.

with that of the composer. A host of unskilful verse-makers allied themselves with Weisse, Michaelis, and Gotter, and threatened to degrade the operetta to the lower level of the opera buffa. A further drawback consisted in the very defective performances, which in most instances resulted from the insufficient powers of the operetta companies.

" We must remember," says Reichardt, in his " History of the Comic Opera," " how much Hiller was hampered by the miserable state of our operatic companies. He was fully aware of this, and what I admire in him is that he never lost sight of the fact that he was writing, not for singers, but for actors, who had scarcely music enough in them to sing over their wine." The state of things had not altered much since Hiller began to write. The Italian operas alone were supported by the courts; the German operettas remained in the hands of private speculators, who did not possess the means of attracting vocalists of artistic cultivation. No singer of any reputation would have thought it consistent with his dignity to appear in German vaudeville. The vaudeville, therefore, remained in the hands of actors, who had seldom any vocal powers and still seldomer any but a superficial cultivation, but who willingly appeared in operettas on account of the high fees[18] and great applause they might reckon upon. Reichardt gives an appalling description of the German opera in Berlin in 1774 ; he heard one of Hiller's operas " sung by a wide-mouthed, screeching woman, and a lover with a voice like a night-watchman," and that before an audience which had " the reputation of very refined taste " ;[19] he was no better pleased at Leipzig.[20] Müller says of a performance of Wolf's " Treuen Kohler " at Dresden in 1776 : " As only two of all the performers were at all musical, you may imagine how the opera was

---

[18] " Operettas are the favourite pieces in Berlin, and cost a great deal of money," wrote Ramler to Knebel, in 1772 (Litt. Nachl., II., p. 36). He paid the actors of the first parts one louis-d'or, of the second one ducat, and the rest two gulden for a first performance (Plümicke, Entwurf e. Theatergesch. von Berlin, p. 274).

[19] Briefe e. Aufmerks. Reisenden, I., p. 147.

[20] Briefe e. Aufmerks. Reisenden, II., p. 94. Burney, Reise, III., p. 46.

rendered." It is conceivable, therefore, that the growing
partiality for German opera was regarded with disfavour by
earnest men, as prejudicial alike to the dramatic interests
which were still struggling to assert themselves in Germany,[21]
and to the artistic development of operatic music proper.[22]
The actor Müller, during his professional tour in 1776, made
himself acquainted with the views of competent judges as to
the admissibility of German operettas; the different opinions
which he collected are characteristic enough. Lessing—
who held the union of poetry and music as the most perfect
in existence, " so that nature herself appears to have destined them not so much for union as to be considered as one
and the same art "[23]—was against vaudevilles. "They are
the ruin of our stage. Such works are easily written; every
comedy affords material to the author; he scatters a few
songs about, and the thing is done. Our new dramatic poets
find this a far easier task than writing a good character
piece." Gleim was even more violently opposed to vaudeville than Lessing, and gave Müller an epigram upon the
" Witch " :—

> Die, schlau wie Schlang' und Krokodill,
>   Sich schleicht in aller Menschen Herzen
> Und drinnen sitzt, als wie ein Huhn
> Auf seinem Nest, und lehrt : Nur *kleine* Thaten thun
>   Und über *grosse* Thaten scherzen ! "

Weisse smiled when Müller repeated the lines to him, and
declared himself, as became the founder of German opera,
in its favour. He was too modest, however, to maintain that
operettas were dramatic works of art, or to hope thereby to
raise the taste of his countrymen; he could only disclaim all
intention of degrading it or of doing more than encouraging

---

[21] " Comic operas push out all tragedies and legitimate drama," complained
Ramler in 1771 (Knebel, Litt. Nachl., II., p. 33). Boie writes to Knebel to the
same effect in 1771 (Litt. Nachl., II., p. 108): " I do not like operettas. The
taste which our public is developing for them threatens to extinguish all hope
of the revival of true comedy." So also Schubart, Teutsche Chronik, 1774,
pp. 349, 478; Knigge, Ephemer. d. Litt. u. d. Theat., 1785, II., p. 98.

[22] A. M. Z., III., p. 327.

[23] Lessing's Werke, XI., p. 152.

German people to come together, and providing pleasant and popular entertainments for them when they did so.[24] Gotter preserved a discreet neutrality on the subject, since he had had a direct interest in more than one operatic libretto; he would not declare for either side, and was of opinion that variety was the root of all pleasure. Wieland was more explicit, and declared that the national stage could only be rendered of importance by German music; comic and serious German vaudevilles were wanted, but good poets would soon come forward to supply the need. He was not only able to point to his own "Alceste," and the success it had obtained; he had developed his views on the cultivation of German vaudeville with a lively acknowledgment of the achievements of Schweitzer, and he possessed genuine feeling and interest for music. Even a musician like Reichardt declared himself against the operetta, but thought as it was there it ought at least to be improved, and made as useful as possible.[25]

The interest which was taken by great poets in the elevation of the vaudeville is exemplified by Goethe; after "Erwin und Elmire" and "Claudina von Villabella" were written, his intercourse with his early friend Christoph Kayser[26] (b. 1736) caused him to attempt the construction of vaudeville after the received type of the Italian operetta. His first experiment was "Scherz, List und Rache," which he began in 1784, and sent at once to Kayser for composition;[27] the two first acts were ready the following year, and were well thought of in Weimar;[28] in Rome, whither Goethe was followed by Kayser at the end of 1787, they finished the operetta together.[29] But Goethe thought that the operetta

---

[24] Weisse, Selbstbiogr., p. 103. Engel says the same in the preface to the "Apotheke," p. viii. Cf. Schmid, Das Parterr, p. 155.

[25] Briefe eines Aufmerks. Reisenden, I., p. 141. Ueb. d. Com. Opera, p. 6. Cf. Mus. Kunstmag., I., p. 161. Geist des Mus. Kunstmag., p. 94.

[26] Riemer, Mitth., II., p. 111.

[27] Riemer, Mitth., II., p. 194.

[28] Goethe, Br. an Frau von Stein, III., pp. 181, 191. Knebel, Litt. Nachl., I., p. 149.

[29] Riemer, Mitth., II., p. 192. Briefw. m. Zelter, II., p. 121.

was extravagantly mounted,[80] and complains himself that a defective conception of the intermezzo had led him to spin out the trivial subject into innumerable musical pieces, which had been treated by Kayser quite after the old-fashioned models. "Unhappily," says Goethe, "adherence to the old principles caused it to suffer from poverty of parts; it never went beyond a terzet, and one felt inclined to wish that the doctor's medical books might be endowed with life to form a chorus. All the pains we took, therefore, to confine ourselves within narrow and simple limits went for nothing when Mozart appeared. The 'Entführung aus dem Serail' threw all else into the shade, and our carefully worked-out piece was never heard of again at any theatre."[81]

A closer examination of Mozart's opera will make it clear to us why it threw all others into the shade. The plot of Bretzner's[82] "Entführung aus dem Serail," written for André in 1781, is simple and in no way original:—

Constanze, the beloved of Belmont, is in the power of the Pasha Selim, who has confined her in his seraglio, and sues in vain for her love. Belmont has been made aware of her place of confinement by Pedrillo, his former servant, who has also fallen into the hands of the Pasha, and become the overseer of his gardens; Belmont hastens to liberate his beloved. In seeking Pedrillo he stumbles upon Osmin, overseer of the country-house in which the action takes place; and both he and Pedrillo (who is even more obnoxious to Osmin from his known love to Blondchen, Constanze's waiting-maid, whom Osmin seeks to win) are rudely repulsed by Osmin. In the meantime Pedrillo succeeds in recommending Belmont to his master as an accomplished architect; Selim takes him into his service, and Osmin is reluctantly obliged to admit him to the country-house. In the second act Blondchen makes short work of Osmin's arrogant jealousy in respect of her, and Constanze remains constant against the renewed attempts of the Pasha. Hereupon Pedrillo inveigles Osmin into drinking with him, and renders him harmless by means of a sleeping potion; the freedom thus obtained is employed by the lovers in an interview at which their flight the following night is determined on. In the third act this is put into effect. Pedrillo

---

[80] Goethe, Werke, XXI., p. 6. Cf. Br. an Frau von Stein, III., p. 235.

[81] Cf. Goethe, Briefw. mit Zelter, II., p. 121. Riemer, Mittheil., II., p. 292.

[82] "Belmont und Constanze, oder die Entführung aus dem Serail." Eine Operette in drey Akten von C. F. Bretzner (Leipzig, 1781). A French adaptation, "L'Enlèvement" was made by Ch. Destrais, Strasburg, 1857.

gives the sign, Belmont escapes with Constanze; as Pedrillo is carrying off Blondchen, Osmin enters still half asleep; they contrive to escape but he causes them to be pursued, and both couples are brought before the Pasha. They are condemned to death, but the Pasha, moved at last by their self-sacrificing love and fidelity, pardons and unites them.

The original libretto is arranged for a genuine vaudeville. All the dramatic interest lies in the spoken dialogue; the songs are, with a few exceptions, superfluous additions, and imply a very moderate amount of execution. Mozart undertook to indicate to Stephanie where and how, in the interests of the composer, alterations should be made, and only left to him the framing of the text, with which it was not necessary to be so particular, if only the situations were well arranged in their main features. The principal point, next to giving to the musical element of the piece its due prominence as the most fitting expression of lyric sentiment, was the proper consideration of the individualities of the performers themselves. Fortunately this task was not complicated in the way which had so often been the case. Madame Cavalieri was certainly more of a bravura singer than anything else, and neither her appearance nor her acting was effective; but Adamberger and Fischer were just as Mozart would have had them, both as singers and actors, and Fischer especially was an extraordinarily gifted artist. The part of Osmin, which was created for him, shows the influence of a congenial spirit on the conceptions of the creating artist. When Mozart was fairly embarked in the work, he wrote to his father about the libretto and the alterations already made in it (September 26, 1781):—

The opera began with a soliloquy which I have begged Herr Stephanie to turn into a little ariette, and also, instead of the two chattering together after Osmin's song, to make a duet out of the dialogue. As we have given the part to Fischer, who has an excellent bass voice (although the Archbishop once told me he sang too low for a bass, and I assured his grace that he would sing higher next time), we must give him something to do, especially as he is such a favourite with the public. In the original book Osmin has only one little song, and nothing else but the terzet and finale. I have given him an aria in the first act, and he is to have another in the second. I have trusted the aria altogether to Stephanie, the music was ready before he knew a word about it.

These alterations were of specially good dramatic effect in the first scene, and Osmin's song called to life the first German comic aria which deserves to be called great. In the second act the dialogue between Blondchen and Osmin becomes a duet; on the other hand, a superfluous duet between Constanze and Blondchen is very rightly omitted. Instead of it Constanze has the great bravura song "Martern aller Arten," chiefly as a concession to the singer; for the repetition of the scene in which she scornfully rejects the Sultan's, proposals is in every way superfluous. Blondchen's second song—newly inserted—is, however, quite appropriate; in it she expresses her joy at her approaching deliverance; so that the original duet is really embodied to a certain extent in these two songs.

But the chief alteration which Mozart contemplated was in the conclusion of the second act. In Bretzner's text the abduction scene is treated as a grand ensemble movement, with which the third act commences. A long and elaborate duet between Belmont and Pedrillo, who are lying in ambush, makes the beginning, and then Constanze appears and is carried off by Belmont. After Pedrillo has climbed up to Blondchen in the window, Osmin comes out of the house still heavy with sleep; but he sees the fugitives and has them pursued and brought back by his guard ; they beg for mercy, seek to regain their liberty by bribery—in vain; Osmin rages, and all the characters are in a state of excitement.

Mozart's quick eye saw that this scene, bringing together all the characters in a succession of rapidly varying and contrasting situations, forms the culminating point of the opera ; he wished, therefore, that this "charming quintet, or rather finale, should be placed at the close of the second act." He also saw that this transposition would necessitate other important alterations. The second act could be kept together very well by the mutual understanding of the two lovers; but the third act, for which nothing was reserved but the unravelling of the knot by the clemency of the Sultan, if it was to have any substance or interest, "must be provided with an entirely new intrigue." The difficulty of finding this seems to have put a stop to the alteration, and the original arrangement remained. But for Bretzner's insignificant finale to the second act there was substituted an elaborate quartet, which expresses in music the reunion of the lovers in its various aspects of joy and jealousy, of disputes and reconciliation. An air for Belmont precedes this; it is well-fitted for the situation, and is intended also as a concession to the singer, for in this act, where all the other characters come to the front, Belmont had originally nothing to sing but the ensemble music.

Mozart began the composition of the ensemble movement at the commencement of the third act. The greater part of the duet between Belmont and Pedrillo before the romanze was sketched out by him in his usual way, the voices and bass written in full, the accompaniment indicated here and there. It breaks off, however, in the middle; and Mozart appears to have purposely laid it aside, convinced that the scene must be differently treated.[33] The ensemble was given up; Mozart saw that it would throw the whole opera out of gear, and would concentrate the interest and the action at the wrong place. The abduction scene was confined to dialogue, only Pedrillo's romanze being left; in addition, songs for Belmont and Osmin were inserted, both highly characteristic. The duet for Belmont and Constanze, which follows, is altered only in the words, not in the situation; the closing catastrophe it was thought well to modify. In Bretzner's version the Pasha Selim, who is a renegade, recognises in Belmont his son, which leads to the *dénouement;* but Stephanie makes him pardon the lovers from generosity and magnanimity, which, as a critic remarked, were the fashion of the day in Vienna.[34] Constanze's song of gratitude at the close is very rightly omitted, and replaced by the then customary vaudeville, in which all the characters declare in turn: "Wer solche Huld vergessen kann, den seh man mit Verachtung an!"

---

[33] Jul. André has lately published this interesting relic: duet, "Welch ängstliches Beben," zur Oper "Die Entführung aus dem Serail" von Mozart. Offenbach: André (389 K.).

[34] Cramer, Magazin der Musik, II., p. 1057.

Mozart's father had raised objections to the libretto, and the alterations in it; he was particularly concerned that the verses were not in regular rhyme throughout. Thereupon his son made him the following remarkable answer (October 13, 1781):—

Now about the text of the opera. As far as Stephanie's work is concerned, you are quite right, but the poetry is very well suited to the character of the stupid, boorish, and malicious Osmin. I am quite aware that the versification is not of the best; but it goes so well with my musical thoughts (which were running in my head long before) that I cannot but be pleased; and I would wager that no fault will be found in performance. Belmont's aria, "O wie ängstlich," could scarcely be written better for the music. Constanze's aria too is not bad, with the exception of the "Hui,"[35] and the line "Sorrow reposes in my bosom," for sorrow cannot repose. After all, in an opera, the poetry must be the handmaid of the music. Why do Italian comic operas always please, in spite of their wretched librettos—even in Paris, as I was witness myself? Because the music is supreme, and everything else is forgotten. All the more then will an opera be likely to please in which the plan of the piece is well carried out, and the words are written simply to suit the music; not turned and twisted so as to ruin the composition for the sake of a miserable rhyme, which God knows does far more harm than good in a dramatic representation.[36] Verse, indeed, is indispensable for music, but rhyme is bad in its very nature: and poets who go to work so pedantically will certainly come to grief, together with the music. It would be by far the best if a good composer who understands the theatre, and knows how to produce a piece, and a clever poet, could be (like a veritable phœnix), united in one; there would be no reason to be afraid as to the applause of the ignorant then. The poets seem to me something like trumpeters, with their

---

[35] In Constanze's aria the words run:—

"Doch im Hui schwand meine Freude
Trennung war mein banges Loos;
Und nun schwimmt mein Aug' in Thränen
Kummer ruht in meinem Schooss."

Mozart had previously written to his father (September 26, 1781): "I have altered *Hui* into *schnell*, thus: 'Doch *wie schnell* schwand meine Freude.' I do not know what our German poets are thinking of. Even if they do not trouble themselves to understand what is best fitted for dramatic or operatic treatment, they need not make human beings converse like pigs."

[36] Reichardt finds special fault with the rhyming in his Briefe über die musikalische Poesie, p. 115 (an appendix to his pamphlet on the German Comic Opera, Leipzig, 1774).

mechanical tricks—if we composers were to adhere so closely to our rules (which were well enough as long as we knew no better) we should soon produce music just as worthless as their worthless books."[37]

"Now I think I have talked nonsense enough for this time"—so Mozart concludes this interesting letter, as he was fond of doing when his desire to justify himself had led him into general æsthetic questions, on which he was averse to expatiating at any length. His opinion as to the relative positions of music and poetry in operatic works is unusually interesting. In complete opposition to Gluck, who considered music as subordinate to poetry, Mozart requires that poetry shall be the handmaid of music. In the sense in which the context shows him to have meant it, he is undoubtedly right. He exacts that the plan of the piece shall be well laid out; that is, that the plot shall be interesting, and shall as it proceeds afford dramatic situations fitted for musical expression. He requires further that the words shall be written merely for the music, that is, that the poetical conceptions shall be of a kind to stimulate the composer, to elevate and support him, while allowing him perfect freedom of thought and action. He had mentioned Osmin's song to Stephanie, and the music was ready before the latter had written a word of the poetry; the words he then prepared accorded so admirably with the musical ideas which had been running in Mozart's head, that faults here and there in the versification did not seem to him of much consequence.

The impulse he required for his musical conceptions was the representation of the *dramatis personæ* in certain definite situations, not the verbal framing of the poet's ideas.[38] The

---

[37] It must be kept in mind that German operatic poets confined themselves to imitating Italian opera libretti, which were all cast in the same mould. Krause's pamphlet, highly esteemed by contemporaries, Von der musikalischen Poesie (Berlin, 1752) takes this for granted; Hiller (Ueber Metastasio, 1786, p. 6) refers the German librettists to Metastatio; even Goethe, although in another way, endeavoured to form German vaudeville after an Italian type. Views of the subject, similar to those of Mozart and Reichardt, are carried out in detail in Cramer's Magazin der Musik, II., p. 1061.

[38] Gluck's intentions were unquestionably the same. He warred against the mechanical formalism of musicians, and strove to free the composer from the fetters of form and make him a poet. But he was in some danger of going too far, and making the musician merely the interpreter of the poet.

points which were contained in the verse, and influenced the construction of the musical idea, were to him co-operating but not dominating elements. The words of an opera have a definite object; they provide foundation and support for the musical expression, and are not therefore absolutely independent, as in the drama,[89] but are obliged to recognise and respect the laws of music, as well as those of poetry. To attain this end a compromise is as indispensable as in every other union of the sister arts. Architecture, in her highest achievements, turns for embellishment to sculpture and painting; and no one has ever doubted that in such co-operation each art must make some concession to the other. The architectural plan must be so conceived as to afford fitting space and position for the sculpture and painting; these, on the other hand, must be introduced with a view to the essential conditions of the building; the pediment, the arch, the metope are not freely selected forms, but constitute the limitations which arise from the necessities of the building. The sculptor modifies his style to suit the character of the building, the painter knows how to give significance to the whole design by skilful composition and combinations of colour on the flat surface of the walls. Doubtless architecture, with her severe laws and inflexible forms, imposes restrictions on the fancies of the artist; but who can imagine that Phidias in the sculptures of the Parthenon, Raphael in the Loggia of the Vatican, renounced their freedom of design or their independence of execution in obedience to the will of the architect? The relation between poetry and music is of the same kind. Mozart saw the necessity for co-operation between the musician and the poet, if the right effect was to be given in its just proportions. The musician must be ready to "give some hints" which shall put the poet in possession of his intentions and of the conditions necessitated by the rules of his art; the poet must be "intelligent," clever, and cultivated enough to fall in with the intentions of the musician, and poet enough to retain his poetical powers in spite of these limitations.

---

[89] Cf. Hanslick, Vom Musikalisch-Schönen, p. 27.

Mozart is quite right in asserting that co-operation of this kind is the surest pledge for an altogether satisfactory opera; unhappily he is quite right also in declaring such a co-operation to be attainable only by "a veritable phœnix."

To a certain degree a mutual understanding is of course indispensable, but it confines itself, as a rule, to an unwilling concession on this or the other side.[40]   Music finally assumes the mastery in opera, where it is the actual medium of expression; no one could deny that good music would make the poorest verse pass muster, whereas bad music could not be made acceptable even when "wedded to immortal verse." But the very fact that music appeals direct to the senses gives it an advantage when opposed to poetry, which reaches the imagination through the intellect; just as a poetical description of a work of art falls far short of the effect produced directly on the mind by contemplation of the work itself. Music works on the sense of hearing in an as yet inexplicable manner, rousing emotions and fancies with an instantaneous power surpassing that of poetry. Even if this be disputed, it must be allowed that music does not appeal immediately to the intellect as language does. Even the species of music which is said to occupy the intellect most especially, viz., music in strict forms of counterpoint, does not do it in such a way as to enable the hearer to discover the meaning of the composition by means of its actual utterances; it exercises his intellect otherwise by rousing the desire in him to grasp and hold the artistic forms as such, and the laws upon which they depend.[41] Music must borrow from poetry what it does not possess for itself, namely, the ability to call forth a well-defined image which shall identify itself with the sentiment evoked by the music and give to this its exact significance. This point is, of course, of special importance in opera, although the fact must not be lost sight of that the stage accessories

---

[40] The same difficulty has led composers of the present day to write their own libretti. But it is not in nature that the highest aims can thus be attained. Burney quotes Metastasio's utterances on this point (Reise, II., p. 222). Cf. O. Jahn, Ges. Aufs. üb. Musik, p. 70.

[41] Cf. Hanslik Vom Musikalisch-Schönen, p. 78.

and pantomimic representation come greatly to the aid of the music, so that it is quite possible for an audience to follow an opera with interest and gratification without understanding the language in which it is written. This is a further proof that, important as the poetic details doubtless are, the plot and situations are the really essential points. For the paradox that a libretto if it is to be musical cannot be poetical, but can only have certain external forms of poetic delivery, is certainly false. The conditions of poetic delivery and musical execution are essentially the same, and 'a distinction between them is impossible. But the means of delivery which the poet has at his disposal are manifold and varied, and not all applicable in the same place ; if the poet is master of his art, and has a clear conception of what he is striving after, he will know what are the particular means he ought to employ to be in accord with the musical part of the work.[42]

Bretzner was very indignant at the proposed alterations in his libretto, and inserted the following notice in the " Berliner Litteratur und Theater-Zeitung " (No. 1783) :—

> It has pleased some hitherto unknown person in Vienna to take in hand my opera, " Belmont und Constanze," or " Die Entführung aus dem Serail," and to publish the piece in a very altered form. The alterations in the dialogue are not considerable, and may be passed over; but the adapter has inserted a vast number of songs, the words of which are in many cases edifying and touching in the highest possible degree. I would not willingly deprive the improver of the glory belonging to his work, and I therefore take this opportunity of specifying these inserted songs as belonging to the Vienna edition and Mozart's composition.

In conclusion, and after giving " a specimen of the improver's work from the quartet," Bretzner exclaims : " And this is called improvement ! " Nevertheless the text was improved, and although far from first-rate, it had been rendered a fairly satisfactory and practicable libretto, which has not yet been very far surpassed in the literature of German comic opera. The plot is certainly not thrilling, but it

---

[42] Lessing has some excellent observations on the relations of music to poetry in the continuation of his Laokoon (Werke, XI., p. 153).

allows the natural development of a succession of musical situations. It was, as we have seen, Mozart's merit to recognise these in his musical representation, to make them available in such a way as to distinguish the "Entführung" from all earlier vaudevilles and operettas.

Mozart's performance was not confined to the adoption of certain ready-developed forms of Italian opera, pressed into the service of the German opera, partly from necessity, partly from the narrow principle that the songs were to be sung by personages of supposed high position.[43] This would have been no sufficient reason for substituting the aria for the *Lied;* it was done to give full scope to musical construction, and to make the standard and measure of the execution to consist only in the artistic conditions of the dramatic situations, and in the nature of the musical expression.[44]

At home as he was in Italian, French and German opera, in sacred and instrumental music, he had obtained such a mastery over musical forms as gave him a freedom of action which his favourable circumstances in Vienna allowed him to make use of, and the fact that he was composing a German opera gave him a sense of a still higher freedom. He was German in every thought and feeling, and German music was his natural way of expressing himself as an artist, requiring no unusual form, no special characterisation, nothing but freedom of thought and action. In the "Entführung," German sentiment, emotion, and disposition found expression for the first time at the hands of a true artist. It is easy to understand how the fulness of life and truth in such a work would throw into the shade all who believed solely in those forms which were borrowed from foreign

---

[43] Hiller, Wochentl. Nachr., I., p. 256. Lebensbeschreibungen, I., p. 312. Reichardt, Ueb. d. Com. Oper, p. 8.

[44] He was perfectly aware that comic opera must follow its own laws. "You cannot imagine," he wrote to his father (June 16, 1781), "that I should write an opéra comique in the same style as an opera seria. Just as in an opera seria there must be a display of much learning and good sense, and very little playfulness, so in an opera buffa there must be very little display of learning and a great deal of playful merriment. It cannot be helped if people will have comic music in an opera seria; but there is a great difference. I believe that buffoonery is not quite rooted out of music yet; and in this case the French are right."

II.

Q

sources, and only superficially remodelled.[45]   This truly
German and truly Mozart-like style is nowhere more decidedly exemplified than in the part of Belmont.   It is only
necessary to note the contrast between the male sopranos of
the opera seria, or the comic lovers of the opera buffa, and
this Belmont, who expresses manly love in all its force and
intensity.   It is plain that his love is not the wild and transitory gleam of passion, but an emotion having its roots
deep in the heart, sanctified by sorrow, and held with the
constancy of a true moral nature.   Manliness is the ground-
tone of all his agitated sentiments; the steady glow of a well-
balanced mind penetrates every expression of his feelings.   It
is an easier task to portray the wild excitement of passion
than to depict a mind and character in its totality by means
of each separate expression;[46] and the conception of love, the
essential motive power of musical drama, from this point of
view, marks an era in musical representation, important
alike for its national character and its artistic construction.
It was not by mere chance that Mozart made the tenor voice,
which had been virtually deprived of its proper province in
Italian opera, into the organ of manly love and tenderness.
Belmont has become a type in German opera.   Adamberger,
judging from contemporary testimony was the most fitting
representative of such a character.[47]   Various songs composed
for him by Mozart characterise him as a singer of noble and
expressive delivery.[48]

---

[45] The autograph score of the " Entführung" (384 K.), in three volumes (458
pages), was presented by Mozart to his sister-in-law, Madame Hofer, one
evening when she had especially gratified him by her singing; it is now in the
possession of Paul Mendelssohn-Bartholdy, of Berlin.   Some of the odd sheets
are in André's collection.   Wolfgang writes to his father (July 20, 1782): "You
will find many erasures, because I knew that the score would be copied at
once : so I let my ideas have free play, and made my alterations and abbreviations before sending it to the copyist."

[46] The ancients indicated this distinction by the terms *pathos* and *ethos*.

[47] Meyer (L. Schröder, I., p. 368) speaks of his nasal tones in the high notes.

[48] These are the beautiful air, " Per pietà non ricercate " (420 K., part 8) ;
the air written in 1785 for the oratorio " Davidde Penitente " (469 K., 6), " A
te fra tanti affanni"; and a grand air belonging to 1783 (431 K., part 3), which
is one of the most beautiful.   It supposes a faithful lover awaking to find
himself in prison, and expressing his surprise and anger in an agitated recitative,

Belmont's character and tone of mind are drawn in firm lines in his first cavatina (1). His state of anxious suspense is implied rather than fully indicated by his expression of secret devotion. But this little song, which none but a master-hand could have thrown off so lightly and so surely, is of most significance, by reason of its connection with the overture. Mozart makes no remark to his father on the overture except that it was short, and that "it alternates between *forte* and *piano*, the Turkish music being always *forte*, modulated by changes of key, and I do not think any one can go to sleep over it, even if they have lain awake all the night before" (September 26, 1781). As usual, when he speaks of his compositions, he only indicates the means employed and the external effect, and does not attempt any verbal description of the music itself. It is certainly true that a lively and incessant suspense is kept up by the constant modulatory changes, especially from major to minor, and by sharp contrasts of *forte* and *piano*. But this is not all; the character of the overture is so singularly fanciful that a few bars suffice to place the hearer in an imaginative mood. The most varied emotions of joy and sorrow are lightly touched, but never held, the tone of the whole is so fresh and cheerful that the listener involun-tarily yields to the spell; and the impressions of the new world in which he finds himself are heightened by the highly original tone-colouring. Then comes a slower movement, expressing longing desires in the tenderest, most appealing tones. It has scarcely died away before we are again whirled along our fantastic course, which ends in an appealing cry, followed without a pause by Belmont's cavatina, "Hier soll ich dich denn sehen, Constanze!" We recognise at

---

"Misero! O sogno!" In the andante, "Aura che intorno spiri," his thoughts turn to his beloved one, for whom he is suffering; a simple and dignified cantilene, full of warm, deep feeling. The allegro, expressive of his horror at his position, is full of wild excitement and anguish. The whole song is simple and full of manly dignity without bravura, which seems to have been Adam-berger's ,peculiar style. The musical treatment is rich in interesting detail; the wind instruments—flutes, bassoons, and horns—are employed to give individual colouring.

once the middle movement of the overture, but changed from the minor to the major key. This change, and the difference of shading between the arrangement for the voice and that for the orchestra, give to the charming little movement two distinct expressions, just as the same landscape has two different aspects seen at noon or in the moonlight. The overture renders us free to receive the effect of the work of art as such, prepared by what forms the starting-point of the work; and the first song sets the crown on the overture, while it transports us at once into the frame of mind which predominates throughout the opera. Still more important in its climax and composition is Belmont's second song (4). The situation is more definitely developed; Belmont knows now that Constanze is there, that he will soon see her, and this certainty condenses all the emotions roused by the memory of a sorrowful past, and the prospect of a perilous future, into the one feeling of their speedy reunion. Mozart was so taken with this song that he wrote it down as soon as he received the libretto. " This is the favourite song of all who have heard it—myself included," he wrote to his father (September 26, 1781), " and is exactly calculated for Adamberger's voice. 'O wie ängstlich, o wie feurig!' You can imagine how it is expressed, with the very beating of the heart—the violins in octaves. One can see the trembling, the hesitation, the very swelling of the breast is expressed by a crescendo, one can hear the sighs, the whispers, rendered by the violins muted, with one flute in unison."

It would be doing Mozart an injustice to consider this sound-painting as his first object; it is in reality but a subordinate, although a very effective and useful element of the whole musical conception. Belmont's two other songs—one in the second act, before the meeting with Constanze (15),[49] and the other at the beginning of the third act, before the

---

[49] This air was considerably abbreviated by Mozart. In the adagio there was originally a distinct middle movement following the second occurrence of the subject; it passed into the key of E flat major, and at the seventeenth bar closed in D minor, whereupon the first subject recurred. The allegro was also shortened.

abduction (17)[50]—are much quieter in tone, and are characterised by manly composure combined with warm sensibility. These qualities are visible also in the musical construction of the broad and expressive cantilene, which allows free scope for the display of a full tenor voice in its best position. The structure of the melodies diverges in a remarkable degree from that which predominates in Mozart's Italian operas, and approaches nearer to that employed in his instrumental music. And yet the national character of the melodies is not so pronounced in the "Entführung" as in the "Zauberflöte," nor are the songs in their whole design so completely absolved from Italian forms.

The part of Constanze, so far as musical characterisation is concerned, is not nearly so well thought out as that of Belmont. " I have been obliged," writes Mozart to his father (September 26, 1781), " to sacrifice Constanze's song (6) in some degree to the voluble organ of Mdlle. Cavalieri. But I have sought to express 'Trennung war mein banges Loos und nun schwimmt mein Aug' in Thränen' as far as is compatible with an Italian bravura song."[51] We shall readily allow that he has been so far successful; and that, apart from the inserted bravura passages, the song is not only fine from a musical point of view, but appropriate to the situation. But in the great bravura song of the second act everything has been sacrificed to Mdlle. Cavalieri's voluble organ, and, as Gluck would have said, it *smells of music*.[52] It is, as we have seen, inserted without reference to the plot, and this may have led to the further consequence of treating it altogether as an extraneous piece. As regards length and difficulty, it is one of the greatest of bravura songs, and is accompanied by four obbligato instruments—flute, oboe, violin, and vio-

---

[50] This air also was considerably altered by Mozart.

[51] The same may almost be said of the air " Tra le oscure ombre funeste," which Mozart composed in 1785 for Mdlle. Cavalieri in the oratorio, " Davidde Penitente " (469 K., 8). The first movement is expressive of earnest feeling; the second has more of bravura.

[52] Salieri narrates that Gluck was dissatisfied with one part of his " Danaides" without knowing the reason why; after many repetitions he exclaimed at last, " I have it ! the passage *smells of music !* " (Mosel, Salieri, p. 79).

loncello.[53] Considered as a concert piece it is of importance
by reason of the plan, artistic in design and execution, which
permits the treatment of the five obbligato parts as integral
divisions of the whole, while making due provision for
sound effects and musical interest. The song is still often
sung, although the glitter surrounding mere execution has
passed away. But it does not belong to the " Entführung."
Together with the brilliant execution there is a certain heroic
tone in the song which is quite out of keeping with the opera
and with the character of Constanze in it. The true Constanze, as Mozart imagined her, is found in the second air
(10), which expresses with much truth and intensity the ardent
longing of the maiden sorrowing for her lover. Firmness
and assurance are manly attributes, but a dreamy resigned
absorption in the contemplation of vanished happiness is
proper to a woman, and to this maidenly sentiment Mozart
has given beautiful expression. This feminine tone gives
the song a certain resemblance to that of Ilia in "Idomeneo"
(Vol. II., p. 151); but the latter is, as the situation requires,
drawn in darker lines, and takes more hold on the mind.
Here as elsewhere the same point is noticeable, viz., that
when Mozart works outward from the heart of an individual
situation, the separate elements of the musical construction
are more striking, and the form is freer and more lifelike than
it would otherwise be.[54]

The instrumentation also is peculiarly effective, especially
by the employment of the wind instruments, which shed a
gentle glow over the whole. Mozart, against his custom,

---

[53] The bravura part was originally extended into eleven bars (from bar 5,
p. 153), with the voices and instruments contending; the close was also
longer, fifteen bars being inserted at p. 175, bar 7. Rochlitz asserts (A. M. Z.,
I., p. 145) that in later years Mozart undertook a searching revision of the
"Entführung," making numerous alterations, especially abbreviations. "I heard
him play one of Constanze's principal airs, after twofold revision, and deplored
some of the omitted passages. 'They may do for the piano,' said he, 'but not
on the stage.' When I wrote that I was too fond of hearing myself, and did
not know when to leave off." This is the only instance known of such hyper-
criticism on Mozart's part.

[54] It has already been remarked that Mozart made use of a motif from
Zaide " for this air (Vol. II., p. 121).

makes use of the basset-horn instead of the clarinet in this song. In the part of Belmont, too, the instrumentation is modified to some extent. The second song (4) is very delicate and tender in its instrumentation, the wind instruments being treated as solos, although not concertante; in the others there is a very pithy forcible tone, which in the last (16) becomes almost brilliant.

The duet (20), owing to the singularity of the situation, differs materially in character from an ordinary love duet. Within sight of death each of the lovers has the painful consciousness of having led the other to destruction; and their mutual endeavour to console one another with the certainty of their love, which death may consummate but cannot destroy, raises them to the height of enthusiastic inspiration. This sentiment is excellently well expressed in the first calm movement with fervour and clearness, and a perceptible blending of painful emotion and loving consolation; the second movement does not quite reach the same high level. Not only do some of the passages, and the very tedious conclusion, make concessions to passing effect, but the expression does not rise to the ecstatic strain which is implied in the situation.[55]

The noble forms of the two lovers stand in the sharpest contrast to that of Osmin, which is altogether Mozart's creation, and certainly one of the most original characters of dramatic music. The very way in which he is introduced is masterly. After Belmont has sung his cavatina, which breathes the noblest love and constancy, Osmin comes out of the house to gather figs; he sings a song for his pastime; it is a love song, but one suggested by painful jealousy. The minor key of Osmin's song gives it a wild, desolate expression, in strong contrast to the cheerful candour of the cavatina; many popular songs have this expression, and Osmin's song is successfully imitated from the popular style. The phrasing is clumsy in spite of the marked rhythm, but the effect is quite startling when Osmin in a complacent hum

---

[55] Tieck, Dramaturg. Blätter, II., p. 315 : " The duet is one which may draw tears from the eyes of the most insensible." Even Berlioz (À Travers Chants, p. 243) thought highly of it.

repeats the last words an octave lower, and then at once breaks out into a wild "Trallalera!" The uncouth fellow lolls and stretches so completely at his ease that there cannot be a moment's doubt of how unamiable he will prove to be if any one should venture to cross his path.[56] This is soon put to the proof. He refuses with assumed indifference to answer Belmont's repeated inquiries, and on the latter interrupting him (involuntarily, as it were, with the melody of his own song, which has so irritated Belmont), the unabashed rudeness of Osmin breaks out in speech. It is as interesting as instructive to note how in this duet the simplest and easiest means of musical representation are used to produce a continuous climax and the most lively characterisation. While it is still in full train Pedrillo enters, and Osmin turns upon him with a fresh outbreak of rage in the song which Mozart had spoken of to his father (3). Again changing his tactics, he endeavours to repress his opponent with all the weight of his dignity and cleverness. Gravity and importance, expressed by the rhythm, the pompous intervals, the syncopated accompaniment, alternate with impatience and haste, when the singer becomes irritated. Very characteristic is the demeanour of Osmin as he complacently nurses the thought: "I have my wits about me!" ("Ich hab' auch Verstand!"). He works himself gradually up into a rage, and the threats which he pours forth in a breath fall like blows on the head of the hapless Pedrillo. The effect is produced by the accentuation given to the rapid flow of words; the first fourth of every bar is forcibly given by the orchestra, and the second is taken up by the voice in fifths, and then in octaves. At last he comes to a triumphant close, and one thinks it is all over. But he has only stopped to take breath, and at once resuming his furious course, he ends by completely overpowering his opponent. Mozart writes to his father on the conclusion of this song (September 26, 1781): "The 'Drum beim Barte des Propheten' is in the same time, but the notes are more rapid, and as his anger grows one imagines the climax must be close at hand; the allegro assai

---

[56] Cf. Lobe, A. M. Z., XLVIII., p. 537.

follows in quite a different time and key, and has an excellent effect. A man in such violent rage oversteps all bounds of moderation, and loses all command over himself, and so must the music. But since," he continues, expressing in simple words that wherein lies the charm of all true art, "since the passions, violent or not, must never be carried to the point of producing disgust, and the music, however thrilling, must never fail to satisfy the ear, consequently must always remain music, I have not chosen a distant key to follow the F (the key of the song) but an allied one; not the nearest key of all, D minor, but the farther one of A minor." In point of fact, the effect of the minor key is extraordinary, both here and in other places where it is only cursorily touched. It adds to the frenzied wildness of the character in which lust and cruelty are blended, and it is emphasised by the strongly marked though monotonous rhythm. And how wonderfully all these characteristics are enhanced by the instrumentation!

"Osmin's rage," writes Mozart, "acquires a comic element by the introduction of the Turkish music." The effect is enhanced by the simplicity which has hitherto characterised the instrumentation. The oboes (with bassoons and horns) predominate until, in the last verse: "Sonderlich beim Mondenscheine," a flute insinuates itself with very good effect. There are many characteristic touches in spite of the scanty means at disposal, as for instance, the mocking entry of the oboe at the words, " Ich hab' auch Verstand."

The Turkish music serves for far more than local colour and characterisation. The expression of fanaticism is coloured as well as heightened by the shrill sound of the piccolo flute, the blows of the drum and cymbals, and the tingle of the triangles.[57] The bewilderment produced by these

---

[57] A singular effect is given by the sustained notes of the oboes and bassoons with the appoggiatura:—

Mozart has made a similar use of them in the Wedding March in " Figaro," where he was equally desirous of imparting peculiarity of colouring.

instruments, the breathless rapidity of the movement, and the monotony of the rhythm make one feel that giddiness must ensue if it goes on much longer. But Mozart never makes us giddy, he makes use of the most forcible means for characterisation, but never to the point of becoming painful, and all with so much cheerfulness and humour that the total effect is decidedly pleasing.

We make acquaintance with Osmin's boorish character in many different situations; he is true to himself in them all. The second great song (19) contrasts in some measure with the first. He is triumphant, he has his enemies in his power, and he is beside himself with joy; but he retains the same savage nature, and in the midst of all his rejoicing the main point for him is that he can now loll and stretch himself comfortably, which he proceeds to do to his heart's content on the long-sustained A and D, to which he easily carries his scale. Especially characteristic is the middle movement of this song. One seems to see a wild beast, now yawning and stretching, now crouching for a spring; grim cruelty and lustful indolence are wonderfully characterised by the alternation of octaves and dissonant suspensions in the accompaniment, as well as by the triplet passages which are given by the orchestra in unison, as if there could be no harmony here; the expression of joy is mingled with unspeakable brutality, and comes to a climax in the shrill note of exultation at the close.[58] But Osmin shows himself a true poltroon in the duet with Blondchen (9)—her snappish impudence completely gets the better of him, and although he endeavours to overawe her with the deepest notes of his deep bass voice, her persiflage drives her unwieldy antagonist quite out of the field. The lament which he thereupon sings: "Ihr Engländer, seid ihr nicht Thoren, ihr lasst euren Weibern den Willen !" (" You Englishmen, what fools you are, to leave your wives their freedom ! ") is in contrast to his love song, and completes the conception of it. Here there is nothing of

---

[58] Mozart has used only the piccolo flute here, as specially adapted for the tattoo-like principal subject, and its wild, shrill conclusion. The clarinets are very originally treated, particularly in those places where they are apart from the other wind instruments and support the voice with sustained notes.

the barbarous nature which showed itself in lust and jealousy, but only the pitiful whining of a slavish soul which trembles before a resolute woman's will. The characterisation of the last movement—when Osmin gives up all appearance of superiority and yields upon every point—is charming, and produced by the simplest musical means. He displays another side of his character in the duet (14) in which Pedrillo induces him to drink.[59] His senses are soon overcome, and he endeavours to outvie Pedrillo. It is of advantage to the situation that the personality of the singers required that even here Osmin must be considered the chief person; one only needs to hear the arrogance with which he delivers the principal subject in order to feel sure on whom the wine will take strongest effect,[60] and even when the rapidly concluded *entente cordiale* is expressed in unison, Osmin's low-pitched octaves keep the upper hand. But here, too, Mozart keeps within bounds, and never goes beyond a joke; Osmin's drunken sleep is excluded from his representation. Osmin's character is least strongly characterised in the terzet (7), of which Mozart writes to his father as follows (September 26, 1781):—

Now for the terzet which concludes the first act. Pedrillo has represented his master as an architect, which affords him an opportunity of meeting his Constanze in the garden. The Pasha has taken him into his service; and Osmin, as overseer, and knowing nothing of this, is insolent to him as a stranger, being himself an unmannerly churl and the arch-enemy of all strangers, and refuses to allow him to enter the garden. The first movement is short, and as the words allowed of it I

---

[59] Mozart's expression, in his letter to his father (September 26, 1781), "The drinking duet, which consists entirely of my Turkish tattoo (Zapfenstreich)," leads to the conclusion that he has here made use of an earlier composition, with which I am not acquainted. The Turkish music, in conjunction with trumpets (no drums), is admirably suggestive of Osmin's excited, half-tipsy state.

[60] This motif was evidently composed just as Osmin sings it. Fischer's flexible and melodious voice made it doubly effective in contrast to the less voluble tenor, so characteristic of the insignificant Pedrillo. At the outset, an admirable effect is produced by the violins, strengthened by piccolo and ordinary flutes, which gently accentuate the melody detached from its simple but agitated accompaniment. There is something peculiarly seductive in this melodious rippling sound, of which there is another instance in the Moor's song in the "Zauberflöte."

have kept the three voices fairly well together; but then begins the major *pianissimo*, which must go very fast, and the conclusion will draw many tears, which is just what the conclusion of a first act should do; the more tears the better—but the shorter the better, so that the audience may not forget the applause.

We see from this that Mozart thought more in this instance of a vivid expression of the situation than of minute characterisation, and all the three characters are alike in their urging and scolding. The advisability, therefore, of keeping the three voices "fairly well" together, their imitative arrangement keeping up the impression of great excitement, is indicated by the situation, although, owing to the necessity for stricter attention to form, the individual characterisation is thereby limited.

Osmin's last appearance in the finale is very amusing. While all the other characters are expressing their gratitude in the favourite form of a round, Osmin tries in vain to keep in the same track; but the round sticks in his throat, and his angry spite will have vent; the hunting-song of the first act with the obbligato janizaries' music rushes once more past our ears. Although some elements borrowed from the conventional forms of the Italian bass buffo are discernible in the part of Osmin, yet Mozart has made use of them in such an entirely original manner that they are closely interwoven in his own creation. It is, however, the consistency of the individual characterisation which distinguishes the part of Osmin and raises it far above the ordinary buffo parts, causing it to afford a striking instance of Mozart's eminent talent for dramatic construction.

The part requires a performer such as Fischer, of whom Reichardt writes: "He is an excellent bass singer; his voice has the depth of a violoncello, and the height of an ordinary tenor; its compass is—

so that his deep notes are never harsh, nor his high ones shrill; his voice flows with ease and certainty, and is full of charm. In praise of his style I need only say that he is a worthy pupil of the great tenor Raaff, who was, and still is considered, the best tenor in all Europe. Fischer has a more flexible organ than perhaps any other bass singer, and his acting is as good in serious drama as in comic."

Such materials as this are calculated to bring forth good effects. Among them may be noted the original sense of climax which Mozart produces by repeating a passage an octave lower; this is done in the *Lied* and in both of Osmin's airs at the words "Ich hab' auch Verstand" (3), and "Denn nun hab ich vor euch Ruh!" (19). The same effect occurs in the beautiful song "Non sò d' onde viene," composed also for Fischer; an expressive and sustained passage is repeated an octave lower, and the effect is very beautiful.

In order to give an adequate idea of Fischer's powers, the two serious songs composed for him by Mozart must be considered along with this decidedly comic part. The above-mentioned, "Non sò d' onde viene" (512 K.), broad in conception and style, displays the whole compass and wealth of Fischer's organ in the most favourable light. The other, "Aspri rimorsi atroce" (432 K.), composed in 1783, is remarkable for the expression of a gloomy, agitated mood, not illumined by any ray of light.

An expressive recitative is followed by a single movement (allegro, F minor) in incessant agitation, the almost uninterrupted triplets of the stringed instruments giving it the character of trembling unrest. The voice part is very striking by reason of its decided rhythm and frequent dissonant intervals; but it is mostly declamatory, and there is no appearance of a cantilene proper; the wind instruments give effect to the strong accents. The whole song pursues its rapid course like a gloomy nocturne, and dies away at last in a dull moan. This song is distinguished among all that Mozart has written by its uninterrupted expression of gloomy passion, and it would be almost inconceivable that he intended it for concert singing, did we not know that Fischer was to sing it : he was unsurpassed in every species of delivery.

The parts of Blondchen and Pedrillo are not by any

means so important in their characterisation as those of
the principal personages, neither have they much influence
on the development of the plot. Blondchen, besides her
share in the duet with Osmin, has two songs, of which the
first (8) is in no way remarkable, written evidently for a
seconda donna. The only point to be noted is a passage
going up to—

which gives proof of Mdlle. Teyber's vocal powers.[61] The
second song (12) is far fresher and more original, and
expresses heartfelt joy in so lively and charming a manner,
without ever overstepping the province of a good-humoured
soubrette, that the hearer is involuntarily beguiled into the
same cheerful frame of mind. A German element is unmistakably present (we are reminded of the " Zauberflöte "), and
we may note the first appearance of those naïve girl-parts
common to German opera.[62]

Mozart has given to Pedrillo's song (15) somewhat of a
military tone, suggested perhaps by the opening words
" Frisch zum Kampfe ! " and although his servile nature
is indicated here and there in the accompaniment, the
effect of the whole is too forcible and brilliant for the
character.[63] On the other hand, the romanze (18) which he
sings in the third act to the guitar is a jewel of delicate
characterisation. Not, however, with any reference to
Pedrillo himself, for he sings the song, not from personal
impulse, but as something he has heard and learnt ; but the
strange effects of harmony and rhythm, the mixture of bold

---

[61] In its first design this air was considerably longer; the second part began
at p. iii, bar 9, instead of p. 109, bar 19 ; it was in D major, instead of A
major, and led back into the first subject, bringing the whole to a conclusion
after twenty-nine interpolated bars.

[62] The instrumentation of this air; full, and the orchestral parts carefully
worked out; the accompaniment at the words " ohne Aufschub will ich eilen"
is unusually charming and animated. It also has been shortened by Mozart.

[63] Arnold (Mozart's Geist, p. 375) interprets the words as though Pedrillo
was trying to assume a courage which he did not possess.

knightly impulse with timid dismay, is so fantastic, so unreal, that we seem to be ourselves in Moorish lands, and are readily persuaded that we are listening to genuine Moorish music. But we are listening, in fact, to no music but Mozart's, whose own mind evolved the music which the situation demanded, without any previous philological study of Moorish national melodies. The two choruses of janizaries (so Mozart calls them in the score[64]) are not only characterised by the Turkish airs they embody, but by original harmonies and rhythm which give them a foreign and national character, without any special regard as to whether it is actually Turkish or not.[65]

We have already had occasion to remark how the ensemble movements proceed naturally from the exigencies of the situation, and are therefore essential to the musical characterisation of the work. This is especially true of the quartet (16), which forms the conclusion of the second act. Belmont and Constanze meet for the first time in the Pasha's garden, where are also Blondchen and Pedrillo. The meeting of the lovers is the more significant, since it is in anticipation of their approaching flight. An unusually elevated tone of sentiment is therefore common to them all; but the particular circumstances produce many different shades of feeling, and each character has its own distinct peculiarities. It is the task of the composer to combine this multifariousness into an artistic whole. The scenic accessories come very happily to his aid. The two pairs of lovers wander about the garden in close converse, so that they are heard sometimes apart, sometimes one after the other, sometimes together, according to the requirements of the situation and of the musical grouping. The beginning is a simple matter. Constanze and Belmont ex-

---

[64] He writes to his father of the first (September 26, 1781): "The janizary chorus is all that can be desired, short and merry, and very well suited for the Viennese public."

[65] Ulibicheff, who makes some striking observations on this chorus, notices its many points of resemblance (such as the alternation of relative major and minor keys) to Russian national melodies, with which Mozart may have become acquainted at Prince Gallitzin's (II., p. 375).

press their feelings in a short duet-like movement, full of heart, such as Mozart has made proper to lovers. When they turn aside Pedrillo and Blondchen advance, deep in consultation on the flight, so that the music assumes a lighter and more cheerful tone. But their thoughts are also occupied with the approaching happy turn in their fortunes, and when Belmont and Constance draw near, they all spontaneously join in the expression of joyful emotion. Small touches betray the master. The consultation between Pedrillo and Blondchen is in A major, and closes with an easy phrase on the words : " Wär' der Augenblick schon da !" (" O, that the moment had come !"), very expressive of the girl's character. The orchestra at once takes up this phrase with great emphasis, produced both by the sudden change to the key of D major and by the forcible unison of the instruments, as if they were exclaiming, "It has come!" and then leads back simply and expressively to the leading motif, which now for the first time asserts its full significance :—

wär der Au-genblick schon da!

But now the tone grows troubled. Belmont cannot repress a feeling of jealousy, and, embarrassed and confused, he seeks to express his doubts to Constanze, who does not understand him. Pedrillo follows in the same direction to Blondchen, who is far more ready in apprehending his meaning. The oboe gives charming expression to the feelings which the jealous lovers scarcely dare to clothe in words. Then Belmont and Constanze came forward again. The two men speak together, each after his manner— Belmont noble and open, Pedrillo with chattering haste. Constanze bursts into tears, Blondchen answers Pedrillo with a box on the ears ; the women lament together, and the men are aware that they have gone too far. After the lively expression of these contrasting emotions in rapid alternation, the lovers emerge from the confusion, explain themselves as to their true feelings, and so prepare for the reconciliation. The short ensemble movement in which Mozart consummates this *dénouement* (andante 6-8) is one of those passages of which a friend used to say that "der liebe Gott" himself could not have done it better; the purest beauty and a truly holy expression of satisfaction penetrates the simple and unpretending phrase. The magic of such conceptions cannot be rendered in words, nor can it be satisfactorily indicated by what actual means the effect is attained, and yet it is always of interest to see the master in his workshop.

It is easy to see in this case that the key selected (A major) combines with the rhythm and the harmonic treatment to produce the wished-for effect. It gives the voices a pitch allowing of the clearest and most melodious tones, heightened in their effect by the deeper pitch of the accompanying stringed instruments, and it also, although in fact the nearest key to the principal one, produces an impression of surprise as great as though it were a more distant one. This is due to what precedes the adoption of the A major key. The first movement in D major is followed by one in G minor, which leads to E flat major, B minor, F major; D minor is just touched, but only to pass again through C minor and B flat major into G minor, with a rapid transition into E major. After this restless change of key, the passage into A major has a wonderfully tranquillising effect, and the adherence to the key throughout the movement gives it a peculiar charm. But the reconciliation has not yet taken place; the lovers sue for pardon, but the two women allow them first to feel their injustice, and here Blondchen assumes the lead by virtue of her fluent tongue, while the men supplicate more and more earnestly, until at last peace is concluded. This movement is a model of dramatic characterisation. An excellent effect is produced by Blondchen's singing throughout in triplets (12-8 against 4-4), in contrast to the calm flowing melodies for the other voices. The movement only acquires its full significance by contrast with what has preceded it.

II.

R

When pardon has been granted, every trace of past sorrow is obliterated by the feeling of complete satisfaction. After so much mental strain a complete relaxation is necessary from a musical point of view. The last movement is therefore very simple, although appropriately brilliant and fiery. It seldom departs from the principal key, and is frequently in canon form; very light passages for the voices, rapid instrumentation, and an unusually effective *crescendo* at the close, give it an impulsive and quickening effect. This was the first really dramatic ensemble movement in a German opera, and in it we find concentrated all Mozart's services to the German opera—a full and free employment of all the means afforded by song and orchestra to give musical expression to emotion, without subservience to any more binding forms than those laws which are founded on the nature of music.

The masterly treatment of the orchestra in the " Entführung has been repeatedly pointed out, and there is no need to repeat that Mozart turned to account all the advantages offered to him by the Vienna orchestra. In comparison with " Idomeneo " the instrumentation is not exactly scantier, but it is clearer and simpler; the tendency to employ the different instruments independently, to bring forward subordinate subjects, &c., is held in check, and the details are more lightly treated on account of stage effects. " I think I may venture to lay down," says Weber, " that in the ' Entführung ' Mozart's *artist experience* came to maturity, and that his *experience of the world* alone was to lead him to further efforts. The world might look for several operas from him like ' Figaro ' and ' Don Juan,' but with the best will possible he could only write one ' Entführung.' I seem to perceive in it what the happy years of youth are to every man; their bloom never returns, and the extirpation of their defects carries with it some charms which can never be recovered."[66]

---

[66] C. M. von Weber, Lebensbild, III., p. 191. Cf. A. Wendt, Leipzig Kunstbl., 1817, p. 189. (Heinse, Reise- und Lebensskizzen, I., p. 298.)

CHAPTER XXVI.

COURTSHIP.

IT has often been pointed out that Mozart wrote the "Entführung" as an accepted lover; and many analogies have been drawn between his own love affairs and those represented in the opera, with the view of accounting for the depth and truth of his expression of the tenderest of passions. It is true that Mozart could not have rendered love so truly without having felt it in its full intensity. But if we stop to realise the difficulties and vexations with which Mozart had to struggle as a lover, we shall rather wonder that he could compose at all under such circumstances, and the "Entführung" becomes a striking proof that creative genius sets the artist free from the pressure of life, and raises him into the region of beauty in which true art is begotten.

We have already seen the relief it was to Mozart, when obliged to quit the house of the Archbishop, to find a lodging with Madame Weber, his old Mannheim friend. After Aloysia's marriage to the actor Lange, the mother lived in somewhat reduced circumstances with her other three daughters, and was glad to let her spare rooms; it was a comfort to Mozart to be relieved by friendly hands of the little housekeeping cares which he was ill-fitted to attend to himself. But his father was averse to the arrangement; he feared that the Webers would make a tool of him, as they had, in his opinion, in Mannheim. He was not at all satisfied with Wolfgang's reassurances on the subject, and pressed him to take another lodging; Wolfgang declared himself quite willing if he could find one equally comfortable. As this did not seem likely, and a report reached Salzburg that Mozart was engaged to be married to one of Madame Weber's daughters, his father insisted on compliance with his desire. Wolfgang answered (July 25, 1781) :—

I repeat that I have long wished to take another lodging, if only to stop people's chatter; and it annoys me to have to do it for the sake of

R 2

absurd gossip, in which there is not a word of truth. I should like to know what pleasure it can be to certain people to spread such baseless reports. Because I am living with the family I must, forsooth, marry the daughter! There is no talk of affection—they jump over all that; I simply go to the house, and then get married. If ever in my life I was far from thinking of marriage, it is at this moment. I wish for nothing less than a rich wife; and even if I could make a good marriage now I must perforce wait, for I have other things in my head. God has not given me my talent that I might cripple it with a wife, and waste my prime in inactivity. Shall I embitter my life at its very opening? I have nothing to say against matrimony, but for me at present it would be an unmitigated evil. Well, if there is no other way, false as it all is, I must avoid even the appearance of it, although the appearance has no foundation except my lodging in the house. No one who does not live in the house can imagine how very little intercourse I have with them; for the children seldom go out—never except to the play—and I cannot accompany them because I am seldom at home at that hour. We have been on the Prater once or twice, but the mother was with us; being in the house I could not avoid going, and I heard no such foolish gossip then. I must tell you, too, that I paid only *my own* share;[1] and the mother, having become aware of the gossip from others as well as from myself, objects to our going anywhere together again, and has herself advised me to move my quarters to avoid further annoyance, for she says she would not willingly injure me, however innocently. This is my only reason for leaving, and this is no valid reason; but people's mouths must be stopped. It would not be difficult to find a better room, but very difficult to meet with such kind and obliging people. I will not say that I am uncivil and never speak to the young lady to whom report has wedded me, but I am not in love with her; I chat and joke with her when I have time—that is in the evenings, when I sup at home; in the morning I write in my own room, and in the afternoon I am nearly always out—and so that is really all about it. If I am to marry all the girls I have made fun with, I shall have at least a hundred wives. Now farewell, my dear father, and trust your son, who has really the best intentions towards all honest people! Trust him, and believe him sooner than certain people who have nothing better to do than to calumniate honest folk.

An unfinished allegro to a clavier sonata (400 K.) remains as a curious and amusing instance of the influence exerted on a composer by his immediate surroundings. After a very

---

[1] K. R[isbeck] says (Briefe über Deutschland, I., p. 193) it was considered proper in Vienna to treat the ladies of the party, even when they were in no way related to their escort. Mozart must have been thinking of his former liberality to the Webers, so severely blamed by his father (Vol. I., p. 418).

cheerful first part, a plaintive tone is struck in the second, and a very strongly accentuated musical dialogue occurs. The names of the two sisters Weber are written against the characterising phrases of the music :—

The Messmer family had offered Mozart apartments in their house in the suburbs, but he could not make up his mind to accept the offer: "The house is not what it was," he writes to his sister (December 15, 1781). Messmer had staying with him at the time Vinc. Righini (1756-1812), formerly an opera-buffa singer and then a composer; they were on very intimate terms, and Madame Messmer was especially friendly to Righini. The latter, as Mozart informs his father in answer to his inquiries, makes a great deal of money by giving lessons, and his cantata (probably "Il Natale d' Apollo") had been given twice during Lent with great success. " He writes *prettily ;* is not superficial, but a great thief. He gives back his stolen goods so unblushingly and in such overflowing abundance that people can hardly digest them " (August 29, 1781).[2]

Another musical family would have been glad to receive him as an inmate, and his father appears to have been not unwilling that he should form a closer connection in this case. Wolfgang had been introduced to Herr Aurnhammer, whose "fat lady-daughter" Josephine was considered one of the first clavier-players of the day. They received him kindly, and often invited him, as he informs his father (June 27, 1781) : "I dine almost daily with Herr Aurnhammer; the young lady is a horror—but she plays divinely ; she seems

---

[2] Zelter says that Righini's position in Berlin was almost identical with that of Salieri in Vienna; " he may have been of a rather more lively disposition, but he was of about the same height and breadth " (Briefw. m. Goethe, II., p. 29). Cf. A. M. Z., XVI., p. 875.

to lose her really refined taste in singing, however, and drags everything."[8]

It would have been convenient to them that Mozart should be in their immediate neighbourhood. But he was far from satisfied with the quarters which they offered him ; it was a room "for rats and mice, but not for human beings. The stairs need a lantern to light them at noonday; and the room might be called a *cell*. The wife herself called the house a rat's nest—in fact it was really dreadful." Nor did he feel any inclination for closer intercourse with this family, whose motives in wishing for him he believed that he saw through. Seeing that his father had set his mind upon his going, he felt constrained to set the two sides of the question before nim. The description which follows is somewhat "schlimm" certainly, but too characteristic of the writer to be omitted :—

He is the best-natured man in the world; too much so, indeed, for his wife—a stupid, silly chatterer—has quite the upper hand, so that when she speaks he has not a word to say. Whenever we go for a walk together he begs me not to mention in his wife's presence that we took a fiacre or drank some beer. Now I cannot possibly have confidence in such a man. He is a good fellow and my very good friend, and I can dine with him when I please, but I am not used to be paid for *my civilities;* indeed a dinner would scarcely be fitting payment, but people like these think so much of what they do. I will not attempt to describe the mother to you; one has enough to do at table to refrain from laughing at her. You know Frau Adlgasser ? This creature is worse, for she is ill-natured as well as stupid. As for the daughter, if a painter wanted a model for the evil one he might have recourse to her face. She is as fat as a peasant-girl, and once seeing her is enough to make one wretched for the whole day. *Pfui Teufel!*

I wrote to you how she plays the clavier, and why she begged me to assist her.[4] She is not content that I should pass two hours every day

---

[8] She used to give a concert every year "as a proof of her existence and industry," according to the notice for 1799 (A. M. Z., I., p. 523); "the latter quality is all that she can now truthfully boast of" (Cf. A. M. Z., VI., p. 471; VII., p. 469. Reichardt, Mus. Ztg., I., p. 128). As late as 1813 she ("who had once reigned supreme as a pianoforte-player in Vienna") appeared in public, and was pronounced "an accomplished and correct player, but cold and old-fashioned" (A. M. Z., XV., p. 300).

[4] She wished to perfect herself in playing for some years longer, and then go to Paris and "make her fortune." Cramer's Magazin der Musik says (1787, II., p. 1274), "Madame Aurnhammer is an excellent teacher of the piano, on

with her, she would like me to spend the whole day there, and then she makes herself agreeable! or rather, worse than that, she is seriously in love with me. I thought it was a joke, but I know it for certain now. When I first observed it (for she took liberties, reproaching me for coming later than usual, or not staying long enough, and other such things) I felt constrained to tell her the truth politely, for fear she should make a fool of herself. But it was of no use, she became more deeply in love. Then I tried being very polite until she began her non-sense, when I turned cross. Then she took me by the hand and said, "Dear Mozart, do not be so angry, and you may say what you like, I am so fond of you." It was the talk of the whole town that we were going to be married, and people wondered at my choice. She told me that when anything of the kind was said to her, she laughed at it; but I know from a certain person that she acknowledged it, with the addition that we should set out on our travels together as soon as we were married. That made me really angry. I gave her my true opinion on the subject, and reproached her with abusing my kindness. I have left off going there every day, and only go every other day, so as to break it off by degrees. She is an infatuated fool. Before she knew me, she said when she heard me at the theatre, "He is coming to me to-morrow, and I shall play him his variations in the same style." For this very reason I did not go. It was a conceited speech, and an untrue one, for I had had no intention of going there the following day.

All this did not prevent Mozart from assisting Fräulein Aurnhammer in his usual amiable manner. At a concert at Aurnhammer's (November 24, 1781) he played the Concerto a due (365 K.) with her, and a sonata which was composed expressly, and "went remarkably well" (381 K.).

A few months later he played a duet with her at one of his own concerts (May 25, 1782), and postponed a journey to Salzburg because he had promised to play at her concert in the theatre (October 26, 1782). He also dedicated to her the sonatas for piano and violin which appeared in 1781 (376-380 K.).

In September he actually found a new lodging, but he was far from comfortable there; "it was like travelling in a post-chaise instead of one's own carriage." He had made

---

which she gives lessons; I have not heard her play for long. It is she who superintended the engraving by Herr Artaria of many of Mozart's sonatas and varied airs." She attempted variations herself, which she used to play at her concerts and to have printed (Mus. Corresp., 1791, p. 362; 1792, p. 195). She had arrived at Opus 63 in 1799 (A. M. Z., II., p. 90).

the sacrifice for his father's sake, and he now took occasion to beg the latter not to listen to gossip, but to believe that he meant "to remain the same honest fellow as ever" (September 5, 1781). But the discomfort of his domestic circumstances in the midst of incessant work only increased his desire to set up an establishment of his own. The gossip of the town and his father's exhortations had produced a contrary effect to that intended, and his liking for Constanze Weber grew more decided day by day. He felt persuaded that she would make him happy, and, since she returned his affection, they became betrothed lovers. He could not disguise from himself that his father would certainly disapprove of this step, and he laid before him with great candour all that had led to it. After setting forth his prospects of an assured position, and the steps which he had taken towards obtaining it, he continues (December 15, 1781) :—

My desire is to have something certain to fall back upon, and then one can live very well on chance here—and to get married. Nature speaks as loud in me as in any other, perhaps louder than in a great heavy blockhead. I have no inclination to live like most young men of the present day. In the first place I have too much love for religion, and in the second too much love for my neighbour, and too much good feeling to lead astray an innocent girl. I can take my oath I have never done so. But I know that this reason, strong as it is, is not elevated enough. But my temperament, which is inclined for a quiet domestic life —my want of habit of attending to my clothing, washing, and other such things—make a wife indispensable to me. I am quite persuaded that I could live better on the same income with a wife than as I am now. And how many unnecessary expenses would be done away with ! True, others would arise ; but one knows them and can calculate on them—in fact, one leads a regular life. An unmarried man only half lives, in my opinion. That is my opinion—I cannot help it ; I have reflected and considered enough, and have quite made up my mind. But who, you will ask, is the object of my love ? Do not be horrified, I beg. What ! not a Weber ! Yes, a Weber ; not Josepha, nor Sophia, but Constanze, the middle one. I have never seen such dissimilarity of mind in any family as in this. The eldest, Josepha, is lazy and cross ; Aloysia Lange is a false, unprincipled woman and a coquette ; the youngest, Sophie, is too young to be anything yet but the good thoughtless creature she is. God keep her from temptation ! But the middle one, my dear good Constanze, is the martyr of the family, and on that very account, perhaps, the best-natured, the cleverest—in a word, the best of them all. She looks after everything in the house, and yet can never do right. She is not ugly, but she is far from being beautiful. Her whole beauty consists in her dark eyes and good figure. She is not intellectual, but has common sense enough to fulfil her duties as a wife and mother. She is not inclined to extravagance, that is quite untrue; on the contrary, she is always badly dressed, for the little her mother can do is done for the two others, never for her. True, she likes to be neat and clean, but not smart; and almost all that a woman needs she can make for herself; she understands housekeeping, has the best heart in the world—she loves me and I love her—tell me if I could wish for a better wife? I must tell you that when I wrote before love was not there, but was born of her tender care and attention when I was living in the house. My earnest wish now is to get something settled to do (of which, God be praised, I have great hope), and I shall then hasten to beg your permission to rescue my poor darling, and make her and myself—indeed, I may say, all of us—happy, for does not my being happy render you so?

This confirmation of the news which had already reached him from other quarters was a heavy blow to L. Mozart. The perspective of " dying on a sack of straw in a room full of starving brats " which he had once before held out to his son (Vol. I., p. 426) opened itself to him anew; marriage without a certain and sufficient income was, in his opinion, and knowing his son as he did, the first step to certain ruin. And then the Weber family! The description which Wolfgang gave of them was not calculated to inspire confidence; if he had been so completely deceived in Aloysia, who could answer for his better judgment with respect to Constanze? But his father knew more than he had learnt from Wolfgang; he knew that the latter had given a written promise of marriage, and, from all the communications he received, he could not but believe that both mother and daughter had been playing upon the young man's inexperience and sense of honour to entice him into their net. L. Mozart sought by every means in his power to influence his son; he demanded information as to the written agreement, that he might be satisfied that it did not exist, and that Wolfgang was bound only by his word. But Wolfgang showed himself firmer and more independent at this juncture than ever before; he had made up his mind, and it was not to be shaken.

He did not hesitate to explain the circumstances of the

marriage contract (December 22, 1781). After the death of their father, the Weber children had been placed under the guardianship of Johann Thorwarth, court manager and inspector of the theatrical wardrobe, a man of considerable influence in matters theatrical, and well thought of by Count Rosenberg and Baron Kienmayer—"a sworn enemy of the Italians."[5] This man had been prejudiced against Mozart by calumniators, who represented that he had no certain income, and that he did not mean honestly by Constanze; this so disturbed the mother that she did not rest until she had induced Mozart to request an interview with the guardian. The interview took place, but the guardian was so little satisfied that he insisted on all intercourse with Mozart being broken off unless he would agree to a written contract. Madame Weber declared that this could not be; that all the intercourse consisted in Mozart's coming daily to their house, and that she could not possibly put a stop to it, seeing that she was under much obligation to him as a friend, and that she placed every confidence in his truth and honour; if the guardian thought such a step necessary, he must undertake it himself. Hereupon Thorwarth prohibited all intercourse unless Mozart would give a written agreement. He must make his choice. Having no intention of giving up Constanze or affording ground for suspicion to her friends, he signed an agreement by virtue of which he bound himself to espouse Mdlle. Constanze Weber within three years, or "in case of such an impossibility as his changing his mind," he was to pay her three hundred florins a year. He assured his father that there was no sort of risk in this, as he was finally resolved never to forsake her; but if such an unheard-of event were to occur, he would think himself easily bought off with three hundred florins; besides that his Constanze would, he knew, be far too proud to accept a price. "And what did the devoted girl do?" he continues; "as soon as the guardian had gone, she took the agreement from her mother, tore it up, and said: 'Dear Mozart, I need no written assurance

---

[5] Da Ponte, Mem., II., p. 104.

from you; I can believe your simple word!'" It was thought best by them all to keep this transaction secret; but it gradually oozed out, until all Vienna knew of it. It might be wrong, and this part of the affair was blameable—thus much he acknowledged to his father; but neither the guardian nor the mother deserved to be branded as misleaders of youthful innocence; it was a falsehood that they had made him free of the house and then bound him in spite of himself—it was quite the contrary, and he would have known better than to give in to such conduct.

His indignation was raised to the highest pitch when he heard from his father that the most disgraceful falsehoods as to his dealings with Constanze had reached Salzburg by way of Munich, and were attributable to "that scoundrel" Winter, who had always hated him on Vogler's account.[6] Winter had been staying in Vienna with the bassoonist Reiner, and Mozart had sought him out as an old acquaintance. It was all the more infamous, since this very Winter, who "deserved the name neither of a man nor a human being," and to whose "infamous lies" Mozart would not condescend to oppose "infamous truths," had once said to him: "You will be foolish to marry; you can earn enough—why should you not keep a mistress? What prevents you? Is it your d——d religion?" (December 22, 1781). But against such calumnies he was powerless. "My maxim is," he says (January 9, 1782), "that what does not concern me is not worth the trouble of talking about; I am ashamed to defend myself from false accusations, for I always think that the truth is sure to come to light." He therefore refused to stir in the matter, and left free course to all the falsehood and misrepresentation.

---

[6] Cf. I., p. 389. Winter was avowedly hostile to Mozart (Biedenfeld, Kom. Oper, p. 86); he used to reproach him with stealing from Handel (A. M. Z., XXVIII., p. 468), with forcing up soprano voices (Biedenfeld, Kom. Oper, p. 212); and his scorn at piano-playing opera composers (A. M. Z., XXVIII., p. 467) was especially directed against Mozart. It is generally acknowledged that Winter was not the simple, unsophisticated being that he appeared (cf. Biedenfeld, p. 212), and I have been assured by those who knew him well that he was quite capable of spiteful intrigue.

L. Mozart was naturally not much reassured by this
explanation. He called his son's attention to Madame
Weber's failings, which rendered a good education of her
daughters very unlikely, and Wolfgang could not deny (April
10, 1782) that "she is fond of drink, and takes more than a
woman should. But I have never seen her intoxicated; I
can quite deny that. The children drink nothing but water."
His father further pointed out that she would certainly be a
burden on him after his marriage, and that she made no
secret of her intentions in this respect. Wolfgang could
not but perceive for himself that the mother was seeking her
own advantage in the marriage of her daughter (January 30,
1782), "but she will find herself very much mistaken. She
wished us (when we were married) to lodge with her—but
that will come to nothing, for I would never agree to it, and
Constanze still less. *Au contraire*, she intends to see very
little of her mother, and I shall do my utmost to prevent it
—we know her." But Wolfgang was deeply wounded at his
father's depreciation of Constanze herself (January 30,1782):—

Only one thing more (and without saying it I could not sleep quietly)
—do not ascribe such motives to my dear Constanze; believe me, I
could not love her as I do if she deserved your censure. My dear, good
father, I only wish that we may soon meet; for that you will love her,
as you love all true hearts, I know for certain.

He remained proof against all his father's remonstrances
(January 9, 1782) :—

I cannot be happy without my beloved Constanze, and I should be
only half happy without your consent; make me quite happy then, my
dearest, best of fathers!

He confided to his sister (whom he had befriended in her
own need) what he and Constanze had to suffer from her
mother's temper. He used to work until nine o'clock in the
evening, he writes (February 13, 1782):—

And then I go to my beloved Constanze; but our pleasure in being
together is often embittered by her mother's angry tongue, as I shall
explain to my father in my next letter, and make it the ground of my
wish to liberate and rescue her as soon as possible. I go home at half-
past ten or eleven; it depends upon her mother's powers of holding out,
or mine of resisting.

Constanze, at Wolfgang's instigation, sought to gain his sister's affection by many little acts of attention; she sent her caps made by herself after the latest Vienna fashion, and on another occasion a little cross of no great value, but of a kind very much worn in Vienna; and again, a heart with an arrow that Wolfgang thought particularly appropriate to his sister (March 23, 1782). She "took courage at last" in a letter (April 20, 1782), "to petition for her friendship as sister of her very worthy brother;" she felt that " she half deserved it already, and would try to deserve it altogether," as well as to gain the good opinion of the father of them both. Both the lovers were delighted at the favourable reception of these overtures, although the father's views were not thereby anywise altered. He was especially against any idea of marriage before Wolfgang had some secure means of livelihood, and in spite of many attempts and tedious negotiations there did not seem much likelihood of this at present. " If I could only have it in writing from 'der liebe Gott,'" he writes to his father (January 23, 1782), "that I should continue in good health and never be ill, oh, would I not marry my dear, faithful sweetheart this very day!" His three pupils brought him eighteen ducats a month; if he could only get one more it would make 102 florins 24 kreutzers, on which he and his wife could maintain themselves "quietly and plainly, as we wish to live." In case of sickness, indeed, his income would cease altogether; but he could write an opera once a year, give a concert, publish some compositions, or raise subscriptions for them; accidents could not always be taken into account. " But," he concludes, "if we cannot succeed we must just fail, and I would rather we did so together than wait any longer. I cannot be worse off—things must improve with me. My reasons for not waiting any longer are not so much on my own account, as on hers. I must release her as soon as possible." The father did not grant the urgent necessity, and seeing in Wolfgang's calculations on the possibilities of an uncertain future a sure proof that he had not yet learnt what the foundation of a well-ordered household should be, he persisted in his refusal to consent to an immediate marriage.

Difficult as Mozart's position was rendered by the displeasure   his father and the ill-temper of Frau Weber, his beloved Constanze herself did not always improve matters; the violence of her feelings sometimes put his constancy to the trial, and added to his perplexities. The lovers' quarrels soon blew over, but Mozart's position became daily more insupportable as his affairs became known and talked of. Even the Emperor, who felt a warm interest in the family affairs of the artists who had access to him,[7] had expressed himself graciously as to Mozart's marriage when the latter played before him with Clementi; his condescension raised hopes which were not destined to be fulfilled.

When the success of his opera had directed public attention towards him, the curiosity as to his relations with Constanze became still more general. "What are we to do?" he writes mournfully to his father (July 27, 1782). "Most people believe that we are married already: the mother is wild about it, and the poor girl and myself are tormented to death." The earnest tone of mind in which he passed through this time of trial is illustrated in a later letter to his father (August 17, 1782), where he says that he has long since heard mass and confessed with Constanze, "and I found that I never prayed so heartily or confessed and communicated so devoutly as by her side. She felt the same, and it would really seem that we are made for each other, and that God, who orders all things, has ordained our union also, and will not forsake us."

At this juncture a distinguished musical patroness espoused the cause of the lovers. The Baroness von Waldstädten, famous as a clavier-player as early as the year 1766,[8] was one of the ladies who had taken Mozart under their protection from his first arrival, and interesting herself, womanlike, as much in his affairs of the heart as in his musical performances, she sought by every means in her power to bring his relations with Constanze to a happy con-

---

[7] A striking instance is Salieri's account of how Joseph II. assisted him to marry (Mosel, Salieri, p. 57).

Hiller, Wochentl. Nachr., I., p. 100.

clusion. In order to withdraw Constanze from the tyranny of her mother, and to facilitate Wolfgang's intercourse with his betrothed, she took the latter more than once for a considerable time into her own house in the Leopold Strasse. There were, indeed, reasons which rendered this intimacy undesirable. The Baroness had led an unhappy life, and sought to indemnify herself for it by indulgence in the frivolous habits then only too frequent among the higher ranks of society; her reputation was not of the best. Mozart knew this, as all Vienna knew it; he had reason to dread the influence of such a friendship for Constanze, but he was convinced that the Baroness meant well by them both, and he felt that he had no resource but to accept her help, and to be very grateful for it. But Constanze's mother had at least some show of right in forbidding her daughter to continue in communication with the Baroness, and, fearful lest she should be taken altogether out of her power, she endeavoured to force her to return home. An undated letter, addressed in great tribulation to the Baroness, gives us full insight into Mozart's trying circumstances :—

Most honoured Baroness,—I received my music by the hands of Madame Weber's maid, and was obliged to give a written receipt for it. The servant confided to me what, if true, is a lasting disgrace to the whole family; I can only believe it from my knowledge of Madame Weber's character, and it afflicts me greatly. Sophie had come out weeping, and when her maid asked her the cause of her tears, she said: " Tell Mozart in secret that Constanze had better return home, for my mother insists upon sending the police for her." But surely the police would not dare thus to enter any house. Perhaps it is only a ruse to get her home again. If this threat is really fulfilled, I see nothing for it but to marry my Constanze early to-morrow, or, if it can be done, to-day; for I would not allow of this affront to my beloved, and it could not happen to my wife. Another thing: Thorwarth was appointed to his place to-day. I beg your ladyship to give me your kind advice, and to render us poor creatures all the assistance you can. I am always at home. In the greatest haste. Constanze knows nothing of all this. Has Herr von Thorwarth waited on your ladyship already? Is it necessary that we should both go to him after dinner to-day?

Under these circumstances Mozart was ready to espouse his Constanze without a moment's delay; he reiterates his entreaties for his father's consent (July 31, 1782):—

You will have received my last letter by this time, and I have no doubt that your next will bring your consent to our union. You can have nothing really to object to in it, and your letters show that you have not; for she is a good honest girl, and I am in a position to provide her with bread. We love each other and wish for each other, so there is no reason for delay.

But his father still withheld his consent. He was so deeply affected by the affair that he scarcely took proper interest in the success of the " Entführung," and Wolfgang complained of the coolness with which his father received his opera. The latter retorted that he was making himself detested in Vienna by his arrogant manners. Wolfgang answered (July 31, 1782):—

And so the whole world declares that my boasting and criticising have made enemies for me of all the professors of music and others. What world? Presumably the Salzburg world; for whoever was here would hear and see enough to the contrary: and that shall be my answer to the charge.

The Baroness Waldstädten had in the meantime (by what means we know not) smoothed away all difficulties, and the wedding was celebrated on August 4, before the arrival of the father's formal consent, for which they had waited two post-days. Wolfgang's conviction that the consent could not now be withheld was justified;[9] on the day after the wedding the longed-for letters from the father and sister arrived, and Wolfgang answered in his overflowing happiness (August 7, 1782):—

I kiss your hand, and thank you with all the tenderness which a son can feel for his father for your very kind consent and paternal blessing. My dear wife will write by the next post to beg our best of fathers for his blessing, and our beloved sister for the continuance of her valued friendship. There was no one present at the ceremony except the mother and the youngest sister, Herr von Thorwarth as guardian and supporter (Beistand) to us both, Herr Landrath von Cetto supporting the bride, and Gilowsky supporting me. When we were actually united

---

[9] L. Mozart writes to the Baroness (September 13, 1782): "I am heartily glad that his wife does not take after the Webers, as otherwise he would be miserable; your ladyship assures me that she is a deserving person, and that suffices me " (Hamburg. Litter. u. Krit. Blätter, 1856, No. 72, p. 563).

my wife and I both began to weep. Every one, including the officiating priest, was moved to tears by the sight of our happiness. Our wedding festivities consisted solely in a supper given us by the Baroness von Waldstädten, which was rather princely than baronial.[10] Now my dearest Constanze is rejoicing in the thought of a journey to Salzburg, and I wager—yes—I will wager that you will be happy in my happiness when you have learnt to know her, as I do, for the most upright, virtuous, and loving wife that ever made the happiness of a man.

The father considered it necessary to draw attention to the fact that he could no longer expect Wolfgang to assist in extricating him from the debts he had incurred on his son's behalf; on the other hand, Wolfgang must neither now nor at any future time reckon upon him for support; and he begged him to make his bride fully aware of this circumstance. Mozart answered (August 7, 1782):—

My dear Constanze—now, thank God, my own lawful wife—has long known my circumstances and all that I have to expect from you. But her friendship and her love for me were so great that she willingly sacrificed her whole future life to my destinies.

Such was Mozart's courtship, such was his "Entführung aus dem Auge Gottes," as he used jokingly to call his marriage, because the house in which Madame Weber lived on the Petersplatz was called "Zum Auge Gottes." Truly this time brought him none of the peaceful happiness which the certainty of mutual love bestows under more prosperous circumstances, but it afforded him abundant opportunity for the display of his freedom as an artist, and of his inflexible constancy to what he thought true and right. Unaffected by the vulgarity from the atmosphere of which he had resolved upon rescuing his Constanze, unchanged by the violence and hastiness of his beloved herself, unmoved by the hard and often unjust judgment of his father, he preserved both the firmness of his conviction and will, and the tender susceptibility and charm of his affectionate heart. The mental and moral development of every man depends in no small

---

[10] During the supper, according to Nissen, a "sixteen-part harmony" of his own composition was performed as a surprise to him. This must be a mistake, for even the great serenata (361 K.) is only in thirteen parts.

II.   S

degree upon whether his course of life has been smooth and his happiness easy of attainment, or whether he has obtained the conditions of his existence only after a long and severe struggle. We must not, therefore, turn aside our glance from the trials and troubles which have beset the lives of great artists and noble men; it was through adversity that they became what they were.

CHAPTER XXVII.

MARRIED LIFE.

THE newly married couple began their housekeeping upon an uncertain and barely sufficing income, and so it remained to the end. Limited means, sometimes even actual want, failed either to increase the carefulness or to damp the spirits of husband or wife.

Mozart's sincere and upright love for his wife has been clearly demonstrated already; it was the talk of Vienna. One day, soon after his marriage, as he and his wife were walking in the public gardens, they amused themselves by playing with her little pet dog. Constanze told Mozart to make believe to beat her, in order to see the indignation of the dog. As he was doing so, the Emperor came out of his summer-house and said, "What! only three weeks married, and come to blows already!" whereupon Mozart laughingly explained the joke. Later, in 1785, when there was much talk, even in the newspapers, of the unhappy relations between Aloysia Lange and her husband,[1] the Emperor met Constanze Mozart, and said, after some remark on the sad position of her sister: "What a difference it makes, to have a good husband!"[2] At about the same time the English tenor, Kelly, was introduced at a musical party to Mozart and his wife, "whom he loved passionately."[3] His affection betrays itself in many amiable

---

[1] Cf. Friedel, Briefe aus Wien (1784), p. 409.

[2] Mozart himself wrote this to his father, who communicates it to Marianne September 17, 1785).

[3] Kelly, Reminisc., I., p. 225.

traits, and most clearly in the letters addressed to his wife on his later journeys, to which she herself expressly appeals as proofs of his " rare affection and excessive tenderness for her."[4] An expression of Nissen's that Constanze cared "perhaps more for his talent than himself" might lead to a belief that his love was not returned in full measure ; but against this view we have the testimony of worthy Niemet- schek, who knew them both, and says: " Mozart was happy in his union with Constanze Weber. She made him a good, loving wife, who accommodated herself admirably to his ways, and gained his full confidence and a power over him which she often used to restrain him from rash actions. He loved her sincerely, confided all to her, even his faults, and she rewarded him with tenderness and faithful care. All Vienna knew of their mutual affection, and the widow can never think without emotion of her days of wedded life." Constanze had, as Mozart had written before their marriage, " not much intellect, but enough common sense to fulfil her duties as a wife and mother." It can, indeed, be gathered from contemporary letters and notices[5] that she had neither

---

[4] A. M. Z., I., p. 855.

[5] I cannot undertake to give anything like a comprehensive description of Mozart's wife, although I have received many communications from trust- worthy persons who have known her personally. Their knowledge is of her later years only, and their accounts are often inconsistent. This inconsistency arises from the conflict in the widow's mind between pride in the fame of the husband, of whose greatness she was fully aware only after his death, and a painful remembrance of the hardships of their married life. These hardships she was inclined to ascribe solely to his want of capacity for practical affairs, and an injured feeling was often mingled with her unbounded pride in Mozart's artistic achievements and her belief in his love for her. The peculiarities of her second husband, Nissen, a business man, painfully accurate and precise, tended no doubt to intensify the contrast. Nissen's was an honourable, although a commonplace nature, and he had earned Constanze's gratitude by his care for her in her widowed and destitute condition, and by placing her in a good worldly position as his wife ; so that it is not surprising that Mozart's memory should have passed into the background, with the exception of his musical fame, which Nissen could not rival. At any rate, we find Constanze con- tinually posing as the patient martyr, suffering from the thoughtlessness of a man of genius, who remained a child to the end of his days. This is unjust to Mozart, but it would be equally unjust to Constanze to make her mainly responsible for the family difficulties.

natural capacity nor what we call education enough to render her on an equality with Mozart, or to elevate him by her intellectual influence; nay, rather, she failed fully to appreciate or understand him. Like all the Weber family, she had musical talent, which had been cultivated up to a certain point. "She played the clavier and sang nicely."[6] At the Mozarteum, in Salzburg, there is the commencement of a "Sonata à deux Cembali," unfinished, with the superscription "Per la Signora Constanza Weber—ah!" A sonata for pianoforte and violin, in C major, which only wants the concluding bars of the last movement (403 K.), belonging to the year 1782, is inscribed "Sonate Première, par moi, W. A. Mozart, pour ma tres chère épouse." In a letter to Härtel (February 25, 1799), the widow mentions a march for the piano which her husband had composed for her. Although her voice was not so fine as those of her sisters Aloysia and Josepha, she sang very well, especially by sight, so that Mozart used to try his compositions with her. Solfeggi by Mozart are preserved, with the inscription—"Per la mia cara Constanze," or "Per la mia cara consorte" (393 K.), some of them exercises of a few bars' length, others elaborate passages in varied tempo and style, which give abundant practice for execution and delivery. There is a song also— "In te spero o sposo amato," (Metastasio, "Demofoonte"), mentioned by the widow in a letter to Härtel (February 25, 1799), as composed "per la cara mia consorte," which implies a compass and volubility reminding us of her sister Aloysia. It was natural, therefore, that Constanze should take the soprano parts in any private performances among their friends, and we know that she once sang the soprano soli of the Mass in C minor (427 K.) at Salzburg, which require a first-rate singer.

We must also give her credit for more than ordinary musical taste and cultivation, from her partiality for fugues, of which Mozart writes to his sister (April 20, 1782), when he sent her a prelude and fugue (394 K.), which he had composed for her:—

---

[6] Jahrb. d. Tonkunst. (1796), p. 43.

The cause of this fugue coming into the world is in reality my dear Constanze. Baron van Swieten, to whom I go every Sunday, allowed me to take home all the works of Handel and Sebastian Bach, after I had played them to him. When Constanze heard the fugues, she quite fell in love with them; she cares for nothing but fugues now, especially those of Handel and Bach. Having often heard me play fugues out of my head, she asked me if I had never written any down? and when I said no, she scolded me roundly for not writing the most artistic and beautiful things in music; she would not leave me any peace until I had written down a fugue, and so it came to pass.

Mozart would hardly have been happy with a wife who possessed neither taste nor understanding for music. But neither would his creative power have been strengthened by an intellectually excitable and exciting wife; it was far more beneficial for him to find womanly sympathy in his household affairs, and to be soothed rather than urged to greater efforts. She patiently bore his abstraction when his mind was intent upon musical ideas, and gave in to many little whims, which in Mozart seldom proceeded from ill-temper. He was never disturbed by the conversation and noise going on around him when he was writing down his compositions; it was rather agreeable to him to have his attention so far occupied in other directions that his excessive productivity was held, as it were, in check. His wife would sit by him and tell him stories and nursery tales, over which he would laugh heartily, working all the time; the more ludicrous they were the better he was pleased.[7] She was always ready to cut up his meat for him at table, an operation which he tried to avoid, lest in his abstraction he should do himself an injury[8]—an oddity which is only mentioned as a proof how much of a child Mozart always remained in many of the ways of life.

He was severely tried by his wife's delicacy; her health was undermined by frequent and often dangerous confinements, and she was often, especially in the year 1789, for many months in a critical condition. He bestowed the tenderest care upon her, and spared nothing that was likely to benefit

---

[7] Nissen, p. 689.

[8] Shlichtegrolls Nekrolog. Cf. Zelter, Briefw. mit Goethe, VI., p. 61.

her, even when the remedy proposed (as for instance, repeated
visits to Baden for some years) was a severe tax upon his
slender resources. Instances of liberality like that displayed
to him on one occasion of his wife's illness by a comparative stranger were few and far between. A certain
honest tripe-boiler, Rindum by name, who knew nothing of
Mozart personally, but who delighted in his music, heard that
his wife, suffering from lameness, had been ordered foot-
baths of the water in which tripe had been cooked; he
begged her to go to his house for them as often as she
pleased, and at the termination of the cure he could not be
induced to accept any payment either for them or for board
and lodging during a considerable time.[9] As for Mozart himself, the care that he bestowed upon her was tender and
loving to an uncommon degree. He used to ride every
morning at five o'clock, but he never went without leaving a
paper in the form of a prescription upon his wife's bed, with
some directions of this kind :—

Good morning, my darling wife, I hope that you have slept well, and
that nothing has disturbed you; I desire you not to get up too early,
not to take cold, not to stoop, not to stretch, not to scold the servants,
not to fall over the doorstep. Do not be vexed at anything until I
return. May nothing happen to you! I shall be back at —— o'clock.[10]

The tenderest anxiety for his wife's health is expressed in
his letters, and he especially cautions her to spare her weak
foot. Frau Haibl (Sophie Weber) narrates :[11]—

How troubled Mozart was when anything ailed his dear little wife!
On one occasion she had been ill for fully eight months, and I had
nursed her. I was sitting by her bed, and so was Mozart. He was composing, and I was watching the sleep into which she had at last fallen;
we were as quiet as the grave for fear of disturbing her. A rough maid-
servant came suddenly into the room. Mozart, fearing that his wife
would be awakened, wished to beckon for silence, and pushed his chair
backwards with an open knife in his hand. The knife struck between
his chair and his thigh, and went almost up to the handle in his flesh.
Mozart was usually very susceptible of pain, but now he controlled him-

---

9 Niemetschek, p. 97.   Nissen, p. 686.
10 A. M. Z., I., p. 291.   Nissen, p. 687.
11 This letter was made use of by Nissen.   I obtained it from Köchel.

self, and made no sign of pain, but beckoned me to follow him out of the room. We went into another room, in which our good mother was concealed, because we did not wish Mozart to know how ill his wife was, and yet the mother's presence was necessary in case of emergency. She bound the wound and cured it with healing oil. He went lame for some time, but took care that his wife should know nothing of it.

He became so accustomed during this long illness to receive every visitor with his finger on his lip, and the low exclamation "Chut!" that even some time after her recovery, when he saw an acquaintance in the street, he would walk on tiptoe, and whisper " Chut! " with his finger on his lip.[12] The contemplation of such deep-seated affection as this causes us to be more surprised to hear that Mozart, whose unmarried life had been without a blemish, was, nevertheless, unfaithful to his wife. She told herself how Mozart acknowledged his indiscretions to her, and how she forgave him : " He was so good, it was impossible to be angry with him ; one was obliged to forgive him." Her sister, however, betrays that Constanze was not always so patient, and that there were occasional violent outbreaks, which is quite conceivable ; but it is also abundantly evident (and Mozart's letters to his wife fully confirm the fact) that the close and tender relations of each to the other were not seriously disturbed by these failings.[13] They might on this account alone be lightly dismissed, and in addition it must be remembered that rumour was busy among the public and in the press, and magnified solitary instances of weakness on Mozart's part into distinguishing features of his character. He was credited with intrigues with every pupil he had, and every singer for whom he wrote a song; it was considered a witty remark to designate him as the actual prototype of his Don Juan ; and his dissipated life was even considered as the proper confirmation of his artistic genius. Exceptional gifts and accomplishments cannot do away with the equality of all men before the moral law ; transgressions of the moral law may be judged leniently or severely, as the case may be,

---

[12] A. M. Z., I., p. 291. Nissen, p. 687.
[13] On this point I have accepted the verbal testimony of trustworthy Salzburg friends, confirmed by Niemetschek, p. 98 (Nissen, p. 690).

but weaknesses, which in ordinary men are judged lightly, or
passed over altogether, must not be measured by another
standard, or made the sign of complete moral degradation
when they are committed by an artist and a genius whose
very faults interest us more than the virtues of other men.
Nor should implicit confidence be placed in the gossip
and chatter which surround this side of a great man's
private life, and turn errors into crimes.   The free and easy
manners and ideas of the day, which found special favour in
Vienna,[14] the peculiar temptations to which an artist's temperament and mode of life expose him, make Mozart's
failings conceivable.   If it be remembered further how im-
prudently Mozart behaved, how professional envy and mean-
ness designedly tarnished his fame, it will be readily conceded
that better grounds for a fair estimate of Mozart's character
are to be found in numerous well-authenticated and consistent instances of his true nobility of mind than in idle and
malicious gossip.   The earnest spirit in which he looked upon
these things is well displayed in a letter to his best and dearest
friend, Gottfried von Jacquin (Prague, November 4, 1787) :—

Now, my dear friend, how are you ?   I hope that you are all as hale
and hearty as we are ; you cannot but be content, dear friend, since you
possess all that you can desire at your age and in your position ; especially
since you seem altogether to have renounced your former somewhat
unsettled life.   Do you not daily grow more convinced of the truth of
my little lecture ?   Is not the pleasure of a fickle and capricious love a
thousand times removed from the blessedness accompanying a sincere
and rational affection ?   I am sure you often thank me in your heart
for my advice !   You will make me quite proud !   But without a joke—
you owe me a little gratitude if you have really made yourself worthy
of Fräulein N——, for I played no unimportant part in your improvement or reformation.

---

14 Forster, Sämmtl. Schr., VII., p. 268.   The French traveller [K. Risbeck]
says a great deal about the dissoluteness of the Viennese.   " All the great towns
are alike in this respect.   The courts are more or less corrupt, and the nobility
universally so ; those who can do as they like abuse their privileges, and act
unworthily.   But it is not always fair to consider freedom of manner as a sign
of licentiousness, as those who live in small towns are apt to do.   If a pretty
girl permits a kiss on her hand, or even her lips—if, when she loves a man, she
is not ashamed to say so—these are not deadly sins, and the shame rests with
those who take advantage of her openness."

Hummel, who was received into Mozart's house as his pupil, wrote in 1831, when he lay dying at Kissingen: "I declare it to be untrue that Mozart abandoned himself to excess, except on those rare occasions on which he was enticed by Schikaneder, which had chiefly to do with the "Zauberflöte."[15] His intimacy with the notorious profligate Schikaneder during the summer of 1791, when his wife was an invalid at Baden, and the excesses to which he then gave way, have been magnified by report, and made the foundation of the exaggerated representation of Mozart's thoughtless life.[16] The further reproach brought against him of extravagance and bad management of his household must not be left altogether unnoticed, illiberal as it may seem to hold up for the examination of posterity the trivial cares of housekeeping and money-getting which, when ordinary mortals are concerned, are kept sacred within the four walls of the home. But this part of Mozart's life has been intruded so often into the foreground, that a concise statement of the facts belonging to it seems indispensable. By some his contemporaries have been condemned for allowing his mind to be hampered by unworthy cares, by others he has himself been reproved for having brought himself to poverty by thoughtless extravagance; both these views are exaggerated and in this sense unjust.

It is true that Mozart was not so highly esteemed in Vienna during his life as after his death. The general public admired him chiefly as a pianoforte-player, the downfall of German opera prevented his continuance along the successful path which his "Entführung" had opened to him, and his Italian operas did not obtain so great a measure of

---

[15] From a MS. biographical notice of Hummel, by M. J. Seidel, communicated by Preller.

[16] The length to which the calumny went is shown by Suard (Mél. de Litt., II., p. 339): "J'ai entendu dire qu'il n'avait fait la 'Flûte Enchantée' que pour plaire à une femme de théâtre dont il était devenu amoureux, et qui avait mis ses faveurs à ce prix. On ajoute que son triomphe eut des suites bien cruelles, et qu'il en contracta une maladie incurable dont il mourut peu de temps après. Ce fait me paraît peu vraisemblable: la 'Flûte Enchantée' n'est pas le dernier de ses opéras, et lorsqu'il l'a composée sa santé était déjà fort altérée."

applause as the lighter ones of his contemporaries ; when the "Zauberflöte" made its effect it was too late. It is scarcely surprising, therefore, that he failed to reach the position before the world which should by right have been his. But though it is easy for posterity to decide that Mozart had just claims to a place by the side of Gluck and above Bono, Salieri and Starzer, it must not be forgotten that his contemporaries had before them a young and struggling artist, and that those veterans had long been in possession of their distinguished places. Without laying too much stress upon the intrigues of opponents, or the Emperor's parsimony, it is plain that Mozart could not readily attain a position which had first to be created for him. He himself was encouraged by the brilliant success of the "Entführung" and the universal applause which he received as a pianist to hope for a secure and respectable position, and he was bitterly disappointed that his good recommendations failed to procure him the post of teacher to the Princess Elizabeth. In his usual impulsive style he resolved on quitting Vienna at once, and wrote to his father (August 17, 1782):—

The Vienna gentlemen (among whom the Emperor comes foremost) shall not imagine that I have nothing to do in the world outside Vienna. It is true that I would rather serve the Emperor than any other monarch, but I will never stoop to beg for any service. I believe myself to be in a position to do honour to any court. If Germany, my beloved father-land, of which, as you know, I am proud, refuses me, then must France or England be the richer for a clever German—to the disgrace of the German nation. I need not tell you that the Germans have excelled other nations in almost every art—but where did the artists make their fortunes or their fame? Certainly not in Germany ! Even Gluck—did Germany make him the great man he is ? Alas, no ! The Countess Thun, Count Zichy, Baron van Swieten, and Prince Kaunitz are all vexed with the Emperor for not encouraging men of talent to remain in his service. Prince Kaunitz said to the Archduke Maximilian, speaking of me, that such men only came into the world once in a hundred years, and ought not to be driven out of Germany, especially when the monarch is so fortunate as to possess them in his capital. You cannot think how kind and polite Prince Kaunitz was in an interview I had with him ; he said when I took leave : " I am indebted to you, my dear Mozart, for taking the trouble of calling on me, &c." You would not believe either how anxious the Countess Thun, Baron van Swieten, and other great people are to retain me here; but I cannot wait long, and *will* not wait on charity, as it were. Emperor though he be, I would rather dispense with his favours than accept them in such a way.

His idea, as he let fall now and then in conversation, was to go to Paris for the following Lent. He wrote on the subject to Le Gros, and was of opinion that if he could only obtain engagements for the " Concert spirituel " and the " Concert des amateurs," he would have no lack of pupils, and could also do something in the way of composition; his main object would of course be an opera.[17] With this end in view he had been for some time studying the French language, and had also taken lessons in English, in the further expectation of making a tour in England; he thought he should understand the language fairly well in three months.[18] His father was not a little disturbed by this new idea; he opposed it with every argument he could find to his son, and even wrote on the subject to the Baroness von Waldstädten (August 23, 1782) :[19]—

I should be quite reconciled (to the marriage), if I did not discover a great fault in my son: he is too indolent and easy-going, perhaps occasionally too proud, and all these qualities united make a man inactive; or else he grows impatient and cannot wait for anything. He is altogether ruled by opposite extremes—too much, or too little, and no medium. When he is in no pressing need he is quite content, and becomes indolent and inactive. Once set going, he is all on fire, and thinks he is going to make his fortune all at once. Nothing is allowed to stand in his way, and unfortunately it is just the cleverest people, the exceptional men of genius, who find continual obstacles in their path. What is there to prevent his having a prosperous career in Vienna, if he only has a little patience ? Kapellmeister Bono is an aged man. Salieri will be promoted at his death, and will leave another place vacant. And is not Gluck also an old man ? Honoured madam, exhort him to patience, and pardon me for asking the favour of your ladyship's opinion on the matter.

---

[17] Salieri was recommended by Gluck as a composer for the Grand-Opéra in Paris, in 1784, when he had himself refused to undertake the composition of " Les Danaides " (Mosel, Salieri, p. 77).

[18] A book of exercises and letters in English was used by Mozart as an account book in 1784 (André, Vorr. zu Mozart's Themat.-Catalog., p. 3).

[19] Hamburg. Litt. u. Krit. Blätt, 1856, No. 72, p. 563.

His remonstrances had the desired effect upon Wolfgang;
he was obliged to acknowledge to his father (August 24,
1782) that it would be better to prolong his stay at Vienna;
that he could go to France or England at any time.
L. Mozart, reassured, wrote to the Baroness (September 13,
1782): "My son has relinquished his intention of leaving
Vienna at present, in consequence of my letters; and as he
now intends to visit me in Salzburg, I shall be able to make
the strongest and most necessary representations to him on
the subject."

These representations were all the more effective since
Mozart had at this juncture every reason to be satisfied with
the sympathy and applause of the Vienna public.   It is true
that on the revival of Italian opera his works were excluded
from the theatre; but in the year 1786 the Emperor proved
that he had not forgotten him by commissioning him to
compose the "Schauspieldirector" and "Figaro."   But
when Mozart, nevertheless, failed to obtain a permanent
post, the idea again seriously presented itself of leaving
Vienna and going to England.

An Englishman named Thomas Attwood (1767-1838) had
come from Italy to Vienna in the year 1785, and become
Mozart's pupil.   By a singular coincidence also the English
tenor, Michael Kelly, and the English prima donna, Nancy
Storace, were engaged at the Italian Opera.   Stephen Storace,
the brother, was also resident in Vienna as a composer for a
considerable time.   Mozart was on very friendly terms with
them, and his design was thereby strengthened.   At the
beginning of November, 1786, he wrote to his father that he
intended in the latter part of the Carnival to undertake a
journey through Germany to England if his father would
consent to receive and take charge of his two children and
the servants.   Constanze was to accompany him.

"I have written pretty strongly," L. Mozart informs his
daughter (November 17, 1786), "and promised to send him
the continuation of my letter by the next post.   It is not a
bad idea, in truth.   They may go away quietly—they may
die—they may stay in England.   Then I may run after them
with the children; and as to the payment which he is to give

me for the children and servants, &c., Basta ! My refusal
is explicit and instructive, if he chooses to take it so." We
see how prejudiced the once tender father had become
against his son and his son's wife; whereas his daughter,
who had married in 1784, came to his house to be confined,
and he afterwards took entire charge of her son Leopold, a
fact which he concealed from Wolfgang. Wolfgang's plan
was given up immediately on receipt of this letter from his
father. But when his English friend left Vienna at the
beginning of February, 1787, and returned to England, the
wish to accompany him rose strong in Mozart. He had
become more prudent meanwhile. Attwood was to prepare
a settled post for him in London, and to procure him a commission to write an opera or subscriptions for a concert, and
then only he would come. He hoped that his father would
in this case relieve him of the care of his children until he
should have decided whether he would remain there permanently or return to Germany. The English travellers
passed through Salzburg, and made L. Mozart's acquaintance, to their mutual satisfaction;[20] but his objections against
Wolfgang's journey were not by any means removed. He
wrote to him in a fatherly way, as he informs his daughter
(March 1, 1787), " that he would make nothing by a journey
in summer, and would go to England at a wrong time; he
would spend about two thousand florins, and would certainly
come to want, for Storace is sure to write the first opera.
Wolfgang would lose heart very soon."

Mozart again abandoned his intention, but not before
rumours of it had reached the public ear,[21] rumours which
showed the Emperor the necessity for giving him a per-

---

[20] Kelly, Reminisc., I., p. 277. L. Mozart gives his daughter a long account
of the English visitors who were invited to a State concert by the Archbishop,
and very well received.

[21] A Viennese correspondent of January 25, 1787, says (Cramer's Musik.
Magaz., II., p. 1273): " Mozart left Vienna some weeks ago on a professional
tour to Prague, Berlin, and, it is even said, to London. I hope that it will be
productive both of pleasure and profit to him." And Leopold Mozart wrote
to his daughter (January 12, 1787): " The report that your brother intends
going to England is confirmed from Vienna, Prague, and Munich."

manent post, in order to keep him in Vienna.[22]   Unhappily,
Mozart's father did not live to see this end to all his anxieties.
He died on May 28, 1787.

As there was no kapellmeister's place vacant, the Emperor
appointed Mozart his "private musician," (Kammermusicus)
with a salary of eight hundred florins.   The smallness of the
sum was ascribed to the influence of Strack; he was, as
usual, appealed to for advice, and humoured the Emperor's
inclination to parsimony.   The appointment was made on
December 7, 1787; in August, 1788, Mozart assures his
sister that he is really appointed, and that his name appears
on the official theatrical list as "kapellmeister in the actual
service of his imperial majesty."   Gluck, who had been
appointed "private composer" (Kammercompositeur) by
Maria Theresa on the 7th of October, 1774, with a salary of
two thousand florins, died on November 15, 1787.   Mozart
naturally took his place; but it does not seem to have
occurred to the court that a corresponding rise of salary
would have been no undeserved distinction.

Mozart himself was not dissatisfied with his pay, since
none of the musicians attached to the imperial household
received more; but he was justly annoyed, at a later date,
when he was suffered to draw his pay without having the
opportunity given him of producing any important work.
He looked upon it as an alms doled out to him, while the
opportunity of distinguishing himself as a composer was
denied, and wrote bitterly after the customary entry of his
income on the official return: "Too much for what I do;
too little for what I could do."[23]   This was not the right
way to remind those in authority that a promise of "promotion" on the first seasonable opportunity had been held
out to him.   The cares which beset the closing years of the
Emperor Joseph are explanation sufficient of the decline of
his interest in music and the drama and his care for the
great composer; this, however, the latter failed to perceive.
It was clear also that he did not know how to turn his

---

[22] Niemetschek, p. 44. Rochlitz's account, founded on information from
Mozart's widow (A. M. Z., I., p. 22), is confirmed by Nissen (p. 535).
[23] A. M. Z., I., p. 291.

opportunities to advantage, when, in May, 1789, he refused the offer of Frederick William II. to make him kapellmeister in Berlin with three thousand florins salary. With unselfish emotion Mozart exclaimed: "How can I desert my good Emperor?" The King wished him to reconsider the proposal, and promised to hold to his word for an indefinite period if Mozart would consent to come.[24]

Once returned to Vienna, Mozart thought no more of the matter, and only after much persuasion from his friends was induced to lay it before the Emperor and tender his resignation. In unpleased surprise Joseph asked: "What, do you mean to forsake me, Mozart?" Whereupon Mozart answered with emotion: "May it please your majesty, I will stay." Upon the question of a friend as to whether he had not taken the opportunity of demanding some compensation, he exclaimed angrily: "Who the devil would have thought of that at such a time?"

At the end of 1789 he received the commission to write the opera of "Così fan Tutte," but Joseph II. died (February 20, 1790) before Mozart's position had been permanently provided for. After the accession of Leopold II. he appears to have made an attempt to obtain the post of second kapellmeister under Salieri (old Bono had died in 1788, and Salieri had been promoted to his place),[25] but this also was unsuccessful. Convinced that he must now, for the present at least, renounce all hope of promotion at court, he applied to the civic authorities for the post of assistant to the Kapellmeister Hofmann at the Stephanskirche. The application was granted, with the promise of Hofmann's lucrative post in case of his death; but the old man survived Mozart, and this hope of an independence fell through with the rest.[26] Under these circumstances Mozart

---

[24] Rochlitz expressly states that the King repeated this conversation to various persons, among others to Mozart's widow, during her stay in Berlin, in February, 1796.

[25] Mosel, Salieri, p. 132.

[26] The story that after his return from Prague (September, 1791), as Niemetschek has it (p. 36), or on his death-bed, as it is usually embellished, Mozart received his appointment as actual kapellmeister, with all its emoluments, is

was thrown back for a means of livelihood upon lessons, concerts, and composition. We know how much he disliked lesson-giving (Vol. I., p. 411), and his dislike was more likely to increase than diminish, and yet he was obliged to lay himself out to give lessons. In May, 1790, he wrote to his friend Puchberg: "I have two pupils now, and should like to make the number up to eight; try to spread it about that I give lessons." Mozart was never a fashionable and well-paid music-master in Vienna, such as Steffan, Kozeluch, or Righini. This may excite surprise, since he was so distinguished as a pianist, but he was wanting in the patience and pliability necessary, and perhaps also in steadiness and regularity. When he met with talent or enthusiasm, or when he was personally attracted, he was fond of giving lessons; as, for instance, to Franziska (afterwards Frau von Lagusius), the sister of his friend Gottfried von Jacquin, to whom he writes from Prague (January 14, 1787):—

I kiss your sister's hand a thousand times, and beg her to practise industriously on her new pianoforte — but the recommendation is unnecessary, for I must own that I never had so industrious and zealous a pupil as herself—and I rejoice in the expectation of giving her further instruction, according to my poor ability.

She was considered an excellent pianiste, and one of Mozart's best pupils; he wrote the trio with clarinet and tenor (498 K.) for her (August 5, 1786).[27] He also sent her the grand Sonata for four hands in C major (521 K.) as soon as it was finished (May 29, 1787), with a message through her brother that "she must set about it at once, for it was somewhat difficult." They were mostly ladies to whom he gave lessons, for the ladies of high rank in Vienna were cultivated enough to be considered as leaders of fashion,

---

evidently unfounded. In the widow's petition for a pension (in the Mozarteum at Salzburg) only "the expected appointment to the post of cathedral kapellmeister" is mentioned, and in a magistrate's order of December 12, 1791 (in the collection of Al. Fuchs), "Joh. Georg. Albrechtsberger, imperial court organist, appointed to the post of assistant kapellmeister at the metropolitan church of St. Stephan, as successor to the late Herr Mozart." Hoffman died in 1792, and then Albrechtsberger succeeded him.

27 Caroline Pichler, Denkwürd, I., p. 180.

more especially in music.[28] Among them were students in
the genuine sense of the word, such as Frau von Trattnern,
to whom Mozart addressed elaborate written communications
on the execution of his clavier compositions, more especially
on his Fantasia in C minor, composed for her.[29] For Barbara
Ployer he composed (February 9, 1784) the Concerto in E
flat major (449 K.), which he did not consider as among his
great ones, and the more difficult one in G Major (453 K.);
and he writes to his father (June 9, 1784):—

> To-morrow there is to be a concert at Herr Ployer's country-house in
> Döbling; Fräulein Babette is to play her new concerto in G, I the
> quintet [with wind instruments, in E flat major, 452 K.], and then both
> of us the grand sonata for two pianos [in D major, composed early in
> 1784, 448 K.]. I am to take Paesiello, who has been here since May
> on his return journey from St. Petersburg, in order that he may hear my
> compositions and my pupils.

No doubt the greater number of his pupils either—like
Fräulein Aurnhammer—cared more for social intercourse
with Mozart than for actual instruction, or took lessons for
a short time only that they might be able to speak of the
great performer as their teacher. The celebrated physician,
Jos. Frank, relates that he took twelve lessons from him in
1790:[30]—

> I found Mozart a little man with a large head and plump hand, and
> was somewhat coldly received by him. "Now," said he, "play me
> something." I played a fantasia of his own composition. "Not bad,"
> said he, to my great astonishment; "but now listen to me play it." It
> was a miracle! The piano became another instrument under his
> hands. It was strengthened by a second piano, which served him as a
> pedal.[31] Mozart then made some remarks as to the way in which I should
> perform the fantasia. I was fortunate enough to understand him. "Do

---

[28] K. R[isbeck], Briefe, I., p. 292. G. Forster, Sämmtl. Schr., VII., p. 268.
Meyer, L. Schröder, I., p. 360. Schink, Dramaturg. Monate, II., p. 542.

[29] Niemetschek, p. 92. According to a letter of Nissen's to Härtel (November
27, 1799), they were in the possession of Gelinek, and are apparently lost.
Journ. d. Lux. u. d. Mod., 1808, II., p. 802.

[30] Prutz, Deutsch. Museum, II., p. 27. Frank was well known as a "great
musician." Briefw. Carl Augusts mits Goethe, I., p. 302.

[31] L. Mozart wrote to his daughter from Vienna (March 12, 1785): "He has
had a great *fortepiano pedal* made, which stands under the harpsichord, three
spans long, and fearfully heavy."

you play any other pieces of my composition ? " " Yes," answered I ;
" your variations on the theme ' Unser dummer Pöbel meint ' (455 K.),
and a sonata with accompaniments for violin and violoncello." "Good !
I will play you that piece ; you will profit more by hearing me than by
playing them yourself."

It is plain that he had the tact and skill to manage even
such pupils as these. He treated those who had the power
and the wish to become true artists under his guidance in
quite another fashion, and they profited not only by his
regular instruction, but still more by his encouragement and
incitement ,to exertion.

Johann Nepomuk Hummel came to Vienna in 1785, with
his father, who afterwards undertook the conductorship of
the opera, under Schikaneder ; at seven years of age the
young Hummel already created great expectations by his
clavier-playing. A pupil of Mozart's, named Freystädter,
brought Hummel to him in 1797 ; the boy played one of the
easier sonatas (with which Mozart had no fault to find,
except as to the hurried *tempo*), and then one of his newest
concertos by heart.[82] Thereupon Mozart decided to undertake Hummel's instruction, but only on condition that he
resided with them altogether. We are not told how often or
with what regularity he received lessons ; but he heard
Mozart play, and had to play over to him any clavier music
that came into the house. One evening Mozart returned
late from some entertainment with his wife, and found a
piece of music which he was curious to hear. Young
Hummel, who had been awaiting their return, had lain down
on a couple of chairs and fallen asleep. " Stanzerl," said
Mozart, to his wife ; " wake Hans, and give him a glass of
wine." No sooner said than done ; and the boy played the
new piece of music, late at night as it was.[83]

Mozart's musical instruction was sure to be desultory.
Freystädter relates that he generally received Mozart's
directions and corrections of his musical exercises sitting at
side-table, while a game of bowls was going on.[84] Attwood

[82] Allgem. Wiener Mus. Ztg., 1842, p. 489. Seidel, Handschr. Notiz.
[83] Holmes tells the story on trustworthy family authority (p. 258).
[84] Allgem. Wien. Mus. Ztg., 1842, p. 489.

also tells us that Mozart sometimes persuaded him to join in a game of billiards instead of taking a lesson.[85] The pupils did not consider their master guilty of caprice and neglect; but felt themselves spurred to activity by their intercourse with him.

Mozart took young Hummel everywhere with him, made him play, played duets with him, and declared that the boy would soon excel himself as a pianist. Hummel was greatly attached to Mozart, both then and ever after; he remained in his house for two years, until in November, 1788, his father set out with him on a professional tour.

Mozart also gave lessons in the theory of music, sometimes even to ladies; we hear of a cousin of the Abbé Stadler as Mozart's pupil in thorough-bass. The exercise-book which he used for instruction in thorough-bass in 1784 is now in the Imperial library at Vienna.[86] Mozart wrote down a very characteristic melody, or a bass, or both, which the pupil was to arrange in several parts; then Mozart corrected the passage with short remarks on the various mistakes, alternately Italian or German, sometimes of a comic nature—for instance: "Ho l' onore di dirla, che lei ha fatta la scioccagine (da par Suo) di far due ottave tra il 2do Violino ed il Basso"; or in German: "This E is very forced here; it shows that it has only been put in to prevent too rapid a passage from one consonance to another—just as bad poets often do stupid things for the sake of rhyme. You might have gone gradually from C to D very prettily by inserting thirds." These remarks are purely grammatical; and it is evident that Mozart's teaching was of the good old-fashioned kind, which strives first to give the pupil a thorough knowledge of the grammar of his art. From exercise-books of this kind, of which Zelter saw one in Vienna,[87] a little hand-

---

[85] Holmes, p. 259. Cf. Fétis, Curios. Hist. de la Mus., p. 212.

[86] Stadler (Vertheidig. der Echtheit des Req., p. 13) says: "When I turn over these leaves, I never fail to remember the great master, and rejoice in observing his manner of working."

[87] Zelter, Briefw. mit Goethe, V., p. 85. In the Wiener Zeitung, 1796, p. 1038, Jos. Haydenreich advertises for sale at a price of 4 fl. 30 kr., "Ein noch unbekanntes geschriebenes Fundament zur erlernung des Generalbasses von Mozart."

book of thorough-bass was afterwards printed under Mozart's name, and was much in use for some time.[88] With more advanced pupils he naturally proceeded differently. Attwood preserved an exercise-book with compositions, which he had submitted to Mozart shortly after his arrival in Vienna. Mozart had crossed out whole passages, and rewritten them with the remark, " I should have done this so."[89] When Kelly, the tenor, who made pretty little songs which Mozart admired, imagined that he could make himself into a serious composer by means of studies in counterpoint, Mozart said to him, " If you had studied counterpoint long ago in Naples, you would have done well; now that you have to give your mind to your education as a singer, you will make nothing of it. Remember that half-know-ledge is a dangerous thing. You have considerable talent in the invention of melodies ; a smattering of theory would ruin that, and you can always find some musician who can help you when you want it. Melody is the essence of music. I should compare one who invents melodies to a noble racehorse, and a mere contrapuntist to a hired post hack. So let it alone ; and remember the old Italian proverb ' Chi sa più, meno sa.' "[40]

Lesson-giving might fail greatly to increase either Mozart's fame or his income, but his success as a virtuoso was brilliant and lasting. His father warned him, when he talked of settling in Vienna, of the fickleness of the public, but Wolfgang answered cheerfully (June 2, 1781) :—

The Viennese certainly love change—*but only at the theatre,* and my line is too popular not to be supported. This is, in truth, *Clavierland !* and, even supposing they were to tire of me, it would not be for several years, and in the meantime I should have made both money and reputation.

In this expectation he was not disappointed; the applause which greeted him on his first appearance was repeated as often as he appeared in Vienna.

---

[88] It has been published several times in Vienna by Steiner & Co. with the title of " Kurzgefasste Generalbass-schule von W. A. Mozart," and as " Funda-ment des Generalbasses von W. A. Mozart," by J. G. Siegmeyer (Berlin, 1822).

[89] Holmes, p. 316.

[40] Kelly, Reminisc., I., p. 228.

The proper season for concerts, and also for private musical parties, was Lent, when the theatres were closed; the concerts were generally given in the theatre.[41] Mozart invariably gave a concert in Lent. After the success of the first (1782) he used to make a common undertaking every spring with a certain Phil. Jac. Martin. He was a native of Regensburg, who had studied with good old Bullinger at the Jesuit College in Munich, and supported himself with difficulty: "quite a young man, who tries hard to get on in the world by his music, his beautiful handwriting, and especially by his clever head and strong intellect" (May 29, 1782). Martin had established an amateur musical society, which gave concerts every Friday during the winter.[42] Mozart writes to his father (May 8, 1782):—

You know that there are a number of amateurs here, and very good ones, both male and female ; hitherto there has been no organisation among them. This Martin has now received permission from the Emperor, with expressions of the highest approbation, to give twelve concerts in the Augarten and four grand evening concerts on the finest open spaces in the city.[43] The subscription for the whole summer is two ducats. You can well imagine that we shall get subscribers enough, all the more for my being associated with him. Even supposing that we only get one hundred subscribers, and that the expenses amount to two hundred florins (an outside sum), that means three hundred florins profit for each of us. Baron van Swieten and the Countess Thun are taking it up warmly. The orchestra is entirely amateur, with the exception of the bassoons, trumpets, and drums.

---

[41] Nicolai, Reise, IV., p. 552. C. Pichler, Denkw., I., p. 127.

[42] Nicolai (Reise, IV., p. 552) dilates upon the announcement of these great amateur concerts, and especially upon paragraph 6, which runs : " Card-tables will be placed in the ante-rooms, and money for play provided at discretion; the company will also be provided with every kind of refreshment." He asserts that this was not so at the private concerts of true connoisseurs, at which he had been present.

[43] Wien. Ztg., 1782, No. 44. K. R[isbeck], Briefe, I., p. 276. " The entertainments I most enjoyed during the nights of last summer, were the so-called ' lemonade-tents.' Great tents were erected on one of the largest open spaces in the city, and there lemonade was dispensed at night; several hundred seats were occupied by ladies and gentlemen. A band of music was placed at a little distance, and the perfect silence which was maintained by the numerous assembly had an indescribable effect. The charming music, the solemn silence, the confidential mood engendered by the night, all combined to give the scene a peculiar charm " (Jahrb. d. Tonk., 1796, p. 78).

The Imperial Augarten replaced the old "Favorite" established by Joseph I. in the Leopold Vorstadt of Vienna. It was laid out by Joseph II, and opened to the public for their free use in 1775, with the well-known inscription over the entrance: "Public place of recreation dedicated to all men, by one who esteems them."[44] The principal building was used as an hotel, and the Emperor built for himself a simple little house, surrounded by wooden palings, where he sometimes spent several days, and amused himself by walking freely among his people. On Sunday afternoons in especial, all the fashionable population of Vienna strolled there,[45] so that the speculation promised to be a successful one.

It provided plenty of occupation for its promoters. Mozart writes (May 25, 1782):—

To-morrow is our first entertainment in the Augarten. At half-past eight Martin is to call for me in a hackney-coach, and we have six visits to make; I must be ready by eleven o'clock to go to Rumbeck; then I dine with the Countess Thun; we are to rehearse the music in her garden in the evening. There is to be a symphony by Van Swieten, and another by me; Mdlle. Berger, an amateur, is to sing; a boy named Türk[46] is to play a violin concerto, and Fräulein von Aurnhammer and I the duet concerto in E flat (365 K.).

The first concert went off well; among the audience were the Archduke Maximilian, the Countess Thun, Wallenstein, Baron van Swieten, and many other musical connoisseurs, but we hear nothing further of the undertaking, which cannot have been so brilliant a success as had been hoped.[47] There was no doubt, however, as to the success which Mozart achieved during the Lenten concerts of 1783. He contributed greatly towards the success of a concert given by his sister-in-law, Aloysia Lange, at the theatre on

---

[44] Hormayr, Wien., V., I., pp. 41, 50.

[45] Nicolai, Reise., III., p. 12.

[46] Franz Türke is mentioned later as a distinguished amateur (Jahrb. d. Tonk., 1796, p. 63).

[47] In 1791, Martin, "directeur des concerts d'amateurs," announced his great concerts in the Imperial Augarten in the Prater, and at court, in a somewhat doleful manner (Wien. Ztg., 1791, No. 45 Anh.). They were afterwards continued under the conductorship of the vice-president, Von Keess (Jahr. d. Tonk., 1796, p. 74. A. M. Z., III., p. 46).

March 11. His Parisian symphony for the Concert spirituel (297 K., Vol. II., p. 49) was performed on this occasion, after which Madame Lange sang the song which he had composed for her in Mannheim : " Non sò d' onde viene " (294 K., Vol. I., p. 419), with new variations for the voice. How many memories it must have awakened in them both! " Gluck had the box next to the Langes," he informed his father (March 12, 1783), "in which was also my wife. He could not praise enough either the symphony or the song, and he invited us all to dinner next Sunday." In addition Mozart played a concerto of his own composition. "The theatre was very full; and I was so well received by the public, that I could but feel happy and content. After I had gone away the clapping was so persistent that I was obliged to return and repeat the rondo. It was a perfect storm of applause." For his own concert on March 22 every box was taken, and the theatre "could not have been fuller." The programme of this concert, which he copied for his father, gives us an idea of what Mozart's concerts were. There were performed:—

1. The new Hafner symphony, composed the previous summer (385 K., Vol. II., p. 210).

2. Air from "Idomeneo," "Se il padre perdei" (366 K.), sung by Madame Lange.

3. The third subscription concerto, then just published, in C major (415 K., No. 5).

4. The Countess Baumgarten's scena (369 K., Vol. II., p. 168), sung by Adamberger.

5. The short Sinfonia-concertante of the last "Final-musik" (320 K., Vol. II., p. 87).

6. The favourite concerto in D (175, 382 K., Vol. I., p. 324).

7. Scena, "Parto, m' affretto," from "Lucio Silla" (135 K., Vol. I., p. 180), sung by Mdlle. Teyber.

8. Impromptu fantasia by Mozart, beginning with a short fugue, "because the Emperor was there" (Vol. II., p. 173), followed by variations on an air from the opera of "Der eingebildete Philosoph" by Paesiello ("Salve Tu, Domine"), and when the thunder of applause obliged him to play again, he chose the air "Unser dummer Pöbel meint," from Gluck's "Pilgrims of Mecca," as a theme for variations.

9. A new rondo, composed for Madame Lange, and performed by her (416 K.).

10. The last movement of the first symphony.

This programme makes it evident that the demands on a concert-giver were far greater then than now, and the public were undoubtedly more patient listeners. "What pleased me most," wrote Wolfgang to his father (March 29, 1783), "was the sight of the Emperor, and how pleased he was, and how he applauded me. It is always his custom to send the money for his box to the pay-place before he comes to the theatre; otherwise I might certainly have expected more (than twenty-five ducats), for his delight was beyond all bounds." A short time after Mozart played a concerto at Mdlle. Teyber's concert.[48] Again the rondo was encored, but when he sat down to the piano again, he had the desk removed in order to improvise. "This little surprise delighted the audience immensely; they clapped, and cried 'Bravo, bravissimo!'" The Emperor did not leave this concert until Mozart had quite finished playing. So the latter in high glee informs his father (April 12, 1783). In Lent, 1784,[49] besides a concert in the theatre, which took place in April, Mozart proposed to give six subscription concerts, and he begs his father to send him the score of "Idomeneo," because he intended to produce it (December 6, 1783).

The pianoforte teacher Richter had established Saturday concerts, which were attended by the nobility only upon the understanding that Mozart was to play; after playing at three of them he raised subscriptions (six florins) for three concerts of his own, which took place on the three last Wednesdays in Lent (March 17, 24, and 31), in a fine hall belonging to Trattnern, a bookseller.[50] The list of subscribers

---

[48] Cramer, Magazin d. Musik, I., p. 578: "A concert was given this afternoon in the National Theatre for the benefit of the celebrated Herr Chevalier Mozart, the performance including several pieces of his own composition. The concert was attended by a very numerous audience, and the two new concertos and various fantasias, which Herr Mozart performed on the pianoforte, were received with loud and general applause. Our gracious Emperor, contrary to custom, remained through the whole performance, and joined in the unprecedented applause of the public. The receipts are said to amount to 1,600 florins."

[49] Wien. Ztg., 1784, No. 28, Anh.

[50] Nicolai, Reise, II., p. 636.

numbered 174 names,[51] thirty more than were procured by the partners, Richter and Fischer; the latter was a violin-player, married to Storace, the singer.[52]

"The first concert, on the 17th," Mozart writes (March 20, 1784), "went off well; the hall was crammed full, and the new concerto, which I played, was very well received; every one is talking about the concert." The succeeding performances were equally successful, so that he was able to assure his father that they had been of considerable service to him. Besides the subscription concerts, he gave two others in the theatre, which also went off well. "To-morrow should have been my first concert in the theatre," he writes (March 20, 1784), "but Prince Louis Liechtenstein has an operatic performance which would have taken half the nobility from my audience, besides some of the chief members of the orchestra. So I have postponed it, in a printed advertisement, to April 1." He wrote two great concertos[53] and the quintet for piano and wind instruments, which was enthusiastically applauded. "I myself," he adds, "consider it the best thing I ever wrote in my life. I do wish you could have heard it! And how beautifully it was performed! To tell the truth, I grew tired of the mere playing towards the end, and it reflects no small credit on me that my audience did not in any degree share the fatigue."

In the following year Leopold Mozart visited his son in Vienna, and was an eye-witness of his popularity. He

---

[51] This imposing list includes not only the names of Mozart's avowed patrons, Countess Thun, Baroness Waldstädten, Count Zichy, Van Swieten, but also of the Duke of Würtemburg, the Prince of Mecklenburg, the Princes C. Liechtenstein, Auersperg, Kaunitz, Lichnowsky, Lobkowitz, Paar, Palm, Schwarzenberg, and the famous names of Bathiany, Dietrichstein, Erdödy, Esterhazy, Harrach, Herberstein, Keglewicz, Nostiz, Palfy, Schaffgotsch, Stahremberg, Waldstein; besides the Ambassadors of Russia, Spain, Sardinia, Holland, Denmark, the great bankers, Fries, Henikstein, Arenfeld, Bienenfeld, Ployer, Wetzlar, high officers of state and scholars, such as Isdenczy, Bedekovich, Nevery, Braun, Greiner, Keess, Puffendorf, Born, Martini, Sonnenfels—in very truth the most distinguished society of Vienna.

[52] Kelly, Reminisc., I., p. 231. Pohl, Mozart in London, p. 169.

[53] At the same time Mozart wrote the two concertos for Barb. von Ployer (Vol. II., p. 279), a concerto in B flat major (No. 4, 450 K.) on March 15, a concerto in D major (No. 13, 451 K.) on March 22, and the quintet (452 K.) on March 30.

writes to his daughter (January 22, 1785): "I have this moment received a line from your brother, saying that his concerts begin on February 11, and are to continue every Friday." He arranged to be in Vienna for this concert, which was given on the Mehlgrube, with a subscription list of over one hundred and fifty at three ducats each. He wrote to Marianne at the conclusion of the concert (February 11, 1784): "Wolfgang played an admirable new concerto, which was in the copyist's hands when we arrived yesterday; your brother had not even time to try over the rondo. The concerto is in D minor" (466 K., No. 8). The second concert, too, "was splendid"; and at a benefit concert in the theatre for which Wolfgang wrote the Concerto in C major (467 K., No. 1) he made 559 florins, "which we had not expected, as the list for his subscription concerts numbers one hundred and fifty persons, and he has often played at other people's concerts for nothing," as L. Mozart writes (March 12, 1785). He played at Madame Laschi's concert on February 12, 1785, a splendid concerto which he had composed for the blind pianiste in Paris, Marie Thérèse Paradies (1759-1824); this is probably the Concerto in B major (456 K., No. 11) dated September 30, 1784. "When your brother made his exit," writes the father, "the Emperor bowed to him, hat in hand, and called: 'Bravo, Mozart!' He was very much applauded on his entrance."

During the Lent of 1786 Mozart had, as he wrote to his father (December 28, 1785), three subscription concerts, with one hundred and twenty subscribers; for these he wrote three new concertos. One in E flat major (482 K., No. 6) on December 26, 1785, another in A major (488 K., No. 2) on March 2, 1786, and the third in C minor on March 24, 1786, the andante of which he was obliged to repeat at the concert of April 7, the last given in the theatre.[54] In Advent of the same year, as he informs his father (December 8, 1786), he gave four concerts at the Casino, for which he composed a new Concerto in C major (503 K., No. 16), dated December 4, 1786; in January of the same year he

---

[54] Wien. Ztg., 1786, No. 28, Anh.

journeyed to Prague, where he was received with enthusiasm as the composer of "Figaro." In obedience to the
general desire, he played at a great concert in the Opera-
House, to a very crowded audience; Mozart was recalled
three times, and when at last he improvised variations on
"Non più andrai" there was no end to the applause; a
second concert was attended with eqally brilliant results.
Madame Storace informed L. Mozart, who wrote the news
to his daughter (March 1, 1787), that Wolfgang had made
one thousand florins in Prague.

Even if it be granted that the honour and profit of these
concerts did not equal that which was accorded to celebrated
vocalists of the day,[55] yet it would be unjust to maintain that
Mozart was not appreciated by the public, and that they
failed to express their appreciation in hard cash. Any comparison with the unexampled success attained by great
performers of a later day ought not to leave out of sight that
the concert-visiting public has enormously increased since
that time, when this enjoyment was the exclusive privilege
of the higher ranks.

The growing interest for literature and art was then just
beginning to awaken in the citizen class some desire for participation in theatrical performances and concerts; but still
the concert public of that time had very little resemblance
to that which we now expect to find. The difference shows
itself in the private concerts. During the winter, and particularly during Lent, musical performances were the chief
means of entertainment among the nobility and wealthy
citizens. Amateur theatricals were also very fashionable,
and even operas were often given in private.[56] An opera
by Prince Liechtenstein has been mentioned before (Vol. II.,
p. 287); Mozart's "Idomeneo" was given in 1786 at
the private theatre of Prince Auersperg, where in 1782
an Italian opera had been given in honour of the Grand

---

[55] Storace and Coltellini had a salary of 1,000 ducats, besides free quarters
and travelling expenses; and to this was added the profit accruing from
benefits, concerts, and other sources. Marchesi received 600 ducats and a
valuable ring for six performances (Müller, Abschied, p. 8).

[56] Theaterkal., 1787, p. 95. C. Pichler, Denkw., I., p. 124.

Duke ;[57] Kelly had heard the Countess Hatzfeld[58] sing Gluck's "Alceste" there incomparably well.[59]

Noblemen of high rank often maintained their own musical establishments ; and though this did not often consist, as in the case of Prince Esterhazy or the Prince von Hildburghausen,[60] of a complete orchestra, yet the retinue of most of the nobility (especially in Bohemia) were capable of taking part in orchestral music,[61] or there was at least a band of wind instruments to play during meals or in serenades.[62] But for the private performances of which we have just spoken a complete orchestra was always employed,[63] which was an easier matter then than it would be now that orchestras are so much more fully appointed. This arrangement was of the greatest importance for the musical profession. The frequent concerts gave opportunity for a large number of musicians to educate themselves into good orchestral players, and the composers found constant employment in every branch of their art. Patrons vied with each other in the production of new works by distinguished masters, and above all in the acquisition of celebrated performers. The expense of musical soirées was very great, but custom made it a point of honour among the aristocracy to patronise the art which then surpassed all others in public estimation.

Mozart's popularity as a pianist would, as a matter of course, render him much in request at these private concerts. As early as the winter of 1782 he was engaged for all the concerts given by Prince Gallitzin, the Russian ambassador, who " placed his carriage at my disposal both going and returning, and treated me in the handsomest

[57] Wien. Ztg., 1782, No. 82.

[58] Jahrb. Tonk., 1796, p. 25.

[59] Kelly, Reminisc., I., p. 201. A performance of " Axur " is mentioned (Jahrb. f. Tonk., 1796, p. 38). According to the Thematic Catalogue, Mozart wrote a concluding chorus " für Dilettanti," to Sarti's opera, " Le Gelosie Villane," on April 20, 1791.

[60] Dittersdorf, Selbstbiogr., pp. 7, 49.

[61] Gyrowetz, Selbstbiogr., p. 8.

[62] Cf. pp. 307, 627.

[63] C. Pichler, Denkw., I., p. 45.

manner possible' (December 21, 1782). During the following winter he again played regularly for Prince Gallitzin, also for Count Johann Esterhazy, Count Zichy, &c. He calculates for his father's benefit that, from February 26 till April 3, he would have to play five times for Gallitzin, and nine times for Esterhazy, to which might be added three of Richter's concerts and five of his own, besides chance invitations. "Have I not enough to do?" he asks. "I do not think I shall be allowed to get out of practice." When his father was in Vienna in 1785, he wrote to his daughter that Wolfgang's harpsichord had been to the theatre and to different private houses quite twelve times between February 11 and March 12.[64] What amount of fee Mozart received for his performances in private we have no means of ascertaining; in general, however, the aristocracy were accustomed to reward distinguished artists according to their deserts, and the exceptional position of the Viennese nobility enabled the artists to accept their liberality without loss of dignity; the more so as it was usually founded on sentiments of esteem and consideration. That the friendly demeanour of persons of high rank was highly prized by the artists themselves, there can be no doubt; nor would there be wanting some who sought to merit it by servile adulation. From any tinge of this Mozart was absolutely free; not only was he unfettered by the forms of social class distinctions, but he moved in society with all the independence of a distinguished man, without laying claim to the license usually accorded to artists of genius. The etiquette of rank was no bar to his intimacy with Prince Karl Lichnowsky; and another of his true friends was Count August Hatzfeld, who had carefully cultivated a considerable musical talent, and was a first-rate quartet violinist. He became so imbued with the spirit of Mozart's quartets, that the latter was said to have declared that he liked nobody's execution of them so well as Count

---

[64] Mozart's concert harpsichord is now in the Mozarteum at Salzburg, a little instrument by Anton Welter, in a walnut-wood case with black naturals and white flats and sharps. It has five octaves, is light in touch, and tolerably powerful in tone.

Hatzfeld's.[65] The song in "Idomeneo" with obbligato violin
was composed for him. His noble character won for him
universal esteem, which was intensified by the calmness with
which he met death in his thirty-first year (Bonn, 1787).
Mozart wrote to his father in a very serious letter (April 4,
1787) :—

> On this subject (death and dying) I have already expressed my mind
> to you on the occasion of the melancholy death of my best and dearest
> friend, Count von Hatzfeld. He was thirty-one—just my age. I do
> not mourn for *him*, but for myself and for all those who knew him as I
> did.

Mozart also gave regular musical performances every
Sunday morning in his own house; he used to invite his
friends, and musical amateurs were admitted on payment.
Kelly relates[66] that he never missed one of these. I find them
mentioned elsewhere also, and have heard of them from old
people who took part in them during the last years of
Mozart's life. They were always well attended; but whether
Mozart's public concerts were continued with unabated
success after the year 1788, or whether the time had come
when he was to experience "the fickleness" of the Viennese,
I have no means of determining with exactitude. He wrote
three symphonies in June, July, and August of 1788, whence
it may be concluded that he was giving concerts during that
time; and, by the same reasoning, the absence of any symphonies or concertos composed during the years immediately
following would prove that no concerts were then given.
His pecuniary embarrassments during those years tell the
same tale; and the cutting off of this important contribution
to his income seems to have occasioned his journeys to
Berlin and Frankfort.   Not until January, 1791, do we meet
with another pianoforte concerto in B flat major (595 K.,
No. 15) that was no doubt intended for a Lenten concert.

The publication of his compositions, which in the present
day would have been Mozart's chief dependence, was by no
means profitable, as matters then stood. The music trade

---

[65] Cramer's Mag. d. Musik, II., p. 1380.
[66] Kelly, Reminisc., I., p. 226.

of the day was small and insignificant; indeed, the first
impulse was given to it by the publication of an edition of
all Mozart's works soon after his death. During his life,
however, compositions were more often copied than printed;[67]
and the composer was obliged to keep careful watch lest
copies should be distributed which were not ordered from
him, and which in consequence he was never paid for. It
need scarcely be said that caution such as this was not in
Mozart's nature, and that copies of his works were frequently
made and sold without his knowledge. Different musical
firms (Joh. Traeg, Lausch, Torricella, &c.) advertised copies
of his compositions for sale under his very eyes; nor was
this conduct, however undesirable, thought unworthy of a
respectable tradesmen. He was careful only of his concertos; too much depended on his keeping possession of
them, and not allowing any one to play them who chose.
His three first concertos, indeed, he thought it advisable to
publish himself by a subscription of six ducats (December
23, 1782). He offered them afterwards to the "highly
respectable public" for four ducats, "beautifully copied and
revised by himself."[68] Even this his father thought too dear;
but Mozart thought that the concertos were worth the
money, and could not be copied for it.

When sending his father those composed in the following
year, he wrote (May 24, 1784): "I can wait patiently until
you send them back, so long as they do not fall into any one
else's hands; I might have had twenty-four ducats for one
of them to-day; but I think it will be to my advantage to
keep them a couple of years by me, and then to have them
printed." He used to take only the orchestral parts with
him on his journeys, and to play himself from a clavier part
of most extraordinary appearance, according to Rochlitz.[69]
It consisted of only the figured bass and the principal

---

[67] Mozart's printed composition only extended during his lifetime to Op. 18
(Klavierconcert, 451 K., No. 13), without counting variations and songs.

[68] Wien. Zeit., 1783, No. 5, Anh. These three concertos in A major
(414 K., No 10), F major (413 K., No. 12), and C major (414 K., No. 5),
were then printed in Vienna as Œuvre IV.

[69] A. M. Z., I., p. 113.

motifs, with hints for the passages, runs, &c.; he depended on his memory, which never by any chance failed him. In 1788 he advertised copies of three quintets for four ducats.[70]

As far, then, as concertos and symphonies were concerned, the composer made his principal profit by his own perform-ance of them ; but he was also called upon to write different things for other people. Mozart wrote many compositions for his pupils, an extraordinary number for his friends and acquaintance, and not a few to order on particular occasions. Among the latter class are the quartets written for Frederick William II., in 1789 and 1790 (575, 589, 590, K.), for which he was doubtless well paid ; it was said that he received for the first a valuable gold snuff-box and a hundred friedrichs-d'or.[71] It is well known that one hundred ducats were paid in advance for the Requiem, and something may have come in for the adaptation of Handel's oratorios, ordered by Van Swieten in 1788 and 1789, as well as for here and there a commission or dedication. But a closer examination of the long list of Mozart's compositions of this class makes it probable that they were not for the most part profitable to him. A cha-racteristic anecdote is related of him by his widow, which bears out this supposition.[72] At one of Mozart's Sunday matinées there was present a Polish Count, who was very much delighted with the new (composed March 30, 1784) piano-forte quintet with wind instruments. He commissioned Mozart to write a trio with obbligato flute, which the latter promised to do. As soon as he arrived at home, the Count sent Mozart a hundred half-louis with a very polite note, repeating his thanks for the pleasure the music had given him. The terms of the note left Mozart no doubt that the money was a generous gift, and he returned the politest acknowledgment, at the same time sending the Count, con-trary to his custom, the original score of the quintet he had so much admired. A year after the Count came again to Mozart and inquired after the trio. Mozart excused himself by saying he had not yet found himself in the humour to

[70] Wien. Ztg., 1788, No. 27, Anh.
[71] N. Berl. Musikzeitg., 1856, p. 35.
[72] A. M. Z., I., p. 289.

write anything worthy of the Count's acceptance. "Then, no doubt," answered the Count, "you will find yourself still less in the humour to return me the hundred half-louis which I paid you for it." Mozart returned the money, but the Count kept the score of the quintet, which was soon after printed in Vienna without Mozart's permission. Against such persons and such behaviour Mozart had no weapons but a shrug of the shoulders, and a—"The rascal!" It may well be supposed that others besides this Polish Count took advantage of such easy-going good-nature. But the publishers must not be credited with more than their share of blame.[73] Variations and similar trifles were doubtless often printed without the composer's consent, and brought in considerable profits in which he had no share. But the more important of his works which appeared during his lifetime were either printed by subscription or trusted for publication to Torricella, Artaria, and Hoffmeister. I have only in one case been able to discover the amount paid to him; he wrote to his father, who communicated it to his daughter (January 22, 1785) that he had sold his quartets dedicated to Jos. Haydn to Artaria for one hundred ducats. This was a considerable sum for those days, and the reception given to the quartets on their appearance might well cause the publisher to fear he had paid too dear for them. It is said that the two beautiful pianoforte quartets in G minor (478 K., composed in July, 1785) and in E flat major (493 K., composed in June, 1786), were only the commencement of a series bespoken by Hoffmeister; but the public finding them too difficult, and refraining from buying them, he allowed Mozart to retain the money he had paid in advance, and gave up the continuation.[74] The popularity gained by Mozart's greater works must always have been of gradual growth, since they were considered in every respect too difficult, and it is quite credible that Hoffmeister said, as was reported of him:[75] "Write more popularly, or else I can neither print nor pay for anything more of yours!"

---

[73] Rochlitz's account (A. M. Z., I., p. 83) does not tally.
[74] Cf. Nissen, p. 633.
[75] Rochlitz, A. M. Z., XV., p. 313. Für Freunde der Tonkunst, I., p. 148.

nor is it less credible that Mozart should have answered: "Then I will write nothing more, and go hungry, or may the devil take me!"

A note written to Hoffmeister on November 20, 1785, is indeed in quite another tone:[76]—

> Dear Hoffmeister,—I have recourse to you, and beg you to assist me with a little money, of which I am much in want at present. I earnestly entreat you to send me what I require as soon as possible. Pardon my troubling you so much, but you know me, and are aware how much I have your affairs at heart, so that I am convinced that you will not be offended at my importunities, but will be as ready to show yourself my friend as I am yours.

A very enterprising publisher, Commerzienrath Hummel, of Berlin, maintained that, though not musical, he could tell by the look of a composition whether it would suit him. He had a poor opinion of Mozart, and used to boast of having sent him back various works.[77]

Rochlitz relates, as an instance of Mozart's ill-treatment at the hands of theatrical managers,[78] that Schikaneder paid nothing for the "Zauberflöte," and even, contrary to the agreement, sold the score without his knowledge. Seyfried,[79] on the other hand, maintains that Schikaneder paid Mozart a hundred ducats, and resigned the net profits of the sale of the score to his widow. Be this as it may, Schikaneder's treatment of Mozart must not be considered illustrative of that which he usually received from his managers. A hundred ducats was then the usual payment in Vienna for an opera. This sum Mozart received for the "Entführung," for "Figaro," and no doubt also for "Così fan Tutte." For "Don Giovanni" he had 225 florins. To this were usually added the proceeds of a benefit performance (and another for the poet), which of course depended on the popularity of the composer with the public. Mozart does not mention the benefit performance of the

---

[76] Endorsed by Hoffmeister: "Den 20 Nov., 1785, mit 2 Dukaten." N. Ztschr. Mus., IX., p. 164.

[77] A. M. Z., I., p. 547.

[78] A. M. Z., I., p. 83; cf. p. 147. Nissen, p. 548.

[79] Neue Zeitschr. Mus., XII., p. 180.

"Entführung"; but both in this case and that of "Figaro" it must have had considerable results.[80] Bondini paid a hundred ducats for "Don Giovanni." The Bohemian States, who ordered the "Clemenza di Tito" for their coronation festival, can scarcely have offered him less remuneration; even the manager Guardasoni, who was famous for his parsimony, "almost agreed" in the year 1785 to give Mozart "two hundred ducats for an opera and fifty ducats travelling expenses," as he informs his wife—an agreement, however, which was never carried out.[81]

In this respect, therefore, Mozart was not behind contemporary composers. With regard to performances on foreign stages, we have no definite information as to whether his permission was asked or paid for,[82] but we may gather something from the ordinary usages of the time. It was the traditional custom in Italy that whoever ordered the opera should pay for it; what became of the score afterwards was generally left to chance. The impresario remained in possession of it, and usually allowed the copyist to make what profit he could out of the sale of it (Vol. I., p. 131); but the composer also kept the score, and seems to have distributed it wherever he thought he might gain honour or profit by it. In Germany the case was altered, since there the composer had generally to do with a court theatre. In Mannheim and Munich he retained undivided possession of the score (Vol. II., p. 141).[83] Mozart rejoiced that Baron Riedesel had asked him for the "Entführung" and not the copyist (Vol. II., p. 213). As a matter of course foreign theatres took the easiest course open to them to obtain possession of the score. When they applied to the composer it was only because they saw no other way of getting it, or for some special reason. Any question of

---

[80] Dittersdorf says that the profits from his benefit performance of the "Doktor and Apotheker" amounted to 200 ducats (Selbstbiogr., p. 243).

[81] Rochlitz's account is confused and uncertain. (Für Freunde d. Tonk., II., p. 258., II).

[82] He expected a gift from the Prussian Ambassador; whether he received it, or what it was, is not known.

[83] Count Seeau must have sold for his own profit the pieces which were only purchased for representation; Schröder and Beecké complain of this in unpublished letters to Dalberg.

the composer's rights or the theatrical manager's obligations
seems never to have occurred to either party. A careful
hold of the score and watchful supervision of the copyist
were the only means of protection. These did not go far,
nor was Mozart the man to make use of them. When,
therefore, his operas appeared on foreign boards without any
compensation to himself, he only shared the fate of most of
his contemporaries, nor does he seem to have complained of
it. He is glad to write to his father (December 6, 1783)
that his "Entführung" had been well and successfully performed in Prague and Leipzig; and he rejoiced again when
"Figaro" was given in Prague and "Don Giovanni" in
Vienna; but there is no mention of payment.

If we summarise these financial remarks, we shall arrive
at the conclusion that in view of the importance of his
works, and the profits afterwards made on them both by the
theatres and the publishers, Mozart was very inadequately
paid; but this standard cannot be unreservedly applied to
them. The conditions and fluctuations of profit to which
even artists are subject are ruled by the prevalent type of
living among citizens and the higher classes; the close-
fisted organisation of a community of merchants and traders
cares little for the comet-like course of an artistic genius,
and is only too likely to give it an altogether wrong direction
or to ruin it at the outset. From a pecuniary point of view
we must acknowledge that Mozart was on the whole as
well treated as the majority of his fellow-artists; that
both as a composer and a performer he was sometimes no
worse, sometimes better, paid than others; that he had no
lack of opportunities for earning money, and that in point of
fact he had a very good income. If Mozart had possessed
the same capacity for business as his father or Joseph
Haydn, he would no doubt have reaped far greater advantages from his position in Vienna; but even on what he
actually earned he might have lived in ease and plenty.
Without ourselves going into calculations on the subject,
we have a trustworthy witness for it in Leopold Mozart.
During his visit to Vienna, in 1785, he had a watchful eye
on the earnings and expenditure of his son, and wrote to his

daughter (March 19, 1785): "I believe that, *if he has no debts to pay*, my son can now lay by two thousand florins; the money is certainly there, and the household expenses, so far as eating and drinking are concerned, could not be more economical." How far removed was Mozart from such providence! From the time of his marriage we find him in constantly recurring money difficulties; a long list of melancholy documents lets us into the vexations, cares, and humiliations which were the inevitable consequences of his improvidence. Scarcely six months after their marriage the wedded couple were obliged to apply to the Baroness von Waldstädten in the following note, in order to avert a threatened action-at-law by one of their creditors :—

Most honoured Baroness,—I find myself in a fine position, truly! We agreed with Herr von Tranner lately that we should have a fortnight's grace. As this is customary with every merchant, unless he be the most disobliging fellow in the world, I thought nothing more of it, and hoped, if I could not pay the amount myself, at least to be able to borrow it. Now Herr von Tranner sends me word that he positively refuses to wait, and if I do not pay him between to-day and to-morrow he will bring an action against me! I cannot pay him even the half of it. If I had had any idea that the subscriptions for my concert would come in so slowly, I would have fixed the payment for a later date. I pray your ladyship, for Heaven's sake, to help me to preserve my honour and my good name! My poor little wife is feeling poorly, and I cannot leave her, or else I would come myself and beg this favour of you by word of mouth. We kiss your ladyship's hand a thousand times, and beg to remain your ladyship's obedient children,

February 15, 1783. W. A. AND C. MOZART.

In July of the same year, when he was setting out for Salzburg, and actually in the act of entering his carriage, he was stopped by an importunate creditor for the paltry claim of thirty florins, which, nevertheless, he found it difficult to satisfy.[84] And not long after his return to Vienna he was disagreeably surprised by a demand for twelve louis-d'or, which he had borrowed at Strasburg in 1778. He was obliged to write to his father :—

---

[84] Nissen, p. 475.

You will remember that when you came to Munich, where I was writing the great opera, you reproached me for having borrowed twelve louis-d'ors from Herr Scherz, at Strasburg, with the words, "Your want of confidence in me disappoints me—but enough; I suppose I shall have the honour of paying the twelve louis-d'or." I travelled to Vienna, you to Salzburg. What could I suppose from your words but that I need think no more of the debt—or at least, that you would write to me if you did not pay it, or speak about it when I saw you in Salzburg? I ask nothing further of you, my dear father, than that you will be my security for a month. Had he demanded payment during the first year I could have done it at once and with pleasure; and I will pay him as it is, only I am not in a position to do so at this moment.

In the very same year that his father boasts of his finances, we find him in a difficulty which necessitated his applying to his publisher, Hoffmeister, who put him off with a couple of ducats. But the saddest insight into the embarrassed and humiliating position in which Mozart found himself after the year 1788 is afforded by his letters to his friend, Michael Puchberg, a wealthy merchant,[85] musical himself, and with two daughters, one of whom distinguished herself as a clavier-player. He was a Freemason, and it seems to have been through the lodge that an intimacy was founded close enough to warrant Mozart's constant application to him for assistance. His wish to borrow a sum sufficiently large to be of permanent benefit to him, either from Puchberg himself or by his instrumentality, was not granted. So that when his rent became due, or his wife's doctor's bill, or a stay in the country had to be provided for, he was constantly obliged to claim assistance from his friend. Whenever it was possible Mozart strove to meet his household embarrassments in a joking mood. In the winter of 1790 Joseph Deiner, the landlord of the "Silver Serpent," who was of use to Mozart in many of his household affairs, called upon him one day and found him in his workroom dancing about with his wife. On Deiner's asking him if he was giving his wife dancing lessons, Mozart answered, laughing, " We are

---

[85] He was called a "Niederlagsverwandter," that is, he belonged to the privileged society of merchants, for the most part Protestants, who had the right, subject to certain restrictions, of keeping warehouses and trading wholesale (Nicolai, Reise, IV., p. 447).

warming ourselves, because we are very cold, and have no money to buy fuel." Thereupon Deiner ran home and brought them some wood, which Mozart accepted and promised to pay him for as soon as he made any money.[86] But dancing will not satisfy every need, and the faithful Puchberg was never weary of assisting Mozart. He sent him larger or smaller sums, which Mozart was never in a position to repay, so that after his death his liabilities amounted to one thousand florins. Puchberg, who was of great service to Mozart's widow in the ordering of her affairs, postponed his claims for several years, so as to give her the opportunity of paying him by degrees, as her circumstances improved.[87] Mozart had recourse to other friends besides Puchberg; in April, 1789, he borrowed one hundred florins from an aspirant to Freemasonry, named Hofdemel, as is testified by the existing letter and note of hand.[88] It was not likely that assistance of this kind would materially improve Mozart's position. In 1790, when he undertook the journey to Frankfort, in the result of which he had placed great hopes, he was obliged to raise his travelling expenses by pawning plate and ornaments;[89] and the financial transaction of which he speaks in his letters to his wife, whereby somebody was to hand him over one thousand florins on Hoffmeister's endorsement, shows clearly enough that he had fallen into the hands of usurers, from whom he had striven in vain to free himself by Puchberg's intervention. These facts prove only too clearly that from the time of his marriage Mozart became gradually entangled in a net of embarrassments, without any hope of permanent extrication. His letters show how deeply he felt the cares and humiliations of his position. The circumstances of so public a character could not remain long concealed in Vienna, even had he been less injudiciously open than he was; after his death ill-natured gossip exaggerated his debts to a sum of thirty thousand florins, and the rumour reached the ear of the Emperor Leopold. The widow, informed of this by a

---

[86] Wiener Morgenpost, 1856, No. 28.

[87] Nissen, p. 686.

[88] O. Jahn, Aufs. üb. Musik., p. 234.

[89] Nissen, p. 683.

friend of high rank, explained the calumny to the Emperor, and assured him that three thousand florins would cover all Mozart's debts. The Emperor gave her generous assistance as soon as the facts and extenuating circumstances had been made known to him,[90] but he refused a pension.

The same charitable dispositions which settled the amount of Mozart's debts were also busy in accounting for the fact of their existence. How could they have been contracted but by dissipation, irregular living, and extravagance ?[91] Against such accusations we must listen to Mozart himself, who would hardly have had the face to appeal to his manner of life and well-known habits in applying for help to his intimate friend Puchberg, if he had been conscious of such improprieties as those with which he was charged. Leopold Mozart's testimony is unimpeachable as to the economy of the housekeeping in the matter of eating and drinking, and it was confirmed by Sophie Haibl. It may be thought that the father purposely limits his praise of Wolfgang's economy to matters of eating and drinking, and this is no doubt quite possible. Mozart was very neat and particular in his dress, and fond of lace and watch-chains.[92] Clementi

---

[90] Niemetschek, p. 57. Nissen, p. 580.

[91] How far Mozart was misjudged in this respect is shown by such expressions as those in Schlichtegroll's Nekrolog: "In Vienna he married Constanze Weber, who made a good mother to his two children and a careful wife, striving to restrain his folly and extravagance. His income was considerable, but his excesses and want of economy in household affairs caused him to leave nothing to his family but the fame of his genius and the observation of the world." It is not surprising that Mozart's widow should have bought up a whole impression of this notice in 1794. Rochlitz warmly condemns such shameless calumny. Arnold is much coarser (Mozart's Geist, p. 65), accounting for his premature death by saying : " Besides this [excessive work] he was a husband, brought up two children, and had many intrigues with lively actresses and other women, which his wife good-naturedly overlooked. He must often have starved with his wife and children, if the threats of impatient creditors had been carried into effect. But when a few louis-d'or made their appearance the scene changed at once. All went merrily, Mozart got tipsy on champagne and tokay, spent freely, and in a few days was as badly off as ever. The liberties he took with his health are well known; how he used to drink champagne with Schikaneder all morning, and punch all night, and go to work again after midnight, without any thought of his bodily health."

[92] Nissen, p. 692.

took him for a valet-de-chambre on account of his elegant
appearance, and his handsome attire is referred to on various
occasions.   His father writes mockingly to his daughter
from Vienna (April 16, 1785) that Wolfgang and Madame
Lange had intended going with him to Munich, but nothing
was likely to come of it, "although each of them have had
six pairs of shoes made, which are all standing there now."
It may well be then that Mozart was not over-economical
in his dress; at the same time there is no reason to accuse
him of extravagant foppery.

The excess of which Mozart was mainly accused, however,
was not of this kind at all, but lay more in the direction of
sensual indulgence.   He had always been extremely fond of
cheerful society and the manifold distractions it brought
with it; nay, it was quite a necessity to him, as a refreshment after long-sustained mental efforts.   Mozart gave no
parties at home, but his wife used to organise little musical
performances on family festivals or to amuse her husband;
few friends were present on such occasions, and Haydn's
music was generally preferred by Mozart himself.[93]

There can have been no lack of opportunities for intercourse with his fellow-artists and with the numerous
accomplished and wealthy amateurs then in Vienna, and we
can well imagine that Mozart's social impulses found constant and lively exercise.   Music was the principal object of
meeting, and Mozart brought his tribute to the entertainment
in the form of improvisation, both grave and gay; he was a
lively and cheerful companion, too, in other respects, always
ready for a joke, and fond of exercising his gift for improvising comic doggerel verses.[94]

Of all amusements, Mozart was fondest of dancing, and

---

[93] Niemetschek, p. 99.

[94] Niemetschek, p. 93.   Mozart was very accessible to the pleasures of society
and friendship.   "Among his friends he was as open as a child, and full of merriment, which found vent in the drollest tricks.   His friends in Prague have a
pleasant remembrance of the hours passed in his company, and are never weary
of praising his good, innocent heart; when he was present, one forgot the artist
in the man" (Cf. Rochlitz, A. M. Z., III., p. 494).   His brother-in-law, Jos.
Lange, remarked that Mozart was generally in most jesting mood when he was
busy with some great work (Selbstbiogr., p. 171).

found ample opportunity for indulging his passion in Vienna, where dancing was at that time an absolute rage.[95] His wife confided to Kelly, who saw Mozart dance on the occasion of their first meeting, that her husband was an enthusiastic dancer, and thought more of his performances in that line than in music; he was said to dance the minuet very beautifully.[96] His letters have many indications of this partiality, and he gives his father a merry and complacent account of a ball at his own house (January 22, 1783):—

Last week I gave a ball in my own house; but of course the gentlemen paid two florins each. We began at six o'clock in the evening and left off at seven. What! only one hour? No, no; seven o'clock in the morning! You will scarcely believe that I could find room for it.

He had lately moved, and had taken apartments with Herr von Wezlar, a rich Jew:—

There I have a room a thousand paces long, and a bedroom, then an anteroom, and then a fine large kitchen; there are two fine large rooms next to ours, which stand empty at present, and these I made use of for the ball. Baron Wezlar and his wife were there, so were the Baroness Waldstädten, Herr von Edelbach, Gilowsky the boaster, young Stephanie, Adamberger and his wife, the Langes, &c.

Still more exciting entertainments were the masked balls; and we have already seen (Vol. I., p. 337) that Mozart possessed both inclination and talent for disporting himself in assumed characters. He writes from Vienna (January 22, 1788), begging his father to send him his harlequin's dress, because he would like to go on the Redoute as harlequin: "but so that nobody should know it; there are so many here (chiefly great asses) who go on the Redoute." Several good friends associated themselves into a "compagnie-masque," and performed a pantomime on Whit Monday, which filled up the half-hour before dancing began. Mozart was Harlequin, Madame Lange Columbine, Lange played Pierrot, an old dancing-master named Merk, who "drilled" the company, took Pantaloon, and the painter Grassi the Doctor. The plot and music were by Mozart, the doggerel verses

---

95 Kelly, Reminisc., I., p. 204.
96 Kelly, Reminisc., I., p. 226. Nissen, p. 692.

with which the pantomime was introduced by the actor
Müller; it might have been better, Mozart thought, but he
was satisfied with the acting: " I assure you we played very
well," he informs his father (March 12, 1783). Of the music
for this pantomime thirteen numbers for stringed instruments in parts are preserved, the first violin written by
Mozart (446 K.) It is, as may be imagined, very unpretending, as are also the briefly indicated situations ; for instance :
"Columbine is sad—Pantaloon makes love to her—she is
angry—he is gay—she angry—he angry too."

Another passion of Mozart's was billiard-playing; Kelly
relates that he often played with Mozart, but never won a
game.[97] He had a billiard-table in his own house, and played
with his wife in case of need,[98] or even quite alone. This was
certainly a luxury, though far from an unusual one in Vienna
at that time, and it was occasioned not solely from love of
the game,[99] but, as Holmes rightly remarks, from the care of
the physicians for Mozart's health.

In the spring of 1783 he was seized with cholera, which
was raging as an epidemic,[100] and in the following summer
he was again seriously ill, as Leopold Mozart informs his
daughter (September 14, 1784):—

My son has been very ill in Vienna. He was very much overheated at
Paesiello's new opera, " Il re Teodoro," and was obliged to go into the
open air to look for the servant who had charge of his overcoat, because
orders had been given that no servants should be admitted to the theatre
by the ordinary entrance. This brought on rheumatic fever, which without
careful attention might have turned to typhus. Wolfgang writes: " I have
had raging colic every day for a fortnight at the same hour, accompanied
by violent vomiting. My doctor, Herr Sigmund Barisani, was in the habit
of visiting me almost daily even before this illness; he is very clever, and
you will see that he will soon make himself a name."

Barisani was the son of the Archbishop's physician at
Salzburg, an intimate friend of the Mozart family. He was

---

[97] Kelly, Reminisc., I., p. 226.
[98] Niemetschek, p. 100.
[99] Nicolai, Reise, V., p. 219.
[100] He wrote to his father (June 7, 1783): " God be praised, I am quite well
again, only my illness has left a cold in the head behind as a remembrance—
very good of it!"

distinguished in his profession, becoming later chief physician at the general hospital, and a warm friend and admirer of Mozart. A charming memorial of their friendship is preserved at the Mozarteum in Salzburg, in the form of some affectionate verses addressed to Mozart by Barisani, bearing date April 14, 1787. Underneath Mozart has written the following lines :—

To-day, September 3 of this same year, I was so unfortunate as to lose by death this noble-natured man, my dearest, best friend, and the saviour of my life. It is well with him! but with me—us—and all who knew him—it can never be well again, until we are so happy as to meet him in another world *never to part again.*

Barisani, seeing the impossibility of altogether weaning Mozart from the habit of writing far into the night, and very often as he lay in bed in the morning, endeavoured to avert the hurtful consequences in another way. He recommended him not to sit so long at the clavier, but at all events to compose standing, and to take as much bodily exercise as he could.[101] His love of billiard-playing gave the doctor a welcome pretext for turning this motive into a regular one; Mozart was equally fond of bowls, and he was the more ready to follow the doctor's directions with regard to both games since they did not interfere with his intellectual activity. It happened one day in Prague that Mozart, while he was playing billiards, hummed an air, and looked from time to time into a book which he had with him; it appeared afterwards that he had been occupied with the first quintet of the "Zauberflöte."[102] When he was writing down the score of "Don Giovanni" in Duschek's garden, he took part at the same time in a game of quoits ; he stood up when his turn came round, and sat down again to his writing after he had thrown.[103]

But what of Mozart's inclination for strong drink, so often talked of? There can be no doubt that he was very fond of punch; Kelly speaks of it,[104] and Sophie Haibl does not

---

[101] Giesinger, Biogr. Not. üb. J. Haydn, p. 30.

[102] Nissen, p. 559.

[103] Bohemia, 1856, pp. 118, 122.

[104] Kelly, Reminisc., I., p. 226.

disguise that her brother-in-law loved a "punscherl," but she also asserts that he had never taken it immoderately, and that she had never seen him intoxicated.[105] That he was capable of wild excess is contradicted by his whole nature and by his conduct through life ; but these make it probable that he did not disdain the *poculum hilaritatis* in cheerful society, and that he gave vent to his spirits in a manner more unrestrained than it should have been.[106]

But Mozart also fortified himself with a glass of wine or punch when he was in the throes of composition. In one of his apartments his immediate neighbour was Joh. Mart. Loibl, who was musical and a Freemason, consequently intimate with Mozart; he had a well-filled wine-cellar, of the contents of which he was never sparing in entertaining his friends. The partition wall between the houses was so thin, that Mozart had only to knock when he wished to attract Loibl's attention ; whenever Loibl heard the clavier going and taps at his wall between the pauses, he used to send his servant into the cellar, and say to his family, " Mozart is composing again ; I must send him some wine."[107] His wife made him punch, too, when he was writing the overture to " Don Giovanni " the night before its performance. Whoever casts a glance over Mozart's scores will see that they could not have been written in the excitement caused by wine, so neat and orderly are they even to the smallest details, and in spite of the most rapid execution ; and those who are in a position to examine any one of his compositions will not need to be told that no intellect overstrained and excited by artificial means could possibly have produced such perfect clearness and beauty. Whether Mozart was right in providing a bodily stimulus in the form of strong drink during a continuous intellectual strain may well be doubted ; experience and opinions differ widely on this point. Goethe advised that there should be no forcing an

---

[105] Nissen, p. 672.

[106] Rochlitz suggests that Mozart sought forgetfulness of anxious thoughts in wine (A. M. Z., III., p. 495).

[107] Frau Klein, of Vienna, Loibl's daughter, related this and many other characteristic traits from her childish remembrances to my friend Karajan.

unproductive mood into activity by external means of any
kind; but he answered Eckermann's remark that a couple
of glasses of wine were often of great service in clearing the
mental vision, and bringing difficult subjects to a solution,
as follows: "You know my Divan so well that you will
remember that I said myself—

> Wenn man getrunken hat,
> Weiss man das Rechte,

and that I entirely agree with you. There exist in wine
inspiring forces of a very important kind; but all depends
upon circumstances and times and places, and what is
useful to one does harm to another."[108]

Let us now gather into one the separate traits which we
have been constrained to discuss, owing to the wide dissemi-
nation of those injurious reports against which Niemetschek
has already rightly protested.

We have before us the picture of a cheerful, pleasure-
loving man, capable of such exertions of productive power
and such intellectual industry as have seldom been surpassed
in the history of art, and seeking his necessary recreation in
social intercourse and the pleasures of the senses to a degree
which was equalled by the majority of his contemporaries in
Vienna without exciting any attention at all. He was not
by any means a thoughtless, dissipated spendthrift. But a
spendthrift he was, if the word be taken to signify one who
fails to control his wants and luxuries, so that they may be
in proportion to the actual state of his finances. His
most dangerous qualities were a good-natured soft-hearted-
ness, and a spontaneous generosity. He gave, as it were,
involuntarily, from inner necessity. Rochlitz relates that
he not only gave free admissions to the chorus-singers at
Leipzig, to which they had no claim, but that he privately
pressed a considerable present into the hands of one of the
bass singers who had specially pleased him. When a poor old
piano-tuner, stammering with embarrassment, begged for a
thaler, Mozart pressed a couple of ducats into his hand and

---

[108] Eckermann, Gespräche mit Goethe, III., p. 234, &c., especially p. 220.

hurried from the room.[109] When he was in a position to give
help, he could not see any one in want without offering relief,
even though it entailed future difficulties on himself and his
family; repeated experiences made him no more prudent in
this respect.   That he was often imposed upon there can
be no doubt.   Whoever came to him at meal-time was his
guest, all the more welcome if he could make or understand
a joke, and Mozart was happy if only his guests enjoyed
their fare.   Among them were doubtless, as Sophie Haibl
relates, " false friends, secret blood-suckers, and worthless
people, who served only to amuse him at table, and intercourse with whom injured his reputation."[110]   One of the
worst of this set was Albert Stadler, who may serve as an
example of the way in which Mozart was sometimes treated.
He was an excellent clarinet-player, and a Freemason; he
was full of jokes and nonsense, and contrived so to ingratiate
himself with Mozart that the latter constantly invited him
to his house and composed many things for him.   Once,
having learnt that Mozart had just received fifty ducats, he
represented himself as undone if he could not succeed in
borrowing that very sum.   Mozart, who wanted the money
himself, gave him two valuable repeater watches to put in
pawn upon condition that he should bring him the tickets
and redeem them in due time ; as he did not do this, Mozart
gave him fifty ducats, besides the interest, in order not to
lose his watches.   Stadler kept the money, and allowed the
watches to remain at the pawnbroker's.   Nowise profiting
by this experience, Mozart, on his return from Frankfort, in
1790, commissioned Stadler to redeem from pawn a portion
of the silver plate which had been pledged for the expenses
of the journey and to renew the agreement for the remainder.
In spite of a very strong suspicion that Stadler had pur-
loined this pawn-ticket from Mozart's open cashbox, the
latter was not deterred from assisting him in the following
year towards a professional tour, both with money and
recommendations, in Prague, and from presenting him with

---

[109] A. M. Z., I., p. 81.
[110] Nissen, p. 673.

a concerto (622 K.), composed only a few months before
Mozart's death.[111]

No doubt all this shows culpable weakness on Mozart's
part—weakness incompatible with his duty to himself and
his family.   His household burdens were increased by many
misfortunes, especially by the repeated and long-continued
illnesses of his wife, necessitating an expensive sojourn in
Baden for many successive summers.   Her delicacy doubtless prevented such personal supervision of the household
as was essential to its economical management.   She failed
also to acquire such an intellectual influence over her
husband as to strengthen his capacity for the proper conduct
of his affairs, and she had not strength of mind or energy to
take the management of the household entirely into her own
hands.   She felt the discomfort keenly, saw the causes of
it, but could not strive against them for any length of time.
Without wishing to reproach her, we may say at least that
had Constanze been as good a housekeeper as Mozart was
a composer, things would have gone well with him.

It must not be supposed that Mozart was blind to the
advantages of good household management or wanting in
the will to effect it; from time to time he made earnest
endeavours after economic reform.   In February, 1784, he
began an exact catalogue of his compositions, in which he
carefully entered every one of his works, until a short time
before his death, with suggestions of the theme;[112] at the same
time he began to keep an account book of his income and
expenditure.   André observes as to this account, which
unhappily I have not been able to see, that Mozart entered
his receipts—which included the profits on some concerts, on
lessons to different persons of rank, and on a few of his
compositions—on a long piece of paper.   His expenditure
he noted in a little quarto book, which he afterwards used

---

[111] Nissen, p. 683.

[112] This document, invaluable for the history of Mozart's compositions, leaving
no doubt as to important points from the year 1784 onwards, has been published
by André under the title, " W. A. Mozart's thematischer Catalog " (Offenbach,
1805, 1828).   It is my authority for all assertions as to the date of his works,
except where otherwise specified.

for writing English exercises and translations. His entries, while they lasted, were exact and minute. For instance, on one page we find:—

May 1, 1784. Two lilies of the valley ... 1 kreutzer.
May 27, 1784. A starling ... ... 34 kreutzers.

Then comes the following melody—

with the remark, "Das war schön!" It is easy to discover what so delighted him. On April 12 he had composed his pianoforte concerto in G major (453 K.), and soon after played it in public. The subject of the rondo is:—

The pleasure he felt at hearing it piped so comically altered induced him to buy the bird. He grew very much attached to his "Vogel Stahrl," as indeed he was to all animals, especially birds, and when it died he erected a gravestone to its memory in his garden, with an epitaph in verse.[113]

The excessive neatness of the account-books leads us to fear that they were not persevered with for any very long time, and indeed it is almost surprising that Mozart should have kept them for a whole year, from March, 1784, to February, 1785. After that he handed them over to his wife, and the entries soon cease.

Certainly Niemetschek is right in saying that "even if the same indulgence be granted to Mozart that we must all wish to see extended to ourselves, he cannot be put forward as an example of carefulness and economy." Whoever, like Mozart, begins his housekeeping with nothing at all, or even with debts, and is dependent upon an uncertain and fluctuating income, has need of the strictest economy and regularity, amounting even to parsimony, if he is to extricate himself from his difficulties or attain to com-

---

[113] Niemetschek, p. 91.

petence; otherwise occasional strokes of good fortune are seldom of use—indeed are sometimes positive hindrances." Regularity and economy were, as we have seen, qualities not in Mozart's nature, and he never acquired them. Their absence sufficiently accounts for his constant financial embarrassments. He atoned for his errors and weakness by poverty and want, by sorrow and care, by shame and humiliation; he was spared none of the punishment which life ruthlessly inflicts on those who do not conform to the laws of her iron necessity. But death has wiped out the stain, and the misrepresentations of envious detractors and petty fault-finders have no power to touch that which is immortal.

CHAPTER XXVIII.

MOZART'S FAMILY AND FRIENDS.

MOZART'S relations to his father, which had hitherto, one may say, filled his whole mental life to a most uncommon degree, had been seriously affected by his marriage. It was not till after long opposition that Leopold Mozart voluntarily, although most unwillingly, gave his consent, and how deeply he was wounded will appear from the answer he made to a conciliatory letter addressed to him by the Baroness Waldstädten (August 23, 1783):—

I thank your ladyship most heartily for the interest you are pleased to take in my affairs, and more especially for your ladyship's extraordinary kindness in celebrating so handsomely my son's wedding-day.[1] When I was a young fellow I imagined that those were philosophers who spoke little, laughed seldom, and maintained a surly demeanour towards all the rest of mankind. But my own experience has now fully convinced me that I am myself a philosopher without knowing it; I have done my duty as a father—have made the clearest and most comprehensible statements in many letters—and I am convinced that he knows my painful circumstances, made doubly so by my advanced age and unworthy position in Salzburg—he knows that I am sacrificed

---

[1] At Wolfgang's request he sent the Baroness a couple of Salzburg tongues, which were esteemed a delicacy.

morally and physically by his behaviour—and there now remains no resource to me but to leave him (as he has so willed it) to himself, and to pray the Almighty to bestow my paternal blessing on him, and not to withdraw His Divine mercy. As to myself, I will endeavour to preserve what remains of my native cheerfulness, and still to hope for the best.[2]

Putting ourselves in the place of Leopold Mozart, we must acknowledge that his reproaches and misgivings were in some respects well founded; but, nevertheless, he went too far in that he could not make up his mind to recognise his son's independence, and gave way to a bitterness of feeling which made him hard and unjust, and which, unhappily, was never altogether effaced from his heart. Wolfgang, on the contrary, betrayed no shadow of resentment—his love and reverence for his father remained the same to the end, unabated by unsparing and often unjust fault-finding. If his letters were less frequent or shorter than formerly he had ample excuses to offer, either of illness or the numerous occupations and distractions which were unavoidable in his position.[3] When, for any of these reasons, customary congratulations were neglected, an apology was sure to follow—for instance (January 4, 1783): "We both thank you heartily for your New Year's wishes, and willingly acknowledge ourselves stupid blockheads for having forgotten our duty in this respect; being so far behindhand, we will dispense altogether with a New Year's wish, only offering you our general every-day wish, and so let it pass." Being quite convinced that his Constanze could not fail to impress his father and sister favourably, and that personal acquaintance would efface all unpleasant feeling, he was very anxious to

---

[2] Hamburger Litt. u. Krit. Blätter, 1856, No. 72, p. 563.

[3] Unfortunately Wolfgang's letters to his father are only preserved in anything like completeness up to his visit to Salzburg (July, 1783); after that we have only detached ones. His sister believed, so Nissen says (Vorr., p. XVI.), that the later letters were destroyed by the father, on account of containing allusions to Freemasonry, which is probable enough. There is no sort of evidence that Mozart ever actually neglected his father's correspondence; but it was not in his power to continue to keep a journal such as he had been in the habit of writing while travelling, or such as the daughter kept up after her marriage.

take her to Salzburg as soon as possible. But many difficulties came in the way, for which his father did not always
make due allowance. Mozart was particularly desirous of
passing his father's fête-day in Salzburg (November 15, 1782),
but the time was too short for him. He had promised to play
at a concert for Fräulein Aurnhammer on November 3, and
he must be in Vienna again at the beginning of December,
that being the best season for lessons and concerts; to these
objections might be added the impassable state of the
roads, and such severe cold as rendered it undesirable to
travel with his wife. In short, the journey must be postponed
until the spring; in spring, however, the approaching confinement of his wife again put it out of the question. At the
last moment Mozart invited his father to stand godfather
(June 7, 1783):—

I had no idea that the joke would so soon turn into earnest, and therefore postponed falling on my knees, clasping my hands and humbly
begging you, my dearest father, to stand godfather to my child. But as
there may still be time for it, I do so now. Nevertheless, in sure hope
that you will not refuse my request, I have taken care that in case of
need somebody shall stand at the font in your name. Whether the child
shall be *generis masculini* or *feminini!* it is to be called Leopold or
Leopoldine.

Soon after the birth of the child,[4] however, at the end of
July, 1783, they actually set out. Mozart and some of his
friends had misgivings lest the Archbishop should seek to
detain him in Salzburg, because he had never received any
formal dismissal from service—"for a priest is capable of
anything." With this idea, he proposed a meeting in
Munich, but his father appears to have reassured him.[5]

Before Mozart was married, he had "made a vow in his
heart" that, if he succeeded in bringing Constanze to Salzburg, he would compose a mass to be performed there. "A
proof of the sincerity of this vow," he wrote to his father
(January 4, 1783), "is afforded by the score of the half of

---

[4] The firstborn son, Leopold, "der arme dicke fette and liebe Buberl," as
he is called in a letter (December 10, 1783), died in the same year.

[5] On January 19, 1786, L. Mozart wrote to his daughter that the Archbishop
had opened a letter of Wolfgang's, but without finding anything in it.

my mass, which is laying before me in full hope of completion." He took with him to Salzburg only the Kyrie,
Gloria, Sanctus, and Benedictus, composed on a scale of
great splendour (427 K.). The missing movements were
probably supplied from an older mass, and the whole was
rehearsed at the Kapellhaus on August 23, and performed at
St. Peter's church (the Archbishop having apparently
refused the cathedral) on August 25, Mozart's wife taking
the soprano part.[6]

Mozart was not by any means idle during this visit to
Salzburg. The revival of Italian opera had suggested to
him to look about for a libretto for an opera buffa, and
even before he came to Salzburg he had entered into
negotiations with Varesco through his father. Varesco declaring himself quite ready, it only needed the visit to Salzburg to concert the plan of the opera, "L'Oca del Cairo."
Varesco prepared a detailed account of the plot, and carried
out the first act in full; Mozart set himself with equal zeal
to its composition, and took back to Vienna a sketch of
part of the act. We shall have to do later with the fate of
this opera.

At the same time he found leisure for a service of love to
Michael Haydn. Hadyn had been ordered by the Archbishop to compose some duets for violin and tenor, perhaps
for his special use, but owing to a violent illness, which
incapacitated him for work during a lengthened period, he
was unable to finish them at the time appointed ; the Archbishop thereupon threatened to deprive him of his salary.
When Mozart heard of the difficulty he at once undertook
the work, and, visiting Haydn daily, wrote by his bedside to
such good purpose that the duets were soon completed and
handed over to the Archbishop in Hadyn's name.[7]

These two duets (423, 424, K.) show no signs of hasty
composition, but are worked out with evident affection, partly
no doubt from desire to do credit to himself and his friend,
but partly also from the interest which the difficulties of the

---

[6] Nissen, p. 476.
[7] A. M. Z., I., p. 291. Biograph. Skizze von Mich. Haydn (Salzburg, 1808), p. 38.

task presented. There is no small amount of art required to give the clear-cut outline and well-defined divisions which are essential in works of this kind, and yet to bestow full attention on light and shade and delicate touches of detail. The art consists chiefly in the free disposition of parts, which is partly imitative (where independent movement is necessary) and so managed as also to bestow an original and striking character on the passages which form the accompaniment. This is all the more striking because the limited number of parts only occasionally gives scope for full harmonies, the effect of which must be attained by means of skilful adjustment. It is a task requiring all the resources of art and genius to employ the stiff monotony of broken chords, and at the same time to gratify the sense of hearing by such a sense of harmony as can only be given by the absolutely free play of the different parts. This task is here accomplished with as much ease as was compatible with the limited means at disposal. Variety in form is carefully provided for. The first Duet in G major consists of a broadly designed allegro, a short, beautiful adagio, and an animated, but more than usually serious rondo; in the second, in B flat major, a light allegro is introduced by a short adagio; then follows an adagio in the form of a Siciliana, and the conclusion is made by very graceful variations. The melodies and harmonies are free and original, the composition is broad, fresh and lively, and a multitude of delicate touches betray the master's hand. Michael Haydn treasured the original as a memorial both of artist and friend, and Mozart himself set considerable store by the work.

Mozart found several new inmates in his father's house. My son is in Vienna, and intends to remain there," writes L. Mozart to Breitkopf (April 29, 1782); " I have therefore arranged that two pupils shall reside with me for their education, viz., the son, twelve years of age, and the daughter, fourteen, of Herr Marchand, theatrical manager in Munich. I hope to make a great violinist and pianist of the boy, and a great singer and pianiste of the girl." These pupils were joined by another of nine years old, Johanna Brochard, daughter of the celebrated actress, who profited by L.

Mozart's instruction during 1783 and 1784.[8] Wolfgang
took a lively interest in all this youthful talent. He says of
Margarethe Marchand, whom he met afterwards in Munich
as Frau Danzi (October 31, 1783) : " Her grimaces and
affectations are not always pleasant. Only blockheads would
be taken in by them. I myself would rather have the most
boorish manners than such exaggeration of coquetry." According to what we hear of her performances afterwards, she
must have followed good advice and altered her style.[9]

Wolfgang took great interest in her brother Heinrich, and
sent him word (December 6, 1783) that he had spoken in
his favour both at Linz and Vienna. "Tell him to rely
chiefly on his staccato; for that is the only way in which he
can avoid comparison with La Motte at Vienna." There
was also in Salzburg at that time the blind pianiste,
Marie Thérèse Paradies, who was an acquaintance of L.
Mozart, and now became known also to Wolfgang,[10] who
afterwards wrote a concerto for her (Vol. II., p. 288). But
the object of Mozart's visit, which lay nearest his heart, was
the establishment of friendly relations between his wife and
his father and sister; and this unfortunately in great measure failed. A superficial friendship seems to have resulted
from the visit; but there are many indications that neither
the father nor sister felt attracted by Constanze. Mozart
appears to have been aggrieved that his wife was not presented with any of the trinkets that had been given him in
his youth.[11] This trait is characteristic as a proof that
Leopold Mozart thought himself justified in showing in the
plainest manner disapproval of his son's marriage, and of
the wife he had chosen; and it can scarcely be wondered at
that Constanze, conscious of the want of anything like
sympathy in her husband's family, should not have encouraged his sense of dependence on their advice and opinions.
But this sense was too deeply implanted in his heart to be
ever altogether eradicated; and his letters, though not so

---

[8] Lipowsky, Bayersch. Mus. Lex., p. 36.
[9] Rochlitz, Für Freunde d. Tonk., III., p. 179.
[10] Wien. Mus. Ztg., 1817, p. 289.
[11] Nissen, Vorr., p. 18.

frequent as formerly, continued to the end to breathe the
same spirit of childlike love and reverence.   After a stay
of almost three months the young couple returned home.
Mozart sends his father the following account of their journey from Linz :—

> We arrived here safely yesterday, October 30, at nine o'clock in the
> morning. We passed the first night at Böcklbruck. The following
> forenoon we arrived at Lambach, and I was just in time to accompany
> the Agnus Dei of the office on the organ. The " Herr Prälat " [who
> had received Mozart kindly in 1767] was very delighted at seeing me
> again. We remained there the whole day, and I played on the organ
> and a clavichord. I heard that at Ebersperg, on the following day, Herr
> Steurer was to give an operatic performance at which all Linz would be
> present, so I determined to proceed there at once. Young Count Thun
> (brother to the Thun at Vienna) called on me, and said that his father
> had been expecting me for the last fortnight, and that I was to stay
> with him. The next day, when we arrived at the gate of Linz, we were
> met by a servant to conduct us to the residence of old Count Thun. I
> cannot say enough of the politeness with which we are overwhelmed.
> On Tuesday, November 4, I shall give a concert in the theatre here, and
> as I have not a single symphony with me, I am writing one for dear life
> to be ready in time. My wife and I kiss your hands, and beg your
> forgiveness for having troubled you during so long a time ; once more
> we thank you heartily for all the favours we received from you.[12]

What symphony it was which Mozart composed at Linz
cannot be exactly ascertained.   Holmes conjectures that it
may be a Symphony in C major (425 K., score 6), which,
according to Niemetschek, was dedicated to Count Thun ;
this fact would support the conjecture.   André, however,
believes that the unprinted Symphony in G major (444 K.)
may be the one composed in Linz, the more so as the score
is in Mozart's handwriting only as far as the first half of the
andante, and has then been completed by a copyist ; this is
very probably because Mozart, in order to gain time, only
wrote out the parts of the last half, as was his custom when
in haste.   The smaller orchestra also, the narrower dimen-
sions and the lighter character of this symphony, all point
to it as the one in question ; that in C major is more

---

[12] On L. Mozart's return from Vienna in 1785, he stopped at Linz, as the
guest of Count Thun; here he met the new Bishop, Count Herberstein (I., p. 25).

striking and important both in style and treatment.   Nevertheless the two symphonies both belong to the same time
and style, and indicate in a curious way a transition in
Mozart's instrumental music ; the positive influence of
Haydn's symphonies is nowhere so clearly apparent as in
these two works.   The very fact that in both cases the
allegro is preceded by a pathetic, somewhat lengthy adagio
is very significant ; this is a well-known arrangement of
Haydn's, but was only exceptionally made use of by Mozart.
The same influence is visible everywhere ; in the lively,
rapid, and brilliant character of the whole, in the effort to
please and amuse by humorous turns and unexpected contrasts of every kind in the harmonies, in the alternations of
f and p, and in the instrumental effects.   A remarkable instance of this is the andante of the Symphony in G major.
The very theme, the simple bass, the triplet passage for the
second violin, then the minor with the figure in the bass,
and the sharp accentuation, are all completely Haydn-like
features.   The counterpoint of the finale of both symphonies
reminds us of Haydn's manner.[18]   It need scarcely be said,
however, that there is no trace of servile imitation in either
work, and that Mozart's originality asserts itself here as
elsewhere.   A comparison of the Symphony in E flat major
(543 K., composed June 26, 1788) shows also many more
points of resemblance to Haydn's style than other works
of the same date ; but Mozart's individuality is here so overpowering as to have given its distinguishing stamp to these
very features.

The fact that Mozart wrote a symphony within the course
of a few days will excite no surprise ; it is worthy of note
that during his stay in Linz he copied an " Ecce Homo"
which made a great impression on him, for his wife, with
the inscription "Dessiné par W. A. Mozart, Linz, ce 13
Novembre, 1783; dédié à Madame Mozart son épouse"; she

---

[18] Instances might be multiplied on closer examination; I content myself with
quoting from the C major symphony the unexpected entry of E minor (p. 6, bar 8)
and C major (p. 6, bar 12), the loud notes for the wind instruments (p. 25, bars
3, 4), the original theme with which the basses interpose (p. 28, bar 5), and most
especially the mocking conclusion of the minuet (p. 36, bars 12-16).

preserved it as a proof "that he had some talent for draw-ing," as she wrote to Härtel (July 21, 1800).

In the year 1785 Leopold Mozart returned the visit of his son and daughter-in-law, and remained their guest from February 10 to April 25. He convinced himself that their income ought to be more than sufficient for the support of the household, and took great delight in his second grandchild Carl, now six months old, "a healthy, lively, merry child."

But on the whole he appears to have been dissatisfied with his visit, and very little inclined to accede to Wolfgang's wish that he should take up his residence with them in Vienna.[14] His pleasure in his son's performance and admi-ration of his genius were as great as they had ever been. During the whole of his visit, one concert followed close on another, and Wolfgang was engaged almost as a matter of course for them all; his father took equal pride in his playing and his compositions. At one concert Wolfgang played the splendid concerto he had composed for Paradies (456 K.). "I had a very good box," writes his father to Marianne, "and could hear every gradation of the instru-ments so perfectly, that the tears came to my eyes for very joy"—so thoroughly did the old man appreciate and relish artistic beauty. The day after his father's arrival, Mozart invited Haydn to a quartet party at his house. On such occasions Mozart, who in later years discontinued his practice of the violin, usually took the tenor part. Kelly tells of a quartet party at Storace's, when Haydn took the first violin, Dittersdorf the second, Mozart tenor, and Van-hall violoncello—a cast unique of its kind.[15] L. Mozart writes to his daughter:—

They played three of the new quartets, those in B flat, A, and C major (458, 464, 465 K.). They are perhaps a little easier than the other three,

---

[14] Nissen asserts (Vorr., p. 18) that L. Mozart's letters from Vienna to his daughter (of which I have unfortunately only seen a few), betray considerable coldness towards his son.

[15] Kelly, Reminisc., I., p. 240. Holmes conjectures that as Haydn was a good violinist, but no solo-player, Kelly has substituted him for Mozart by a slip of memory (p. 267); it is more probable that Dittersdorf, the most celebrated violin-player of the day, played first violin, and Haydn second.

but admirable compositions. Herr Haydn said to me: *"I assure you solemnly and as an honest man, that I consider your son to be the greatest composer of whom I have ever heard; he has taste, and possesses a thorough knowledge of composition."*

L. Mozart knew the value of such an opinion from such a man; it afforded him a confirmation of his faith, and of the conviction to which he had sacrificed the best powers of his life. Such a testimony to his son's genius was the father's best reward, and one of the brightest spots of his life. L. Mozart obtained much credit also through his pupil Heinrich Marchand, who accompanied him, and played with great success at several concerts.

Nor were other entertainments and enjoyments altogether wanting. He heard Aloysia Lange, whose beautiful voice had once been a source of anxiety to him, in Gluck's "Pilgrims of Mecca" and in Grétry's "Zemire and Azor" (her favourite part): "She sang and played admirably on both occasions." He visited the Baroness Waldstädten, whose acquaintance had gratified him so much, in the convent of Neuburg, where she was then staying; but we do not hear anything of the future course of their friendship.

It is an important fact, and one of grave significance in the case of a man of L. Mozart's tone of mind and thought, that he was led by his son's influence to enter the order of Freemasonry. The strong national feeling which existed in him, side by side with devotion to the tenets of his church, regulating his conception of moral duties, and influencing all his critical judgments, makes it conceivable that he should seek for enlightenment through an association which numbered among its members some of the most considerable and highly esteemed of his friends. I am not aware how far he was satisfied by the disclosures made to him, nor whether he remained an active member of the order after his return to Salzburg; his daughter saw grounds for believing that his subsequent correspondence with Wolfgang turned mainly on topics connected with Freemasonry. From Vienna Leopold Mozart travelled by way of Munich, where he had a pleasant visit, back to Salzburg. There he found awaiting him an announcement from his gracious master

that, as he had already exceeded his six weeks' leave of
absence, if he did not report himself before the middle of
May, "no salary should be paid to him until further notice."
We can enter into the complaints he made to his daughter
of the dulness of his life in Salzburg. He never saw his
son again. A faint hope, expressed to Marianne (September 16, 1785), that Wolfgang, not having written for a considerable time, meant to surprise him with a visit, was not
fulfilled ; he himself, accompanied by Heinrich Marchand,
paid a flying visit to Munich in February, 1787, but did not
go on to Vienna. His paternal pride was gratified by the
intelligence of Wolfgang's brilliant success in Prague ; and
he did not neglect to inform his daughter when Pater
Edmund, who had been on a visit to Vienna, declared on
his return that Wolfgang had the reputation of being the
first of living musicians (February 3, 1786). He watched
with anxious sympathy over the course of his son's worldly
affairs, but refused with consistent severity any substantial
support, the right to which Wolfgang had clearly forfeited
by his independent attitude ; paternal advice, in its most
unsparing form, was always at his service. Leopold Mozart
transferred to his daughter the tenderness and active participation which was now denied to him in his intercourse with
his distant son. Thus he remained to the end true to his
principles, but not untouched by the weakness and suffering
of old age ; he answers one of Marianne's anxious inquiries
after his health (February 24, 1787) :—

> An old man must not expect anything like perfect health ; he is always
> failing, and loses strength just as a young man gains it. One must just
> patch oneself up as long as one can. We may hope for a little improve-
> ment from the better weather now. You will, of course, find me very
> much thinner, but, after all, that is of no consequence.

He had still a pleasure to come in the visit of the Storaces
and Kelly ; Mdlle. Storace had packed up Wolfgang's letter
intrusted to her so carefully, that she could not get at it, but
verbal intercourse with such intimate friends of his son must
have been ample compensation for this. Soon afterwards
he fell ill, on hearing which Wolfgang wrote as follows
(April 4, 1787): —

I have this moment heard what has quite overwhelmed me—all the more since your last letter allowed me to imagine that you were quite well—and now I hear that you are really ill! How earnestly I long for reassuring news from your own hand, I do not need to tell you, and I confidently hope for it, although I have learnt to make it my custom to imagine the worst of everything. Since death (properly speaking) is the true end of life, I have accustomed myself during the last two years to so close a contemplation of this, our best and truest friend, that he possesses no more terrors for me ; nothing but peace and consolation ! and I thank God for enabling me to discern in death the *key* to our true blessedness. I never lie down in bed without remembering that perhaps, young as I am, I may never see another day ; and yet no one who knows me can say that I am melancholy or fanciful. For this blessing I thank God daily, and desire nothing more than to share it with my fellow men. I wrote to you on this point in the letter which Mdlle. Storace failed to deliver *à propos* of the death of my dearest friend Count von Hatzfeld ; he was thirty-one—just my own age ; I do not mourn for him, but for myself, and all those who knew him as I did. I hope and pray that even as I write this you may be already better; but if, contrary to all expectation, this should not be the case, I conjure you by all that we hold most sacred, not to hide the truth from me, but to write at once, in order that I may be in your arms with the least possible delay. But I hope soon to receive a reassuring letter from yourself, and in this hope, I, with my wife and Carl, kiss your hands a thousand times, and am ever,—Your most dutiful son.

This letter puts the seal on the beautiful, genuinely human relations existing between the father and son ; in the presence of death, they stand face to face like men, calm in the assurance that true love and earnest efforts after truth and goodness reach beyond the limits of our earthly existence. Leopold Mozart apparently recovered from this attack, and wrote to his daughter on May 26, that he should expect her and her family to spend Whitsuntide with him ; but this pleasure was denied to him. On May 28, 1787, a sudden death[16] ended the career of a man who had accomplished, by means of a singular union of shrewdness and industry, of love and severity, the difficult task of educating a child of genius into an artist.

---

[16] Mozart lost no time in communicating the sorrowful news to his friend, Gottfried von Jacquin : " I must inform you that on my return home to-day I received the sad intelligence of the death of my dear father. You can imagine the state I am in."

The personal relationships which resulted from Mozart's marriage not only affected his mental and social condition, but had also considerable influence on him as a composer; it is indispensable therefore to take them into account in any consideration of his artistic career.

His relations with his mother-in-law were, as might have been expected, unfavourable enough at first. She did not indeed live in the same house with them, as Mozart writes for his father's consolation (August 31, 1782);[17] but even at the second visit which he paid her with his wife, she scolded and disputed until Constanze was reduced to tears, and they resolved in consequence only to visit her on family fête-days. This state of affairs was afterwards improved, since we can well understand that it was impossible for a man of Mozart's genial and loving nature to keep up offence. " Mozart and our late mother became more and more attached to each other," writes Sophie Haibl. " He used often to come running to our house with little packets of coffee and sugar, saying as he handed them out : ' Here, mamma dear, take a little *Jause'* (afternoon coffee). He never came to us empty-handed." Constanze's youngest sister, Sophie, was in very frequent intercourse with them ; her sister's constant illness rendered her help in nursing, which she was always most willing to bestow, quite invaluable ; and during Mozart's last illness we find her constant in attendance at his bedside. Mozart's intercourse with Aloysia Lange and her husband[18] seems to have been friendly and unembarrassed. The Langes did not live happily together, and though Lange himself laid the blame upon backbiters,[19] it was notorious that their disunion arose from his unreasonable jealousy, a jealousy for which his wife had

---

[17] " My son wrote to me some time ago," writes L. Mozart to the Baroness Waldstädten (August 23, 1782), "that as soon as he was married he would cease to live with the mother. I hope he has already actually left the house ; if not, it will be a misfortune both for him and his wife."

[18] Prefixed to the first volume of the "Ephemeriden der Literatur und des Theaters" (Berlin, 1785), are the portraits of Lange and his wife in a medallion. Her features are regular and good, but, probably owing to her delicate health, less youthful than one might have expected.

[19] Lange, Selbstbiogr., p. 118.

far more cause than he.[20] But as far as Mozart was concerned
Lange's jealousy must have been unprovoked, or he would
hardly have taken the part of Pierrot in the pantomime already noticed (Vol. II., p. 304), allowing his wife to play Columbine to Mozart's Harlequin. She acknowledged later that,
as a young girl, she had under-estimated Mozart's genius,
and she learnt to look upon his music with admiration and
reverence, and upon himself with friendship and esteem.[21]
We find many indications in the letters of friendly intercourse
between the Mozarts and the Langes. It was natural,
therefore, that they should have afforded each other professional help whenever opportunity arose. On April 10, 1782,
Mozart composed a song (383 K.)[22] for his sister-in-law, the
words of which show it to have been intended for a benefit
performance by way of farewell :—

> Nehmt meinen Dank, ihr holden Gönner
> So feurig als mein Herz ihn spricht.

Whether Madame Lange was about to leave Vienna on a
tour, or had merely come to the end of an engagement, I
cannot say. The composition (in G major) takes the form of
a ballad in two verses, and is very simple, easy and pleasing.
Original features are not wanting, as for instance, suspensions
and transition notes on an organ point, which even modern
musicians would find piquant. The accompaniment is
easy, but delicate ; the stringed instruments play *pizzicato*
throughout, a device not often employed by Mozart ; the
flutes, oboe, and bassoon, employed as solo instruments, but
without any bravura, enliven the simple design. In the
following year (January 8) he composed a Rondo (416 K.,
part 1), "Mia speranza adorata," which she first sang at a
concert at the Mehlgrube ; the distinguishing qualities of
this song are delicacy and tenderness ; it depends for effect
more upon a sympathetic delivery than on the compass and

---

[20] Friedel, Briefe aus Wien, p. 409.

[21] A. M. Z., III., p. 659.

[22] On the same day Mozart writes to his father full of anxiety about his own
circumstances, thus proving again that the true artist can divest himself during
his hours of production of the cares and anxieties of his ordinary life.

executive powers of the singer.   In March of the same year, Madame Lange and Mozart mutually supported each other at their concerts.

After the revival of the Italian opera, it often happened that Mozart was requested to compose detached pieces for insertion.   When, in 1783, Anfossi's opera of " Il Curioso Indiscreto," composed in 1778, was represented, Madame Lange and Adamberger, who, as German singers, had to contend with much opposition, knew that they could not fail to make an effect in music of Mozart's composition, and begged him to write two songs for their *début*.   He was, as ever, quite ready to grant their request; but he had yet to learn that even in Italian opera he could not assert his claims without opposition.   We have his own account in a letter to his father (July 2, 1783) :—

The opera was given the day before yesterday, Monday ; none of it pleased except my two songs, and the second, a bravura song, was encored.   But you must know that my enemies were ill-natured enough to spread about beforehand that Mozart had undertaken to correct Anfossi's opera.   I heard of this, and sent word to Count Rosenberg that I would not produce the songs unless the following notice in German and Italian was printed in the opera-book : " Notice.—The two songs, page 36 and page 102, are composed, not by Signor Anfossi, but by Herr Mozart, at the desire of Madame Lange.   This announcement is made out of respect and consideration for the fame of the celebrated Neapolitan composer." This was done, and I handed over the songs, which did as much credit to myself as to my sister-in-law.[28]   So my enemies are caught in their own trap !   Now I must tell you of one of Salieri's tricks, which did not hurt me so much as poor Adamberger.   I think I wrote to you that I had also composed a rondo for Adamberger.   At one of the early rehearsals, before the rondo was ready, Salieri called Adamberger aside, and told him that Count Rosenberg was not pleased at the idea of his inserting a song, and he should advise him as a friend to abandon it.   Adamberger, exasperated against Rosenberg, answered with a stupid display of ill-timed pride : " I flatter myself that Adamberger's fame is so well established in Vienna that he has no need to seek the favour of the public by songs written on purpose for him ; I shall sing what is in the

---

[28] The Berl. Litt. u. Theat. Ztg., 1783, p. 559, announces from Vienna : " June 30, 1783, ' Il Curioso Indiscreto ' was performed for the first time.   Madame Lange sang to-day for the first time in the Italian opera, and the public. in spite of all cabals, showed their appreciation of her talents." Cf. Lange's Selbst· biogr., p. 119.

opera, and never insert any song as long as I live." And what was the consequence? Why, that he made no effect at all, and now repents, but too late; for, if he were to come to me to-day for the rondo, I would not give it to him. I can use it very well in one of my own operas. But what most provokes him is that my prophecy and his wife's turns out correct, viz., that neither Count Rosenberg nor the manager knew a word of the affair, so that he was simply tricked by Salieri.

Adamberger might certainly have made a brilliant display of his powers in the song (420 K., part 8) "Per pietà non ricercata."[24] It is broad in design, and affords the singer opportunities for a display of voice, delivery, and execution; it maintains a certain dignity of tone throughout. A very effective use is made of the wind instruments; and a comparison of their full satisfying sound with that of the wind instruments in the song quoted (Vol. II., pp. 232, 233) will show how closely connected in a true work of art are the tone-colouring of the instruments and the nature and development of the motifs.

The first of Madame Lange's two songs, "Vorrei spiegarvi, oh Dio!" (418 K.), was composed on June 20, and is broad in outline, the first slow movement in especial being delicately elaborated in detail. It expresses the painful hesitation of a mourner who would fain express her grief, but dares not; and this idea is well expressed by the broken phrases of the voice part, leaving the thread of the music to be carried on by the accompanying orchestra. A simple accompaniment, delivered *pizzicato* by the second violins and tenors, forms the canvas for the design, in which the oboe supports the principal motif, sometimes accompanying the voice, sometimes relieving it; an easy figure twines round the chief subject, sustained throughout by the first violins muted; while the horns and bassoons in sustained chords give consistency and shading to the whole. The situation and subject of the song necessitate restless and varied modulation; and this opening movement affords an example of Mozart's art in projecting a design and maintaining it

---

[24] Written on the autograph is (June 21, 1783): "All the parts are to be extracted and augmented—the *parte cantante* to be done at once, and returned to Herr Adamberger."

throughout with the utmost delicacy and variety of detail. The allegro which follows is more directly suggestive of opera buffa in its impulsive haste and in its dramatic characterisation ; but the skill is worthy of note with which the elevated tone of the first movement is preserved and the bravura of the singer is placed in the most favourable light.[25] The second song, "No che non sei capace" (419 K.), which is allotted to the same character, Clorinda, is a bravura song, in the very fullest acceptation of the term. The passages of two allegro movements mount to the highest heights like rockets, bursting from a ground-work of declamatory and dignified melody. The orchestra, too, is tolerably noisy, but so managed as always to spare the voice.

Mozart was very much gratified when the Langes selected his " Entführung aus dem Serail " for their benefit performance prior to a month's leave of absence, and he takes care to acquaint his father with the fact (December 10, 1783).[26] The choice was of course made chiefly in their own interests, since the opera was a favourite, and the part of Constanze might have been written for Madame Lange. Kelly, who admired her as one of the first vocalists of the day, and repeats Stephen Storace's comparison of her voice and execution to those of the Bastardella, was of opinion that the part of Constanze was of " the exact compass " for her voice.[27] When she reappeared, after a severe illness, in the same opera, on the 25th of November, 1785,[28] she was " deservedly well received,"[29] and the part was one which she

---

[25] The completely written-out melody of a soprano air (178 K.) is preserved, the words of which, " Ah spiegarti, oh Dio vorrei," differ very little from the above; it is probably a first attempt abandoned. The voice part of Adamberger's air sketched in the same way still exists, and the bravura air is on the same leaf.

[26] The performance took place on January 25, 1784, and was repeated on February 1 (Wien. Ztg., 1784, No. 7, Anh., No. 9, Anh.).

[27] Kelly, Reminisc., I., p. 253.

[28] The notices of her professional tour in the year 1784, from Berlin, Dresden, Leipzig, Schwedt, and Hamburg, are full of admiration (Berl. Litt. u. Theat. Ztg., 1784, I., p. 160; II., p. 138).

[29] Wien. Ztg., 1785, No. 97.

frequently played later with the greatest applause, bestowed especially on the bravura songs.[80]

Mozart wrote another song for her on March 14, 1788 (538 K.), " Ah se in ciel benigne stelle " (from Metastasio's " Eroe Cinese,") apparently as a concert-piece.   It is long and elaborate, well calculated to display great compass of voice, and more of bravura than the previous songs ; but, as regards invention and mechanism, it is of less importance than those already noticed.   It is not wanting in interesting harmonic details nor in expressive passages, but they stand apart, and are not blended into a harmonious whole in Mozart's usual manner.

A very favourable idea of Aloysia's vocal powers may be formed from the songs composed for her in Vienna ; the promise of the young girl had been amply fulfilled.[81]   The fabulous height of her voice, which reached with ease to—

was moderated in the second song to—

but the low notes appear to greater advantage, and we are surprised by intervals such as—

The flexibility of the voice appears to have been cultivated to an astonishing degree in every direction, and though the merit was chiefly Mozart's that these passages were interesting, expressive, and in good taste, yet their execution required a cultivated and   accomplished singer.   Hufeland wrote in 1783 that Madame Lange's voice was one of the finest he

[80] It was so in Amsterdam in 1798 (A. M. Z., III., p. 659), and in Paris in 1802 (A. M. Z., IV., p. 322).
[81] Cf. Jahrb. d. Tonk., 1796, p. 39.

had ever heard, unusually pleasing and sympathetic, although somewhat weak for the stage,[82] and in this judgment Cramer concurs.[83] It was no doubt from consideration for the distinctive tone-colouring of the voice that Mozart did not make use of the whole body of wind instruments, particularly not of the clarinets, but allowed the gentler oboe to predominate in the accompaniment.

Mozart's eldest sister-in-law, Josepha, made her first appearance as a singer at Schikaneder's theatre, after her marriage with the violinist Hofer. With the exception of a high and flexible voice (a common inheritance, apparently, of all the Webers), she had no special gifts nor musical cultivation, and Mozart seems to have taken great pains in practising her parts with her. He wrote a bravura song for her on September 17, 1789 (580 K.), "Schon lacht der holde Frühling," which she, as Rosina, was to insert in the German adaptation of Paesiello's "Barber of Seville"; only portions of the score remain. It has no special significance, and reminds us in its embellishments of the Queen of Night's songs, which it resembles in other respects. Mozart interested himself also in his brother-in-law Hofer, studying his quartets with him, although Hofer was an indifferent musician; he took him with him on his last professional journey to Frankfort, that the name of Mozart might facilitate his public appearance, and be of use to him in his very narrow circumstances.

Mozart was always ready to lend a helping hand, even where family considerations had no influence. When Nancy Storace, the original Susanna, in "Figaro," was leaving Vienna, he composed for her the beautiful song with obbligato pianoforte (505 K., part 6), which he played himself at her concert.[84] He selected the words of the song which had been composed for Idamante in the Vienna performance of "Idomeneo," "Non temer amato bene." The circumstance that Idamante addresses laments and endearments to Ilia, who is

---

[82] Alsatia, 1853, p. 92.

[83] Magaz. d. Mus., II., p. 185.

[84] The autograph has on the title-page "Composta per la Sgra. Storace dal suo servo ed amico W. A. Mozart, 26 di Dec., 1786."

present, perhaps suggested the appropriateness of an obbligato accompaniment, and, in point of fact, the piano part represents the lover in the most charming and expressive manner, appearing now to assent, now to reply to the expressions of the singer. In this respect, as well as in its tone and sentiment, this song is far in advance of the earlier one with obbligato violin; the spirit of " Figaro " moves over it, and we seem to recognise the depth of feeling and the tinge of sentimentality which characterise the Countess.

Mozart's comparative failure in his attempt to insert songs in Anfossi's " Curioso Indiscreto" did not prevent his coming forward as soon as another opportunity of the same kind offered itself. On November 28, 1785, Bianchi's " Villanella Rapita" was produced for the first time, and Mozart was induced to give the opera the support of some ensemble movements of his composition.[35] The beautiful Celestine Coltellini (second daughter of the poet Coltellini, who had written the libretto of Mozart's first opera) was engaged in 1783 by the Emperor Joseph II. himself at Naples, where she had been singing with great success since 1779.[36] She first appeared on April 6, 1785, in Cimarosa's " Contadina di Spirito," [37] and took the place of Mdlle. Storace (who had temporarily lost her voice) [38] in the first performance of Storace's opera, " Gli Sposi Malcontenti," on June 1, 1785.[39] Her voice was not first-rate, and her compass only moderate, but she had been thoroughly well trained, sang with ravishing expression, and fascinated her audience by her acting, especially in comic parts.[40] These qualities were made

---

[35] Wien. Ztg., 1785, Nr. 97, Anh. I do not know whether Bianchi wrote his opera for Vienna or Venice. The statement (A. M. Z., XXIV., p. 485) that the Emperor Joseph II. caused it to be composed in the form of a pasticcio is incorrect. The overture, which was given in Leipzig (A. M. Z., XIII., p. 168) and Vienna (A. M. Z., XXIV., p. 485) as having been composed by Mozart for this opera, is the one which was written in Salzburg in 1779 (319 K.; Cf., I., p. 516).

[36] Kelly, Reminisc., I., p. 48.

[37] Wien. Ztg., 1785, No. 29, Anh.

[38] Wien. Ztg., 1785, No. 46, Anh.

[39] Kelly, Reminisc., I., p. 234.

[40] Cramer, Mag. d. Mus., II., p. 62. Reichardt, Musik. Monatsschr., p. 38. Scudo, Mus. Anc. et Mod., p. 18

prominent in Mozart's charming terzet and quartet; her part is that of a peasant-girl, simple even to silliness, who receives presents from a Count, without being in the least aware of his intentions, nor of the rage and jealousy of her betrothed and her father. In the terzet (450 K.) "Mandina amabile" (composed November 21, 1785), the delight with which she accepts the money, and, at the request of the Count, gives him her hand with the words, "Ecco servitevi!" is not given with any particular refinement by the poet; but Mozart has thrown so much grace and roguery into the action that it becomes an excellent point for a clever actress. The opening has a certain resemblance to the duet between Don Giovanni and Zerlina, although the latter stands several degrees higher, in accordance with the different characters of the personages; a comparison of the two pieces affords a proof of Mozart's skill in basing his characterisation on the conditions of the dramatic situation. Even when the lover interferes with jealous violence, and the Count seeks to excuse himself with as good a grace as possible, she fails to perceive what is passing before her; and Mozart does not neglect the opportunity of combining these opposing elements into a well-proportioned animated whole. The effect is excellent when the key, after the duet has pursued its rollicking course in A major and the nearly related keys, passes into A minor, and then with rapid transition into C major; even when it has reverted into A major the minor key constantly recurs in discords suggestive of jealousy. The quartet (479 K.) "Dite almeno, in che mancai" (composed November 15, 1785), has a less strongly marked situation. Mandina confronts her indignant lover and father with innocent simplicity; when the Count enters, a violent altercation arises between the men, of which she cannot understand the cause, but, anxious at any sacrifice to restore peace, she begs with really touching earnestness for pity and forgiveness. Her calmness, in opposition to the voluble excitement of the men, gives the movement its distinguishing character, which it was the task of the performer to throw into relief; her part, especially in the tender and beseeching passages, is full of feeling and charm. As to

the other parts, the ever-increasing tumult of an animated
dispute is represented with very simple, well-calculated
expedients in a manner which is thoroughly Italian; a
striking instance of this is the joining in of the orchestra
when the wrangling is at its height, with the preservation of
all the delicate comic effects.   The masterly treatment of
the orchestra, both in detail and in effects of grouping,
would alone suffice to raise these two pieces far above
similar movements of the then commonly received opera
buffa type.   More excellent even than the brilliant and
characteristic sound effects is the independent and copious
construction of the instrumental parts, which nevertheless
are kept within their proper provinces as foils to the voices.
Of the voice parts it need scarcely be said that they are
delicately and characteristically treated, and move freely
and with animation side by side, producing at the same
time an effective whole.   There is no bravura, and the treatment of the voices indicates moderate capabilities on the
part of the singers.   Coltellini's part never goes above—

rarely so high, and calls for no great amount of execution.
Among the male singers Mandini was by far the most important; the part of Almaviva was afterwards written for
him, and the passionate expressions of the lover Pippo in
the terzet remind us of that part.   The tenor Calvesi (Count)
and the second bass Bussani (Biaggio) were of less account.
These ensemble pieces were the mature and graceful products
of Mozart's fully developed genius, and nothing but their
simplicity of design and construction points them out as pieces
inserted in an opera, and dependent upon it for their peculiar
character.

   We can well believe that Mozart composed songs to please
the singers, male and female, who appeared in his operas.
He was not only ready to write additional pieces for them in
his own operas, but frequently offered songs as an acknowledgment to the performers who sang for him.   Louise
Villeneuve appeared on June 27, 1789, as a new performer

in Martin's "Arbore di Diana," and was received with well-deserved and genuine applause on account of her pleasing appearance, her expressive acting, and her artistically beautiful singing.[41]   When she was about to appear as Dorabella in "Così fan tutte," in August, 1789, Mozart wrote for her an aria to Cimarosa's opera, "I Due Baroni" (578 K.), "Alma grande e nobil cuore," of forcible expression without making any great demands on the voice.[42]   More original, although not very deep, are the two songs composed for the same singer in October, 1789, for insertion in Martin's "Burbero di Buon Cuore." The first (582 K.), "Chi sa, chi sa qual sia," is a single andante movement very moderate in tone. The second (583 K.), "Vado, ma dove," begins with a short, passionate allegro, with which is connected an andante simple in design and construction, but with a wonderfully beautiful and expressive cantilene, the effect of which is much heightened by the splendid instrumentation.

A bass song, composed for Signor Franc. Albertarelli in Anfossi's "Le Gelosie Fortunate" (May,1788), was occasioned by the singer's connection with the performance of "Don Giovanni." It is a cheerful, thoroughly buffo aria, and the principal melody—

Voi siete un po ton - do, mio ca - ro Pom - pe - o, l' u - san - ze del
mon - do an - da - te a stu - diar, an - da - te, an - da - te, an - da - te a stu - diar.

has been employed again by Mozart, with a slight but expressive alteration, in the first movement of the C major symphony, the only instance of the kind known to me. Similar demands were made upon Mozart's generosity when he came into connection with Schikaneder's theatre. He composed (March 8, 1791) for the bass singer, Gerl, who sang Sarastro in the "Zauberflöte," an aria (612 K.), "Per questa bella mano," with an obbligato double-bass accompaniment,

---

[41] Wien. Ztg., 1789, No. 52, Anh.
[42] It is only known to me in an old copy among Mozart's remains.

which was played by Pischlberger with extraordinary execution. The combination reminds us of other similar Schi-
kaneder-like effects, and the interest of the song depends
mainly on the executive powers of the double-bass player,
which are nevertheless confined within narrow limits. The
limitation has in some degree influenced the treatment of the
voice part, and this pleasing and, for a powerful bass voice,
effective song can only be regarded as a curious occasional
piece. Another occasional composition is Gleim's German
war song, " Ich möchte wohl der Kaiser sein "[43] (539 K.),
composed March 5, 1788, for performance by the favourite
comedian, Friedrich Baumann, jun., at a concert in the
Leopoldstädter Theatre on March 7, with special reference,
no doubt, to the Turkish war which had just broken out.[44]
This accounts for the running accompaniment of Turkish
music to an otherwise simple and popular song.[45] To sum
up : it would appear that during Mozart's residence in
Vienna, from 1781 to 1791, he completed five ensemble
movements of different kinds, besides at least thirty separate songs for various occasions,[46] among which there is not
one which does not possess artistic interest, and a great
number which may be placed in the first rank of works of
the sort.

His genius was at the service of others besides vocalists.
We have already seen that he wrote a pianoforte concerto for
the blind performer Mdlle. Paradies (Vol. II., p. 288). An
artist similarly afflicted from early youth was Marianne
Kirchgässner (b. 1770), who had attained extraordinary pro-
ficiency on the harmonica under Schmittbauer's instruction.[47]
When, in the course of a grand professional tour, she came
to Vienna (May, 1791) she excited Mozart's interest so greatly

---

[43] Müller, Abschied, p. 156.

[44] It was just noticed in the Wien. Ztg., 1788, No. 23, Anh.

[45] The song: " Beim Auszug in das Feld," dated August 11, 1788, in the
Thematic Catalogue, was probably written for a similar use; but I am not
acquainted with it.

[46] A German air, " Ohne Zwang aus eigenem Triebe " (569 K.), noted by
Mozart, under date " Jenner, 1789," has quite disappeared.

[47] Mus. Corr., 1790, p. 170 ; 1791, p. 69.

by her playing, that he composed a quintet for her, which she frequently afterwards performed with great success.[48] The combination of instruments—flute, oboe, tenor, and violoncello, with the harmonica—produces an originality of sound effect which is seriously impaired when, as usually happens, the piano is substituted for the harmonica. The latter instrument is limited in compass, having no bass notes,[49] and requires for its due effect a melodious and expressive style of execution. Mozart has given the adagio a sentimental, love-sick tone, which is sometimes a good deal overdrawn, but the second movement is cheerful and pleasing, and, without forming too strong a contrast, it leads to a sound and agreeable conclusion. With just discrimination he has given the piece a very well-defined and firmly constructed form, relying for original effect on the tone-colouring and harmonic transitions, which are often extremely bold.

Mozart gave his support to another young artist, who had no such claim to pity as the two just mentioned. Regina Strinasacchi, of Ostiglia (1764-1839), was a pretty, amiable girl, and an accomplished violin-player, who came to Vienna in 1784. Mozart extols her taste and feeling to his father, who confirmed the praise when Strinasacchi appeared at Salzburg in December, 1785: " Every note is played with expression, even in symphonies, and I have never heard a more moving adagio than hers; her whole heart and soul is in the melody which she delivers, and her power and beauty of tone are equally remarkable.[50] I believe, as a rule, that a woman of genius plays with more expression than a man." "I

---

[48] She announced (Wien. Ztg., 1791, No. 66, Anh.) that in her concert on June 19, she would play "an entirely new and beautiful 'Konzertantquintet,' with wind instruments, accompanied by Herr Kapellmeister Mozart." Cf. Mus. Correspondenz, 1792, p. 146. A. M. Z., III., p. 127. Among the sketches in the Mozarteum at Salzburg is the commencement of another quintet for the same instruments in C major.

[49] Both in Berlin and Leipzig complaints were made that Mar. Kirchgässner had sought to attract admiration by a rapidity and an affected manner quite out of keeping with the character of the harmonica (Reichardt, Mus. Monatsschr., p. 25. Berl. Mus. Ztg., 1793, p. 150. A. M. Z., II., p. 254).

[50] Cf. Schink, Litt. Fragm., II., p. 286.

am just writing," continues Wolfgang, "a sonata (454 K.)[51] which we shall play together at her concert on Thursday" (April 24, 1784). But the sonata was not ready in time, and Strinasacchi with difficulty extorted her own part from Mozart the evening before the concert, and practised it without him on the following morning; they only met at the concert. Both played excellently, and the sonata was much applauded.[52] The Emperor Joseph, who was present, thought he could distinguish through his glass that Mozart had no music before him; he had him summoned and requested him to bring the sonata. It was blank music paper divided into bars, Mozart having had no time to write out the clavier part, which he thus played from memory, without even having heard the sonata.[53]

Mozart found an old Salzburg acquaintance at Vienna in the person of the horn-player Joseph Leutgeb. He had settled in Vienna, as Leopold Mozart writes (December 1, 1777), and bought a "snail-shell of a house" in one of the suburbs, upon credit; here he set up business as a cheese-monger, from the profits of which he promised to repay a loan, which, however, was still owing when Wolfgang came to Vienna; he begs his father's indulgence for Leutgeb, who was then wretchedly poor (May 8, 1782). He was a capital solo-player on the French horn,[54] but was wanting in higher cultivation. Mozart was always ready to help him, but he frequently made him the butt of his exuberant sprits. Whenever he composed a solo for him, Leutgeb was obliged to submit to some mock penance. Once, for instance, Mozart threw all the parts of his concertos and symphonies about the room, and Leutgeb had to collect them on all fours and put them in order; as long as this lasted Mozart sat at his

---

[51] It is entered in the Thematic Catalogue under April 21, 1784.

[52] In the Wiener Zeitung (1784, No. 54, p. 1560), Torricella announces the composition by the celebrated Kapellmeister Mozart of three new clavier sonatas, the third of which, with a violin accompaniment, had a short time before been played with great success in the theatre by the celebrated Mdlle. Strinasacchi and Herr Mozart, which is sufficient recommendation in itself.

[53] The story is told by the widow (A. M. Z., I., p. 290), and more in detail by Rochlitz (Für Freunde der Tonk., III., p. 285).

[54] Dittersdorf, Selbstbiogr., p. 50.

writing-table composing. Another time, Leutgeb had to kneel down behind the stove while Mozart wrote.[55] The manuscripts themselves bear traces of good-humoured banter. One (417 K.) has the superscription: "Wolfgang Amadé Mozart takes pity on Leutgeb, ass, ox, and simpleton, at Vienna, March 27, 1783"; another (495 K.) is written alternately with black, red, blue, and green ink. While he is writing down a rondo he amusingly imagines the player before him, and keeps up a running commentary on the supposed performance. The tempo, too, is jokingly indicated as adagio for the horn part, while the accompaniment is allegro; Leutgeb's inclination to drag is alluded to in the remark at the close of the ritornello: "A lei Signor Asino"—in the ejaculations on the theme: "Animo—presto—sù via—da bravo—coraggio—e finisci già" (at the conclusion). He goes on the same strain: "Bestia—oh che stonatura—chi—oimè (at a repeatedly recurring F sharp)—bravo poveretto! —Oh seccatura di coglioni! (when the subject recurs)—ah che mi fai ridere!—ajuto (at a repeated E flat)—respira un poco! (at a pause)—avanti, avanti!—questo poi va al meglio (when the theme reappears)—e non finisci nemmeno?—ah porco infame! Oh come sei grazioso!—Carino! Asinino! hahaha—respira!—Ma intoni almeno una, cazzo! (at a repeated C sharp)—bravo, evviva!—e vieni à seccarmi per la quarta, e Dio sia benedetto per l' ultima volta (at the fourth repetition of the theme)—ah termina, ti prego! ah maledetto —anche bravura? (at a short run) bravo—ah! trillo di pecore (at a shake)—finisci? grazie al ciel!—basta, basta!" Leutgeb was quite willing to submit to his friend's banter as the price of four concertos (412, 417, 447, 495, cf. also 514 K.). They are rapidly put together and easy of execution, without any great originality. Their brevity enables the instrument to preserve its true character as one unsuited for display of execution; in the last movement, which is the regulation rondo in 6-8 time, the original nature of the horn as a hunting instrument is made apparent, which at that

---

[55] According to a communication of Sonnleithner's, who also asserts that Leutgeb died in good circumstances on February 27, 1811.

time, when hunting music was thought more of than at
present, was no doubt found very entertaining. In other
respects, the customary concerto form is preserved. The
first movement is an allegro in sonata form, kept within
narrow limits, the second is a simple romanza, followed
by the rondo. The accompaniment is simple, to allow
due prominence to the horn as the solo instrument, but
Mozart seldom refrains from adding touches of life and
character to the whole by means of a freer movement in
the accompaniment. The quintet for the horn, violin, two
tenors, and bass (407 K.), was also written for Leutgeb,
who possessed the autograph.[56] The horn part is throughout concertante, the stringed instruments serve only as accompaniment, but are very independent and characteristic,
so that the whole has some approach to the quartet style.
The piece is altogether more important and finer than the
concertos.

Far more important both as to compass and substance is
the concerto for clarinet in A major (622 K.), which Mozart
wrote or adapted for Stadler, towards the close of his life
(between September 28 and November 15, 1791). There
exist six pages of a draft score of the first movement, composed much earlier for the basset-horn, in G major, and
available for the clarinet with a few alterations in the deeper
notes. It has not been ascertained whether this concerto
was ever finished, but it is scarcely probable.

It was to be expected that Mozart, who was the first to
do justice to the capabilities of the clarinet as a solo instrument, would deal with it with peculiar partiality ; the more
so, as he had so distinguished a performer to work for.[57]
The brilliant qualities of this splendid instrument are in
point of fact thrown into the strongest relief. The contrasts
of tone-colouring are made use of in every sort of way, especially in the low notes, here much employed in the accompaniment passages, whose wonderful effect Mozart was, as
far as I know, the first to discover.

---

[56] Cäcilie, IV., p. 306; VI., p. 203.
[57] Schink, Litt. Fragm., II., p. 236. Musik. Wochenbl., p. 118.

The capacity of the clarinet for melodious expression, tunefulness, and brilliant fluency, and for the union of force with melting tenderness, is skilfully taken into account; and as Mozart invariably brings the external into harmony with the internal, we find in this work that the grander and broader forms and the greater execution are the natural outcome of brilliant and original ideas. It is not too much to say that this concerto is the basis of modern clarinet-playing. Mozart composed on September 29, 1789, for the same fickle friend, the "Stadlersquintett ' for clarinet and strings (582 K.), which was first performed at the concert for the Musicians' Charitable Fund on December 22, 1789.

The distinct and frequently overpowering effect of the clarinet, in conjunction with stringed instruments, would necessitate its treatment as a solo instrument; and Mozart's loving efforts to display to the full its singular beauties and rich powers serve to isolate it still more completely. Although he avoids with equal taste and skill the danger of treating the stringed instruments as mere accompaniment, or of emphasising the clarinet unduly, and combines them to a whole often with touches of surprising delicacy, yet the heterogeneous elements are not so completely incorporated as are the stringed instruments when they are alone. The whole mechanism is therefore loose and easy, the subjects are more graceful than important, and their development less serious and profound than usual. This quintet therefore, cast as it is in the most beautiful forms, and possessed of the most charming sound effects—fully justifying the praise bestowed upon it by Ambros ("Limits of Music and Poetry") in Goethe's words, "its whole being floats in sensuous wealth and sweetness"—yet falls below the high level of the stringed quintets.

The Andante in A major to a violin concerto, dated in the Thematic Catalogue April 1, 1785 (470 K.), must certainly have been written for a virtuoso; perhaps for Janiewicz, who was then in Vienna.

Mozart sometimes bestowed improvised compositions in the form of alms. One day a beggar accosted him in the street and claimed a distant relationship with him.   Mozart, having no money, went into the nearest coffee-house, wrote a minuet and trio, and sent the beggar with it to his publisher, who paid him what it was considered worth.[58]

His ever-ready good-nature must have made Mozart a great favourite among his fellow-artists, and yet he had only too often to complain of the ingratitude to which his very good-nature subjected him.   Between him and the majority of Italian opera-singers there existed, nevertheless, an innate antagonism ; they complained of his compositions as being far too difficult and not telling enough.   There can be no doubt that he made many concessions to display of execution, but these were not considered extensive enough at the time, and Mozart, scorning so cheap and easy a way of gaining the applause of the public, sought to attain his end by other and better means.[59]   It is not to be wondered at, therefore, that the Italians in Vienna for the most part objected to singing in Mozart's operas, the more so as their disinclination was fostered by outsiders ; Mozart, on his part, disliked the then prevalent style of singing : "They rush at it, and shake and make flourishes," he said, "because they have not studied, and cannot sustain a note."[60]

He was fond of mocking in his sarcastic style at this kind of composition and performance, and used to imitate off-hand at the piano grand operatic scenas in the style of well-known masters, with the most telling effect.[61]   Such exhibitions would not tend to increase the number of his friends.   Mozart was "cutting" (*schlimm*), as we know, and took no pains to restrain his jesting moods, which were doubtless often taken in far worse part than they were meant.   But he also pronounced many a sharp censure in earnest upon artists who felt the more bitter as his own

---

[58] So Parker asserts, Mus. Mem., II., p. 179, "from authentic sources."

[59] Cf. Niemetschek, p. 75.   Rochlitz, A. M. Z., I., p. 115.

[60] Rochlitz, A. M. Z., III., p. 591.   Compare Mozart's remarks on Gabrielli and Aloysia Weber, I., p. 427.

[61] Rochlitz, whose opinions were identical, describes a bravura scena for a prima donna, which Mozart has also recorded (A. M. Z., III., p. 591).

superiority made itself incontestably felt.[62]   Soon after his
settlement in Vienna his father was informed that his
boasting and criticisms were making him enemies among
musicians and others, but this accusation Wolfgang indignantly repelled (July 31, 1782).

Nevertheless, we find him writing not long afterwards
(December 23, 1782): "I should like to write a book—a
short musical criticism with examples ; but of course not in
my own name."   There was a rage at Vienna for the discussion and criticism of all imaginable subjects by means of
pamphlets and brochures.[63]   That which tempted Mozart to
take pen in hand was the downfall of German opera, which
was a serious blow to him.   He was conscious of what he as
a German might have accomplished for German art, and it
pained him to see the universal preference for Italian art and
artists.

From early youth he had been aware of the unworthy
devices often employed in Italian music, and his aversion to
"all Italians" continually betrays itself, but very seldom to
the extent of making him unjust towards individual persons
or performances.   His healthy judgment and inexhaustible
flow of human kindness preserved him from this danger.
Jos. Frank relates[64] that, finding Mozart continually engaged
on the study of French opera scores, he once asked him if
he would not do better to devote himself to Italian music,
which was then the fashion of the day in Vienna.   Mozart
answered: "As regards the melodies, yes ; but as regards
the dramatic effects, no ; besides which, the scores that you

---

[62] " Deceit and flattery were alike foreign to his artless character," says
Niemetschek (p. 96), " and any restraint upon his intellect was insupportable to
him.   Free and unreserved in his expressions and answers, he frequently
wounded the susceptibilities of self-love, and made many enemies."   An article
upon him after his death contains the following passage (Reichardt, Musik.
Wochenbl., p. 94): " Now that he is dead, the Viennese will know what they
have lost in him.   During his life he was much harassed by cabals, whose
hostility he sometimes provoked by his *sans-souci* manner."

[63] Blumauer, who mentions this characteristic in his observations on the
culture and literature of Austria, asserts that within eighteen months 1,172
publications of this kind appeared at Vienna (Pros. Schr., I., p. 72).

[64] Prutz, Deutsch. Museum, II., p. 28.

see here are by Gluck, Piccinni, Salieri, and, with the
exception of those by Grétry, have nothing French in them
but the words."[65] This was true, and we may allow that
Mozart did not require to learn melody from the Italians.
His judgments of various composers might offend at the time,
but we are now ready to endorse them as not only striking
but fair. We have already learnt his opinion of Righini
(Vol. II., p. 251). Of Martin, the universal favourite, he said:
" Much in his works is really very pretty, but ten years
hence he will be quite forgotten."[66] How ready he was to
acknowledge merit in any performance " which had something in it " is plainly shown in a letter to his father
(April 24, 1784) :—

> Some quartets have just appeared by a man named Pleyel; he is a
> pupil of Jos. Haydn. If you do not already know them, try to get them,
> it is worth your while. They are very well and pleasantly written, and
> give evidence of his master. Well and happy will it be for music if
> Pleyel is ready in due time to take Haydn's place for us.

This was just at the time when he was busy with his
own quartets, where he showed how one master learns from
another. When he found nothing original in any work he
put it aside with the words, " Nothing in it," or vented his
mocking humour on it. Rochlitz relates that once at Doles'
he made them sing the Mass of a composer "who had evident
talent for comic opera, but was out of place as a composer
of sacred music," parodying the words in a very entertaining
manner.[67]

The description which Mozart gives to his father of the
celebrated oboist, J. Chr. Fischer (1733-1800), is characteristic of his sharp and involuntarily comic criticism.
Fischer had come to Vienna from London, where he enjoyed
an extraordinary reputation (April 4, 1787) :[68]—

---

[65] The few opera scores found among Mozart's remains are Gluck's " Arbre
Enchanté," " Le Diable à Quatre," Grétry's " Zemire et Azor," " Barnevelt,"
Mich. Haydn's " Endimione."

[66] Rochlitz, A. M. Z., I., p. 116. Cf. Siever's Mozart u. Süssmayer, p. 22.

[67] A. M. Z., III., p. 493. He did not think highly of Jomelli as a church
composer, although he admired his operas (A. M. Z., I., p. 116), while of Gassmann he formed an exactly opposite opinion (A. M. Z., XX., p. 247).

[68] Burney, Reise, I., p. 22. Busky, Gesch. d. Mus., II., p. 584.

If the oboist Fischer did not play better when we heard him in
Holland (1766) than he plays now, he certainly does not deserve the
reputation which he has.   But, between ourselves, I was then at an age
incapable of forming a judgment.   I can only remember that he pleased
me, as he pleased all the world.   It would be quite reasonable to contend that taste has altered since then to a remarkable degree, and that
he plays after the old school—but no! he plays, in fact, like a miserable
learner; young André, who used to learn from Fiala, plays a thousand
times better.   And then his concertos of his own composition!   Every
ritornello lasts a quarter of an hour—then enter the hero—lifts up one
leaden foot after another, and plumps them down on the ground alternately.   His tone is all through his nose, and his tenuto is like the
tremulant stop on the organ.   Could you have supposed all this? and
yet it is nothing but the truth, the real truth, which I tell you.

Mozart's amiability and good-nature prevailed in his
personal intercourse with fellow-artists, even where reserve
or irritated feeling would have been excusable.   When the
Italian Opera was reopened, from which Mozart had been
purposely excluded, he did not withdraw his friendship from
the composers, whom he might justifiably have considered
as interlopers.   When Paesiello came to Vienna from
St. Petersburg in 1784 he was treated with a distinction
never bestowed upon German masters.   His "Barbiere di
Seviglia" was at once put upon the stage, and the Emperor
lost no time in commissioning him to compose an opera,
for which Casti, as the most distinguished comic poet, was
to provide the libretto.   The opera was "Il Re Teodoro,"
for which Joseph himself suggested the subject as a satire,
it was said, on the visit of Gustavus III. of Sweden to
Venice in the year 1783.[69]   Such active participation from the
Emperor assured the maestro a brilliant position, both
pecuniary and social, during his stay in Vienna.   Mozart,
whose judgment of Paesiello's light music was very favourable,[70] made friendly advances towards him.   Kelly was
present at their introduction, and testifies to their mutual
courtesy and esteem;[71] and we have already seen (Vol. II.,

---

[69] So Jos. Frank asserts in Prutz, Deutsch. Museum, II., p. 24.   There are
interesting notices in Kelly's Reminisc., I., p. 238.

[70] Rochlitz, A. M. Z., I., p. 115.

[71] Kelly, Reminisc., I., p. 238.

p. 279) how pleased Mozart was to have his compositions performed before Paesiello by a talented pupil. Paesiello, on his part, begged for the score of "Idomeneo" for his own study.[72] Mozart was equally complaisant to Sarti, who was in Vienna at the same time, on his way to St. Petersburg. "If Maestro Sarti had not been obliged to set out to-day for Russia," he writes to his father (June 9, 1784), "he would have gone out with me. Sarti is a straightforward, honest man. I have played a great deal to him, ending with variations on one of his airs (460 K.),[73] which gave him great pleasure."

The "honest" man afterwards wrote a most malicious criticism on some passages in Mozart's quartets, concerning which, indignant that "barbarians, without any sense of hearing should presume to think they can compose music," he exclaims, "Can more be done to put performers out of tune?" ("Si può far di più per far stonar i professori?"). He points out error after error "which could only be made by a clavier-player, who can see no difference between D sharp and E flat"; and concludes with a flourish, "This is, in the words of the immortal Rousseau, 'De la musique pour faire boucher ses oreilles!'"[74]

A charming instance of Mozart's benevolence towards younger artists is supplied by Gyrowetz. He relates in his autobiography, how he was introduced to the most distinguished artists of Vienna, at some grand soirée:—

Mozart appeared to be the most good-natured of them all. He observed the youthful Gyrowetz with an expression of sympathy which seemed to say: "Poor young fellow, you have just embarked on the ocean of the great world, and you are anxiously looking forward to what fate may have in store for you." Encouraged by so much affability and sympathy the young artist entreated the master to cast a glance over his compositions, which consisted of six symphonies, and to give his

---

[72] Bridi, Brevi Notiz., p. 47.

[73] The theme "Come un agnello" is from Sarti's opera, "Fra i Due Litiganti il Terzo Gode," which was then the rage in Vienna, and is the same which is made use of in the second finale of "Don Giovanni."

[74] Sarti's "Esame acustico fatto sopra due frammenti di Mozart" has, as far as I know, never been printed; an extract was given in A. M. Z., XXXIV., p. 373 (cf. XXVI., p. 540).

opinion of them. With true benevolence, Mozart granted the petition, went through the works, commended them, and promised the young artist to have one of his symphonies performed at his concert in the hall at the Mehlgrube, where Mozart gave subscription concerts during that year (1785). This took place on a Thursday. The symphony was performed with great applause. Mozart, with his native courtesy and kindness, took the young composer by the hand, and introduced him to the public as the author of the symphonies.

Beethoven made his appearance in Vienna as a youthful musician of promise in the spring of 1787, but was only able to remain there a short time;[75] he was introduced to Mozart, and played to him at his request. Mozart, considering the piece he performed to be a studied show-piece, was somewhat cold in his expressions of admiration. Beethoven remarking this, begged for a theme for improvisation, and, inspired by the presence of the master he reverenced so highly, played in such a manner as gradually to engross Mozart's whole attention; turning quietly to the bystanders, he said emphatically, "Mark that young man; he will make himself a name in the world!"[76]

Mozart does not appear to have become intimately acquainted with Dittersdorf, who at that time was paying only passing visits to Vienna; but his way of mentioning Mozart shows appreciation and esteem. The same may be said of Gluck, who, as we have seen, showed himself on several occasions well disposed towards Mozart (Vol. II., pp. 212, 285); but the difference of their natures—perhaps also Salieri's close connection with Gluck—prevented anything like intimacy between them.

That, notwithstanding so much goodwill, Mozart should

---

[75] According to a letter from Bonn of April 8, 1787 (Cramer's Magaz., II., p. 1,386) he was still in Bonn at that time, and returned home just before the death of his mother, on July 17, 1787.

[76] Schindler (Biogr. Beethoven, I., p. 15) apparently did not know of this interview, which Beethoven was fond of alluding to; the above account was communicated to me in Vienna on good authority. The anecdote is embellished in Beethoven's Studien (Anh., p. 4), and alludes to studies in counterpoint and theory which Beethoven had not even attempted at the time. According to Ries (Biogr. Not., p. 86) he received a few lessons from Mozart, but never heard him play.

have met with envious critics and detractors[77] among the artists of Vienna is scarcely to be wondered at. We have already noticed one of his most determined opponents, Kreibich (Vol. II., p. 203); another, equally implacable, was Leopold Kozeluch, a pianist of some brilliancy, and a fashionable teacher, especially after he gave lessons at court; he had a passing reputation, too, as a composer, but vanity and stupidity were his chief claims to distinction. He was fond of magnifying his own merits by paltry criticism of his fellow-artists, especially of Haydn. Once, when a new quartet of Haydn's was being performed in a large company, Kozeluch, standing by Mozart, found fault, first with one thing and then with another, exclaiming at length, with impudent assurance, " I should never have done it in that way!" " Nor should I," answered Mozart; " but do you know why ? Because neither you nor I would have had so good an idea."[78] Henceforth Kozeluch became Mozart's avowed and determined opponent; and what better revenge could be taken by the man " who never praised any one but himself," than to pronounce the overture to " Don Giovanni " " good, but full of faults ";[79] and to exclaim condescendingly, after hearing the full rehearsal of the overture to the " Zauberflöte," " Ah, our good friend Mozart is trying to be learned this time!"[80] When they were both at Prague, at the coronation of Leopold, Kozeluch expressed his enmity to Mozart so obtrusively, that he forfeited a great share of the interest " with which hitherto every Bohemian had been proud to own him as a fellow-countryman."[81]

---

[77] " Mozart willingly listened to criticism, even when it was adverse," says Rochlitz (A. M. Z., I., p. 145) ; " he was susceptible only to blame of one kind, and that was the kind which he most often received—that is, blame for his too fiery imagination and intellect. This sensitiveness was but natural ; for if the blame were justifiable, then all that was most original and characteristic in his music was valueless."

[78] The anecdote is given by Niemetschek, p. 94 ; Rochlitz (A. M. Z., I., p. 53) ; Griesinger (Biogr. Notizen über J. Haydn, p. 105) ; Nissen, p. 681, who names Kozeluch.

[79] Bohemia, 1856, p. 127.

[80] This remark was communicated to me by Neukomm, who heard it from Haydn.

[81] A. M. Z., II., p. 516.

The most charming instance of Mozart's reverence and love for Joseph Haydn is the dedicatory epistle wherein he offers him his six quartets as the fruit of long and painful study inspired by his example, as a father intrusts his children to a tried and valued friend, confident of his protection and indulgence towards them. These expressions of reverence came from the very depths of Mozart's heart: to a friend who made some remark on the dedication he answered: "It was due from me, for it was from Haydn that I learned how quartets should be written."[82] "It was quite affecting," says Niemetschek" (p. 94) "to hear him speak of the two Haydns or any other of the great masters; one would have imagined him to be one of their enthusiastic pupils rather than the all-powerful Mozart." The Haydn so honoured of Mozart was not by any means the "Father Haydn" of a later time, reverenced and loved by all. It was not until after his residence in London that Haydn met with general admiration and veneration in the Austrian capital; in earlier years the opposition to his originality was nowhere stronger than in Vienna. His very position in the service of Prince Esterhazy, and his residence in Hungary, prejudiced the musicians of the capital against him. The music-loving public enjoyed his fresh and jovial creations with unrestrained delight, but the artists and connoisseurs took grave exception to them. Humour in music was as yet unrecognised, and the dispute as to whether and in what degree it could be justified had just begun; the freedom, well considered as it was, with which Haydn treated traditional rules, was looked upon as a grave fault. At the head of his opponents stood the Emperor Joseph;[83] he would have nothing to say to his playful oddities, and we can scarcely wonder that the royal example was widely followed, and that Haydn had good cause to complain of his critics and enemies.[84] It required

---

[82] Rochlitz, A. M. Z., I., p. 53 ; cf. p. 116.

[83] So Reichardt asserts, A. M. Z., XV., p. 667 (Schletterer, Reichardt, I., p. 325). Reise nach Wien, II., p. 91, and Dittersdorf (Selbstbiogr., p. 238).

[84] Sending a sonata to Artaria, he writes (February 8, 1780): "I hope at least to gain credit for this work with people of cultivation ; it is sure to be criticised by the envious (who are very numerous) "; and similar remarks frequently occur.

an artist as genial and as incapable of envy as Mozart fully
to understand and appreciate him. And Haydn was equally
prompt to discover the greatness of Mozart, and to accord
him his full share of admiration and esteem. We have seen
the testimony which he bore of Mozart to his father (Vol. II.,
p. 321); and he lost no opportunity of expressing his conviction
of Mozart's artistic greatness.[85] When it was proposed to
produce an opera by Haydn at Prague, together with
Mozart's "Figaro" and "Don Giovanni," Haydn wrote to
the Commissary Roth:[86]—

> You wish an opera buffa from me. With all my heart, if it will give
> you any pleasure to possess some of my vocal compositions. But if it
> is your intention to place the opera on the stage in Prague I am sorry
> that I cannot oblige you. My operas are inseparable from the company
> for whom I wrote them, and would never produce their calculated effect
> apart from their native surroundings. It would be quite another
> matter if I had the honour of being commissioned to write a new opera
> for the theatre in question. Even then, however, it would be a risk to
> put myself in competition with the great Mozart. If I could only
> inspire every lover of music, especially among the great, with feelings
> as deep, and comprehension as clear as my own, in listening to the
> inimitable works of Mozart, then surely the nations would contend for
> the possession of such a jewel within their borders. Prague must strive
> to retain the treasure within her grasp—but not without fitting reward.
> The want of this too often saddens the life of a great genius, and offers
> small encouragement for further efforts in future times. I feel indignant
> that Mozart has not yet been engaged at any imperial or royal court.
> Pardon my wandering from the subject—Mozart is a man very dear to
> me.

This letter was written in December, 1787, and the news
of Mozart's appointment as Imperial private composer had
not yet reached Haydn in Esterhaz; the uncertain position
of his friend evidently affected him greatly. In the year
following, when controversy was rife in Vienna on the subject of "Don Giovanni," Haydn found himself one evening
in the midst of a company discussing the faults of omission

---

[85] Parke, Mus. Mem., I., p. 170.
[86] Niemetschek, p. 78 (A. M. Z., I., p. 182; XI., p. 780. Nissen, p. 643.
Wien. Musikzeitg., 1817, p. 218. Nohl, Musikerbr., p. 101). Griesinger asserts
by mistake (Biogr. Notizen, p. 104), followed by Carpani (Le Haydine, p. 202),
that in 1791, Haydn (who was then in London) was summoned to Prague for
the coronation of Leopold II., but refused the invitation in the words, " Where
Mozart is, Haydn cannot show himself."

and commission of the new opera; at last he was asked for his opinion. "I cannot decide the questions in dispute," said he; "but this I know, that Mozart is the greatest composer in the world."[87] It must not be imagined that because Haydn set so high a value on Mozart's operatic compositions, he had by any means a small opinion of his own. Forgotten as they now are, he himself was not inclined to rank them below the performances of the majority of his contemporaries. He writes to Artaria (May 27, 1781):—

> Mons. Le Gros, directeur of the Concert spirituel, writes me many compliments on my "Stabat Mater," which has been performed four times with great success. The management were surprised at this revelation of my powers as a vocal composer; but they had had no previous opportunity of judging of them. If they would only hear my operetta "L' Isola Disabitata," and my last opera "La Fedeltà Premiata"! I assure you, such works have never yet been heard in Paris, and perhaps not in Vienna; but it is my misfortune to live retired in the country.

He says of the "Armida," in March, 1874, that it has been produced with signal success, and is considered his best work.[88] It is doubly significant, therefore, that Haydn should have acknowledged himself so completely overshadowed by Mozart as an operatic composer. And not in this branch of their art alone did he accord him superiority; he gave way even where they might justly be considered as rivals, and declared that, if Mozart had written nothing but his violin quartets and the "Requiem," he would have sufficient claim to immortality.[89] He assured a friend, with tears in his eyes, that he could never forget Mozart's clavierplaying; "It came from the heart!"[90] To the end of his life he missed no occasion of hearing Mozart's music, and used to assert that he had never heard one of his compositions without learning something from it.[91] In 1790, when he had returned to his solitude at "Estoras," he writes how

---

[87] Rochlitz, A. M. Z., I., p. 52.
[88] Nohl, Musikerbr., pp. 84, 93. Cf. Griesinger, Biogr. Not., p. 25.
[89] Stadler, Vertheidigung der Echtheit des Mozartschen Requiem, p. 27.
[90] Griesinger, Biogr. Not., p. 104.
[91] Carpani, Le Haydine p. 201.

the north wind had waked him from a dream of listening to the " Nozze di Figaro."[92]

The personal intercourse between the two was simple and hearty. Mozart used to call Haydn " Papa," and both Sophie Haibl and Griesinger mention their use of the pronoun *du* to each other, a habit less frequent in those days than at present between friends of such difference in age. But while Mozart lived in Vienna, Haydn had his fixed residence at Eisenstadt or Esterhaz, and only came to Vienna for a few months at a time with his princely patron, who was not fond of the capital, and shortened his stay there as far as was practicable; Haydn sometimes obtained leave of absence for a flying visit to Vienna, but the Prince always gave it unwillingly.[93]

It was not until the Kapelle was broken up, on the death of Prince Nicolaus in 1790, that Haydn took up his abode in Vienna; and in December of the same year Salomon persuaded him to undertake the journey to London. Mozart agreed with others of Haydn's friends in considering this expedition a great risk, and drew his attention to the difficulties he was sure to encounter as an elderly man, unused to the world, amidst a strange people whose language he did not understand. Haydn replied that he was old, certainly, (he was then fifty-nine), but strong and of good courage, and his language was understood by all the world.[94] Mozart spent the day of Haydn's departure with him, and as they took leave he was moved to tears and exclaimed: " We are taking our last farewell in this world ! " Haydn himself was deeply moved, thinking of his own death, and sought to console and calm Mozart.[95]

A letter from Haydn to Frau von Gennzinger (October 13, 1791) shows that calumniators sought to sow enmity between the friends in their separation: " My friends write, what I cannot however believe, that Mozart is doing all he can to

---

[92] Karajan, Haydn in London, p. 66. Nohl, Musikerbr., p. 114.
[93] Griesinger, Biogr. Not., p. 23.
[94] Griesinger, Biogr. Not., p. 35. Dies, Biogr. Nachr., p. 75.
[95] Dies, Biogr. Nachr., p. 77.

disparage me. I forgive him. Mozart must go to Count von Fries to inquire about the payment."[96] When the news of Mozart's death reached London, Haydn lamented his loss with bitter tears.[97]

The sight of these two great and noble men extending to each other the hand of brotherhood, and remaining true to the end, untouched by professional envy or intrigue, is as pleasant as it was rare in the Vienna of those days. Each understood and appreciated the other, each freely acknowledged his indebtedness to the other from a musical point of view, and each, in his own consciousness of power and independence, found the standard for estimating the worth of his brother-artist. Those who strove to raise the dust of dissension between them are, for the most part, forgotten or relegated to their due position in the background of musical history: Mozart and Haydn stand side by side on the heights, witnessing for ever to the truth that the greatness of a genuinely artistic nature attracts and does not repel its like.

CHAPTER XXIX.

SOCIAL INTERCOURSE.

FIRST among the group of friends in intercourse with whom Mozart found entertainment and refreshment of the highest kind, must be named the Countess Thun, *née* Uhlefeld. She was one of the musical ladies who took him under their protection from the first, and it was she more especially who introduced him in Vienna, and furthered his advancement by every means in her power. The prominent position which was hers more in virtue of her cultivation and amiability than of her rank and wealth, pointed her out as

---

[96] Karajan, J. Haydn in London, p. 97. Nohl, Musikerbr., p. 135.

[97] I have heard from Neukomm that Haydn spoke of it with emotion (Cf. Wien. Ztg. für Theat., 1808, III., p. 107). "I am childishly glad to be at home," he wrote (December 20, 1791), "and welcomed by my old friends. I only regret to miss the greeting of the great Mozart, whose death I deplore. Posterity will not see such talent for a century to come" (Karajan, p. 102; Nohl, Musikerbr., p. 140).

a fitting protectress for genius. She was one of the few
ladies with whom the Emperor Joseph continued ·in later
years on a footing of intimacy, and he took leave of her in a
touching letter from his death-bed.[1] Music had the place of
honour in her entertainments. She played the pianoforte herself with "that grace, lightness, and *délicatesse* to which no
fingers but a woman's can aspire," as Burney says;[2] he was
delighted with her gay, natural manners, her witty sallies, and
her pleasant irony, as well as with her taste, knowledge, and
serious interest in all things musical.[3] Her favourite composer at that time (1772) was Beecké (Vol. I., p. 367), who
mentions to Dalberg having composed in 1785 a sonata for
three pianofortes for the Countess Thun and her daughters.

Reichardt also, whom she took under her protection on
his arrival in Vienna in 1783, extols her as the most intellectual and most charming woman in Vienna, and adds that
her musical receptions were frequented both by the Emperor
and the Archduke Maximilian.[4] Georg Forster became her
enthusiastic admirer during his stay in Vienna in 1784. He
enumerates in a letter to Heyne[5] the distinguished men
whose favour and patronage he enjoyed, and we recognise
among them many of Mozart's friends and patrons. Such
were the good old Counsellor von Born, Baron Otto von
Gemmingen—the intimate friend of Van Swieten, who had
come to Vienna in the summer of 1782[6]—the old Councillor
von Spielmann[7]—a man of learning and at the same time

---

[1] Besides the Countess Thun, these were the Princesses Liechtenstein,
Schwarzenburg, Lobkowitz. Kelly, Reminisc., I., p. 209. Car. Pichler, Denkwürd., I., p. 141. Hormayr, Gesch. Wiens., V., p. 94. Vehse, Gesch. des
österr. Hofes, VIII., p. 304.

[2] Burney, Reise, II., p. 160. She told him that she had formerly played
much better, but that she had borne six children, each of whom had carried
away something of her musical power.

[3] Burney, pp. 188, 215.

[4] A. M. Z., XV., p. 668. Schletterer, Reichardt, p. 327.

[5] G. Forster, Sämmtl. Schr., VII., p. 272.

[6] Meyer, L. Schröder, I., p. 380.

[7] He possessed a house with a beautiful garden, on the high road. At a
concert there given, Nicolai admired the promising pianoforte-playing of
Spielmann's little daughter, who had been instructed by her talented mother
(Reise, IV., p. 554; cf. III., p. 37, 291).

more deeply versed in the affairs of the department of Prince Kaunitz than any other statesman—the great minister Kaunitz himself (Vol. II., p. 212), good, simple Count Cobenzl (Vol. II., p. 173), Field-Marshal Haddik, "a splendid old soldier, plain and plump,"[8] and to this list Forster adds the name of the Countess Thun, "the most virtuous and enlightened woman of Vienna." He gives a more particular account of his intercourse with her to Thérèse Heyne :—

You cannot imagine how condescending and friendly every one is. One scarcely remembers that one is among persons of high rank, and one feels quite on the footing of an intimate friend. This is especially my case with the Countess Thun, the most charming woman in the world, and her three graces of daughters, each of them an angel in her own way. The Countess is the best mother that I know ; the children are all innocence, joyful as the morning light, and full of natural sense and wit, at which I wonder in silence, just as I wonder at the sense and wit of a certain maid on the Leine. This charming family combine the most refined discourse, and the most extensive reading and liberal know-ledge, with a pure, heartfelt religion, free from all superstition, the reli-gion of gentle and innocent hearts familiar with the secrets of nature and creation. Almost every evening between nine and ten, these [above-named] people assemble at the Countess Thun's, and enjoy brilliant conversation or music, either clavier-playing, or German or Italian singing ; sometimes, when the humour seizes them, they dance.

We can well imagine how completely Mozart felt himself at home in this circle ; Prince Karl Lichnowsky, his friend and pupil, was the Countess Thun's son-in-law.

Greiner's house was another in which learning was honoured and cherished, and which formed a meeting-point for all celebrities. Greiner's daughter, Caroline Pichler, an admirable pianiste,[9] thus describes it :[10]—

Besides the poets Denis, Leon, Haschka, Alxinger, Blumauer, &c., whose names were then famous, our house was frequented by men of severer science. No foreign scholar or artist visited Vienna without bringing introductions to Haschka or to my parents themselves. Thus we entertained the celebrated traveller Georg Forster, Professors Meiners and Spittler, Becker, Gögking, the actor Schröder, and many

---

[8] G. Forster, Sämmtl. Schr., VII., p. 269.
[9] Jahrb. d. Tonk., 1796, pp. 19, 70.
[10] Car. Pichler, Denkw., I., p. 92.

musicians and composers such as Paesiello and Cimarosa; I need not say that our native artists, Mozart, Haydn, Salieri, the brothers Hickl, Füger, and others were frequent guests.

The house of the Martinez brother and sister, which has become by association a true temple of the muses for the Viennese, was another rendezvous for musicians. Metastasio, on his arrival at Vienna in 1730, took up his residence with Nicolai Martinez, Master of the Ceremonies to the Apostolic Nuncio, and remained with him until his death in 1782. He became the intimate friend of the family, and carefully superintended the education of the children. One of the daughters, Marianne (born about 1740), by reason of her talent, and her lively, pleasant manners, attracted his special attention.[11] Through his instruction she became well versed in the Italian, French, and English languages and literature, and in all the branches of a liberal education. Nor was this all; Metastasio perceived that she possessed considerable musical talent, and took care that she should receive a thorough musical education. Joseph Haydn, who, on being dismissed from the Kapellhaus a penniless young man, had taken a miserable garret in the same house, was engaged to give Marianne lessons in playing and singing, for which he was boarded free for three years by way of payment,[12] a more important result for him being that he thus became acquainted with Porpora, who interested himself in Marianne's education out of friendship for Metastasio. Afterwards, under the careful guidance of Bono and of Metastasio himself, she developed gifts as a singer, player, and composer which excited general admiration,[13] and won applause from Hasse.[14] In 1773 she was made a member of the Philharmonic Academy at Bologna,[15] and afterwards received a " Dictor-diplom " both from Bologna and Pavia; in 1782 her oratorio " Isaaco" was performed at the " Societätsconcert."[16] She

---

[11] Cristini, Vita di Metastasio, p. 206.
[12] Griesinger, Biogr. Not., p. 13. Carpani, Le Haydine, p. 86.
[13] Burney, Reise, II., pp. 181, 227, 254. Jahrb. d. Tonk., 1796, p. 41.
[14] Burney, Reise, II., p. 260.
[15] Mancini, Rifl. Prat. sul Canto Fig., p. 229.
[16] Wiener Musikzeitg., 1842, p. 70.

lived with her brother (Imperial librarian) after the death
of Metastasio, whose property she inherited;[17] she gave receptions, which were frequented by all the intellectual and
musical celebrities of the day.[18] Kelly, who brought an introduction to her, declared that, in spite of her advanced age,
she retained all the animation and cheerfulness of youth,
and was pleasant and talkative. He says that Mozart (who
had been warmly received by Metastasio on his early visits
to Vienna) was very intimate with her, and that he had
heard them play duets of her composition at her musical
parties.[19]

One of the most distinguished musical dilettanti of the day
at Vienna was the Geheimrath Bernh. von Keess (d. 1795).
This "well-known lover of music and patron of musicians"
took the amateur concerts in the Augarten (Vol. II., p. 284,
note 47) under his protection, and possessed a rare and costly
collection of musical objects.[20] He gave private concerts
twice a week in his own house, as Gyrowetz relates:[21]—

The best virtuosi in Vienna, and the first composers, such as Jos.
Haydn, Mozart, Dittersdorf, Hoffmeister, Albrechtsberger, Giarnovichi,
&c., assembled at these concerts. Haydn's symphonies were performed
there, Mozart used generally to play the pianoforte, and Giarnovichi, the
most celebrated violin virtuoso of the day,[22] usually played a concerto;
the lady of the house sang. It happened one evening that Mozart was
late in arriving, and they waited for him to begin, because he had promised to bring with him a song for the lady of the house. One servant
after another was sent to find him, and at last he was discovered in a
tavern; the messenger begged him to come at once, as all the company
was waiting to hear the new song. Mozart thereupon recollected that
he had not written a note of it. He sent the messenger for a sheet of
music paper, and set to work in the tavern to compose the song. When
it was finished he went his way to the concert, where the company were
waiting for him with great impatience. After a little gentle reproach for
his delay he was most affectionately received; the lady of the house sang
the new song, a little nervously, it is true, but it was enthusiastically
received and applauded.

---

[17] Cristini, Vita di Metastasio, p. 211.
[18] Jahrb. d. Tonk., 1796, p. 71.
[19] Kelly, Reminisc., I., p. 252.
[20] Wien. Ztg., 1796, No. 29.
[21] Gyrowetz, Selbtsbiogr., p. 9. Cf. Nohl, Musikerbr., pp. 116, 136, 145.
[22] Dittersdorf (Selbstbiogr., p. 233) is of this opinion.

Mozart's boyish fancy of only playing before connoisseurs naturally disappeared as he grew older and more sensible. He took pleasure in playing to all who took pleasure in hearing him, and was so far from the affectation of requiring to be pressed, that many persons of rank in Vienna reproached him with being too ready to play to anybody who asked him. One requirement, indeed, he made which seems difficult of attainment in musical society, viz., the silence and attention of his audience. " Nothing irritated him so much," says Niemetschek (p. 88), "as restlessness, noise, or talking over music. On such occasions the usually gentle, courteous man completely lost patience, and expressed his annoyance without reserve. He has been known to rise in the middle of his playing, and leave an inattentive audience." In some cases his satirical humour led him to show his disgust in other ways.[23] When he was playing to real musicians and connoisseurs he was indefatigable.[24] After his concert in Leipzig, where he had alternately played and conducted, he said to the good old violin-player Berger : " I have only just got warm. Come home with me, and I will play you something worthy of an artist's ears." And after a hasty supper, his ideas and imaginations streamed from the instrument till close on midnight. Then suddenly springing up, as his manner was, he cried : " Now, what do you think of that? You have heard Mozart after his own fashion ; something less will do for the others."[25]

The family with whom Mozart appeared most completely at home in Vienna was that of the celebrated botanist Freih. von Jacquin. We have an attractive description of it (1844) from Caroline Pichler, who was intimate there from her youth :[26]—

This family had for sixty or seventy years been a shining light in the scientific world, both in and out of Vienna, and their house was visited by many for the sake of the pleasant social intercourse there to be enjoyed. While the learned, or would-be learned, paid their respects to

---

[23] Rochlitz gives a comical example (A. M. Z., I., p. 49).
[24] Niemetschek, p. 95.
[25] Rochlitz, A. M. Z., XIV., p. 106. Für Freunde der Tonkunst, III., p. 222.
[26] Car. Pichler, Denkw., I., p. 179.

the famous father and his worthy son, Jos. Frz. v. Jacquin,[27] the more youthful assembled round the younger son Gottfried, whose lively intellect, striking talent for music, and charming voice made him the centre of the gay circle, together with his sister Franziska, the still-surviving Frau von Lagusius. On Wednesday evenings—which from time immemorial, were dedicated by the family to society, even in winter when the Jacquins lived in the Botanic Gardens[28]—learned talk went on in the father's room, while we young people chattered, joked, made music, played games, and entertained ourselves entirely to our satisfaction.

How thoroughly happy and at home Mozart was with this family may be seen from a letter to Gottr. von Jacquin, written in the full glow of his happiness at the brilliant reception he had met with in Prague (January 14, 1787) :[29]—

At last I am fortunate enough to find a moment in which to inquire after your dear parents, and all the Jacquin family. I can only hope and pray that you are all as well and happy as we two are. I can assure you, however, that (although we have been received here with extreme politeness and all possible honour, and Prague is really a handsome, pleasant city) I long very much for Vienna, and most particularly for *your* house. When I reflect that after my return I shall enjoy the pleasure of your society again for a short time, and then perhaps lose it for ever, I feel to its full extent the friendship and esteem which I bear to your whole family. Now farewell! Present my respects to your revered parents, and embrace your brother for me. I kiss your sister's hand a thousand times. But now it is time I close, is it not? Long ago, you will think. Write to me soon, very soon; if you are too lazy to do it yourself, send for Salmann, and dictate a letter to him; but it never comes straight from the heart unless you write yourself. Well —I shall see whether you are as much my friend as I am, and always shall be, yours.

During his second stay in Prague Mozart acquaints his friend with the good reception of " Don Giovanni " (November 4, 1787),[30] and adds :—

---

[27] On April 24, 1787, he wrote in Mozart's album : " Tibi qui possis blandus auritas fidibus canoris, ducere quercus in amicitiæ tesseram.—Jos. FRANC. A JACQUIN."

[28] The Botanic Garden was laid out by Maria Theresa, in the suburbs (Nicolai, Reise, III., p. 34) ; Mozart lived in the neighbourhood, which facilitated his intercourse with the Jacquins.

[29] Wien. Zeitschr., 1842, No. 79, p. 627.

[30] Wien. Zeitschr., 1842, No. 79, p. 625.

I wish that all my friends (especially Bridi and you) could be here just for one evening to participate in my pleasure.

And then he ends in his mocking way :—

My great grandfather used to say to his wife, my great grandmother, and she to her daughter my grandmother, and she again to her daughter, my mother, and she finally to her daughter, my dear sister, that it was a great art to be able to speak well and fully, but that it was perhaps a still greater art to know when to leave off speaking. I will, therefore, now follow the advice of my sister due to our mother, grandmother, and great grandmother, and bring my moral reflections and my letter to a close together.

And when, to his " delighted surprise," he received a second letter from Jacquin, he answers in a postscript :—

Can it be that neither your dear parents, nor your sisters and brother keep me in remembrance ? That is incredible ! I put it down to your forgetfulness, my friend, and I flatter myself that I may safely do so.

Gius. Ant. Bridi, of whom Mozart speaks in the above letter, was a young merchant of Roveredo, who was a favourite in musical circles[81] alike for his fine, well-trained tenor voice, and for his amiable character.[82] On the production of " Idomeneo " at the Auersperg theatre, he took a part, probably that of Idomeneo.[83] He too enjoyed, as he afterwards gratefully recorded, Mozart's friendship and confidence.[84] Gottfried von Jacquin wrote the following characteristic words in Mozart's album (April 11, 1787) :—

Genius without heart is a chimera—for it is not intellect alone, not imagination, not even the two combined which make genius—love! love! love! is the soul of genius.

He was endeared to Mozart by his musical talent and sympathy. A memorial of their friendship exists in the song composed for Jacquin on March 23, 1787: " Mentre di lascio, o figlia," from Paesiello's " Disfatta di Dario " (513 K., part 9). A comparison of this with the song composed

---

[81] Jahrb. d. Tonk., 1796, p. 10. Reichardt, Reise n. Wien, I., p. 466.
[82] He was Kelly's companion on a visit to Haydn (Reminisc., I., p. 221).
[83] A. M. Z., XXVI., p. 92.
[84] Brevi Notizie int. ad alc. compositori di musica (Rover., 1827), p. 51.

for Fischer shows how well Mozart understood the art of adapting himself to given conditions. There is no presupposition here of such a compass and flexibility of voice, nor of such force of passion as give the earlier song its original stamp; all that is required is a bass voice of moderate compass and no great depth, a certain volubility of voice, and a considerable amount of feeling and cultivation. The situation excludes any expression of violent emotion, and moderates the sentiment without rendering it less hearty; we are called on to sympathise with the sorrow of a father taking leave of his daughter at a moment pregnant with fate, not with that of a youth parting from his beloved. Here again external conditions have been utilised in the production of a song which is worthy by its beauty of form and grace of expression to take a high rank among others of its class.[35] Mozart composed other songs for his friend and his friend's family; ballads, for instance, for particular occasions and friends. Concerning one of these, he writes: " If the song *en question* is to be a test of my friendship, have no more doubt on the subject, here it is. But I hope that you do not need the song to convince you of my friendship" (Prague, November 4, 1787). Another, "Erzeugt von heisser Phantasie" (520 K.) is inscribed: " Den 26 Mai, 1787, in Hrn. Gottfried von Jacquin's Zimmer, Landstrasse." Several charming little canzonetti for two sopranos and a bass, with Italian words, were also written for this circle. Mozart indicates one of them, " Più non si trovano " (549 K.), under date July 16, 1788, and there are five other notturni of the kind existing in autograph, viz.: "Luci cari luci belle " (346 K.); " Ecco quel fiero istante," by Metastasio (436 K.); "Mi lagnerò tacendo," by Metastasio (437 K.); " Se lontan

---

[35] It is illustrative of Mozart's way of working that at the place where a very bold and striking harmony occurs in the otherwise simple air, the bass is figured in the transcription—

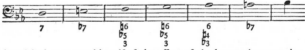

as if he wished to assure himself of the effect of the harmonic succession.

ben mio tu sei " (438 K.), " Due pupille amabili " (439 K.).
To these exists in Mozart's handwriting wind-instrument
accompaniment, for two clarinets and a basset-horn, or three
basset-horns, a combination often employed by Mozart,
apparently without any special reason. The accompaniment
may be dispensed with, the canzonetti being properly intended
for the voices alone. They are extremely simple, but full of
grace and charm, and betray the master in their harmonic
turns and disposition of parts. It may be inferred that these
compositions were primarily intended for the Jacquin family,
from the fact that several of them passed as the composition
of Gottfr. von Jacquin in Vienna, as was the case with more
than one solo song concerning whose authenticity there can
be no doubt. Mozart set little store by such occasional compositions; they passed from hand to hand, and as Jacquin
himself composed songs, which were put in circulation from
his house, some of Mozart's might easily, without any fault
on his part, be ascribed to him. As a set-off to these, the
bass song, " Io ti lascio, o cara, addio " (245 K. Anh.), composed by Jacquin, is to this day included among Mozart's
works. In the " Allgemeine Musikalische Zeitung," where
it was first printed, it was expressly stated that the original
was in Mozart's handwriting, and was written by him in
a few minutes, as he took leave of a lady friend; the scene
was afterwards variously laid at Prague and Mayence,
and elaborated into a love episode. But in a letter to
Härtel (May 25, 1799), Mozart's widow protested against
the genuineness both of the song and of the story, and
emphatically asserted, supported by the Abbé Stadler, that
the song was composed by Gottfr. von Jacquin as a farewell to
the Countess Hatzfeld, and that Mozart put the accompaniment to it. The song contains Mozart-like phrases, but no
characteristic touches of his genius.

Kelly relates that he composed Metastasio's " Grazie
agl' inganni tuoi," that Mozart was pleased with the simple
melody, and wrote variations upon it.[86] These do not exist,
but we have a sketch by Mozart in which Kelly's melody,

---

[86] Kelly, Reminisc., I., p. 226.

with some slight improvements, and a new middle phrase, is arranged for two soprano voices and a bass, with a wind instrument accompaniment (flute, two clarinets, horns and bassoons) no doubt for some special occasion (532 K.).

Concerted songs of this kind were then a favourite pastime in musical circles; they were often comic, and sometimes coarse. No one will doubt that Mozart was always ready for this species of fun, and his comic "Bandl-Terzett" (441 K.) was known, not only among his Vienna friends,[37] but far and wide among lovers of music and fun. Mozart had made his wife a present of a new belt ribbon which she wished to wear one day when she was going for a walk with Jacquin. Not finding it she called to her husband: "Liebes Mandl, wo ists Bandl?" (Where is the belt, my dear?) They both looked for it in vain till Jacquin joined them and found it. But he refused to give it up, held it high in the air, and being a very tall man, the Mozarts, both little, strove in vain to reach it. Entreaties, laughter, scolding, were all in vain, till at last the dog ran barking between Jacquin's legs. Then he gave up the ribbon, and declared that the scene would make a good comic terzet. Mozart took the hint, wrote the words in the Vienna dialect (which is essential for the comic effect), and sent the terzet to Jacquin.[38] Well sung, it never fails of its effect. A four-part pendant to the terzet "Caro mio Druck und Schluck," was in the possession of Mozart's widow, as she informed Härtel (May 25, 1799); it seems to have been a canon with a comic bass part (Anh. 5 K.).

Canons were in special favour at the social gatherings of

---

[37] Mozart writes to Gottfr. von Jacquin (Prague, February 14, 1787): "You may be sure that we managed to get up a little quatuor in *caritatis camera*, and the 'schöne Bandl hammera'." Allusions are also made to it in his letters to his wife.

[38] I was informed in Vienna that Mozart's widow related the circumstance in this way, only Van Swieten was erroneously substituted for Jacquin. A fragment of the original score (with quartet accompaniment) gives the names of Constanze, Mozart and Jacquin as singers. In the short preliminary notice to the published "Terzett" (Œuvres, V., 8), the detail was omitted as unnecessary to be made public. A quintet which appeared in Vienna in 1856, as Canto a 5 voci di Mozart, "Oh, come lieto in seno" (244 Anh. K.), is from Ant. Cartellieri's opera, "Il Segreto," composed in 1804 (Bohemia, 1860, No. 50, p. 448).

which we have been speaking. It may always be taken for
granted that children and persons of slight musical cultivation will take peculiar pleasure in this severest form of
musical mechanism, if the persistent regularity with which
each part pursues its independent course is combined with
a general effect of harmony and satisfaction. For the enlightened few, the interest arises from such a skilful handling
of forms confined within the strictest rules as shall emphasise
epigrammatic points in the most vivid and telling manner.
So in poetry, the sonnet, the triolet, and other similar forms
serve by their very limitations to emphasise the conceits
which they express. The same sort of contrast, produced
without departing from a strict adherence to rule, forms the
chief effect of the canon. The sharp definition of its various
parts gives it abundance of means for accentuating particular
points, aided by their constant recurrence in different positions and different lights. The canon, therefore, is the
epigrammatic form of music, the most suitable vehicle for
a moral sentence or a witty phrase, and it is capable of
expressing alike the most serious and the most comic ideas.
It requires, indeed, the firm hand of a master so to triumph
over the difficulties of the form as to produce not only a
masterpiece of counterpoint for the satisfaction of the learned,
but also a melodious self-sufficing vocal piece, whose most
studied difficulties shall leave the impression of lucky accidents. The greatest masters seem to have turned for recreation to the composition of canons,[39] and even grave men like
Padre Martini[40] and Michael Haydn[41] did not disdain to write
comic canons. Mozart cultivated the style, and a long list may
be placed under his name. In the " Œuvres " (XV., XVI.)
two two-part, nine three-part, nine four-part, and one six-part

---

[39] Jos. Haydn hung his rooms round with forty-six canons of his own composition, framed and glazed (Griesinger, Biogr. Notizen, p. 97. Carpani, Le
Haydine, p. 121. Cf. Biogr. Skizze von Mich. Haydn, p. 29.

[40] His *canoni bernesche* were, according to Carpani (Le Haydine, p. 113),
widely disseminated.

[41] Neukomm informed me that a canon by Mich. Haydn, ascribed to Mozart,
was composed in Salzburg with reference to a particular person ; another of his
comic canons, suggested by the joking rhymes of the organ-builder Egedacher
in Salzburg, is given in facsimile in the Cäcilia (XVI., p. 212).

canons are printed; but they are certainly not all genuine. In the Thematic Catalogue, the following are noted as composed by Mozart :—

> XV. 1. Difficile lectu [Nimm ists gleich warm] three-part (559 K.).
> 2. Caro bell' idol, three-part (562 K.).
> 5. Ave Maria, four-part (554 K.).
> 6. Lacrimoso son io, four-part (555 K.).
> XVI. 1. O du eselhafter [Gähnst du Fauler], four-part (560 K.).
> 2. Alleluja, four-part (553 K.).
> 3. Grechtelseng [Alles Fleisch], four-part (556 K.).
> 4. Gemma in Prater [Alles ist eitel], four-part (558 K.).
> 6. Bona nox [Gute Nacht], four-part (561 K.).

Besides these there must have been four more published from Mozart's autograph, for the widow writes (November 30, 1799) that she has sent thirteen canons in the original. But of these one (XV. 12) "O wunderschön" (227 K.) was by W. Byrd (d. 1623), published by Mattheson (Vollk. Kapellm. p. 409), and only copied by Mozart, and the same may have been the case with others. We recognise Mozart with some certainty in :—

> XV. 4. L. m. d. A. r. s. [Nichts labt. mich mehr.], four-part (233 K.).
> XVI. 5. Lieber Freistädler, lieber Gaulimauli [Wer nicht liebt], four-part (232 K.).
> 7. L. m. i. A. [Lasst uns froh sein], six-part (231 K.).
> 9. [Lass immer] two-part (410 K.). But this canon exists in Mozart's handwriting as an adagio for two basset-horns with a bassoon, perhaps as an accompaniment to a vocal piece.

Concerning the others I can speak with no certainty; but those which are well authenticated seem to me by far the finest. Some genuine canons by Mozart are omitted from this collection, such as the four-part canon, called in the Thematic Catalogue " Nascoso " (557 K.), which is particularly fine.[42]   There are serious canons,[43] cheerful canons,[44] and an overwhelming majority of comic canons.   The words

---

[42] One, known as " Im grab ists finster," is very doubtful, and one mentioned by Zelter (Briefw., II., p. 128) ; " Hätts nit gedacht das Fischgraten so stechen thaten," is by Wenzel Müller.

[43] Especially 553, 554 K.

[44] Especially 555, 562 K., and the above-mentioned " Nascoso " (557 K.).

to these last were generally his own; they are almost always
in the Vienna dialect, and not a few of them are too coarse
for publication, although they are preserved in verbal tradition. The original words of two of the most authentic may
serve as an example of the rest:—

Grechtelseng, grechtelseng, wir gehn in Prater. In Prater ? itzt, lass
nach, i lass mi nit stimma. Ei bei Leib. Ei ja wohl. Mi bringst nit
aussi ! Was blauscht der ? was blauscht der ? Itzt halts Maul, i gieb
dir a Tetschen ! (556 K.).

Gemma in Proda, gemma in d' Hetz, gemma in Kasperl. Der Kasperl
ist krank, der Bär ist verreckt, was thät ma in der Hetz drausst, in
Prater giebts Gelsen und Haufen von Dreck (558 K.).

The fun consisted essentially in the dialogue form and
colloquial expressions of the text—as will be evident to
all who compare the newly substituted versions, which,
unexceptionable and correct as they are, neutralise the
whole comic effect—of the canons. Mozart's mastery of
form and his wonderful power of transforming everything he
attempted into a complete and well-rounded work of art, are
displayed in all the canons without exception ; each one
contains the clear expression of a particular mood, together
with a melodious beauty, so thoroughly consistent with
the form in which they are embodied as to appear inseparable from it. Finding eight four-part and two three-part
canons under one date (September 2, 1788) in the Thematic
Catalogue, we may be inclined to imagine that Mozart was
seized with a sort of periodical canon-fever ; but it is more
probable that some circumstance led to his noting on that
day all the works of the kind that he had either in hand
or in prospect. No doubt most of them were composed
on the spur of the moment, as we know was the case with
two among the list. The tenor singer, Joh. Nepomuk Peierl,
" a man of refinement," according to Schröder,[45] who had
sung with his wife for several years at the Salzburg theatre,
paid a short visit to Vienna in 1785, and became acquainted
with Mozart. He had a peculiar pronunciation which often
made him the subject of raillery, and Mozart made it the

---

[45] Meyer, L. Schröder, II., 1, p. 81.

text for a three-part canon of wonderfully comic effect.[46] This was scarcely ended when the singers turned over the leaf, and began another four-part canon (560 K.) on the words: "O du eselhafter Peierl! o du peirlischer Esel! du bist so faul als wie ein Gaul, der weder Kopf noch Haxen hat, mit dir ist gar nichts anzufangen, ich seh dich noch am Galgen hangen; du dummer Gaul! du bist so faul! du dummer Peierl bist so faul als wie ein Gaul; O lieber Freund—— verzeihe mir! Nepomuk! Peierl! verzeihe mir!"[47] There is nothing particularly refined or amusing about the jest except the very excellent and effective canon. This was so highly applauded that it was employed on other occasions with more emphatic invectives, addressed to other individuals.[48] Mozart's marvellous gift of improvisation, showing itself in this form among others, is illustrated by an anecdote vouched for by Rochlitz. The evening before Mozart left Leipzig for Berlin, whence he intended to return in a few days, he supped with the Precentor Doles, with whom he was very intimate. His entertainers, melancholy at the prospect of parting, begged for a few lines of his writing by way of remembrance. Mozart was in a merry mood, laughed at their "whining," and declared he would rather go to bed than write music. At last he took a sheet of note-paper, tore it in half, sat down and wrote—at the most for five or six minutes. Then he handed one-half to the son, the other to the father. On one page was a three-part canon in long notes without words, and when sung very melancholy and melodious. On the second page was also a three-part canon without words, but in quavers, and full of drollery. When they had discovered

---

[46] 559 K.: " Difficile lectu mihi Mars et jonicu" (the last word is so managed that it becomes *cujoni* in singing).

[47] The leaf on which Mozart has hurriedly written down the two canons is given in facsimile in the Cäcilia (I., p. 179), where a more detailed account of them is also to be found. The time may be conjectured from the information which Lipowsky (Baiersches Musik-Lexicon, p. 239) gives about Peierl.

[48] It appears in the Thematic Catalogue as: " O du eselhafter Martin," and is generally known as such. André, and afterwards Prof. Dehn, of Berlin, possessed this canon in Mozart's handwriting, but with *Jacob*, *Jacobisch* substituted throughout for Martin, Martinsch; and in this way the quizzing may have been extended to several persons.

that the two might be sung together, Mozart wrote to the first the words, " Lebet wohl, wir sehn uns wieder!" To the second, " Heult noch gar wie alte Weiber"—and so they were sung.[49] Unhappily this double canon is not preserved.

Many comic compositions of this kind are ascribed to Mozart wrongly or on insufficient grounds.[50] One most diverting example of his love of humour exists in the " Musikalische Spass," as he calls it himself—the " Bauern-symphonie," as it is sometimes designated—which was probably written for a special occasion on June 11, 1787; owing, no doubt, to pressure of time it was only partially scored. Ignorant composers and unskilful performers are ridiculed together in this piece, which is in the form of a divertimento (Vol. I., p. 303) in four movements for string quartet and two horns. The ridicule of the players is very broad, as, for instance, when the horns, where they should come in solo in the minuet, play actual wrong notes, or when the first violin at the close of a long cadenza, consisting of a number of trivial disconnected passages, finishes off with an ascending scale, and goes at least half a tone too high. But the most amazing confusion occurs at the end, where, in the midst of a fanfare in F major for the horns. the stringed instruments strike in one after another, each in a different key. A semitone higher or lower is treated as a matter of small importance, thirds are carried on even where they are out of place; but sometimes, when a part seems to come in too soon, or when nothing but accompaniment is heard for several bars, as if the principal parts were pausing too long, or when at a particular point a note occurs which sounds excruciatingly false, it is only by the context that we can be assured that no actual mistake has happened, and that the composer does not deserve to be hissed on his own

---

[49] A. M. Z., III., p. 450.

[50] I will only mention the three-part comic or " schoolmaster " mass which goes under Mozart's and also under Haydn's name; Carpani asserts (Le Haydine, p. 112) that it is by Aumann, an Augustine monk of St. Florian, and a learned musician. He also says that it was formerly customary in Vienna to perform this kind of comic music on St. Cecilia's Day, at musical parties.

account. This is repeatedly the case also in the plan and
treatment of the movements as a whole ; they are after the
usual pattern, turns and passages occur of the customary
kind, with here and there a striking modulation, but there is
a complete lack of power to grasp or carry out an idea ; two
or three bars bring each effort to an end, and there is a
constant recurrence to the traditional formula of the closing
cadence. The attempt after thematic elaboration in the
finale is very ludicrous ; it is as though the composer had
heard of such a thing, and strove to imitate it in a few
phrases, greatly to his own satisfaction. The art is most
remarkable whereby the pretended ignorance never becomes
wearisome, and the audience is kept in suspense throughout.
The effect rests partly on the shrewd conception of what is
truly comic in ignorant pretension (for nowhere is irony more
dangerous than in music, the impression of discord being
one difficult of control), partly on the perfect mastery of the
instruments displayed by the composer.[51]

Among the compositions resulting mainly at least from
friendship or social circumstances may be included the songs
or ballads (*Lieder*) of which we have already noticed some
examples.[52] In Vienna and South Germany the "Lied" was
far from having attained, at that time, the importance it
afterwards possessed. Even in social circles, classical and,
therefore so far as song was concerned, Italian music pre-
dominated, and aspiring dilettanti sought exclusively for songs
which should display their artistic cultivation. Dilettantism
was then just beginning to bear sway, especially over the
pianoforte, and its dominion speedily extended to vocal music,
where the "Lied" became its peculiar form of expression.
In North Germany the state of affairs was somewhat different.
Italian opera in Dresden and Berlin was too isolated to

---

[51] An anonymous quartet "for people who know their notes, and who,
without moving their fingers, only move their bows up and down the open
strings," published with the title "Neugebornes musikalisches Gleichheitskind"
(Prague: Haas), and ascribed to Mozart by the Breslauer Zeitung (1835
No. 170, p. 1090), with a very unlikely anecdote, is but a dull affair.

[52] Reissmann, Das deutsche Lied in seiner histor. entwickelung, p. 77. K. E.
Schneider, Das musikalische Lied in geschichtl. Entwickelung, III., p. 195.

have much influence; the want of practised singers had caused the cultivation of the operetta, which fell back on the confined form and simple expression of the "Lied," and in its turn raised the "Lied," which had lingered only in taverns[53] and the domestic circle, to higher significance and cultivation. Weisse expressly declared that his operas were intended to incite the Germans to social song. Nor had earlier and greater composers, such as Telemann, Graun, Ph. Em. Bach, and others, disdained to compose ballads, or odes as they were then called, for domestic practice. In Berlin this tendency was especially active, and Marpurg, in his "Critical Letters," treats of the musical ode ("Chanson, Strophenlied") historically and æsthetically, and appends a long list of examples. The influence of the operetta upon the development of the "Lied" is unmistakable. It was something more than chance which caused the simultaneous rise of German lyric poetry in many parts of North Germany, which produced such lyric poets as Weisse, Uz, Gleim, Hagedorn, Jacobi, &c., and the "Dichterbund" of Gottingen, with Hiller as their special composer. Klopstock had little to do with the movement. His odes have found composers, especially (not to mention Reefe) Gluck, who followed his principles in keeping close to the words of the poet, and aiming at declamatory effect.[54] He was followed by Reichardt, a warm admirer of Klopstock,[55] who wrote an essay on the composition of Klopstock's odes.[56] But they had little influence, and the musical treatment of lyrical poetry received its chief impulse when Herder awoke the taste for national songs, and Goethe produced genuine German lyric poems: Reichardt[57] and Schulz[58] were the two composers who felt

---

[53] Sacred songs do not come within the scope of this observation.

[54] W. H. Riehl, Gluck als Liedercomponist (Augsb. Allg. Ztg., 1861. Beil. Echo, 1862, No. 1-3).

[55] A. M. Z., XVI., p. 22. Schletterer, Reichardt, pp. 157, 164.

[56] Musik. Kunstmagazin, I., p. 22.

[57] Reichardt drew attention in 1782 (Musik. Kunstmagazin, I., p. 3) to the national songs, to which the composer ought to turn for materials (Cf. Schletterer, Reichardt, I., p. 408).

[58] The first collection of national songs by J. A. P. Schulz appeared in Berlin, 1782. The character indicated by the title is more definitely stated in the preface.

this impulse most strongly, and mainly strove for the development of the German ballad in its own simple popular style.

But this phase of musical influence had, in Mozart's day,
hardly penetrated to Vienna. Hofmann, Steffan, Beecké,
Haydn, and others had indeed composed Lieder, but they
laid claim to nothing higher than the amusement of social
circles; the words are generally of mediocre merit, and the
music so simple as to make it evident that the song did not
intend to intrude into good society. Mozart only occasionally
composed Lieder.[59] He was in the habit, as his wife writes to
Härtel, of writing down in a book kept for the purpose any
poem which he admired, or which incited him to composition; but his reading was not extensive, and there was little
to attract him in Vienna at that time. He had his own
opinions on this subject as on others, and we are struck with
his remarks in a letter to his father (December 23, 1782) :—

I am at work upon a very difficult matter, viz., the setting of an ode on
Gibraltar, by Denis.[60] But it is a secret, for a Hungarian lady wishes to
surprise Denis with it. The ode is dignified—fine, if you like—but too
pompous and exaggerated for my taste. How can it be otherwise?
Truth and moderation are hardly known and never valued nowadays.
If a thing is to succeed it must either be so easy that a hackney-coach-
man could imitate it, or so incomprehensible that, just because they do
not understand it, everybody is ready to praise it.

Every competent critic will endorse Mozart's opinion on
Denis's ode ;[61] but how many then in Vienna were as independent and candid in their judgment on the favourite poet
as the young composer? A facsimile of Mozart's hasty
sketch of part of this ode is taken from the archives of the
Mozarteum at Salzburg. Whether the ode was ever finished
I do not know.

---

[59] Schneider gives a criticism of Mozart as a song-writer (Das musikal. Lied,
III., p. 282).

[60] The news of the repulse of the Spaniards by the English at the siege of
Gibraltar, in 1782, excited the greatest enthusiasm in Vienna, where sympathy
was entirely on the side of the English. Mozart wrote to his father (October
19, 1782) : "I have, indeed, heard the news of the English victory, to my great
delight, for you know that I am an arch-Englishman !"

[61] Wiener Realzeitg., 1782, p. 765. Retzer, Nachlese zu Sineds Liedern
(Wien, 1784), p. 84.

We may gather that Mozart's Lieder were the result of occasional impulses, from the fact that they occur at long intervals, and that he usually wrote several at one time. On May 7, 1785, he composed three poems by Weisse; on the autograph (472-474, K.) is noted, "Weisse, erster Band, p. 18, 14, 29"; Weisse's lyrical poems (Leipzig, 1772) formed part of Mozart's modest library. The year 1787, however, was most fruitful, owing doubtless to his constant intercourse with Jacquin; we find four in May (517-520, K.), two on June 24 (523, 524, K.), two at Prague on November 6 (529, 530, K.), and another on December 11 (531 K.). Then there is a pause until January 14, 1791, when three ballads (596-598, K.) were composed, according to Nissen, for a children's publication.[62] Mozart published but few of these compositions;[63] they generally remained in the possession of those for whom they were written, and were circulated in MS. copies, which explains why many were attributed to him which he never wrote, while some of his own composition were attributed to others.[64] The greater number of them

---

[62] Three songs (390-392 K.), date unknown, were, judging by the handwriting, composed early in the Vienna period, if not before Mozart left Salzburg.

[63] Das Lied der Freiheit (506 K.) appeared in the Wiener Musenalmanach for 1786. Besides this, so far as I am aware, no songs of Mozart appeared in his lifetime, except the "Veilchen" (476 K.) and "Trennung und Wiedervereinigung" (519 K.), with the title, "Zwei Deutsche Arien zum Singen beim Klavier in Musik gesetzt von Herr Kapellmeister Mozart" (Wien bei Artaria, 1790); perhaps, also, "An Chloë" (524 K.) and "Abendempfindung" (523 K.) (with the same title).

[64] Soon after Mozart's death, many songs, genuine and unauthentic, appeared singly or in collections. A professedly complete collection, entitled: "Sämmtliche Lieder und Gesänge beim Fortepiano von Kapellm. W. A. Mozart" (Berlin: Rellstab), contains thirty-three songs, of which only five are genuine (Cf. A. M. Z., I., p. 744). The collection in the fifth volume of the "Œuvres" (Breitkopf and Härtel) is supported by the authority of the widow, and is thoroughly to be relied on; it contains, exclusive of compositions not strictly belonging to our category, twenty-one songs, properly so-called. Of these, the "Gesellenreise" (468 K.) and two other Freemasons' songs (483, 484, K.) were originally written with organ accompaniments: the "Zufriedenheit" (349 K.), and an unpublished "Komm liebe Zitter" (351 K., composed "1780 für Herr Lang") with accompaniment for the mandoline. A "Wiegenlied" with pianoforte accompaniment, "Schlafe mein Prinzchen" (350 K.), was published subsequently by Nissen (Nachtrag, p.

are true "Strophenlieder," such as the ballads from Campe's
"Kinderbibliothek" (595, 598, K.), to which also belongs
the ballad for little Fritz's birthday (529 K.), to which very
unsuitable words have been adapted. These are all mani-
festly easy and simple, and possess the same charm from the
mouths of children as "Komm lieber Mai." Hagedorn's
little song, "Zu meiner Zeit bestand noch Recht und Bil-
ligkeit" (517 K.), is jestingly treated; Mozart himself has
written over it, "A little through the nose," to emphasise
the proper comic delivery. The quality which distinguishes
these songs from the majority of those contemporary with
them is not so much their perfect form and finish, their
attractive melodies, or their harmonious delicacy (though
these exist in full measure) as their vivid expression of a
poetic mood, be it cheerful, earnest, or passionate. The
poems of Hagedorn, Weisse, Jacobi, Overbeck, Hölty,
Miller, Claudius, and others whose names are unknown,
seem to us little calculated to stir the poetical productivity of the composer; and the passionate expression and
forcible accentuation of some of the songs strike us as
being almost in opposition to the words of the poem. Look
only at the close of the second song, "Zufriedenheit"
(473 K.), "Und angenehm ist selbst mein Schmerz, wenn
ich vor Liebe weine"; or the words in the "Betragenen
Welt" (474 K.), "Es wird ein prächtig Fest vollzogen,
bald hinkt die Reue hinterdrein." We must not leave
out of account, however, that the standpoint of literary
cultivation accepted by Mozart and his contemporaries
had its own conceptions and standard of poetic representation;[65] a perhaps not very distant future will doubtless
feel equal wonder at some of the poems set to music in
our own day. It is more important to note Mozart's exposition of his own poetic nature, which led him to grasp
and embody, not so much the words and the form, as
the animating idea of the poem before him. Therefore

---

[65] Reichardt regrets that his "Lieder geselliger Freude" (1796) can include
none of the compositions of "men so highly esteemed as Haydn, Mozart, and
Dittersdorf," on account of the coarseness of the words (Vol. I., p. viii.).

it is that he gives us in his music a depth and truth of emotion which are wanting in the words. Take, for example, the first song by Weisse, "Der Zauberer." Divest it of the pastoral costume, which is strange to us, and of the tame, somewhat clumsy expression, and retain the situation of a young girl awaking to her first consciousness of love with timid amazement. This we shall find in Mozart's composition; certainly not in Weisse's shepherdess.

In one song of passionate and sorrowful expression—"Trennung und Wiedervereinigung;" by Jacobi—two verses, in which the sentiment is considerably modified, have a fresh setting, and the first melody recurs only at the close. Others have each verse the same. One of these is the song "An Chloë" (524 K.), perhaps the best known and liked of all Mozart's pleasant, easy melodies; but it is the least significant and song-like of any, being formed after the manner of Italian canzonetti. "Abendempfindung" (523 K.) is more original and finer in its expression of emotion and in its form, which appears to yield to its changing moods, but is in reality both finished and well defined; "Unglückliche Liebe" (520 K.) is passionate and almost dramatic, a definite situation being indicated by the poet in the superscription: "Als Louise die Briefe ihres ungetreuen Liebhabers verbrannnte."

But the crown of all the songs, by virtue of its touching expression of emotion and its charming perfection of form, is unquestionably Goethe's "Veilchen" (476 K.).[66] In other songs we discern musical genius divining and bringing to light the poetic germ which lies hidden in the words; here we have the impression made upon Mozart by true poetry. It may seem remarkable that so simple a lyrical poem should have been treated by Mozart as a romance, giving a certain amount of dramatic detail to the little story; and yet it must not be overlooked that the masterly touch which repeats the closing words: "Das arme Veilchen! es war ein herzigs

---

[66] The facsimile of the song, after the original in the possession of my friend Wilh. Speyer, of Frankfort, is appended to this work.

Veilchen!" fully reasserts a genuine lyric element.[67] A
tendency to dramatic effect was inherent in Mozart's nature
as an artist, and Goethe's clear and plastic presentation of a
simple image, true in every feature, could not fail to impress
him deeply. The poem must have fallen into his hands by
some accident; had he known others of them, he would
certainly have preferred them to Weisse's. Why did he not
seek them out ? He does not seem to have sought out any
poems for composition, but took what came, and Goethe had
scarcely penetrated to the circle in which he lived. Had
the springtime of German poetry been opened before his day,
what inspirations might he not have drawn from its source!

Mozart's labours as a song composer are not by any
means on a level with those in the other branches of his art,
although even here his artistic nature could not fail to make
itself felt. Beethoven followed him closely in his manner of
song-writing, and walked steadily to the last in the path
indicated by Mozart.

CHAPTER XXX.

VAN SWIETEN AND CLASSICAL MUSIC.

GOTTFRIED, Baron van Swieten, was a man who exercised, in more than one respect, an important influence on Mozart's career. He was born in 1734, the son of
the Empress Maria Theresa's celebrated and influential
physician Gerhard van Swieten, who had removed with his
family from Leyden to Vienna in 1745. Gottfried devoted
himself to the study of the law, and pursued a diplomatic
career,[1] but from his youth up he had been passionately fond
of music, and had turned his studies in the art to practical,

---

[67] A reviewer in the Musik Realzeitung (1790, p. 1), extolling the "Tren-
nungslied," and the "Veilchen," remarks on the taste and delicate feeling they
display, and adds: "Very striking is the treatment of the words at the close
of the song, the pathetic repetition of 'Das arme Veilchen! es war ein herziges
Veilchen!'" Cf. Reissmann, "Das deutsche Lied," p. 146.

[1] He travelled with the Duke of Braganza, in 1768 (Zimmermann, Briefe,
p. 96).

though not very successful account. In 1769 Favart's
" Rosière de Salency " was produced in Paris with music by
different composers; Van Swieten wrote several of the songs,
but they failed to attract much praise.[2]   He also composed
eight symphonies " as stiff as himself," as Haydn said.[3]   In
1771 Joseph II. appointed him ambassador to the Court of
Prussia,[4] and there Nicolai made his acquaintance, and speaks
of him as " an enthusiastic amateur and connoisseur, and
even a composer."[5]   His residence in Berlin was important
for the development of his musical taste and the ideas which
he afterwards undertook to introduce in Vienna.

In 1740, Frederick the Great had erected the Berlin Opera
House, and produced the Italian opera seria of the time with
all the brilliancy of first-rate performers and scenic accessories.[6]   Grand operas (interrupted, however, by the Seven
Years War) were regularly given; the King used to sit in the
pit immediately behind the conductor, so as to be able to
look over his score.[7]   He held firm to his original principles
of taste ; would admit nothing but opera seria, and no new
works except those of Hasse and Graun. The Kapellmeister
Carl Heinrich Graun (1709-1759) was obliged to compose
the operas (to which the King furnished libretti in French, to
be turned into Italian[8]), and hurried over his uncongenial task ;
they were always submitted to the King, and what he disapproved of had to be altered.[9]   He preferred Hasse's composition on account of his greater fire and passion, while Graun
(highly prized as a singer by his royal master)[10] heard little
but blame for his shortcomings as a composer.

Notwithstanding this, he had to produce his opera year

---

[2] Grimm, Corr. Litt., VI., pp. 263, 314.

[3] Griesinger, Biogr. Not., p. 66. One was performed by Mozart (Vol. II.,
p. 284).

[4] Müller praises the liberal support which he received from him in Berlin, in
1776 (Abschied, p. 116).

[5] Nicolai, Reise, IV., p. 556.

[6] Schneider, Gesch. d. Oper in Berlin, p. 14.

[7] Burney, Reise, III., p. 67.

[8] N. Ztschr. für Mus., IX., p 130.

[9] Zelter, Fasch, p. 22.

[10] Reichardt, Kunstmagaz., I., p. 158.

after year, and matters continued unchanged.[11] Johann Friedrich Agricola (1720-1774), who succeeded Graun in 1760, wrote little himself, except some pieces for insertion in old operas, which are kept in the same style. The King would have nothing to say to any other composers, and received Reichardt with the advice: " Have a care of the new Italians; the fellows write like pigs."[12]

Reichardt, in applying for Agricola's post after the death of the latter in 1775, was obliged to support his claims by the production of an opera, " modelled on the pattern of Graun and Hasse";[13] as kapellmeister, he must not dream of striking out in any other direction. For the last ten years of his life the King took little interest in musical matters; Italian opera lingered on with the pieces of Graun and Hasse, but it sank lower and lower.[14]

Side by side with the opera, however, which followed so closely the Italian tradition, there arose in Berlin a peculiar form of instrumental music founded on the Saxon school. The King, as is well known, gave a private concert every evening, and performed on the flute pieces composed by himself or his master Quanz, who wrote over three hundred such for Frederick.[15] Johann Joachim Quanz (1697-1773),[16] to whom the King had been much attached from his earliest years, was supreme in all matters musical, and was nicknamed the " Pope of the Berlin music."[17] He was the only man who presumed to cry "Bravo!" to the King's playing.[18] Next after Quanz in Frederick's favour stood Franz Benda (1709-1786),[19] an artist of originality and a first-rate violin-

---

[11] Zelter, Fasch, p. 49. The parallel which Reichardt (Briefe eines aufmerks. Reisenden, I., p. 15) institutes between Hasse and Graun well expresses the general views.

[12] Reichardt, Mus. Monatsschr., p. 69. A. M. Z., XV., p. 610. Schletterer, Reichardt, p. 261, where detailed and interesting information is given.

[13] A. M. Z., XV., p. 605. Schletterer, Reichardt, I., p. 257.

[14] Reichardt, Mus. Zeitg., I., p. 74.

[15] Burney, Reise, III., p. 116.

[16] Autobiographische Mittheilungen s. in Marpurg's Histor. Krit. Beitr., I., p. 197.

[17] Burney, Reise, III., p. 111. Zelter, Fasch, p. 47.

[18] A. M. Z., III., p. 172. Reichardt, Mus. Wochenblatt, p. 70.

[19] His autobiography is given in N. Berl. Mus. Ztg., 1856, No. 32.

player; his manner of execution was peculiar to himself, and rested mainly on a pure and expressive delivery. His brother Joseph (1724-1804) and the sons of both followed in his footsteps, and the Concertmeister J. Gottlieb Graun (1698-1771) highly esteemed as a violin-player and instrumental composer, may be said to have belonged to the same school. By these distinguished artists the Berlin orchestra was formed and trained to a degree of excellence second only to that of Dresden, and not until later surpassed by Mannheim and Vienna.

The highest rank among the artists of Berlin must be accorded to Philipp Emanuel Bach (1714-1788).[20] He was summoned to the Prussian capital in 1738 as accompanist to the then Crown Prince, and after 1756 he shared the office with Fasch. He was an accomplished and tasteful accompanist, but the wearisome monotony of the royal concerts disgusted him, and as an artist he could not but be annoyed at the King's narrow prejudices. He revenged himself by refusing to comply when Frederick, who liked to play in "various times" required his accompanist to give way to him. This led to a dislike on the King's part, which prevented him from duly appreciating Bach;[21] and the latter willingly obeyed a summons to Hamburg in 1767, to fill Telemann's place. His technical studies, founded on J. Sebastian Bach's system of fingering, and his clavier sonatas entitle him to be considered as the father of modern pianoforte-playing, and Haydn acknowledged him alone as his model.[22] He was held in unbounded reverence as a creative and original artist, especially in Berlin and Hamburg,[23] and deserved equal respect as a man of cultivation and good-breeding. Nicolai declares that what Quintilian says of Cicero may be applied

---

[20] His autobiography; s. Burney, Reise, III., p. 199. Cf. Rochlitz, Für Freunde der Tonkunst, IV., p. 273.

[21] Zelter, Fasch, pp. 14, 47.

[22] Griesinger, Biogr. Not., p. 15. Rochlitz, Für Freunde der Tonkunst, IV., p. 274. Bach told him once that he was the only man who had ever quite understood his works (Dies, Biogr. Nachr., p. 38).

[23] Compare, for instance, Burney's account (Reise, III., p. 209) with Reichardt's opinions expressed at different times (Briefe e. aufmerks. Reisenden, I., p. 111; II., p. 7. Kunstmagaz., I., p. 24. Musik. Alman., 1796. A. M. Z., XVI., p. 28. Schletterer, Reichardt, I., p. 163).

with equal truth to Bach: that those who have learnt to appreciate his works above all others have made a marked advance along the path of knowledge.[24]   The school of Joh. Sebastian Bach was represented in all its severity and scholarly learning by his son Wilhelm Friedemann Bach (1710-1784), who passed the later years of his life in Berlin, as much admired as an artist of genius and scholarship[25] as he was dreaded and disliked by reason of his overbearing egotism and eccentric fancies.[26]   Agricola was also a pupil, and like all his pupils, an enthusiastic admirer of Seb. Bach, but Kirnberger was undoubtedly his greatest apostle.   It was he who represented the school of Bach in Berlin, side by side with the operatic school of Hasse and Graun, and he was mainly, though far from exclusively,[27] active in developing the instrumental style, which determined the taste of the Berlin musical world.[28]

The position of music in Berlin was peculiar in that it had gained recognition for itself, even in respect of its literature.   Not a few musicians were cultivated and scientific men, ready with their pen and anxious to employ it in the

---

[24] Nicolai, Reise, IV., p. 558.

[25] Zelter, Briefw. m. Goethe, V., p. 210 : " His extemporising, especially when he was in the vein, was the admiration of men such as Marpurg, Kirnberger, Benda, Agrikola, Bertuch, Ring—most of them excellent organ-players, who all felt how far he surpassed them." He used to say of his brother, Ph. Emanuel, with a compassionate air : " Mein Bruder, der Hamburger, hat einige artige Sächelchen gemacht "; and the latter made use of the same family expression in speaking of the London brother (Reichardt, Musik. Zeitg., II., p. 159).

[26] Forkel, Musik. Alman., 1784, p. 201. Reichardt, Musik. Alman., 1796. Zelter, Briefw., V., p. 209.

[27] I need only allude to the vocal compositions of Ph. Em. Bach; and the union of both schools in Graun's " Tod Jesu " is very apparent.

[28] A. M. Z., II., p. 585 : " Berlin is perhaps the only place in Germany where the most ardent enthusiasm for modern music is still (1800) combined with a zealous defence of the older school. Joh. Seb. Bach and his celebrated sons still strive for pre-eminence with Mozart, Haydn, and Clementi." Zelter writes (Briefw. m. Goethe, V., p. 208) : " I have been accustomed to honour the Bach genius for the last fifty years. Friedemann died here, Emanuel Bach was royal chamber musician here, Kirnberger and Agrikola were pupils of old Bach ; Ring, Bertuch, Schmalz, &c., performed scarcely anything but the old Bach pieces, and I myself have taught here for the last thirty years, and have pupils who play all Bach's music well."

musical cause. Quanz's "Course of Flute-Playing" (1752) was followed by Ph. Em. Bach's "True Art of Playing the Clavier" (1753, 1761) and Agricola's "Introduction to the Art of Song" (1757); and together with these may be noted Marpurg's "Art of Playing the Clavier" (1750), "Introduction to Clavier-Playing" (1755, 1765), and "Introduction to Music and Singing" (1763); it was no small honour for Leop. Mozart's "Violin Method" to find recognition in this circle (Vol. I., p. 16). The writings of the advocate Krause on musical poetry (1752), of Nichelmann on melody (1755), and Marpurg's "Introduction to Vocal Composition" (1758) must not be omitted from the list.

The theory of harmony and counterpoint was studied with equal zeal, and Kirnberger and Marpurg have earned for themselves a place of honour in the history of music.

Joh. Phil. Kirnberger (1721-1783), Kammermusicus to the Princess Amalie, a pupil of Seb. Bach, was of small merit as a composer, but, being a sagacious man, and fond of research, he busied himself in tracing the principles and maxims of composition through the works of his revered master.[29] The gift of literary expression was denied to him by his education and manner of life; and unless he were assisted by friends such as Agricola, Sulzer, or his pupil Schulz, he found it difficult to express his views with clearness.[30] His intellect, knowledge, and study were considerable, his character open and estimable;[31] but he was embittered by the want of the recognition which he believed to be his due. Want of refinement led him to turn his critical acumen into a weapon of attack, which he often used in a manner both spiteful and unjust.[32] Quanz had maintained that a

---

[29] A characteristic instance of this reverence is given by Zelter (Briefw., V., p. 163).

[30] A. M. Z., III., p. 598. Zelter, Briefw., III., p. 17.

[31] This testimony is afforded by his grateful pupil, Schulz, and also by Eberhardt (A. M. Z., II., p. 872) and Z[elter] (Berlin Mus. Ztg., 1793, p. 129. Cf. Zelter, Fasch, p. 59. Rintel, Zelter, p. 116).

[32] Reichardt was badly received by Kirnberger (Schletterer, I., p. 98), who retaliated by a highly coloured picture of a theoretical critic in his "Briefen eines aufmerks. Reisenden" (I., p.128), which was recognised as Kirnberger (A.M. Z., II., p. 597). But in after-times he did him honourable justice (A. M. Z., III., p. 169).

genuine duet admitted of no bass, and published some duets to prove his point; Kirnberger played the duets on the church organ while Quanz was receiving the communion, with a bass added.[33]

Friedr. Wilh. Marpurg (1718-1795) thereupon took up the cudgels, and endeavoured to prove from Kirnberger's fugues that he was the last man who had a right to make himself conspicuous as a critic. This gave rise to a feud, which was carried on with great bitterness on both sides, respecting various principles of musical theory. Marpurg had the advantage of a thorough school and university education. As private secretary to General Bodenberg he had enjoyed intercourse with Voltaire, D'Alembert, and Maupertuis, and a lengthened stay in Paris in 1746 had made him familiar with the French cultivation of the time. After 1749 he lived in Berlin. In his youth he had been the friend of Winckelmann[34] and the companion of Lessing, in his jovial hours as well as in his studies and controversies.[35] Shrewd and thorough in matters of research, and of passionate temper, he could neither brook contradiction nor control his violence;[36] and superior as he was to Kirnberger in powers of expression, he yielded nothing to him in coarseness and virulence of attack.[37]

Yet another influence on musical affairs in Berlin remains to be noted, viz., the musical journals edited by Marpurg and the musicians and scholars associated with him—"The Musical Critic on the River Spree" (1749-1750), "Critical and Historical Contributions to the Study of Music" (1754-1762), and "Critical Letters on Music" (1760-1764).

Music was treated also by literary men from a more general point of view. Sulzer included music in his

---

[33] Thus Reichardt relates (A. M. Z., III., p. 172) what is alluded to in the critical letters (I., pp. 15, 23, 41, 175, 231).

[34] Justi, Winckelmann, I., p. 48.

[35] Spazier, A. M. Z., II., pp. 569, 593.

[36] The anecdotes which he published with the title of "Legende einiger Musikheiligen von Simeon Metaphrastes d. j." (Cölln, 1786), are characteristic of his bitterness and his cynicism.

[37] He spared Ph. Em. Bach as little as the latter spared him (Zelter, Briefw. m. Goethe, VI., p. 321).

"Treatise on the Fine Arts" (1771-1774), and sought counsel of professional men better versed in the art than himself. He selected Kirnberger as the fittest man for his purpose, and after him his pupil J. A. P. Schulz, who was inferior to his master in scholarly acquirements, but far superior to him in clearness and facility.[38] The great influence which Sulzer's work exercised in Germany caused his views upon music therein expressed to be appealed to as a sort of final authority. Fr. Nicolai was exceedingly fond of music, and made it a practical study.[39] He was personally acquainted with all the great musicians, especially Agricola, Marpurg, and Reichardt, and he set himself seriously to form musical opinions founded on his own observation. When he undertook the German Universal Cyclopedia in 1765, he included music in the list of subjects treated. Nicolai's influence in Berlin was great,[40] and a literary organ of so much importance could not fail to give weight and consideration to musical criticism.

The practical result of these musical efforts, so far as they did not proceed immediately from the King, consisted mainly in the "Liebhaberconcert," founded in 1770, and held every Friday evening under Nicolai's direction.[41] All available forces were assembled on these occasions; orchestral works, native or foreign, were performed, vocal and instrumental virtuosi found an audience, and great vocal compositions were frequently produced, such as Graun's and Ph. Eman. Bach's sacred music, and what is more noteworthy, Handel's oratorios, especially "Judas Maccabæus," the "Feast of Alexander," and the "Messiah."[42] Earnest and

---

[38] Schulz gives an account of this himself, which does not altogether agree in details with Reichardt's story (A. M. Z., II., p. 276; III., p. 597).

[39] Göcking, Fr. Nicolai's Leben, p. 95 (cf. 29). Schletterer, Reichardt, I., pp. 97, 140.

[40] Burney, Reise, III., pp. 58, 74.

[41] Reichardt, Brief. e. aufmerks. Reis., I., p. 32. Schletterer, Reichardt, I., p. 139. Müller, Abschied, p. 117. It existed, together with other similar institutions, until the beginning of this century (Cramer, Mag. d. Mus., I., p. 565. A. M. Z., II., p. 586).

[42] Nicolai mentions these three oratorios as well known to him in 1781 (Reise, IV., p. 534). An enthusiastic account of "Judas Maccabæus" after a

upright intention, and efforts after intellectual comprehension
in art, deserve all recognition, even when united with
partiality, pedantry, and quarrelsomeness.   The supremacy
claimed by Frederick the Great's capital, even in music,
extended to South Germany, and especially to Vienna.
Wagenseil and Steffan, at that time men of considerable
note in Vienna, are complacently taken to task by Marpurg.[43]
Nicolai openly says[44] that after Fux's death Vienna had
various good composers, but no extraordinary genius worthy
to rank with Seb. and Ph. Em. Bach, Telemann, Graun,
or Hasse, men who had determined the course of musical
progress in North Germany until Haydn appeared.   The
Viennese, on the other hand, were entirely ignorant of all
that concerned music in North Germany, and especially in
Berlin.[45]

Youthful impulses could not altogether fail, however,
to stir the musical world of Berlin.   The French operetta,
conducted for a long time by Schulz,[46] and still more the
German opera after 1771,[47] had the effect of gradually reform-
ing the taste of the general public.   Prince Henry, who had
an excellent band in his pay, was by no means so devoted to
old music and the old composers as the King.[48]   His concertmeister Joh. Pet. Salomon (1745-1815), whom Reichardt
heard perform Bach's violin solos without accompaniment
exceedingly well,[49] produced Haydn's symphonies and quartets

---

performance at a Liebhaberconcert in 1774, was given by Reichardt in Briefe
e. aufmerks. Reis., I., p. 82. Zelter describes the great effect which a performance of the "Messiah" in 1783 made upon him (Rintel, Zelter, p. 137). The
"Messiah" had been performed in Hamburg as early as 1775 (Joh. Heinr. Voss,
Briefe, I., p. 295).

[43] Marpurg, Krit. Briefe, II., p. 141.
[44] Nicolai, Reise, IV., p. 525.
[45] Reichardt, A. M. Z., XV., p. 666 (Schletterer, Reichardt, I., p. 325).
[46] A. M. Z., III., p. 601. It was certainly not to the taste of Frederick the
Great. When it was proposed to sing the choruses in Racine's "Athalie," the
King put a stop to it with the remark (January 10, 1774): "La musique française ne vaut rien, il faut faire déclamer le chœur, alors cela revient au même
(Preuss, Friedrich der Grosse, III., p. 310).
[47] L. Schnieder, Gesch. der Oper in Berlin, p. 49.
[48] Burney, Riese, III., p. 149.
[49] Schletterer, Reichardt, I., p. 140.

with zeal and energy.[50] His successor, J. A. P. Schulz (1747-1800), a pupil of Kirnberger's, who had made a lengthened tour in Italy, and become personally acquainted with Haydn,[51] followed his natural inclination—to the great dissatisfaction of his master—in composing after the new style,[52] and wishing to produce not only Haydn's but Gluck's music. His attempts were unsuccessful, but Haydn's music was admired by others besides the more youthful of the public. There were, it is true, supporters of the old music, who made a noisy exit whenever Haydn's music was performed; but others, such as Marpurg, laughed at such folly, and did not withhold their recognition of his genius;[53] Nicolai speaks of him with frank and enlightened approbation.[54] Reichardt, as kapellmeister to the king, could not afford an independent judgment;[55] but he endeavoured, by the "Concert spirituel"[56] which he set on foot, and by his compositions and writings,[57] to turn the interest of the public in new directions.[58]

It was into this peculiar musical atmosphere, so different from that of Vienna, that Van Swieten entered at Berlin. His turn of mind being essentially rational and methodical,[59] disposed him to sympathy with the severe Berlin school, and to a partiality for a concise style; he was enchanted with the music of Handel and Bach, which he brought back with him to Vienna, and turned to account by means of his personal

---

[50] Rochlitz, Für Freunde der Tonkunst, III., p. 191.

[51] A. M. Z., III., p. 176.

[52] A. M. Z., III., p. 605. Even the Princess Amalie expressed to Schulz her dislike to his choruses to "Athalie" (A. M. Z., III., p. 614) in two very emphatic letters (Echo, 1857, Nos. 10, 14).

[53] A. M. Z., II., p. 575. Cf. Nohl, Musikerbr., p. 76.

[54] Nicolai, Reise, IV., pp. 526, 534.

[55] He has given some interesting particulars as to his position to Frederick (A. M. Z., XV., pp. 601, 633. Schletterer, Reichardt, I., p. 260).

[56] Cramer, Mag. d. Mus., I., p. 565. Schletterer, I., p. 357.

[57] At the same time he published the Musical Magazine (1-4, 1782), and was concerned in Nicolai's "Allgemeiner Deutscher Bibliothek." Cf. Schletterer, I., p. 432.

[58] The influence exerted by the Crown Prince, afterwards King Frederick William II., upon the musical taste of Berlin, belongs to a later time than that under consideration.

[59] Griesinger, Biogr. Not., p. 69.

friendship with Haydn, Mozart and Beethoven. He commissioned Ph. Em. Bach to compose, in 1774, six grand orchestral symphonies, with the express wish that he would allow his genius full play, without any regard to difficulty of execution.[60] In Berlin also Van Swieten became better acquainted with Haydn than was possible in Vienna, and like Mozart and the youthful Beethoven, he loved and reverenced him next to Handel and Bach. "As far as music is concerned," he writes (December, 1798), " I have gone back to the times when it was thought necessary before practising an art to study it thoroughly and systematically. In such study I find nourishment for my mind and heart, and support when any fresh proof of the degeneracy of the art threatens to cast me down. My chief comforters are Handel and the Bachs, and with them the few masters of our own day who tread firmly in the footsteps of the truly great and good, and either give promise of reaching the same goal, or have already attained to it. In this there can be no doubt that Mozart, had he been spared to us, would have succeeded ; Joseph Haydn stands actually at the goal."[61] On his return to Vienna (which took place about 1778) he at once assumed a position of great importance. He succeeded to his father's office as Prefect of the Imperial Library, was appointed President of the Education Commission in 1781, and intrusted with the conduct of the educational scheme which was introduced throughout the Empire in 1783. Knowledge, intelligence, and zeal he certainly possessed ;[62] but he was wanting in the energy and decision necessary to carry out the projects he conceived.[63] His influential position, rank, and wealth, the hereditary fame of his family, and the importance of his mission at the court of Frederick the Great, gave him the right to a place among the most distinguished society. He exerted all his influence in the cause of music, even for so subordinate an

---

[60] Reichardt, A. M. Z., XVI., p. 28 (Schletterer, Reichardt, I., p. 163).

[61] A. M. Z., I., p. 252.

[62] Nicolai, Reise, III., pp. 358, 363.

[63] G. Forster, Sämmtl. Schr., VII., p. 273. Van Swieten's activity and influence are very differently estimated by R. Kink (Gesch. d. Univers. in Wien, I., p. 539).

end as to enforce silence and attention during musical performances. Whenever a whispered conversation arose among the audience, his excellency would rise from his seat in the first row, draw himself up to his full majestic height, measure the offenders with a long, serious look, and then very slowly resume his seat. The proceeding never failed of its effect.[64] Van Swieten was not liberal in money matters; he always had it in his power to collect money among his friends of high rank for musical purposes, and he did not fail on such occasions to contribute his own quota;[65] but he was not by any means generous for a wealthy and childless man. Haydn's experience supported this view,[66] and the eulogies pronounced on Van Swieten's benevolence to Mozart's family after his death[67] have no foundation; in fact, he did nothing worth mentioning for them. In his intercourse with artists, however highly he might estimate them and their works, his demeanour was always that of a grand seigneur, and he enforced his own views with an air of somewhat overbearing superiority. This was again Haydn's experience,[68] and Mozart can scarcely have escaped some measure of annoyance from the same source.

But such personal failings as these are cast into the shade by the merit which is due to Van Swieten as the man who awoke interest in Vienna for severe and classical music. His influence upon Mozart is unmistakable. At the beginning of 1782 we find them in constant intercourse, and Mozart habitually present at Van Swieten's musical Sunday mornings, at which music in the severe style only was performed. He had, as Mozart writes to his sister (April 20, 1782), "a stock of music good in point of value, but small in quantity"; and in order to add to it, Mozart requests his father to send him both his own church compositions, and

---

[64] So Neukomm informed me. G. Forster was affronted by Van Swieten's stiff, cold manner (Sämmtl. Schr., VII., p. 270). Cf. Jahrb. d. Tonk., 1796, p. 72.

[65] Dies, Biogr. Nachr., p. 158.

[66] Dies, Biogr. Nachr., p. 210. Griesinger, Biogr. Not., p. 66.

[67] Musik. Corresp., 1792, p. 4. Niemetschek, who had called him the father of Mozart's orphan children, omitted this in the second edition.

[68] Dies, Biogr. Nachr., p. 180.

some select works of Michael Haydn and Eberlin, which he
had formerly copied (Vol. I., p. 238); they were performed
with great applause in the little circle,   These performances
were clearly not intended for an audience ; for Van Swieten
sang tenor, Mozart alto (at the same time playing the pianoforte), Starzer[69] tenor, and young Tebery,[70] who had just
returned from Italy, bass (March 12, 1783).   But in this
way they became familiar with the best works of masters
who had been hitherto unheard in Vienna.   "It is a fact,"
writes Mozart (April 12, 1783), " that the change of taste has
extended even to church music, which is much to be regretted ; so it comes that the best church music lies worm-
eaten in the garret."[71]

Clavier music of the same school also found a place in
Van Swieten's musical meetings. Mozart writes to his father
(April 10, 1782) :—

> I wish you would send me Handel's six fugues and the toccata and
> fugues by Eberlin.   I go every Sunday morning to the Baron van
> Swieten, and nothing is played there but Handel and Bach.   I am
> making a collection of the Bach fugues, Sebastian's as well as Emanuel's
> and Friedemann's, and also of Handel's, and I want just these six. Also,
> I should like to let the Baron hear Eberlin's.

Concerning the latter, however, he writes soon after to his
sister (April 20, 1782) :—

> If my father has not yet had Eberlin's works copied, pray countermand
> them.   I have found them here, and see (now that I refresh my memory
> of them) that they are very trivial and unworthy of a place with Handel
> and Bach.   His four-part movement deserves all respect, but his clavier
> fugues are simply *versetti* spun out to great length.

---

[69] He often played at Van Swieten's with the famous lute-player Kohaut
(Griesinger, Biogr. Not., p. 66).

[70] I cannot say whether Anton Teyber (b. 1754), whom Mozart met at
Dresden in 1789, or Franz Teyber (b. 1756) is intended.   Both were natives of
Vienna, probably brothers of the two female singers of the same name (Vol. I.,
p. 69), and they both died at Vienna—Anton as court chamber composer in 1822,
and Franz as kapellmeister and court organist in 1810.

[71] Nicolai's opinion is in accordance with this ; he speaks of the church music
in Vienna, in 1781, as inferior both in composition and performance (Reise, IV.,
p. 544).

We have seen already how Mozart's interest in the study
of these masters was still further kindled by the pleasure his
wife took in fugues (Vol. II., p. 267). When he sent his
sister a three-part fugue with a prelude, he wrote to her
(April 20, 1782) that if time and opportunity served, he
meant to write five more fugues, and present them all to
Van Swieten; she must therefore keep this one to herself,
learn it by heart, and play it; "it is not so easy to play
fugues." A second (39 Anh. K.) has only the theme with
one answer written down :—

A third is rather more finished (40 Anh. K.), and its very
original subject promises an interesting elaboration—

which causes the more regret that it should have stopped
short of completion.

Mozart twice projected arranging Frohberger's "Phantasia
supra Ut, re, mi, fa, sol, la" for the pianoforte,[72] but neither time
did he accomplish his intention (292 Anh. K.). The three-part
fugue in C major, which has been published (394 K.), probably the same that Mozart sent to his sister with a prelude,
gives an idea of his intentions. A four-part fugue in G
minor, wanting only a few bars, was finished and published
by Stadler (401 K.). Only sketches remain of other clavier
fugues. The most finished (26 bars) is a fugue in G major
(23 Anh. K.) :—

---

[72] Kircher, Musurgia, I., p. 466. Weitzmann, Gesch. d. Klavierspiels, p. 214.

To the same time and school belongs the great fugue for two pianofortes in C minor, composed on December 29, 1783 (426 K.). The beginning is preserved of another fugue for two pianofortes in G major of a totally different character (45 Anh. K.):—

We may judge of the manner in which Mozart wished his fugues to be played from an expression to his sister, when he sent her the first of them (April 20, 1782):—

> I have taken care to write "andante maestoso" on it, that it may not be played too fast; for, if a fugue is not played slowly, the recurring subject is not distinctly and clearly heard, and so loses its effect.

Afterwards (in June, 1788) Mozart arranged the C minor fugue for his string quartet, and wrote "a short adagio" as an introduction (546 K.), probably for Van Swieten, with whom he was then in closer intercourse than ever, in consequence of the instrumentation and performance of Handel's oratorios.

The ease and distinctness with which four-part movements of this metrical style could thus be executed, had already suggested to Mozart the arrangement of five fugues from Bach's "Wohltemperirte Klavier," for stringed instruments (405 K.). The handwriting points to 1782 or 1783, when Van Swieten's influence was at its highest. The fugues selected, doubtless with a view to their suitability for the purpose, were (in Breitkopf and Härtel's edition):

No. 2, in C minor; No. 7, in E flat major; No. 9, in E major; No. 8, transposed from D sharp major to D major; and No. 5, in D major.

An interesting illustration of the pleasure with which Mozart sought to follow in the steps of Handel and Bach, is afforded by the unfinished "Klaviersuite" (399 K.) belonging to 1782 or 1783. It begins, according to rule, with an overture (C major) consisting of two movements, a slow introduction in imitation, and a fugued Allegro closing on the dominant. Then follows, after traditional usage, an Allemande (C minor), a Courante (E flat major), and a Sarabande (G minor); of this last, however, only six bars are written. The imitation of the older masters is unmistakable in the design and many of the details of the movements, the only novelty being the changes of key. They may, in this sense, be considered as studies; but Mozart's originality constantly asserts itself, and the Courante in especial is completely imbued with it. Still more original and free is the "Short Gigue for the Klavier," which Mozart wrote on May 17, 1789, "in the album of Herr Engel, court organist in Leipzig" (574 K.), no doubt in remembrance of Bach, whose motetts he had there heard for the first time with unbounded delight. The light and flexible gigue had been transformed by Bach's freer, and at the same time severer, treatment into a fantastic, almost humorous movement, which took the same place in the suite that was afterwards given to the scherzo in the sonata. Mozart selected the severer style, and the intellectual skill with which the strictest forms of counterpoint, harmony, and rhythm are so freely and archly treated, as to make both player and listener hold their breath from surprise, renders this little composition a masterpiece. It causes regret that the suite, containing as it did so many elements capable of development, was not seriously taken up and carried to perfection by Mozart.

It must not be supposed that Mozart's study of Bach and Handel had no result but to teach him to write fugues; his earlier compositions show him to have been no novice in the art of counterpoint. What he found most admirable in

these masters was their power of making forms strict even
to rigidity the medium of a natural expression of their
musical ideas and emotions.; their use of all the available
wealth of contrapuntal combinations was no mere trick of
barren speculation, but a deliberate selection of a means of
expression from the inexhaustible fund of their productive
powers. That this was the sense in which Mozart reverenced his masters is proved by his criticism of Eberlin and
of Hassler, who had learnt Bach's harmonies and modulations by heart, but was unable to work out an original fugue;
and it is proved more satisfactorily still by his own works.

Even in compositions avowedly written as studies, Mozart's
originality appears, and in his later works there is no trace
of any attempt at servile imitation of Bach or Handel.[73]
He imitated, not their work, but their way of working,
drew from the sources to which they had given him access,
and employed that which he received from them in accordance with his own nature and the task before him.[74]

Master-strokes of genius in many pieces of his chamber
music—as also in the last movement of the C major symphony, and in the overture to the "Zauberflöte," where art
reaches its highest pitch in the union of strictest form
with freest fancy—may be ascribed in no small degree to
the impulses arising from his study of Bach and Handel.
But their influence reaches beyond his compositions in the
severe style. The perfection of *polyphonic* composition
which characterises all Mozart's works, and wherein consists one of his chief merits, rests, even in its broadest and
freest development, upon the foundations laid by those

---

[73] Rochlitz's assertion (A. M. Z., I., p. 115) that Mozart wrote a great deal in
Handel's style that he did not publish, is unfounded.

[74] It is observed in Reichardt's Musik. Zeitg., I., p. 200, that J. S. Bach was
in advance of his age, and that long after his death his mantle had descended
upon Mozart, who was the first thoroughly to admire and reverence the spirit of
his art, and to reproduce it in his own works. Zelter also declares that Mozart
is a truer successor of Seb. Bach than his son Philipp Emanuel or Joseph
Haydn (Briefw., IV., p. 188); he recalls how the music of Seb. and Eman. Bach
was at first unintelligible to him; how Haydn was blamed for having travestied
what was intense earnest to them; and, finally, how Mozart appeared and gave
the proper interpretation to all three (Briefw., II., p. 103).

masters. So, too, the fertility and boldness of Mozart's harmonic treatment may be traced back to the same source. Harmonic beauties, novel and striking transitions and turns, are frequent enough in his earlier works, but they are simply harmonic combinations, whereas in his later works they appear as a free and intellectual development of the polyphonic principle.

Again, the influence of the older masters and their works is observable in a certain harshness occasioned by independence in the disposition of parts, which Mozart does not by any means seek to avoid. In this respect he makes demands upon his audience as great and greater than those, for instance, of Bach and Beethoven, and may be compared to Sophocles, who, admired as he justly was by the ancients for his sweetness and charm, did not hesitate upon occasion to startle his hearers with his harsh severity. Mozart's severity is never the result of clumsy workmanship, but is a conscious and deliberate choice of means; neither is it employed as a stimulant, but rather as an incentive to a better appreciation of passages of perfect beauty. The sense of deliverance from conflict and obscurity, and passage into calmness and light, is so striking that it cannot be wondered at if the means whereby it is attained are little analysed.[75]

Among the compositions in precise or metrical style special interest attaches to the three-part pianoforte fugue in C major (394 K.). It opens with an introduction, more elaborate than a prelude, and entitled, therefore, a "fantasia." Such introductions, not always in free form (sometimes called "toccate"), were usually prefixed to a fugue or other composition in order to give it the character of an improvisation; several others by Mozart exist. The one in question, after a few slow bars, is a lively movement, varies its key continually, and does not carry out fully any motif or passage; this agitated unrest gives it a pathetic character, and excites expectation; the whole movement is brilliant and effective. It closes on the dominant, thus announcing its nature as an

---

[75] Rochlitz is mistaken in trying to discover a mixture of Bach's gloominess with Mozart's youthful fire in the latter's Salzburg compositions (A. M. Z., II., p. 642).

introduction. The fugue which follows is in striking contrast,
firm and quiet, yet full of life and latent emotion :—

The two first bars, with their intervals of fourths, announce a
more serviceable than individually expressive subject, but the
agitated motif which follows has a very original character,
heightened by its auxiliary notes and by its rapid succession
of sharp dissonants. A gentle, almost melancholy, tone per-
vades the whole fugue, and is expressed also by its frequent
passage into a minor key. Apart from its interesting technical elaboration, it is important by reason of its characteristic expression, and may serve as an illustration of Mozart's
complete mastery of the fugue form. To this it may be added
that the fugue we are considering is essentially adapted for
the pianoforte both in conception and composition. This is not
the case in the same degree with the G minor Fugue (401 K.),
which is artistically worked out, but not equal to the C major
either in breadth of expression or adaptation to the nature of
the instrument. The same may be said of the three-part fugue
in D major, of which Mozart has written thirty-seven bars
(443 Anh., 67 K.). The effect of the C minor fugue (426 K),
also, rests neither on the sound effects of the pianoforte nor on
those of the stringed instruments. It is so broadly conceived,
so earnestly and with such ruthless severity carried out, that
the external means of expression fall into the background
before the energetic enunciation of the laws of form, obeyed
consciously, but without servility.[76] Quite otherwise is the

---

[76] Beethoven wrote out this fugue in score; the autograph is in the possession
of A. Artaria.

case with the introduction, which, written originally for strings, is expressly adapted to their peculiarities of sound effect. The harmonic treatment, and more especially the enharmonic changes, are of extraordinary beauty and depth, and occasion remarkable effects of suspense and climax. Most admirable is the art with which the character of the movement as an introduction is maintained, and the defiant style of the following fugue clearly indicated, at the same time that the mind is tuned to a pitch of longing and melancholy which makes the entry of the categorical fugue a positive relief and stimulant.

A fugue for four stringed instruments in D minor, of which the first elaboration is indicated in the sketch (76 Anh. K.)—

appears well suited to the instruments. Whether it was to form a movement in a quartet or an independent piece we have no means of ascertaining.

It appears fitting to cast a glance in this place on two works belonging to a later time, but falling within the same school of composition. These are the two " Pieces for an organ in a clock," in F minor,[77] which have been published, and are well known as Fantasia and Sonata for the Piano-forte, for four hands. They both consist of a slow movement and another in lively, metrical style ; their design is similar, but not identical. The first, composed in December, 1790 (594 K), opens with a solemn Adagio, whose impression of great gentleness is not disturbed by some harmonic harsh-ness ; it keeps strictly within the limits of an introduction. The Allegro in F major, formed by the imitative treatment of an agitated motif, is divided sonata-like into two parts, and returns through an harmonic transition to the Adagio, which is modified in a masterly way, and leads to a calm conclusion. The whole piece is marvellously rounded off; and the restlessness of the Allegro contrasts with, but does not oppose, the gentle expression of the Adagio. Each forms the fitting complement to the other.

The second piece (608 K.), composed on March 3, 1791, is more broadly planned, and has a greater depth of feeling. It begins with the Allegro, the first bars of which serve to introduce a fugue, admirably disposed and full of lovely melody, with a general tone of serious contemplation. When the fugue has been brought to a close by a stretto with the subject inverted, a striking harmonic transition leads back to the opening motif, which passes into the Andante in A flat major. Its treatment as a middle move-ment is more weighty and elaborate. A well-developed motif recurs again and again in varied figuration, connected by different interludes, and gives a general impression of pure and satisfied grace, touched with a breath of melancholy recollection, the natural development of the powerful feeling and contemplative spirit of the Allegro. But this happy calm is of short duration. The first movement returns; the fugue re-commences, rendered more animated than before by a counter-subject, and breaks off with a passionate conclusion.

---

[77] Müller, proprietor of the art museum on the Stockameisenplatz, announces (Wien. Ztg., 1791, No. 66, Anh.) that he has on view there " the magnificent mausoleum erected to the memory of the great Field-Marshal Laudon. There will be performed also funeral music composed by the famous Kapellm. Mozart, which is very well suited for the occasion which has called it forth."

These two compositions are a fresh proof of Mozart's deep insight into the nature of the forms of counterpoint, which gave him power to use them as the free expression of his individual nature; he is entitled to the praise of having brought these forms to their fullest perfection, an incalculable gain to the development of music, which has proceeded in other directions since his time. It is sometimes regretted that Mozart should have wasted his genius and his labour upon compositions for a toy clock.[78] We may rather remark how like a true artist he set himself to perform the task before him, and produced a work which, keeping within its given conditions, forms, nevertheless, a great and harmonious whole.

Mozart, having become acquainted through Van Swieten with the vocal compositions of Handel, Bach, and other masters of the church style, turned, as might be expected, with renewed zeal to this branch of musical art. Unfortunately, upon the introduction of the new regulations in church matters in 1783, the Emperor Joseph prohibited the performance of figured or instrumental church music in the churches of Vienna, and it was only at the court chapel or St. Stephen's cathedral, when the Archbishop celebrated, that musical masses could be performed. German congregational singing was substituted in other cases;[79] it was not liked, and many complaints were made that the total abolition of church music should have been deemed the only remedy for its abuses.[80] Thus Mozart was deprived of all hope of success in this direction. But he had undertaken in 1782, in performance of a vow, to compose a Mass for Salzburg; and this work bears distinct traces of the studies which were occupying him at the time. Mozart completed the Kyrie, Gloria, Sanctus, and Benedictus of this Mass in C minor (427 K.); the first movement of the Credo is com-

---

[78] The Andante composed on May 4, 1791, "for a waltz on a little organ" (616 K.), is a graceful little piece, with no pretence after anything deeper, either in execution or expression.

[79] Nicolai, who notices this reformation (Reise, IV., p. 550), has adduced proofs of it (Beil., X., 1, 2).

[80] Forkel, Musik. Alman., 1784, p. 187.

plete as to the choir parts and bass, and the essential points of the accompaniment are indicated; in the same way the voices, obbligato wind instruments, and bass of the Incarnatus are fully written out, the rest of the accompaniment being only indicated. The whole plan and treatment of the Mass differ from those of the earlier ones. In the latter, limitation to a narrow standard and the subservience of the parts to the whole are the prevailing principles, while in the former the effort is evident to give as wide a signification as possible to each part in itself. With this object each section of the text is treated as an independent movement; the Gloria consists of seven completely detached pieces. The mechanism corresponds to its external divisions, and the treatment throughout is thematic and elaborate, for the most part in strict form. A wealth of resource is displayed in the means employed to give the desired effect; several of the choruses are five-part, one is eight-part, and then again four solo voices are introduced in various ways. The orchestra necessarily complies with the usual Salzburg conditions; the brass instruments are completely appointed, but neither flutes nor clarinets are used with the oboes and bassoons—all the effect of independence possible is given, chiefly by the skilful introduction and treatment of obbligato instruments. It cannot be said, however, that the instrumental part of this work is as brilliant and full of colour as others composed at the same period; the tone-colouring is on the whole monotonous; but there are not wanting some original instrumental effects, principally of the wind instruments. Such is the employment of the trombones (usually only a support to the voices), with independent effect in several parts of the Kyrie and Sanctus. The effect of the whole accompaniment consists mainly in the independence with which it contrasts with the voices, and is produced partly by effective passages and partly by skilful contrapuntal elaboration. That which most strikes us on a careful examination of this Mass is the dissimilarity of the movements in many respects, suggesting that it was undertaken as a study. The solo movements are the most important, more especially by reason of their bravura treat-

ment. Bravura was not considered by any means out of
place in church music, and even the classical masters of the
last century—such as Handel and Bach—did not exclude it
from their sacred works. But it is curious that Mozart,
who only introduced bravura into his dramatic music from
complaisance to the singers, should have made concessions
to the taste for it in this Mass. The first grand soprano
solo is quite after the pattern of an old bravura aria, and
displays little or nothing of Mozart's originality. It is so
suggestive of the style of Graun or Hasse that we are
inclined to suspect the influence of these masters through
Van Swieten. More of Mozart's own character is given to
the Incarnatus est, accompanied by the wind instruments,
and containing touches of delicacy and grace ; but the bravura goes beyond all bounds, especially in the twenty-two
bars of cadenza for the voice and wind instruments. The
duet for two sopranos, Domine Deus, and the terzet for
two sopranos and tenor, Quoniam tu solus, are written in
stricter form, both for voice and accompaniment, and are
simpler and more dignified in expression.

But the inflexibility of form has something in it of
pedantry; the work seems to be done as an exercise, and we
seek in vain for the fresh wellings-up of inspiration which
delight us even in less important compositions of Mozart.
The same remark holds good of the choruses. The first
five-part choral movement of the Credo accords most in
design with the style of the earlier Masses. A lively subject
shared between the strings and wind instruments forms, as
it proceeds, the thread which binds the choral passages
together ; the latter are contrapuntally treated, and the
whole movement is more solemn in tone than was usual in
earlier works. The long fugue " Cum Sancto Spiritu " is
admirably worked out, and, in spite of its difficulty, very
clear. Notwithstanding all this, the nervous force of individual life is wanting to the work, and cannot be replaced by
the artistic workmanship displayed in the different parts,
even when these have force and character of their own, as
for instance in the magnificent ending, when the voices in
unison maintain the theme against a florid accompaniment.

The Osanna has more of independent life; it is a long, elaborately fugued movement, the technical interest of which has engrossed the composer longer than was necessary.[81] The Benedictus in four parts, and worked out at length, is remarkable on account of its earnest, somewhat dry tone, which effectually distinguishes it from the same movement in other masses, to which a soft and pleasing character was given. The Kyrie, Gloria, and Sanctus are very fine movements, in which the skilful rendering of strictest form does not overpower the expression of feeling and the truly musical proportions of the work. The varied expression of the different passages is so suitable, so clear and telling, that we may see at once how firm a grasp Mozart had taken of the true spirit of church music. The crown of the composition, however, is the five-part Gratias with the eight-part Qui tollis, which are planned and executed in masterly fashion, and are penetrated with Mozart's spirit and life. Their earnestness, severe even to harshness, their breadth of outline and massive effects, are worthy of the great examples who were vividly present to his mind; and we cannot fail to discern the master who was stimulated by these very examples to draw more deeply on the resources of his own creative genius, and to soar to higher realms of art by the exertion of his own powers.

After the first performance of the Mass in its unfinished state at Salzburg, in 1783, Mozart laid it aside for more pressing work. But when in 1785 he was commissioned to write an oratorio for the concert for the Musical Fund

---

[81] A four-part vocal fugue, "In Te Domine speravi," of which Mozart has written thirty-four bars (23 Anh., K.), appears to belong to this time, and is very fresh and forcible :—

(March 13 and 14; Vol. II., p. 174), he determined to make use of the Kyrie and Gloria to which, with slight alterations, the Italian words of the "Davidde Penitente" (469 K.) were adapted. He added (on March 6 and 11) two new arie for Mdlle. Cavalieri and Adamberger.[82] The work lost in unity of style more than it gained by the addition of these two songs, of which the orchestral accompaniment is in Mozart's later style, and the design and treatment are different from those of the other movements. They are both in the style of the concert arie of the time, and are quite equal to the best in expression and treatment of the voice. The Mozart-like character is more marked than in the rest of the work, but it does not reach its fullest development; and the arie are too florid for an oratorio. Bu the mixture of styles was then customary, and indeed brilliant solos were looked for by the public as a relief to the more serious choral movements.

At the present day there cannot be two opinions as to the impropriety of such a mixture.[83] The important point to be noted, however, is that just at the time when the instrumental and operatic music of Vienna threatened to banish altogether the severer and more classical style, Mozart

---

[82] Rochlitz, A. M. Z., III., p. 230; cf. XXVII., p. 447. The parts of the Mass are made use of in the following manner:—

"Davidde":

1. Chorus, "Alzai le flebili voci"		Kyrie.
2. Chorus, "Cantiam le lodi"		Gloria.
3. Soprano air, "Lungi le cure ingrate" ...		Laudamus (with the remark, "to be sung by the second singer," Mdlle. Distler).
4. Chorus, "Sii pur sempre"		Gratias.
5. Duet, "Sorgi o Signore"		Domine Deus.
6. Tenor Air, "A te fra tanti affanni" ...		New.
7. Chorus, "Se vuoi puniscimi"		Qui tollis.
8. Soprano Air, "Fra le oscure ombre" ...		New.
9. Terzett, "Tutti le mie speranze"		Quoniam tu solus.
10. Chorus, "Chi in Dio sol"		Jesu Christe, cum Sancto Spiritu. Amen.

[83] Reichardt criticises favourably on the whole a cantata composed of the last numbers (8, 9, 10) of the oratorio arranged by Hiller (Musik. Zeitg., I., p. 368; cf. 382); another cantata borrowed from it is mentioned (A. M. Z., IX., p. 479).

became familiar through Van Swieten with the works of the
classical masters. They laid deep hold on his imagination
and intellect, giving him a powerful impulse to classical
studies, without which his genius would not have arrived at
a full mastery of his art; these studies, combined with his
ever-growing powers of production, have impressed their
indelible stamp upon the works of this period.[84]

CHAPTER XXXI.

MOZART AND FREEMASONRY.

A N account of the circumstances which affected Mozart's
social and artistic position in Vienna, as well as his
moral and intellectual development, would be incomplete
without some notice of his connection with Freemasonry.[1]

It is well known[2] that a propensity for secret associations
and brotherhoods, having for their object the furtherance of
intellectual, moral, and political ideas, was very prevalent in
Germany during the latter half of the eighteenth century.
These associations were all more or less closely allied to
Freemasonry, and the traces of their influence are most
apparent in the impulse which they gave to the national
literature.[3] Be the degree great or small in which Free-
masony has advanced the cause of humanity, and granting
that its good effects have often been obscured by the follies,
crimes, and impostures which have hidden themselves behind
the secrecy of its vows; it is still an undoubted fact that

---

[84] Gerber's assertion in the Tonkünstlerlexicon, I., p. 976: "Lucky for him
that he was moulded into perfect form while still young by the pleasing and
playful muses of Vienna; otherwise he could hardly have escaped the fate of
Friedemann Bach, whose soaring flight could be followed by few mortals," is
only half true, for Mozart's deepest studies were made not in Salzburg, but in
Vienna.

[1] The initiated will see at once that an outsider is speaking, and that the
expressions used are on that account additionally cautious.

[2] A survey of the most important phenomena attendant on this movement is
given by Schlosser (Geschichte des Achtzehnten Jahrh., III.; I., p. 278).

[3] Gervinus, Gesch. d. Deutschen Nationalitt., V., p. 274.

princes like Frederick the Great, great and good men like Lessin, Herder, Wieland, and Goethe, have looked upon Freemasonry as a means of attaining their highest endeavours after universal good. It will suffice for our present purpose to quote a passage from Goethe's funeral oration upon Wieland :[4]—

If any testimony were desired in favour of an association which has existed from very ancient days, and has survived many vicissitudes, it would be found in the spectacle of a man of genius—intelligent, shrewd, cautious, experienced, and moderate—seeking his equals among the members of our association, feeling himself at one with us, and, fastidious as he was, acknowledging our fellowship to be the perfect satisfaction of his earthly and social desires.

Wieland himself declared that[5] the " intellectual temple-building" had for its chief and highest object " the earnest, energetic, and persevering efforts of every true and honest mason to approach nearer himself, and to lead his brethren nearer, to the ideal of humanity, and to prove that man is fashioned and appointed to be a living stone in the eternal temple of the Almighty." [6] It was natural that in Vienna, where there was more intellectual life than elsewhere, the form of secret association should have been utilised in the furtherance of these high aims :[7]—

In the year 1781 was formed a society of the most distinguished leaders of thought in Vienna, under the presidency of the noble and intellectual Ignaz von Born. The aim of the society was to give effect to that freedom of conscience and thought so happily fostered by the government, and to combat superstition and fanaticism in the persons of the monkish orders, the main supports of both these evils. Reinhold and the friends of his youth, Alxinger, Blumauer, Haschka, Leon and Ratschky, were the most zealous members of this association. They

[4] Goethe, Werke, XXI., p. 329.

[5] Wieland, Werke, LIII., p. 435.

[6] " To do good, to lighten the burden of mankind, to assist in the enlightenment of his comrades, to cause enmity to decrease among men, and to do all this with indefatigable zeal, is the duty of the mason and the true secret of his order. The ceremonies are minor mysteries, by means of which a man becomes a Freemason outwardly. The part taken by the order in the spread of toleration, especially among Christian sects, has been too plainly demonstrated to need mention here " [Kessler von Sprengseisen] (Anti-Saint-Nicaise, p. 62).

[7] L. Lewis, Gesch. d. Freimaurerei in Oesterreich : Wien, 1861.

adopted the forms of Freemasonry as an outward expression of their mental and spiritual union. Their lodge was entitled "True Harmony,"[8] and, supported indirectly by the favour of the Emperor Joseph, they laboured for a considerable time with energy and success to carry out their preconceived designs. Their weapons were learning and eloquence, and in their use of these, whether in earnest severity or in jesting irony, they were more than a match for their opponents.[9]

From this circle, which contained other distinguished men, such as Sonnenfels, Retzer, and Gemmingen, proceeded the satires of Born and Blumauer against monasticism, which had so extraordinary an effect at the time. The scientific organ of the Freemasons was the Vienna "Real-zeitung," edited by Blumauer, which endeavoured to drive superstition and prejudice from the domain of science in the same insidious way in which they had entered it—Blumauer's principle[10] being that the work of enlightenment is a very gradual one, and that a far harder task than that of learning is the unlearning of what has been once hammered into the heads of ordinary mortals. As might have been expected, Freemasonry became after a time an affair of fashion in Vienna, and many abuses crept in :—

The order of Freemasonry pursued its course with an amount of publicity and ostentation almost ludicrous. Freemasons' songs were composed, published, and sung everywhere. Their symbols were hung as charms upon watch-chains; ladies were presented with white gloves by novices and associates, and various articles of fashion were christened *à la franc-maçon*. Many members joined the order from curiosity, or in order to enjoy the pleasures of the table. Others had still more interested views. It might be of material advantage to belong to a brotherhood which had members in every rank, and had made a special point of gaining the adhesion of powerful officials, presidents, and members of the government. One brother was bound to help another; and those who did not belong to the brotherhood were often at a serious disadvantage; this fact enticed many to join. Others again, more

---

[8] There were eight lodges in Vienna in 1785. The oldest of them, "Zur gekrönten Hoffnung," was the one to which Mozart belonged; it contained many rich and noble members, and was said to lay great stress on gorgeous banquets (Briefe eines Biedermanns üb. d. Freimäurer in Wien: Münch., 1786, p. 40).

[9] K. L. Reinhold's Leben, p. 18.

[10] Blumauer, Pros. Schr., I., p. 69.

sincere or more ignorant, thought they had found a key to higher mysteries—such as the philosopher's stone, or intercourse with disembodied spirits. The Freemasons were unquestionably very benevolent; collections for the poor brethren were often made at their meetings.[11]

The proceedings against the Illuminati in 1785 led to a commencement of persecution of the Freemasons, but on December 11 of the same year the Emperor Joseph issued a decree in which, while disclaiming any knowledge of the secret vows of the order, or any approval of its juggleries, he gave it his countenance upon condition of certain reforms, and placed it under the protection of the state.[12] This decree, which was extolled by some as a proof of the highest wisdom and clemency, and bewailed by others as the ruin of genuine Freemasonry, gave occasion to violent disputes, intensified by the carrying out of the Emperor's order for the reduction of the existing eight lodges to three. Born, who disapproved of the reform, had, in spite of his previous popularity, to suffer numerous personal attacks. An unpleasant encounter with Jos. Kratter, nicknamed the "freemason's auto-da-fé," called forth a multitude of malignant pamphlets, and in 1786 Born retired altogether from the lodge.[13] His loss was a serious one for its intellectual influence, and his example was followed by others. The imperial recognition of the lodge did not preserve it from increasing attacks and suspicions, which afterwards proceeded to publicly expressed disapproval on all sides. But many steadfast spirits still held out. Loibl, for instance, placed his dwelling at the disposal of the lodge for their meetings. His daughter still remembers (1867) how her father spent hours clothed in his robes, sitting before a crucifix with lighted tapers, reading the Bible in preparation for the sittings, at which the children, peeping through the keyhole, wondered to see the gentlemen seated round the table conversing with earnest mien. Mozart was among these enthusiasts, and maintained his connection with the

---

[11] Car. Pichler, Denkw., I., p. 105.

[12] Wien. Ztg., 1785, No. 102.

[13] Cf. Voigt an Hufeland (Aus Weimars Glanzzeit, p. 46. Baggesen's Briefw., I., p. 304).

lodge until his death; he even conceived the idea of founding a secret society of his own—" The Grotto "—and drew up rules for its guidance.[14]

It can scarcely have occurred to Mozart to consider his connection with Freemasonry as a means of worldly advancement; such calculations were foreign to his nature, and would have been in no degree realised. His connection with the order was of no practical advantage to him. The high standing of the order when Mozart came to Vienna—the fact that the most distinguished and cultivated men, moving in the best society, were counted among its members, renders it natural that he should have desired to attach himself to it. His need for intercourse with earnest and far-seeing intellects would lead him to the same conclusion. So, too, in a still greater degree, would his genuine love for mankind, his warm sympathies both in joy and sorrow, his sincere desire to help and benefit others, which amounted even to a weakness; and perhaps the greatest attraction of all would be the satisfaction of his truly exceptional longing for friendship. Even his boyish years are full of instances of enthusiastic devotion and attachment—to young Hagenauer (Vol. I., p. 50), to Father Johannes at Seeon (Vol. I., p. 58), to Thomas Linley (Vol. I., p. 119), and others; and as a man his loving, sympathetic friendship was accorded to many, among whom I may remind the reader of Bullinger (Vol. I., p. 335), of Barisani (Vol. I., p. 305), of Gottfried von Jacquin (Vol. II., p. 357), of Count Hatzfeld (Vol. II., p. 291). An order which made the brotherhood of its members the chief reason of its existence was sure to have strong attractions for him, the more so that the spirit of independence which he possessed in common with all other gifted natures was gratified by the equality of every brother within the circle of his

---

[14] Mozart's widow, who communicated his plan for this order to Härtel (November 27, 1799; July 21, 1800), stated that Stadler, with whom Mozart had discussed the whole subject, could give more information, but hesitated to reveal the circumstances connected with it. Although it says little for Mozart's knowledge of mankind that he should have chosen such a man for a confidant, the general interest taken in all matters relating to secret societies may serve to explain Mozart's partiality for them.

order. Again, the position which he had at that time assumed in relation to the priestly and monkish orders gave him a powerful impulse towards Freemasonry. Notwithstanding his strict religious training, he had inherited from his father a decided aversion to these institutions. L. Mozart writes to his daughter (October 14, 1785) :—

There is an appalling difference between these sisterhoods and true Christianity. It would be an undoubted gain if the nunneries were dissolved. They exist neither by virtue of true vocation, nor supernatural calling, nor spiritual zeal, nor as the true discipline of devotion and abnegation of desires, but are the result of compulsion, hypocrisy, dissimulation, and childish folly, leading in the end to confirmed wickedness.

The effects of his connection with Freemasonry upon Mozart are as plainly discernible as his reasons for joining the order. Carefully and well as his early training laid the foundation of his after-development, it was impossible but that the narrow circumstances of his Salzburg life should cramp his intellectual energies ; and his visits to great cities, important as they were in inciting him to fresh efforts for self-improvement, were too transitory to have much practical effect. Earnest endeavours after freedom of moral and intellectual development were at that time the special characteristic of Freemasonry in Vienna, and the effect must needs have been a salutary one which followed the entrance of a young man into a circle which busied itself in solving, both theoretically and practically, the highest problems of the universe. It would be difficult to say how far the secrecy and mystery of the order worked on his imagination and attracted him ; but some such influence is quite conceivable in a nature so artistic and excitable as his.

That Mozart was quite in earnest in his fidelity to his order is proved by the pains he took to induce his father to become a Freemason. The letter, already quoted (Vol. II., p. 323), in which, anticipating his father's speedy death, he speaks of the true meaning of death from a mason's point of view, bears ample testimony to his earnestness. His lodge recognised it in the oration pronounced after his death,[15] of which the passages immediately relating to him may here be quoted :—

> It has pleased the Almighty Architect of the Universe to take from among us our best-beloved and most estimable member. Who did not know, who did not respect, who did not love our worthy brother, Mozart? Only a few weeks ago he was in our midst celebrating the dedication of our masonic temple with entrancing tones. Who of us that saw him then, my brethren, would have supposed his days to be numbered? Who would have thought that in three weeks we should be mourning his loss? How true it is that man's sad destiny often cuts short his career in the very prime of life! Kings perish in the midst of their ambitious plans, which go down to posterity incomplete. Artists die, after devoting all that was granted them of life to the glorification of their art. The admiration of all mankind follows them to the grave, nations mourn for them, and yet the universal fate of these great men is—to be forgotten of their admirers. It shall not be so with us, my brethren! Mozart's early death is an irreparable loss to art. His genius, displayed in earliest childhood, rendered him the wonder of his age—half Europe was at his feet—the great ones of the earth called him their darling—and we called him—brother. Fitting as it is, however, to call to our remembrance his abilities in his art, we must not forget to give our strongest testimony to his excellent heart. He was a zealous supporter of our order. The main features of his character were brotherly love, devotion to the good cause, benevolence and genuine satisfaction in using his talents for the good of his fellows. He was estimable alike as husband, father, friend of his friends, brother of his brothers; he wanted only wealth to make hundreds happy after his own heart.

Mozart owed many of his impulses as a composer to his connection with Freemasonry. We shall see later that the "Zauberflöte" came directly under its influence; in this place it will be fitting only to mention those compositions which he composed for particular festivities within the lodge; they are, of course, exclusively for male voices, and betray in other ways enforced compliance with certain conditions.

The "Gesellenreise" (468 K.), composed on March 26, 1785, is a social song, elevated and pleasing in tone; two others are intended for the opening and closing of a lodge

---

[15] Maurerrede auf Mozart's Tod. Vorgelesen bei einer Meisteraufnahme in der sehr ehrw. St. Joh. zur gekrönten Hoffnung im Orient von Wien vom Bdr. H . . . . r. Wien, gedruckt beym Br. Ignaz Alberti, 1792, 8.

(483, 484, K.) : [16] all three have organ accompaniments. The two last conclude with a chorus for two tenors and a bass voice. Similar three-part choruses are introduced in other Freemason cantatas, and are easy and popular, suitable to amateurs. The tenor solos, on the other hand, are adapted to a trained singer, Adamberger, who was a member of the lodge.

An unfinished cantata (429 K.) was probably intended for some masonic purpose. The first chorus, " Dir Seele des Weltalls, Sonne, sei heute das erste der festlichen Lieder geweiht," for two tenors and bass, with accompaniment for the quartet and flute, clarinet, two oboes and two horns, is written out in full for the voices with a figured bass, and the accompaniment is sketched in Mozart's usual way. The same is the case with the long-drawn-out tenor aria which follows, " Dir danken wir die Freude." Only seventeen bars of a second duet for tenor voices, intended as a conclusion, are written out. The three-part male chorus, the solos exclusively for tenor voices, and the limited orchestra, all suggest masonic influence; I will not attempt to give an opinion on the symbolism of the words. The first chorus is fine, spirited and solemn.[17] Two other cantatas certainly fall within this category. The first of these is the Maurerfreude (471 K.) composed on April 20, 1785, shortly before the departure of his father, in whose presence it was first performed. The lodge were giving a banquet in honour of Born, who had been highly complimented by the Emperor for his invention of a new kind of amalgam.[18] The cantata, with words by Petran, was afterwards published in score, with a title-page engraved by Mansfeld, representing " Wisdom and Virtue," as the text says, " addressing themselves to their disciple"; it was sold for the benefit of the poor.[19] The main substance of the work consists of a long

---

[16] Lewis, Gesch. d. Freim. in Oesterreich, p. 162.

[17] In the Salzburg Mozarteum there is a complete autograph score of the first chorus and part of the first air ; but the chorus is in four parts, for soprano, alto, tenor, and bass, and the wind instruments are limited to two oboes and two horns ; no doubt a subsequent arrangement.

[18] Wien. Ztg., 1785, No. 32.

[19] Lewis, Gesch. d. Freim. in Oesterreich, p. 119.

tenor solo worked out in free form for Adamberger, the first and greater part being after the fashion of the allegro of a concert aria. There is nothing of the Italian form in it, but deep and genuine feeling is expressed in Mozart's familiar and purely German manner. The animation of the expression reaches its climax in a recitative leading to a serious and rhythmical song of two verses, the concluding lines of which are repeated by the chorus. In the accompaniment to this cantata, a clarinet is introduced in addition to the quartet, two oboes and two horns, and treated with evident partiality, the deeper notes being employed in Mozart's favourite triplet passages; Stadler had no doubt something to do with this.[20] The second, "Kleine Freimaurercantate" (623 K.), with words by Schikaneder,[21] was composed on November 15, 1791, and performed a few days afterwards at the consecration of a new masonic temple: it is the last work which Mozart completed. There is somewhat more of variety in its conception; a short chorus interrupted by solos is followed by a recitative and aria for the tenor, which leads to another recitative divided between tenor and bass; then follows a duet, after which the first chorus is repeated. It is very pleasing and popular in tone, but not equal to the previous cantata in depth and energy of expression.[22] The cantata, "Die ihr des unermesslichen Weltalls Schöpfer

---

[20] In the library of the Munich Conservatoire there is a manuscript score of this cantata, in which the original words, "Sehen, wie dem starren Forscherauge," are changed into "Sehen jenes Irrthums Nacht verschwinden," for use in church services; also the final chorus is arranged in four parts, for soprano, alto, tenor, and bass, and strengthened by trumpets and drums.

[21] Lewis, p. 39.

[22] Wien. Ztg., January 25, 1792, No. 7, p. 217: "Reverence and gratitude for the departed Mozart caused a number of his admirers to announce the performance of one of his works for the benefit of his necessitous widow and children; the work may be termed his *swan's song*, composed in his own inspired manner, and performed by a circle of his friends under his own direction two days before his last illness. It is a cantata upon the dedication of a Freemasons' lodge in Vienna, with words by one of the members." The score, with the original words, appeared at Vienna, with the title, "Mozarts letztes Meisterstück eine Cantata gebeben vor seinem Tode im Kreise vertrauter Freunde." Appended to the cantata is a song, "Lasst uns mit verschlungnen Händen," which may also be by Mozart. The cantata was published later, with other words, and the title, "Das Lob der Freundschaft."

ehrt " (619 K.), composed in July, 1791, is not certainly the immediate result of Mozart's connection with Freemasonry, but it is evidently an expression of the state of mind which it was the object of Freemasonry to produce.[23] Frz. Hein. Ziegenhagen, a wealthy merchant of Hamburg, incited by the study of the Encyclopedists, especially of Rousseau, felt himself called upon to take part in the various attempts which were made towards the close of the last century to abolish the pedantry of the schools ; and his efforts to bring education back to a state of natural simplicity were more energetic and daring than those of less ardent reformers. He published, out of love for humanity and paternal tenderness, as he said, an elaborate treatise in which he sought to prove,[24] by a criticism of the biblical tradition, that existing religions could not satisfy the inquirer into the nature of things, and then laid down rules for the theoretical and practical education of human beings.   He hoped, in all seriousness, " to induce wise princes and enlightened universities to introduce the study of the relations of things to each other, which is so unmistakably superior to ordinary religious teaching ; and he hoped also to make the acquaintance of such parents as wished to devote their children to husbandry and the management of a colony which he proposed to found, in accordance with his views, in the neighbourhood of Strasburg."   In order to render his book attractive from every point of view he adorned it with eight copperplate engravings by Chodowiecki, and requested Mozart to compose a song to be sung with orchestral accompaniment in the meeting-houses of his colony.

Mozart was certainly not acquainted with the entire con-

---

[23] The inducement to this composition was briefly hinted at in the A. M. Z. I., p. 745, and afterwards given at greater length by G. Weber (Cäcilia, XVIII., p. 210).

[24] This book of 633 pages bears the title: " Lehre vom richtigen Verhältnisse zu den Schöpfungswerken und die durch öffentliche Einfürung derselben allein zu bewürkende allgemeine Menschenbeglückung herausgegeben von F. H. Ziegenhagen.   Hamburg, 1792, 8." Mozart's composition is appended, printed on four pages.   Ziegenhagen was born in 1753, at Salzburg ; late in life he fell into bad circumstances, and put an end to his life at Steinthal, near Strasburg, in 1806.

tents of this eccentric, almost crazy work; Ziegenhagen gave him a few general hints of his Utopian scheme, in which he was doubtless perfectly sincere, and sent him the words of the hymn. These words emphatically express the effort after truth, brotherhood, and happiness which was the final object of Freemasonry, and Mozart could not but treat them after the same manner that he treated similar poems avowedly masonic. Ziegenhagen's lines are so deficient in poetic spirit, and even in poetic metre, that it required a more than ordinary amount of genius and cultivation to give them the impress of a musical work of art. A work of art this cantata undoubtedly is; it is more free in conception than usual, the arie, and especially the recitatives, being allowed considerable scope, in order to fall in with the unequal and rhetorical words. The union of such an accentuation as was necessary to the sense of the words with the full expression of warm emotion and the subservience of both to appointed musical forms, are the essential features of this composition, and are the more likely to strike us, who are so entirely out of sympathy with the ideas suggesting the work. A style of music specifically belonging to Freemasonry is of course inconceivable; but in the finest passages of works such as this, and in the "Zauberflöte," something is expressed of the essence of the masonic character, of *moral convictions* (I had almost said of *virtue*, but fear to be misunderstood), which appears outside the province of music, but which has sometimes been made very effective, especially by Beethoven. The "Maurerische Trauermusik bei dem Todesfalle der Br. Br. Meklenburg und Esterhazy" (477 K.), composed in July, 1785, is an orchestral composition of wonderful beauty and originality. The combination of instruments is unusual; besides the stringed instruments there are two oboes, one clarinet (only one again), three basset-horns, one horn in E flat, one horn in C, and a double bassoon.[25] The deep tones of the wind

---

[25] The employment of three basset-horns, as in the vocal terzet (Vol. II., p. 361) and in an adagio for two clarinets and three basset-horns (411 K.), is no doubt the result of circumstances. The beginning of an adagio and allegro for these instruments exists among the fragments (93, 95 Anh., K.).

instruments give a peculiarly solemn expression to the
work.   After a few introductory chords they are joined by
the strings, and the first violins maintain throughout the
same character, contrasting with the wind instruments in
free rhapsodic passages, expressive of grief in all its varied
shades.   This is most striking when a Cantus firmus, following the introduction[26]—

is first delivered *piano* by the oboes and clarinet, and at the
sixth bar is taken up by the full force of the wind instruments. The violins in the meantime have graceful passages,
expressive of gentle sorrow, which rise to a gradual climax
of passionate regret.   As this storm abates, we are led back
to the introductory motif, which prepares the way in another
climax for the conclusion, preceded by a singularly bold harmonic transition of deeply sorrowful expression:—

If we compare the contrapuntal treatment of this Cantus
firmus with similar works of earlier date, such as the

---

[26] Mozart has jotted this melody hastily down upon an extra leaf, in order to
make no mistake in the working-out. According to my colleague Heimsoeth
the first six bars render the first psalm-tune with the first difference (from the
Cologne Antiphonary) ; what follows is very probably a local compilation of
several psalm-tunes for the penitential psalm " Miserere mei Deus," different
tunes being customary in different places. The melody of the first phrase is
from the beginning of the first psalm-tune, the melody of the second phrase
occurs in the seventh tune.

" Betulia Liberata,"[27] we are struck with its development of technical mastery as well as of depth of sentiment and freedom of expression; the same is the case also with the " Zauberflöte" and the " Requiem." Mozart has written nothing finer than this short adagio in technical treatment, sound effects, earnest feeling, and psychological truth. It is the musical expression of that manly calm which gives sorrow its due, and no more than its due, in the presence of death, and which was expressed by Mozart in another form in the letter to his father already quoted (Vol. II., p. 323).

CHAPTER XXXII.

MOZART AS AN ARTIST.

TO those who realise the excitement and want of repose of Mozart's life in Vienna, and the variety of occupations and distractions which beset him, it must appear matter of wonder that he was able to produce so large a number of compositions, each bearing an individual character of maturity and finish. The wonder increases as the conviction grows that not only was he ready as each occasion arose to prove, as Goethe says every artist should, that his art came at his command, but that he had the power of bringing forth at will his deepest, best conceptions, so that the external impulse appeared only as the momentum given to an artistic inspiration. It must at the same time be remembered that Mozart was not fond of writing, and generally waited until the last moment to give shape to his ideas. He was occasionally, therefore, late with his compositions, as with the sonata for Strinasacchi (Vol. II., p. 337), or had only time to write the parts without scoring them (Vol. II., pp. 318, 366), or scarcely allowed the copyist time to finish his work (Vol. II., p. 327); it is only necessary to look through his Thematic Catalogue to see that most of his compositions were written as short a time as possible before they were actually wanted. His

---

[27] Vol. I., p. 197 ; cf. also pp. 272, 277.

father, who, as a man of business, considered the proper disposition of time as a matter of vital importance, often called
his son's attention to this failing. " If you will examine
your conscience closely," he writes (December 11, 1777),
"you will find that procrastination is your besetting sin;"
and when Wolfgang was at work on "Idomeneo " in Munich,
he warned him " not to procrastinate" (November 18, 1781).
After his stay in Vienna, convinced that his son was in this
respect unchanged for the better, he writes to Marianne, on
hearing from Wolfgang that he was over head and ears at
work on the " Nozze di Figaro " (November 11, 1785), " He
has procrastinated and thrown away his time after his usual
habit, until now he is forced to set to work in earnest, in
compliance with Count Rosenberg's commands."

It cannot be denied that Leopold Mozart was right, and
that a judicious and methodical distribution of time is as
desirable in an artist or a genius as in any one else ; it is true
also that perseverance and care may enable even an artist to
overcome his inclination to procrastination.

But a glance at the extraordinary fertility of Mozart's
genius, at the burning zeal and intensity with which he
worked, will suffice to show the injustice of accusing him of
idleness, or of never working unless he was actually driven
to it. He was perfectly justified in writing to his father
from Vienna (May 26, 1781) : " Believe me, I do not love
idleness, but rather work." The father's injustice was the
result of a want of comprehension of the peculiar creative
process of his son's genius. He did not appreciate the
activity and industry of his mind, because it made no show,
and, indeed, often hid itself behind a careless demeanour; he
failed to perceive that the disinclination to write generally
arose from the feeling that the workings of the mind were
not yet in a shape to be expressed by the pen.

A conception of Mozart's work, almost equally mistaken, is
that which takes as a measure of his genius his wonderfully
rapid production, which often made his grasp of an artistic
idea coincident with his embodiment of it in music. The
overture to " Don Giovanni" is most often quoted as an example of this extraordinary speed. Niemetschek says (p. 84):—

Mozart wrote "Don Juan" at Prague in 1787; it was finished, rehearsed, and announced for performance in two days' time, before the overture was begun to be written. The anxiety of his friends, increasing every hour, appeared to entertain him; the more apprehensive they became, the less he would consent to hurry himself. It was not until the night before the performance, after spending the merriest evening imaginable, that he went to his room at near midnight, began to write, and completed the admirable masterpiece in a few hours.

This very credible account is corroborated by Mozart's wife :[1]—

The evening before the performance of "Don Juan" at Prague, the dress rehearsal having already taken place, he said to his wife that he would write the overture at night, if she would sit with him and make him some punch to keep his spirits up. This she did, and told him tales about Aladdin's Lamp, Cinderella, &c., which made him laugh till the tears came. But the punch made him sleepy, so that he dozed when she left off, and only worked as long as she told tales. At last, the excitement, the sleepiness, and the frequent efforts not to doze off, were too much for him, and his wife persuaded him to go to sleep on the sofa, promising to wake him in an hour. But he slept so soundly that she could not find it in her heart to wake him until two hours had passed. It was then five o'clock; at seven o'clock the overture was finished and in the hands of the copyist.

This musical myth has received a stronger colouring in the account of the elder Genast, then a young actor at Prague. According to him, Mozart partook so freely of the hospitalities of a certain gentleman on the evening in question that Genast and a friend brought him home, laid him senseless on his bed, and themselves went to sleep on the sofa. On awakening, they heard Mozart lustily singing, as he composed his overture, and "listened in reverential silence as the immortal ideas developed themselves."[2] A good instance, this, of the way to manufacture an anecdote.

Niemetschek, who had previously remarked with justice that Mozart's work was always ready in his head before he sat down to his writing-table, was no doubt of the correct opinion that the overture was only written down in this haste, not composed. Whether the wife believed this or not

---

[1] A. M. Z., I., p. 290 ; cf. p. 52. Nissen, p. 520.
[2] Genast, Aus d. Tageb. e. alten Schausp, I., p. 3.

is doubtful, since she adds ingenuously : " Some will recognise
the dozings and rousings in the music of the overture." An
evident repetition of some one else's words, and a very
ingenious idea. One can only say with Hoffman : " Some
people are fools ! "[8]

An unprejudiced examination soon disposes of the not only
foolish but detrimental idea[4] that rapidity of workmanship is
a sign of true genius; but it is not by any means so easy a
task to gain a clear and comprehensive insight into the workings of an artist's nature.[5] Fortunately for our purpose,
however, averse as Mozart was to talk much of himself or his
compositions, he has left us characteristic traits and expressions sufficient to enable us to realise his individualities in
this respect.[6]

It is a matter of universal experience that the great men
of every art and science, who have left any enduring proofs
of their genius, have worked the more zealously and the
more earnestly in proportion as their genius surpassed that
of other men. That this holds true of Mozart no one who
has studied his life and works will wish to deny. In his
youth, as long as he remained under the direct control of his
father, his studies were regular and severe. And as a man
and a fully developed artist he had no ambition to be considered one who threw off his compositions with the carelessness of genius, or who was ashamed of his honest efforts and
labours. His dedication of his quartets to Haydn speaks of
them as the fruit of long and painful labour, and in a conversation with the orchestral conductor Kucharz, at Prague,

---

[8] Hoffmann, Fantasiestücke (Ges. Schr., VII., p. 68). The story has lately
been discussed (cf. Signale, 1862, p. 531).

[4] C. M. von Weber deduces from his own experience " the ill results upon the
student's youthful mind of these marvellous anecdotes concerning the masters
whom he reverences and strives to follow." (Lebensb., I., p. 177.)

[5] Rochlitz has frequently expressed correct views as to Mozart's method of
working, especially in the article " Ein guter Rath Mozarts " (A. M. Z., XXII.,
p. 297. Für Freunde der Tonk., II., p. 281).

[6] A letter from Mozart to a certain Baron von P. upon this subject, first printed
by Rochlitz (A. M. Z., XVII., p. 561), and often subsequently, is incontestably
a fabrication as it stands. As it is impossible to determine how far it is founded
upon truth, it must remain entirely out of the question.

before the performance of "Don Giovanni," he expressed himself as follows: " I have spared neither labour nor pains to produce something worthy of the reputation of Prague. It would be a great mistake to imagine that my art is an easy matter to me. I assure you, my dear friend, no one has given more trouble to the study of composition than myself. It would not be easy to find a celebrated musician whose works I have not often and laboriously studied." And in point of fact, the narrator continues, even when he had attained to 'classical perfection, the works of great masters were always to be seen lying on his desk.[7] We have already seen how eagerly and with what good result he studied Bach and Handel, when once Van Swieten had given him the impetus. Rochlitz[8] declares that he was as familiar with the works of Handel as if he had been all his life director of the Ancient Concerts in London. He had arrived in Leipzig just after arranging "Acis and Galatea" and the "Messiah" for Van Swieten, and the impressions of these works were fresh upon him. "Handel," Rochlitz heard him say, "knows better than any of us what will make an effect; when he chooses he strikes like a thunderbolt."[9] He admired not only Handel's choruses, but many of his arie and solos, which were not thought much of at that time. "Although he is often prosy, after the fashion of his time," said he, " there is always something in his music."[10]

At Leipzig Mozart became acquainted with the vocal compositions of Sebastian Bach. Doles made the St. Thomas choir sing him the wonderful eight-part motett, " Singet dem Herrn ein neues Lied." His surprise at the flow of melody, wave upon wave, passed all bounds; he listened with rapt attention, and exclaimed with delight: "That is indeed

---

[7] Niemetschek, p. 84.

[8] Rochlitz, A. M. Z., I., p. 115. Für Freunde der Tonkunst, IV., p. 239.

[9] Beethoven's expression is well known: " Handel is the unrivalled master of masters; go and learn from him how with limited resources to produce such grand results!" (Studien, Anhang, p. 22). Gluck took Kelly (Reminisc., I., p. 255) into his bedroom, and showed him Handel's portrait hanging near his bed, which he used reverently to greet each morning on awaking.

[10] Haydn declared that Handel was grand in his choruses, but mediocre in vocal solos (Griesinger, Biog. Not., p. 115).

something to take a lesson from!" When he heard that the St. Thomas school possessed several other motetts by Bach, he begged to see them, and no score being accessible he surrounded himself with the parts, and was buried in study until he had worked them all out ; then he asked for copies of the motetts.[11] His interest in Benda's monodramas (Vol. II., p. 74) and his expressions on the importance of French opera, prove that he had profited by the study of living masters; all his works bear traces of the kind of influence which is exercised upon a genial and receptive nature by the great performances of others.

Of a different kind to these general preparatory studies, is that which may be properly be called the labour of production : such a technical skill and perfection as enables an artist to clothe his ideas in form. It is impossible in any art (and more especially so in music) to separate absolutely form and substance, and to treat each as a self-sufficing element, and equally impossible to divide at any given point the creative, inventive force of an artistic production from its formative, executive force. The process of production, whether physical or mental, is a mystery to mankind; whence and how the artist is inspired as by a lightning flash with an idea, he knows himself as little as he can trace in his completed work the actual momentum of its conception.

The characteristics of the gradual formation and perfection of artistic ideas vary greatly in different artists ; even in great and highly organised natures the mental powers are variously endowed and developed. Statements as to the easy or painful, rapid or deliberate, methods of working of different artists, vague and unsatisfactory in themselves, are for the most part the result of superficial observation and knowledge. It is of little consequence whether an artist at his work is easily distracted by external impressions, or whether he pursues his train of thought undisturbed by what is going on around him. It is of little consequence whether an artist feels necessitated or has made it his habit, to regulate his intellectual labours, and to give a written

---

[11] Rochlitz, A. M. Z., I., p. 117.

form to every creative impulse, or whether he renounces external aids, and shapes, proves, elaborates and connects his ideas in his own mind only. That which is of consequence, that which no true artist is without, is the power to carry on a train of thought from its earliest germs to its full development, unhindered by interruptions and distractions; and the further power to realise the idea of the whole at every point, as the determining element of the details of conception and form. It is difficult to know whether to admire more the steady flow of invention and form as it proceeds from some minds, or the gradual evolution of a unique self-contained whole out of an apparent waste of disconnected ideas which is characteristic of others. Mozart displayed from every point of view an exceptionally happy organisation. His copious and easily excited productive power was supported by a delicate sense of form, which was developed to such perfection by thorough and varied study that he employed the technicalities of musical form as if by a natural instinct. In addition to this he possessed the gift of so detaching his mind from what was going on around him that he could work out his ideas even to the minutest detail; his wonderful memory enabling him to retain in its completeness whatever he had thus inwardly elaborated, and to reproduce it at any moment in a tangible form.

The impulse which drives an artist to production is seldom consciously felt by himself and is never capable of definition. In most cases this signifies but little, for external impulse usually furnishes only the occasion for a work of art, and even when the impulse happens to be a visible one our attention is concentrated on the creation which it has called forth. 'This is especially true of music, which draws its immediate inspiration neither from nature nor from the world of thought. It would be of the highest interest to follow the process by means of which impressions made on the artist's mind produce well-defined musical ideas. This, however, is impossible; the idea and its musical development are simultaneous efforts of the mind; the work of art thus called into being cannot be immediately referred to any impulse from without.

Nor is it by any means essential that it should. It is of far greater psychological interest to consider those characteristics of the artist which give a clearer insight into his disposition and ways of feeling, although it may not be possible to trace them in the details of his works. Thus we are told that the sight of beautiful nature stirred Mozart's productive powers to activity. Rochlitz writes on Constanze's authority:[12]—

When he was travelling with his wife through beautiful scenery, he used to gaze earnestly and in silence on the scene before him; his usually absent and thoughtful expression would brighten by degrees, and he would begin to sing, or rather to hum, finally breaking out with: "If I could only put the subject down on paper!" And, when I sometimes said that he could do so if he pleased, he went on : "Yes, of course, all in proper form! What a pity it is that one's work must all be hatched in one's own room!"

He always endeavoured to pass the summer in the country or where there was a garden; it is well known that it was chiefly in a garden that he wrote "Don Juan" in Prague and the "Zauberflöte" in Vienna; and in 1758, having taken a country residence for the summer, he wrote to Puchberg (June 27): "I have done more in the ten days that I have been here than I should have done in two months anywhere else." This love of nature is not surprising in a man of Mozart's healthy tone of mind, who had been brought up amid the beautiful surroundings of Salzburg. But he was by no means wedded to these, or to any other influences from without. Wherever he was he was incessantly occupied with musical thoughts and labours. "You know," he writes to his father (Vol. II., p. 43), "that I am, so to speak, steeped in music—that it is in my mind the whole day, and that I love to dream, to study, to reflect upon it." Those who knew him well could not fail to be aware of this. His sister-in-law Sophie describes him well:[13]—

He was always good-humoured, but thoughtful even in his best moods, looking one straight in the face, and always speaking with reflection, whether the talk was grave or gay; and yet he seemed always to be carrying on a deeper train of thought. Even when he was washing his

---

[12] A. M. Z., I., p. 147.   [13] Nissen, p. 627.

hands in the morning, he never stood still, but walked up and down the room humming, and buried in thought. At table he would often twist up a corner of the table-cloth, and rub his upper lip with it, without appearing in the least to know what he was doing, and he sometimes made extraordinary grimaces with his mouth. His hands and feet were in continual motion, and he was always strumming on something—his hat, his watch-fob, the table, the chairs, as if they were the clavier.

Karajan tells me that his barber used to relate in after-years how difficult it was to dress his hair, since he never would sit still; every moment an idea would occur to him, and he would run to the clavier, the barber after him, hair-ribbon in hand. We have already observed that musical ideas occupied him during all bodily exercises, such as riding, bowls, and billiard-playing; his timidity in riding may have arisen from the frequent distraction of his attention from the management of his horse. General conversation, as Frau Haibl says, did not disturb his mental labours, and his brother-in-law Lange was particularly struck by the fact that when he was engaged on his most important works he took more than his usual share in any light or jesting talk that was going on; this resulted from an involuntary impulse to find a counterpoise for his intellectual activity. Even when music was going on, provided it did not particularly interest him, he had the power of carrying on his own musical thoughts, and of ignoring the music he heard, as completely as any other disturbance. His elder sister-in-law, Frau Hofer, told Neukomm that sometimes at the opera Mozart's friends could tell by the restless movements of his hands, by his look, and the way in which he moved his lips, as if singing or whistling, that he was entirely engrossed by his internal musical activity.

The abstraction and absorption of men of genius appears natural and comprehensible, and is respected even by those whose intellectual activity is not concentrated in the same way. But few are able to enter into the workings of a mind which is ever conceiving and shaping ideas in its hidden recesses, without severing its connection with what is going on around; such a mind has a sort of double existence, and appears able to follow two paths leading in different directions at the same time. If, as sometimes happens, the outer activity fails to keep pace with the inner, a superficial observer possesses himself of this fact, and makes it the basis of his judgments, leaving out of account the inner and true activity of which the outer is but a manifestation. Even Mozart's father failed to comprehend his peculiar organisation, and refused to recognise any results of his labour but those which were written down, and which had thus, after a long and uninterrupted chain of intellectual exertions, received the seal of their artistic completion. To Mozart himself, on the contrary, this part of his labour seemed unimportant and even burdensome, his productive powers having little share in it. He postponed it as long as possible, not only because he wished to retain his power over the work which occupied him, until it was fully matured in his own mind, but also because he took far more pleasure in creating than in transcribing. It cannot be denied that he sometimes postponed this least congenial part of his task too long. To the methodical man of business this appears all the more blamable, since Mozart was always able at need to execute commissions accurately and punctually ; to speak of idleness, or of forced industry, shows complete ignorance of the man. It is true that Mozart laid himself open to the imputation by the speed at which he wrote when he actually set to work; those who observed this could not conceive why a man with such "gifts of Providence" did not "compose," as people say, from morning to night. His wife said truly:[14] "The greater industry of his later years was merely apparent, because he wrote down more. He was always working in his head, his mind was in constant motion, and one may say that he never ceased composing." Although his wife was constantly called on by his admirers to urge him to work, she considered it her duty far oftener to restrain and moderate his activity.

The wonderful harmony of different artistic qualities in Mozart, which Rossini expressed so finely by saying that Mozart was the only musician who had as much genius as

---

[14] Nissen, p. 694.

knowledge and as much knowledge as genius, may be traced in many particulars. The more subordinate power of grasping the idea of a strange composition at a glance, and of executing it on the spot, he possessed as a matter of course. His playing at sight has already been noted many times (Vol. I., pp. 37, 109, 363, 365), and his criticism of Sterkel and Vogler show his own view of the matter (Vol. I., p. 387). " It must be," Umlauf said, as Mozart writes to his father (October 6, 1782), " that Mozart has the devil in his head and his fingers—he played my opera, which is so badly written that even I cannot read it, as if he had composed it himself." To this power of seeing at a glance the details and whole conception of a musical work was added a marvellous memory, capable of retaining all that was so seen. As a boy he gave proof of this by his transcription of the Miserere (Vol. I., p. 119); in later years he used to play his concertos by heart when he was travelling; not merely one or another that he had practised, but any or all; he was known to play a concerto from memory that he had not seen for long, because he had forgotten to bring the principal part.[15]   At Prague he wrote the trumpet and drum parts of the second finale in " Don Juan " without a score, brought them himself into the orchestra, and showed the performers a place where there would certainly be a mistake, only he could not say whether there would be four bars too much or too little; the mistake was found just as he had said.[16]   But this proves only the power of remembering what was finished and impressed on the mind. A more remarkable instance of musical memory was his writing only the violin part of a sonata for piano and violin to perform with Strinasacchi (Vol. II., p. 337), and playing the piano part from his head without ever having heard the piece; or writing a composition at once in parts, without having scored it (Vol. II., p. 366). This displays the astonishing clearness and precision with which he grasped and retained compositions he

---

[15] Niemetschek, p. 85. Rochlitz, A. M. Z., I., p. 113. Für Freunde der Tonkunst, II., p. 287.
[16] Nissen, p. 560.

had once thought out, even in their minutest details, and we can now account for the rapidity of his transcription from the fact of its being mere transcription. External distractions, so far from annoying him, served to divert his mind during the mechanical labour with his pen.[17] He made Constanze tell him stories, or played bowls; his wife tells us herself how she was confined of her first child while he was composing the second of his quartets, dedicated to Haydn (421 K.). This was in the summer of 1783, and he sat at work in the same room where she lay; indeed, he generally worked in her room during her frequent illnesses. When she complained of pain, he would come to her to cheer and console, resuming his writing as soon as she was calm. This is a striking proof how unshackled Mozart's musical activity was by external circumstances; it is not given to many to remain so completely master of their ideas and powers during an event which would naturally appeal to the tenderest feelings of the heart. Still more striking is his expression to his sister when he sends her the prelude and fugue before mentioned (Vol. II., p. 321). He apologises for the prelude being placed improperly after the fugue: "The reason was," he says, "that I had already composed the fugue, and wrote it down while I was thinking out the prelude."

Such mental powers as these reduced the mere writing to an almost mechanical operation; nevertheless, he did not rely so completely as he might have done on his memory, but made occasional notes for his better convenience and certainty. Rochlitz tells us, no doubt on Constanze's authority:[18]—

Mozart, when in company with his wife or those who put no restraint on him, and especially during his frequent carriage journeys, used not only to exercise his fancy by the invention of new melodies, but occupied his intellect and feeling in arranging and elaborating such melodies, often humming or singing aloud, growing red in the face and suffering no interruption. The briefest indications in black and white sufficed to preserve these studies in his memory; his easily kindled imagination, his complete mastery of the resources of his art, and his extraordinary

---

[17] Niemetschek, p. 82.
[18] Rochlitz, A. M. Z., XXII., p. 298. Für Freunde der Tonkunst, III., p. 283.

musical memory needed little aid; he used to keep scraps of music paper at hand (when travelling, in the side-pocket of the carriage) for such fragmentary notes and reminders;[19] these scraps, carefully preserved in a case, were a sort of journal of his travels to him, and the whole proceeding had a sort of sacredness to his mind which made him very averse to any interference with it.

These notes, having served their purpose,·seem to have been thought unworthy of preservation ; the few that remain are interesting and suggestive. The sketch which is given in facsimile of Denis's ode (Vol. II., p. 370) gives an outline of the whole work in writing so hasty as scarcely to be recognised for Mozart's. The voice part is written entire as well as the bass of the accompaniment, and the other parts have all their characteristics so clearly noted that there could be no doubt as to their further elaboration. It is evident that the composition was finished in Mozart's brain when the sketch was written, so that it does not appear as one attempt among several to give shape to his conception, but as an aid to the memory when it should be necessary to write down the whole in detail. Similar, but still slighter, is the sketch for one of the songs in "L' Oca del Cairo," which is given in fac-simile in Jul. André's edition in pianoforte score. Here again the voice part is given from beginning to end, but the bass is not shown, and the accompaniment only here and there (once with the direction that the clarinets are to be used). The piece was simple enough to require very slight reminders for its elaboration. It would not be easy to decide whether such a sketch should be considered as the result of much previous reflection and study, or whether it was the immediate fruit of a moment of inspiration. These two sketches never having been elaborated, so far as we are aware, we can make no comparison which will show how far such sketches were modified before the completion of the work. There is considerable difference between the first hasty sketch of the terzet (5) from the "Sposo Deluso" (430 K.), which Jul. André has given in the

---

[19] An old leather case which was used for the purpose was jokingly called by him his portfolio, for the preservation of his valuable documents.

preface to his pianoforte edition, and the later elaboration of it. Nothing remains but the first motif—

but so differently applied that this sketch cannot have been taken as the point of departure for the working-out, but must be considered as an earlier and rejected conception. On the other hand, the sketches for a song from "Idomeneo" (Vol. II., p. 148) and for a tenor song (420 K.) are almost identical in the voice part with the score as it stands.

Peculiar interest attaches to Sketch I., given in facsimile. The three first lines are noted for a clavier composition; then follows the sketch of a terzet (434 K.) for two bass voices and a tenor, from an opera buffa, on which Mozart was apparently at work in 1783. A fair copy of the work is partially preserved, and gives an idea of the way in which Mozart arranged his scores. The sketch contains only the voice parts, with slight hints for the accompaniment, showing how in one place the first idea was rejected and then again resumed. It is evident from the way in which the space is employed that the notes were made very hastily.

The score, on the contrary, is a fair copy of the work accidentally left unfinished. It has the proper number of parts for the voices and orchestra, with the corresponding title before each. The ritornello is first given, which is long, because it serves as an introduction to the first scene of the opera. It is formed of motifs which recur later, and it is plain that this independent introduction was written after the completion of the terzet, in which the motifs have each their special signification. The principal parts (first violin and bass), are written in full, but only those parts of the wind instruments in which they have independent motifs; all that was intended to give colouring and shading to this simple outline is omitted. The voice parts are all inserted in proper order, and the bass is given in full; but there are few hints for the accompaniment. It is all written firmly and neatly, showing plainly enough that it was finished. The deviations from the sketch are unimportant in the bass voice, more striking in the tenor, where the primary design of the melody remains, but the elaboration is modified and the conclusion lengthened. Where the voices are together nothing has been altered, so far as we can discover. The first sketch breaks off a few bars sooner than the score, which itself is a comparatively small fragment of the whole terzet.

It is evident, therefore, that the true artistic work was done before the first sketch was made, and that the elaboration of the latter into the score was no mere mechanical adoption of the motif (which seems to have been rejected upon critical revision and, so to speak, born again), but the final reduction to form of what was already complete in conception. This is still more the case in the elaboration of the accompaniment in detail; the well-defined outline which is given keeps it within certain limits without imposing on it any hampering restraint.

Further instances may be found in those works of which the plans of the scores, generally unelaborated, are preserved. Particularly instructive are the unelaborated movements of the Mass in C minor (427 K.) and of the "Requiem" (626 K.) in André's edition; also the pianoforte score of the duet (384 K.) from the "Entführung" and the unfinished opera "L' Oca del Cairo," edited by Jul. André, are examples of similar sketches. They possess peculiar interest to students, since they show those points which Mozart considered as containing the germ of the whole conception. The different stages of the elaboration can be traced in most of Mozart's autograph scores. The voices and bass are invariably written first, and enough of the accompaniment to show its characteristic points; this fact can be recognised, even in scores afterwards fully elaborated, by the differences in ink and handwriting, which is generally more hasty in the elaboration than in the earlier sketch. When once this was made, the elaboration was often long deferred; the whole of the first act of "L' Oca del Cairo" was thus projected, and, the design of the opera being abandoned, was never elaborated; so, too, all the movements of the "Requiem," from the Dies iræ to the Quam olim were written entire for the voices with a figured bass, while the

instrumentation was only suggested.   He waited for time
and inclination to continue the work thus begun, and needed
more urging to it than to any other, for once having fixed the
outline of his design, it required a mere mechanical effort to
reproduce it in his mind with details of form and colour.   A
striking example is that mentioned on p. 360 (Vol. II.), where,
by the figuring of the bass, he supplied an aid to his memory
of a peculiar harmonic succession which perhaps flashed across
him at the moment of transcription in his compositions.

Important alterations were seldom made by Mozart, unless
at the instance of the singer or the instrumentalist.   He sent
his father the score of the "Entführung" with the remark
that there were many erasures, because the score had to be
copied at once, and he had therefore given free play to his
ideas, and then altered and curtailed them before giving
the score to be written; it is evident from this that the
alterations were almost all made with reference to external
circumstances.   The improvements made as the work proceeded were usually only trifling, such as modifications in
pianoforte passages, or unimportant turns of expression in
vocal parts.   Thus, for instance, the close of the Count's
song in " Figaro " was originally simpler—

Fà   e   giu - bi - lar,   e   giu - bi - lar,

whereas later four bars of flourish were inserted instead of the
second bar.   It is still more striking that in the last finale,
where Figaro makes a feigned declaration of love to Susanna
in disguise, it originally ran thus—

Un   ri - sto - ro al mio cor   con - ce · de - te

which Mozart, not considering sufficiently expressive of the
affected pathos of the situation afterwards altered to the
exaggerated :—

Un   ri - sto - ro al mio cor   con - ce · de · te

In the duet for the two girls in "Così fan Tutte" (4),
Dorabella's part had the bars—

Se fiamma, se dar - da, non sem - bra scoc - car,

which were altered to—

Se fiamma, se dar - da, non sem - bra scoc - car.

The decided heroic style of the first version, which would
be fitting enough for Fiordiligi, is thus toned down, and an
expression of greater elegance given to the passage.

It is worth remarking that the characteristic motif of
Donna Anna's song in "Don Giovanni"—

Or sai chi l'o-no-re ra - pi-re a me vol-se, chi fu il tra - di - to - re,

was originally—

Or sai chi l'o-no-re ra - pi-re a me vol-se, chi fu il tra - di - to - re,

and every one must feel how greatly it has gained by the
alteration. In every case Mozart's self-criticism has been
founded on true feeling and discrimination, even when it has
not been called for on definite technical grounds. In the
Countess's song in "Figaro" (19) the first division of the
allegro, from bar eight, concluded originally thus :—

giar l'in - gra - to cor . . l'in - gra - - - - - to cor.

The phrase as it is now known was written underneath and
the bass scratched out. In the further course of the allegro
the three bars—

Ah! se al - men la mia co - stan - za

were originally simply repeated after the interlude, and then went on :—

Nel lan - gui - re a-man-do og - nor mi por - tas - se.

Mozart appears to have felt when he surveyed the whole song that such an untroubled expression of a fresh joyous impulse was not altogether appropriate to the character of the Countess, and he therefore inserted seven bars on the repetition of the motif, which give the passage an altogether different colour :—

Ah! se al-men la mia co - stan - za nel lan - guir a - -
- man - - - do og-nor . . mi por - tas - se u - na . . spe -
- ran - za di can - giar l' in - gra - to cor, mi por - tas - se.

The strongly accented change to C minor expresses such a depth of sorrow and yearning pathos that the lively tone of the allegro seems to be covered with a veil, and the whole emphasis of the song falls upon this place. Certainly, none would have suspected this passage of being an interpolation. The concluding bars of the Andante of the C major symphony (551 K.) originally ran thus :—

How beautifully this passage is replaced by the eleven closing bars, which now lead back to the chief theme, and give emphasis and dignity to the close! In the terzet from "Tito" (14) the andantino originally closed with a simple passage for the strings :—

This is now replaced by a passage divided among all the instruments—

which, with its agitated motion, is more sharply character-istic of the situation. All these are examples, not of improve-ments to a finished work, but of a free act of production giving a new disposition to the passages in their relation to the whole work. But Mozart sometimes hesitated at the moment of decision, and made repeated experiments before he was satisfied, as in the case of the conclusion of Su-sanna's charming song in "Figaro," which seems to belong so naturally to its position that one cannot imagine it other than it is ; yet the sketches and alterations of the original show that many earlier experiments were made.   Worthy of note also are the two bars in the overture to the "Zauberflöte" (p. 10, André), in which the clarinet leads the repetition of the second subject—

and which Mozart, with just discrimination, has struck out of the finished work.

It is a curious fact that Mozart was sometimes uncertain as to his rhythm. The quartet in "Così fan Tutte" (21) was originally written :—

At the eighth bar Mozart saw that this was incorrect, and altered the first bars—

and continued it so. There is an exactly similar case in the duet in the "Zauberflöte" (8) which Mozart wrote at first thus—

Bei Män - nern, wel - che   Lie - be,

and did not find out his mistake until quite the end, when
he carefully scratched out all the bar lines and put in the
correct ones :—

Bei Män - nern   wel - che   Lie - be.

Again, in Sesto's air in " Tito " (19), the adagio originally
began—

Deh per   que - sto i-stan - te   so - lo,

but the bar lines were afterwards erased and fresh ones
supplied in red chalk, making the first bar full. Another
very singular mistake in the duet in the " Zauberflöte " consists in the omission in the second and third bars of the two
chords for clarinets and horns, which Mozart has evidently
merely forgotten to transcribe. Now and then, but very
rarely, important alterations are made in the instrumentation of his works. One instance occurs in the introduction
to the "Zauberflöte," at the beginning of which the trumpets
and drums were in C, and were so carried on to the entrance
of the three ladies; then Mozart seems to have thought that
trumpets and drums could be used with effect as accompaniment, and he has struck through all that he had previously
written, and noted the trumpets and drums upon a loose
sheet in E flat; he has then continued them for seven bars
as an accompaniment to the opening trio. At the beginning
of Leporello's great songs in " Don Giovanni " (1, 4) trumpets
and drums were indicated, but they were afterwards struck
out when it came to be performed. In a long comic air,
which was intended for " Così fan Tutte " (584 K.), he has
struck out the horn part, after writing the whole of it. In
Dorabella's air (28) the fundamental bass of those parts
where only wind instruments are now employed was intrusted to the double-bass; Mozart afterwards struck this
out, and expressly noted "senza basso." In the second finale

of the "Zauberflöte" the *piano* chords which follow Pamina's
words, "Ich muss ihn sehen" were first given by the strings,
but flutes and clarinets were afterwards substituted.   In the
G minor symphony he at first intended to have four horns, but
after a few bars he struck them out, and limited himself to two.
In the terzet in the " Zauberflöte " (20), the first bar of the
accompaniment was given to the violins, thus—

which was afterwards erased, and a single crotchet used on
the unaccented part of the bar, with great gain to the effect.
But these are solitary instances. The individual tone-
colouring of the instruments is an essential element of
musical construction, which cannot be added afterwards,
but is contemporaneous with the conception, and has its
own share in the working-out of the musical idea.   When,
therefore, the composer develops his work in his own mind,
he hears not only certain abstract sounds, but definite individual tones embodied in the voices and instruments; the
whole image glows with vivid colouring in his mind, and
only needs to receive its outward form.   Besides, it must be
remembered that Mozart himself created the orchestra as it
was employed with increasing effect from " Idomeneo " onwards; the full use of wind instruments, their combination
with each other and with the strings; the consequent radical
change of colouring in the instrumentation as a whole, and the
wealth of charming detail in the blending of the tone-colours,
are all due to Mozart.[20]   He had never heard the effects he
strove to produce; they existed in the orchestra, it is true, as
the statue exists in the marble; but just as the sculptor must
have seen with his spiritual eye what he strives to reproduce
in the stone, so Mozart can have heard only with his spiritual
ear the sounds which he drew from his orchestra.[21]

---

[20] Cf. Niemetschek, p. 73.

[21] When Stadler once complained to him of an awkward passage, and wished
it altered, Mozart said : " Have you the notes in your instrument ? " "Yes,"
said he. " Then," answered Mozart, " it is your business to bring them out."
Neukomm told me this anecdote.

The alterations which have been mentioned are not to be considered as selected from among many similar instances, they are the only ones of any consequence with which my researches have acquainted me. In forming our idea of Mozart's method of writing his score, we may remark further, that he did not content himself with such hasty outlines beforehand as might suggest the course of the whole by a few touches, but sketched out fully those parts where he thought well to give particular attention to the details. Canons, fugues, passages in counterpoint, with a complicated disposition of parts or some other difficulty, were worked out upon scraps of music paper or sheets which had been previously used but not quite filled, and then transferred to the score. An accurate sketch for the first finale in " Don Giovanni," for instance, where the three dance melodies occur together in different measures, was shown to me by Al. Fuchs, who had procured one such sketch from each of Mozart's great operas. There was another also of the three-part canon in the second finale of " Così fan Tutte," in which only the canon, not the voice part belonging to it, was noted. There exists also, in addition to the rough draft of the score of " L' Oca del Cairo," sketches of those parts of the quartet (6) and finale (7) which demand particular attention on account of the contrapuntal disposition of the parts. Unfortunately but few of these sketches have been preserved, but those few show Mozart's method very clearly, and leave no doubt that they were made in order that his conception might be fully developed and arranged in his own mind before its final reduction to writing. They testify, too, of the thoughtfulness and deliberation with which he worked, of the severe demands which he made upon himself, and the conscientiousness which prevented his trusting to the lucky inspiration of the moment or to his own well-tried readiness of resource. Our idea of Mozart as an artist is no longer that which has been so commonly received and admired, and which shows us a spendthrift of his artistic powers, who was only driven by dire necessity to collect the fruits which his genius cast unbidden into his lap. The prerogative of genius is not a dispensation from labour and painful exertion, but the power of attaining the highest aims of such labour, and of obliterating every trace of effort in the perfection of the work.

The external characteristics of Mozart's scores show also great care for order and clearness. His handwriting was small, but though often rapid, and sometimes hasty, always clear, decided, and individual.[22] The smaller details, in which copyist's errors might easily creep in, are specially cared for; all the instructions for delivery are carefully given in each part. In short, Mozart's scores leave an impression, not of pedantry, which magnifies what is unimportant and loses time in an exaggerated regard for method and uniformity, but of a well-considered order and careful arrangement of details in their due relation to the whole work.

Admirably illustrative of Mozart's method, as we have endeavoured to portray it, are the numerous unfinished compositions of which frequent mention has been made; many of these were found after his death,[23] and some are preserved in the Mozarteum at Salzburg. Among these rough draughts of scores are several beginnings of masses belonging to his Salzburg days, as also some songs and many unfinished instrumental compositions, but by far the greater part were written in Vienna. Among them we may note :—

> 6 fragments of string quintets.
> 2 quintets for clarinet and strings.
> 1 quartet for English horn and strings.
> 9 drafts of violin quartets.
> 9 drafts of pianoforte concertos.
> 1 pianoforte quartet.
> 2 drafts of pianoforte trios.
> 1 sonata for pianoforte and violoncello.
> 2 sonatas for pianoforte and violin.
> 4 movements for two pianofortes.
> 9 movements for the pianoforte.

These are none of them roughly sketched drafts, but fair copies of unfinished scores, the completion of which was prevented by outward circumstances. Again we meet with

---

[22] The facsimile of the "Veilchen" affords an instance of Mozart's handwriting during the time of the Vienna visit.

[23] The list compiled by Abbé Stadler (Rechtf. der Echth. d. Req., p. 9) is given by Nissen (Anh., p. 18), and carefully revised by Köchel (Anh., 12-109).

confirmation of the fact that Mozart never began to write until his composition was in all essential points completed in his own mind. When only a few bars are written they offer a perfected melody, a motif only requiring its further development. When the sketches are longer they form a well-rounded, continuous whole, that is evidently interrupted, not because the continuation is not ready to hand, but because some chance has prevented its further transcription. It may be plainly discerned also that not only are detached ideas put into shape, but the different characteristic traits of execution are indicated in the usual way, so that the chief effects and capabilities of the motifs may be clearly inferred.

It appears as if Mozart, when once interrupted in the transcription of a composition, was very loth to return to it again. That he might have done so cannot for a moment be doubted. His memory was infallible; but his interest was concentrated on the work with which he was concerned at the moment. He was easily impelled to write what he had already completed in his head, and this led him naturally to the next piece of work; to return to what he considered as over and done with was contrary to his nature and habit. There is no reason whatever to suppose that any of these sketches, preliminary notes, or unfinished compositions were ever subsequently made use of. This not only testifies of the wealth and ease of his productivity, which scorned to borrow even from himself, but it proves that his creations proceeded immediately from spontaneous impulses, each having independent birth, and owing its development to the singular fecundity of his artistic nature. The individual truth and fresh life of Mozart's works are founded in this natural spring of ever-welling spontaneity. Their artistic perfection rests on the skill with which the conception is developed; but in what consists the peculiar charm and beauty which is acknowledged and enjoyed by us all as inseparable from Mozart's music is, and will ever remain, an unsolved mystery.

However carefully Mozart, as a rule, prepared his compositions before writing them, we, who are acquainted with his nature and education, can scarcely doubt that he was

able on occasion to compose as he wrote. Such a song as
that which he wrote in the tavern for Frau von Keess
cannot well have been ready in his head. When he was in
Prague at the beginning of 1787 he promised Count Joh.
Pachta to write a country dance for a public ball, but failed
to produce it. At last the Count invited him to dinner an
hour earlier than his usual time, and when Mozart appeared
placed all the requisite materials before him, and entreated
him to compose the dance on the spot, seeing that it was
required for the following day. Mozart set to work, and
before dinner had composed nine country dances, scored for
full orchestra (510 K), which he certainly had not prepared
beforehand.[24] These and similar instances refer to easy pieces
in free form ; but we have already seen (Vol. II., p. 366), that
he could improvise canons and double canons of an unusual
kind ; and what further proof can be required than reference
to his marvellous gift of executive improvisation ?

In composing Mozart never had recourse to improvisation.
" He never came to the clavier when he was writing," says
Niemetschek (p. 82) ; " his imagination pictured the whole
work when he had once conceived it." His wife also says
naïvely, but graphically : " He never composed at the
clavier, but wrote music like letters, and never tried a movement until it was finished."[25] When his compositions were
completed he used to rehearse them, singing or playing,
with his wife or any one else who happened to come in.
Kelly narrates that Mozart greeted him one evening with,
" I have just written a little duet for ' Figaro.' You shall
hear it." He sat down at the pianoforte, and they sang it
together ; it was the duet (16) " Crudel perchè finora " ; and
Kelly often remembered with keen delight how he had first
heard and sung this charming composition.[26]

---

[24] Nissen, p. 561. Bohemia, 1856, No. 22, p. 118. There are four quadrilles,
each with a country dance ; some of them are specially named, " La Favorite,"
" La Fenice," " La Piramide." In one of them a theme is delivered by the piccolo
and big drum, which Weber has employed as an Austrian grenadier march in
" Kampf und Sieg " (Schr., III., p. 97). He had probably heard it in Prague.
[25] A. M. Z., I., p. 855 ; Nissen, p. 473.
[26] Kelly, Reminisc., I., p. 258.

In one sense, it is true, Mozart felt the necessity for an external vent to his musical ideas; and for this he had frequent recourse to his own special instrument, the clavier or pianoforte. "Even in his later years," says Niemetschek (p. 83), "he often spent half the night at the piano;[27] these were the hours that witnessed the birth of his divinest melodies. In the silent calm of night, when there was nothing to distract the mind, his imagination was kindled into supernatural activity, and revealed the wealth of melodious sound which lay dormant in his nature. At such times Mozart was all emotion and music, and unearthly harmonies flowed from his fingers! Only those who heard him then could know the depth and extent of his musical genius; his spirit, freed from every impediment, spread its bold pinions, and soared into the regions of art." It could scarcely fail to be the case that in such hours as these the subject of his improvisation should often be the work of which his mind was full at the time; but it would be a mistake to consider the improvisation as an express preparation for a subsequent work, or as the actual source from which it sprang. The improvisation was the embodiment of the mood of the moment, its form and extent were limited by the conditions of the instrument on which it was played, and it could by no means serve as an immediate foundation to a work to be performed under entirely different conditions and with a definite object.

Mozart carefully separated his time for writing and his time for improvising. To the end of his life he kept to his early habit of writing in the morning (Vol. II., p. 208), and even when he had been out the evening before, or had played far into the night, he was accustomed to begin work at six or seven o'clock; in later days, however, he indulged himself by writing in bed. After ten he usually gave lessons, and never returned to the writing-table unless there were urgent occasion. Such occasion arose often enough, it is

---

[27] "From his childhood," says the article in Schlichtegroll's Nekrolog, "he preferred playing at night; he seated himself at the clavier at nine o'clock in the evening, and would remain at it until midnight, having to be forced away even then; otherwise he would have played through the whole night."

true. When he was composing " Figaro," his father tells
Marianne (November 11, 1785) how he postponed all his
pupils until the afternoon, so as to have the whole morning
free for writing, and we have already seen that he sometimes
wrote in the evening, and even at night. Mozart's marvellous improvisations were not confined to hours of solitude
and calm, nor to the satisfaction of his inner cravings; he
showed himself equally master of the art when the impulse
came from without, as was frequently the case, for people
loved to hear him improvise. There is a peculiar charm in
this accomplishment which, while it at once identifies the
artist with his creation, requires the highest concentration
of artistic energy to satisfy the varied conditions on which
the production of a work of art depends. The improvising
musician and his audience act and react upon each other;
the latter receive the direct impression of the artist's individuality and power, and feel themselves, as it were, let into
the secret of his method of producing the works which
delight them, while the former is inspired to fresh efforts of
genius by his consciousness of possessing the sympathy of
his hearers. Mozart was always ready to play when he
thought he should give pleasure, but he improvised in his
best vein only " when he spied out among the crowd surrounding him one or more of the privileged few who were
capable of following the flights of his genius; oblivious
of all others, he addressed the elect in the hieroglyphics of
his art, and poured forth for them alone his richest streams
of melody."[28] We have much contemporary testimony as to
the impression made by Mozart's improvising. Ambros
Rieder, who died in 1851 at eighty years of age in Percht-
tolsdorf—an enthusiastic musician and a worthy man—
writes in his " Recollections ":[29]—

---

[28] So a contemporary asserts (Wien. Allg. Mus. Ztg., 1818, No. 3, p. 62).
Rochlitz speaks of Mozart's humour as one of his special characteristics
(A. M. Z., III., p. 590): "I have heard most of the distinguished performers
on this instrument since Mozart, except Beethoven; the playing of many of
them was admirable, but the inexhaustible *wit* of Mozart was never approached
by any."

[29] N. Wien. Mus. Ztg., 1856, No. 25.

In my youth I had opportunities of hearing and admiring many distinguished virtuosi, both on the violin and the harpsichord; but I cannot describe my amazement and delight in hearing the great and immortal W. A. Mozart play variations and improvise on the pianoforte before a numerous and aristocratic audience. It was to me like the gift of new senses of sight and hearing. The bold flights of his imagination into the highest regions, and again down to the very depths of the abyss, caused the greatest masters of music to be lost in amazement and delight. I still, in my old age, seem to hear the echo of these heavenly harmonies, and I go to my grave with the full conviction that there can never be another Mozart.[30]

And Niemetschek, when an old man, said to Al. Fuchs: "If I dared to pray the Almighty to grant me one more earthly joy it would be that I might once again hear Mozart improvise; those who have not heard him can form no idea of his extraordinary performances."[81] Repeated mention has already been made of Mozart's readiness and skill in playing " out of his head," as he used to call it (Vol. I., pp. 385-386). He avoided the common error of improvising virtuosi in the introduction of long cadenzas, " making a hash in the cadenza of what had sounded well enough in the concerto," as Dittersdorf says (Selbstbiogr., p. 47). A new fashion came into vogue about this time; instead of a long cadenza, a simple theme was delivered, and then varied according to every rule of the art; but Mozart used also frequently to improvise a free fantasia in his concertos (Vol. II., p. 285). Rochlitz narrates[82] how at Leipzig the audience wished to hear him alone at the close of one of his concerts, and though he had already played two concertos and an obbligato scena, and accompanied for nearly two hours—

He sat down at once, and played to the delight of all. He began simply and seriously in C minor—but it is absurd to attempt to describe it. As he was playing with special reference to the connoisseurs who were present, he brought the flights of his fancy lower and lower, and closed with the published variations on "Je suis Lindor." (Vol. II., p. 174).

---

[80] Cf. Schink, Litt. Fragm., II., p. 288. An article on Beethoven says (A. M. Z., I., p. 525): " He shows to the utmost advantage in improvisation. Since Mozart's death, *who will always remain to my mind the non plus ultra in this respect*, I have never had so much enjoyment as from Beethoven."

[81] Deutsche Mus. Ztg., 1861, p. 322.

[82] A. M. Z., I., p. 113.

Stiepanek, writing of the concert which Mozart gave in Prague (February, 1787), says :—

At the close of the concert Mozart improvised on the pianoforte for a good half-hour, and raised the enthusiasm of the delighted Bohemians to its highest pitch, so that he was obliged to resume his place at the instrument in compliance with their storm of applause. His second stream of improvisation had a still more powerful effect, and the audience again tumultuously recalled him. Their enthusiasm seemed to inspire him, and he played as he had never played before, till all at once the deathlike silence of the listeners was broken by a voice from among them exclaiming, " Aus 'Figaro'!" whereupon Mozart dashed into the favourite air, " Non più andrai," and improvised a dozen of the most interesting and artistic variations upon it, ending his wonderful performance amid a deafening storm of applause.[33]

Niemetschek also speaks of this concert (p. 40) :—

A sweet enchantment seized upon us in listening to Mozart's improvisation on the pianoforte, which he continued for more than half an hour, and we gave vent to our delight in a perfect storm of applause. His playing surpassed anything that could be imagined, uniting all the qualities of first-rate composition and perfect ease of execution.

Such moments of inspiration as this gave his countenance an expression which betrayed the artist within him.[34] At other times, his appearance was in no way striking or distinguished. His head was somewhat too large in proportion to his body; his face was pale, though not unpleasing, but in no way uncommon, and the Mozart family nose asserted itself very plainly as long as he continued to be thin. His eyes were tolerably large and well shaped, with good eyelashes and bushy brows, but they were not bright, and his look was absent and restless. He had a great dislike to hearing his appearance commented on as insignificant (Vol. I., p. 381), and was seriously angry once when the Prussian ambassador gave him a letter of introduction, in which he said that he hoped Mozart's insignificant personal appearance would cause no prejudice against him.[35] " This absent creature," says the notice in Schlichtegroll's " Nekrolog," " became another being as soon as he sat down to the piano.

---

[33] Nissen, p. 517.
[34] Cf. Nissen, p. 622.   Niemetschek, p. 66,
[35] Nissen, p. 692.

His spirit seemed to soar upwards, and his whole mind was absorbed in what seemed the proper object of his being, the harmony of sound." "His whole countenance would change," says Niemetschek, "his eye became calm and collected; emotion spoke from every movement of his muscles, and was communicated by a sort of intuitive sympathy to his audience."

CHAPTER XXXIII.

MOZART'S PIANOFORTE MUSIC.

THERE can be no reason to doubt what has often been asserted and maintained with proof, that Mozart was the greatest pianoforte-player of his time. Although, however, the fame of a virtuoso among his contemporaries is more brilliant and universal than that of a composer, yet posterity can form but a vague idea of the performances which were so enchanting to the hearers. It is impossible to give an accurate or very intelligible account of Mozart's playing, but it will not be without interest to note such of its characteristic features as are still within our grasp.

"He had small, well-shaped hands," says Niemetschek (p. 66), "and moved them so gently and naturally over the keys, that the eyes of his hearers were charmed no less than their ears." Like most pianoforte-players, his hands used involuntarily to assume the position they would have had in playing. The notice in Schlichtegroll's "Nekrolog" even observes that constant practising had rendered his hands awkward in ordinary use, and that it was only with extreme difficulty that he could cut up his meat at table! "It was wonderful that he could do so much with them, particularly in left-hand stretches. A great deal of his perfection must be ascribed to the admirable fingering, which according to his own acknowledgment he owed to a diligent study of Bach's works."[1] Mozart certainly appears to have played Bach's clavier music from a very early age (in his

---

[1] Cf. A. M. Z., I., p. 157.

letters to Breitkopf the father frequently orders Bach's last compositions); and once at a party at Doles', when the conversation fell upon Bach's playing, Mozart declared: " He is the father; we are the lads. Those of us who can do anything owe it to him; and whoever does not admit that is a ———." [2]

Mozart's criticisms on the playing of Nanette Stein (Vol. I., p. 361) and Vogler (Vol. I., p. 387) prove the value he attached to good fingering as the foundation of firm and expressive execution. It is well known that Ph. Em. Bach's [3] practical development of his father's principles [4] laid the foundation of the present system of the art of fingering, and it is equally certain that Mozart, and with and after him Clementi, were the first to tread in the path so marked out. [5] He insisted mainly that the player should have a " quiet, steady hand," the natural ease, flexibility, and smooth rapidity of which should be so cultivated that the passages should "flow like oil" (Vol. I., p. 361); he did not counsel the practice of *tours de force* which might be prejudicial to these qualities. His first requirements were the delivery of "every note, turn, &c., correctly and decidedly, and with appropriate expression and taste" (Vol. I., p. 387). He cautions players against over-rapidity of execution, not only of passages where the harmony is strictly connected, but also of those where offences against strict time seem more allowable. He was strongly opposed to violations of time. [6] He believed (Vol. I.,

---

[2] So Rochlitz says (Für Freunde der Tonk., IV., p. 309), and the expression sounds very like Mozart. But when he speaks of a visit paid by Mozart to Bach in Hamburg, shortly before he went to Leipzig (1789), he forgets that Bach died in 1788, and Mozart was never in Hamburg.

[3] His " Versuch über die wahre Art das Klavier zu spielen " appeared first in the year 1752; his numerous and widely known pianoforte compositions aim principally at the enforcing of practical principles.

[4] An account of J. S. Bach's scientific method is given by Forkel (Ueb. J. S. Bach, p. 11); a notice of the system of fingering formerly in use will be found in Becker (Hausmusik in Deutschland, p. 58).

[5] A. E. Müller, in his " Anweisung zum genauen Vortrag der Mozartschen Klavierkonzerte " (Leipzig, 1796), has applied the principles of Bach's fingering to the more difficult passages of five concertos of Mozart.

[6] "Nothing made Mozart so angry as the maltreatment of his operas in public performances, principally by exaggerating the rate of the tempos," says Rochlitz (A. M. Z., I., p. 84).

p. 361) that Nanette Stein would never acquire the power of playing in time, because she had not been accustomed to it from childhood. His own playing always excited admiration from his accurate time, never giving way to a *tempo rubato* in the left hand, while at the same time playing with perfect expression and deep feeling—and without making grimaces, to which he had a great aversion (Vol. I., p. 361).

He placed correctness first in the list of qualities essential to first-rate playing, and included among them ease and certainty in the execution of unusual technical difficulties, delicacy and good taste in delivery, and, above all, that power of breathing life and emotion into the music and of so expressing its meaning as to place the performer for the moment on a level with the creator of the work before him. We must be content to accept the enthusiastic testimony of the public, of connoisseurs, and of accomplished fellow-artists,[7] who all agreed that Mozart indisputably ranked highest among virtuosi, by virtue of his fulfilment of all these conditions.[8] When we find Clementi declaring that he never heard any one play so intellectually and gracefully as Mozart, Dittersdorf finding art and fine taste united in his playing, and Haydn asserting with tears in his eyes that he could never forget Mozart's playing, because it came "from the heart" (Vol. II., p. 350), the simple expressions of such men are more eloquent than the most emphatic hyperbole.

The union in Mozart of the virtuoso and the composer caused his performances as a virtuoso to be more directly influenced by his compositions than was usually the case. His pianoforte compositions have left us only an imperfect image of these combined accomplishments, partly because

---

[7] "It was his greatest and oft-lamented grievance," says Rochlitz (A. M. Z., I., p. 49), "that he was generally expected to perform mechanical juggling tricks and tight-rope antics on the instrument, which it amused people to *see*." (Cf. I., p. 387).

[8] "Mozart is the most finished and best pianoforte-player that I have ever heard," writes a correspondent from Vienna in 1787 (Cramer, Mag. f. Mus., II., p. 1273). "Never shall I forget the divine pleasure afforded me," says Rochlitz (A. M. Z., I., p. 113), "partly by the spirituality of his compositions, partly by the brilliancy, as well as the heart-melting tenderness of his execution."

the living breath of genius cannot be reproduced, partly because the greater number of these works were written under the influence of external cirumstances, which denied free scope both to the composer and the performer.[9]

Variations upon a well-known theme were at that time a favourite form of improvisation, so much so that varying and improvising were terms often used synonymously.[10] It is easy to understand the interest which even a less educated public took in this form. A simple theme, either familiar or of a kind to be easily understood, gives the hearers something to be laid hold of, and it amuses them to recognise and follow the air in its manifold disguises. The regular development and elaboration of a motif, obliging constant attention from the hearers in order to trace the connection of its different parts, was not expected in these fashionable variations. What was looked for was such a prominence given to some characteristic elements of the subject (whether in the harmonic succession, in the rhythm or the melody) as should serve constantly to suggest it to the mind, while affording a basis for a free play of musical fancy. Such variations on a given subject may be in some measure compared with arabesque and similar ornamentations in architecture, which display complex and fantastic varieties of animal and vegetable forms, but behind their apparent irregularities maintain a constant reference to the constructive design.

Mozart never cultivated any other than this easy style of variation ; and we find a contemporary critic expressing the wish that he would write, "not only these florid variations, but others in the style of the two Bachs, with scientific inversions and imitations, and in counterpoint."[11] But amateurs were fond of the easier form, and he found frequent occasion to write variations for his pupils or other friends. He did not care about them himself, and took no pains to have them published. But finding favour with

[9] Frz. Lorenz, W. A. Mozart als Clavier-Componist (Breslau, 1866); a fine description, rich in characteristic traits.

[10] Cf. Vol. I., pp. 177, 200, 285.

[11] Mus. Real-Ztg., 1788, p. 49.

the public, they were eagerly sought after and published,[12] often with many inaccuracies; nor were all genuine that appeared under the name of Mozart.[18] The following variations belong to the Vienna period, and probably to the year 1784 :—

1. " Unser dummer Pöbel," from Gluck's " Pilgrims of Mecca " (Vol. II., p. 285, 455 K.)

2. " Come un agnello," from Sarti's " Fra Due Litiganti " (Vol. II., p. 345, 460 K.).

In 1785 were composed :—

3. September 12 (500 K.)
4. Duet, November 4 (501 K.)

Then follow : —

5. " Upon a Minuet by Dupont," composed April 9, 1789 (573 K.)
6. " Ein Weib ist das herrlichste Ding," from the second part of the " Two Antonios," by Schikaneder, composed March 8, 1791 (613 K.)

The following were announced in 1785, but some of them certainly belong to an earlier date :[14]—

---

[12] In 1785 Torricella announced " Neueste Fantasie-Variationen von Mozart," as follows: " The eagerness with which the works of this famous master are everywhere looked for, and the certainty with which they command the esteem of the connoisseur by their art and elegance, and touch the hearts of all by their tender melodiousness, have induced me to publish these very beautiful variations for the benefit of the most fastidious lovers of music, to whom I offer a new work calculated to do honour to its author. I shall endeavour from time to time to place all the remaining variations of this admirable master in the hands of an appreciative public." Fräulein Aurnhammer supervised the publishing of several of Mozart's variations (Cramer, Magaz. d. Mus., II., p. 1274).

[18] The variations on a theme by Dittersdorf (287 Anh., K.) are by Eberl, according to his assertion in the Hamburg Correspondent (July 25, 1798, No. 118, Beil.), and his are also the variations so often printed under Mozart's name on the theme, " Zu Steffen sprach im Traume " (288 Anh., K.). The variations on a theme from Sarti's " I Finti Eredi " (289 Anh., K.) are by Förster. Mozart's widow, in letters to Härtel (May 25, June 15, 1799), appealed to well-informed friends to support her assertion that the variations " Une fièvre brûlante " (285 Anh., K.), whose genuineness had already been doubted by Siebigke (Mozart, p. 68), were not by Mozart, and she is undoubtedly right. 54 K. (after 547 K.) and 137 Anh., K. (after 581 K.) are arrangements.

[14] The following should certainly be placed earlier : 14, 15 (24, 25 K.), composed in his ninth year. 16 (179 K.), on Fischer's minuet, composed in 1774 (Vol. I., p. 323). 17. " Mio caro Adone," from Salieri's " Fiera di Venezia " (180 K.). 18. " Je suis Lindor," from Beaumarchais' " Barbier " (354 K.). The two latter were published in Paris (Vol. II., p. 70). In July, 1781, Mozart mentions three airs with variations, without specifying them more exactly.

7. " Lison dormoit " (264 K.).

8. " La Belle Françoise " (353 K.).

9. " Salve tu Domine," from Paesiello's "Eingebildete Philosoph "
(398 K.).

10. " La Bergère Silimène," with violin (359 K.).

11. " Hèlas, j'ai perdu mon amant," with violin (360 K.).

In 1786 :—

12. " Marche des Mariages Samnites," by Grétry (352 K.).

In 1787 :—

13. " Ah, vous dirais-je maman? " (265 K.).

In all these, even the more pretentious of them, there is
no appearance of a higher object than passing amusement,
secured by means of the contrast of the different variations
in time and measure, major and minor, prominence of the
right hand or the left, with all of which devices we are now
so over-familiar. It never occurred to Mozart to give a
deeper meaning to his variations by the grouping of the
movements, nor still less to torture a simple theme into all
sorts of fantastic forms. He confined himself to a tasteful
embellishment of the subject; harmonic and contrapuntal
treatment was not altogether absent, but it was little more
than suggested as a sort of seasoning to the music. In
many of the earlier variations mechanical difficulties are
brought into the foreground. Certain favourite difficulties,
such as the passing over of the hands, long shakes or chains
of shakes in one hand, while the other has the subject, were
always to be found; passages which now offer neither novelty
nor difficulty display nevertheless, upon closer inspection,
both elegance and originality. The equal use made of the
two hands is worthy of remark; a considerable amount of
execution in the left hand is presupposed in these as in most
of Mozart's compositions. In the later variations (3, 5, 6,
17) there is little or no bravura. The theme is easily and
gracefully treated; and no attempt is made to invest with
undue dignity what is merely a light and passing expression
of fancy. As one of the most interesting and successful
compositions of this kind may be mentioned the four-handed
variations (4), which are both graceful and amusing. Some-

times variations form a component part (the middle or last movement) of a sonata, either with[15] or without accompaniment (284, 331, K.). This has caused no essential difference in their treatment; they are neither wider in conception nor freer in execution, nor are they connected by intermediate passages so as to form one whole—a device often and successfully employed by Haydn and Beethoven.

Mozart's original themes are, for the most part, fresher and more graceful than those he has borrowed. The accompanied sonatas give greater scope for originality by the multiplication of the parts; and very often the simple enunciation of the theme by one of the parts allows a better defined expression of free contrapuntal treatment to be given to it by the other parts. But, as we have said, these modifications are unimportant; the form of the variation is here, as elsewhere, simply light and entertaining.[16]

Various short pianoforte pieces, for particular occasions and persons, were written during Mozart's Vienna period, as, for instance, the three rondos :—

1. In D major, composed January 10, 1786 (485 K.).
2. In F major, composed June 10, 1786 (494 K.).[17]
3. In A minor, composed March 11, 1787 (511 K.).[18]

The two in F and D major are easy of comprehension and execution—cheerful, but not striking music; the latter is peculiar in that the oft-repeated theme recurs in different keys, thus necessitating changing modulations in the episodes.[19] The third, in A minor, is very original and beautiful.[20] The theme is somewhat piquant in its rhythm and harmonic treatment, and suggestive of a national melody—

---

[15] In the sonatas for piano and violin (377, 379, 481 K.), and in the trios (496, 564 K.).

[16] Compare the remarks by Marx on Mozart's variations (Lehre von der Musik. Kompos., III., p. 84).

[17] It has been arbitrarily but not altogether unsuitably combined into one sonata with two other movements, composed on January 8, 1788 (533 K.).

[18] The second Rondo in F major (616 K.) was originally written for a musical box.

[19] Cf. Widmann, Formenlehre, p. 111.

[20] This Rondo is analysed by Marx (Lehre v. d. Mus. Kompos., III., p. 150).

a mode of characterisation not often used either by Mozart or Beethoven. Its original modifications cause fresh surprise each time that it recurs. The second theme, effective by contrast with the first, is in itself both fine and expressive, and gives occasion for much appropriate and interesting treatment. The short middle movement, in A major, is lighter in style, but accords well with the chief theme, and leads back to it by a striking modulation. The whole piece is original in character; and the tone of melancholy which runs through it and constantly asserts itself forms a most attractive contrast to the restless movement of some of its parts.

The short Adagio in B minor (540 K.) (composed March 9, 1788) is also very beautiful, serious and even sad in tone, and otherwise interesting by reason of its harmonic inflections. Although this piece is written in perfectly regular form, in two parts with a coda, it reminds us in its whole style of an improvisation. This is still more the case with the so-called fantasias. It has already been remarked that preludes or fantasias were often prefixed as introductions to various kinds of compositions, either in the form of free improvisations or elaborate pieces that could be used on different occasions. A fantasia of this kind, prefixed to the beautiful fugue in C major, has already (Vol. II., p. 391) been noticed.

Mozart sent to his sister from Paris (July 20, 1778) a short prelude, " not a prelude to lead from one key to another, but a sort of capriccio, to try the clavier," leaving the style of playing to her own judgment. " She received it at four o'clock," writes the father (August 13, 1778), " and at five, when I came home, she said she had thought of something, and if I liked it, she would write it down. She then began to play the prelude by heart. I rubbed my eyes and said : 'Where the deuce did you get that idea?' She laughed and drew your letter from her pocket." This is, no doubt, the unpublished prelude in C major (395 K.) which was in the possession of Mozart's sister. The essential character of this, as of the prelude in C minor (396 K.), is modulatory. There is no delivery of a regular melody, or working out of a definite motif, but the whole consists of varied and skilfully grouped passages and arpeggios, keeping both hands in equal activity, and displaying an abundance of rapid and often curious and striking changes of harmony. But even in this apparently unfettered straying through harmonies we cannot fail to be aware of organisation in the succession of the modulations, in the connection of the passages, and in the whole conception. The C major is in several detached contrasting movements, the C minor is founded on the definite form of a two-part sonata movement, but very freely treated.

The fantasia in D minor (337 K.) is of somewhat different design, in so far that the melodic element is more prominent, but at first only in oft-repeated phrases, which are continually prevented from developing into a perfect cantilene by the occurrence of a contrasting motif, or the outbreak of a quick stormy passage. The character of a gradual concentration of force is very clearly expressed. The tender and graceful theme which is at last allowed to assume its due proportions, can, however, be in no way considered as the proper result of such a preparation ; it is not worked out, but first interrupted, and then brought to a rapid but not a satisfying conclusion, so maintaining the character of the piece as an announcement of something greater which was to come.

The well-known fantasia in C minor (475 K.), Mozart's performance of which so surprised Jos. Frank (Vol. II., p. 279),[21] is better worked out, and in every respect a more important work. Five movements, in various keys and tempos, are closely bound together into a whole by connecting passages or harmonic inflections. Each movement, though not completely separate, has yet a certain independence, with melodies of its own rounded into a simple song-like form ; there is no attempt at the elaboration, or even the full development, of a motif, but everything presses onwards, each section leading as of necessity to the next, which is intended to form a lively contrast to what has preceded it. In spite of the predomi-

---

[21] It was composed May 20, 1785, and published by Mozart, together with the sonata in C minor (457 K.), as Op. 11.

nance of a slow tempo, the whole work has a restless character, and the recurrence at the end of the serious and
sustained commencement leads only to a provisional and
unsatisfying conclusion.   Here again, the essence of the
fantasia is modulatory.   The changes of harmony are
frequent—often bar by bar—rapid and striking; the passages
and even the melodies are so constructed as to lend themselves to this method.   In spite of its length the fantasia
preserves the character of an introduction, though not of
necessity to the sonata with which it is printed.   The mood
which is so distinctly expressed in the two first bars of the
adagio is preserved throughout the fantasia; it is a sad and
sorrowful mood of doubting and questioning, of struggling
and striving, of longing for deliverance from a heavy burden,
for freedom from doubt and care; disheartened by failure,
unrefreshed by consolation, it sinks at last into itself, and is
heard no more.   But there is no hopeless despair, no cynical
irony in this music.   It is expressive throughout of the composure of a man who even in combat never loses command
over himself.   The boldness of its harmonies, and the consistency of its tone were of unusual significance at the time
of its composition.   It is much to be regretted that the letter
concerning it, which Mozart addressed to Frau von Trattnern
(Vol. II., p. 279), has not been preserved.[22]

Above and beyond such detached movements as these,
the form of pianoforte composition chiefly cultivated by
Mozart was the sonata, either with or without the accompaniment of one or more instruments.[23]   The foundation of
the sonata proper, and of the definite form in which the chief
movement of the sonata, at least, was cast—was laid by
Kuhnau and Dom. Scarlatti, the latter of whom brought his
extraordinary technical knowledge to bear with effect on the
treatment and style of pianoforte music.   From the middle
of the last century the piano as a solo instrument has been
increasing in favour, especially among amateurs, and it

---

[22] A poetical exposition of this fantasia is given by Kanne (Wien. Mus. Ztg.,
1821, p. 386).

[23] Cf. Im. Faiszt, Beiträge zur Geschichte der Klaviersonate bis C. P. Em.
Bach (Cäcilia, XXV., pp. 129, 201; XXVI., pp. 1, 73).

naturally followed that this species of composition should be cultivated with corresponding attention. Ph. Em. Bach and his disciple Jos. Haydn fixed the form of the sonata in all essential respects, and by the intrinsic worth of their compositions, and the charm of their execution, brought the germ of perfection therein contained to the point of vital development. To them succeeded Mozart, carrying on their work in his own original manner.

It has already been demonstrated (Vol. I., p. 292) that the clavier sonata in its free development forms the basis of independent instrumental composition, and that every advance in the one direction acts favourably in the other; it will suffice here, therefore, to touch briefly on the main points of this species of composition.

The sonata now signifies a composition for a solo instrument, consisting of several movements, differing in time, measure, and key, but sufficiently allied in design and grouping to form a coherent whole. In its earlier stage two movements often composed a sonata, but afterwards three or four became the rule. One of the movements is in slow time, and forms the appropriate expression of a calm, serious, or tender mood. It soon became usual to place this movement in the middle, with the instinctive feeling that a composed and self-concentrated mood ought to succeeed to a demonstrative or passionate one. If the more animated movement were preceded by the slow one, the latter would lose its independent character, and become a mere introduction to the former. The second of the lively movements served as a conclusion, and was invariably cheerful, sometimes even merry in tone. The music being principally intended for social entertainment, was so constructed as to leave a pleasant, cheerful impression. When a fourth movement was added it was generally in the same tone, and sometimes preceded, but more often followed, the slow movement. During his Vienna period Mozart's sonatas, both solo and accompanied, have but three movements, while his symphonies, quintets, and quartets are always furnished with minuets.

The three movements of the sonata have only gradually

assumed their present form. One of Mozart's earlier sonatas, in A major (331 K), consists of an andante with variations, a minuet, and rondo ; another, in D major (284 K.), has a middle movement, consisting of a rondo *en polonaise*, followed by a theme with variations. Afterwards, however, he adhered to the regular sonata form, with the first movement as its most characteristic part, forming the point of departure for the development of all modern instrumental music. It has already been remarked that the essential elements of the sonata movement consist in the treatment of the principal motif in the first part, and in its working out in the second.

The contrapuntal elaboration of a theme in strict form was the groundwork of the first part, and was followed by the characteristic treatment of well-defined motifs, side by side with a free use of figures and passages. An important point was the delivery of a second theme, independent of the first and sharply distinguished from it. This was always in the dominant of the principal major key (C major —G major), or in the relative major of the principal minor key (C minor—E flat major). These are the two main pillars of the movement. Their further development, their connection by means of interludes, and the conclusion of the part, are not further hampered by rule, except that the part must close in the dominant. The province of the second part was the working out of one or more motifs employed in the first part, or altogether new. The treatment was either mainly harmonic or mainly thematic, and had for its object the organic development of the given elements, the enhancing of the interest, and the effective return to the first part. Upon this elaboration, and leading back to the first theme, were concentrated all the power and genius of the master. The repetition of the first part entailed many modifications, partly because the second theme was obliged to appear in the principal key in which the movement closed ; it allowed also of alterations in grouping the different phrases, of amplifications or curtailments, and especially of such a long-drawn climax at the close as should almost entitle the repeated second part to be considered as a third part.

Mozart found these elements ready to hand, and gave them the stamp of his own individual nature. In his hands the second subject, distinctly enunciated, became not only an independent but a counter-subject rising in characteristic relief from the body of the part. But his originality is principally displayed in the formation of the themes. Their predominant characteristic is songlike melody, which Nägeli (Vorlesungen üb. Musik, p. 156), with a mistaken view of the nature of instrumental music, considered to be the degradation and ruin of pianoforte-playing. With truer judgment Mozart has followed the injunctions of Ph. Em. Bach, and after him Haydn, and has striven to write melodiously. Mozart's musical training was founded on song —and his inclinations led him to song—in a greater degree than was the case with his two predecessors. When once the pianoforte composer had renounced the severe polyphonic method—when once he had come to regard his theme not as material for pedantic elaboration, but as a free melody capable of giving expression to his artistic perceptions, then song became the point of departure for all his melodies. A transference to the instrument of the forms expressly constructed for the voice was impracticable; they could only be employed by analogy, in conformity with the nature of the instrument. Mozart never employed the form of the Italian cantilene in his pianoforte compositions, nor in his instrumental works generally; a glance at his Italian operas will show the difference in the treatment of the melodies. Wherever a comparison of instrumental with vocal works is possible, it must be made with the German operas, especially with the "Zauberflöte." In his instrumental works Mozart gave his emotions their natural expression without binding himself to any such set forms as those of Italian opera; with equal freedom he treated song in his German operas as the immediate outcome of his feelings. The developed forms of German instrumental music suggested this treatment. The essential conditions of a beautiful melody, founded on the relations of intervals, rhythm and harmonies, were perfectly fulfilled in Mozart's pianoforte compositions. Each melody is complete, uniform and full of his own charm of grace and euphony. The delivery of such melodies must have given special prominence to those qualities in Mozart's playing which Haydn declared came from his heart; we are sometimes surprised in the concertos, for instance, to find the chief effect depending on a long, simply sustained melody, which he must have played in masterly fashion. This song-like and expressive treatment of the separate melodies was accompanied by an extraordinary wealth of melody. Instead of the connecting phrases which generally led out of the principal motif or were formed by free passages, Mozart introduced new melodies. This was made an occasion of reproach to him, as Dittersdorf says ("Selbstbiographie," p. 237): "Mozart is unquestionably a great original genius, and I know of no composer who possesses such an astonishing wealth of ideas. I only wish he were a little less prodigal of them. He gives his hearers no time to breathe; as soon as one beautiful idea is grasped, it is succeeded by another and a finer one, which drives the first from the mind; and so it goes on, until at the end not one of these beauties remains in the memory." We shall certainly not echo this complaint of Mozart's prodigality of ideas; but it cannot be denied that though the formation of independent melodies is an important and necessary step in advance, it does not reach the last stage of development. Mozart's melodies are not strung together without connection, both external and internal; but, in the shorter sonatas especially, where they are not worked out, they strike us as the indicated points in a design wanting as yet the detail of which it is capable.[24]

The gain was important in two respects. The close juxtaposition of melodies excluded, or greatly limited, the employment of connecting passages without sense or meaning. Of these Mozart makes comparatively little use. He used figures and passages chiefly as ornaments, and not as independent members of the movement. But where this form of transition seemed inevitable, he used it without ceremony, just as in architecture supports are worked into the artistic design,

---

[24] Cf. the excellent remarks by Marx (Lehre von der Musik. Kompos., III., p. 588), and for a more profound criticism (Ibid., III., p. 215).

without any disguise of their structional importance. We may instance the broad and expressive treatment of his closes and half-closes, which are now so striking as to appear to many a special peculiarity of Mozart's style. This, however, they are not ; they were then in general use, and proceeded from the desire to maintain the key with firmness and decision. The greater freedom of modern music in this respect, and the substitution of graceful and original transition phrases for dry commonplaces is an undoubted progress. Mozart's transition phrases were, however, often elegant and interesting, as may be proved from a reference to his returns to the theme in the second parts, and to the varied development which he gives to the simple ground form of the organ point.

The second respect in which Mozart's method was a gain to music was in the clearness which it gave to his designs. This clearness is an inseparable adjunct of Mozart's art ; by means of it the main points of his structure were as clearly defined as an architectural ground-plan, and became the supports for elaboration and development. Mozart himself was far from exhausting the resources of the method which he founded; others have followed in his footsteps, and Beethoven, his intellectual heir, has displayed all the depth and wealth of that which he has inherited.

In the choice and arrangement of his melodies Mozart invariably displays delicate taste and discrimination. He is particularly happy in surprising his hearers with a new melody when they least expect it—at the close of the first theme, for instance, which generally brings with it a certain sense of satisfied completeness. But his most inimitable effect is produced when, just as the movement is drawing to a close, a perfect melody starts up in all its charm of fresh sweetness, reviving the interest of the hearers, and often giving an entirely new turn to the whole. As a striking example, I may remind my readers of the first movement of the Symphony in C major (551 K.). Who has not been charmed again and again by the last melody, which, like a shining meteor, sheds light and cheerfulness around? Similar, though not perhaps equally brilliant, effects are of constant occurrence ; they have not been achieved, have scarcely even been attempted by any other musician. On the other hand, however, the partiality with which Mozart has treated the close and other less prominent points of his movements has been prejudicial to the so-called second subject; this is usually the weakest part. It should have a light and tender character, in contrast to the principal subject; it is frequently, however, insignificant in comparison to the other motifs, and gives the impression of having been neglected.

The further development of the fundamental scheme was accomplished by means not of the insertion of phrases connecting its principal members, but of the thematic treatment of these members themselves. Mozart's study of Bach and Handel led him in this direction, as was particularly shown in his later pianoforte works; an interesting example is afforded by the two movements in the Allegro and Andante in F major (553 K.), which are throughout in counterpoint. This work must not be considered as a relapse into the strict forms of counterpoint, such as the canon and the fugue, but as the free development of the laws to which polyphonic and contrapuntal forms are alike subject. Instrumental and especially pianoforte music, freed from the fetters of strict form, was in danger of advancing exclusively in the direction of homophonic development, and so becoming insipid. It is Mozart's merit to have brought polyphonic and thematic treatment, modified according to the altered character of the music and the nature of the instrument, to its freest and most beautiful expression. This is particularly noticeable in the "working-out" divisions of the movements, on which the main emphasis must necessarily fall, and which can only attain their full significance by means of this treatment. Mozart does not indeed develop them in length and breadth as Beethoven does, but he makes them, even when they are so condensed as to appear mere transition movements, the culminating point of the whole movement, the concentration of all its force and action. The mode of treatment is as free as the choice of subject ; but the effect generally depends upon a thematic treatment which is often very artistically designed and woven together.

Not that the harmonic element is neglected—the boldest

and most original modulations occur in the very places where close examination discloses the thematic as the vivifying element, the true impulse of the work. This free and intellectual treatment of the polyphonic method was distasteful to many of Mozart's contemporaries, who only accepted the traditional forms of counterpoint. Thus, a critic expresses himself as follows concerning the E flat sonata for violin and piano (481 K.) :—

The pleasing style of this sonata by Herr M. will cause it to find favour with all lovers of the art. It is to be wished, however, that Herr M. would attach himself less closely to the passing taste of the day ; his works would thereby gain a more universal and lasting worth. That Herr Mozart is not wanting either in the knowledge of harmony or the wealth of imagination which would enable him to offer us stronger meats is sufficiently vouched for by this and many other of his well-known works.

The same critic considered the working-out movement far too long :—

Although musical science has no actual rule in such cases, yet a difference of three pages is out of all reason.[25]

The slow middle movement and the last movement have not the accurate and well-defined form of the first. Two essentially easier forms are mainly employed, with many modifications, namely, variations and the rondo. The slow movement is, as a rule, founded upon the song form, and is therefore often designed in two parts ; but the design is only very seldom developed as broadly and fully as in the first movement; the repetition of the theme more than once, with the then customary additions and embellishments,[26] led naturally to the adoption of variations. But in every case the first requirement was the composition of a movement melodious in form and substance, and owing its expression not to its connection with any other, but to its own intrinsic

[25] Musik. Real-Ztg., 1788, p. 50.
[26] Ph. E. Bach says in the preface to his six sonatas for the piano, with altered repetitions (Berlin, 1759) : " The alteration at the repeat is in the present day indispensable. It is expected from every performer that he should change every idea in repetition, without any allowance being made for the construction of the piece or the ability of the performer."

feeling. The tone of sentiment then existing was favourable to the production of just such movements, and they therefore undoubtedly belong to Mozart's finest creations. These simple and expressive melodies, exquisitely formed and firmly handled, full of warm and deep emotion or of sentimental tenderness, seem to be the precious legacy of the time to which we also owe the purest strains of our lyric poetry. The calm with which they are for the most part permeated expresses in a rare degree the enjoyment and satisfaction of artistic activity. The very ease with which these movements are constructed, by means of the development of the main idea of variations on it and of freely treated and often contrasting secondary parts, shows how freely and naturally they proceeded from the heart of the musician. As an instance of detail we need only mention the delicacy and grace with which Mozart leads up to the conclusion, and leaves his hearers with a parting impression of perfect satisfaction.

The last movements are not by any means of equal merit with the other two. A large majority are in the easy rondo or variation form. The incredible ease with which Mozart poured forth melodies is more than ever apparent in these movements, but they are often loosely strung together without development, and sometimes trivial in character. The original intention of the movement, of enlivening the audience by a cheerful dance or something similar, is generally kept in view; the tone is one of more or less excited merriment, without depth or true humour. Mozart's enjoyment of dances, games, and jests of all kinds found expression in such performances as these. Their purity and grace of form shows however that, like a true artist, he lifts every manifestation of his nature into a higher sphere. Many of his last movements form exceptions to what has been said above, both by reason of their stricter form and of their more elevated tone.

The list of sonatas for pianoforte alone which Mozart composed in Vienna is not a very long one.[27] Of the first which appeared—

---

[27] An analysis of them is given by Kanne (Wien. Mus. Ztg., 1821, Nos. 3-8, 19-30, 44-50). Cf. Lorenz, Deutsche Mus. Ztg., 1861, p. 321.

Three sonatas, Op. 6 (330-332, K.), in C, A, F major.

Three sonatas, Op. 7 (333, 284, K.), dedicated to the Countess Therese Cobenzl, in B flat and C major; the third is with the violin (454 K.)—

some must certainly have been composed earlier; then follow :—

C minor, composed October 14, 1784 (457 K.), with the fantasia (475 K.) published in 1785 as Op. 11.

F major, composed January 3, 1788, in two movements (533 K.).

"A Short Pianoforte Sonata for Beginners," in C major (545 K.), composed June, 1788.

B flat major, "for pianoforte alone," composed February, 1789 (570 K.).[28]

B flat major, composed July, 1789 (576 K.).

Most, if not all, of these appear to have been composed for special occasions. The most important is unquestionably the celebrated one in C minor, the fire and passion of which, especially in the last movement, surpass all previous efforts, and point to what Beethoven was to achieve in the piano-forte sonata. The second, in B flat major, is pleasing and gay; the working out of the first movement is free and full. The third, in D major, is easy and cheerful, with more passages than usual.

Three four-handed sonatas[29] are also preserved :—

D major, composed November, 1781, for Aurnhammer's Soirée (381 K.).

F major, composed August 1, 1786 (497 K.).

C major, composed May 29, 1787 (521 K.).

Pianoforte music for two performers was then far from having attained the popularity which it now possesses, especially among amateurs. Those who wished to play for the sake of playing, and to give full effect to their perform-ance, would not readily shackle themselves with a fellow-performer, and lose their absolute sway over the instrument. Duets were considered an exceptional kind of amusement, not without its peculiar charm. This charm consisted in the richer elaboration of material which they allowed, and in such a division and alternation of the parts as should set the

---

[28] An *ad libitum* violin part has been added to this sonata.

[29] The variations for four hands in G major (Œuvr., VIII., 3) have already been noticed (Vol. II., p. 446).

two players in competition. Mozart, who excelled in this
kind of treatment, often employed it, and even transfers
entire cantilene with their accompaniments to the bass part,
not always, as Marx rightly observes ("Lehre von der
Musikalischen Composition," III., p. 601), with a good
sound effect. Of the two great sonatas, that in F major is
by far the most striking; the emphasis is not here laid upon
the first movement. The adagio, and still more the rondo,
are specially interesting from their beautiful motifs and the
seriousness—even to grandeur—of their treatment. The
other Sonata in C major is not trivial in conception, but
depends more upon brilliant execution, and leaves a cheerful,
pleasant impression.

Compositions for two pianofortes were more popular, as
affording more scope for display to the performer, but the
inconvenience attending their performance has prevented the
cultivation of this branch of composition. It appears at one
time to have been a favourite one with Mozart, owing, no
doubt, to some special circumstances. The Fugue in C
minor (426 K., Vol. II., p. 392) was composed on December
29, 1783, and the Sonata in D major (448 K.) at the beginning
of 1784; the latter is a capital bravura piece for the time at
which it was written, effective even now, and interesting
from the interweaving of the two parts. The first movement
is the best, the working-out forcible and effective, though
not elaborate; the andante is somewhat tedious, owing to
the repetition of the entire first part. Several commence-
ments now among the sketches in the Salzburg Mozarteum
fall within this period. A second fugue, in G major (45 Anh.
K.), has already been noticed (Vol. II., p. 388); the commence-
ments of an Allegro in C minor (44 Anh. K.) and of an Adagio
in D minor (35 Anh. K.) are so grand and forcible as to
cause regret that they were not continued ; a last movement
in B flat major (43 Anh. K.) is calmer and more cheerful in
character. It is remarkable how these few bars confirm the
observation that the choice of a minor key was with Mozart
an invariable sign of a special effort of his productive powers.

The sonatas with violin accompaniment composed by
Mozart in Vienna were few in number. The first collection

which appeared in November, 1781 (Vol. II., p. 187), Six
Sonatas, Op. 2 (376, 296, 377-380, K.), in F, C, F, B flat, G,
E flat major, comprise some sonatas written at an earlier date
—those in C and B flat major undoubtedly were, both upon
external and internal evidence. That they were all intended
for one collection is evidenced by the differences in their
designs, probably for the sake of variety. Thus, the Sonata
in C major begins with an elaborate Adagio leading into the
Allegro in G minor (in depth of feeling these are the finest
movements in the set) ; the last movement is in variations.
In the Sonata in F major, variations are placed in the middle,
and the last movement is a tempo di minuetto, treated rondo
fashion. The first movement is especially prominent in the
Sonatas in F major and E flat major. A Sonata in C major
begun in 1782, " Pour ma tres chère épouse " (404 K.), is
unfinished. The fragment of a Sonata in A major, with an
introductory Andante, followed by a Fugue in A minor (402
K.), only half worked-out, and completed by Stadler, belongs
unquestionably to the period of Mozart's intercourse with
Van Swieten. These were followed by :—

B flat major, composed April 21, 1784, for Strinasacchi (Vol. II., p. 336),
(454 K.).
E flat major, composed December 12, 1785 (481 K.).
A major, composed August 24, 1787 (525 K.).
F major, " Short Violin Sonata for Beginners," composed July 10,
1788 (547 K.).

The greater number of these were composed for pupils.
The majority of amateur pianists were then ladies, and it
was usual for them to be accompanied on the violin by
their teachers or other friends ; this kind of music found
favour also in social reunions.[30] It follows, therefore, that
these sonatas have no great depth of passion or scholarly
treatment, but are well supplied with beautiful melodies and
startling harmonic inflections, and are made interesting,
sometimes even brilliant, to please the performers. A notice
of the first six sonatas soon after their appearance says :[31]—

---

[30] Cf. the account in C. Pichler's Denkwürdigkeiten, I., p. 90.
[31] Cramer, Magaz. d. Musik, I., p. 485.

These sonatas are unique of their kind; rich in new ideas and signs of the genius of their author, very brilliant and well suited to the instrument. Besides this, the violin accompaniment is so artistically combined with the pianoforte part that both instruments are kept in constant activity, and the sonatas require a violin-player of equal skill with the pianist. But it is impossible to give a full description of this very original work. The connoisseur must play it through for himself, and he will then be ready to acknowledge that we have not exaggerated its merits.

It appears from this that the violin part was usually treated as subordinate, exclusively intended for accompaniment; but not so with Mozart: his violin parts are completely independent, on an equality with the piano, and composed with special reference to the idiosyncrasies of the instrument. Indeed, the whole design of these sonatas avoids any interweaving of the parts, which are generally in strict counterpoint; even the simple form of imitation is comparatively seldom employed; the parts relieve one another, exchange melodies and passages, or move freely together. If, however, we compare the violin part so skilfully added to the Sonata in B flat major (570 K.), we shall find that it is no essential part of the design, but an evident addition; while in the violin sonatas proper, simple as the violin part may be, it cannot be subtracted without injury. The principal charm of these sonatas lies in the rich development of their harmonies. In this respect, too, the later sonatas are, as usual, superior to the earlier. With the exception of the short sonata for beginners (547 K.), that in E flat major (481 K.) is the easiest, but it is remarkably clear and pretty. The working-out of the first movement is formed by the delicate harmonising of the favourite subject already known to us (Vol. I., p. 259)—

which recurs free in the second part, and is therefore judiciously used to bring the whole movement to a close. In the B flat major sonata also (454 K.) the interest of the working-out is essentially harmonic; the return to the first subject is as striking to those who hear it now as it could have

been to Mozart's contemporaries. There are many similar
touches which suffice to convince us how great an effect of
novelty and boldness these sonatas must have produced.
The first place must again be accorded to the slow middle
movements by reason of their beautiful melodies, in the
steady flow of which the art of not merely beginning well,
but of maintaining the interest, and knowing where to leave
off, may be admired and studied. In all of them a delicate
and tasteful accompaniment, a rich and bold harmonic treat
ment—I need only mention the effective enharmonic changes
in the andante of the B flat major sonata (454 K.), and
in the adagio of the E flat major (481 K.)—give to the simple
outlines a delicate warmth of colour. Each of these movements is fine of its kind, but the andante of the Sonata in
A major (526 K.) is specially attractive from the earnestness
of its tone.

In the same class may be reckoned the trios, or, as
Mozart called them, terzets for piano, violin, and violoncello, which were also principally intended for the social
circle of amateurs. Their composition for special occasions
may be inferred from the fact that they all five fall within the
summer and autumn of 1786 and 1788:—

G major, composed July 8, 1786 (496 K.).[82]
B flat major, composed November 18, 1786 (502 K.).
E major, composed June 22, 1788 (542 K.).[83]
C major, composed July 14, 1788 (548 K.).
G major, composed October 27, 1788 (564 K.).

In June of the latter year Mozart asked his friend Puchberg if he did not intend to give a musical party soon, for he
had written a new trio. This was the trio in E major; and
a later distinct mention of a trio written for Puchberg
probably refers to the same. There can at least be no
question as to the superiority of this trio in design and
originality, as well as in the effective treatment of the
instruments. The first movement is full of fire and energy,
the imitative working-out of the second subject being

[82] Notes and alterations have been inserted by Mozart in red ink.
[83] The finale is extant in a second and unfinished arrangement.

wonderfully heightened in effect by a bold harmonic inflection. The second movement, with something of the character of a national melody, is fresh and charming, and has rhythmic and harmonic points which give it a piquancy altogether modern. The last movement, though not devoid of expression and delicacy, is inferior in vital energy to the first, and seems somewhat too long, perhaps because an exclusive attention to brilliancy loses its effect upon hearers of our day. External influences account for the fact that the succession of the trios is not in accordance with their merit and importance. The two last are inferior not only to that just mentioned, but also to the two first. In these, as usual, the middle movements stand highest; in the first movement of the trio in B flat major (2) there is no new second subject, but the first is employed again with some modification; the second part, therefore, opens with an entirely new and independent melody. The trio in C major (548 K.) is very easy, and seems to have been intended for some particular person. The last (564 K.) was first written by Mozart as a sonata for pianoforte alone. When he had occasion to add the two stringed instruments, he had the original composition copied, added the violin and violoncello parts, and altered what had to be altered for the piano. The original sonata may be easily traced, except here and there, where the alterations have gone deeper, and the different instruments, except in the variations, have little independence. In contrast with the emancipation of the violin part in the violin sonatas, the violoncello part of the trios is always in the background. It is treated as a bass instrument, and only exceptionally leads the melody or takes an independent part; of bravura it has little or none, and thus the original effects of which the combined instruments are capable seldom occur. One remarkable instance of such an effect, however, is in the last movement of the first trio (496 K.) at the passage in G minor, where the violin repeats four times the melancholy bar—

and then slides on to the G, while the violoncello carries out an expressive bass passage in crotchets, and the piano in two parts moves above both instruments in quavers; an effect of sound and motif which has often been laid claim to in recent days as something new and original.   An insurmountable obstacle to the fuller development of the trio (in which Beethoven later put forth all his creative powers) consisted in the want of good violoncellists among the musical circles for whom Mozart composed these works.

A trio in E flat major, for pianoforte, clarinet, and viola (498 K.), composed on August 5, 1786, for Franziska von Jacquin, is very original (Vol. II., p. 278).   The unusual combination of instruments necessitated unusual treatment. The viola is not a bass instrument, and is only available for middle parts, so that the usual violoncello part could not be given to it; this necessitated an altogether original design and execution, and a dependence for effect upon a peculiarly light colouring and transparent clearness.   The viola, whether accompanying or leading the melody, is treated throughout with special partiality, and has even a certain amount of bravura.   Mozart was fond of taking the viola himself in his later years, and Franziska von Jacquin was an excellent pianiste, so that we can understand his providing himself with a good part to perform with his friends.   The deeper tones of the clarinet are not used, out of consideration to the viola; its full liquid tones are particularly well adapted for the delivery of the melody.   The plan of the movements deviates from the ordinary course.   The first is not an Allegro, but an Andante 6-8 (signifying formerly a moderately agitated tempo) which is played straight through with no repetition of the first part.   It is in three tolerably equal divisions, in each of which the two beautiful subjects are enlarged upon in an easy but attractive manner, the first of them especially—

being scarcely ever lost sight of; the movement ends with a short coda.   The second movement is a minuet, the only one of the kind in Mozart's pianoforte pieces, serious and broad in tone, somewhat elaborated in the trio, the motif of which is taken up in the coda; on the whole, a fine and characteristic movement. The concluding rondo is full of pretty melodies and brilliant passages, and the different parts are delicately and independently treated.

A relatively much higher rank than that of the majority of the trios is taken by the two quartets for pianoforte, violin, viola and violoncello, of which the first, in G minor (478 K.), was composed on October 19, 1785; the second, in E flat major, on June 3, 1786 (493 K.). They are, suitably to their enlarged resources, grander and broader in design, the motifs are fuller, and thematic treatment comes to the foreground. The details of the work are developed from within, and are made subservient to the plan of the whole. Notwithstanding, therefore, their more elaborate treatment, the mode of expression is more definite, the contents weightier, the expression more forcible and clearer.

The inclination of the present day, since Beethoven has raised chamber music both in substance and form to a hitherto unapproachable height, is to make beauty of form[34] predominate over force and depth of original expression; it will be instructive, therefore, to cast a glance over a criticism by Rochlitz, written in the year 1800 :[35]—

In these compositions, written for a select and limited circle, the spirit of the artist is displayed after a rare and singular manner, with the grandeur and sublimity of an appearance from another world; there are moments, it is true, of melting sadness or cheerful humour, but they are only moments, and the composer breaks forth again in the greatness, even fierceness, of his strength, or writhes in bitter sorrow— the struggle ending, as it were, only in victory or death. That this may not be taken for mere empty raving, let any one hear, well-executed— (which can only be by persons who possess, together with the requisite skill, both a heart and an understanding for music)—Mozart's quartet for pianoforte, violin, viola and violoncello, in E flat major. Let it be heard, studied, and then heard again.

---

[34] By way of example I may remind the reader of the tender, yearning, almost dreamlike impression made by the wonderful harmonic progression in the larghetto of the Quartet in E flat major.

[35] A. M. Z., III., p. 27.

As an illustration of passionate feeling, amounting even to harshness in the force of its expression, we should rather quote the first movement of the quartet in G minor. The following account from Vienna of "the latest musical novelties at grand concerts," written in 1788, will give some idea of the reception which these quartets met with on their first appearance, and of the difficulties they presented to contemporary performers: [36] —

The favourite pianoforte composer among lady amateurs is Kozeluch, but Pleyel is beginning to be a dangerous rival to him. Pleyel's music contains humour and more of original invention than Kozeluch's, although the latter possesses elegance, regularity of form, and a certain flow of ideas. Mozart is at present residing in Vienna as imperial kapellmeister. He is considered as a remarkable man by every philosophic lover of music. His genius was precocious, and he both composed and played in his eleventh year (even earlier) to the admiration of all who heard him. But what is truly remarkable is that this precocious child should have blossomed into maturity as an accomplished musician. We know the usual rapid course of such a prodigy by sad experience! We look in vain for its fruits, for its stability. Not so with Mozart! But now a few words on a curious phenomenon which he (or his celebrity) has brought to pass. A short time ago appeared a solitary quartet (for piano, violin, viola, and violoncello), very artistically arranged, requiring extreme accuracy of delivery in all the four parts, but even under the most favourable circumstances not likely to please any but musical connoisseurs in a *musica di camera*. The report, "Mozart has written a new and very remarkable quartet, and such or such a princess possesses it and plays it!" was soon spread abroad, excited curiosity, and caused the indiscretion of the production of this original composition at a grand noisy concert. Many pieces can sustain their reputation even under a mediocre performance; but this work of Mozart's in the hands of indifferent amateurs, carelessly rendered, is simply unendurable. It was so performed innumerable times last winter; at almost every place which I visited I was taken to a concert, and there entered a town-bred miss, or some other conceited amateur, to play this quartet to the noisy company who pretended to find it the *goût*. But it gave no real pleasure; every one gaped with *ennui* at the long *tintamarre* of four instruments who did not keep together for four bars, and whose contradictory *concentu* gave no impression of unity of sentiment. The obstinacy with which it was forced down everywhere was indescribable. It is not enough to stigmatise this folly as an ephemeral *manie du jour*, for

[36] Journal des Luxus und der Moden, 1788, p. 230.

it lasted throughout a whole winter, and (as far as I can learn) is still only too often repeated. What a contrast if this masterpiece were to be performed by four skilful musicians, in a quiet room where the listening ear might catch the suspension of every note, in the presence of only two or three attentive listeners! But this would give no opportunity for display or the applause of the vulgar.[87]

The quintet in E flat major (452 K.) for pianoforte, oboe, clarinet, horn, and bassoon is a composition of peculiarly charming effect; it was composed by Mozart on March 30, 1784, for a concert which he gave in the theatre, and, being excellently performed, was received with great applause. He himself considered it, as he tells his father (Vol. II., p. 287), to be the best thing he had ever written, and he selected it to play before Paesiello (Vol. II., p. 279). It must not be judged from the various arrangements which have been made of it; it is accurately and exclusively fitted for the instruments for which it was written. The sound effects produced by the well-considered combinations of the wind instruments are of surprising beauty, and the pianoforte maintains its ground against its melodious rivals by means of its power of quicker motion. The whole work is clear and easy in each of its multitudinous details, and from beginning to end it is a true triumph of the art of recognising and adapting the peculiar euphonious quality of each instrument. This harmony of sound, combined with a somewhat strongly accentuated harmonic treatment, constitutes the principal charm of the work, which is not rich in thematic invention. Here and there Italian echoes are heard in the melodies, but the German style predominates, as it does in the quartets previously noticed.[88] Beethoven is known to have emulated this work of Mozart's in his quintet (Op. 16); in no other of his works, perhaps, does he so plainly appear to have set a

---

[87] Forkel, who otherwise takes no notice of Mozart, says of this article that it is evident that the author is a dilettante, without any knowledge of art, and therefore only capable of judging from outward appearances (Musik. Alman., 1789, p. 119).

[88] A second quintet for piano, oboe, clarinet, basset-horn, and bassoon, was only commenced by Mozart (54 Anh., K.).

pattern before him for imitation; for once he has not succeeded in surpassing it. [89]

The pianoforte concertos, of which Mozart wrote seventeen in Vienna, must be considered from a somewhat different point of view.[40] They are as follows :—

F major, composed end of 1782 ⎱ ⎰(413 K., part 12).
A major, composed early in 1783 ⎰Op. 4⎱ (414 K., part 10).
C major, composed early in 1783 ⎰ ⎱(415 K., part 3).
E flat major, composed February 9, 1784, Op. 23 (449 K., part 14).
B flat major, composed March 15, 1784, Op. 67 (450 K., part 14).
D major, composed March 22, 1784, Op. 18 (451 K., part 13).
G major, composed April 12, 1784, Op. 15 (453 K., part 9).
B flat major, composed September 30, 1784, Op. 21 (456 K., part 11).
F major, composed December 11, 1784, Op. 44 (459 K., part 10).
D minor, composed February 10, 1785, Op. 54 (466 K., part 8).
C major, composed March 9, 1785, Op. 82, 6 (467 K., part 1).
E flat major, composed December 16, 1785, Op. 82, 4 (482 K., part 6).
A major, composed March 2, 1786, Op. 82, 5 (488 K., part 2).
C minor, composed March 2, 1786, Op. 82, 5 (491 K., part 7).
C major, composed December 4, 1786, Op. 82, 1 (503 K., part 16).
D major, composed February 24, 1788, Op. 46 (537 K., part 20), "Krönungsconcert."
B flat major, composed January 5, 1791, Op. 82, 2 (595 K., part 15).

The greater number of these were composed between 1783 and 1786, when Mozart played much at concerts, and were intended for his own use ; some of them also for that of others (Vol. II., p. 294).[41] This accounts for their great diversity of character and design. Of the three first which were intended to come before the public together (Vol. II., p. 293),

---

[89] A kind of legend has grown up among reminiscence hunters, to the effect that the few and unimportant motifs which recall Mozart, especially in the second movement, were introduced by Beethoven as a homage to Mozart. A comparison of the two quintets is given after his fashion by Lenz (Beethoven, III., p. 160).

[40] The most complete collection of Mozart's concertos in score, agreeing with Breitkopf and Härtel's issue of the parts, is that published in Paris by Richault; the collection begun in Offenbach by André is not finished.

[41] Sketches of pianoforte concertos (56-61 Anh., K.) bear further testimony to Mozart's lively interest in this species of composition. A Concerto Rondo in A major belonging to October 19, 1782, is completed, with the exception of some gaps in the instrumentation (386 K.).

Mozart wrote to his father, while still at work upon them (December 23, 1782) :—

> The concertos are a happy medium between too easy and too difficult; they are very brilliant, pleasing to the ear, without, of course, being empty. Here and there are places which appeal exclusively to connoisseurs, but even ignoramuses will be pleased with them without knowing why.

It is plain that he knew what he intended. Of the later concertos he writes (May 24, 1784) :—

> I cannot make a choice between the two concertos in B flat and D (450, 451, K.). I consider them both tough morsels for the performers *(Concerte die schwitzen machen)*: but the one in B flat is more difficult than the one in D. I am very curious to hear which of the three concertos in B flat, D, and G major (453 K.) you and my sister like best; that in E flat does not belong to them, being quite peculiar of its kind, and written for a small rather than a large orchestra. So that we have only to do with the three concertos, and I am curious to find whether your opinion agrees with the universal one here, and with my own. They ought, it is true, to be heard with all the parts, and well played.

The emphasis which Mozart laid on the orchestra is very noticeable. The essential merit and originality of his concertos consists in his combination of the orchestra and the solo instrument into a whole, by means of the co-operation of all their separate and independent elements.[42] The prominence given to the orchestra (which, it must be remembered, owed to Mozart its richer composition, both of wind and stringed instruments) in those larger portions of the work where it occurs independent of the piano, as in the tutti of the ritornelli, gives a symphonic character to the concertos. Even in those places where the pianoforte asserts itself as the solo instrument the orchestra participates so directly in the course of the pianoforte part as to form a not disjointed whole ; in fact, the concertos have been aptly designated as symphonies with a part for the pianoforte.[43] Mozart's art of blending the tone-colouring of the orchestra, which drew

---

[42] This is with justice emphasised by Rochlitz (A. M. Z., III., p. 28). Nägeli also testifies how Mozart " broke new ground for orchestral compositions with his pianoforte concertos " (Vorles., p. 159).

[43] Siebigke, Mozart, p. 69.

tears from his old father at the hearing of one of his new
pianoforte concertos, shows his delicate sense of euphony
and accurate knowledge of instrumental effects. The
pianoforte, with its comparative want of sustained tone, is
at a disadvantage even with solo stringed or wind instruments, far more so with a combination of them. This was
still more the case at that time, in consequence of the
defective mechanism of the instrument; and both art and
ingenuity were required to make it at all effective. When,
after an elaborate ritornello, which has given a sense of
fulness and satisfaction to the hearers, the pianoforte enters,
Mozart aims at producing such a contrast, either by means
of extreme simplicity or of a brilliant pianoforte passage, as
shall gain over the listener to the peculiar charm of the new
element, and excite his attention, which is then kept up by
the competition of the rival forces. The composer has no
intention of confining the orchestra within the narrow limits
of a modest accompaniment (for in that case why should
he have appointed it so fully?); he means it to put forth its
whole strength, as well as to support and raise the pianoforte
part. An inexhaustible succession of fine effects is thus
produced. The delivery by the orchestra of the melody in
sustained chords supports, as it were, the tendrils thrown
out by the pianoforte, and gives a firm basis for figures and
passages containing bold harmonic successions. But while it
thus seems subservient to the solo instrument, the intensive
strength and the tender fragrance of its sound effects are
made to form an admirable contrast to the light and brilliant
versatility, the sharpness, and clearness of the pianoforte.
It seems scarcely necessary to illustrate by an example the
universal characteristics of the species, but I may instance
the wonderfully fine andante of the Concerto in C major
(467 K.) Here the orchestral part is rich in striking
harmonic detail, and in fine and original sound effects, which
so completely enchant and satisfy the ear as scarcely to
allow of a climax. In contrast to this we have a sur-
prisingly simple pianoforte part, displaying the distinctive
properties of the instrument without effort or difficulty, and
hovering, as it were, like a higher spiritual element over the

orchestral accompaniment, with which it is nevertheless inseparably connected. Even Beethoven (who made a profound study of Mozart's pianoforte concertos) cannot be said to have surpassed him in this combination from within of different instrumental forces. The superiority of his great pianoforte concertos rests upon other grounds.

It must not be supposed, however, that Mozart had no higher qualities than a finely cultivated sense for the blending of tone colours. The invention, elaboration and distribution of the motifs were governed by the nature of the resources at his command; these had to be taken into account in the first sketch of the work, that so justice might be done them in its completed form ; the germ must contain the capacity for development under the most varied conditions. There is scarcely one instance in the concertos of an important motif confided to the orchestra or the pianoforte alone ; they are all shared in common. But when a subject is broadly and elaborately treated by the orchestra, it is naturally kept in the background by the pianoforte, while other motifs, merely announced by the orchestra, are rendered with their full effect and embellishments by the solo instrument. This competition of the two forces is most evident in the alternating effects given to the working-out of the different subjects, but even in the brilliant figures and passages the orchestra appears like a well-proportioned edifice, decked with a profusion of arabesque-like ornament by the pianoforte. Thus the charm of these concertos, most rightly so called, depends upon the active co-operation of the contrasted elements, by means of which the whole work is richly and brilliantly grouped, as a picture is grouped by a judicious disposition of light and shade.

The division of the concertos into three movements, as well as the formation of the movements after the analogy of the sonata, were found ready to hand, and only further developed by Mozart. The first and principal movement contains the essential ingredients of the sonata form, namely, a second well-defined subject, and the working-out division; but it is freer, and, owing to its improved resources, more fully appointed. A distinct first part with a repetition does not exist; in its place there appears the first ritornello, with the solo movement belonging to it. The principal subjects, with their working-out, are shared between the orchestra and the piano; but the solo is no mere repetition of the orchestral part; it differs both in the grouping and treatment of the subjects, and leads up to an inevitable climax. A short ritornello brings this section to a close, and introduces the working-out part, equally shared between the pianoforte and orchestra. The severer forms of counterpoint are only sparingly used, the harmonic element being the main support of an animated figure treatment; the polyphonic and homophonic manner are so blended throughout as to display the principal subjects from ever-varying points of view, and to keep the interest alive and active from first to last. This middle movement, on which as usual the main interest is concentrated, leads back to the principal key and the introductory ritornello. The latter is generally shortened, and the first part is not literally repeated, but undergoes modifications in arrangement and elaboration. The conclusion is formed by the customary cadenza, which might also be introduced at other pauses, but was invariable here. It gave opportunity for a free improvisation, consisting of brilliant passages wrought into a sort of capriccio with the addition of an elaborate variation on one of the subjects, or of several subjects so condensed as to form a *résumé* of the whole movement.[44] The cadenza thus forms the concluding coda of the pianoforte part, and the orchestra brings the movement to an end in similar fashion by a more or less elaborate ritornello. In this way the first movements of the concertos are developed out of the general sonata form, with such a regard to the relative claims of the orchestra and the pianoforte as serves to distinguish them from corresponding movements of the quartet and the symphony.

---

[44] A collection of cadenzas to several concertos (175, 271, 414, 415, 449, 451 453, 456, 459, 488, 537, 595 K.) is preserved, and partially published (624 K.). They appear to have been written down by Mozart for pupils; they are neither difficult nor elaborate, and certainly give no idea of his improvised cadenzas. Beethoven wrote cadenzas of his own to the D minor concerto (466 K.) (Wie Modeztg., 1836, Beil., 10. Werke, 70A, 11, 12).

The two other movements are altogether simpler in design and execution. The slow movement is in song-form, its working out sometimes that of a rondo, sometimes varied, but always simple and clear, and abounding in charming detail. Here again Mozart has displayed a fund of deep and noble sentiment in its purest form, and the fantastic and romantic elements, mingled with a dreamy resignation, and an earnest endeavour after the expression of individual feeling, are more apparent in these movements than in any other of his compositions. Startling harmonic progressions, scattered touches of piquancy contrasting with vague sentimentality, and rhythmical whimsicalities, give all the greater charm that they in no way interfere with simplicity of conception or purity of form. I need only adduce by way of illustration the simple and beautiful romanze of the Concerto in G major (453 K.), or the pleasing and highly original Siciliana of the Concerto in A major (488 K.). The andante of the C major concerto already mentioned is, however, incomparably the finest (467 K.). The emotion is so pure and lofty that the sorrowful impulses which prompt it, harshly expressed though they may be in places, such as the following—

penetrate the music like memories of a long since vanquished grief that has no more power to trouble the pure serenity of a mind which has mounted from resignation to holy joy. This example, among many others, should teach us that beauty does not consist in the mere rejection of all that is harsh or keen, but in the maturity of the conception which gives birth to the work, and in the harmony of the conditions under which it is represented. Such fruits as these can only be offered by an artist who has discovered the true secret of life.

The last movement of the concertos is always the easiest; it is generally in rondo form, sometimes in variations, lively and cheerful in tone; its predominant 2-4 time preserves its original character of a dance; or sometimes it is in 6-8 time, after the fashion of a hunting song, as in the rondo of the Concerto in B flat major (450 K.) which closes in a long crescendo with a regular hunting flourish of trumpets.[45] On the whole these last movements are more inte-

---

[45] The last movement of the Concerto in F major (413 K.) is a rondo-like "Tempo di menuetto," after the old style (Vol. I., p. 325), similar to one in a violin sonata (377 K.).

resting than those of the other pianoforte compositions, and full of graceful, even humorous, passages, of which the last movement of the C minor Concerto (491 K.) may serve as an illustration.   The peculiar harmonic treatment gives the subject a character entirely its own, and a new transition at the close invests it with a surprising charm.   The Concerto in D minor also (466 K.) confirms the oft-repeated observation that Mozart's compositions in the minor keys are his deepest and most important, for its last movement is distinguished above all others by its fire and intensity of expression.[46]   On the other hand, the middle movements of these two symphonies (in E flat and B flat major), although not wanting in grace, are inferior to their other two movements in force and passion.   It is true that the andante of the C minor symphony was encored on its first performance (Vol. II., p. 288), but the effect it made depended not so much on its melodies, charming as they are, as on the obbligato treatment of the wind instruments, which was an entire novelty at that time.

There can be no doubt that Mozart's concertos afford the best standard for our judgment of him as a pianoforte composer.   The majority of them, written for himself in his best days, take the highest rank among his works.   The first three (413-415 K.) intended for large audiences are, as Mozart rightly indicates, light in character; so is the Concerto in E flat major (449 K.), written for Fräulein Ployer, and the Concerto in B flat major, probably intended for Fräulein Paradies (456 K.); next to these may be placed the Concertos in D major (451 K.) and F major (459 K).   They are all distinct in their main characteristics; some, such as those in B flat major (450 K.), G major (453 K.), A major (414, 488 K.), are cheerful and graceful; others, as the D minor (466 K.) and C minor (491 K.), are passionately agitated; others again, serious and self-contained, as the E flat major (452 K.)

---

[46] The sketch of the beginning of a rondo first intended for this concerto is prefixed to the Offenbach score of the Concerto in B flat major (450 K.). Mozart rightly gave the preference to the very dissimilar fiery theme of the present rondo.

and B flat major (595 K.); brilliant and stately, as the C
and D major (503, 537 K.); or impetuous even to grandeur,
as the oft-mentioned Concerto in C major (467 K.).

Each of them may be regarded as a well-organised whole,
to be as such apprehended and rendered; in addition to this
the music is genuine pianoforte music, sympathetic and
brilliant, although at the present day presenting no technical
difficulties. "The astonishing rapidity, particularly in the
left hand, which may be termed unique,"[47] would scarcely
be much thought of now, although an imperfectly trained
executant would still find difficulties in Mozart. He exacts
a clear song-like delivery of the long-drawn melodies, and a
"quiet steady" hand, which should make the passages
"flow like oil," and his passages almost all depend upon
scales and broken chords; real feats of bravura, such as
jumps, crossings, &c., only occur in exceptional cases.
Mozart has undoubtedly done much to improve the pianoforte, and has laid the foundation of its future development,
but he has not by any means exhausted the resources of the
instrument. He avoided, as we have seen, passages in
octaves, sixths or thirds, with which Clementi excited so
much astonishment, because he feared that they would prejudice what he looked on as the chief requisites of good
execution. Generally speaking, his aim was not chord-
playing or the production of massive effects, but clearness
and transparency, qualities which especially belonged to the
instruments of his day. While the tendency of modern
execution is to turn the piano into a sort of independent
orchestra, Mozart's endeavour was rather to reveal the
specific qualities of the piano in clear and unmixed contrast
with the orchestra. His was, at least, the right path for the
development of pianoforte execution. The principal excellence of the concertos lies, however, not in their executive
difficulties, but in their musical substance. In conception
and workmanship they display lofty impulse and perfect
freedom.

The means at command were considerable enough to

---

[47] Niemetschek, p. 32.

incite the composer to unwonted efforts; and Mozart went to
work with special good-will on what was destined for his own
performance.   Since also they were to make a more immediate impression on the audience than other works, Mozart
has made more use than was his custom of attractive means
of expression, and it is very characteristic that he does this,
not by virtuoso-like pianoforte effects, but by an elevation of
the musical expression.   A careful survey of the details will
show much to be here prefigured which is of great effect in
our most modern music; but such points are only intended
by Mozart to give a passing piquancy of flavour to his music.
There is in his concertos so much that is daring and striking
in harmonic treatment, in organ points, suspensions, and
transitions, that Ulibicheff, even if he did not actually con-
demn the concertos, would certainly have found traces in
them of the "chimera-chords," which he professed to have
discovered in Beethoven.[48]

---

[48] In Reichardt's Musik. Wochenblatt (1791, p. 19) C. Spazier has a notice on
Herr C. Rick, "who played a pianoforte concerto by Mozart, and gave admirable
expression to the sentimental passages and original ideas of the great master,
who, like all great geniuses that strive to make art obedient even to their
mental vagaries, sometimes falls into the most. singular paradoxes.   It is with
feelings of pleasure that we behold an artist of this stamp pursuing with ease a
course which would cost others the most stupendous exertions."